FREEDOM OF RELIGION

The scale and variety of acts of religious intolerance evident in so many countries today are of enormous contemporary concern. This timely study attempts a thorough and systematic treatment of both Universal and European practice side by side. The standards applicable to freedom of religion are subjected to a detailed critique, and their development and implementation within the UN is distinguished from that within Strasbourg, in order to discern trends and obstacles to their advancement and to highlight the rationale for any apparent departures between the two systems. This dual focus also demonstrates the acute need for the European Court to heed the warnings from various patterns of violation throughout the world illustrated by the Human Rights Committee and the Special Rapporteur on freedom of religion or belief.

PAUL M. TAYLOR is a Barrister (Lincoln's Inn).

D1564394

FREEDOM OF RELIGION

UN and European Human Rights Law and Practice

PAUL M. TAYLOR

CAMBRIDGE
UNIVERSITY PRESS

CAMBRIDGE UNIVERSITY PRESS

Cambridge, New York, Melbourne, Madrid, Cape Town, Singapore, São Paulo

CAMBRIDGE UNIVERSITY PRESS

The Edinburgh Building, Cambridge CB2 2RU, UK

Published in the United States of America by Cambridge University Press, New York

www.cambridge.org
Information on this title: www.cambridge.org/9780521672467

First published 2005

Printed in the United Kingdom at the University Press, Cambridge

A catalogue record for this book is available from the British Library

ISBN-13 978-0-521-85649-2 hardback
ISBN-10 0-521-85649-3 hardback
ISBN-13 978-0-521-67246-7 paperback
ISBN-10 0-521-67246-5 paperback

CONTENTS

FOREWORD

This study of the United Nations and European international human rights law guaranteeing freedom of religion addresses issues of great contemporary concern. There are many places in the world where the followers of a particular religion may not lawfully worship or practise their religion in their daily lives. Apostacy and proselytism may be criminal acts, as may artistic speech that causes offence to religious feelings. Religious intolerance continues to fuel a high proportion of the situations of armed conflict around the world, thus being the seemingly intractable cause of so much human suffering. Since 9/11, incitement to religious hatred has increased in significance, with Muslims being the targets of general blame. Religion is as the heart of the debate about multiculturalism, exemplified by the heated controversy in France about the wearing of headscarves by Muslim women. The relationship between Church and State remains a contentious issue in some other societies. In a watershed and contentious judgment in *Refah Partisi v. Turkey*, the European Court of Human Right has ruled that a state legal order that is founded on Shariah Law is not consistent with democracy in Europe, so that the banning of a political party that seeks to introduce such an order is not in breach of the guarantee of the right to freedom of association in the European Convention on Human Rights. And the return to strict Christian religious values in the United States has raised moral questions and issues of separation of Church and State for the courts.

This book is likely to become the place of first recourse on the international human rights law on freedom of religion that govern these and other situations and issues. It offers a comprehensive analysis and evaluation of the relevant international law standards that have evolved within the United Nations and the Council of Europe. The book is distinctive in its reliance upon both the – sometimes differing – jurisprudence and practice of the United Nations and European human rights systems. At the United Nations level, what is of great value is the author's use not only of the practice of the Human Rights Committee, but also of the reports of the UN Special Rapporteur on Freedom of Religion or Belief. These reports are a depressingly revealing mine of information about the large extent and different forms of the ongoing violations of freedom of religion perpetrated or tolerated by States around the world.

DAVID HARRIS
Professor Emeritus and Co-Director of the
Human Rights Law Centre,
School of Law,
University of Nottingham
April 2005

PREFACE

The escalating religious intolerance of recent years, both through State violation and by non-State entities, is most conspicuous in events following the collapse of the former Soviet Union, in religious conflict in many parts of the world and, of course, in the attacks of 11 September 2001. This has caused speculation whether the international instruments which were developed more than half a century ago, and those which followed but were shaped by those instruments, are sufficient to meet present and foreseeable demands. The array of religious violations visible in so many countries today could not have been anticipated by the drafters of the core freedom of religion Articles in the foundational instruments, namely the Universal Declaration on Human Rights and the European Convention. The development of comparable provisions in later instruments, such as the International Covenant on Civil and Political Rights and the United Nations Declaration on the Elimination of all Forms of Intolerance and of Discrimination based on Religion or Belief ('the 1981 Declaration'), suggests that the issues which fashioned the text of those later provisions did not depart significantly from those faced by the original drafters, except perhaps in the intensity with which they were debated.

Among recent patterns of violation, particularly in countries of the former Soviet Union, are measures such as prohibitive registration formalities and bans on proselytism aimed at the protection of a traditional State religion or the preservation of national identity in reaction to the influx of new religious movements. Many other countries have recently adopted preventive policies against so-called 'sects' as a result of exaggerated fears of their activities. The xenophobia and discrimination directed at Muslims following September 11 has been far more widespread and anxieties about 'extremism' have, for example, led various countries to react more unfavourably than ever towards Muslim dress. Hostility towards Muslims has added impetus to moves which had already begun in certain countries for legislation designed to prohibit religious vilification or religious hatred. It remains to be seen whether this will be at the expense of religious practice such as teaching and proselytism.

One other development of recent years has been the emergence of political parties with an overtly religious agenda, the most radical advocating the introduction of a system of government based on religious law.

It is therefore timely to reflect on whether existing instruments are capable of meeting immediate expectations and, as we approach the 25th anniversary of the 1981 Declaration, to consider in particular the contribution to the development of current standards made by that Declaration and by the Special Rapporteur on freedom of religion or belief appointed to examine incidents and governmental action inconsistent with the Declaration. The 1981 Declaration is of unique significance in the development of the freedom of religion since it was the first, and remains the only, United Nations instrument dedicated solely to that freedom. This work pays tribute to the specialist role of the Special Rapporteur in providing a wealth of material on recurring patterns of violation worldwide and in serving to uncover contemporary sources of intolerance and obstacles to the promotion of international obligations.

The purpose of this book is to provide a detailed survey of the elements of the freedom of thought, conscience and religion as developed within both the United Nations and European systems and to offer an analysis of trends at a time when the freedom faces a number of important challenges. It provides a critique of United Nations and European practice in order to identify and explain apparent departures between the two systems, to help to discern obstacles to the advancement of standards and to guage the level of recognition given to different aspects of the freedom. The aim is to enable an immediate appreciation of the United Nations or European system for those familiar with only one, and to provide coverage of the law and practice of both United Nations and European institutions for those familiar with neither system.

I would like to acknowledge and thank Professor David Harris, who has been extremely generous in his support for this work and whose assistance I value enormously. I would also like to thank, among many others who have helped in its preparation, the librarians at Cambridge University's Squire Law Library for their patient assistance with many queries and the kind provision of facilities beyond all expectation. I am also greatly indebted to Wolfson College Cambridge for a Visiting Fellowship that offered a stimulating environment for the completion of this work, to Finola O'Sullivan of Cambridge University Press who throughout has never been anything but extremely helpful, and to the anonymous referees appointed by Cambridge University Press for their very useful recommendations for improvement of the text.

TABLE OF CASES, APPLICATIONS, AND COMMUNICATIONS

The European Court of Human Rights

The European Commission of Human Rights

Views and Decisions of the Human Rights Committee

The Human Rights Chamber for Bosnia and Herzegovina

TABLE OF TREATIES, DECLARATIONS, AND OTHER INTERNATIONAL INSTRUMENTS

ABBREVIATIONS

AC	Appeal Cases
AIR	All India Reporter
Am J Int'l L	*American Journal of International Law*
Brigham Young UL Rev	*Brigham Young University Law Review*
BYBIL	*British Yearbook of International Law*
Cambridge LJ	*Cambridge Law Journal*
Case W Res J Int'l L	*Case Western Reserve Journal of International Law*
CD	Collected Decisions of the European Commission of Human Rights
CHR	Commission on Human Rights
CIL	*Contemporary Issues in Law*
Con & Lib	*Conscience & Liberty*
Cornell Int'l LJ	*Cornell International Law Journal*
Ecc LJ	*Ecclesiastical Law Journal*
Ec Rev	*Ecumenical Review*
ECtHR	European Court of Human Rights Judgments and Decisions
Ed & Law	*Education and the Law*
EHRLR	European Human Rights Law Review
EHRR	European Human Rights Reports
Emory Int'l L Rev	*Emory International Law Review*
Emp Lawyer	*Employment Lawyer*
ESCOR	United Nations Economic and Social Council Official Records
ETS	European Treaty Series
Eur L Rev	*European Law Review*
GA Res.	General Assembly Resolution
GAOR	General Assembly Official Records
Harv Int'l LJ	*Harvard International Law Journal*
Harv L Rev	*Harvard Law Review*

Harv WLJ	*Harvard Women's Law Journal*
HR & UKP	*Human Rights and UK Practice*
HRLJ	*Human Rights Law Journal*
HRQ	*Human Rights Quarterly*
HRJ	*Human Rights Journal*
ICCPR	International Covenant on Civil and Political Rights (1966)
IHRR	International Human Rights Reports
ILM	International Legal Materials
Int JLP & F	*International Journal of Law, Policy and the Family*
Int'l & Comp Law Q	*International and Comparative Law Quarterly*
Int'l Bull Miss Res	*International Bulletin of Missionary Research*
Int'l Comm'n Jurists Rev	*Review, International Commission of Jurists*
Isr YB Hum Rts	*Israel Yearbook on Human Rights*
J Church & St	*Journal of Church and State*
J Civ Lib	*Journal of Civil Liberties*
J Soc Wel Law	*Journal of Social Welfare Law*
KCLJ	*King's College Law Journal*
Med Sc & L	*Medicine, Science and the Law*
Neth Int'l L Rev	*Netherlands International Law Review*
NLJ	*New Law Journal*
Northern Ireland LQ	*Northern Ireland Legal Quarterly*
Northw UL Rev	*Northwestern University Law Review*
NYUJ Int'l L & Pol	*New York University Journal of International Law and Politics*
ODIHR	Office for Democratic Institutions and Human Rights
OSCE	Organization for Security and Co-operation in Europe, formerly the Conference for Security and Co-operation in Europe
Oxford J Leg Stud	*Oxford Journal of Legal Studies*
Pac Rim L & Pol'y J	*Pacific Rim Law and Policy Journal*
Pat of Prej	*Patterns of Prejudice*
PL	*Public Law*
Plen. Mtg	Plenary Meeting

Pol Quart	*Political Quarterly*
RADIC	*African Journal of International and Comparative Law*
Rat Jur	*Ratio Juris*
RCADI	*Receuil des Cours de l'Académie de Droit International de la Haye*
Santa Clara L Rev	*Santa Clara Law Review*
SCR	Supreme Court Reports
U Chicago L Rev	*University of Chicago Law Review*
UN	United Nations
UNTS	UN Treaty Series
Vand J Transnat'l L	*Vanderbilt Journal of Transnational Law*
Virginia J Int'l L	*Virginia Journal of International Law*
WCRP	World Conference on Religion and Peace
William Mary L Rev	*William and Mary Law Review*
WLR	Weekly Law Reports
YBECHR	Yearbook of the European Commission of Human Rights
Yearbook	Yearbook of the European Convention on Human Rights

1

Introduction

Overview

An appraisal of the development and content of the freedom of thought, conscience and religion has never been more challenging. Events since the collapse of the former Soviet Union and the aftermath of the attacks of 11 September 2001 have confronted the traditional concept of freedom of religion with an entirely new range of demands. These could not have been anticipated by the drafters of the core freedom of religion Articles in the foundational instruments. In the United Nations context these are Article 18 of the Universal Declaration on Human Rights (the 'Universal Declaration')[1] and Article 18 of the International Covenant on Civil and Political Rights ('the ICCPR').[2] Within the

---

[1] The full text of the Universal Declaration is at Annex 1. Article 18 of the Universal Declaration reads as follows:

> 'Everyone has the right to freedom of thought, conscience and religion; this right includes freedom to change his religion or belief, and freedom, either alone or in community with others and in public or private, to manifest his religion or belief in teaching, practice, worship and observance.'

> (Universal Declaration on Human Rights, adopted and proclaimed by GA Res. 217A(III) of 10 December 1948, UN Doc. A/3/810 (1949)).

[2] The key Articles of the ICCPR are set out in Annex 2. Article 18 of the ICCPR reads as follows:

> 1. 'Everyone shall have the right to freedom of thought, conscience and religion. This right shall include freedom to have or to adopt a religion or belief of his choice, and freedom, either individually or in community with others and in public or private, to manifest his religion or belief in worship, observance, practice and teaching.
> 2. No one shall be subject to coercion which would impair his freedom to have or to adopt a religion or belief of his choice.
> 3. Freedom to manifest one's religion or beliefs may be subject only to such limitations as are prescribed by law and are necessary to protect public safety, order, health, or morals or the fundamental rights and freedoms of others.

Convention for the Protection of Human Rights and Fundamental Freedoms ('the European Convention'), adopted under the auspices of the Council of Europe, the key provision is Article 9.[3] Even the Declaration on the Elimination of all Forms of Intolerance and of Discrimination Based on Religion or Belief ('the 1981 Declaration'),[4] which was concluded much later and was the first international instrument dedicated solely to freedom of religion, did not contemplate recent patterns of violation which are emerging globally.

Those texts constitute the basic building blocks of the freedom of religion and were inevitably shaped by the issues which faced the original drafters. Prominent areas of contention in the early debates were resistance to an explicit right to change religion (from various Islamic countries), doubts about proselytism as an adjunct to the right to practise a religion and, more generally, the ideological opposition from numerous Communist countries to the assertion of rights of the individual over the interests of the State. The extent to which neutrality should be preserved in State education was also a fundamental, though more recent, concern (in the ICCPR and the 1981 Declaration).

However, since those instruments were concluded a number of trends have tested whether the text of the core provisions is sufficient to address the immediate and foreseeable challenges of the future. Among such

---

4. The States Parties to the present Covenant undertake to have respect for the liberty of parents and, when applicable, legal guardians to ensure the religious and moral education of their children in conformity with their own convictions.'

(International Covenant on Civil and Political Rights (1966), New York, 16 December 1966, in force 23 March 1976, 999 UNTS 171)

[3] The key Articles of the European Convention are set out in Annex 4. Article 9 of the European Convention reads as follows.

1. 'Everyone has the right to freedom of thought, conscience and religion; this right includes freedom to change his religion or belief and freedom, either alone or in community with others and in public or private, to manifest his religion or belief, in worship, teaching, practice and observance.

2. Freedom to manifest one's religion or beliefs shall be subject only to such limitations as are prescribed by law and are necessary in a democratic society in the interests of public safety, for the protection of public order, health or morals, or for the protection of the rights and freedoms of others.'

(European Convention on Human Rights and Fundamental Freedoms (1950), Rome, 4 November 1950 in force 3 September 1953, 213 UNTS 221)

[4] The full text of the 1981 Declaration is at Annex 3 (Declaration on the Elimination of all Forms of Intolerance and of Discrimination Based on Religion or Belief (1981), proclaimed by GA Res. 36/55 of 25 November 1981, UN Doc. A/36/51 (1982)).

trends is the political momentum in many countries of the former Soviet Bloc to protect traditional State religion in response to the influx of new religious movements. New religious movements filled the vacuum left by the abrupt exodus of Communism and are seen as a threat to the process of rebuilding the national identity of those countries. Obstacles imposed to prevent the emergence of new religious movements include prohibitive registration formalities required for their establishment, as well as widespread prohibitions on religious practice, particularly proselytism. The protection of traditional State religion as a means of reigniting national identity is a relatively new issue. Until recently, the protection of State religion has more commonly been a feature of many Islamic countries where national law is inseparable from religious law and preservation of the orthodoxy of State religion is paramount.

Another recent trend has been the pronounced incidence of religious hatred against Muslims. The xenophobia, intolerance and discrimination towards Muslims which followed the events of September 11 caused the Commission on Human Rights to react with calls for appropriate control of the mass media to prevent incitement to violence and intolerance towards Islam.[5] This gave strength to moves which were already afoot in certain countries (for example, Australia) to enact legislation to prohibit vilification on grounds of religion and has since given rise to initiatives in other countries (notably the United Kingdom) to create religious offences such as incitement to religious hatred. However, there have been concerns that such a low threshold could, in practice, be applied to this type of legislation so as to interfere directly with fundamental aspects of freedom of religion, particularly religious practice through teaching and proselytism. The risks are inherent in the teaching of any religion which amounts to the denial of other religions but are greater in the case of comparative teaching or teaching by one religious group of the beliefs of another.

At same time, there has been misplaced concern that the overt practice of Islam is a proxy for 'extremism'. This has influenced certain European States (notably France and Switzerland) to react against traditional Muslim observance, such as the wearing of religious headdress in State schools, relying on the obligation of neutrality of States in education and (in the case of Switzerland) prohibiting religious headwear as a form of proselytism. The same issue has a different dimension in Turkey where principles of secularity are enforced more generally.

---

[5] CHR Res. 2002/9 (2002) of 15 April 2002.

Fears of extremism, coupled with a lack of understanding of the requirements of Islam has resulted in a widespread failure on the part of many
European States to appreciate the importance to Muslims of straightforward religious practice and observance. The 1981 Declaration has
done much to correct this by providing a detailed explanation of different
forms of manifestation of religion or belief.

One other phenomenon of note has been the emergence of political
parties adopting an overtly religious agenda, with the most radical
parties advocating the introduction of a system of government based
on religious law. The aspirations of some religious political parties have
given rise to concerns over the imposition of religious law on non-
adherents. Outside the political sphere positive endorsement has
undoubtedly been given recently to the collective, rather than individual, aspects of religious manifestation through religious association
and church membership (and this goes some way towards dismantling
the impediments to religious association posed by registration
requirements).

Recent years have also witnessed a steady growth in recognition of the
conscientious implications of compulsory military service. This has
served to demonstrate just how undeveloped are the general principles
concerning various forms of coercion, particularly coercion to act contrary to one's religion or belief and compulsion to disclose one's beliefs.
Of the core freedom of religion Articles, Article 18(2) of the ICCPR and
Article 1(2) of the 1981 Declaration offer explicit protection against
coercion but only against coercion in religious choice. It remains to be
seen what future direction these developments will take.

Another dimension of recent change has been the escalation of religious intolerance by non-State entities and the corresponding role of the
State in combating intolerance. Greater emphasis has been placed on the
positive obligations on States to protect rights and freedoms by appropriate means and it is expected that this principle will see greater
practical recognition in future years.

All these issues will be discussed in detail in later chapters, which will
address the origins of the text of each of the core freedom of religion
Articles and the development of standards applicable to each constituent
freedom.

One other observation worth making at the outset concerns the
obvious differences between the United Nations and European frame-
works. The textual similarities between Article 9 of the European
Convention and Article 18 of the Universal Declaration from which it

stemmed are self-evident. However, the relative homogeneity of legal and democratic systems across European countries contrasts with the vast range of ideological, religious and cultural foundations of the systems of government of the nations represented within the Universal system. In some countries these foundations even go the root of their basic conception of the freedom of thought, conscience and religion. Following more than half a century of experience of both the European and United Nations systems, and in the face of new patterns of religious intolerance in recent years, it is timely to examine critically the paths taken by each system in developing the standards applicable to religious freedom since the Universal Declaration was adopted in 1948, and since the European Convention entered into force in 1953.

This work therefore aims to provide an appraisal of the development of the right to freedom of thought, conscience and religion at both United Nations and European levels. Standards within the United Nations system are reflected principally in the work of the Human Rights Committee and the Special Rapporteur ('the Special Rapporteur')[6] appointed by the Commission on Human Rights to examine incidents and governmental action inconsistent with the 1981 Declaration. In addition, wider sources such as the *travaux préparatoires* of most instruments touching upon freedom of religion play an essential part. Within European jurisprudence, the practice of the European Court on Human Rights ('the European Court') and the former European Commission on Human Rights ('the European Commission') provide the basis for evaluating developing European standards under the European Convention. Although this work is primarily aimed at the conclusions to be drawn from a critique of the practice of the United Nations and European institutions, occasional reference will be made to other regional initiatives found in the Council of Europe Framework Convention for the Protection of National Minorities and the Organization for Security and Co-operation in Europe ('OSCE', formerly the Conference for Security and Co-operation in Europe), as well as certain systems of national law where they have particular relevance.

The United Nations and the European systems were selected for examination because of the historical interrelation between the two

---

[6] The title of the 'Special Rapporteur on religious intolerance' was changed to 'Special Rapporteur on freedom of religion or belief' by CHR Res. 2000/33 of 20 April 2000.

(given that Article 9 of the European Convention was taken from the text of Article 18 of the Universal Declaration). However, it is important to appreciate fully the significance of any apparent departures between United Nations and European standards and to distinguish genuine from supposed paths of divergence. Some differences may be explained merely by the different role and function played by each of the various organs from which applicable standards of religious freedom may be derived or through which they are expressed. Limitations of legal competence and technical expertise are also relevant. Some differences are explicable only in terms of policy (for which historical trends are particularly important) while others are attributable to the different contexts in which Universal and European standards apply.

A thematic approach will be followed as closely as possible throughout this work in order to discern the advances and reversals on particular issues of recurring importance. An in-depth evaluation of apparent discrepancies within particular themes will help to expose the significance of points of divergence. A thematic approach also lends itself to an assessment of the future development of standards of religious freedom in such a way that might achieve better consistency between the United Nations and European institutions, and may point to the most effective means of utilising the existing organs.

Of the major recent works on freedom of religion, that by Tahzib[7] represents the most comprehensive survey of United Nations instruments, and those by Malcolm Evans[8] and Carolyn Evans[9] both provide penetrating insight into the decision-making of the European Court and European Commission. However, none attempts any detailed thematic evaluation of both European and Universal standards beyond coverage of the separate historical developments of the major United Nations and European instruments and the occasional comparison between the two.[10] Given the importance of such an evaluation this work attempts to develop a framework for the discussion of both United Nations and

---

[7] B. G. Tahzib, *Freedom of Religion or Belief: Ensuring Effective International Legal Protection*, The Hague/London: Martinus Nijhoff Publishers (1996).

[8] M. D. Evans, *Religious Liberty and International Law in Europe*, Cambridge: Cambridge University Press (1997).

[9] C. Evans, *Freedom of Religion Under the European Convention on Human Rights*, Oxford: Oxford University Press (2001).

[10] A useful overview of the role of UN and regional systems in protecting freedom of religion is found in N. Lerner, *Religion, Beliefs and International Human Rights*, Maryknoll, New York: Orbis (2000).

European jurisprudence. Extensive use will be made of the Special Rapporteur's reports in order to demonstrate the value of the role of the Special Rapporteur in offering more in-depth understanding of religious conflict and violation than the barest outline available in the Human Rights Committee's review of State reports or the specific instances considered in individual communications. The Special Rapporteur's reports offer, in the Universal context, a better appreciation of the dynamics of the freedom of religion which, it will be argued, are all too often overlooked in the decisions of the European institutions. It is important to be aware of emerging trends in religious intolerance and to heed the warnings that can only be discerned from an examination of situations worldwide in which the widest variety of cultures, religions and values interact. It is suggested that the European Court might take into account, far more than hitherto, the different sources and guises of intolerance evidenced globally and anticipate more fully the implications and potential reach of its decisions.

Interrelation between the UN and European systems

The historic connection between the Universal Declaration and the European Convention from which it stemmed deserves special comment at this stage. It is also important to note some of the practical obstacles faced by the development of freedom of religion in the Universal context, which arguably have less relevance to Europe in isolation.

Article 9 of the European Convention drew its inspiration and its text from Article 18 of the Universal Declaration in pursuance of the express aim of the European Convention in taking 'the first steps for collective enforcement of certain rights stated in the Universal Declaration'.[11] Article 9 was to be based as far as possible on Article 18 of the Universal Declaration to reduce the risk of devising definitions that were at odds with those in United Nations instruments. The *travaux préparatoires* of Article 18 of the Universal Declaration,[12] and those of subsequent United

---

[11] Preamble to the European Convention. For the drafting of the European Convention, see Council of Europe, *Collected Edition of The 'Travaux Préparatoires' of the European Convention on Human Rights*, 8 vols., The Hague: Martinus Nijhoff (1975–85). For commentary, see A. H. Robertson and J. G. Merrills, *Human Rights in the World*, Manchester: Manchester University Press (1996).

[12] For commentary on the drafting of Article 18 of the Universal Declaration, see: N. Robinson, *Universal Declaration of Human Rights: Its Origins, Significance, Application*

Nations instruments in the field of freedom of religion, demonstrate that some of the influences that fashioned the text of Article 18 may be said to have little relevance to Article 9 of the Convention. Some of the most significant issues debated in the formulation of Article 18 of the Universal Declaration, such as the right to change religion, accentuate the differences between instruments intended for Universal and European application, were raised with greater force (and were to have lasting impact) in the debates that led up to Article 18 of the ICCPR[13] and the 1981 Declaration.[14] Divergence in the basic conception of the freedom of religion at Universal level was particularly marked when impetus was given to a United Nations initiative on religious intolerance following various anti-Semitic incidents in the early 1960s. The General Assembly passed a resolution calling for the preparation of a draft declaration and a draft convention on the elimination of religious intolerance. Simultaneously, a draft declaration[15] and a draft convention[16] were advanced on the elimination

and Interpretation, New York: Institute of Jewish Affairs (1958); R. Cassin, *La Déclaration Universelle et la Mise en Oeuvre des Droits de l'Homme*, 79 RCADI (1951) 241; B. Kaufmann, *Das Problem der Glaubens- und Uberzeugungsfreiheit im Völkerrecht*, Zürich: Schulthess Polygraphischer Verlag (1989), pp. 124–46; M. Scheinin, 'Article 18', in A. Eide (ed.), *The Universal Declaration of Human Rights: A Commentary*, Oslo: Scandinavian University Press (1992); A. Verdoodt, *Naissance et Significance de la Déclaration Universelle des Droits de l'Homme* (1964), Lourain: Paris Société d'études morales, socials et juridiques, Editions Nauwelaerts (1964).

[13] M. J. Bossuyt, *Guide to the 'Travaux Préparatoires' of the International Covenant on Civil and Political Rights*, Dordrecht/Lancaster: Martinus Nijhoff (1987). For commentary on the drafting of Article 18 of the ICCPR, see: T. van Boven, *De Volkenrechtelijke Bescherming van de godsdienstvrijheid*, Assen, Netherlands: Van Gorcum (1967); K. J. Partsch, 'Freedom of Conscience and Expression, and Political Freedoms', in L. Henkin (ed.), *The International Bill of Rights The Covenant on Civil and Political Rights*, New York/Guildford: Columbia University Press (1981).

[14] For commentary on the drafting of the 1981 Declaration, see S. Liskofsky, 'The UN Declaration on the Elimination of Religious Intolerance and Discrimination: Historical and Legal Perspectives', in J. E. Wood (ed.), *Religion and the State: Essays in Honour of Leo Pfeffer*, Waco, Texas: Baylor University Press (1985).

[15] United Nations Declaration on the Elimination of All Forms of Racial Discrimination, proclaimed by GA Res. 1904 (XVIII) of 20 November 1963 (1963), UN GAOR, 18th Sess., Supp. No. 15, 1261 Plen. Mtg at 35, UN Doc. A/5515 (1963).

[16] International Convention on the Elimination of All Forms of Racial Discrimination (1965) (New York, 21 December 1965, in force 4 January 1969, 660 UNTS 195, reprinted in 5 ILM 352 (1966); UN GAOR, 20th Sess., Supp. No. 14, 1406 Plen. Mtg at 47, UN Doc. A/6014 (1964). See: E. Schwelb, 'The International Convention on the Elimination of All Forms of Racial Discrimination 1965', 15 Int'l & Comp Law Q (1966) 996; N. Lerner, *The U.N. Convention on the Elimination of All Forms of Racial Discrimination*, Alphen aan den Rijn: Sijhoff & Noordhoff (1980); M. Banton, *International Action Against Racial Discrimination*, Oxford: Clarendon Press (1996).

of racial discrimination in the knowledge that issues of racial discrimination could be progressed swiftly with the removal of content relating to religious intolerance, given opposition expected from Communist countries on ideological grounds.[17] Also by then the requirements of certain Middle East countries were better appreciated than during the drafting of the Universal Declaration. The result was that the Declaration on Racial Discrimination was adopted in 1963, followed rapidly by the adoption of the Convention on Racial Discrimination in 1965. By contrast, it was not until nineteen years after the General Assembly called for preparation of a convention on religious intolerance that, at best, a declaration could be adopted, while a convention still remains an aspiration.[18]

In short, it may be speculated whether developments in Universal standards since the Universal Declaration was adopted, and developments in European standards since the Convention entered into force mean that the two systems have, in certain respects, followed different trajectories. It is important to understand any resulting differences between Universal and European standards. In doing so, it is also necessary to appreciate the differences between various sources of interpretation (both within the United Nations and European systems) that reflect emerging standards of religious freedom.

The institutions and their contribution to standard-setting

From United Nations sources, specific guidance on the Human Rights Committee's understanding of Article 18 of the ICCPR is found in

---

[17] For further insight into these parallel developments, see: N. Lerner, 'Toward a Draft Declaration Against Religious Intolerance and Discrimination' 11 Isr YB Hum Rts (1981) 82; N. Lerner, 'The Final Text of the UN Declaration against Intolerance and Discrimination Based on Religion or Belief' 12 Isr YB Hum Rts (1982) 185; A. Cassese, 'The General Assembly: Historical Perspective 1945–1989', in P. Alston (ed.), *The United Nations and Human Rights: A Critical Appraisal*, Oxford: Clarendon Press (1992); W. McKean, *Equality and Discrimination under International Law*, Oxford: Clarendon Press (1983).

[18] For further detail concerning the background to the draft declaration and draft convention, see: J. Claydon, 'The Treaty Protection of Religious Rights: UN Draft Convention on the Elimination of All Forms of Intolerance and of Discrimination Based on Religion or Belief' 12 Santa Clara L Rev (1972) 403; T. van Boven, 'Advances and Obstacles in Building Understanding and Respect between People of Diverse Religions and Beliefs' 13 HRQ (1991) 437.

General Comment No. 22[19] and, in the case of those countries which accepted the right of individual petition under the first Optional Protocol, the Human Rights Committee's consideration of individual communications.[20] More general sources of interpretation of Universal standards under the ICCPR include the *travaux préparatoires* (which are recorded in some detail) and the results of examination of State reports submitted under Article 40 of the ICCPR. Unfortunately, State reports have limited interpretative value in relation to specific Articles and there has been a relative shortage of communications from countries with a non-European conception of freedom of religion. The work of the Special Rapporteur, by contrast, provides a wealth of information on a variety of violations but its emphasis is more factual than interpretative.

As far as European sources of interpretation are concerned, the *travaux préparatoires* of the European Convention are incomplete although, given that the origins of Article 9 are so clearly found in Article 18 of the Universal Declaration, this is not a significant handicap. Furthermore, the decisions of the European Commission and the European Court are so clearly documented with supporting reasoning that they themselves represent a thorough reflection of developing standards, even if the reasoning is open to criticism for its lack of rigour.

The role and function of each organ determine not only the authoritative status of its findings but also the context and limitations of its own operations. Each of the United Nations and European institutions will now be considered briefly in turn, so that standards expressed by them may be seen in the context of their function. This will help to explain some of the apparent differences in emphasis, and substantive divergences, between the United Nations and European systems.

The Human Rights Committee

As the body charged with monitoring the implementation of the ICCPR, the Human Rights Committee is extremely influential. Its eighteen members are elected from candidates nominated by each State party (they must be nationals of that State) though relatively few countries in reality make

---

[19] General Comment No. 22 (48), UN Doc. CCPR/C/21/Rev.1/Add.4 (1993). The text of General Comment No. 22 is at Annex 5.

[20] For the most thorough account of Optional Protocol procedures, see P. R. Ghandhi, *The Human Rights Committee and the Right of Individual Communication, Law and Practice*, Aldershot: Ashgate (1998).

the necessary nominations and it has been suggested that groups of countries act in concert before nominating candidates.[21] Under Article 31 of the ICCPR, in the election of the Committee, 'consideration shall be given to equitable geographical distribution of membership and to the representation of the different forms of civilisation and of the principal legal systems'. Boerefijn has observed from a regional analysis (of African, Asian, Latin American and Caribbean, Central and Eastern European and Western European regions) that between 1977 and 1997 African and Asian States have become increasingly under-represented.[22] In fact together they are represented by six members in most years (occasionally seven). It is also worth noting that most members broadly speaking come from countries with a Western tradition. Even in the case of those countries of Central and Eastern Europe constituting part of the former Communist Bloc, their aspirations during the 1990s began to focus on membership of the European Community and this might be said to have given the Committee more of a Western European bias. Having said that, the Human Rights Committee's independent status has been described as 'its most prized possession'.[23] Members act in their personal capacity, not under the direction of their nominating State. Members of the Committee are also independent from other treaty bodies.

The role of the Human Rights Committee in examining State reports stems from the mandatory obligation of States under Article 40 of the ICCPR to 'submit reports on the measures they have adopted which give effect to the rights recognized herein and on the progress made in the enjoyment of those rights'.[24] The Human Rights Committee follows an Article-by-Article approach to examining State reports. This means that out of the substantive Articles 1 to 27, Article 18 is low in the list

[21] I. Boerefijn, *The Reporting Procedure under the Covenant on Civil and Political Rights: Practice and Procedures of the Human Rights Committee*, Antwerp: Hart Intersentia (1999), at p. 40. Boerefijn discusses at length in Chapter 2 the composition and election of members of the Committee. For further insights of a former Human Rights Committee member, see T. Opsahl, 'The Human Rights Committee', in P. Alston (ed.), *The United Nations and Human Rights: A Critical Appraisal*, Oxford: Clarendon Press, (1992), pp. 369–443.

[22] Boerefijn, *The Reporting Procedure under the Covenant*, pp. 53 and 54.

[23] UN Doc. CCPR/C/SR. 1385 (1994), p. 7, para. 37 (per Mrs Higgins).

[24] See: D. McGoldrick, *The Human Rights Committee: Its Role in the Development of the International Covenant on Civil and Political Rights*, Oxford: Clarendon Press (1994); R. Higgins, 'The United Nations Human Rights Committee', in R. Blackburn and J. Taylor (eds.), *Human Rights for the 1990s: Legal, Political and Ethical Issues*, London: Mansell (1991), pp. 67–74; M. Nowak, *CCPR Commentary*, Kehl: N. P. Engel

chronologically and requires expertise in religious matters of considerable sensitivity and variety, which perhaps few members of the Human Rights Committee possess. In addition, it is likely that earlier Articles might be considered to be of more general importance (particularly Articles 1 to 10) and as they fall within the familiarity and general competence of most Committee members they are more likely to be selected for detailed consideration in preference to later Articles. As a result, issues under Article 18 may be relatively low in the priorities of most members. In examining Article 18 issues in State reports, the comments of members might therefore be said to have particular strength given the pressures of time and the relative importance of other issues of public emergency, arbitrary deprivation of life, genocide, torture, slavery, arbitrary arrest and detention and so on, considered in earlier Articles of the ICCPR.

Comments may be given by individual members or by the entire Committee, questions may be asked of States (whether from individual members or the Committee as a whole), and requests may be made for further information but only when clearly elicited within the Committee's competence.[25] Since 1992 the Committee has provided its collective view by means of concluding observations.[26] Concluding observations are the most authoritative since they reflect consensus across all members. Concluding observations have typically included recommendations for the review of legislation to bring it in compliance with the ICCPR and to ensure appropriate domestic application pursuant to Article 2. It is likely that the recent suggestion that a single committee might undertake the function of reviewing State reports under all six United Nations treaties (while another deals with individual petitions and inter-State communications) would result in an even less detailed consideration of Article 18 issues by members and be detrimental to the reporting process, at least as far as freedom of religion is concerned.[27]

When States prepare reports for the Human Rights Committee, as Boerefijn has pointed out, the Committee's guidelines offer no details on

---

(1993); P. Alston and C. Crawford (eds.), *The Future of UN Human Rights Treaty Monitoring*, Cambridge: Cambridge University Press (2000).

[25] However, the summary records do not bear out whether questions and requests for further information were all put within the Committee's competence and therefore with a basis in the Covenant. See Partsch, 'Freedom of Conscience and Expression', p. 448.

[26] See UN Doc. A/49/40 (1994), pp. 12–13, paras. 54–6 for an explanation of the new format.

[27] This suggestion was discussed by T. Buergenthal in 'A Court and Two Consolidated Treaty Bodies' in A. F. Bayefsky (ed.), *The UN Human Rights Treaty System in the 21st Century*, The Hague/London: Kluwer Law International (2000), pp. 299–302.

the specific aspects of each Article on which the Committee wishes to receive information.[28] If States are allowed too much latitude in reporting on matters covered by Article 18, there is the risk that in those countries where religious freedom is most under threat, State reports may consist of no more than bare assertions that cited legislation meets the State's obligations. If so, members of the Human Rights Committee would be given little material on which to base their criticism of religious practices. Prompted by its concern that States might also consider themselves to be discharging their reporting obligations merely by including constitutional or legal enactments, the Human Rights Committee has emphasised that 'instead of simply paraphrasing the law, States should focus on its practical application'.[29] The Human Rights Committee has therefore endeavoured to ensure that State reports are meaningful and that its comments in response have greatest value.

As far as General Comments are concerned, the Committee is expressly entrusted under Article 40(4) of the ICCPR with the obligation to study the reports submitted by States and to transmit to all States its reports and such General comments as it may consider appropriate.[30] General Comments 'represent the HRC's accumulated experience of years of consideration of a particular article ... they have the potential to be profoundly influential ... [and] ... perform a key function of giving some substantive content to the articles concerned'.[31] Their purpose is to make available the Committee's experience in handling State reports in order to promote more effective implementation of the ICCPR (in

---

[28] Boerefijn, *The Reporting Procedure under the Covenant*, p. 83.

[29] UN Doc. A/51/40 (1997), p. 8, para. 36. A. H. Robertson reviewed the value of the reporting system in the light of the tendency of States to provide the best available account of the situation in their country – A. H. Robertson, 'The Implementation System: International Measures' in L. Henkin (ed.), *The International Bill of Rights: The Covenant on Civil and Political Rights*, New York/Guildford: Columbia University Press (1981), pp. 337–69. The full text of the amended guidelines for State reports (which are non-binding) is included in UN Doc. A/56/40 vol. 1 (2001), Annex III.A. For commentary on an earlier version of the guidelines for the submission of reports, see Boerefijn, *The Reporting Procedure under the Covenant*, pp. 178–82.

[30] See generally: T. Opsahl, 'The General Comments of the Human Rights Committee' in Jekewitz, Jürgen et al. (eds.), *Des Menschen Recht Zwischen Freiheit und Verantwortung: Festschrift für Karl Joseph Partsch*, Berlin: Dunker & Humblot (1989); *Reporting Obligations of States Parties to the United Nations Instruments on Human Rights*, UN Doc. A/44/98 (1989); 'Effective Implementation of United Nations Instruments on Human Rights and Effective Functioning of Bodies Established Pursuant to Such Instruments', UN Doc. A/45/636 (1990); Work of the Human Rights Committee under Article 40 of the Covenant on Civil and Political Rights, UN Doc. A/CONF.157/TBB/2 (1993).

[31] McGoldrick, *The Human Rights Committee*, p. 471.

particular, through a clear appreciation of the requirements of the ICCPR), to publicise the shortcomings evident in State reports, and more generally to stimulate States Parties and international organisations in the promotion and protection of human rights.[32] The Committee has, for example, emphasised that 'its General Comment on Article 18 should be reflected in government policy and practice'.[33] The new Consolidated Guidelines for State reports require the terms of all Articles of the ICCPR, together with General Comments issued by the Committee, to be taken into account in preparing the report.[34] The Committee often refers to its General Comments when reviewing State reports[35] but General Comments are of wider significance than State reports given their extensive distribution both within and beyond the United Nations.[36] General Comments also alert States to the true nature of the obligations to be undertaken by them prior to becoming parties. Even if the composition of the Human Rights Committee is criticised from time to time for not being geographically representative, much of the content of General Comments is drawn from experience gained in the examination of State reports from diverse cultures and, if necessary, after consultation with experts. Since the content of each General Comment is debated extensively within the Human Rights Committee, and since General Comments cover issues that are well-settled and represent a form of 'judicial commitment',[37] it may be concluded that they have considerable value. General Comments also to some extent make up for the exclusion of any *actio popularis* claims under the Optional Protocol which might otherwise have generated statements of broader principle than individual communications.

The Human Rights Committee's function in reviewing State Reports and formulating General Comments is therefore seen as a particularly important supervisory tool, which provides a greater measure of continuity and uniformity in the treatment of particular issues than can be found in the examination of individual communications alone. However, it is also

---

[32] UN Doc. A/36/40 (1981), Annex VII, p. 107.

[33] CCPR/C/79Add.43 (1994), para. 20 (Tunisia).

[34] UN Doc. A/56/40 vol. 1 (2001), pp. 162–7, Annex III (Consolidated Guidelines for State reports under the International Covenant on Civil and Political Rights (as amended at the seventieth session, October–November 2000 (CCPR/C/GUI/Rev.2)), effective for all reports to be presented after 31 December 1999.

[35] UN Doc. A/49/40 (1994), p. 44, para. 242 (Jordan), and p. 58, para. 351 (Slovenia).

[36] N. Lerner, 'Religious Human Rights under the United Nations' in J. van der Vyver and J. Witte (eds.), *Religious Human Rights in Global Perspectives: Legal Perspectives*, The Hague/London: Martinus Nijhoff (1996).

[37] UN Doc. CCPR/C/133 (1997), p. 9, para. 57.

clear that the role of the Special Rapporteur on religious intolerance is a necessary complement to that of the Human Rights Committee given the inevitable reluctance on the part of States to highlight areas of non-compliance with Article 18 in their reports.

The Role of the Special Rapporteur

The Special Rapporteur was first appointed by the Commission on Human Rights in 1986 and given a specialist task (unlike the Human Rights Committee) to 'examine incidents and governmental actions inconsistent with the provisions of the Declaration on the Elimination of All Forms of Intolerance and of Discrimination Based on Religion or Belief, and to recommend remedial measures for such situations'.[38] The work of the Special Rapporteur is particularly valuable in supplementing some of the inherent deficiencies of the ICCPR reporting system noted above. It has been suggested that the 1981 Declaration might serve as a guide in measuring compliance with Article 18 of the ICCPR.[39] Certainly the Special Rapporteur makes frequent reference to General Comments of the Human Rights Committee. The critical difference between the roles of the Special Rapporteur and the Human Rights Committee obviously lies in the different bases of accountability though there is nothing to prevent the Human Rights Committee from utilising information provided by the Special Rapporteur to supplement information from State reports and Optional Protocol communications,[40]

---

[38] CHR Res. 1986/20, 42 UN ESCOR Supp. (No. 2) at 66, UN Doc. E/CN.4/1986/65 (1986). The following have been appointed as Special Rapporteur: Mr Angelo d'Almeida Ribeiro (Portugal), 1986–93; Mr Abdelfattah Amor (Tunisia), 1993–2004; and Ms Asma Jahangir (Pakistan), 2004.

[39] United Nations Seminar on the Encouragement of Understanding, Tolerance and Respect in Matters Relating to Freedom of Religion or Belief, UN Doc. ST/HR/SER. A/16 (1984), para. 93.

[40] Optional Protocol material has been used extensively in order to complete the inadequate information provided by Uruguay in its reports, as pointed out by Boerefijn: Boerefijn, *The Reporting Procedure under the Covenant*, p. 211. It has been maintained by some that the Human Rights Committee (unlike the Special Rapporteur) does not have fact-finding competence. Schwelb has suggested that the Human Rights Committee is not authorised to use any material other than State reports (E. Schwelb, 'Civil and Political Rights: the International Measures of Implementation', 62 Am J Int'l L (1968) 827, at 843). However, Boerefijn, *The Reporting Procedure under the Covenant*, p. 210 cites the Committee's Report on the Informal Meetings Procedures (CCPR/C/133, para. 9) to conclude that Committee members are now positively encouraged to broaden the range of information provided by States to include that provided by non-governmental sources. The Special Rapporteur draws from information from a wider range of sources than the governments concerned,

including examples of non-co-operation with the Special Rapporteur.[41] In reality, there is very little interaction between the Human Rights Committee and the different special rapporteurs.

The Special Rapporteur is entrusted with limited powers. According to van Boven,[42] the Special Rapporteur cannot do more than 'expect' a dialogue with countries under enquiry. Nevertheless, '[t]he common expectation is that these supervisory efforts will foster more tolerance for people holding different religions and beliefs and bring about better ways of life in a spirit of peace and justice'.[43]

The European Convention treaty organs

The merger of the functions of the European Court and European Commission into a single Court effected by Protocol 11[44] was aimed

particularly from non-governmental organisations, and assumes a more specialist role in that only certain aspects of the ICCPR are within his purview.

[41] See for example the questioning of Niger over its non-co-operation with the special rapporteur on summary and arbitrary executions (UN Doc. CCPR/C/SR. 1208 (1993), p. 5 para. 20.

[42] van Boven, 'Advances and Obstacles' 437.

[43] *Ibid.*, at 446. The Special Rapporteur's role has been wide-ranging. For example, the Special Rapporteur has long recognised that the school, as an essential element in the educational system, may also constitute a fertile and highly suitable terrain for lasting progress in the area of tolerance and non-discrimination in matters of religion or belief, and conducted a survey supported by CHR Res. 1995/23 of problems relating to freedom of religion and belief from the standpoint of the curricula and textbooks of primary or elementary and secondary educational institutions (UN Doc. E/CN.4/1998/6 (1998), para. 33). In November 2001, The International Consultative Conference on School Education in Relation to Freedom of Religion or Belief, Tolerance and Non-discrimination convened in Madrid to consider a strategy as a preventive measure in the curricula of primary or elementary and secondary schools (for a summary, see UN Doc. A/56/253 (2001), pp. 31–4, paras. 107–21). See also CHR Res. 1998/21, entitled 'Tolerance and pluralism as indivisible elements in the promotion and protection of Human Rights'.

[44] Protocol 11 to the European Convention on Human Rights and Fundamental Freedoms (1994), 155 ETS, opened for signature on 11 May 1994. For further discussion on the effectiveness of the European Convention mechanisms, see Council of Europe, *In Our Hands, The Effectiveness of Human Rights Protection 50 Years after the Universal Declaration*, Strasbourg: Council of Europe Press (1998). For further detail concerning Protocol 11, see: R. Bernhardt, 'Current Developments – Reform of Control Machinery under the European Convention on Human Rights: Protocol 11', 89 Am J Int'l L (1995) 145; A. Drzemczewski and J. Meyer-Ladewig, 'Principal Characteristics of the New European Convention on Human Rights Mechanism, as established by Protocol 11, signed on 11th May, 1994', 15 HRLJ (1994) 81; H. Schermers, 'The Eleventh Protocol to the European Convention on Human Rights', 19 Eur L Rev (1994) 367; A. R. Mowbray, 'A New European Court of Human Rights', PL (1994) 540. Mowbray comments on the facets of negotiation in reaching the final text of Protocol 11 and provides a useful summary of the changes associated with the new Court.

at enhancing confidence in a system which had begun to suffer from undercapacity and extensive delays as a result of the escalating number of applications received both by the European Commission and the European Court.[45] Until 31 October 1998 the European Commission was able to make a determination that a claim was inadmissible (under Articles 25 and 26 of the European Convention) or, as a means of eliminating claims with no merit, determine the claim to be manifestly ill-founded or an abuse of the right of petition even if technically admissible (Article 27). After that date, the European Commission was effectively replaced by a new Court. The Court assumed the European Commission's previous function in determining issues both of admissibility and merit, through Committees comprising three judges (to determine admissibility according to the pre-existing criteria) and through Chambers (to determine admissibility if the Committee does not reach a unanimous admissibility decision, and to determine separately the merits of the claim).[46] Serious issues of interpretation may be transferred by the Committee (if a party does not object) to the Grand Chamber,[47] which also acts as an ultimate appeal forum for the parties in exceptional cases for hearing serious questions of interpretation and consistency in the application of the Convention, as well as serious issues of general importance.[48] The Court also assumed the European Court's earlier function of providing advisory opinions and the European Commission's role in facilitating the amicable settlement of claims. At the same time, the powers of the politically-oriented Committee of Ministers of the Council of Europe, to make a binding decision on the issue of substantive breach of a European Convention provision, was abolished and its function is now confined to the implementation of the Court's judgments. Although Article 45 requires reasons for judgments and inadmissibility decisions to be given, the Explanatory Report[49] supports the previous practice of providing summary reasoning. Although this will expedite the handling of claims, it has led to a certain amount of confusion in the interpretation of Article 9. Accordingly, it is suggested that summary reasoning should be applied with care by the Court.

---

[45] D. J. Harris, M. O'Boyle and C. Warbrick, *Law of the European Convention on Human Rights*, London: Butterworths (1995), pp. 706–14.

[46] Article 29(1).   [47] Article 30.   [48] Article 43.

[49] *The Explanatory Report to the Eleventh Protocol*, Council of Europe, pp. 5–17 (reprinted in 17 EHRR 514 (1994) at para. 105). See also Harris, O'Boyle and Warbrick, *Law of the European Convention*, pp. 360–2.

Throughout this work, unless otherwise stated, mention of the
European Commission or the European Court in decision-making
before 1 November 1998 should be taken as a reference to each respective body as it functioned before that date, and mention of the European
Court in decisions made after that date should be taken as a reference to
the newly constituted European Court.

Under the European Convention there is no direct equivalent to
Article 2 of the ICCPR (beyond the broad reference in Article 1 that
Parties 'shall secure' Convention rights and freedoms to everyone within
their jurisdiction). The supervisory function of the Human Rights
Committee only has limited counterpart in the role of the Secretary
General under Article 52 (formerly Article 57) of the European
Convention and in the newly established European Commissioner for
Human Rights.[50] Little use has been made of the Secretary General's
powers to request States to furnish explanations of the manner in which
domestic law achieves effective implementation of Convention obligations, with only a handful of such requests ever having been made. The
creation of the office of Commissioner for Human Rights is welcomed
given the importance of the task of enhancing dialogue with States.[51]
However, arguably the most effective monitoring of religious liberty
issues in Europe is provided by means of non-treaty organs, most
notably the OSCE,[52] spanning Europe (other than Albania), the
United States and Canada where the norms established by participating
States 'are not legal norms, but political ones'.[53]

---

[50] Resolution (99) 50 (1999) adopted by the Committee of Ministers on 7 May 1999 at
104th session, Budapest. For further discussion on the need for such a role, see
M. O'Boyle, 'Reflections on the Effectiveness of the European System for the Protection
of Human Rights' in A. F. Bayefsky (ed.), *The UN Human Rights Treaty System in the 21st
Century*, The Hague/London: Kluwer Law International (2000), pp. 169–80.

[51] Note also that periodic reporting to the Committee of Ministers is provided for by Articles
24–6 of the Framework Convention for the Protection of National Minorities (Council of
Europe Framework Convention for the Protection of National Minorities (Strasbourg
1 February 1995, in force 2 January 1998), 34 ILM (1995) 351). For an explanatory report
on the Framework Convention, see 2(1) IHRR (1995) 225.

[52] See: T. Buergenthal, 'The CSCE and the Promotion of Racial and Religious Tolerance',
22 Isr YB Hum Rts (1992) 31; D. McGoldrick, 'The Development of the CSCE after the
Helsinki 1992 Conference', 42 Int'l & Comp Law Q (1993) 411.

[53] J. Helgesen, 'Between Helsinki and Beyond' in A. Rosas, J. Helgesen and D. Gomien
(eds.), *Human Rights in a Changing East–West Perspective*, London: Pinter (1990),
p. 261. For the effectiveness of OSCE monitoring mechanisms, see: A. Bloed, 'The
OSCE and the Issue of National Minorities' in A. Phillips and A. Rosas (eds.),

Chapter structure

This work is divided into three core chapters. Chapter 2 ('Freedom of religious choice') and Chapter 3 ('The scope of the *forum internum* beyond religious choice') are closely related in that they both attempt to discern the true reach of the unrestricted *forum internum*, as distinct from the external right of manifestation which is considered in detail in Chapter 4 ('The right to manifest religious belief and applicable limitations'). The architecture of all core freedom of religion Articles makes the same inescapable and immutable distinction between the unrestricted *forum internum* and the right to external manifestation. It is for this reason that it is vital to know precisely where the boundaries of each are to be drawn. The *forum internum* is taken to denote the internal and private realm against which no State interference is justified in any circumstances, while the *forum externum*, or right of manifestation, may be restricted by the State on specified grounds. The focus of Chapter 2 is on the right to freedom of religious choice. Chapter 3 considers the true extent of the remaining rights comprised within the *forum internum*, by reference to the various means by which those rights have been recognised.

Chapter 2 therefore introduces discussion on the scope of the *forum internum* with what is commonly accepted as the unrestricted freedom of religious choice. The chapter begins with the origins of the text found in Article 18(2) of the ICCPR (guaranteeing freedom from coercion that would interfere with that choice). Article 18(2) may be regarded as adding little to the substantive freedom of choice until it is appreciated from the *travaux préparatoires* of the ICCPR that the purpose of its initial inclusion was to provide a counterpart to the express right to change religion, by offering a right to maintain a previous choice of religion. Concerns that this might justify coercive measures to maintain an existing religion when an individual wished to change it led to the amendment of Article 18(2) so as to preserve the individual's choice,

Universal Minority Rights, London: Minority Rights Group (International) (1995); A. Bloed, 'Monitoring the CSCE Human Dimension: In Search of its Effectiveness' in A. Bloed et al. (eds.), *Monitoring Human Rights in Europe*, Dordrecht/London: Martinus Nijhoff in co-operation with the Helsinki Federation for Human Rights (1993); S. Kandelia, *Implementing the OSCE's Human Dimension Since 1995*, Papers in the Theory and Practice of Human Rights, No. 26, London: University of Essex, Human Rights Centre (1999); Karen S. Lord, 'What Does Religious Liberty in the OSCE Mean in Practice?' 5(2) *OSCE Bulletin* (1997) 9.

rather than to justify any coercive measure that may undermine that choice. Chapter 2 will discuss whether proselytism and missionary work constitute coercion and whether Article 18(2) is the anti-proselytism measure which it is commonly considered to be. The European Court has been confronted with the issue of religious choice primarily in relation to State restrictions on proselytism (in Greece). Relatively little attention has been given to the importance of religious choice (or United Nations debates on proselytism and religious choice) in the decision-making of the European Court. The Court accepted that proselytism is an acceptable manifestation of religion or belief that may take the form of bearing witness to one's faith. The Court also observed the possibility that proselytism could take 'improper' forms. However, the Court used the mere possibility of the existence of extreme and corrupt forms of proselytism to support State claims that a legitimate aim was pursued by more general restrictions on proselytism, namely the protection of 'the rights and freedoms of others'. The scope of this limitation ground is an issue which spans all chapters. It will be argued that a narrow construction of 'the rights and freedoms of others' is generally appropriate in the case of proselytism, to protect against coercion that would deprive the individual of free religious choice.

Freedom from coercion in Article 18(2) of the ICCPR is limited to issues of impairment of religious choice without extending more generally to coercion to act contrary to one's religion or belief. Broader principles of coercion are taken up in Chapter 3 in an attempt to define the controversial scope of the *forum internum* beyond the issue of religious choice. It is widely taken to include freedom from certain forms of coercion to act contrary to one's beliefs, freedom from being required to reveal one's beliefs, and protection against the imposition of penalties for holding particular beliefs. Chapter 3 therefore begins by addressing the limits of coercion permitted in the exercise of recognised State functions (for example, in raising taxes and implementing a defence policy) and coercion resulting from the voluntary assumption of employment obligations. Following a long period of reluctance by both the European and United Nations organs to admit that compulsion to act contrary to one's beliefs raises issues of conscience, recent developments suggest that recognition is emerging for the conscientious implications of certain forms of coercion. Claims based on coercion have historically been shoe-horned awkwardly into the framework of manifestation (and justifiable State restriction on manifestation) so as to admit essential State compulsion in the implementation of general tax, pension and military policies. In spite of developments that suggest this early approach has been revised, a survey of United Nations and European standards does not reflect a coherent pattern of protection for the *forum internum* that enables the individual to resist compulsion to act contrary to belief and, indeed, the other facets of the *forum internum* do not appear to be consistently developed. Inappropriate support is still often given by the European Court to State reliance on limitation provisions without an easily identifiable form of manifestation underpinning such analysis. This is less evident in the practice of the Human Rights Committee.

Chapter 3 also separately examines the less obvious or indirect sources of protection for the *forum internum*, such as the generous interpretation given by the European Court to the limitation ground 'the rights and freedoms of others', which suggests, for example, that there exists a right within Article 9 of the Convention to 'respect' for one's religious beliefs or feelings. Such a right, if it exists at all, must fall primarily within the *forum internum* since it cannot readily take the form of manifestation. The European Court's willingness to extend a limitation ground to embrace a *forum internum* right that is not well recognised contrasts starkly with the Court's hesitancy to render protection to certain better established *forum internum* rights. The practice of the Court suggests a sustained preference for analysis based on manifestation (rather than *forum internum* rights) in order to admit the application of limitation provisions as claimed by States. There is therefore a close interrelation between the *forum internum* rights discussed in Chapters 2 and 3 and the analysis to be undertaken of issues of manifestation and justifiable limitations covered in Chapter 4.

Discussion concerning different forms of manifestation of religion or belief in Chapter 4 continues with a detailed examination of the individual's right to manifest religion or belief in worship, teaching, practice or observance, with particular attention to the permissible limitations that may be imposed by States. There is a danger that the principles developed within the particular context of each decision might be over-generalised where, for example, the need for discipline and order in prison or military institutions, or even the need for respect for parental convictions in education, allow greater restriction on rights of manifestation than would otherwise be justified. The threshold for upholding limitation provisions might be perceived as unduly low and the recognition of different forms of manifestation undeveloped unless the environment in which individual decisions were made is taken into consideration. Inevitably the issues raised by individual petitions before the European institutions and the Human Rights Committee are limited in scope and arise in specific circumstances, so there is much to be gained from a thematic analysis of the widest range of relevant sources in order to allow general principle to emerge above the individual background of each decision. Also, many early decisions are unreliable. In any event, it is clear that individual decisions alone offer an incomplete representation of current standards, particularly those of the Human Rights Committee which are few in number (compared with those of the European institutions) and span a relatively confined range of subject matter. It is only by evaluating United Nations and European sources side-by-side that a more complete evaluation may be made of substantive differences between UN and European organs in practice and standard-setting.

This task is greatly facilitated by the work of the Special Rapporteur under the mandate given in connection with the 1981 Declaration. Although neither the Human Rights Committee nor any of the European institutions is strictly bound to pay regard to the 1981 Declaration, the rich variety of illustrations of incompatibility worldwide offers a perspective which is frequently lacking in individual decisions and could usefully serve to warn decision-makers of the contemporary challenges to religious freedom in emerging global patterns. The use of the Special Rapporteur's material wherever possible in this work therefore provides greater practical context for each issue under consideration. This is particularly important for identifying recognised forms of manifestation of religion or belief, isolated from issues that bear on the appropriateness of State restriction in particular circumstances. Article 6 of the 1981 Declaration offers a detailed list of various forms of manifestation going well beyond the condensed formula of 'teaching, practice, worship and observance' found in Article 9 of the European Convention and Article 18 of the ICCPR. The Special Rapporteur's reports help to cultivate an awareness of the significance of various forms of manifestation across the full spectrum of religions and assist the better appreciation of rights which may seem unimportant purely in the European context. However, even Article 6 of the 1981 Declaration cannot be regarded as comprehensive and must be supplemented by other sources so that, for example, the omission from Article 6 of any explicit reference to the wearing of religious apparel was made good by General Comment No. 22. This work aims to pay tribute to the specialist mandate of the Special Rapporteur, which is often underestimated in theoretical approaches to freedom of religion.

One further aim of this work, in view of the inherent limitations of any scheme for protecting religious freedom, is to evaluate the striking conclusion reached by Lillich on Article 18 of the Universal Declaration that, 'one is forced to acknowledge that the right of religious freedom, is one of the weakest – from the point of view of its recognition and its enforcement – of all the rights contained in articles 3–18 of the Universal Declaration'.[54] This conclusion is alarming given that it has been maintained by some that the 'twentieth century is pre-eminently the century of religious persecution'.[55]

---

[54] R. B. Lillich, 'Civil Rights' in T. Meron (ed.), *Human Rights in International Law: Legal and Policy Issues*, Oxford: Clarendon Press (1984), at p. 160.

[55] G. Weigel, 'Religion as a Human Right', 77 *Freedom at Issue* (1984) 3.

2

Freedom of religious choice

Introduction

The focus of this chapter is principally that part of the *forum internum* concerned with the freedom of each individual to choose a particular religion, to maintain adherence to a religion or to change religion altogether at any time, and the right to be free from restrictions or coercive forces that impair that choice. Personal choice in such matters is unrestricted for reasons of principle and because of the impossibility of providing otherwise. Pfeffer had this in mind when commenting, 'as the common-law adage has it, the devil himself knows not the thoughts of man'.[1] Similarly, as Krishnaswami noted, '[f]reedom to maintain or to change religion or belief falls primarily within the domain of the inner faith and conscience of an individual. Viewed from this angle, one would assume that any intervention from outside is not only illegitimate but impossible.'[2]

Nevertheless, the right to freedom of choice of religion or belief has been one of the most controversial and contested aspects of the right to freedom of thought, conscience or religion. The different formulations of the freedom found in United Nations texts reflect differences in emphasis and intention between those States, on the one hand, which sought unrestricted freedom for the individual to change religion (without considering it necessary to contemplate a right to 'maintain' a religion) and, on the other hand, those for whom a right to maintain religion was paramount.

The drafting history of Article 18 of the Universal Declaration on Human Rights ('Universal Declaration') and of the International

---

[1] L. Pfeffer, *Religious Freedom*, Skokie: National Textbook Company for the American Civil Liberties Union (1977), at p. 33.

[2] A. Krishnaswami, *Study of Discrimination in the Matter of Religious Rights and Practices*, UN Doc. E/CN.4/Sub.2/200/Rev.1 (1960), reprinted in 11 NYUJ Int'l L & Pol (1978) 227, at 231.

Covenantion on Civil and Political Rights ('ICCPR') is particularly important to understand because the freedom from coercion as expressed in Article 18(2) of the ICCPR (and in its counterpart in Article 1(2) of the Declaration on the Elimination of all Forms of Intolerance and of Discrimination Based on Religion or Belief (the 1981 Declaration)) is often misunderstood as justifying measures against the propagation of religion. For example, it has been suggested by Partsch that the purpose of inclusion of the words, 'the freedom to have or to adopt a religion or belief of his choice' in Article 18(2) of the ICCPR was to protect against zealous proselytisers and missionaries.[3] Such protection was certainly one of a number of reasons proposed for the inclusion of Article 18(2), though one that was not widely accepted. Among other reasons for opposing an explicit right to change religion were concerns about the political and social dimensions of a change of religion, as well as its doctrinal implications. However, States that advocated the widest scope for the freedom to change religion were more likely to treat as coercive any measures directed at maintaining an individual's religion and were more inclined to consider proselytism as an integral part of the practice or manifestation of religion, if not an enabling factor in promoting fuller choice of religion.

Consistent with this latter interpretation of Article 18(2) is the Human Rights Committee's General Comment No. 22,[4] paragraph 5, which illustrates coercive measures by reference principally to matters falling within the State's function and makes no reference at all to private sources of proselytism as coercive. Nothing in General Comment No. 22 seems to equate proselytism with coercion. In addition, some have argued that the appropriate conditions for complete freedom of choice of religion are met by a prevailing culture of tolerance that permits, rather than prohibits, exposure to different religious disciplines. Dickson[5] notes that the emphasis given in the ICCPR is positive in extending the freedom to have or to adopt a religion or belief of choice to the prohibition on coercion which would interfere with this freedom, because Article 18 not only prohibits States from interfering

---

[3] K. J. Partsch, 'Freedom of Conscience and Expression, and Political Freedoms in L. Henkin (ed.), *The International Bill of Rights: The Covenant on Civil and Political Rights*, New York/Guildford: Columbia University Press (1981), at p. 211.

[4] General Comment No. 22 (48), UN Doc. CCPR/C/21/Rev.1/Add.4 (1993). The text of General Comment No. 22 is at Annex 5.

[5] B. Dickson, 'The United Nations and Freedom of Religion', 44 Int'l & Comp Law Q (1995) 327.

with the individual's freedom of religion but also requires States to create appropriate conditions to allow for the full enjoyment of the freedom.[6]

In reality, there remains uncertainty as to what precisely constitutes coercion under Article 18(2) of the ICCPR and, as Sullivan observes, the wording of the 1981 Declaration similarly does not elucidate what conduct, conditions or forms of communication would constitute coercion.[7] Nowhere is the term 'coercion' defined. There is therefore much to be gained from a close examination of the preparatory works of the United Nations instruments in which such issues were debated at length.

The text of Article 9 of the European Convention for the Protection of Human Rights and Fundamental Freedoms ('European Convention') does not include a provision equivalent to Article 18(2) since it was drawn from Article 18 of the Universal Declaration without being shaped by the same concerns that initially led to proposals for Article 18(2) of the ICCPR. The European Court has considered the issue of coercion in the context of State restrictions on proselytism (notably in *Kokkinakis v. Greece*)[8] and found that a legitimate aim was pursued by those restrictions on the basis of the limitation ground 'the protection of the rights and freedoms of others'. Precisely what rights and freedoms of others are at issue remains unclear although it may be argued that what is contemplated is that part of the *forum internum* concerning religious choice and freedom from coercion that would impede religious choice. This would be consistent with Article 18(2). However, there is some ambiguity in the way in which the European Court approached proselytism. If 'the protection of the rights and freedoms of others' in Article 9 is to be construed more broadly than protection for that part of the *forum internum* concerning religious choice (and freedom from coercion that would impede religious choice), the European Court's approach could support the purported aim of a wide range of State restrictions on proselytism that at this stage is indeterminate. This has serious implications for all religions which disseminate their beliefs. Added to this is a recent development in the

---

[6] *Ibid.*, at 341.

[7] D. J. Sullivan, 'Advancing the Freedom of Religion or Belief through the UN Declaration of the Elimination of Religious Intolerance and Discrimination', 82 Am J Int'l L (1988) 487. For discussion on those acts likely to amount to coercion, see the Human Rights Committee debates on General Comment No. 22, UN Doc. CCPR/C/SR. 1166 (1992), pp. 11–14, paras. 76–97.

[8] *Kokkinakis v. Greece* (Ser. A) No. 260–A (1993) ECtHR.

practice of the European Court when deciding whether restrictions on freedom of expression under Article 10 pursue a legitimate aim. The European Court appears to be prepared to give undue breadth to the notion of the 'protection of the ... rights of others' (as provided in Article 10) on the basis that Article 9 contains a right to 'respect for the religious feelings of believers'.[9] Article 9 does not, on its face, include any such right and subsequent decisions suggest that this approach is misplaced.[10] No such right is recognised at United Nations level. The consequence of this approach would be inconsistency between United Nations and European standards and a potential curb on proselytism going well beyond the need to protect against coercion.

One way in which to avoid an incongruous gap between Universal and European standards would be for the European Court to address proselytism and other aspects of religious choice in full view of the historic development of United Nations instruments and emerging United Nations practice, conscious of all the challenges to religious freedom that are posed in the Universal arena. Given the range of obstacles to the advancement of standards at Universal level, the European Court has opened itself to criticism for its developing juris-prudence under Articles 9 and 10. This chapter will offer a basis for interpreting European decisions in such a way as to allow for the consistent development of European jurisprudence in line with Universal standards.

Freedom to change or maintain religion

Human rights instruments differ subtly, but critically, in the drafting which defines the scope of an individual's freedom to change or main-tain a religion. Article 18 of the Universal Declaration expressly states that the right to freedom of thought, conscience and religion 'includes freedom to change his religion or belief'.[11] This phrase was repeated in the text of Article 9 of the European Convention. Although such an explicit right to change religion in the Universal Declaration was opposed by certain Middle-Eastern countries,[12] their efforts to delete it

---

[9] *Otto-Preminger-Institut v. Austria* (Ser. A) No. 295–A (1994) ECtHR, para. 47.

[10] *Wingrove v. United Kingdom* (1997) 24 EHRR 1.

[11] For the Third Committee debates on the Universal Declaration, see UN Doc. A/C.3/3/SR. 127 (1948).

[12] For further discussion, see O. El Hajje, 'Islamic Countries and the International Instruments on Human Rights', 3(1) Con & Lib (1991) 46.

did not avail until in the drafting of the ICCPR Islamic nations sought a shift in the balance in Article 18 away from freedom to change religion towards greater emphasis on freedom to maintain a religion.[13] The resulting text of the ICCPR reflects various compromises to accommodate this, although in such a way as to avoid permanence in the choice of religion (suggested by freedom to 'maintain' or to 'have' a religion). Article 18(1) of the ICCPR ultimately includes the text: 'This right shall include freedom to have or to adopt a religion or belief of his choice'. As a result of continued opposition from Middle-Eastern countries in the drafting of the 1981 Declaration to delete freedom to 'change one's religion', and the implication that it is repeated within the wording 'or to adopt',[14] and in the face of pressure from Soviet countries for greater emphasis on atheistic belief, the text of Article 1 of the 1981 Declaration refers instead to 'freedom to have a religion or whatever belief of his choice'. However, given an ostensible slackening of Universal standards and in order to prevent the 1981 Declaration being interpreted as changing any previous United Nations instruments, it was necessary to add the saver in Article 8.[15] Those who resisted a different version from that in Article 18 of the ICCPR conceded in order that the draft could win more widespread acceptance, but only on the understanding that the Article as amended was still

[13] For drafting reports of the Commission, see: UN Doc. E/CN.4/SR. 116–17 (1949); UN Doc. E/CN.4/SR 161 (1950). For Third Committee debates on the ICCPR, see: UN Doc. A/C.3/5/SR. 288–290, 302, 306, 367 and 371 (1950–1); UN Doc. A/C.3/9/SR. 563–566 (1954); UN Doc. A/C.3/15/SR. 1021–1027 (1960).

[14] The text adopted by the Commission (Resolution 20 (XXXVII of 10 March 1981) and the Council (Resolution 1981/36 of 8 May 1981) included, in the preambular para. 2, reference to the right to change one's religion or belief, and, in Article I, reference to freedom to adopt a religion or belief of his choice. For reports of the Working Group appointed by the Commission concerning both the draft declaration and the draft convention on religious intolerance, see: UN Doc. E/CN.4/874 (1964); UN Doc. E/CN.4/891 (1965); UN Doc. E/CN.4/1154 (1974); UN Doc. E/CN.4/1179 (1975); UN Doc. E/CN.4/1213 (1976); UN Doc. E/CN.4/1257 (1977); UN Doc. E/CN.4/1292 (1978); UN Doc. E/CN.4/1347 (1979); UN Doc. E/CN.4/1408 (1980); UN Doc. E/CN.4/1475 (1981). For the Third Committee debates, see: UN Doc. A/C.3/22/SR. 1507–1510 (1967); UN Doc. A/C.3/28/SR. 2013 (1973); UN Doc. A/C.3/33/SR. 61 (1978); UN Doc. A/C.3/36/SR. 27–37 and 43 (1981).

[15] This reads: 'Nothing in the present Declaration shall be construed as restricting or derogating from any right defined in the Universal Declaration of Human Rights and the International Covenants on Human Rights.' This arose from a proposal made by the Byelorussian S.S.R. and a counter-proposal by the Netherlands (UN Doc. E/1981/25 (1981), p. 149, at p. 150).

understood to entitle everyone to have or adopt their religion of choice.[16]

By following the text of Article 18 of the Universal Declaration it is clear that Article 9 of the European Convention benefited from the successful inclusion of an express right to change religion which could not be repeated in later United Nations instruments.

Objections to the explicit right to change religion in Muslim countries were rooted in domestic laws (which either constitutionally adopted religious law or were inspired by it) and the implications that a change of religion would have in countries whose laws were religious in origin. The most sustained opposition to an express right to change religion was from the Saudi delegate (Mr Baroody), highlighting the importance of this issue to the Muslim world.[17] Although not specifically referring to matters of doctrine, various grounds were advanced for the deletion of the explicit right to change religion in the preparation of the ICCPR. First, it was superfluous since everybody had the right 'to maintain or to change his religion' at will and there seemed to be no point in placing stress on it.[18] Secondly, freedom of thought, conscience and religion was proclaimed but specific mention was only made of the right to change religion and not thought or conscience,[19] or even

[16] The Swedish delegate, for example, explained that Sweden had agreed to participate in the adoption of the draft declaration without a vote 'on the understanding that the declaration in no way restricted or derogated from the already established right to freedom of thought, conscience, religion or belief, including the right to choose and practise a religion or belief or to change it for another', UN Doc. A/C.3/36/SR. 43 (1981), p. 13, para. 77. For statements on adoption, see UN Doc. A/36/684 (1981), at 2–3, and for post-adoption statements, UN Doc. A/C.3/36/SR. 43 (1981) and UN Doc. A/36/PV.73 (1981). For a first-hand account of the Third Committee proceedings in the final drafting stages of the 1981 Declaration, see J. A. Walkate, 'The Right of Everyone to Change His Religion or Belief – Some Observations', 30 Neth Int'l L Rev (1983) 146. See also J. A. Walkate, 'The U. N. Declaration on the Elimination of All Forms of Intolerance and Discrimination Based on Religion or Belief (1981) – An Historical Overview', 1(2) Con & Lib (1989) 21.

[17] See, for example, statements made by the Saudi delegate in the context of the Universal Declaration: UN Doc. A/C.3/3/SR. 127 (1948) at pp. 403–4.

[18] UN Doc. A/C.3/5/SR. 289 (1950), p. 115, para. 42; UN Doc. A/C.3/9/SR. 563 (1954), p. 11, para. 11.

[19] UN Doc. A/C.3/5/SR. 289 (1950), p. 115, para. 42 (Saudi); UN Doc. A/C.3/9/SR. 563 (1954), p. 100, para. 11 (Saudi); UN Doc. A/C.3/9/SR. 566 (1954), p. 117, para. 34 (Saudi); UN Doc. A/C.3/15/SR. 1021 (1960), p. 197, para. 8 (Saudi) – similarly in the context of the Universal Declaration, see UN Doc. A/C.3/3/SR. 127 (1948), p. 391 (Saudi).

political opinions[20] – as if deliberately to avoid the undeniable contra-dictions between, for example, capitalist and communist philosophies.[21] Thirdly, the words, 'to maintain or to change' were incomplete and failed to address various states of mind in between.[22] It was the Afghan representative who openly stated the attitude of a Muslim country in giving his objections to Article 18 based on religious belief: 'Moslems permitted non-Moslems to become Moslems but did not allow Moslems to leave Islam.'[23]

The Saudi delegate explained later that his criticism of Article 18 had no connection with differences of opinion between Muslims about the interpretation of Koranic law, although he elaborated on the signifi-cance of Koranic law in the domestic jurisdiction of certain countries where it was the equivalent of a constitution and the Article would accordingly permit the interference in the domestic affairs of Muslim States.[24] Yemen also foresaw difficulties in achieving legislative compli-ance as required by the ICCPR given that national legislation was largely religious in origin and the Articles concerning freedom of religion and non-discrimination raised great difficulties for the Arab countries with regard to an express right to change religion, as well as non-discrimination in matters of marriage, divorce and inheritance.[25]

It was therefore argued that a text intended to affirm the individual's right to change religion would be more generally acceptable as long as it was not explicit,[26] even in such a country as Saudi which 'would be the last to deny the right to change one's religion'.[27] The Iraqi delegate

---

[20] UN Doc. A/C.3/5/SR. 306 (1950), p. 224, para. 47 (Saudi).

[21] UN Doc. A/C.3/9/SR. 563 (1954), p. 100, para. 11 (Saudi). See also in the context of the Universal Declaration UN Doc. A/C.3/3/SR. 127 (1948), p. 391 (Saudi).

[22] UN Doc. A/C.3/15/SR. 1023 (1960), p. 206, para. 12 (Saudi). For counter-arguments, see the comments of Pakistan, UN Doc. A/C.3/15/SR. 1024 (1960), p. 211, para. 25 (Pakistan).

[23] UN Doc. A/C.3/9/SR. 565 (1954), p. 108, para. 12 (Afghanistan).

[24] UN Doc. A/C.3/9/SR. 571 (1954), p. 145, para. 62 (Saudi).

[25] UN Doc. A/C.3/5/SR. 290 (1950), p. 122, para. 62 (1950) (Yemen). He concluded: 'It would be impossible to force a State to abandon traditional legislation which it had applied for centuries and which was known to be in conformity with the aspirations and needs of the people', *ibid.*, at para. 63.

[26] UN Doc. A/C.3/5/SR. 302 (1950), p. 203, para. 7 (Egypt).

[27] UN Doc. A/C.3/5/SR. 306 (1950), p. 224, para. 47 (Saudi). See also the comment of the Saudi delegate denying the accusation made by other delegations that those such as Saudi who did not agree to the inclusion of the words 'to maintain or to change' were opposed to changes in religion, 'That was not at all the case' – UN Doc. A/C.3/15/SR. 1025 (1960), p. 214, para. 9 (Saudi).

similarly considered an express right to change religion to be superfluous, not objectionable in principle and of universal application.[28]
Nevertheless, the inclusion of such an express right had earlier caused
Saudi to abstain from voting for the Universal Declaration altogether,[29]
and Egypt had only been able to vote in favour of its inclusion in the
Universal Declaration if Egypt's concerns about proclaiming freedom to
change religion appeared in the summary record.[30]

The Saudi proposal to delete from paragraph 1 of Article 18 of the
ICCPR the words 'to maintain or to change his religion or belief and
freedom'[31] was withdrawn in view of the Brazilian and Philippine
amendment substituting the words 'to maintain or to change his religion or belief' with 'to have a religion or belief of his choice'.[32] However,
this gave rise to concern, expressed by France, that a choice could not be
reversed and effectively became final or permanent,[33] until the compromise version proposed by the United Kingdom was generally accepted,
adding the words 'or to adopt' after 'to have'.[34] The idea of choice was
already present but the words 'or to adopt' would more clearly apply the
Article to those who did not already have a religion. In addition, it
overcame the static connotation highlighted by France. Accordingly,
Article 18(1) of the ICCPR came to include the words: 'This right shall
include freedom to have or to adopt a religion or belief of his choice'.

There is little doubt that in spite of the immense struggle over the
drafting of Article 18(1) of the ICCPR, it embraces freedom on the part
of the individual at all times either to change or to maintain religious
belief or adherence. In voting in favour of the two-power amendment,
the Italian delegate was convinced that, with the addition of the words
'or to adopt', suggested by the United Kingdom representative, 'the right
to change one's religion or belief was now as much assured by the
amendments as by the text of the Commission on Human Rights'.[35]

---

[28] UN Doc. A/C.3/9/SR. 577 (1954), p. 176, para. 9 (Iraq).
[29] UN Doc. A/C.3/6/SR. 367 (1951), p. 124, para. 41 (Saudi); UN Doc. A/C.3/9/SR. 566
(1954), p. 116, para. 34 (Saudi).
[30] UN Doc. A/PV/3/183 (1948), p. 913 (Egypt).   [31] UN Doc. A/C.3/L.876 (Saudi).
[32] The Philippine amendment read: 'This right shall include freedom to have a religion
of his choice ...' until Mrs Dembinska (Poland) pointed out the omission of
the words 'or belief' (UN Doc. A/C.3/15/SR. 1024 (1960), p. 211, para. 27) (Poland).
The joint proposal of the Philippines and Brazil (A/C.3/L877) corrected this – ibid., at
p. 210, para. 8.
[33] UN Doc. A/C.3/15/SR. 1026 (1960), p. 220, para. 7 (France).
[34] UN Doc. A/C.3/15/15/SR. 1027 (1960), p. 225, para. 2 (United Kingdom).
[35] UN Doc. A/C.3/15/15/SR. 1027 (1960), p. 226, para. 11 (Italy).

In reviewing the debates on the Universal Declaration and the ICCPR, Partsch commented that '[i]n the extended discussions, one element stands out as of utmost importance. No one who favoured deleting the express mention of the right to change one's religion denied that right'.[36] Even after further challenges in the preparation of the 1981 Declaration (discussed below), Benito suggests that in spite of the differences between the United Nations instruments, they 'all meant precisely the same thing: that everyone has the right to leave one religion or belief and to adopt another, or to remain without any at all'.[37] The Human Rights Committee has also construed Article 18 as if it contained an express right to change religion, consistent with Benito's view. Paragraphs 3 and 5 of General Comment No. 22 touch on the freedom to change religion or belief by affirming in paragraph 3 that Article 18 'does not permit any limitations whatsoever on the freedom of thought and conscience or on the freedom to have or adopt a religion or belief of one's choice. These freedoms are protected unconditionally, as is the right of everyone to hold opinions without interference in article 19(1)'.[38] In paragraph 5 of General Comment No. 22, the Human Rights Committee also 'observes that the freedom to "have or to adopt" a religion or belief necessarily entails the freedom to choose a religion or belief, including the right to replace one's current religion or belief with another or to adopt atheistic views, as well as the right to retain one's religion or belief'. This restates in effect the explicit language of Article 18 of the Universal Declaration, which had been reformulated in the ICCPR to avoid reference to freedom to change religion.

The importance of General Comment No. 22 is reinforced by the Human Rights Committee's requirement that States take into account the recommendations contained in it.[39] Furthermore, the Committee has referred to the issue of freedom to change religion in considering numerous State reports. For example, the Committee noted the

---

[36] Partsch, 'Freedom of Conscience and Expression,' p. 211.

[37] E. O. Benito, *Elimination of all Forms of Intolerance and Discrimination Based on Religion or Belief*, Human Rights Study Series No. 2, UN Sales No. E. 89. XIV.3, Geneva: United Nations Centre for Human Rights (1989), p. 4, para. 21.

[38] For an unusual recent communication see *Kang v. Korea*, Communication No. 878/1999 (views of 15 July 2003) UN Doc. A/58/40 vol. 2 (2003), p. 152. The use of a coercive 'oath of law-abidance system' by Korea with a view to altering the political opinion of a prison inmate by offering inducements of preferential treatment and improved possibilities of parole resulted in a finding of violation of Article 18 in conjunction with Article 26 (para. 7.2).

[39] See Chapter 1 under the heading 'The Human Rights Committee' (p. 14).

practical limitations in Jordan to the right to have or adopt a religion or belief of one's choice, which should include the freedom to change religion.[40] Members likewise asked Tunisia whether it was permissible for a person, including a Muslim, to change his religion.[41] Similarly concerns were expressed to Libya,[42] Iran[43] and Yemen.[44] The issue has not only arisen with Muslim countries. For example, the Committee has observed as a principal area of concern the excessive restrictions that apply in Nepal to changing religion.[45] The Human Rights Committee's interpretation of Article 18 of the ICCPR is therefore unequivocal.

Muslim countries appear to acknowledge tacitly ICCPR standards in relation to the right to change religion before the Human Rights Committee. The only clear objection has come from Sudan claiming that priority should be given to Islamic law over international standards when questioned about its laws of apostasy. In its concluding observations, the Human Rights Committee pointed out that many States in the Islamic world had participated in the drafting of the ICCPR and that if certain of its provisions had been deemed irreconcilable with Islamic law, States could have entered reservations but did not do so.[46] In fact no reservations to Article 18 were entered by any State.

The members of the Human Rights Committee who actively participated in the drafting of paragraph 5 of General Comment No. 22[47] represent a variety of States, including Muslim countries, yet not one voiced any opinion that stands contrary to the ultimate wording of that paragraph. They include Japan (Mr Ando), France (Ms Chanet), Yugoslavia (Mr Dimitrijević), Egypt (Mr El-Shafei), Austria (Mr Herndl), the United Kingdom (Ms Higgins), Mauritius (Mr Lallah), USSR (Mr Mullerson), Senegal (Mr Ndiaye), Ecuador (Mr Prado Vallejo), Jordan (Mr Sadi) and Sweden (Mr Wennergren).

The Human Rights Committee has extended its concern over the right to religious choice to children as well as adults. For example, it asked Jordan whether a child of Muslim parents could change religion, and it was pointed out that if not, there might be some conflict with

---

[40] UN Doc. A/49/40 vol. 1 (1994), p. 43, para. 235 (Jordan).
[41] UN Doc. A/42/40 (1987), p. 36, para. 137 (Tunisia).
[42] UN Doc. A/50/40 vol. 1 (1996), p. 29, para. 135 (Libya).
[43] UN Doc. A/37/40 (1982), p. 71, para. 316 (Iran).
[44] UN Doc. A/57/40 vol. 1 (2002), p. 75, para. 83(20) (Yemen).
[45] UN Doc. A/50/40 vol. 1 (1996), p. 19, para. 70 (Nepal).
[46] UN Doc. A/46/40 (1991), p. 127, para. 517 (Sudan).
[47] UN Doc. CCPR/C/SR. 1166 (1992).

Article 18 of the Covenant,[48] and it noted that in Finland under the Act on Freedom of Religion, minors under the age of fifteen were obliged to be members of the religious community of their parents.[49] Similar questions on the age at which children could choose their religion were asked of Japan,[50] Barbados,[51] Jamaica[52] and Norway,[53] among others. The opportunity was not taken to mention in General Comment No. 22 the advances in the standards applicable to the rights of the child which had occurred since the drafting of the ICCPR through the United Nations Convention on the Rights of the Child.[54] Instead, although this subject was raised,[55] the nearest proposal (which was not ultimately adopted in General Comment No. 22) was that parents and guardians should give 'due regard' to the right of the child not to be subject to coercion in his or her religious education.[56] There does not appear to be any inconsistency between General Comment No. 22 and the Convention on the Rights of the Child since the latter makes rather limited provision in Article 14(1) for States to 'respect the right of the child to freedom of thought, conscience and religion' but otherwise places greater emphasis on the rights and duties of parents bearing in mind, as Article 14(2) puts it, the 'evolving capacities' of the child.[57] No instrument gives the child an explicit right to choose a religion.[58]

---

[48] UN Doc. A/37/40 (1982), p. 40, para. 180 (Jordan).

[49] UN Doc. A/41/40 (1986), p. 44, paras. 210–11 (Finland).

[50] UN Doc. A/37/40 (1982), p. 15, para. 70 (Japan).

[51] UN Doc. A/36/40 (1981), p. 35, para. 162 (Barbados).

[52] UN Doc. A/36/40 (1981), p. 57, para. 269 (Jamaica).

[53] UN Doc. A/36/40 (1981), p. 76, para. 359 (Norway).

[54] New York, 20 November 1989, in force 2 September 1990 (GA Res. 44/25 of 5 December 1989). For final text, see 28 ILM (1989) 1448. See generally, G. van Bueren, *The International Law on the Rights of the Child*, Dordrecht/London: Martinus Nijhoff (1998).

[55] UN Doc. CCPR/C/SR. 1207 (1993), p. 8, para. 47 (Mr Wennergren), and para. 50 (Mr Pocar).

[56] UN Doc. CCPR/C/SR. 1207 (1993), p. 9, para. 55 (Mr Dimitrijević).

[57] For commentary concerning freedom of religion and the Convention on the Rights of the Child, see B. G. Tahzib, *Freedom of Religion or Belief: Ensuring Effective International Legal Protection*, The Hague/London: Martinus Nijhoff Publishers (1996), pp. 99–105.

[58] Middle-eastern countries were generally opposed to the inclusion within the Convention on the Rights of the Child of any right of the child to choose a religion. For further detail see C. P. Cohen, 'Freedom of Religion or Belief: One of The Human Rights of Children', paper submitted at the conference on Building Understanding and Respect between People of Diverse Religions or Beliefs, Warsaw, 14–18 May 1989 (cited by Tahzib, *Freedom of Religion or Belief* p. 83) and C. P. Cohen, 'United Nations Convention on the Rights of the Child: Introductory Note', 44 Int'l Comm'n Jurists Rev (1990) 36.

Those provisions that do address the position of children confer rights on parents and guardians rather than on children themselves even if, in the case of the 1981 Declaration, the best interests of the child operate as the guiding principle in certain matters.[59]

The Human Rights Committee has therefore provided consistent guidance in its interpretation of the scope of the freedom to change religion or belief, and corrects any doubts that might have been introduced in the debates on Article 18 of the ICCPR.

The inclusion of an explicit right to change religion came under renewed opposition in the drafting of the 1981 Declaration, in which Article 1 represents the counterpart to Article 18(1) of the ICCPR, with two significant points of departure. The first is that instead of referring to 'freedom to have or to adopt a religion or belief of his choice', Article 1(1) refers to 'freedom to have a religion or whatever belief of his choice'. (Article 1(2) adopts a similar formula omitting the word 'whatever'). Pressure for this change came from Muslim countries appealing to arguments that were almost identical to those advanced in the debates on the equivalent provisions of the Universal Declaration and the ICCPR. The reference to 'the right to choose, manifest and change one's religion and belief' in paragraph 2 of the Preamble,[60] and the words 'or to adopt' in Article 1,[61] were not acceptable to those countries (and were deleted) given that the Koran forbids a Muslim to change religion.[62] (There were in fact surprisingly few public statements concerning the Muslim position. Most of the debate instead occurred in unofficial discussions. Such statements as there were criticised the United Nations for its secularism.)[63]

---

[59] For discussion in the preparation of the 1981 Declaration concerning a change of religion by children, see UN Doc. A/C.3/28/SR. 2010 (1973), p. 176, para. 22 (Morocco).

[60] Preamble, para. 2 reads: 'Considering that the Universal Declaration of Human Rights and the International Covenants on Human Rights proclaim the principles of non-discrimination and equality before the law and the right to freedom of thought, conscience, religion and belief, *including the right to choose, manifest and change one's religion or belief'* (emphasis added), UN Doc. E/1981/25 (1981), Annex, p. 150.

[61] Article 1(1) and (2) each included the phrase, 'freedom to have *or to adopt* a religion or belief of his choice' (emphasis added), *ibid.*, at p. 151.

[62] For further detail, see A. A. An-Na'im, 'Religious Minorities under Islamic Law and the Limits of Cultural Relativism', 9 HRQ (1987) 1.

[63] See the statement of Iran, UN Doc. A/C.3/36/SR. 29 (1981), p. 4, para. 11. For further commentary on the compromises reached during negotiation, see N. Lerner, 'The Final Text of the UN Declaration against Intolerance and Discrimination Based on Religion or Belief', 12 Isr YB. Hum Rts (1982) 185. In reference to text which included the words 'and change', the representative of Egypt proposed that they be omitted as they were already implicit in the words 'to choose' – UN Doc. E/CN.4/1292 (1978), p. 61, para. 27.

The right to 'have a religion or belief of his choice' was nevertheless acceptable to those Islamic countries most opposed to the words 'change' or 'adopt' (namely, Egypt, Iraq, Kuwait and Saudi) even though the phrase implies the right to change from any religion and the right to adopt a different religion from that previously held or to adopt a religion for the first time. Those countries which resisted a different version from that in Article 18 of the ICCPR agreed to compromise in order that the form of the draft could win more widespread acceptance throughout the Islamic world that was represented, but only on the understanding that the Article as amended still entitled everyone to have or adopt their religion of choice.

In order to prevent the 1981 Declaration being interpreted as changing any previous United Nations instruments and the norms subsequently established, Article 8 was added.[64] The origins of Article 8 are found in a Byelorrussian proposal made in the Working Group intended to avoid improvement upon the standards laid down in previous instruments[65] but the text was later adapted at the suggestion of Sweden to avoid a lowering of standards set in previous instruments.[66] Article 8 merely preserves the Universal Declaration and the twin Covenants,[67] from any interpretation that restricts or derogates from the rights they enshrine.[68] As Walkate put it, Article 8 'underlines the validity of the rights defined in the Universal Declaration and the Covenants'.[69]

---

[64] See n. 15 above.

[65] 'Nothing in this, or any other, article of the Declaration shall be interpreted as affecting, modifying or adding to the provisions of the International Covenant on Civil and Political Rights or any other international instrument relating to the elimination of all forms of intolerance and of discrimination based on religion or belief.' The Netherlands responded with the proposal: 'There shall be no restriction upon and derogation from any of the provisions of the International Covenant on Civil and Political Rights or any other international instrument relating to the elimination of all forms of intolerance and of discrimination based on religion or belief on the pretext that the present declaration does not recognize such rights or that it recognizes them to a lesser extent' UN Doc. E/1981/25 (1981), pp. 149–50.

[66] The compromise was accepted provided that the Declaration was not, as a matter of procedure, required to be put to the vote in the Third Committee.

[67] The ICCPR and the International Covenant on Economic, Social and Cultural Rights (1966).

[68] As to the normative character of the 1981 Declaration, see T. Meron, *Human Rights Law-Making in the United Nations: A Critique of Instruments and Process*, Oxford: Clarendon Press (1986), pp. 153–4.

[69] Walkate, 'The Right of Everyone to Change His Religion' 146, at 155.

In the conclusions and recommendations to the 1997 report, the Special Rapporteur focused on the right to change religion confirming for the purposes of that mandate that this right is absolute. He cited Article 18 of the Universal Declaration and then, while acknowledging that the ICCPR and the International Convention on the Elimination of all forms of Racial Discrimination (1965) do not explicitly restate the right to change religion found in the Universal Declaration, added that they nevertheless follow in the direction set by it. The omission of an express statement of the right to change religion in the 1981 Declaration,

> 'cannot be taken as betokening an intention to dilute the provisions of 1948 Declaration ... The variety of formulations used to refer to the acknowledgement and development of religious freedom do not amount to a denial of the right to change religion ... It is now established that religious freedom cannot be dissociated from the freedom to change religion ... The Special Rapporteur therefore emphasizes once again the right to change religion as a legally essential aspect of religious freedom.'[70]

In earlier reports, the Special Rapporteur cited as an example of legislation aimed at preventing a change of religion Article 306 of the Mauritanian Penal Code of 1983 by which any Muslim who abandons his faith and does not repent within three days is liable to the death sentence.[71] Allegations of a range of restrictions against a change of religion have been communicated to Indonesia,[72] Iran,[73] Sudan,[74] Kazakhstan,[75] Pakistan,[76] and Algeria.[77] Unusual restrictions were found to exist in Mexico when at least 454 members of various Protestant communities and Catholics of the San Juan Chamula municipality were reportedly expelled by force for having abandoned the Chamula religion and converted to Christianity.[78] The Special Rapporteur also reported on a variety of measures taken in the following countries: Azerbaijan,

---

[70] UN Doc. E/CN.4/1997/91 (1997), paras. 73–80.
[71] UN Doc. E/CN.4/1990/46 (1990), p. 26, para. 60 (Mauritania). See also UN Doc. E/CN.4/1990/46 (1990), p. 26, para. 59 (Malaysia).
[72] UN Doc. E/CN.4/2000/65 (2000), para. 50 (Indonesia).
[73] UN Doc. E/CN.4/1999/58 (1999), para. 66 (Iran).
[74] UN Doc. E/CN.4/1999/58 (1999), para. 96 (Sudan).
[75] UN Doc. E/CN.4/2000/65 (2000), para. 60 (Kazakhstan).
[76] UN Doc. E/CN.4/2000/65 (2000), para. 79 (Pakistan).
[77] UN Doc. E/CN.4/2003/66/Add.1 (2003), p. 16, para. 81 (Algeria).
[78] UN Doc. E/CN.4/1995/91 (1994), p. 62 (Mexico). See also UN Doc. E/CN.4/2001/63 (2001), p. 28, para. 100 (Mexico).

where a recently converted Jehovah's Witness had been arrested and threatened with deportation if he did not give up his belief;[79] India, following attacks on Christian leaders by Hindu militants, which resulted in local police arresting nine Christians on charges of converting Hindus;[80] Bhutan, where it was alleged that Christians were compelled to fill in forms about the circumstances of their conversion and threatened with expulsion from the country if they refused to abandon the Christian faith;[81] the Lao People's Democratic Republic, where it was alleged that twelve Christians were detained for not signing a statement that they 'would stop following Christ';[82] and Viet Nam, where several Montagnards were allegedly forced to denounce their faith in front of other villagers.[83]

In short, the Special Rapporteur has interpreted the 1981 Declaration in such a way that, consistent with the Human Rights Committee's interpretation of Article 18 of the ICCPR, an express right to change religion is imputed in spite of any counter-suggestion from its ambiguous wording.

Consistent with the above interpretation of United Nations instruments, countries of the Organization for Security and Co-operation in Europe (OSCE) affirmed in the Copenhagen Concluding Document of 1990 that, 'everyone will have the right to freedom of thought, conscience and religion. This right includes freedom to change one's religion or belief'.[84] It was as a result of the follow-up meetings of 1992 and 1994 in Helsinki and Budapest that a series of Human Dimension

---

[79] UN Doc. E/CN.4/2000/65 (2000), para. 13 (Azerbaijan).

[80] UN Doc. E/CN.4/2000/65 (2000), para. 47 (India). In Orissa State the Government reportedly adopted an order in the form of an amendment to the Freedom of Religion Act, prohibiting all conversions without prior authorisation from the local police and the district magistrate (UN Doc. E/CN.4/2001/63 (2001), p. 18, para. 53 (India)). India replied that only an intimation is required by way of prior information to the district magistrate. The purpose of the amended rule is to restrict forcible, unlawful, immoral and fraudulent inducement for conversion (UN Doc. E/CN.4/2001/63 (2001), p. 19, para. 54 (India)). See also UN Doc. E/CN.4/2004/63 (2004), p. 12, para. 60 (India).

[81] UN Doc. A/57/274 (2002), p. 11, para. 59 (Bhutan), UN Doc. E/CN.4/2002/73 (2002), para. 68 (Bhutan).

[82] UN Doc. E/CN.4/2004/63 (2004), p. 15, para. 81 (Lao People's Democratic Republic). See also E/CN.4/2005/61/Add. 1 (2005), p. 41, para. 163 (Lao People's Democratic Republic).

[83] UN Doc. A/58/296 (2003), p. 18, para. 108 (Viet Nam); UN Doc. E/CN.4/2005/61/Add. 1 (2005), p. 93, para. 368 (Viet Nam).

[84] Paragraph 9.4, Section II of the Document of the Copenhagen Meeting of the Conference on the Human Dimension of the OSCE 1990 29 ILM (1990) 1311.

seminars were held regularly, the first of direct importance to freedom of religion being the Human Dimension Seminar on Constitutional, Legal and Administrative Aspects of the Freedom of Religion held in Warsaw in April 1996[85] at which '[t]here was broad agreement that the freedom of conscience and belief is an absolute right under the OSCE commitments. This includes the right to believe and the right to change one's faith from one religious tradition to another'.[86]

In the context of the European Convention, as Article 9 includes express freedom to change religion or belief, there would be little need for interpretation by the European Court. The European Court and European Commission have not been faced with restrictions comparable to those illustrated by the Special Rapporteur but there have been decisions involving proselytism and involving the administrative consequences of leaving a particular religion (*Gottesmann v. Switzerland*[87] and *Darby v. Sweden*[88]).

Proselytism and the right to change religion are inextricably linked. In *Kokkinakis v. Greece*,[89] the applicant was a Jehovah's Witness who had been convicted under the Greek law prohibiting proselytism as a result of discussions initiated by him during a visit to the home of an Orthodox cantor. The applicant pointed to the logical and legal difficulty of drawing any even remotely clear dividing-line between proselytism and freedom to change one's religion or belief.[90] The European Court decided in favour of the applicant on the basis of the insufficiently reasoned decision of the Greek appeal court in supporting the applicant's criminal conviction.[91] However, Judge Martens (partly dissenting) was concerned that the European Court's decision failed to draw attention to the pressing nature of the fundamental freedom to change religion. He criticised the European Court for dealing only incidentally with what he regarded as the crucial issue under Article 9, namely whether Article 9 allows member States to make it a criminal offence to attempt to induce somebody to change his religion. He was firmly of the view that it did not:

'The Convention leaves no room whatsoever for interference by the State . . . These absolute freedoms explicitly include freedom to change

---

[85] ODIHR, 'The Human Dimension Seminar on Constitutional, Legal and Administrative Aspects of the Freedom of Religion' held in Warsaw, 16–19 April 1996, *Consolidated Summary*, ODIHR (1996).

[86] *Ibid.*, at p. 16.

[87] *Gottesmann v. Switzerland*, App. No. 101616/83 (1984) 40 D&R 284.

[88] *Darby v. Sweden* (Ser. A) No. 187 (1990) ECtHR annex to the decision of the Court.

[89] *Kokkinakis v. Greece* (Ser. A) No. 260–A (1993) ECtHR.   [90] *Ibid.*, para. 29.

[91] *Ibid.*, at para. 49.

one's religion and beliefs. Whether or not somebody intends to change religion is no concern of the State's and, consequently, neither in principle should it be the State's concern if somebody attempts to induce another to change his religion.'[92]

The potential for State interference in religious choice also exists in those countries which make administrative arrangements for the collection of church taxes and in the apparently harmless administrative requirement to be informed of religious adherence in certain circumstances. In *Gottesmann v. Switzerland*,[93] the European Commission held that the imposition of the legal requirement to notify the State of a change of religion in order to administer the payment of levies to a particular denomination did not constitute violation of Article 9(1). The applicants complained that the domestic authorities arbitrarily imposed formalities governing notification of their decision to leave the Roman Catholic Church when none were prescribed in national law. In rejecting this claim, the European Commission established that for the purposes of Article 9, domestic authorities have 'a wide discretion to decide on what conditions an individual may validly be regarded as having decided to leave a religious denomination'.[94] Although this is consistent with its other decisions upholding the need for a change of church membership to be notified in order to avoid liability for such levies (for example, *E. & G.R. v. Austria*),[95] these decisions failed to take account of two issues. The first concerns the formalities to be completed before the State recognises a change of religion. The second concerns compulsory revelation of one's beliefs. In *Gottesmann v. Switzerland* the expression of non-allegiance to the State Church indicated on a tax declaration by scoring through the relevant space with a double line did not satisfy the authorities' formalities, even though insertion of the word 'none' in later tax declarations did. It would have been useful if the European Commission had offered guidance on the imposition of such formalities, to ensure that they are not capable of being misapplied by States. This is necessary given the use of administrative hindrances in many

---

[92] *Ibid.*, at para. 14.
[93] *Gottesmann v. Switzerland*, App. No. 101616/83 (1984) 40 D&R 284.   [94] *Ibid.*, at 289.
[95] *E. & G. R. v. Austria*, App. No. 9781/82 (1984) 37 D&R 42. It was held, at p. 45, that the applicants' freedom of religion was not jeopardised by payment of a similar levy in view of their freedom to leave the Church, a right which the State legislation had expressly provided.

countries to resist a change from the State religion.[96] The furthest that the European Commission was prepared to go was in its report in *Darby v. Sweden*,[97] concerning the payment of a special tax to the Swedish Lutheran Church on the basis of the applicant's residence, when it confirmed that 'a State Church system must, in order to satisfy the requirements of Article 9, include specific safeguards for the individual's freedom of religion. In particular, no one may be forced to enter, or be prohibited from leaving, a State Church'.[98]

Krishnaswami considered that 'the mere existence of certain prescribed procedures for formally joining a religion or belief, or for leaving it, is not necessarily an infringement of the right to maintain or to change: the real test is whether or not in fact these procedures constitute a restraint upon this freedom'.[99] This is broadly consistent with the European Commission's position. However, he added the warning that '[t]here is, however, a possibility that such formalities might in fact be employed as a means of dissuading an individual from changing his religion or belief'.[100] The European Commission could therefore have taken greater account of such a possibility, particularly as significant obstacles to a change of religion had previously been recognised in European countries.[101]

The related issue which received little attention from the European Commission in the church tax cases concerns compulsion to reveal

---

[96] This is discussed more extensively below under the heading 'Pressure to Maintain a Religion or Belief'. For an example of the refusal by authorities to record religious conversion cited by the Special Rapporteur, see UN Doc. E/CN.4/1995/91(1994), p. 35 (Egypt). It was reported that Muslims cannot change their identity document in order to record their conversion to another religion. See also *X. v. Iceland*, App. No. 2525/65 (1967) 18 CD 33.

[97] *Darby v. Sweden* (Ser. A) No. 187 (1990) ECtHR, annex to the decision of the Court.

[98] *Ibid.*, at pp. 17 and 18, para. 45.

[99] A. Krishnaswami, 'Study on Discrimination in the Matter of Religious Rights and Practices', 11 NYUJ Int'l L & Pol (1978) 227, at 232.

[100] *Ibid.*, at 240.

[101] Sweden commented in response to the circulated Draft Declaration and Convention that according to Swedish law any member of the Swedish State Church who wished to relinquish his membership was legally unable to do so, unless he became a member of certain other congregations recognised by the Swedish State. It was thus legally impossible for a Swedish citizen to leave the Swedish State Church for the reason of joining a religious group not recognised by the State or for that of remaining outside of any confessional organisation. A new law liberalising these provisions was immediately prepared (UN Doc. E/CN.4/82/Add.11 (1948)).

one's beliefs. In order to avoid the levy, individuals are compelled to reveal their beliefs. The sensitivity of such compulsion is not obvious in the European context but is something which the Human Rights Committee has stressed both in its review of periodic reports[102] and in paragraph 3 of its General Comment No. 22, although it has only done so since those particular European decisions were made. Future European decisions might therefore take account of the importance of compulsion to reveal one's beliefs, even if only for apparently harmless administrative purposes following a change of religious membership. In the drafting of paragraph 3, which emphasises that 'no one can be compelled to reveal his thoughts or adherence to a religion or belief', exceptions to this principle were deliberately omitted. This is in spite of suggestions made by certain members of the Human Rights Committee that requests might be made by States to disclose religious beliefs for the purposes of planning the education of a child, identity documents and medical care,[103] or for the purpose of taking an oath in court or avoiding church tax.[104] Ultimately, given the risks to the individual as a consequence of revealing beliefs, and given that the right to refuse to divulge one's ideas was part of the right to hold an opinion, the statement in paragraph 3 prohibiting compulsion to reveal thoughts or religious adherence remained unqualified.[105] Although notification of a change of religion may be an innocuous stipulation in most European countries, in certain countries it could result in exposure to discrimination.

In short, the right to change one's religion seems firmly established in both the United Nations and European systems. Difficulties have been encountered over the last fifty years in developing standards on this particular issue at Universal level. Even though the right has faced little challenge in the context of Article 9 of the European Convention, a reassertion of the absolute character of the right to change religion would be welcomed (should the European Court have opportunity), particularly in the context of proselytism, coupled with a more careful treatment of the administrative requirements following a change of religion.

---

[102] UN Doc. A/47/40 (1994), p. 57, para. 247 (Ecuador). Members of the Committee asked Ecuador in which cases individuals were required under Article 19(15) of the Constitution to declare their religion or belief.

[103] UN Doc. CCPR/C/SR. 1166 (1992), p. 2, para. 5 (Mr Sadi).

[104] UN Doc. CCPR/C/SR. 1166 (1992), pp. 4–5, para. 20 (Mr Lallah).

[105] UN Doc. CCPR/C/SR. 1166 (1992), pp. 3–4, paras 17 and 22 (Mr Dimitrijević).

Pressure to maintain a religion or belief

Origin of the freedom from coercion

The explicit right to freedom from coercion in the choice of religion in Article 18(2) of the ICCPR was sought by those Muslim countries advocating the right to maintain an individual's religion, for the same reasons as were given for resisting an express right to change religion. In its final form, Article 18(2) reads: 'No one shall be subject to coercion which would impair his freedom to have or to adopt a religion or belief of his choice'.

Article 18(2) stems from a two-part amendment proposed by Egypt during the Commission's eighth session in 1952,[106] the first being, 'This right shall include freedom to maintain or to change his religion or belief' and the second, 'No one shall be subject to any form of coercion which would impair his freedom to maintain or to change his religion or belief'. The purpose of the amendment was described by the sponsor as 'mainly psychological',[107] prompted by the imbalance of the existing drafting which referred only to a change of religion with no mention of freedom to maintain a religion (which suggested that freedom existed only to change religion). It was hoped that the Egyptian amendment might allay doubts expressed by representatives of various Islamic countries during the Third Session of the General Assembly, which had led Saudi to abstain from voting on the entire Universal Declaration.[108] Saudi had also recently argued in the Third Committee that to single out a right to change religious beliefs 'might be interpreted as giving missionaries and proselytizers a free rein'.[109] The rationale for the amendment was said to be Articles 12, 13 and 16 of the Egyptian constitution, which permit conversion from Islam only after three conversations with a minister on the subject.[110]

The amendment won widespread acceptance but only if it was given just one of two of its possible interpretations, namely that it merely made explicit something that was already implicit in the original text

---

[106] For the draft under discussion, see UN Doc. E/1992 (1951), annex I. The amendment is at UN Doc. E/CN.4/L.187.
[107] UN Doc. E/CN.4/SR. 319 (1952), p. 3 (Egypt).
[108] UN Doc. E/CN.4/SR. 319 (1952), p. 4 (France).
[109] UN Doc. A/C.3/6/SR. 367 (1951), p. 124, para. 41 (Saudi).
[110] UN Doc. E/CN.4/SR. 319 (1952), p. 3 (Egypt).

and was not more restrictive.[111] It might otherwise be interpreted so as to jeopardise freedom of teaching, worship, practice and observance or, more importantly, as limiting a person who sought to maintain or change his religion or belief.[112] The Australian delegate wanted it clearly understood 'that the expression "coercion" would not include persuasion or appeals to conscience'.[113] Similarly, the Lebanese delegation would only support the Egyptian amendment if it confirmed the right of others to preach and seek to influence a person either to maintain or to change his religion,[114] as would the United Kingdom delegate provided that it could not be interpreted as imposing limitations or restrictions on argument and discussion. From the use of the word 'coercion', that possibility in any event seemed to be excluded.[115] It is evident then that appeals to conscience, preaching and seeking to influence a person either to maintain or to change his religion were not to be regarded as coercive. Both parts of the Egyptian amendment were adopted unanimously by the Commission and nothing was said in the debates to admit the interpretation that the prohibition against coercion as drafted could operate to permit coercion of any form on an individual to maintain a religion.

In the preparation of the ICCPR a number of arguments were advanced for the proposition that as freedom of religion entails the right to maintain a religion, legitimate steps might be taken to ensure the maintenance of an individual's religion and to dissuade a change of religion (in contrast to missionary activities and proselytism which encourage a change of religion). For example, in the Third Committee the Afghan delegate explained that giving an individual permission to change religion might,

> 'be considered to be interfering with his beliefs ... Freedom of religious belief could be achieved if the individual was left free to maintain the belief that he had freely accepted ... If an individual who had freely accepted a certain religion was told that he was free to change it, the idea was put into his mind that he was believing in something which he could change if given the right to do so. Doubt would be instilled and his belief

---

[111] UN Doc. E/CN.4/SR. 319 (1952). For the comments of the delegates of the Commission of the Churches on International Affairs, Lebanon, USSR, the United Kingdom, and Greece, see pp. 5, 8, 8, 9 and 11 respectively.

[112] UN Doc. E/CN.4/SR. 319 (1952), p. 6 (the Commission of the Churches on International Affairs).

[113] UN Doc. E/CN.4/SR. 319 (1952), p. 7. (Australia).

[114] UN Doc. E/CN.4/SR. 319 (1952), p. 8 (Lebanon).

[115] UN Doc. E/CN.4/SR. 319 (1952), p. 9 (United Kingdom).

damaged. That would be tantamount to interference with his freedom of thought and conscience.'[116]

The Saudi delegate took up the same issue when referring to the dangers of religions organised for proselytising activities:

'A powerful State with a proselytizing State religion, if it had mass media of information at its disposal, might well use them to cast doubt in the minds of members of other faiths. The Third Committee should not lend itself to such practices ... To give the sanction of the Covenants to ideological proselytizing in foreign countries might well bring about the disruption of the social order.'[117]

The Saudi delegate contemplated State, rather than private, sources of proselytism, which would also be consistent with fears about the possible political motivation behind proselytism and missionary activities. However, he later referred to more subtle dangers against which the individual needed protection in order fully to enjoy true religious freedom, in the form of pressure, proselytism, errors and heresies.[118] The Saudi delegate also based his opposition to an express right to change religion in Article 18 on the possibility that 'it would raise doubts in the minds of the ordinary people to whom their religion was a way of life'.[119]

Towards the end of the drafting of the ICCPR, the Italian delegate, Mr Capotorti, gave his understanding of the interrelation between the first and second part of Article 18, that 'paragraph 2 of Article 18 prohibited any form of coercion, while paragraph 1 ensured freedom of religious instruction',[120] and Liberia concluded that '[a] man who could not change his religion in fact had a religion imposed on him'.[121] It may be concluded that whatever the origins of the anti-coercion provision, its interpretation as a provision endorsing steps to impair the individual's choice to leave a religion is not supported.

Interpretation of the freedom from coercion

Although Article 9 of the European Convention does not contain a provision equivalent to Article 18(2), it has been suggested that

---

[116] UN Doc. A/C.3/9/SR. 565 (1954), paras. 12–13 (Afghanistan).
[117] UN Doc. A/C.3/15/SR. 1021 (1960), paras. 11 and 12 (Saudi).
[118] UN Doc. A/C.3/15/SR. 1022 (1960), para. 27 (Saudi).
[119] UN Doc. A/C.3/15/SR. 1025 (1960), para. 12 (Saudi).
[120] UN Doc. A/C.3/15/SR. 1027 (1960), para. 12 (Italy).
[121] UN Doc. A/C.3/15/SR. 1024 (1960), para. 7 (Liberia).

Article 17 of the European Convention could be deployed in a manner equivalent to Article 18(2) to prevent coercion in the individual's choice of religion, since Article 17 prevents the European Convention being interpreted as 'implying for any State, group or person any right to engage in any activity or perform any act aimed at the destruction of any of the rights and freedoms set forth herein'.[122] The fact that Article 5(2) of the ICCPR contains a provision almost identical to Article 17 (in addition to Article 18(2)) does not undermine this argument, particularly if it is remembered that the genesis of Article 18(2) of the ICCPR and the right to maintain a religion were introduced to 'balance' (rather than substantially alter) text which at that stage included only an express right to change religion. Article 17 of the European Convention and Article 5 of the ICCPR appear to span both public and private sources of coercion in their reference to 'State, group or person' whereas it may be argued that Article 18(2) of the ICCPR only refers to public sources of coercion. The most direct statement of the Human Rights Committee on the subject of coercion is to be found in paragraph 5 of General Comment No. 22, which adopts a very one-sided emphasis on State-sponsored coercion, highlighting in paragraph 5 that:

> 'Article 18(2) bars coercions that would impair the right to have or adopt a religion or belief, including the use or threat of physical force or penal sanctions to compel believers or non-believers to adhere to their religious beliefs and congregations, to recant their religion or belief or to convert. Policies or practices having the same intention or effect, such as for example those restricting access to education, medical care, employment or the rights guaranteed by article 25 and other provisions of the Covenant are similarly inconsistent with article 18(2). The same protection is enjoyed by holders of all beliefs of a non-religious nature.'

The emphasis of this paragraph is on State coercion (or coercion by those emulating State functions). The expression, 'policies and practices having the same intention or effect' is illustrated by reference to the denial of facilities generally within the public realm (such as education, medical care and employment) and rights which are to be safeguarded by the State (noting in particular Article 25 with its focus on

---

[122] See M. Shaw, 'Freedom of Thought, Conscience and Religion', in StJ. McDonald, F. Matscher and H. Petzold (eds.), *The European System for the Protection of Human Rights*, Dordrecht/London: Martinus Nijhoff (1993), at pp. 452–3 (discussed by C. Evans, *Freedom of Religion Under the European Convention on Human Rights*, Oxford: Oxford University Press (2001), at p. 99).

participation in democratic and public life). Paragraph 5 therefore suggests that Article 18(2) is confined to coercion exercised by or on behalf of the State in denying facilities of a public nature and it does not apparently contemplate private missionary activity as a source of coercion. It was acknowledged by some members of the Human Rights Committee that policies or practices that restrict access to education, medical care, employment or that restrict other guaranteed rights raise issues relating less to the provisions of Article 18(2) than State discrimination.[123] Two members of the Human Rights Committee in particular gave their understanding of 'coercion', both emphasising coercion in the context of public functions. One cited the historic position in Mauritius where at one time schools were administered by the Roman Catholic Church and children were accepted in schools only if they were prepared to observe the precepts of that religion.[124] Another distinguished coercion from discrimination by suggesting that, in general, discrimination was not an end in itself, in contrast to coercion. For example, in the case of racial discrimination it would be impossible to tell a person that if he changed race he would no longer suffer discrimination, whereas coercion could be exercised against a person by telling him that if he adhered to a particular belief he could become a public employee or send his children to a particular school.[125] However, in view of States' obligations under Article 2(1) of the ICCPR to 'respect and to ensure' the rights recognised in the ICCPR, the distinction between public and private sources of coercion is less important.[126]

---

[123] For example, UN Doc. CCPR/C/SR. 1166 (1992), p. 11, para. 76 (Mr El Shafei), and *ibid.*, at p. 12, para. 84 (Mr Lallah). This resulted in the proposal that the issue be dealt within the context of discrimination as well as coercion, *ibid.*, at p. 12, para. 81 (Mr El Shafei).

[124] UN Doc. CCPR/C/SR. 1166 (1992), p. 13, para. 85 (Mr Lallah).

[125] UN Doc. CCPR/C/SR. 1166 (1992), p. 13, para. 86 (Mr Dimitrijević).

[126] In the context of the drafting of the Convention on religious intolerance, the representative of the United States, without proposing an official amendment, considered that the Sub-Commission had omitted an essential element of clarification from para. 1(a). He observed that the word 'coercion' could mean only coercion by a public authority, since it was very difficult to protect an individual from being subject to coercion by groups or other individuals. In view of this he suggested that the words 'by public authorities' be inserted after the word 'coercion' in para. 1(a) and in any other place in the Article where the word 'coercion' appeared (UN Doc. E/CN.4/891 (1965), p. 58, para. 253). Other representatives did not consider this necessary, or recognised that coercion was often exerted by individuals and accordingly considered that the State should have an obligation to protect its citizens from such coercion (UN Doc. E/CN.4/891 (1965), p. 59, para. 256).

Nevertheless, the substance of paragraph 5 of General Comment No. 22 indicates that private sources of proselytism were not evident in the Human Rights Committee's conceptualisation of 'coercion'.

In its review of periodic reports, the Human Rights Committee has raised issues concerning coercion to maintain a religion in a number of instances not involving apostasy (which is discussed separately under the next heading ('Apostasy')) but overall comparatively few. The Committee asked Cyprus whether the statement in its report to the effect that 'the use of physical or moral compulsion for the purpose of making a person change, or preventing him from changing, his religion is prohibited', was compatible with the Covenant for it was possible in the case of certain religions such as Islam to resort to persuasion to prevent someone from changing his religion.[127] Similarly, the Committee noted the impediments placed upon the freedom to change one's religion, for example, in Morocco[128] and Libya.[129]

It is unfortunate that in drafting paragraph 5 the Human Rights Committee failed to be more explicit on the subject of proselytism, in spite of the fact that its importance was raised even in the earliest debates and it continues to be a live issue throughout many parts of the world. However, there is nothing to suggest that it was the Human Rights Committee's view that proselytism and missionary work did constitute coercion within the terms of Article 18(2). The issue had also been raised in the Krishnaswami study and the resulting sixteen Rules, of which Rule I(3) reads: 'No one should be subjected to coercion or to improper

---

[127] UN Doc. A/34/40 (1979), p. 92, para. 388 (Cyprus). An important issue that arises in the context of coercion to maintain a religion is the extent to which religions should be free to regulate their own internal affairs free from State control. In his study, Krishnaswami acknowledged that some religions often do not recognise the right of a member to leave a particular faith, or at least view such a change with extreme disfavour. He commented that '[i]n such a situation the State cannot remain indifferent and may have to limit the authority of the group to determine its membership, even though this might result in some curtailment of its right to manage its religious affairs' (Krishnaswami, 'Study of Discrimination', p. 227, at p. 265). The only basis might be the voluntary assumption of disciplinary steps when agreeing to submit to the internal authority of a religious institution. The closest analogy would be with those cases concerned with the voluntary restriction of human rights pursuant to contracts freely entered into, such as employment contracts with religious institutions. In the European context, see such cases as *X. v. Denmark*, App. No. 7374/76 (1976) 5 D&R 157. For discussion on the 'voluntary model' and State Churches, see C. Evans, *Freedom of Religion Under the European Convention*, pp. 128–9.

[128] UN Doc. A/50/40 vol. 1 (1996), p. 25, para. 112 (Morocco).

[129] UN Doc. A/50/40 vol. 1 (1996), p. 29, para. 135 (Libya).

inducements likely to impair his freedom to maintain or to change his religion or belief'. The Draft Principles on Freedom and Non-Discrimination in the Matter of Religious Rights and Practices[130] prepared by the Sub-Commission on Prevention of Discrimination and Protection of Minorities on the basis of the Krishnaswami study refer in Principle I(3) to 'material and moral coercion'[131] instead of 'coercion or . . . improper inducements'. At the same time the Sub-Commission emphasised that, in the event of conflicting religious interests, 'public authorities shall endeavour to find a solution reconciling these demands in a manner such as to ensure the greatest measure of freedom to society as a whole'.[132] It is likely that Principle I(3) was not intended to embrace proselytism and missionary activity particularly given that Principle I(1) refers to freedom 'to adhere, or not to adhere, to a religion or belief, in accordance with the dictates of his conscience', and Principle II (8)(a) asserts that '[e]veryone shall be free to teach or to disseminate his religion or belief, either in public or in private', omitting the qualification found in Krishnaswami's Rule 10 that only acknowledged the individual's freedom to disseminate 'in so far as his actions do not impair the right of any other individual to maintain his religion or belief'. If anything, the Sub-Commission's Draft Principles suggest that freedom of choice in matters of religion or belief would be diminished if it meant that the individual could not be exposed to ideas and beliefs, in addition to those already held, so as to enable an informed choice to be made between them.

In comparison, the approach of the European Court in applying Article 9 of the European Convention may seem unduly restrictive.

---

[130] UN Doc. E/CN.4/800, UN Doc. E/CN.4/Sub.2/206 (1960), paras. 51–160. The text of the Draft Principles may be found in Krishnaswami, 'Study of Discrimination', p. 227, Annex 1.

[131] This shaped the proposals for what ultimately became Article 1(2) of the 1981 Declaration. The representative of Cyprus proposed that this provision should read: 'The use of physical or moral compulsion for the purpose of making a person change or preventing him from changing his religion is prohibited' (UN Doc. E/CN.4/1347 (1979), p. 72, para. 18). In order to distinguish coercion from persuasion and in order to promote religious tolerance, the Indonesian delegate proposed that Article 1(2) should read: 'No one shall be subject to coercion or any kind of persuasion which would impair his freedom to have or to adopt a religion or belief of his choice. Therefore, any act which leads to such practices is inadmissible' (UN Doc. A/C.3/36/SR. 34 (1981), p. 9, para. 32).

[132] Principle IV(1), discussed at: UN Doc. E/CN.4/Sub.2/SR. 299 (1960); UN Doc. E/CN.4/Sub.2/SR. 301 (1960); UN Doc. E/CN.4/Sub.2/SR. 302 (1960).

In *Kokkinakis v. Greece*[133] the European Court examined a law prohibiting proselytism, which was devised to protect disciples from being enticed away from the dominant religion, that of the Christian Eastern Orthodox Church.[134] The applicant noted that it would surpass 'even the wildest academic hypothesis' to imagine the possibility of a complaint being made by a Catholic priest or by a Protestant clergyman against an Orthodox Christian who had attempted to entice one of his flock away from him.[135] This case will be discussed at greater length below under the heading 'Pressure to Change Religion' but in the context of pressure to maintain a religion or belief the underlying aim of the Greek legislation is crucial. However, this particular aim of the legislation received little attention and the European Court instead found that a legitimate aim had been pursued, namely 'the protection of the rights and freedoms of others', in view of the risks of what the Court termed 'improper proselytism'. The European Court then only criticised the Greek Government for its lack of detailed reasoning in the criminal conviction of the applicant.[136] (Other Greek legislation applied with a similar aim was considered in *Manoussakis and others v. Greece*.)[137] The European Court seemingly chose to overlook the nature of measures that were designed to ensure denominational allegiance.

Apostasy

One of the most direct forms of coercion to maintain one's religion exists in those countries in which a change from a particular religion constitutes apostasy. Apostasy has not been an issue on which the Human Rights Committee has focused much attention but Sudan is one country which has been the focus of examination. In reviewing Sudan's periodic reports, members of the Committee asked whether

---

[133] *Kokkinakis v. Greece* (Ser. A) No. 260–A (1993) ECtHR.

[134] *Ibid.*, at paras. 15 and 17.   [135] *Ibid.*, at para. 29.

[136] Gunn criticised the European Court's decision in *Kokkinakis* – T.J. Gunn, 'Adjudicating Rights of Conscience under the European Convention on Human Rights', in J. van der Vyver and J. Witte (eds.), *Religious Human Rights in Global Perspective: Legal Perspectives*, The Hague/London: Martinus Nijhoff (1996), pp. 305–30. See also B. Lynn, et al. (eds.), *The Right to Religious Liberty: The Basic ACLU Guide to Religious Rights*, Carbondale: South Illinois University Press (1995).

[137] *Manoussakis and others v. Greece* (1997) 23 EHRR 387. In a review of the proselytism law in Greece, Ferrari draws a stark distinction between the State's treatment of Orthodox and foreign religions – S. Ferrari, 'The New Wine and the Old Cask, Tolerance, Religion and the Law in Contemporary Europe', 10 Rat Jur (1997) 75.

the crime of apostasy in Sudan, defined as advocating abandonment of Islam by a Muslim, was considered by Sudan to be compatible with Article 18.[138] The State representative accepted that the crime of apostasy was punishable by death and explained that Islam should not only be seen as a religion but as a complete set of precepts for private and public life. Persons committing apostasy therefore were a danger to the fabric of society and could be compared to traitors in countries with a different legislation.[139] In the view of members of the Committee, domestic provisions regarding the crime of apostasy were not compatible with Article 6 of the ICCPR.[140] The Human Rights Committee also asked Iran whether it was possible for a Muslim to renounce his religion, to become an atheist or to convert to another religion or whether measures were applied in such a case according to Islamic law.[141] Similarly in relation to Egypt, the Committee noted that under the Muslim Code of Religious Law it appeared that Muslims who converted to another religion were considered legally dead. Accordingly, members requested information on the legal status of such converts.[142] The Human Rights Committee's approach to apostasy seems clear even if the issue has not been raised with great frequency.

The Committee against Torture, in a decision that at first sight appears to be inconsistent with the Human Rights Committee's practice, declared inadmissible an Iranian citizen's claim in *M.B.B. v. Sweden*[143] when appealing against his forced return to Iran following Sweden's refusal of asylum. He was a former member of the Iranian Revolutionary Guard (*Pasdaran*) who, having converted to Christianity, claimed that he would no longer be able to carry out his work and would be in danger of execution if returned to Iran. Accordingly, he alleged violation of Article 3 of the Convention Against Torture and Other Cruel, Inhuman or Degrading Treatment or Punishment (1984),[144] on the basis of his change of religion. However, the Committee against Torture decided that the author had failed to substantiate his claim in

---

[138] UN Doc. A/46/40 (1991), p. 125, para. 501 (Sudan).   [139] *Ibid.*, at p. 127, para. 514.

[140] UN Doc. A/53/40 vol. 1 (1998), p. 23, para. 119 (Sudan). For section 126 of the Sudan Criminal Act 1991, see UN Doc. E/CN.4/1993/62 (1993), p. 89, para. 55.

[141] UN Doc. A/37/40 (1982), p. 71, para. 316 (Iran).

[142] UN Doc. A/39/40 (1984), p. 57, para. 301 (Egypt).

[143] *M.B.B. v. Sweden*, Communication No. 104/1998, UN Doc. CAT/C/22/D/104/1998 (views of 5 May 1999) (2000) 7(2) IHRR 400.

[144] New York, 10 December 1984 in force 26 June 1987, GA Res. 39/46, annex, 39 UN GAOR Supp.

view of doubts about his credibility (forged documents were apparently presented by him as evidence). More importantly for these purposes, the Committee also decided that the author had failed to substantiate his claim that there existed 'substantial grounds' (i.e. that the risk of torture on return was 'foreseeable, real and personal')[145] and that 'deserters from the *Pasdaran* who leave the country, as well as converts to Christianity, in general face a risk of being subjected to torture ... if, in the case of the latter, they are not prominent members of the Christian community'.[146]

The Special Rapporteur has reported on the implementation of apostasy laws with particular attention to the treatment of apostasy as a capital offence.[147] In the case of Iran, for example, the Special Rapporteur noted that the death sentence had been passed in instances of apostasy.[148] He reiterated the provisions of Article 18 of the ICCPR

---

[145] *M.B.B. v. Sweden*, Communication No. 104/1998, UN Doc. CAT/C/22/D/104/1998 (views of 5 May 1999) (2000) 7(2) IHRR 400, 406, para. 6.8. See also *C. v. Australia*, Communication No. 900/1999 (views of 28 October 2002), UN Doc. A/58/40 vol. 2 (2003), p. 188. The author claimed a violation of his rights under Article 7 in that his proposed deportation to Iran would expose him to a real risk of a violation of his Covenant rights. Australia argued that official interference with Christian religious activities is limited to those Christian faiths that proselytise and Muslim individuals who abandon Islam to become Christians, asserting that Assyrian Christians do not actively engage in conversions and, in fact, tend to discourage Muslims from joining their faith – this means that they are subject to far less scrutiny and harassment than members of other Christian and minority faiths (*ibid.*, para. 4.15). The Human Rights Committee attached weight to the fact that the author was originally granted refugee status on the basis of a well-founded fear of persecution as an Assyrian Christian (coupled with evidence about the effects of continued detention on the author's mental health) and concluded that Australia had not established that the current circumstances in Iran were such that the grant of refugee status no longer holds validity (*ibid.*, para. 8.5). In a similar context in relation to New Zealand, the Human Rights Committee recently expressed its concern about the impact of measures to implement the UN Security Council's anti-terrorism resolution 1373 (2001) on asylum-seekers by 'removing the immigration risk offshore'. The expulsion of those suspected of terrorism to their countries of origin could pose risks to the personal safety and lives of the persons expelled (UN Doc. A/57/40 vol. 1 (2002), p. 65, para. 81 (New Zealand)). See also *Ahani v. Canada*, Communication No. 1051/2002 (views of 29 March 2004), UN Doc. A/59/40 vol. 2 (2002), p. 260.

[146] *Ibid.*, at p. 406, para. 6.7.

[147] For government explanations of why apostasy is punishable, see UN Doc. E/CN.4/1994/79 (1994), pp. 47–52, para. 45 (Egypt), and for the rationale for apostasy as a capital offence, see UN Doc. E/CN.4/1991/56 (1991), p. 109, para. 76 (Mauritania).

[148] UN Doc. E/CN.4/1995/91/Add.1 (1995), p. 41, para. 15 (Iran). See also: UN Doc. E/CN.4/1992/52 (1992), p. 33, para. 50; UN Doc. E/CN.4/2001/63 (2001), p. 36, para. 147 (Yemen).

and Article 1 of the 1981 Declaration and requested details of the measures to be taken to give effect to these provisions.[149] Perhaps the clearest statement by the Special Rapporteur on apostasy is found in the conclusions and recommendations following a visit to Sudan. The Special Rapporteur considered it 'essential that any conversion should be the result of free choice and not of constraint. Similarly, the conversion of Muslims to another religion should not give rise to any kind of pressure, restriction or deprivation of freedom with respect to the converted believers and the religious officials of their community'.[150]

The position of both the Human Rights Committee and the Special Rapporteur towards the compatibility of apostasy with United Nations instruments is straightforward. The issue has never arisen before the European institutions although the approach of the European Court may be confidently predicted to be in line with Universal standards.[151]

Summary

The settled position of Article 18(2) of the ICCPR in the context of the right to maintain one's religion or belief was put succinctly by Krishnaswami:

> 'Although the [Universal] Declaration does not explicitly mention free-
> dom to maintain religion or belief, as does the draft covenant, the
> omission does not appear to involve any question of substance: it
> would be strange indeed to acknowledge the right to change one's religion
> or belief without admitting the right to maintain it. But the converse is
> not correct: it does not follow from the mere acknowledgement of one's
> right to maintain a religion or belief that the right to change it is also
> conceded, and there are instances in which a change is prohibited while
> the right to maintain is recognized ... If it is to be considered that
> freedom to maintain or to change religion or belief does not admit of
> any restraint – and it seems to be rightly considered by the consensus
> of world opinion – any instance of compelling an individual to join or of
> preventing him from leaving the organization of a religion or a belief in

---

[149] UN Doc. E/CN.4/1995/91/Add.1 (1995), pp. 41–2, para. 16 (Iran); UN Doc. E/CN.4/ 1995/91 (1995), p. 52 (Iran).

[150] UN Doc. A/51/542/Add.2 (1996), para. 147 (Sudan).

[151] For a discussion of this and similar issues, see D. Little, J. Kelsay and A. Sachedina, *Human Rights and the Conflict of Cultures. Western and Islamic Perspectives on Religious Liberty*, Columbia SC: University of South Carolina Press (1988).

which she has no faith must be considered to be an infringement of the
right to freedom of thought, conscience and religion.'[152]

Although proposals were made in the drafting of Article 18(2) of the
ICCPR for a basis to oppose influences to change religion, and for an
explicit right to maintain a religion, the characterisation of proselytism
and missionary work as coercive was not sustained and instead
Article 18(2) focused predominantly on State coercion in religious
choice rather than private acts of proselytism. This is supported by
paragraph 5 of General Comment No. 22 which makes no reference at
all to such activities but instead treats them as manifestations of religion
or belief, subject to applicable limitations. Missionary activity and
proselytism will now be considered in the context of pressure to change
religion to weigh contemporary claims that such practices constitute
coercion to change religion.

Pressure to change religion

Introduction

During the preparation of the Universal Declaration and the ICCPR the
terms 'missionary activity' and 'proselytism' were directly linked by
some delegates to sectarian warfare in Europe, colonialism and the
Crusades. To other countries, proselytism was not associated with
such aberrations of Christian history but was regarded quite separately
as the expression of religious belief which was to be positively safeguarded. During the Second Session of the Commission in 1948,
Article 15(2) of the Draft ICCPR contained the express right of an
individual to 'endeavour to persuade other persons of full age and
sound mind of the truth of his beliefs' until the Egyptian delegate
successfully proposed its deletion on the basis that freedom of religion
was already assured and that the text might otherwise raise difficulties in
regard to ratification.[153] The strength of objection by those countries
opposed to sources of persuasion that might result in a change of
religion first became fully apparent in the Third Committee debates
on the Universal Declaration and the ICCPR.

---

[152] Krishnaswami, 'Study of Discrimination', 227, at 230–1.
[153] UN Doc. E/CN.4/SR. 37 (1947) at p. 15. The Draft Convention under discussion is at
UN Doc. E/CN.4/56 (1947) and the Draft Declaration at UN Doc. E/CN.4/57 (1947).

Missionary activity, imperialist ambitions, colonialism and war

It was feared by Saudi that reference to an express right to change religion in the ICCPR would encourage missionary activity, no doubt fuelled by a belief that missionary organisations were responsible for the inclusion of such an express right which would favour missionary religions,[154] especially those from countries with large material resources,[155] and would disadvantage Muslims who never undertook missionary work or engaged in systematic proselytising.[156] It seemed incomprehensible to the delegates of certain countries (for example, France) that specific mention of a right to change religion should in any way be interpreted as a threat to Islam[157] (and given the oil wealth of the Middle-East it is unlikely that such concerns would be expressed in that way today). Also, it was claimed that missionaries might act as instruments for infiltration and exploitation by foreign powers given that the activities of missionaries were a form of propaganda.[158] In opposing missionary work, Saudi exemplified the historic harm done by missionaries by reference to the Crusades and wars between Catholics and Protestants in Europe. Missionary activity was believed by Saudi (as expressed in the Universal Declaration debates)[159] to be associated with dangerous political intervention through propagandist means. The power of propaganda had become so strong that it was tantamount to actual pressure.[160] Reminders were also given of 'the yoke of colonialism' and 'foreign domination', which had caused such oppression in the past[161] and of the right of self-determination of peoples and nations.[162] (Fears related to colonialism were repeated by Saudi in the preparation

---

[154] UN Doc. A/C.3/9/SR. 563 (1954), p. 100, para. 11 (Saudi); UN Doc. A/C.3/9/SR. 566 (1954), p. 117, para. 34 (Saudi).

[155] UN Doc. A/C.3/9/SR. 566 (1954), p. 117, para. 34 (Saudi).

[156] UN Doc. A/C.3/9/SR. 563 (1954), p. 100, para. 11 (Saudi); UN Doc. A/C.3/15/SR. 1023 (1960), p. 206, para. 11 (Saudi).

[157] UN Doc. A/C.3/6/SR. 371 (1951), p. 142, para. 18 (France).

[158] UN Doc. A/C.3/5/SR. 306 (1950), p. 224, paras. 47–8 (Saudi).

[159] UN Doc. A/C.3/3/SR. 127 (1948), pp. 391–2 (Saudi). Saudi proposed that the Article be confined to the words 'Everyone has the right to freedom of thought, conscience and religion' (UN Doc. A/C. 3/247).

[160] UN Doc. A/C.3/6/SR. 367 (1951), p. 124, para. 41 (Saudi).

[161] UN Doc. A/C.3/9/SR. 563 (1954), p. 100, para. 14 (Saudi).

[162] UN Doc. A/C.3/9/SR. 566 (1954), p. 117, para. 35 (Saudi). In the Third session plenary meetings, Egypt also 'feared ... the machinations of certain missions, well known in the Orient, which relentlessly pursued their efforts to convert to their own faith beliefs the masses of the population of the Orient', UN Doc. A/PV.183 (1948), p. 913 (Egypt).

of the 1981 Declaration.)[163] There was widespread condemnation of such evils among other States but they were not attributed to the work of missions and in any event such manifest wrongs were thought themselves to justify the article under discussion.[164]

Muslim countries were not alone in criticising what was perceived to be imperialist religious zeal. The delegate from Ceylon, a predominantly Buddhist country, referred to the political expansion of Europe into certain Asian countries by the Portuguese who 'fired by religious zeal, had sought to impose Catholicism on the indigenous peoples'.[165] He also referred to the Catholic–Protestant divide and the Thirty Years' War. However, he understood the principle enshrined in Article 18(1) to be that it was impossible to recognise an individual's right to maintain his beliefs without at the same time giving him the right to change them.[166] China expressed similar comments in the Commission but emphasised that it had never engaged in crusades or holy wars, it had never sought to impose religion on other people and was the opposite of fanatical.[167] Few commentators today would disagree with the remarks made on behalf of Saudi and Ceylon but few would consider that missionary work or proselytism, as understood in the West, bore any relation to such historic events.

When such concerns were repeated by Saudi in the debates leading up to the 1981 Declaration, Costa Rica rejected the characterisation of missionaries as imperialist or enemy agents.[168] The Special Rapporteur aimed to put some perspective on the issue by observing, in a review of relevant political, economic and cultural factors that, because of the links existing between the institutions of a religious community within a country and their counterparts abroad, the members of the community are equated with 'foreign agents' and, depending on the particular case,

---

[163] UN Doc. A/C.3/28/SR. 2009 (1973), p. 171, para. 4 (Saudi).

[164] These comments were expressed most clearly in the Universal Declaration debates: UN Doc. A/C.3/3/SR. 127 (1948), p. 394 (Belgium), p. 396 (Philippines), p. 396 (France), and p. 398 (China).

[165] UN Doc. A/C.3/15/SR. 1022 (1960), p. 202 para. 21 (Ceylon).   [166] Ibid.

[167] UN Doc. E/CN.4/SR. 319 (1952), p. 11 (1952) (China).

[168] Mr Paris (Costa Rica) commented that 'missionaries were subject to the laws of this country and would incur the penalties laid down by them if they violated them … Either there was freedom of religion or there was not; if there was such freedom, the activities of missionaries who respected local laws could not validly be hindered. There was no justification for discrimination against missionaries on the mere suspicion that they might be enemy agents' (UN Doc. A/C.3/28/SR. 2011 (1973), p. 182, paras. 18–19).

regarded as spies, agents of colonialism, imperialism or Zionism.[169] It was the historic attitude of such countries that was regarded as the obstacle and not dangers inherent in non-coercive forms of missionary work or proselytism. However, colonialism is still regarded as the source of undesirable sectarianism or heresy in certain parts of the world, such as in Morocco (where the Baha'i faith is considered to be heretical, of colonial origin)[170] and Algeria (where at independence 'there was a pervasive desire to design a State and society in political terms that drew their inspiration from Islam and broke with the colonial period').[171] Needless to say, human rights instruments are oblivious to matters of doctrine (or heresy) but do draw a critical distinction between 'coercion' and 'propagation' of belief. As Lerner usefully observes:

> 'Coercion in religious matters is always a grave violation of human rights. The use of coercion to induce others to adopt a religion which is not theirs or to abandon their own beliefs has played a particularly horrible role in the history of mankind. The condemnation of coercion in the field of religious rights is thus beyond controversy.
>
> The question of freedom of propagation of one's religion and the legitimacy of attempts to convince others of one's religious truth is different. In modern human rights law, the right to change one's religion, in the absence of coercion and as a result of free will is considered a recognized freedom.'[172]

Nevertheless, propagation of religious belief has never been entirely clear of accusations of coercion. Even social action motivated by religious belief, even if not overtly involving the propagation of religion, is often thought to entail coercive elements.

Social concern and inducements

It is the hallmark of many religions that genuine belief should be practised by a variety of means involving social action, providing relief from hardship and poverty and assisting in education so as not to perpetuate those conditions. In certain parts of Africa, the active role of the Church in education has been acknowledged as a vital tool for

---

[169] UN Doc. E/CN.4/1987/35 (1987), p. 13, para. 39.
[170] UN Doc. A/47/40 (1994), p. 15, para. 67 (Morocco).
[171] UN Doc. E/CN.4/2003/66/Add.1 (2003), p. 12, para. 52 (Algeria).
[172] Lerner, 'The Final Text of the UN Declaration', 185, at 188.

development.[173] Concerns about humanitarian intervention, particularly when combined with missionary work or the propagation of a
particular religion, were voiced during the preparation of both the
Universal Declaration and the ICCPR. Some countries wanted the rights
of missionaries to be specifically safeguarded in the Universal
Declaration. For example, the Netherlands considered that freedom to
perform social work, as well as the right of missionaries to enter, travel
and reside in any country should be explicitly stated.[174] This was successfully opposed and in any event there is no right for aliens to enter a
country.[175] Nevertheless, certain aspects of missionary work have been
applauded even by those set against it. In the Commission's drafting of
the ICCPR, the Egyptian delegate commented that among the positive
contributions of certain religious organisations in the Middle East have
been those involved in education but the fear of many Muslim governments (if too much stress were put on the right to change religion)
would be that those organisations might 'redouble their zeal in fields
other than that of education'.[176]

In the Third Committee debates a distinction was made between
those mission activities which should be safeguarded and those which
should be condemned by the international community. Even though
Afghanistan was opposed to an express right to change religion, its
delegate commented as follows: 'Islam did not approve of missionaries;
but that issue was somewhat irrelevant and, in any case, there were
national and international measures to protect the individual, where
necessary, against their activities'.[177] He later added, when discussing

---

[173] D. Nsereko, 'Religion, the State and the Law in Africa', 28 J Church & St (1986) 269, at 273.

[174] UN Doc. E/CN.4/82 (1948), p. 21 (the Netherlands).

[175] For nationals, the freedom to enter a State is clear. Article 12(4) of the ICCPR prevents
nationals from being arbitrarily deprived of their freedom to enter their own country.
The European Convention's Fourth Protocol, Article 3(2) imposes no such qualification to the right of nationals to enter their own country. As to expulsion, Article 13 of
the ICCPR is silent on the issue of expulsion of nationals. The European Convention's
Fourth Protocol, Article 3(1) expressly prohibits the expulsion of nationals but it was
confirmed that such right does not extend to aliens in *Omkarananda and the Divine
Light Zentrum v. United Kingdom*, App. No. 8188/77 (1981) 25 D&R 105. For further
discussion on freedom of movement within and across States, see P. Sieghart, *The
International Law of Human Rights*, Oxford: Clarendon Press (1990), pp. 174–88.

[176] UN Doc. E/CN.4/SR. 117 (1949), p. 8 (Egypt). For discussion of international and
regional standards in relation to proselytism and missionary work, see M. L. Sandgren,
'Extending Religious Freedoms Abroad: Difficulties Experienced by Minority
Religions', *Tulsa Journal of Comparative and International Law*, (2001), 251.

[177] UN Doc. A/C.3/9/SR. 565 (1954), p. 108, para. 16 (Afghanistan).

the Islamic perspective on Article 18, that he was not intending any specific reference to Christianity: 'Christianity allowed other religions to be presented to followers of the faith. Islam was in perfect agreement with that point of view; the only difference lay in the method of presentation of certain other religions. It could not be said that difference of presentation implied any interference with the free judgement of the human will and conscience.'[178] He reaffirmed that 'his delegation had never viewed the provisions of article 18 in connexion with the activities of missionaries and did not do so now'.[179] He concluded that 'the Committee must do its utmost to protect all persons and all societies against pressures which would interfere with their right to a free choice of religion'.[180]

In the Third Session's plenary meeting at the conclusion of the debates on the Universal Declaration, the memorable statement of Sir Muhammed Zafrullah Khan, the representative of Pakistan, is important for the purposes of clarifying the type of missionary activities that he regarded as acceptable. He commented on Article 18 (then numbered 19) that the,

> 'Moslem religion was a missionary religion: it strove to persuade men to change their faith and alter their way of living, so as to follow the faith and way of living it preached, but it recognized the same right of conversion for other religions as for itself.
>
> Article 19 had given rise to anxiety among certain delegations because of the actions of the missionaries of certain other religions. He was glad to pay tribute to the work carried out by Christian missionaries in the East, especially in the fields of education, hygiene and medicine; nevertheless, it was undeniable that their activity had sometimes assumed a political character which had given rise to justifiable objections. In certain cases, the means employed to bring about conversion had made that conversion a worse remedy than the ill it set out to cure.'[181]

Unfortunately he did not specify what activity assumed a political character giving rise to justifiable objection. Although Saudi did not consider this statement to represent the views of all Muslims, the

---

[178] UN Doc. A/C.3/9/SR. 577 (1954), p. 175, para. 2 (Afghanistan).
[179] UN Doc. A/C.3/15/SR. 1024 (1960), p. 211, para. 28 (Afghanistan).
[180] *Ibid.*, at p. 212, para. 30.
[181] UN Doc. A/PV.182 (1948), pp. 890–1 (Pakistan). Mr Baroody (Saudi) believed Sir Mohammed Zafrullah Khan belonged to a very small Muslim sect which considered that it had a proselytising mission (UN Doc. A/C.3/15/SR. 1025 (1960), p. 214, para. 10).

delegate from Pakistan reiterated its content in the context of the ICCPR, reaffirming that in her opinion: 'Islam was, furthermore, a missionary religion and it therefore yielded to other faiths the free right of conversion. Although the means that had been employed to bring about conversion had often given rise to justifiable objections, it would be the greater evil to deny the freedom of exchange of belief or faith.'[182]

It was the view of the Philippines delegate that at the heart of the right to maintain or change a religion or to have no religion at all was 'the right of an individual to have freedom of choice'.[183] He was not insensitive to the Saudi argument concerning the risk of encouraging certain proselytising activities but 'at the same time it would be wrong to think that the article could ever be interpreted as prohibiting the activities of missionaries'.[184] Similarly, the delegate from Nepal, while acknowledging that religious and ideological friction in the world might be reduced in the absence of proselytism, nevertheless understood that the United Nations was not taking a stand against proselytising.[185]

The Israeli delegate considered the right of the individual to change his religion to be a basic human right and, in supporting paragraph 2 of Article 18, gave her interpretation of the word 'coercion' as:

> 'including both physical coercion and more insidious and indirect forms, including improper inducements. In Israel, as in many other countries, criminal law took cognizance of fraudulent acts or false pretences to bring about a change in an individual's religion, but there could well be acts which were ostensibly innocent or even beneficial, such as the giving of gifts or other material assistance, which constituted an inducement to a person to change his religion.'[186]

She understood the reference to a change of religion to mean, 'a change brought about by sincere ideological conviction'.[187]

In short, it would appear that missionary activities have long been associated in the fears of certain States with Crusade history, political ambitions, colonialism, espionage, insidious inducement and other forcible as well as indirect means of coercion to bring about a change of religion. However, for most States proselytism did not have any such association. On the contrary, proselytism was regarded as something to

---

[182] UN Doc. A/C.3/15/SR. 1024 (1960), p. 211, para. 21 (Pakistan).
[183] UN Doc. A/C.3/15/SR. 1024 (1960), p. 210, para. 8 (Philippines).   [184] *Ibid.*
[185] UN Doc. A/C.3/15/SR. 1023 (1960), p. 205, para. 3 (Nepal).
[186] UN Doc. A/C.3/15/SR. 1025 (1960), p. 217, para. 47 (Israel).   [187] *Ibid.*

be safeguarded for all religions and there remains as a result of these debates considerable doubt as to any basis on which proselytism, missionary activities and social action might constitute forms of coercion. Nevertheless, the stigma of coercion is difficult to dispel for so long as the supposed harmful effects of proselytism are exaggerated.

Krishnaswami noted that through foreign missionaries, 'a fresh culture is introduced which may not harmonize with the existing order'[188] and that in the reaction of States, the 'concept of social stability and national security were over-emphasized with the result that the right to disseminate was unduly limited'.[189] The position of missionaries is aggravated by the inadvertent political dimension of their work directed at alleviating poverty, assisting in education, medicine, farming and in enabling communities to improve their living conditions. Thus, in Guatemala, much of the persecution of Christians (including assassinations and death threats) stems from the social action taken by both Catholics and Protestants amongst *campesinos* in rural areas, which is seen as subversive.[190] Benito similarly observes the accusation that the work of religious leaders in certain Asian countries is that of 'inciting counter-revolution'.[191]

It may be added that nothing in paragraph 5 of General Comment No. 22 permits missionary work and social action easily to fall within the prohibition of Article 18(2) of the ICCPR. Paragraph 5 speaks of coercion by means of restricting access to education, medical care and employment rather than coercion by means which render them more readily available. However, an example of the possible misuse of missionary-funded education may be that provided in the drafting of paragraph 5 by the member from Mauritius, a country where children were once only accepted at Roman Catholic schools if they were prepared to observe the precepts of that faith.[192] (Of course much depends upon the availability of choice, and such a requirement in a country with a surfeit of different denominational schools would not constitute coercion.) Support for the protection of missionary work may be inferred in the Human Rights Committee's review of State reports[193] but is more

---

[188] Krishnaswami, 'Study of Discrimination', 227 at 254.   [189] *Ibid.*, at 255.

[190] K. Boyle and J. Sheen, *Freedom of Religion and Belief: A World Report*, London: Routledge (1997), at p. 132.

[191] Benito, *Elimination of all Forms of Intolerance and Discrimination*, p. 18, para. 77.

[192] UN Doc. CCPR/C/SR. 1166 (1992), p. 13, para. 85 (Mr Lallah).

[193] UN Doc. A/35/40 (1980), p. 22, para. 99 (Mongolia). The Committee asked whether freedom of religious propaganda was protected.

clearly evident in the reporting function of the Special Rapporteur.[194] The Special Rapporteur appears to have been more concerned about restrictions on missionary work than its supposed coercive effect. Even when considering particularly vulnerable categories such as orphans or deprived schoolchildren, Krishnaswami was fully aware of the risk that material inducement might render missionary work open to the accusation of coercion but applauded the work of missionaries, who have achieved remarkable results in many parts of the world where children would not otherwise have been educated. He did not rule out the possibility of isolated cases of improper inducements amounting even to outright bribes but in the wider realm of missionary hospitals, schools and orphanages, he concluded that 'where the prior right of parents or guardians to decide whether or not their children shall attend religious instruction is conceded, and where the institutions in question advance social welfare, the advantages obtained by such educational and humanitarian activities can hardly be considered to constitute a material inducement to a change of religion or belief'.[195] The notion of improper

---

[194] For example, the Special Rapporteur commented that, in Sudan, many obstacles are said to be hampering the work of local priests and missionaries who are endeavouring to bring moral and spiritual comfort to the population near El Obeid and in the Nubian mountain area (UN Doc. E/CN.4/1994/79 (1994), p. 111, para. 75). Similar concerns were addressed by the Special Rapporteur to Bhutan concerning the ban on practising Christianity in Bhutan, which was dismissed by the Government on the basis that '[m]oney, gifts and scholarships were being used as incentives for people to convert to Christianity' (UN Doc. E/CN.4/1995/91 (1995), p. 21). Likewise, in Nepal the Government sought to justify the ban on 'involuntary' conversion from Hinduism resulting from 'financial enticement and other temptations'. The ban supposedly operates 'as a source of guarantee to a weak person in protecting and preserving his fundamental rights' (UN Doc. E/CN.4/1994/79 (1994), p. 100, para. 66). Restrictions on the work of foreign missionaries were also noted by the Special Rapporteur in relation to Bangladesh (UN Doc. E/CN.4/2000/65 (2000), para. 15), Belarus (*ibid.*, at para. 16), India (*ibid.*, at para. 46), and Niger (UN Doc. E/CN.4/2001/63 (2001), p. 29, para. 107). However, the Special Rapporteur also referred to the possibility that minorities themselves may occasionally be sources of the intolerance towards other religious communities (*ibid.*, at p. 34, para. 131 and p. 46, para. 184). The Special Rapporteur recently addressed concern to India at legislation in Gujarat State aimed at preventing religious conversions by 'force, allurement or any other fraudulent means' – terms that the Special Rapporteur noted are very broadly defined – UN Doc. E/CN.4/2004/63 (2004), p. 12, para. 60 (India). For other restrictions on proselytism recently noted by the Special Rapporteur (in spite of assertions that improper inducements were offered), see UN Doc. E/CN.4/2004/63 (2004), p. 16, para. 94 (Sri Lanka) and UN Doc. E/CN.4/2003/66/Add.1 (2003), p. 16, para. 77 (Algeria).

[195] Krishnaswami, *Study of Discrimination*, 227, at 255.

'inducement' is elusive and casts doubt, which is largely unsubstantiated, over missionary and humanitarian work.

Objections to missionary work therefore appear to be twofold. First, missionary work often entails the offer of material assistance to alleviate conditions of suffering or physical hardship, which might be perceived (rightly or wrongly) to be available only on acceptance of the missionary religion. The provision of humanitarian assistance, even overtly in the practice of a particular religion, of itself cannot be said to be coercive. It must, it is submitted, be conditioned in a substantive way on joining or adhering to the precepts of that particular religion in order to amount to coercion, even indirect coercion. In the Universal Declaration and ICCPR debates missionary work was associated, by those opposed to it, with the most barbaric and coercive practices of the most shameful episodes of European history. However, when generalisations from a broad survey of historical aberrations are repeated in the context of contemporary privately-funded humanitarian and missionary work, the suggested risks of coercion are exaggerated if not entirely misplaced. It is appropriate now to re-evaluate missionary work for its truly coercive effect dissociated from such stigma.

This discussion has addressed only the first objection and questioned whether it is appropriate to describe social action carried on under a particular religious banner as coercive within the meaning of Article 18(2) of the ICCPR, concluding that it is not (without direct evidence of coercion in each case).

The second objection to missionary work is that it is often motivated by the opportunity to propagate a particular religion through proselytism. However, it similarly has to be questioned whether proselytism amounts to coercion. Unfortunately, the term 'proselytism' has acquired a strong negative connotation, suggesting a 'kind of evangelistic malpractice'[196] and there is therefore much value in attempting a detailed understanding of the distinction between coercive proselytism (encroaching upon the *forum internum* of each individual, the internal and private realm against which no interference is justified in any circumstances) and non-coercive proselytism constituting a protected form of manifestation of religion or belief.[197]

---

[196] Editorial, 'To Evangelize or Proselytize', 20 Int'l Bull Miss Res (1996), 1.

[197] Sullivan notes that '[p]roselytizing may set the rights of those whose religious faith encourages or requires such activity in opposition to the rights of those targeted to be

Proselytism

Although the opposition to proselytism expressed by certain States in the ICCPR debates led to the proposal for an anti-coercion provision, it is clear that the resulting Article 18(2) of the ICCPR was not accepted as an anti-proselytism measure, as noted above under the heading 'Origin of the freedom from coercion', but a general measure to prevent any coercion such as would interfere with the individual's *forum internum* right to change or to maintain their religion.[198] Both the Human Rights Committee and Special Rapporteur have endorsed proselytism as a proper manifestation of religion. The European Court has also given nominal endorsement to proselytism as a legitimate form of manifestation of religion or belief. More importantly, however, the legitimate aims claimed by States for restrictions on proselytism have all too readily been supported by the European Court and a potentially extremely broad interpretation of the limitation ground 'the rights and freedoms of others' has been developed in such a way as to suggest a fundamental departure from Universal standards.

Grounds of opposition to proselytism

Those countries whose religious laws treat adherence to a particular religion by the individual as sacrosanct, and a change of religion as apostasy, are understandably opposed to initiatives promoting alternative religions, particularly where State law and religious law are inseparable (and a change of religion might lead the individual to abrogate obligations imposed by religious law). It may also be believed that the moral condition of the individual and their eternal future are at stake. In the ICCPR debates on Article 18(2), Saudi considered that for the true enjoyment of religion, protection is necessary against 'pressure, proselytism and also against errors and heresies'.[199] It was felt that too great an emphasis was placed on the right to change one's religion given that '[m]en could in fact be induced to change their religion not only for perfectly legitimate intellectual or moral reasons, but also through

---

free from coercion to change their beliefs. The latter right is not a legitimate basis for denying believers the freedom to engage in *non-coercive* forms of proselytizing, such as mere appeals to conscience or the display of placards and billboards': Sullivan, 'Advancing the Freedom of Religion or Belief' 487, at 494.

[198] Such hostility is discussed by Rigaux (F. Rigaux, *L'Incrimination du Proselytism Face à la Liberté d'Expression*, 17 *Revue Trimestrielle des Droits de l'Homme* (1994) 144).

[199] UN Doc. A/C.3/15/SR. 1022 (1960), p. 204, para. 27 (Saudi).

weakness or credulity'.[200] In response, it was argued that sufficient safeguard existed to enable the individual to resist influences and even pressures that might be brought to bear, by the inclusion of the words 'to maintain' which had already been settled by the Commission. The United Kingdom delegate considered that the words 'to change' themselves enable free discussion and exchange of ideas, allowing for opinion to be modified, and that the combined reference to changing religion and to maintaining religion in Article 18(1) served adequately to address concerns over proselytism and propaganda.[201]

For some countries, distaste of proselytism is rooted in issues of culture or national identity quite separate from matters of doctrine. Examples include Armenia, Bulgaria and Greece, where the Orthodox or State religion is part of the national identity and seen to be threatened by competing religions which proselytise.[202] For example, in the Universal Declaration debates the delegate for Greece wondered:

> 'whether the phrase "freedom ... to manifest his religion or belief" might not lead to unfair practices of proselytizing. He mentioned, in that connexion, that he had had occasion to observe real religious competition in a country where all religions were represented. In fact, free

---

[200] *Ibid.*

[201] UN Doc. A/C.3/15/SR. 1022 (1960), p. 200, paras. 5–6 (United Kingdom). The same point was made in the final stages of drafting the 1981 Declaration. While accepting that the text of the draft before the Third Committee might reveal shortcomings or omissions, 'the fact remained that it affirmed that the right to express one's religious faith was a dimension of human existence', UN Doc. A/C.3/36/SR. 32 (1981), p. 9, para. 28 (Observer for the Holy See).

[202] Resistance against the influx of foreign evangelical denominations is particularly strong in Russia (H. Berman, 'Religious Rights in Russia at a Time of Tumultuous Transition: A Historical Theory', in J. D. van der Vyver and J. D. Witte (eds.), *Religious Human Rights in Global Perspective: Legal Perspectives*, The Hague/London: Martinus Nijhoff (1996), p. 288). However, in many other countries it is associated with the growth of nationalism. For further discussion see: P. Hayden, 'Religiously Motivated "Outrageous" Conduct: Intentional Infliction of Emotional Distress as a Weapon Against "Other People's Faiths"', 34 William Mary L Rev (1993) 579; P. W. Edge, 'Holy War on the Doorstep', 146 NLJ (1996) 190; P. B. Kurland, *Religion and the Law of Church and State and the Supreme Court*, Chicago: Aldine (1962); N. Lerner, 'Proselytism, Change of Religion, and International Human Rights', 12 Emory Int'l L Rev (1998) 477. For an account of the relationship between the Orthodox Church and religious minorities in Romania and Georgia, which bears out this discussion, see UN Doc. E/CN.4/2004/63/Add.2 (2004), p. 11, para. 48 (Romania) and UN Doc. E/CN.4/2004/63/Add.1 (2004), p. 17, para. 88 (Georgia).

lodgings, material assistance and a number of other advantages were offered to persons who agreed to belong to one religion or another.'[203]

He felt that the 'danger of such unfair practices was a threat, not only to the minority groups of a given country … but also to the religious majority. While, admittedly, every person should be free to accept or reject the religious propaganda to which he was subjected, he felt that an end should be put to such unfair competition in the sphere of religion.'[204] Greece did not make a formal proposal on the matter but in its post-vote explanation on Article 18 of the Universal Declaration commented that it had voted for the Article 'on the understanding that it did not authorize unfair practices of proselytism'.[205]

It would appear that delegates had differing impressions of what was acceptable and unacceptable proselytism, or were simply unclear as to what the word meant. Similarly, in the preparation of the draft Convention on religious intolerance, the Turkish delegate commented that freedom to worship or assemble, and to establish and maintain places of worship (ultimately protected forms of manifestation within Article 6(a) of the 1981 Declaration) would encourage proselytising.[206] There has historically been a fundamental lack of consensus on what is meant by 'proselytising' and the basis on which it is to be regarded as 'coercive'. Added to this, many of the fears are exaggerated. As the Special Rapporteur recently noted in the context of Algeria, '[t]he topics of conversion and non-Muslim proselytising tend to be blown up and treated as though they were major threats to the existence of Islam, though Islam is deeply rooted in Algeria'.[207] Far more surprising are the opinions expressed by one of the judges of the European Court (Judge Valticos) in *Larissis and others v. Greece*,[208] a case concerning evangelism by Pentecostal air force officers directed towards fellow airmen and towards civilians. Apart from a mere exchange of views,

---

[203] UN Doc. A/C.3/3/SR. 127 (1948), p. 393 (Greece).
[204] UN Doc. A/C.3/3/SR. 127 (1948), pp. 393–4 (Greece).
[205] UN Doc. A/C.3/3/SR. 128 (1948), p. 406 (Greece).
[206] UN Doc. A/C.3/22/SR. 1487 (1967), p. 120. Some of the controversial grounds for opposing proselytism in the drafting of the 1981 Declaration and confusion with guaranteed rights of manifestation were discussed by R. S. Clark, 'The United Nations and Religious Freedom', 11 NYUJ Int'l L & Pol (1978) 197.
[207] UN Doc. E/CN.4/2003/66/Add.1 (2003), p. 24, para. 137 (Algeria).
[208] *Larissis and others v. Greece* (Ser. A) No. 65 (1998–V) ECtHR 363.

'acts of proselytism may take forms that are straightforward or devious, that may or may not be an abuse of the proselytiser's authority and may be peaceful or – and history has given us many bloodstained examples of this – violent. Attempts at "brainwashing" may be made by flooding or drop by drop, but they are nevertheless, whatever one calls them, attempts to violate individual consciences and must be regarded as incompatible with freedom of opinion, which is a fundamental human right.'[209]

A brief survey of the different attitudes of States towards proselytism serves to highlight, first, the extent of rigorous antagonism against what is widely understood to be a protected form of manifestation of religion or belief, secondly, the different justifications of States in opposing proselytism (such as protection against heresy, preservation of the State Church or national identity – none of which is recognised by any human rights instrument), and thirdly, the lack of firm agreement on the distinction between protected forms of 'proselytism' and those which may be restricted.

It is all the more to be regretted that when given the opportunity to clarify the distinction between acceptable and 'improper' proselytism in *Kokkinakis v. Greece*,[210] the European Court failed to provide workable definitions beyond confirming, rather narrowly, that 'teaching' and 'Christian witness' are safeguarded manifestations of religion. It commented as follows: 'Freedom to manifest one's religion ... includes in principle the right to try to convince one's neighbour, for example, through "teaching", failing which, moreover, "freedom to change [one's] religion or belief" enshrined in Article 9 ... would be likely to remain a dead letter.'[211]

---

[209] Judge Valticos (partly dissenting) joined by Judge Morenilla, *Larissis and others v. Greece* (Ser. A) No. 65 (1998–V) ECtHR 363.

[210] *Kokkinakis v. Greece* (Ser. A) No. 260–A (1993) ECtHR.

[211] *Ibid.*, at para. 31. As Judge Pettiti commented in the *Kokkinakis* case: 'In my view, it would have been possible to define impropriety, coercion and duress more clearly and to describe more satisfactorily, in the abstract, the full scope of religious freedom and bearing witness.' This would have provided 'the member States with positive material for giving effect to the Court's judgment in future and fully implementing the principle and standards of religious freedom under Article 9 (art. 9) of the European Convention'. For further discussion of religious witness, see B. G. Ramcharan, 'Religious Witness and Practice in Political and Social Life as an Element of Religious Liberty', in B. Lynn, et al. (eds.). Judge De Meyer in his concurring opinion in the *Kokkinakis* case even considered that '[p]roselytism, defined as "zeal in spreading the faith", cannot be punishable as such: it is a way – perfectly legitimate in itself – of "manifesting [one's] religion"'.

The case concerned a Jehovah's Witness who had been arrested more than sixty times for proselytism, on the latest occasion for discussing his faith with the wife of an Orthodox Cantor when the applicant visited her house. Drawing on text provided by the World Council of Churches the European Court accepted that Christian witness corresponds to 'true evangelism ... an essential mission and a responsibility of every Christian and every Church'.[212] By contrast, the Court explained that:

> '"improper proselytism" represents a corruption or deformation of it. It may ... take the form of activities offering material or social advantages with a view to gaining new members for a Church or exerting improper pressure on people in distress or in need; it may even entail the use of violence or brainwashing; more generally, it is not compatible with respect for the freedom of thought, conscience and religion of others.'[213]

It is interesting that the European Court never once referred in this case to the term 'proper proselytism', possibly in view of the enduring negative associations of all forms of proselytism with 'improper proselytism'. Nor did it ever determine whether the activities of the applicant in gaining an invitation into a private dwelling to share his beliefs constituted teaching, 'true evangelism' or 'improper proselytism'. This is because the European Court ruled against Greece only on the basis of the national court's finding that the offence had been committed by

---

[212] *Kokkinakis v. Greece* (Ser. A) No. 260-A (1993) ECtHR, at para. 48. As some have noted, it would have been better if the Court had not adopted a formula provided by the World Council of Churches but instead a neutral one, or one that applies to non-Christian religions, particularly in view of the fact that the purpose of the Greek law that secured the applicant's conviction was originally drafted to protect the Christian Greek Orthodox Church. For further discussion on proselytism, see S. S. Juss, 'Kokkinakis and Freedom of Conscience Rights in Europe', 1 J Civ Lib (1996) 246. Juss comments that State deference in the decision 'does not engender confidence in the Court's ability to handle more difficult cases in the future' (at p. 251). This was further discussed by P. W. Edge, in 'Kokkinakis v. Greece: A Response to Dr Juss', 2 J Civ Lib (1997) 41. Unlike Juss, Edge argues that reference to the report of the World Council of Churches does not constitute explicit Christian bias (p. 42). See also J. W. Montgomery, 'When is Evangelism Illegal?' 148 NLJ (1998) 524. (Montgomery was leading Counsel for the applicants in *Larissis*. He described the Greek anti-proselytism law as 'an affront to religious freedom').
[213] *Kokkinakis v. Greece* (Ser. A) No. 260-A (1993) ECtHR, at para. 48. For discussion concerning brainwashing, see: J. Allan, *Shopping for a God: Fringe Religions Today*, Leicester: Intervarsity (1986); G. Nelson, *Cults, New Religions and Religious Creativity*, London: Routledge & Kegan Paul (1987), pp. 173–94; J. A. Beckford, *Cult Controversies, The Societal Response to the New Religious Movements*, London: Tavistock (1985), pp. 218–76.

reference to the wording of section 4 of Law No. 1363/1938 (which makes proselytism an offence) without sufficient consideration of the facts.

The European Court did not decide to impugn Greece's anti-proselytism law (as it could have done and as dissenting judges would have liked it to). This is to ignore the purpose of the law, which was originally expressly to protect the State Orthodox religion from non-Orthodox denominations and other religions,[214] and to ignore the fact that the law was consistently used as a tool of discrimination. Judge Martens, in his partly dissenting opinion, even questioned whether it is appropriate for the State to legislate at all against 'improper proselytism'. He commented that: '[a]dmittedly, the freedom to proselytise may be abused, but the crucial question is whether that justifies enacting a criminal-law provision generally making punishable what the State considers improper proselytism'. He replied emphatically that it does not, first of all because 'the State, being bound to strict neutrality in religious matters, lacks the necessary touchstone and therefore should not set itself up as the arbiter for assessing whether particular religious behaviour is "proper" or "improper"'.[215] Secondly, because:

> 'the rising tide of religious intolerance makes it imperative to keep the State's powers in this field within the strictest possible boundaries. However, the Court achieves quite the reverse in attempting to settle those boundaries by means of so elusive a notion as "improper proselytism", a definition of which the Court does not even attempt to give.'[216]

Unfortunately, the European Court paid lip-service to the right to manifest religion through proselytism, referring to it in the narrowest possible terms and in a way that did not adequately confront the true purpose of the Greek legislation. The European Court accepted that a legitimate aim had been pursued, namely 'the protection of the rights and freedoms of others'. When considering whether the restriction was 'necessary in a democratic society', it was conscious that its task was that of determining whether the restriction was 'justified in principle and proportionate'. The Court scrutinised section 4 of Law No. 1363/1938

---

[214] *Kokkinakis v. Greece* (Ser. A) No. 260-A (1993) ECtHR, at paras. 15 and 29. See also *Larissis and others v. Greece* (Ser. A) No. 65 (1998–V) ECtHR 363, at paras. 9, 10, 15, 17, 19.

[215] Partly dissenting opinion of Judge Martens in *Kokkinakis v. Greece* (Ser. A) No. 260–A (1993) ECtHR, para. 16.

[216] *Ibid.*

and found that it was 'reconcilable with the foregoing' if and only in so far as it was designed to punish improper proselytism.[217] However, since the applicant was subjected to criminal prosecution for what was undoubtedly not 'improper proselytism', and given that there had been a history of similar prosecutions under the same legislation, it must be questioned whether the impugned measure was in pursuit of a legitimate aim.

The European Court found that the Greek court had failed to specify sufficiently in what way the applicant had attempted to convince his neighbour by improper means. Accordingly, the applicant's criminal conviction was not proportionate to the legitimate aim pursued or, consequently, 'necessary in a democratic society ... for the protection of the rights and freedoms of others'.[218] The use of this ground of limitation deserves close examination.

Rights and freedoms of others

The European Court in *Kokkinakis* accepted the legitimate aim of the Greek legislation, namely 'the protection of the rights and freedoms of others, relied on by the Government'[219] and it is important to understand this statement in its proper context. The Greek Government's claim referred to 'the personal freedoms of all those living on its territory', coupled with the contention that '[i]f, in particular, it was not vigilant to protect a person's religious beliefs and dignity from attempts to influence them by immoral and deceitful means, Article 9 para. 2 (art. 9–2) would in practice be rendered wholly nugatory'.[220] The European Court could have been supporting only 'the rights and freedoms of others' as an appropriate head of claim in principle (effectively reciting part of Article 9(2)) or, alternatively, it might be taken as accepting the full breadth of the Greek Government's contention of a legitimate aim in the protection of beliefs and dignity against certain influences, in such a way as to extend 'the rights and freedoms of others' in a novel way. It is a feature of the brevity of the European Court's analysis that important underlying reasoning is often difficult to discern.

The same issue arose in *Larissis and others v. Greece*,[221] a case in which Greek air force officers had been convicted of proselytism in separate counts concerning subordinate members of the armed services, and

---

[217] *Ibid.*, at para. 48.   [218] *Ibid.*, at para. 49.   [219] *Ibid.*, at para. 44.
[220] *Ibid.*, at para. 42.
[221] *Larissis and others v. Greece* (Ser. A) No. 65 No. 1998–V ECtHR 363.

civilians. The European Court did little more than refer to its previous decision in *Kokkinakis* when addressing the legitimate aim of the Greek legislation[222] and no attempt was made to elaborate on the distinction between acceptable and 'improper' proselytism. However, when considering whether the convictions for proselytism were proportionate, and in weighing the requirements of the protection of the rights and liberties of others against the conduct of the applicants, a distinction was made between the lower ranking airmen who were proselytised, and the civilians.

In relation to the proselytising of lower ranking airmen, the Greek Government claimed that the measures taken against the applicants were 'justified by the need to protect the prestige and effective operation of the armed forces and to protect individual soldiers from ideological coercion'.[223] In response, the European Commission found that the interference could be justified on the basis of ensuring that the three airmen's religious beliefs were 'respected' in view of the special character of the relationship between a superior and a subordinate in the armed forces, which rendered subordinates more susceptible to influence in a variety of matters including religious beliefs.[224] When the matter came before the European Court it concluded that the measures were proportionate in relation to proselytism directed at the lower ranking airmen but not in relation to proselytism directed at the civilians. The Court did not follow the Commission's ground of justification, namely that of 'ensuring that the three airmen's religious beliefs were respected' although, like the Commission, the Court did consider the 'particular characteristics of military life and its effects on the situation of individual members of the armed forces' to be decisive.[225] By the same token, in relation to the proselytising of civilians it was crucial that the civilians were not subject to pressures and constraints of the same kind as airmen.[226] Even though one civilian was in a state of distress brought on by the breakdown of her marriage, the European Court decided that her mental condition was not such that she was 'in need of any special protection from the evangelical activities of the applicants'.[227] The difference was expressed as follows: '[W]hat would in the civilian world be seen as an innocuous exchange of ideas which the recipient is free to accept or reject, may, within the confines of military life, be viewed as a form of harassment or the application of undue pressure in abuse of power.'[228]

---

[222] *Ibid.*, at para. 44.   [223] *Ibid.*, at para. 47.   [224] *Ibid.*, at para. 49.   [225] *Ibid.*, at para. 50.
[226] *Ibid.*, at para. 59.   [227] *Ibid.*, at para. 59.   [228] *Ibid.*, at para. 51.

However, the judgment does not clearly explain the particular rights and freedoms of others which are at issue, such as to justify restrictions on certain forms of proselytism. The European Court in these cases seems to be taking one of two possible approaches to 'the rights and freedoms of others': either that phrase is confined only to coercion and other forms of interference with the *forum internum*, or the European Court is admitting further latitude to 'the rights and freedoms of others' within boundaries that are not easy to predict. When considering appropriate limitations on the manifestation of religion or belief, the designated limitation grounds under Article 9 are public safety, order, health or morals or the fundamental rights and freedoms of others. Assuming the proselytism in question is such as to impair the freedom of religious choice of the person proselytised, the 'rights and freedoms of others' would be the right to be free from coercion impairing free religious choice. However, it is difficult to discern precisely what 'rights and freedoms of others' might be at stake in the case of proselytism which is not coercive, especially given the view of some judges of the European Court that '[a]ttempting to make converts is not in itself an attack on the freedom and beliefs of others or an infringement of their rights'.[229]

It is worth observing that when discussion focused on the rights and freedoms of others in the Third Committee's consideration of the Universal Declaration, Sweden pointed to the danger inherent in manifestations of political fanaticism and (unsuccessfully) proposed an amendment that would qualify the external manifestations of religion or belief with the words, 'provided that this does not interfere unduly with the personal liberty of anybody else'.[230] This was aimed at promoting a 'policy of tolerance towards individuals who professed religious beliefs, as well as those who had none'.[231] In considering the possible meaning of the phrase 'interfere unduly with the personal liberty of anybody else', the Belgian delegate commented that in 'professing or propagating a faith one could, to a certain extent, interfere with the freedom of others by seeking to impose an unfamiliar idea upon them. But proselytism was not limited to any one faith or religious group. If it was an evil, it was essentially an evil from which all sides had to suffer'.[232]

---

[229] Judge Pettiti in his partly concurring opinion in *Kokkinakis v. Greece*.
[230] UN Doc. A/C. 3/252 (1948).
[231] UN Doc. A/C.3/3/SR. 127 (1948), at pp. 390–1 (Sweden).
[232] UN Doc. A/C.3/3/SR. 127 (1948), at p. 395 (Belgium).

Consequently, Belgium could not accept the Swedish amendment, particularly in view of its vagueness, and the amendment was not adopted. Similarly, the Philippines delegate agreed with the goal of ensuring effective protection for the individual from the manifestations of religious fanaticism but was sceptical of its application to proselytism: 'It was obvious that so long as attempts at religious proselytism remained within the limits of public order, freedom of thought was not threatened: quite on the contrary, the free exchange of religious ideas was one of the healthiest signs of freedom and democracy.'[233]

In view of the lack of consensus on the rationale for any prohibition on the practice of 'improper' proselytism, and given that other types of proselytism are accepted forms of manifestation, it may be appropriate to interpret the 'rights and freedoms of others' to refer primarily to coercion that impairs religious choice. Such an approach could be developed consistently with existing European case law and would result in better convergence with United Nations standards.

Coercion

It may be argued that the European Court in both the *Kokkiakis* and *Larissis* cases referred only to the need to protect others from coercive influences or coercive means that would impair their free choice of religion. In making its decision in the *Kokkinakis* case, it seems unlikely that the European Court was aware of the Human Rights Committee's discussions the year earlier (on 9 October 1992)[234] on what was to become paragraph 5 of General Comment No. 22, concerning coercion amounting to impairment of religious choice. Those discussions (and the text that resulted from them) did not associate any form of proselytism with coercion, for the reasons given above ('Interpretation of the freedom from coercion'), but instead focused on the threat of physical force or penal sanctions, and the denial of access to education, medical care and employment. If the European Court had followed parallel developments in the Human Rights Committee, it might have observed in *Kokkinakis* that proselytism is not generally regarded by the Human Rights Committee as coercive, which would have enabled it to provide a more positive definition of acceptable forms of proselytism than it did. The Court might also have dispensed with the need for any definition of

---

[233] UN Doc. A/C.3/3/SR. 127 (1948), at p. 396 (Philippines).
[234] UN Doc. CCPR/C/SR. 1166 (1992).

improper proselytism beyond that which is genuinely coercive in relation to religious choice.

Nevertheless, it is possible to interpret the European Court's analysis
of 'the rights and freedoms of others' in terms of coercion impairing free
religious choice, amounting to interference with the *forum internum*.
This is indicated by the description of 'improper proselytism' in paragraph 48 of the Court's judgment in *Kokkinakis* in terms of 'offering
material or social advantages', 'improper pressure on people in distress
or in need' and 'violence or brainwashing', all of which the Court stated
are 'incompatible with respect for the freedom of thought, conscience
and religion of others'. These illustrations are reminiscent of the
descriptions given to such coercion by Krishnaswami (Rule 1(3) refers
to 'improper inducements')[235] and by the Sub-Commission on
Prevention of Discrimination and Protection of Minorities (Draft
Principle I(3) refers to 'material or moral coercion').[236] Similarly,
the Court's references in *Larissis* to 'improper pressure' applied to
subordinate airmen and the equivalent 'pressures and constraints' that
were not applied to civilians is consistent with protecting recipients of
proselytism only from coercion that would impair their free religious
choice.

Judge Pettiti in his partly concurring opinion in *Kokkinakis* suggested that:

> '[b]elievers and agnostic philosophers have a right to expound their
> beliefs, to try to get other people to share them and even to try to convert
> those whom they are addressing. The only limits on the exercise of this
> right are those dictated by respect for the rights of others where there is an
> attempt to coerce the person into consenting or to use manipulative
> techniques.'[237]

Judge Martens (partly dissenting in *Kokkinakis*) usefully explained
what the term 'coercion' means in this context:

---

[235] Krishnaswami, 'Study of Discrimination', 227, at 296.

[236] Draft Principles on Freedom and Non-Discrimination in the Matter of Religious
Rights and Practices, UN Doc. E/CN.4/800, UN Doc. E/CN.4/Sub.2/206, Annex
(1960).

[237] Judge Pettiti's remarks were made in response to the Greek Government's suggestion
that a distinction should be made between proselytism that is 'respectable' and that
which is not, rather than in response to the Court's failure to confine 'improper
proselytism' only to coercion.

'Coercion in the present context does not refer to conversion by coercion, for people who truly believe do not change their beliefs as a result of coercion; what we are really contemplating is coercion in order to make somebody join a denomination and its counterpart, coercion to prevent somebody from leaving a denomination. Even in such a case of "coercion for religious purposes" it is in principle for those concerned to help themselves.'[238]

In paragraph 33 of the *Kokkinakis* judgment, in which the Court first invoked the notion of 'respect' in relation to proselytism, the Court was at pains to differentiate Article 9 from other Convention Articles (namely Articles 8, 10 and 11) by virtue of the absolute nature of that part of the right to freedom of thought, conscience and religion which may not be subject to limitation, i.e. the *forum internum*. By contrast, all rights covered by Articles 8, 10 and 11 are subject to limitation provisions. The right of the applicant in *Kokkinakis* to manifest his religion or belief in Article 9 must inevitably avoid encroaching upon those rights of others in Article 9 which are absolute. The Court recognised: 'that in democratic societies, in which several religions coexist within one and the same population, it may be necessary to place restrictions on this freedom in order to reconcile the interests of the various groups and ensure that everyone's beliefs are respected'.[239]

It may be said that the European Court was simply reiterating the need to respect *forum internum* rights by ensuring that they be protected against interference. It would be appropriate to give 'respect' that meaning (in the context of ensuring that chosen beliefs are 'respected') whenever there is a possibility that the right to free religious choice might be at risk of impairment by means of coercion. 'Respect' in this sense would denote assurance against interference with the *forum internum*. This accords with the analysis of paragraph 48 above, where the examples of 'improper proselytism' ('offering material or social advantages', 'improper pressure on people in distress or in need' and 'violence or brainwashing') were directed at interference with *forum internum* rights.

Few would contest that proselytism is aimed ultimately at bringing about a change in religious choice. The decisive factor is arguably only whether proselytism is 'improper' by virtue of being coercive in

---

[238] Partly dissenting opinion of Judge Martens in *Kokkinakis v. Greece* (Ser. A) No. 260-A (1993) ECtHR, at para. 17.
[239] *Ibid.*, at para. 33.

impairing the religious choice of others (and thereby constitutes 'improper pressure', to use the language of the Court).[240] If so, the *Kokkinakis* judgment may not be said to extend 'the rights and freedoms of others' to include a right to have their beliefs 'respected' in any sense beyond the accepted boundaries of the *forum internum*. The *forum internum* is not generally understood to embrace any right to be free from persuasion by others that falls short of coercion impairing free religious choice, nor even a right not have one's own beliefs criticised. In his (partly) dissenting opinion, Judge Martens in *Kokkinakis* usefully commented on the existence of concurrent rights in situations of proselytism and whether proselytism is appropriate for State intervention:

> 'It is true ... that proselytising creates a possible "conflict" between two subjects of the right to freedom of religion: it sets the rights of those whose religious faith encourages or requires such activity against the rights of those targeted to maintain their beliefs.
>
> In principle, however, it is not within the province of the State to interfere in this "conflict" between proselytiser and proselytised. Firstly, because – since respect for human dignity and human freedom implies that the State is bound to accept that in principle everybody is capable of determining his fate in the way that he deems best – there is no justification for the State to use its power "to protect" the proselytised (it may be otherwise in very special situations in which the State has a particular duty of care, but such situations fall outside the present issue). Secondly, because even the "public order" argument cannot justify use of coercive State power in a field where tolerance demands that "free argument and debate" should be decisive. And thirdly, because under the Convention all religions and beliefs should, as far as the State is concerned, be equal.
>
> That is also true in a State where, as in the present case, one particular religion has a dominant position: as the drafting history of Article 9 (art. 9) confirms.'[241]

---

[240] *Ibid.*, at para. 48.

[241] *Ibid.*, at para. 15. Resolution of conflict between rights has been argued by Meron on the basis of a 'hierarchy' (T. Meron, 'On a Hierarchy of International Human Rights', 80 Am J Int'l L (1986) 1), while Henkin suggests that 'usually conflict will be between a principal right and some peripheral application of another, and it may be possible to derive from the Covenant some evidence as to the choice permitted to the state' (L. Henkin, 'Introduction', in L. Henkin (ed.), *The International Bill of Rights: The Covenant on Civil and Political Rights*, New York/Guildford: Columbia University Press (1981), at p. 30). For resolution of gender issues, see D. J. Sullivan, 'Gender Equality and Religious Freedom: Toward a Framework for Conflict Resolution', 24 NYUJ Int'l L & Pol (1992) 795. In the context of proselytism, see: C. M. Robeck, '*Mission and the Issue of Proselytism*', 20 Int'l Bull Miss Res (1996) 2; C. Gustafson

In short, the use by the European Court of the limitation ground 'the rights and freedoms of others' in the context of Article 9 is consistent with coercion that would impair religious choice and, it is argued, should be confined to that form of coercion.

However, the term 'the rights and freedoms of others' is capable of broader interpretation in the light of parallel obligations attaching to the freedom of expression and guarantees prohibiting hate speech. Certain decisions in the context of freedom of expression suggest the existence of safeguards analogous to 'respect' for the beliefs of others. Those decisions will now be evaluated for two separate, but related, issues. The first, and more general, is the extent to which the term 'the rights and freedoms of others' imposes constraints on proselytism and other forms of persuasion to change religion or belief falling short of coercion that impairs the individual's choice. Secondly, but related, is whether there can be discerned in European and Universal standards any true recognition of a right to have one's beliefs respected and, if so, what relevance it has to the question of proselytism.

Hate speech

One limit to which all forms of religious expression are subject concerns hate speech.[242] Article 20 of the ICCPR imposes a restriction on all

and P. Juviler (eds.), *Religion and Human Rights: Competing Claims?* Armonk, New York/London: M. E. Sharpe (1999).

[242] Certain distinctions are important to make. In the context of the drafting of the Convention on religious intolerance, the point was rightly made that criticism of one religion by the adherents of another religion was not necessarily an incitement to hatred, and that a distinction had to be made between propagating one religion and fostering or inciting hatred against another (UN Doc. E/CN.4/940 (1967), p. 19, para. 61). A different distinction was made in the drafting of the 1981 Declaration when Egypt opposed the USSR proposal which contemplated a right to criticise religious beliefs, on the basis that this gave rise to intolerance (UN Doc. E/CN.4/1292; E/1978/34 (1978), p. 64, para. 39). For a summary of measures to combat racist and hate speech, see D. Türk and L. Joinet, 'The Right to Freedom of Opinion and Expression: Current Problems of its Realization and Measures Necessary for its Strengthening and Promotion', in S. Coliver (ed.), *Striking a Balance: Hate Speech, Freedom of Expression and Non-discrimination*, London: University of Essex, Human Rights Centre (1992). See also: K. Greenawalt, *Speech, Crimes and the Uses of Language*, Oxford: Oxford University Press (1989); R. Genn, 'Legal developments – Helsinki Process – Advance in International Outlawing of Incitement to Racism and Religious Hatred', 24 Pat of Prej (1990) 97; A. Garay, *Liberté Religieuse et Proselytisme: l'Experience Européene*, 17 *Revue Trimestrielle des Droits de l'Homme* (1994) 144; E. Steiner, 'Blasphemy and Incitement to Hatred under the European Convention', 6 KCLJ (1995) 143; and P. Rumney, 'Incitement to Racial Hatred and the Problem of Social Exclusion', 5(2) CIL (2000/2001) 89.

activities amounting to the 'advocacy of national, racial or religious hatred that constitutes incitement to discrimination, hostility or violence'. Paragraph 7 of General Comment No. 22 is taken directly from Article 20 and reiterates the absolute requirement on States to prohibit such activities by law. Article 20 is stricter than Article 18(3) in that it contains a mandatory prohibition on particular forms of speech, rather than the option to impose limitations on specified grounds. In debating General Comment No. 22, the issue of 'respect' for the beliefs and religions of others featured in discussion in paragraph 7, concerning the interrelation between Articles 18(3) and 20, in particular to distinguish the permissible limitations in Article 18(3) from the mandatory prohibition in Article 20.[243] Although it was initially considered that 'respect' for the beliefs and religions of others was limited by the requirements of Article 20, it was quickly realised that Article 20 imposes a restriction not on 'respect' for the beliefs and religion of others but on the freedom to manifest one's religions or beliefs.[244] Paragraph 7 did not therefore support a general requirement of 'respect' for the beliefs or religions of others beyond recognition that in the manifestation of religion or belief under Article 18(3), the prohibition on advocacy of national, racial or religious hatred in Article 20 should operate as a brake on manifestation.[245] Having raised the issue of respect by individuals for the beliefs and religions of others, the Human Rights Committee defined the limits of such respect by reference to the scope of Article 20.[246]

Both the Human Rights Committee[247] and the Special Rapporteur[248] have been vigilant in reminding States of the need to oppose intolerance or advocacy of national, racial or religious hatred. However, neither the Human Rights Committee nor the Special Rapporteur appears to have

---

[243] UN Doc. CCPR/C/SR. 1207 (1993), pp. 4–5, para. 23 (Mrs Higgins).

[244] UN Doc. CCPR/C/SR. 1207 (1993), p. 5, para. 23 (Mr Herndl), p. 5, para. 30 (Mr Pocar).

[245] UN Doc. CCPR/C/SR. 1207 (1993), p. 6, para. 33 (Miss Chanet).

[246] For discussion on the interrelation between Articles 18, 19 and 20 of the ICCPR, see Dickson, 'The United Nations and Freedom of Religion', 327, at 340.

[247] UN Doc. A/57/40 vol. 1 (2002), p. 39, para. 75(14) (United Kingdom); UN Doc. A/57/40 vol. 1 (2002), p. 60, para. 79(14) (Sweden); UN Doc. A/58/40 vol. 1 (2003), p. 35, para. 77(18) (Egypt).

[248] UN Doc. A/57/274 (2002), p. 8, para. 36 (Georgia); UN Doc. E/CN.4/2004/63/Add.2 (2004), p. 22, para. 109 (Romania); UN Doc. A/58/296 (2003), p. 11, para. 59 (Iran); UN Doc. E/CN.4/2003/66/Add.1 (2003), p. 13, para. 59 (Algeria); and, more generally, UN Doc. A/58/296 (2003), p. 23, para. 137.

readily acknowledged notions of 'respect' even in the most extreme cases. For example, the Human Rights Committee has ruled as incompatible with the provisions of the ICCPR, and therefore inadmissible *ratione materiae* under Article 3 of the Optional Protocol, Article 19 claims based on a criminal conviction for reorganising the dissolved fascist party in Italy (*M.A. v. Italy*),[249] and a criminal conviction for transmitting anti-Semitic tape-recordings by telephone, warning callers 'of the dangers of international finance and international Jewry leading the world into wars, unemployment and inflation and the collapse of world values and principles' (*J.R.T. and the W.G. Party v. Canada*).[250] In the former case, the Human Rights Committee relied on Article 5 of the ICCPR (which refers to activities 'aimed at the destruction of any of the rights and freedoms recognised herein') and in the latter on Article 20 (in view of the State's obligation to prohibit hate speech). The Committee's reliance on such provisions emphasises the extreme nature of the authors' activities.[251]

The Human Rights Committee's approach to such issues does not appear to be wholly consistent with that found in European jurisprudence, partly owing to the fact that there is no equivalent protection in the European Convention to Article 20 of the ICCPR and partly because the European Commission decision most directly comparable to the Optional Protocol case of *M.A. v. Italy* was an early one characterised by rather imprecise reasoning. In *X. v. Italy*[252] the European Commission decided that the Italian prohibition against reorganisation of the dissolved fascist party was justified on the grounds both of public safety and the protection of the rights and freedoms of others (within paragraph 2 of each of Articles 9, 10 and 11 of the European Convention without distinguishing between them), rather than under Article 17 (the counterpart to Article 5 of the ICCPR, which formed the basis of the Human Rights Committee's decision in *M.A. v. Italy*). This decision does not

---

[249] *M.A. v. Italy*, Communication No. 117/81 (decision of 10 April 1984), UN Doc. A/39/40 (1984), p. 190.

[250] *J.R.T. and the W.G. Party v. Canada*, Communication No. 104/1981 (decision of 6 April 1983), UN Doc. A38/40 (1983), p. 231 (quoting from para. 2.1).

[251] For discussion on Article 20, see: M. Nowak, *CCPR Commentary*, Kehl: N. P. Engel (1993), at p. 359, and D. McGoldrick, *The Human Rights Committee: Its Role in the Development of the International Covenant on Civil and Political Rights*, Oxford: Clarendon Press, (1994), at pp. 490–2. Both comment on *J.R.T. and the W.G. Party v. Canada*.

[252] *X. v. Italy*, App. No. 6741/74 (1976) 5 D&R 83.

therefore represent very strongly reasoned authority although in other instances the European organs have relied directly on Article 17.

For example, in *Glimmerveen and Hagenbeek v. The Netherlands*[253] a claim was brought by the chairman of *Netherlandse Volks Unie*, a political party promoting the idea of an ethnically homogenous population. He claimed that a two-week prison sentence infringed his right under Article 10, which he received for circulating inflammatory tracts. These included statements such as: 'the major part of our population since a long time has had enough of the presence in our country of hundreds of thousands of Surinamese, Turks and other so-called "guest" workers, who, moreover are not at all needed here'.[254] The European Commission held that the applicant could not avail himself of his Article 10 freedoms, by virtue of Article 17 which prevents totalitarian groups from exploiting in their own interests the principles enunciated by the Convention. The European Court supported the decision in *Glimmerveen and Hagenbeek v. The Netherlands* more recently in *Jersild v. Denmark*,[255] a case in which the applicant, a television journalist, assisted in the dissemination of racist views held by the anti-social youth organisation, 'the Greenjackets'. The journalist and the Greenjackets who made the inflammatory remarks in a television interview were all convicted under Danish law, which gave effect to that country's obligations under Article 4 of the International Convention on the Elimination of All Forms of Racial Discrimination.[256] The Court upheld the Commission's finding of violation of Article 10 in the case of the journalist but indicated that 'the remarks

---

[253] *Glimmerveen and Hagenbeek v. The Netherlands*, App. No. 8348/78 and 8406/78 (1979) 18 D&R 187.

[254] *Ibid.*, at 188.   [255] *Jersild v. Denmark* (Ser. A) No. 289 (1995) ECtHR.

[256] International Convention on the Elimination of All Forms of Racial Discrimination (1965)(New York, 21 December 1965, in force 4 January 1969 660 UNTS 195, reprinted in 5 ILM 352 (1966); UN GAOR, 20th Sess., Supp. No. 14, 1406 Plen. Mtg at 47, UN Doc. A/6014 (1964). Article 4 reads as follows: 'States Parties condemn all propaganda and all organizations which are based on ideas or theories of superiority of one race or group of persons of one colour or ethnic origin, or which attempt to justify or promote racial hatred and discrimination in any form, and undertake to adopt immediate and positive measures designed to eradicate all incitement to, or acts of, such discrimination and, to this end, with due regard to the principles embodied in the Universal Declaration of Human Rights and the rights expressly set forth in Article 5 of this Convention, inter alia: (a) shall declare an offence punishable by law all dissemination of ideas based on racial superiority or hatred, incitement to racial discrimination, as well as acts of violence or incitement to such acts against any race or group of persons of another colour or ethnic origin, and also the provision of any assistance to racist activities, including the financing thereof.'

in respect of which the Greenjackets were convicted ... were more than insulting to members of the targeted groups and did not enjoy the protection of Article 10'.[257] A similar analysis, based on the scope of expressions covered by Article 10, is apparent in the concurring Joint Opinion of Judges Ress and Cabral Barreto in *Vatan v. Russia*,[258] which concerned a political party founded 'to support the renascence of the Tartar nation, to enhance the latter's political activity and to protect Tartars' political, socio-economic and cultural rights'.[259] The conclusion that the application was inadmissible because it was manifestly ill-founded could have been reached, according to that Opinion, not only on grounds of failure to exhaust domestic remedies but because 'the reference to the Russian Federation as a "war party" whose arms should be "shortened" and to Russian institutions as "Nazis" overstepped the boundary of permissible freedom of expression within the meaning of Article 10'.[260]

One source of material in which the notion of 'respect' has played a part (albeit limited) concerns the restriction in a number of countries of the promotion of revisionist ideas, resulting in claims under the European Convention and the ICCPR.[261] These have generally upheld the protection of the reputation of others as an appropriate ground of limitation on freedom of expression. For example, in *X. v. Germany*,[262] since the murder of the Jews was a 'known historic fact', the applicant was prevented from asserting that the Holocaust was a piece of Zionist swindle. The European Commission found that the restriction was justified by the protection of the reputation of others within Article 10 of the European Convention[263] (although it is to be observed that this

[257] *Jersild v. Denmark* (Ser. A) No. 289 (1995) ECtHR, para. 35. See also D. McGoldrick and T. O'Donnell, 'Hate-Speech Laws: Consistency with National and International Human Rights Law', 18(4) *Legal Studies* (1998) 453, at 466, T. van Boven, 'Discrimination and Human Rights Law: Combating Racism', in S. Fredman (ed.), *Discrimination and Human Rights: The Case of Racism*, Oxford: Oxford University Press (2001), p. 129, and K. Boyle and A. Baldaccini, 'International Human Rights Approaches to Racism', in S. Fredman (ed.), *Discrimination and Human Rights: The Case of Racism*, ibid., pp. 165–76.
[258] *Vatan v. Russia* (App. No. 47978/99), Judgment of 7 October 2004.
[259] *Ibid.*, para. 9.
[260] See also *Refah Partisi (the Welfare Party) and others v. Turkey* (2003) 37 EHRR 1.
[261] See J. Cooper and A. M. Williams, 'Hate Speech, Holocaust Denial and International Human Rights Law', EHRLR (1996) 593.
[262] *X. v. Germany*, App. No. 9235/81 (1982) 29 D&R 194.
[263] *Ibid.*, at 198. See also *T. v. Belgium*, App. No. 9777/82 (1983) 34 D&R 158; and *Marais v. France*, App. No. 31159/96, (1996) 86 D&R (1996) 184. For further discussion of the legal implications of revisionist speech, see S. Roth, 'Denial of the Holocaust as an Issue of Law', 23 Isr YB Hum Rts (1993) 215.

ground of limitation is specific to Article 10 and has no equivalent in Article 9). A Similar conclusion was reached in the Optional Protocol case of *Robert Faurisson v. France*.[264] The author was a university professor whose denial of the Holocaust through statements of a highly offensive anti-Semitic nature fell within the criminal provisions of the Gayssot Act, which made it an offence to contest the existence of the crimes against humanity tried at Nuremberg in 1945 and 1946. Although the author did not specify which provisions of the ICCPR were violated, the Human Rights Committee examined the matter under Article 19 and found that France could properly rely on the limitation provision in Article 19(3)(a). Referring to General Comment No. 10, the Human Rights Committee noted that the protection of the rights or reputation of others as a limitation ground may relate not only to the interests of other persons but also those of the community as a whole.[265] The Human Rights Committee concluded that '[s]ince the statements made by the author, read in their full context, were of a nature as to raise or strengthen anti-Semitic feelings, the restriction served the respect of the Jewish community to live free from fear of an atmosphere of anti-Semitism'.[266] The Human Rights Committee's reference to 'respect' in this context must be read with caution since it does not refer to respect for the beliefs of others but instead merely recognises the right of a community to live free from religious hatred. Indeed the Human Rights Committee, unlike the Strasbourg organs, has avoided any concept of respect for the religious beliefs of others as a ground of limitation. In the more recent decision of *Malcolm Ross v. Canada*[267] the Human Rights Committee made no reference at all to 'respect' in the case of an Article 19 claim following restrictions imposed on a schoolteacher's statements which denigrated the faith and belief of Jews and called on others to hold those of the Jewish faith and ancestry in contempt. The restrictions were for the pupose of 'protecting the "rights and reputations" of persons of Jewish

---

[264] *Robert Faurisson v. France*, Communication No. 550/1993 (views of 8 November 1996), UN Doc. A/52/40 vol. 2 (1999), p. 84.

[265] General Comment No. 10(19), UN Doc. A/38/40 (1983) Annex VI, p. 109, para. 4.

[266] *Ibid.*, at para. 9.6.

[267] *Malcolm Ross v. Canada*, Communication No. 736/1997 (views of 18 October 2000), UN Doc. A/56/40 vol. 2 (2001), p. 69. See also *Zündel v. Canada*, Communication No. 953/2000 (decision of 27 July 2003), UN Doc. A/58/40 vol. 2 (2003), p. 483, which concerned a limited restriction on the hiring of the Parliament buildings by the author who had been active for many years in Holocaust denial (held inadmissible *ratione materiae*).

faith, including the right to have an education in the public school system free from bias, prejudice and intolerance'.[268]

From these cases it is difficult to infer the development of jurisprudence that recognises 'respect' for the beliefs of others. Even in the case law concerning activities that do entail hate speech or are aimed at the destruction of recognised rights and freedoms within Article 20 or Article 5 of the ICCPR, or Article 17 of the European Convention, the references to respect are sparse.

In the case of offensive or unpopular speech falling outside these provisions but within the realm of freedom of expression, various members of the Human Rights Committee have warned of the real dangers of allowing limitation clauses to be interpreted to prohibit such speech. The concurring opinion of Mssrs. Evatt and Kretzmer (co-signed by Mr Klein) in *Robert Faurisson v. France*, reflects these concerns:

> 'The power given to States parties under article 19, paragraph 3, to place restrictions on freedom of expression, must not be interpreted as licence to prohibit unpopular speech, or speech which some sections of the population find offensive. Much offensive speech may be regarded as speech that impinges on one of the values mentioned in article 19, paragraph 3(a) or (b) (the rights or reputations of others, national security, ordre public, public health or morals). The Covenant therefore stipulates that the purpose of protecting one of those values is not, of itself, sufficient reason to restrict expression. The restriction must be *necessary* to protect the given value.'

Similarly, Mr Lallah (concurring) would have preferred the decision in *Robert Faurisson v. France* to have been made under the more strict framework of Article 20(2) rather than Article 19(3) since:

> '[r]ecourse to restrictions that are, in principle, permissible under article 19, paragraph 3, bristles with difficulties, tending to destroy the very existence of the right sought to be restricted. The right to freedom of opinion and expression is a most valuable right and may turn out to be too fragile for survival in the face of too frequently professed necessity for its restriction in the wide range of areas envisaged under paragraphs (a) and (b) of article 19, paragraph 3.'

There would certainly appear to be support for choosing to determine restrictions on offensive speech within the scope of Article 20(2) or

---

[268] *Ibid.*, at para. 11.5.

Article 5 of the ICCPR, or Article 17 of the European Convention in severe cases when justified by the content of the speech. However, in considering limitations on freedom of expression in the interests of the protection of the 'reputation' or 'rights of others' outside the realms of hate speech, European jurisprudence appears to have departed from the practice of the Human Rights Committee by widening the concept of 'the rights and freedoms of others' to suggest there may exist a right to have one's religious beliefs respected. This development has been confined to more suitable limits with emerging decisions of the European Court but nevertheless has serious implications for free religious speech unless clarified. Most developments in this area have arisen out of challenges over the restrictions posed by European blasphemy laws (or laws with a similar aim).

Blasphemy, disparagement and gratuitous offence

Neither the ICCPR nor the European Convention includes an explicit right to have one's beliefs respected or a right not to be offended by the expression of religious beliefs by others (beyond the realms of the hate speech provisions discussed under the previous heading). Laws enacted to enshrine such rights could play a role in inhibiting religious practice to an extent that is far-reaching and unsustainable, unless contained within suitable limits.[269] The discussion under this heading aims to explain the operation of the ICCPR and the European Convention on those laws which relate to offending the religious sensibilities of others.

The European Commission in *Gay News Ltd and Lemon v. United Kingdom*[270] examined the United Kingdom's criminal offence of blasphemy in a case arising out of a publication intended largely for a homosexual readership. It contained a poem ascribing promiscuous homosexual practices to Christ, which the charge under section 8 of the Law of Libel Amendment Act 1888 described as 'an obscene poem

---

[269] K. Boyle discusses the limits of freedom of speech in matters of religion or belief in the light of the international standards combating religious discrimination and intolerance – K. Boyle, 'Religious Intolerance and the Incitement of Hatred' in S. Coliver (ed.), *Striking a Balance: Hate Speech, Freedom of Expression and Non-discrimination*, London: University of Essex, Human Rights Centre (1992). For the rationale for excluding group defamation from the concept of freedom of expression, see T. D. Jones, *Human Rights: Group Defamation, Freedom of Expression and the Law of Nations*, The Hague/Boston/London: Martinus Nijhoff (1998). See also P. Kearns, 'The Uncultured God: Blasphemy Law's Reprieve and the Art of Matrix', EHRLR (2000) 512.

[270] *Gay News Ltd and Lemon v. United Kingdom*, App. No. 8710/79 (1982) 5 EHRR 123.

and illustration vilifying Christ in His life and in His crucifixion'.[271] The applicants were convicted and claimed violation of Articles 9 and 10. The European Commission only examined the matter in substance under Article 10 because the applicant had not demonstrated that the publication of the poem constituted the exercise of a religious or other belief within Article 9.[272] It concluded that the main purpose of the law had a legitimate aim, namely 'to protect the rights of citizens not to be offended in their religious feelings by publications'.[273] In deciding whether their conviction was necessary in a democratic society, the European Commission reasoned that, '[i]f it is accepted that the religious feelings of the citizen may deserve protection against indecent attacks on matters held sacred by him, then it can also be considered as necessary in a democratic society to stipulate that such attacks, if they attain a certain level of severity, shall constitute a criminal offence triable at the request of the offended person'.[274] Even though the European Commission referred to 'the right of citizens not to be offended in their religious feelings', nothing in its decision suggests that this is a right within Article 9(1) (and in any event the Commission's comments on Article 9 were *obiter*).[275] Nevertheless, the role of religious offence in the limitation ground 'the protection of the reputation or rights of others' has undergone development in subsequent decisions of the European Court under Article 10.

The European Court's decision in *Otto-Preminger-Institut v. Austria*[276] concerned the forfeiture of a film, *Das Liebeskonzil* (Council in Heaven), due to be shown in the Catholic Tyrol region, involving ridicule of the Eucharist and a portrayal of 'God the Father, Christ and Mary Mother of God', which the national court determined fell within the definition of the criminal offence of disparaging religious precepts as laid down in

---

[271] *Ibid.*, at 124.   [272] *Ibid.*, at 131.   [273] *Ibid.*, at 130.   [274] *Ibid.*, at 130.

[275] The Commission commented that if the publication of the poem constituted the exercise of a religious or other belief (contrary to the Commission's Article 10 finding), the applicants' convictions would still have been justified under Article 9(2) on the same grounds as under Article 10(2). The claim for discrimination under Article 14 failed in the absence of evidence that the applicants were discriminated against on account of their homosexual views – *ibid.*, at 131. See also *Choudhury v. United Kingdom*, App. No. 17439/90 (1991) 12 HRLJ 172. On the discriminatory nature of United Kingdom blasphemy law, see P. R. Ghandhi and J. James, 'The English Law of Blasphemy and the European Convention on Human Rights', EHRLR (1998) 430. Ghandhi and James argue for the abolition of the United Kingdom offence of blasphemy rather than its extension to cover religions other than Christianity.

[276] *Otto-Preminger-Institut v. Austria* (Ser. A) No. 295–A (1994) ECtHR.

section 188 of the Penal Code. The applicant association, responsible for arranging the viewing, claimed that seizure and forfeiture of the film violated Article 10. The Austrian Government claimed that its action had the legitimate aim of 'the protection of the rights of others', particularly the right to 'respect for one's religious feelings'.[277] In citing that part of paragraph 48 of the *Kokkinakis* judgment which refers to 'respect for the freedom of thought, conscience and religion of others',[278] the European Court concluded that the Austrian measure had a legitimate aim in that 'respect for the religious feelings of believers as guaranteed in Article 9 can legitimately be thought to have been violated by provocative portrayals of objects of religious veneration'.[279] The European Court appears to have borrowed the notion of 'respect' from the *Kokkinakis* judgment and combined it with the text of section 188 of the Austrian Penal Code, which reads as follows:

> 'Whoever, in circumstances where his behaviour is likely to arouse justified indignation, disparages or insults a person who, or an object which, is an object of veneration of a church or religious community established within the country, or a dogma, a lawful custom or a lawful institution of such a church or religious community, shall be liable … etc.'[280]

When deciding whether forfeiture of the film was 'necessary in a democratic society', the European Court inevitably had to apply criteria found in Article 10 rather than Article 9, in particular the 'duties and responsibilities' on those exercising their freedom of expression stipulated in Article 10(2). It was in relation to such duties and responsibilities that it considered it appropriate to include 'an obligation to avoid as far as possible expressions that are gratuitously offensive to others and thus an infringement of their rights, and which therefore do not contribute to any form of public debate capable of furthering progress in human affairs'.[281] Accordingly there was no violation of Article 10. An important factor appears to have been that in the Tyrol region, Catholicism played a significant role in everyday life in as much as

---

[277] *Ibid.*, at para. 46.
[278] *Ibid.*, at para. 47: 'In the Kokkinakis judgment the Court held, in the context of Article 9, that a State may legitimately consider it necessary to take measures aimed at repressing certain forms of conduct, including the imparting of information and ideas, judged incompatible with the respect for the freedom of thought, conscience and religion of others.'
[279] *Otto-Preminger-Institut v. Austria* (Ser. A) No. 295–A (1994) ECtHR at para. 47.
[280] *Ibid.*, at para. 25.   [281] *Ibid.*, at para. 49.

87 per cent of the population and the film was an attack on Roman Catholicism. However, this should not mean that the interests only of those of majority beliefs should be taken into consideration (so as to exclude minority religions from protection in the case of attacks of equal severity).[282]

More fundamentally, the European Court's judgment in *Otto-Preminger* is open to criticism for failing to distinguish issues under Article 9 from those under Article 10, even if the Court did so principally in relation to establishing the legitimate aim of the restriction. It referred to those 'who choose to exercise the freedom to manifest their religion' (when only Article 10 was at issue), and 'respect for the religious feelings of believers as guaranteed in Article 9' as if this was indeed a recognised right within Article 9 and thereby constituted a ground of limitation under Article 10:

> 'Those who choose to exercise the freedom to manifest their religion, irrespective of whether they do so as members of a religious majority or a minority, cannot reasonably expect to be exempt from all criticism. They must tolerate and accept the denial by others of their religious beliefs and even the propagation by others of doctrines hostile to their faith. However, the manner in which religious beliefs and doctrines are opposed or denied is a matter which may engage the responsibility of the State, notably its responsibility to ensure the peaceful enjoyment of the rights guaranteed under Article 9 to the holders of those beliefs and doctrines.'[283]

The distinction between Articles 9 and 10 was, importantly, clarified in the case of *Wingrove v. United Kingdom*.[284] The maker of a film entitled *Visions of Ecstasy* claimed that the refusal of a British Board of Film Classification certificate needed for the lawful video distribution of the film amounted to violation of Article 10 of the European Convention. Most of the film's duration was given over to sexual imagery focused on the figure of the crucified Christ. The Board refused classification because of its blasphemous content, measured by the United Kingdom's concept of blasphemy. The Government and the European Commission both followed the reasoning in *Otto-Preminger*

---

[282] For a perspective on religious offence, see T. Marood, 'British Asian Muslims and the Rushdie Affair', 61 Pol Quart (1990) 143, in a collection of essays entitled, 'The Political Revival of Religion: Fundamentalism and Others', *ibid.*, at p. 123.

[283] *Otto-Preminger-Institut v. Austria* (Ser. A) No. 295-A (1994) ECtHR, at para. 47.

[284] *Wingrove v. United Kingdom* (1997) 24 EHRR 1.

concerning the legitimate aim of blasphemy law. However, instead, the European Court departed from that approach and took as its starting point the purpose of the Board in protecting against the treatment of a religious subject in such a manner 'as to be calculated (that is, bound, not intended) to outrage those who have an understanding of, sympathy towards and support for the Christian story and ethic, because of the contemptuous, reviling, insulting, scurrilous or ludicrous tone, style and spirit in which the subject is presented'.[285]

In upholding this as a legitimate aim, the European Court accepted that it undoubtedly corresponded to that of the protection of 'the rights of others' within the meaning of Article 10(2) and noted that this 'is also fully consonant with the aim of the protections afforded by Article 9 (art. 9) to religious freedom'.[286] In doing so the European Court deliberately avoided equating 'respect for the religious feelings of believers' with the guarantees in Article 9, as it had in its decision in *Otto-Preminger*. It also avoided discussion on whether this constituted a ground of limitation for the purposes of Article 9(2). This was confirmed when considering whether the interference was 'necessary in a democratic society'. The European Court emphasised, as it had done in *Otto-Preminger,* that the duties and responsibilities in Article 10(2) in the context of religious beliefs include a duty to avoid as far as possible an expression that is, in regard to objects of veneration, 'gratuitously offensive to others and profanatory'.[287] The European Court then concluded that because the film amounted to an attack on the religious beliefs of Christians which was insulting and offensive, the refusal of a classification certificate was within the State's margin of appreciation under Article 10. In his concurring opinion, Judge Pettiti emphasised the importance of this approach and commented as follows: 'Article 9 (art. 9) is not in issue in the instant case and cannot be invoked. Certainly the Court rightly based its analysis under Article 10 (art. 10) on the rights of others and did not, as it had done in the Otto-Preminger-Institut judgment combine Articles 9 and 10 (art. 9, art. 10), morals and the rights of others.'[288]

Although the European Court in *Wingrove* drew the clearest possible distinction between Articles 9 and 10 (by deliberately avoiding equating 'respect for the religious feelings of believers' with the guarantees in Article 9), that distinction was again obscured by the European Court in

---

[285] *Ibid.*, at para. 15.   [286] *Ibid.*, at para. 48.   [287] *Ibid.*, at para. 52.
[288] *Ibid.*, at page 34.

the recent case of *Murphy v. Ireland*[289] when upholding a limited prohibition on a religious advertisement by radio broadcast on an independent local commercial radio station. This case will now be considered in detail. It is open to criticism for failing to have proper regard for the true content of Article 9, for exaggeration of the term 'respect' as developed in *Otto-Preminger* (compounding the above criticisms made in *Wingrove*), and for failing to take due account of alternative, more appropriate, means open to the European Court to address concerns over potential 'offence' to the listening public when supporting a blanket prohibition on religious advertising through broadcast media.

The text of the advertisement was as follows.

> 'What think ye of Christ? Would you, like Peter, only say that he is the son of the living God? Have you ever exposed yourself to the historical facts about Christ? The Irish Faith Centre are presenting for Easter week an hour long video by Dr Jean Scott PhD on the evidence of the resurrection from Monday 10th – Saturday 15th April every night at 8.30 and Easter Sunday at 11.30am and also live by satellite at 7.30pm.'[290]

The European Court cited paragraph 47 of the *Otto-Preminger* judgment when upholding the aims of the prohibition claimed by the Government, namely 'public order and safety together with the protection of the rights and freedoms of others'.[291] Paragraph 47 of *Otto-Preminger* contains the phrase which the European Court in *Wingrove* appeared to go to some lengths to avoid ('the respect for the religious feelings of believers as guaranteed in Article 9 ...'). The European Court in *Wingrove* supported the remainder of paragraph 47 and derived from paragraphs 46, 47 and 49 of *Otto-Preminger* the duties and responsibilities attaching to the freedom of expression, including a duty to avoid as far as possible an expression that is, in regard to objects of veneration, gratuitously offensive to others and profanatory.[292] The question is whether the European Court in *Murphy* was giving its support to the contentious phrase in paragraph 47 of *Otto-Preminger*.

There are two key elements to paragraph 47 which are relevant to the 'rights of others'. Both elements fit the context in which *Otto-Preminger* and *Wingrove* were decided of severely offensive blasphemous expression (under Article 10) but do not appear to have direct relevance to the

---

[289] *Murphy v. Ireland*, App. No. 44179/98 (2004) 38 EHRR 212.
[290] *Ibid.*, at para. 8.　[291] *Ibid.*, at para. 63.
[292] *Wingrove v. United Kingdom* (1997) 24 EHRR 1, at paras. 48 and 52.

situation addressed by the European Court in *Murphy*. The first element relates to the particular means employed in extreme cases when opposing or denying the religious beliefs of others and the State's responsibility to 'ensure the peaceful enjoyment of the right guaranteed in Article 9'. The second element of paragraph 47 of the *Otto-Preminger* judgment concerns the imparting of information and ideas 'judged incompatible with the respect for the freedom of thought, conscience and religion of others' (taken from paragraph 48 of the *Kokkinakis* judgment). The first element was expressed as follows.

> '[T]he *manner* in which religious beliefs and doctrines are *opposed or denied* is a matter which may engage the responsibility of the State, notably its responsibility to ensure the peaceful enjoyment of the rights guaranteed under Article 9 (art. 9) to the holders of those beliefs and doctrines. Indeed, in extreme cases the effect of *particular methods* of *opposing or denying* religious beliefs can be such as to inhibit those who hold such beliefs from exercising their freedom to hold and express them (emphasis added).'[293]

In *Murphy* there was no opposition or denial of the religious beliefs of others except to the extent that, as the Government put it, 'the simple proclamation of the truth of one religion necessarily proclaims the untruth of another'.[294] However, if this were accepted as opposition or denial, even the most unobtrusive and innocuous forms of outward religious devotion, teaching or practice, even if conducted entirely without reference to other belief systems, could be said to constitute the opposition or denial of the religious beliefs of others. In any event, the Government's characterisation of the advertisement in *Murphy* does not place the aims of the prohibition in the same context as the restrictions in *Otto-Preminger* and *Wingrove*. In *Otto-Preminger* the forfeiture of the film *Council in Heaven* was based on section 188 of the Austrian Penal Code, which was intended to suppress disparaging or insulting behaviour specifically directed against objects of religious veneration and likely to 'arouse justified indignation'. The European Court was satisfied on close examination of the decision of the Austrian court that a legitimate aim was pursued.[295] In *Wingrove*, the refusal to allow distribution of *Visions of Ecstasy* was to protect against 'the treatment of a religious subject in such a manner as "to be calculated

---

[293] *Otto-Preminger-Institut v. Austria* (Ser. A) No. 295–A (1994) ECtHR, at para. 47.

[294] *Murphy v. Ireland*, App. No. 44179/98 (2004) 38 EHRR 212 at para. 38.

[295] *Otto-Preminger-Institut v. Austria* (Ser. A) No. 295–A (1994) ECtHR, at para. 48.

(that is, bound, not intended) to outrage those who have an understanding of, sympathy towards and support for the Christian story and
ethic, because of the contemptuous, reviling, insulting, scurrilous or
ludicrous tone, style and spirit in which the subject is presented".'[296]
The aims of these measures were clear and specific and well scrutinised
in each case by the European Court. The restriction in question corresponded with each aim. By contrast, in *Murphy* the Government
accepted that the advertisement appeared innocuous and that it was to
some extent simply informational (though in the context of explaining
how the advertisement fell within the domestic prohibition on religious
advertising it did suggest that the advertisement was 'based on an
evident belief in, and the propagation of, certain religious beliefs').[297]
The first element of paragraph 47 of the *Otto-Preminger* judgment does
not therefore appear to have had any direct relevance in the case of
Murphy – the religious advertisement in *Murphy* could not in any
meaningful sense be characterised as the opposition or denial of the
religious beliefs of others.

The second element of paragraph 47 of the *Otto-Preminger* judgment
explains that certain other conduct (beyond the manner in which
religious beliefs and doctrines are opposed or denied) may be judged
to be 'incompatible with the respect for the freedom of thought, conscience and religion of others' (and paragraph 48 of the *Kokkinakis*
judgment was cited as appropriate authority).[298] The justification
given in paragraph 47 concerned the 'provocative portrayals of objects
of religious veneration; . . . such portrayals can be regarded as malicious
violation of the spirit of tolerance, which must also be a feature of
democratic society'.

It is difficult to conceive the religious advertisement in *Murphy* as a
provocative portrayal of an object of religious veneration. In short,
paragraph 47 of *Otto-Preminger* arguably offers no support for the
legitimate aim claimed by the Government and upheld by the
European Court.

The notion of 'respect' as developed by *Otto-Preminger* relates directly to
the aim of section 188 of the Penal Code in curtailing forms of disparagement or insult directed at objects of veneration where the behaviour is likely
to arouse justified indignation – this is evident in the second element of

---

[296] *Wingrove v. United Kingdom* (1997) 24 EHRR 1, at para. 48.
[297] *Murphy v. Ireland*, (App. No. 44179/98) (2004) 38 EHRR 212, at para. 38.
[298] *Kokkinakis v. Greece* (Ser. A) No. 260–A (1993) ECtHR, at para. 48.

paragraph 47, which refers to 'provocative portrayals of objects of religious veneration'. Support was given to this aspect of *Otto-Preminger* by the European Court in *Wingrove* when it recognised that among the duties and responsibilities that accompany the exercise of freedom of expression is 'the duty to avoid as far as possible an expression that is, in regard to objects of veneration, gratuitously offensive to others and profanatory'.[299] However, it is difficult to see the justification for the Court invoking such a notion of 'respect' to support the aim in *Murphy* of a blanket prohibition on religious advertising using broadcast media. It may be necessary to avoid all religious content in paid broadcast advertising in Ireland in order to avoid dishar-mony in light of the country-specific religious sensitivities prevailing in that country (although the Government commented that '[i]t might have been that there was no contemporary religious disharmony in Ireland').[300] Nevertheless, it has to be questioned whether it is open to the European Court, in the circumstances presented by *Murphy*, to apply the legitimate aim of restrictions that are appropriate to prevent extreme forms of expression, such as those prohibited by section 188 of the Criminal Code in *Otto-Preminger* or prohibited by the criminal blasphemy laws of England (which underpinned *Wingrove*), to all forms of expression which have any religious content. Paragraph 47 of the *Otto-Preminger* judgment should not so easily be invoked as a mantra to legitimise the aim of restrictions which are not directed at extreme forms of opposition or denial of the religious beliefs of others or the provocative portrayal of objects of religious venera-tion, where the restrictions in question instead serve other more general purposes. As the Government in *Murphy* conceded, 'it was simply the religious nature of the advertisement that constituted sufficient justification for its restriction'.[301]

Other, more appropriate, choices of legitimate aim were open to the European Court in *Murphy*. The European Court could have focused on the Government's justification for banning religious content in paid broadcast advertising based on the principle of impartiality, particularly on sensitive issues.[302] This is supported by the case of *VgT Verein Gegen Tierfabriken v. Switzerland*,[303] concerning a prohibition on political

[299] *Wingrove v. United Kingdom* (1997) 24 EHRR 1, at para. 52.
[300] *Murphy v. Ireland*, App. No. 44179/98 (2004) 38 EHRR 212, at para. 38.
[301] *Ibid.*, at para. 38.   [302] *Ibid.*, para. 40.
[303] *VgT Verein Gegen Tierfabriken v. Switzerland*, (App. No. 24699/94), Judgment of 28 June 2001. See also *United Christian Broadcasters Ltd v. United Kingdom* (App. No. 44802), Judgment of 7 November 2000; *Informationsverein Lentia and others v. Austria* (Ser. A) No. 276, Judgment of 24 November 1993.

advertising. The prohibition prevented the broadcast of a television commercial which opposed intensive farming with the exhortation 'eat less meat, for the sake of your health, the animals and environment!'[304] The European Court was easily satisfied that the prohibition was aimed at the 'protection of the ... rights of others' within Article 10(2) since, as the Government claimed in that case, the refusal to broadcast the commercial was aimed at enabling the formation of public opinion protected from the pressures of powerful financial groups, while at the same time promoting equal opportunities for the different components of society. It was open to the European Court in *Murphy* to support this as the aim of the advertising restriction since the Government argued that, just as the restriction on broadcasting of advertising promoted neutrality and balance, allowing or obliging stations to accept advertising on religious issues would undermine that balance.[305] The Government in *Murphy* also argued that the blanket restriction promoted 'a level playing field' for all religions irrespective of their wealth, their dominance, their power and their current popularity.[306] Alternatively, a legitimate aim may have been found by the European Court in *Murphy* in the risks that religious advertisements may 'lead to unrest' (as noted in the domestic Supreme Court's judgment rejecting the applicant's appeal)[307] within the 'public order and safety' grounds asserted by the Government.[308] The necessity of the restriction could then have been measured against the Government's claims, for example, of a 'potentially incendiary situation' given the broadcast context.[309]

It is therefore submitted that the decision in *Murphy* was wrong in invoking paragraph 47 of *Otto-Preminger* to support (as a legitimate aim of the religious advertising prohibition) 'the rights and freedoms of others' as claimed by the Government, since the prohibition was not directed at the opposition or denial of religious beliefs or doctrines of others or the provocative portrayal of objects of religious veneration, within the confines of paragraph 47. Such would be the role, for example, of blasphemy law which prohibits certain extreme forms of expression.

---

[304] *Ibid.*, para. 10.

[305] *Murphy v. Ireland*, App. No. 44179/98 (2004) 38 EHRR 212, at para. 40.

[306] *Ibid.*, para. 43, following *United Christian Broadcasters Ltd v. United Kingdom* (App. No. 44802), Judgment of 7 November 2000.

[307] *Ibid.*, at para. 13.

[308] *Ibid.*, at para. 35. Is also noteworthy that alongside 'the protection of the rights and freedoms of others' (which para. 47 of the judgment of *Otto-Preminger* supports) the Court appears to have accepted 'public order and safety'.

[309] *Ibid.*, at para. 38.

No purpose falling within the ambit of paragraph 47 was pursued by the restriction in *Murphy*.[310]

It may also be questioned whether the European Court was entitled to avoid a detailed examination of whether the aims of the impugned legislation constituted legitimate aims for the purposes of Article 10(2). It gave only cursory consideration to this issue on the basis that 'the applicant did not directly contest that these aims had been pursued' by the prohibition.[311] This does not appear to be supported by the text of the judgment. Instead, it is clear that the applicant claimed that:

> 'a prohibition on religious advertising regardless of its nature or content could not be justified to protect the religious feeling of others. Such a prohibition would only be justified if the Article 9 rights of others included a right not to be exposed to any religious views different to their own and no such right exists under Article 9 or elsewhere in the Convention. Indeed, the applicant argued that such a position would be contrary to the pluralism, tolerance and broadmindedness required in a democratic society.'[312]

The European Court interestingly accepted much of that argument (at least in the context of Article 10)[313] but in passing over the issue of 'legitimate aim' merely stated that because the applicant did not contest that these aims had been pursued by the prohibition there was no need to doubt the aims of the prohibition.

---

[310] In any event Article 10(2) refers to 'protection of the reputation or rights of others' not 'the rights and freedoms of others' cited by the European Court.

[311] *Ibid.*, at para. 63.   [312] *Ibid.*, at para. 50.

[313] The Court supported the famous dictum in *Handyside v. United Kingdom* that 'even expression which could be considered offensive, shocking or disturbing to the religious sensitivities of others falls within the scope of the protection of Article 10' – *ibid.*, at paras. 61 and 72, citing *Handyside v. United Kingdom* (Ser. A) No. 24 (1976) ECtHR, para. 49. The Court also reiterated that the concepts of pluralism, tolerance and broadmindedness on which any democratic society is based 'mean that Article 10 does not, as such, envisage that an individual is to be protected from exposure to a religious view simply because it is not his or her own' – *ibid.*, at para. 72. The issue of proselytism arose because the domestic decision of the High Court suggested, among the public interest justifications for the ban in Irish society of religious advertising on commercial radio, the fact that 'Irish people with religious beliefs tend to belong to particular churches and that being so religious advertising coming from a different church can be offensive to many people and might be open to the interpretation of proselytising' – *ibid.*, at para. 12. Reminiscent of the theoretical distinction made in *Kokkinakis* between proper and improper proselytism, the Government also wondered whether it was possible to distinguish between the 'passionate and committed preacher' and the 'incendiary proselytiser' – *ibid.*, at para. 43.

There still remains the question whether the rights guaranteed under Article 9 include a right to be protected from expressions that are gratuitously offensive or profane, or whether protection from such expressions stems simply from the duties and responsibilities inherent within all forms of expression under Article 10. On this subject the European Court in *Murphy* was not explicit. It commented as follows.

> 'The Court recalls that freedom of expression constitutes one of the essential foundations of a democratic society. As paragraph 2 of Article 10 expressly recognises, however, the exercise of that freedom carries with it duties and responsibilities. Amongst them, in the context of religious beliefs, is the general requirement to ensure the peaceful enjoyment of the rights guaranteed under Article 9 to the holders of such beliefs including a duty to avoid as far as possible an expression that is, in regard to objects of veneration, gratuitously offensive to others and profane (the above-cited *Otto-Preminger-Institut* judgment, §§ 46, 47 and 49).'[314]

It is submitted that there is little room to conclude that Article 9 includes a general right to be protected from such an expression, though it is clear that the protection of Article 9 provides a basis for restriction where the effect of such an expression is to impair the enjoyment of Article 9 freedoms. In addition, the 'duties and responsibilities' of those exercising the freedom of expression impose additional constraint on the exercise of that freedom which is not found in the freedom of religion Articles. The above survey of cases in which the concept of 'duties and responsibilities' of those exercising the freedom of expression was developed indicates that the duty to avoid expressions that are gratuitously offensive and profane arises under Article 10 quite independently from Article 9 freedoms, even in the context of expression giving rise to religious sensibilities. Those duties and responsibilities inevitably have regard to the rights and freedoms of others. However, it is not necessary to impute to Article 9 a right stemming from an Article 10 duty. In the above passage from its decision in *Murphy* the European Court summarised paragraphs 46, 47 and 49 of *Otto-Preminger* in terms of the duties and responsibilities attaching to Article 10, referring first to the 'requirement' to ensure the peaceful enjoyment of Article 9 freedoms and secondly to the 'duty' to avoid expression that is gratuitously offensive to others and profane. Even if it is right to interpret the

---

[314] *Ibid.*, at para. 65.

passage as suggesting that the 'requirement' to ensure peaceful enjoyment of Article 9 rights *includes* a 'duty' to avoid expression that is
gratuitously offensive and profane (and this would be stretching the
purpose of the passage, which is only a contraction of the two key
elements of paragraph 47 of the *Otto-Preminger* judgment), this does
not alter the accepted parameters of Article 9. In paragraph 47 of its
judgment in *Otto-Preminger* the European Court chose to illustrate a
failure to ensure the peaceful enjoyment of Article 9 rights unequivocally by reference to conventionally accepted Article 9 rights,
namely the right to hold and express religious beliefs (not a right
otherwise to be free from particular forms of expression): 'Indeed,
in extreme cases the effect of particular methods of opposing or denying
religious beliefs can be such as to inhibit those who hold such beliefs
from exercising their freedom to hold and express them.'[315]

Where the effect of a particular form of expression under Article 10 is so
extreme as to inhibit the exercise of Article 9 rights, it is clear that the latter
must be respected. Paragraph 47 of *Otto-Preminger* also refers to paragraph
48 of the *Kokkinakis* judgment which in turn contemplates activities which
violate Article 9 freedoms. It was argued above, under the heading
'Coercion', that in paragraph 48 of the judgment in *Kokkinakis*, the incompatibility with respect for freedom of thought, conscience and religion
referred to by the European Court was interference with the *forum internum*, namely freedom from coercion in religious choice.[316] Consistency
with the traditionally recognised content of Article 9 is maintained if use of
the term 'respect' is confined to ensuring that the *effect* of the exercise of
freedom of expression does not impinge on known Article 9 freedoms (or
indeed other freedoms). This is quite different from a right to 'respect for
one's religious feelings' as such.[317]

Furthermore, the justification for the restriction of freedom of
expression in each of the blasphemy cases discussed above (*Otto-
Preminger* and *Wingrove*) was that the attacks on matters held sacred
to the individual had attained a certain level of severity.[318] In the case of

---

[315] *Otto-Preminger-Institut v. Austria* (Ser. A) No. 295–A (1994) ECtHR, at para. 47.

[316] *Kokkinakis v. Greece* (Ser. A) No. 260–A (1993) ECtHR, at para. 48.

[317] This is discussed further in Chapter 3 under the heading ('The rights and freedoms of others as a ground of limitation') at pp. 161–5.

[318] See, for example, *Gay News Ltd and Lemon v. United Kingdom*, App. No. 8710/79 (1982) 5 EHRR 123, at 131.

Otto-Preminger, it was a feature of the film that it was 'gratuitously offensive', ending with a violent and abusive denunciation of what was presented as Catholic morality,[319] and was offered in 'an unwarranted and offensive manner',[320] particularly likely to offend the overwhelming majority of Tyroleans. In *Wingrove*, the European Court was satisfied that the criminal offence of blasphemy required the extent of insult to religious feelings to be significant, made clear by the adjectives 'contemptuous', 'reviling', 'scurrilous' and 'ludicrous' to depict material of a sufficient degree of offensiveness.[321] This is in spite of the fact that, as reaffirmed in both the *Otto Preminger* and *Wingrove* cases (and more recently in *Murphy*):

> 'a wider margin of appreciation is generally available to the States when regulating freedom of expression in relation to matters liable to offend intimate personal convictions within the sphere of morals or, especially, religion. Moreover, as in the field of morals, and perhaps to an even greater degree, there is no uniform European conception of the requirements of "the protection of the rights of others" in relation to attacks on their religious convictions.'[322]

The wide margin of appreciation cited in this form in Article 10 cases is not directly relevant to cases of proselytism in exercise of Article 9 freedoms. As applied in *Wingrove*, it derives from the Article 10 case of *Müller v. Switzerland*,[323] concerning the criminal conviction of an artist for displaying obscene works openly depicting bestiality, contrary to Article 204 of the Swiss Criminal Code, intended to protect morals. Although the prosecutor considered that the works also contravened Article 261 of the Swiss Criminal Code (concerning freedom of religious belief and worship), the case before the European Court only related to Article 204 of the Swiss Criminal Code and accordingly its consideration focused only on Article 10 of the European Convention.[324] The

---

[319] *Otto-Preminger-Institut v. Austria* (Ser. A) No. 295–A (1994) ECtHR, para. 52.
[320] *Ibid.*, at para. 56.   [321] *Wingrove v. United Kingdom* (1997) 24 EHRR 1, at para. 60.
[322] *Ibid.*, at para. 58. However, as Judge Lohmus commented in his dissenting opinion in *Wingrove*, if the Court makes distinctions within Article 10 (such as to make the margin of appreciation wide in relation to religious convictions but narrow in other matters), it is difficult to ascertain what principles determine the scope of that margin of appreciation (para. 6). See also *Otto-Preminger-Institut v. Austria* (Ser. A) No. 295–A (1994) ECtHR, para. 50.
[323] *Müller v. Switzerland* (Ser. A) No. 133 (1988) ECtHR, para. 35 (in turn referring to *Handyside v. United Kingdom* (Ser. A) No. 24 (1976) ECtHR, para. 48).
[324] *Ibid.*, at para. 12.

European Court in *Wingrove* extended the concept from morals in isolation to include religion but its remarks, at best, were still confined only to issues of freedom of expression under Article 10 and (as in *Müller v. Switzerland*) the significance of the concept stemmed directly from the 'duties and responsibilities' referred to in Article 10(2). It is also noteworthy that no such concept was cited by the European Court in *Kokkinakis* (when it might have been possible to refer to *Müller v. Switzerland*) nor even in *Larissis* (when it would also have been possible to refer to *Wingrove*), suggesting that the concept had no application to the exercise of Article 9 freedoms, or at least was not relevant to justify restrictions on proselytism.

In *Murphy*, after citing its previous case law concerning the wide margin of appreciation generally available to Contracting States when regulating freedom of expression in relation to religious matters,[325] the European Court went on to emphasise the importance of its supervisory role given 'the rather open-ended notion of respect for the religious beliefs of others and the risks of excessive interferences with freedom of expression under the guise of action taken against allegedly offensive material'.[326] The European Court is right to be circumspect about such an open-ended notion. However, it more readily accepted the Government's assertion that the reasons for the prohibition were 'relevant and sufficient' given that 'there appears to be no clear consensus between the Contracting States as to the manner in which to legislate for the broadcasting of religious advertisements ... There appears to be no "uniform conception of the requirements of the protection of the rights of others" in the context of the legislative regulation of the broadcasting of religious advertising.'[327]

The European Court has historically supported the right to propagate doctrines which are not well received. In the context of Article 10, it has acknowledged on several occasions that freedom of expression, as one of the essential foundations of a democratic society, indeed one of the basic conditions for its progress and for the self-fulfilment of the individual, is 'applicable not only to "information" or "ideas" that are favourably received or regarded as inoffensive or as a matter of indifference, but also to those that offend, shock or disturb the State or any section of the population. Such are the demands of pluralism, tolerance and broadmindedness without which there is no "democratic

---

[325] *Murphy v. Ireland*, App. No. 44179/98 (2004) 38 EHRR 212, at para. 67.
[326] *Ibid.*, at para. 68.   [327] *Ibid.*, at paras. 81–2.

society".'[328] Furthermore, the limitation provisions 'must be narrowly interpreted and the necessity for any restrictions must be convincingly established'.[329] In *Otto-Preminger*, the Court emphasised the right to propagate doctrines that are hostile to any given faith, distinguishing between the blasphemous manner in which ideas are conveyed and the doctrines themselves. This is consistent with the definition of blasphemy in the United Kingdom, evident from the *Gay News* appeal in the national court, in which Lord Scarman explained that '[t]he test to be applied is as to the manner in which doctrines are advocated and not as to the substance of the doctrines themselves'.[330] Similarly in *Murphy*, the Court's decision turned primarily on the applicant's 'means of expression' and not the message itself (which was of itself entirely innocuous).[331] The central issue chosen by the European Court was whether, for the purposes of Article 10(2) a prohibition of a certain type (advertising) of expression (religious) through a particular means (the broadcast media) could justifiably be prohibited in the particular circumstances of the case.[332] The European Court considered that the matter primarily concerned the regulation of the applicant's 'means of expression and not his profession or manifestation of his religion'.[333]

The same distinction was made in the European Commission's decision in *Van den Dungen v. The Netherlands*,[334] to uphold an injunction granted against the applicant to restrain him from persuading visitors at an abortion clinic not to proceed with an abortion, by showing them enlarged photographs of foetal remains in combination with images of Christ, by calling abortion 'child murder' and employees of the clinic 'murderers'. The European Commission decided that the applicant's

---

[328] *Müller v. Switzerland* (Ser. A) No. 133 (1988) ECtHR, para. 33 (in turn referring to *Handyside v. United Kingdom* (Ser. A) No. 24 (1976) ECtHR, para. 49). See also *Vogt v. Germany* (Ser. A) No. 323–A (1995) ECtHR, para. 52 (i). For discussion of religious pluralism, see T. S. Orlin, 'Religious Pluralism and Freedom of Religion: Its Protection in the Light of Church/State Relationships', in A. Rosas and J. E. Helgesen (eds.), *The Strength of Diversity – Human Rights and the Pluralist Democracy*, Dordrecht/Boston: Martinus Nijhoff (1992).

[329] *Vogt v. Germany* (Ser. A) No. 323–A (1995) ECtHR, para. 52 (i).

[330] *Whitehouse v. Lemon* [1979] AC 617, at 685.

[331] *Murphy v. Ireland*, App. No. 44179/98 (2004) 38 EHRR 212, at para. 61.

[332] *Ibid.*, at para. 72.

[333] *Ibid.*, at para. 61. The European Court's characterisation of the expression as religious rather than commercial was the result of its focus on an explicit prohibition on religious advertising, rather than the result of any analysis of whether the advertisement constituted the manifestation of religion or belief within Article 9.

[334] *Van den Dungen v. The Netherlands*, App. No. 22838/93 (1995) 80 D&R 147.

activities did not constitute the expression of a belief within Article 9(1) and proceeded to examine applicable limitations under Article 10(2). It considered that a legitimate aim could be found in the protection of the rights of others, namely the abortion clinic and the visitors. Visitors had been so shocked and upset that they often had to postpone their appointments, and this in turn required the clinic to offer extra assistance to its patients.[335] The injunction was found to be proportionate given its limited duration and limited area. However, the manner of delivery of the applicant's message was decisive in view of its consequences, even though the same message delivered at the same place in a different manner might not justify State interference.

This is also consistent with the practice of the European Commission under Article 9. Thus, in *Church of Scientology and 128 of its members v. Sweden*,[336] the applicant Church could not base proceedings under Article 9 on alleged 'agitation' against it. The claim originated in the publication of certain statements made by a professor of theology including one that 'Scientology is the most untruthful movement there is. It is the cholera of spiritual life. That is how dangerous it is.'[337] Without ruling out the possibility that opposition against a church or religious group might reach a level that would engage State responsibility, the European Commission commented that it 'is not of the opinion that a particular creed or confession can derive from the concept of freedom of religion a right to be free from criticism'.[338] Likewise, in *X. v. Sweden*[339] it was the loud-voiced behaviour of the applicant in public places likely to provoke indignation with the public when shouting his messages that justified interference with the applicant's rights to manifest his religious beliefs. The European Commission noted that the applicant was not prevented from conveying his religious message to the public, either by word of mouth or by showing placards, and so the restriction was not intended to apply to the message itself.

Similar principles apply under Article 11. In *Plattform 'Ärzte für das Leben' v. Austria*[340] members of the applicant association were expressing their religious beliefs in protesting at the permissiveness of Austrian abortion law when they organised a march which deliberately took

---

[335] *Ibid.*, at 151.
[336] *Church of Scientology and 128 of its members v. Sweden*, App. No. 8282/78, (1980) 21 D&R 109.
[337] *Ibid.*, at 110.   [338] *Ibid.*, at 111, para. 5.
[339] *X. v. Sweden*, App. No. 9820/82 (1984) 5 EHRR 297.
[340] *Plattform 'Ärzte für das Leben' v. Austria* (Ser. A) No. 139 (1988) ECtHR.

a route past the surgery of a doctor who carried out abortions. Although they later re-routed the march in order to avoid that surgery, the Austrian authorities approved the march as originally planned. In the public disruption of the applicant's march which followed, the European Court had to determine the scope of the State's positive obligation to protect against interference with the applicant's rights under Article 11. The Court emphasised that even when voicing highly controversial issues, applicants should not be deterred in their right to demonstrate even in the face of predictable and strenuous opposition to the views expounded:

> 'A demonstration may annoy or give offence to persons opposed to the ideas or claims that it is seeking to promote. The participants must, however, be able to hold the demonstration without having to fear that they will be subjected to physical violence by their opponents; such a fear would be liable to deter associations or other groups supporting common ideas or interests from openly expressing their opinions on highly controversial issues affecting the community. In a democracy the right to counter-demonstrate cannot extend to inhibiting the exercise of the right to demonstrate.'[341]

A clear pattern therefore emerges from the justifications for restrictions in the case of hate speech, activity aimed at destroying protected rights and freedoms, blasphemous expression and expression which causes gratuitous offence, in each case because the conduct in question is required to reach a sufficient degree of severity. That standard is inherent in Article 20 of the ICCPR in the case of hate speech, and in Article 5 of the ICCPR and Article 17 of the European Convention in the case of the destructive exercise of rights and freedoms. In the case of freedom of expression, the Strasbourg institutions have only justified restrictions on the release of blasphemous material where the offence likely to be caused was extreme. The judgment in *Murphy* stands out as anomalous and has been much criticised above (particularly the European Court's treatment of the aim of the restriction), although the broadcast context was obviously pivotal to the finding that there had been no violation. Apart from *Kokkinakis*, in which the notion of 'respect' made reference only to what appear to be *forum internum* rights, principles of 'respect' for the religious feelings of others have developed in the particular context of freedom of expression and the

---

[341] *Ibid.*, at para. 32.

corresponding duties and responsibilities that attach to that freedom. Equivalent principles to those developed under Article 10 should not be taken to apply within the realms of Article 9 (either to impute a right of 'respect' to Article 9(1) or automatically to extend the limitation provisions in Article 9(2)). In any event, the term 'respect' seems to be confined to ensuring that the effect of the exercise of freedom of expression does not impinge on known Article 9 freedoms and does not constitute a right to 'respect' as such (whether for religious beliefs or feelings).

In the case of proselytism, it is difficult to conceive of forms of proselytism which are capable of matching the aims, or achieving the threshold of offence, appropriate under Article 10 in blasphemy cases. In the non-blasphemy cases under Article 10 discussed above, it is clear that the message itself was not subject to restriction outside the particular form of expression chosen by the applicant. On the contrary, the European Court emphasises that pluralism, which ultimately underpinned its decision in *Kokkinakis*, demands freedom to propagate not only beliefs that are favourably received but also those that offend, shock or disturb.

The Human Rights Committee has frequently raised the issue of blasphemy in its examination of State reports. More often than not this has involved countries where the penalty for blasphemy was not severe, such as the United Kingdom[342] and New Zealand,[343] although concern was expressed at the severity of punishments in Libya for a number of offences including 'heresy' (rather than blasphemy).[344] Although the State reports provide useful factual detail, the Committee's examination of them does not provide a definitive position on the application of Article 18 of the ICCPR to that particular issue.

The Human Rights Committee has taken an interest in domestic measures to prevent hate speech as well as laws which restrict statements against religious groups more generally. For example, members of the Committee requested clarification of Article 188 of the Criminal Code of Austria which was discussed extensively above,[345] they asked why the prohibition in Finland against engaging in anti-religious propaganda

---

[342] UN Doc. A/46/40 (1991), p. 100, para. 401 (United Kingdom).
[343] UN Doc. A/44/40 (1989), p. 90, para. 393 (New Zealand). See also UN Doc. CCPR/C/10 Add.6.
[344] UN Doc. A/50/40 vol. 1 (1996), p. 29, para. 135 (Libya).
[345] UN Doc. A/47/40 (1994), p. 25, para. 111 (Austria).

was applicable only to atheists,[346] whether the right to speak for or against religion was protected in Finland,[347] how the provision relating to the prohibition of written materials insulting to a domestically established church or other religious community was interpreted in the Federal Republic of Germany, whether there were still groups in that country advocating racial hatred and if so what action had been taken against them.[348] The Commission on Human Rights too has recently expressed concern about the negative stereotyping of religions, particularly Islam which is frequently and wrongly associated with human rights violations and with terrorism.[349]

The Special Rapporteur has recently followed up allegations of use of the death sentence for blasphemy[350] and gave particular attention to the use of blasphemy laws in the report of the visit to Pakistan.[351] A proposal

---

[346] UN Doc. A/46/40 (1994), p. 32, para. 130 (Finland).

[347] UN Doc. A/41/40 (1986), p. 44, para. 210 (Finland).

[348] UN Doc. A/45/40 vol. 1 (1990), p. 77, para. 321 (Federal Republic of Germany).

[349] Commission on Human Rights Resolution 2002/9 'Combating defamation of religion' (15 April 2002) UN Doc. E/CN.4/2002/200 (2002). This resolution followed the joint efforts of the member States of the Organization of the Islamic Conference and the United Nations High Commissioner for Human Rights in organising the seminar entitled 'Enriching the Universality of Human Rights: Islamic Perspectives on the Universal Declaration of Human Rights' at Geneva on 9–10 November 1998. See also Commission on Human Rights Resolution 1999/82 entitled 'Defamation of religions'. The Special Rapporteur has been concerned for Muslim minorities who have been the butt of prejudice and stereotyping. It was observed that in countries such as Australia, the United States of America and Germany, Islam is associated with religious extremism and terrorism in the media and in particular the popular press. However, the Special Rapporteur was keen 'to stress another concern relating to efforts to combat defamation: these should not be used to censure all inter-religious and intra-religious criticism. Several other communications from the Special Rapporteur illustrate the danger that efforts to combat defamation (particularly blasphemy) may be manipulated for purposes contrary to human rights' (UN Doc. E/CN.4/2000/65 (2000), paras. 110–11). See also UN Doc. CN.4/2005/61/Add.1 (2005), p. 74, para. 292 (United States of America). Similar forms of xenophobia have also been condemned by the Human Rights Committee (UN Doc. A/59/40 vol. 1 (2004), p. 42, para. 68(20) (Germany) and p. 61, para. 72(27) (Belgium). In the European context see the Framework decision on combating racism and xenophobia, COM (2001) 664 final, OJ C 75 E of 26 March 2002.

[350] UN Doc. E/CN.4/2003/66 (2003), pp. 12–13, paras. 59–61 (Pakistan); UN Doc. A/58/296 (2003), p. 14, para. 84 (Pakistan); UN Doc. E/CN.4/2005/61/Add.1 (2005), p. 50, para. 191 (Pakistan).

[351] In the conclusions and recommendations following his visit to Pakistan, the Special Rapporteur commented that blasphemy as an offence against belief may be subject to special legislation but 'such legislation should not be discriminatory and should not give rise to abuse. Nor should it be so vague as to jeopardize human rights, especially

was made by the Special Rapporteur for a study on blasphemy that might result in specific suggestions for addressing this issue but it has not yet been produced.[352] The Special Rapporteur has also communicated concern to a number of countries about the State disparagement of the religious beliefs of minorities, most notably in Iraq[353] and Egypt.[354]

Laws intended to protect religions from disparagement run the risk of falling foul of the same objections to Greece's anti-proselytism law that were voiced by Judge Martens and Judge Pettiti in the *Kokkinakis* case, the principal one being their imprecision. The dangers of imprecision are unavoidable in the laws enacted in many countries, such as Australia (where the Racial and Religious Tolerance Act 2001 passed in the State of Victoria prohibits religious vilification through 'conduct that incites hatred against, serious contempt for, or revulsion or severe ridicule' of another person or class of persons on the ground of their religious belief or activity),[355] the United Kingdom (creating the offence of 'religiously aggravated harassment')[356] and Canada (creating the offence of publicly inciting hatred).[357] While the aims are obvious, the unintended, indirect effect may be to interfere unduly with the fundamental and universally accepted right simply to teach or convey the tenets of any religion or belief where to do so may offend the beliefs of others. The same may be said of 'proper' proselytism. The potential for claims of vilification or harassment to curtail proselytism is already evident in the cultural opposition to all forms of proselytism in countries such as Greece and Turkey.[358] It also lies in the inherent

those of minorities' – UN Doc. E/CN.4/1996/95/Add.1 (1996), para. 82 (Pakistan). See also: UN Doc. E/CN.4/1996/95/Add.1 (1996), paras. 14–16 (Pakistan); UN Doc. E/CN.4/1999/58 (1999), para. 85 (Pakistan); UN Doc. E/CN.4/2000/65 (2000), para. 79 (Pakistan).

[352] UN Doc. E/CN.4/1995/91 (1995), p. 147.

[353] UN Doc. E/CN.4/1993/62 (1993), p. 45, para. 39 (Iraq).

[354] UN Doc. E/CN.4/1994/79 (1994), p. 45, para. 44 (Egypt).

[355] For a critique of Australia's anti-vilification laws, see P. Parkinson, 'Enforcing Tolerance: Vilification Laws and Religious Freedom in Australia', paper presented at the Eleventh Annual International Law and Religion Symposium: 'Religion in the Public Sphere: Challenges and Opportunities', Provo, Utah, 3–6 October 2004.

[356] Section 39 of The Anti-Terrorism, Crime and Security Act 2001 amended the Crime and Disorder Act 1998 to create the offence of religiously aggravated criminal harassment for hostility based on the victim's membership of a religious group. See also the Religious Offences Act 2002.

[357] Section 319 of the Criminal Code of Canada.

[358] See, for example, UN Doc. E/CN.4/2001/63 (2001), p. 35, para. 139 (Turkey).

conflict between mutually exclusive beliefs, or beliefs that themselves are exclusionary.[359] It is uncertain whether such legislation would put at risk certain 'public' forms of religious debate or activities such as street evangelism. No matter how socially or culturally unacceptable proselytism might be, it was certainly considered by Judge Pettiti to be fundamentally associated with freedom of religion in *Kokkinakis*, and should not be subjected to laws capable of repressive interpretation:

> 'Proselytism is linked to freedom of religion; a believer must be able to communicate his faith and his beliefs in the religious sphere as in the philosophical sphere. Freedom of religion and conscience is a fundamental right and this freedom must be able to be exercised for the benefit of all religions and not for the benefit of a single Church, even if this has traditionally been the established Church or "dominant religion".
>
> Freedom of religion and conscience certainly entails accepting proselytism, even where it is "not respectable". Believers and agnostic philosophers have a right to expound their beliefs, to try to get other people to share them and even to try to convert those whom they are addressing . . .
>
> The wording adopted by the majority of the Court in finding a breach, namely that the applicant's conviction was not justified in the circumstances of the case, leaves too much room for a repressive interpretation by the Greek courts in the future.'[360]

It is the uncertain scope of such laws that renders them open to subjective or inconsistent interpretation and application. They also give opportunity for intolerance to be expressed through legal proceedings against rival groups.

The matter was recently examined in the United Kingdom by the House of Lords Select Committee on Religious Offences in England and Wales, appointed to consider and report on the law relating to religious offences. It enquired, in particular, into whether existing religious offences (such as blasphemy) should be amended or abolished, and whether a new offence of incitement to religious hatred should be created. One important background issue was the hostility felt to have been directed at the Muslim community. Although racist in origin it was often expressed in religious terms and was not unlawful in the United Kingdom. By contrast, Sikhs and Jews (as racial rather than religious

---

[359] Examples might include Christianity (based on the teachings of Christ describing himself as the [only] way, the truth and the life).

[360] *Kokkinakis v. Greece* (Ser. A) No. 260–A (1993) ECtHR, 26.

groups) were protected by the Public Order Act 1986, Part III, which created criminal offences of incitement to racial hatred.[361] In the context of a proposed Religious Offences Bill in the United Kingdom intended to treat religious incitement in the same way as racial incitement under the Public Order Act, the Committee noted that there were many more problems associated with incitement to religious hatred than with incitement to racial hatred. It also usefully questioned the role which such legislation could play, given the range of existing alternative legal mechanisms to protect religious groups:

'In addition to the difficulty of proving intent (against a defence of fair comment) is the implication for society in general. This has been described as the "chilling effect", or self censorship motivated by fear that robust expressions of opinion may be judged to have overstepped an undefined boundary and become the subject of prosecution . . .

The gap between criminal incitement and permissible freedom of expression is narrow, perhaps even more so in the case of religion than of race. There is no difficulty in recognising substantive criminal acts such as those of violence, threats or harassment, or even inchoate offences such as incitement to violence (of any type) or conspiracy, aiding and abetting. But it is more difficult to define the point at which a particular expression takes on characteristics that can reasonably be proscribed in the spirit of Article 10.2 of the European Convention. Trenchant and even hostile criticism of religious tenets and beliefs has to be accepted as part of the currency of a democratic society, and that is not at issue. The words used would have to be directed at the members of a religious group and not at their beliefs or customs to make them criminal, but they would have to fall short of calling for specific criminal acts against those members to be caught by a pure incitement offence. So there is only a limited area in between which seems to deserve attention. It has been identified as vilification of the foundations of the faith. This is a difficult area. The dividing line between criticism, though assertive and hostile, and vilification will be varied and subjectively defined; the dividing line has not yet been pronounced on by any UK court. Is unlikely to retain permanence as society's attitudes and those of the faith communities develop and evolve.'[362]

Added to these difficulties is the inevitable divergence across different religions of the threshold at which statements are likely to cause offence.

---

[361] Report of the Select Committee on Religious Offences in England and Wales, (2003 HL 95-I) p. 8, para. 15.

[362] Ibid., pp. 26–7, paras. 82–3.

(The threshold at which expressions are to be regarded as sufficiently severe in opposing or disparaging religious beliefs as to constitute blasphemy would not be the same across different religions and the concept of blasphemy is not found at all in many belief systems.)[363] It is also worth observing that the United Kingdom Government made clear that it did not expect many additional cases to be prosecuted if the Public Order Act were extended to incitement to religious hatred, though it did expect publication of some of the most inflammatory material would be deterred by extremists' fear of the risks of prosecution. This is an indication of the severity of statements that would be intended to be caught by the legislation. As it is, very few prosecutions have been brought under Part III of the Public Order Act 1986 for incitement to racial hatred. Prosecutions only proceed if the Attorney-General gives consent, the purpose being to prevent vexatious prosecutions and to safeguard against unmeritorious cases proceeding. The Committee report was conscious of the risks of misuse of the legislation without appropriate safeguards and commented as follows on the possibility of extending the Act to incitement to religious hatred: 'In the religious context [the Attorney-General's fiat] would be essential in order to minimise litigation over disputes, for example, between (or within) sections of a particular religion or to protect those who, quite unknowingly, stray into remarks (perhaps when proselytising) which turn out to be religiously offensive to someone.'[364]

It therefore has to be questioned whether such legislation can be justified without appropriate mechanisms for filtering out vexatious litigation, particularly where legislation provides for civil causes of action (according to a lower burden of proof than is required for criminal offences) and favours well organised private groups which are able to fund the litigation against impecunious opponents. Furthermore, where the concept of vilification is used, a high threshold should be imposed before particular forms of expression are able to constitute vilification. Experience with the Public Order Act 1986 suggests that it may be used as a tool for conflict

---

[363] The Committee report noted that most Muslim groups were opposed to the repeal of the law of blasphemy in the United Kingdom but preferred it to be extended to cover all faiths, not just Christianity as at present. By contrast, Buddhists, Hindus and Sikhs, as well as some Christians, advocate its repeal. Blasphemy (and blasphemous libel) is a common law offence with an unlimited penalty though, since the Human Rights Act 1998, this must be interpreted in such a way as to be consistent with the European Convention. There have been no prosecutions since that Act. *Ibid.*, p. 13, para. 35 and p. 15, para. 42.

[364] *Ibid.*, p. 28, para. 91.

between (or even within) religious groups – similarly with the practical operation of the Indian Code. Soli Sorabjee, the Indian Attorney-General, recently commented as follows on the Indian Code, which created a number of offences concerned with maliciously outraging the religious feelings of any class of Indian citizens (the purpose of the offences being to maintain public peace and tranquillity in a country where religious passions were easily aroused an inflamed):

> '[E]xperience shows that criminal laws prohibiting hate speech and expression will encourage intolerance, divisiveness and unreasonable interference with freedom of expression. Fundamentalist Christians, religious Muslims and devout Hindus would then seek to invoke the criminal machinery against each other's religion, tenets or practices. This is what is increasingly happening today in India. We need not more repressive laws but more free speech to combat bigotry and to promote tolerance.'[365]

The Committee report also anticipated difficulties in the practical implementation of Article 10 of the European Convention. In order to meet the requirements of Article 10 of the European Convention it would be necessary for Parliament to spell out the necessity of preventing disorder or crime arising from deliberately provoked hatred of particular religious groups, and the protection of the rights of those groups. It was recognised that even if that were done it would not be an easy test for judges and juries to apply, let alone apply consistently. In searching for a formulation for English legislation which could encapsulate the jurisprudence of Articles 9 and 10 of the European Convention (in particular paragraph 48 of *Otto-Preminger*) the Committee concluded that;

> '[b]oth proportionality and the protection of the rights and freedoms of others seem to indicate a test based on vilification of a community or its faith. The threshold would have to be quite high, so as to allow for critical – even hostile – opposition. But the ceiling would need to be low enough to ensure that those who abide by the beliefs under attack are not discouraged from exercising their freedom to hold and express them. We find this a difficult issue.'[366]

Concern for uncertain provisions which restrict freedom of expression has also been voiced within the Human Rights Committee. In his individual opinion in *Robert Faurisson v. France* Mr Ando expressed

---

[365] S. Sorabjee, 'Freedom of Expression in India', in *Developing Human Rights Jurisprudence*, Commonwealth Secretariat vol. 7 (1999) discussed in the Report of the Select Committee on Religious Offences in England and Wales (2003 HL 95-I), p. 18, para. 52.
[366] *Ibid.*, p. 29, para. 94.

misgivings about the Gayssot Act which he considered to be capable of such loose interpretation that it could encroach too far upon the right to reedom of expression so that it would probably be better to replace the Act with more specific legislation. The concurring opinion of Mssrs Evatt and Kretzmer noted above, and that of Mr Lallah, also point to the dangers of interpreting limitation clauses to prohibit unpopular speech or speech which some sections of the population find offensive.

Examples of legal systems that protect religious doctrine, and which may restrict freedom to teach religion or belief contrary to that doctrine, are apparent *inter alia* in Malaysia and Pakistan and were highlighted by the Special Rapporteur. Restrictions in Malaysia were directed at 'curbing the propagation of non-Islamic doctrines against Muslims'[367] and, as explained by the Malaysian Government, were to protect Muslims from being subjected to attempts to convert them to another religion.[368] The enforcement of these laws has allegedly frequently resulted in arrest and detention merely for 'preaching the gospel'.[369] In Pakistan, laws relating to outraging the religious feelings of others have allegedly been used to prevent minority religious groups professing or teaching the tenets of their faith.[370] In a general review of such measures, the Special Rapporteur observed that:

> '[a]lthough legislation that punishes defamation, including blasphemy, is designed to protect religion and addresses a legitimate concern, particularly with regard to phenomena such as fear of Islam and Christianity, it must be acknowledged that blasphemy or defamation are increasingly used by extremists to censure all legitimate critical debate within religions (Jordan, Egypt, Pakistan) or to bring to heel certain minorities accused of holding erroneous views (Pakistan)'.[371]

It has been a matter of concern to the Special Rapporteur whenever restrictions have been placed on any forms of proselytism, preaching or the

---

[367] Article II, paragraph (4) of the Malaysian Constitution as supplemented by the Control and Restriction of the Propagation of Non-Islamic Religions Enactment – UN Doc. E/CN.4/1989/44 (1989), pp. 24–5, paras. 51–2 (Malaysia).

[368] UN Doc. E/CN.4/1990/46 (1990), p. 25, para. 58 (Malaysia).

[369] UN Doc. E/CN.4/1993/62 (1993), p. 63, para. 44; UN Doc. E/CN.4/1994/79 (1994), p. 96, para. 62.

[370] UN Doc. E/CN.4/1989/44 (1989), p. 29, para. 55; UN Doc. E/CN.4/1993/62 (1993), p. 82, para. 48; UN Doc. E/CN.4/1995/91/Add.1 (1995), p. 53 (Pakistan). Similar issues have arisen in Iraq – UN Doc. E/CN.4/1993/62 (1993), p. 42, para. 37.

[371] UN Doc. E/CN.4/2001/63 (2001), p. 46, para. 187. See also UN Doc. A/55/280 (2000), p. 23, para. 97 for an earlier general review, and for references to individual countries see paras. 29 (Comoros), 31 (Djibouti), 33 (United Arab Emirates), 102 (Yemen) and 104 (Azerbaijan).

propagation of belief, as communicated (among other countries) to China,[372] Malaysia,[373] Iran,[374] Egypt,[375] Nepal,[376] Malawi,[377] Bulgaria,[378] Greece,[379] the Russian Federation,[380] the Maldives,[381] Uzbekistan,[382] Saudi,[383] Israel,[384] Lao People's Democratic Republic,[385] Sudan,[386] Myanmar,[387] Azerbaijan,[388] United Arab Emirates,[389] and India,[390] and Indonesia.[391]

---

[372] UN Doc. E/CN.4/1994/79 (1994), p. 39, para. 41 (China).

[373] UN Doc. E/CN.4/1993/62 (1993), p. 63, para. 44 (Malaysia); UN Doc. E/CN.4/1990/46 (1990), p. 26, para. 59 (Malaysia).

[374] UN Doc. E/CN.4/1993/62 (1993), p. 42, para. 37 (Iran); UN Doc. E/CN.4/1995/91 (1995), p. 51 (Iran); UN Doc. E/CN.4/1996/95/Add.1 (1996), para. 116 (Iran). As a result of a visit to Iran the Special Rapporteur endorsed the recommendations of Mr Abid Hussain, the Special Rapporteur on freedom of opinion and expression, who considered that: 'Any prior restraint on freedom of expression carries with it a heavy presumption of invalidity under international human rights law. Any institutionalization of such restraint adds further weight to this presumption. In his opinion the protection of the right of freedom of opinion and expression and the right to seek, receive and impart information would be better served, not by routinely submitting specific types of expression to prior scrutiny, as is currently the case, but rather by initiating action after publication, if and when required' – UN Doc. E/CN.4/1996/95/ Add.2 (1996), para. 96 (Iran), citing E/CN.4/1996/39/Add.1, para. 40.

[375] UN Doc. E/CN.4/1991/56 (1991), p. 86, para. 57 (Egypt).

[376] UN Doc. E/CN.4/1989/44 (1989), p. 26, para. 53; UN Doc. E/CN.4/1990/46 (1990), p. 27, para. 63; UN Doc. E/CN.4/1991/56 (1991), p. 111, para. 79 (Nepal); UN Doc. A/56/253 (2001), p. 16, para. 54 (Nepal).

[377] UN Doc. E/CN.4/1993/62 (1993), p. 63, para. 43 (Malawi).

[378] UN Doc. E/CN.4/2001/63 (2001), p. 8, para. 22 (Bulgaria).

[379] UN Doc. E/CN.4/1990/46 (1990), p. 17, para. 43; UN Doc. E/CN.4/1993/62 (1993), p. 35, para. 32 (Greece); UN Doc. A/51/542/Add.1 (1996), para. 12 (Greece). In the report on a visit to Greece the Special Rapporteur commented that 'in practice the religious freedom of minorities is severely undermined, given the manner in which proselytism is viewed' – *ibid.*, at para. 25. In the conclusions and recommendations, removal of the legal prohibition against proselytism was very strongly recommended.

[380] UN Doc. E/CN.4/1999/58 (1999), para. 56 (the Russian Federation); UN Doc. E/CN.4/ 2000/65 (2000), para. 35 (the Russian Federation).

[381] UN Doc. E/CN.4/1999/58 (1999), para. 73 (Maldives).

[382] UN Doc. E/CN.4/1999/58 (1999), para. 83 (Uzbekistan); UN Doc. E/CN.4/2005/61/ Add.1 (2005), p. 83, para. 334 (Uzbekistan).

[383] UN Doc. E/CN.4/2000/65 (2000), para. 10 (Saudi).

[384] UN Doc. E/CN.4/2000/65 (2000), para. 56 (Israel).

[385] UN Doc. E/CN.4/2000/65 (2000), para. 88 (Lao People's Democratic Republic).

[386] UN Doc. A/51/542/Add.2 (1996), para. 73 (Sudan).

[387] UN Doc. E/CN.4/2003/66 (2003), p. 12, para. 55 (Myanmar).

[388] UN Doc. A/57/274 (2002), p. 4, para. 14 (Azerbaijan).

[389] UN Doc. E/CN.4/2004/63 (2004), p. 11, para. 45 (United Arab Emirates).

[390] UN Doc. E/CN.4/1997/91/Add.1 (1997), para. 58 (India).

[391] The Special Rapporteur reported allegations that in Indonesia a draft bill drawn up by the Religious Affairs Ministry would ban teachings that 'deviate from the main teachings of that religion' E/CN.4/2005/61/Add.1 (2005), p. 34, para. 132 (Indonesia).

The importance of this issue is self-evident. In an assessment of communications between 1988 and 1995, the Special Rapporteur observed that Article 1 of the 1981 Declaration accounts for the second highest number of violations, 'mainly cases of prohibition of proselytizing, of possessing certain religious objects and cases of forced conversions'.[392]

Conclusion

One of the greatest challenges in the drafting of provisions relating to freedom of religion in the Universal Declaration, the ICCPR and the 1981 Declaration was the express right to change religion. Opposition to it led to arguments concerning coercion to change religion, in particular proselytism, which was associated with Crusade history, the propagandist motives of missionaries, sectarianism, imperialist religious zeal and attempts at foreign domination. However, a distinction was successfully made between the right to propagate one's beliefs (which should be protected) and coercion to change the religion or beliefs of another (which may be restricted). An examination of contemporary missionary activity earlier in this chapter argued against the suggestion that social action in promoting humanitarian welfare itself constitutes coercive inducement to change religion. Similarly, it was argued that only extreme and rare forms of proselytism could be said to be coercive. Negative attitudes towards proselytism in some countries result merely from an attitude of social mistrust of proselytism as an irritating and slightly intrusive practice incurring as much inconvenience as interruptions from unsolicited selling or political canvassing. In other countries restrictions on proselytism are designed to protect particular religions or denominations in order to preserve national identity. In many countries protection of doctrine is essential to the integrity of entire legal systems based on religious law, while in others State ideology is fundamentally atheistic. Whatever the motivation for opposing proselytism, there is no doubt that its supposed coercive effects are frequently exaggerated.

The Human Rights Committee's interpretation of the right to 'have or to adopt a religion or belief of his choice' in Article 18(1) of the ICCPR unequivocally supports, in paragraph 5, the right to replace one's religion with another, or to retain it. Coercion that would impair this right in the illustrations provided by the Human Rights Committee had

[392] UN Doc. E/CN.4/1996/95 (1995), para. 27.

more to do with State functions in providing education, medical care and employment but were not linked with missionary work or proselytism. On the contrary, a review of the Human Rights Committee's interpretation when monitoring State compliance with the ICCPR supports the position that restrictions on missionary work, proselytism and the propagation of one's beliefs constitute interference with Article 18 freedoms. Similar conclusions may be drawn from the extensive material available in the Special Rapporteur's reports. Two observations made early in the drafting of the ICCPR express the fundamental importance of the freedom to change and to maintain one's religion. These are that 'freedom of thought, conscience and religion was meaningless unless everyone was free not only to hold a belief but also to change their religion or belief and to try to persuade others of the truth of their religion or belief',[393] and that in the absence of a right to change one's religion or belief 'there would no longer be liberty or progress in the world'.[394]

While in principle the right to 'teach' and the right to propagate one's beliefs are recognised freedoms within Article 9 of the European Convention, uncertainty as to the true meaning of 'proselytism' (given its negative connotations) led to an unworkable distinction in the *Kokkinakis* case between those recognised rights and 'improper proselytism'. The distinction was not clarified in the subsequent *Larissis* case. The European Court in *Kokkinakis* even avoided applying that distinction altogether by deciding that a violation of Article 9 had occurred by means of the national court's failure adequately to reason its decision. The European Court's apparent policy of non-intervention in such cases of proselytism is only partially offset by its notional support for the right to teach and to propagate one's beliefs. The inducements, such as they are, to join a minority religion through proselytism cannot be equated with the pervasive strength of discrimination in favour of State or majority religions in some countries and of discrimination specifically directed against minority religions, particularly those that proselytise. The situation in Greece provides a vivid illustration. Such discrimination and intolerance might be easier to characterise as coercive than proselytism. Discrimination often takes the form of denying to minority religions the very activities by which State or majority religions are

---

[393] UN Doc. E/CN.4 SR. 116 (1949), p. 3 (Commission of the Churches on International Affairs).
[394] UN Doc. E/CN.4/SR. 116 (1949), p. 8 (Philippines).

preserved or promoted. The conclusion is that even culturally undesirable forms of proselytism should be tolerated, rather than State interference against proselytism, yet the European Court in the proselytism cases has failed to intervene sufficiently, even when the laws in question are open to accusations of obvious discrimination. The lack of clear guidance on the distinction between acceptable and 'improper' proselytism is particularly unjustified when viewed in the light of the historical development of the freedom to change and to maintain one's religion, given the opposition to proselytism so strenuously voiced by its opponents in United Nations debates, on the basis of reasoning which was rejected in those debates and rejected subsequently by the Human Rights Committee and Special Rapporteur.

The European Court has also, in recent years, introduced the concept of 'respect' for the religious beliefs or feelings of others to support restrictions on the manifestation of religion and belief under Article 9, as well as freedom of expression under Article 10. To the extent that the limitation ground 'the rights and freedoms of others' is relevant to proselytism consisting of the persuasive portrayal of beliefs under Article 9, it was argued above that it is generally applicable only to fundamental interference with the *forum internum*, namely freedom from coercion in religious choice. This would produce consistency with Article 18(2) of the ICCPR. However, the limitation provisions applicable generally to freedom of expression are also of concern unless suitably contained. In the case of *Wingrove* the European Court corrected the inappropriate application to Article 9 of principles separately developed under Article 10 (when previous case law, such as *Otto-Preminger*, equated 'respect for the religious feelings of believers' with the guarantees in Article 9). The separation between Article 9 and Article 10 freedoms was not clearly maintained in the more recent decision in *Murphy*, but the European Court was also criticised above for the way it avoided any detailed examination of the aim of the prohibition on paid religious advertising by radio broadcast, and only provided superficial analysis of general principles which might operate to justify such a restriction. The Court mechanically cited key principles relevant to the 'rights of others' which had been developed in the particular context of *Otto-Preminger* and *Wingrove* (of severely offensive blasphemous expression), and which were derived directly from the aims of the prohibitions in those cases. The Court in *Murphy* suggested, without adequate justification, that those principles were of general application to restrictions far removed from such aims – yet in *Murphy* there was no opposition or denial of the religious beliefs of others and nothing amounting to a provocative portrayal of objects of religious veneration of the type referred to in the paragraph of the *Otto-Preminger* judgment relied on by the Court in *Murphy* to invoke those priniciples.

It is likely that the European Court will in the near future face a new range of claims based upon measures prohibiting disparagement or vilification of religious groups or their belief systems. A more rigorous approach will be expected in the reasoning of the European Court than that exhibited in *Murphy* and in the proselytism cases. Whatever the attitude in a country towards proselytism and the aim of a State in restricting proselytism and other forms of religious expression, the issue is put in context by the warning given in connection with OSCE commitments, that '[o]verly restrictive regulation of religious speech prevents the free exchange of ideas which is one of the fundamental pillars of democracy and one of the guarantees underpinning the freedom of religion'.[395]

[395] ODIHR, 'The Human Dimension Seminar', p. 18.

3

The scope of the *forum internum* beyond religious choice

Introduction

This chapter is concerned with establishing the outer limits of the *forum internum* beyond freedom of religious choice. The *forum internum* is taken to denote the internal and private realm of the individual against which no State interference is justified in any circumstances. It comprises not only the individual's absolute freedom of choice of religion or belief (as discussed extensively in Chapter 2) but also a range of additional freedoms (which shall be referred to as the residual scope of the *forum internum*). However, the precise reach of these additional freedoms is uncertain and neither the United Nations nor European institutions have developed clear or consistent principles to enable them to be formally recognised. On the contrary, when faced with the absolute character of the *forum internum*, jurisprudence has developed in order to subject the freedom to State regulation at the expense of the *forum internum* – yet it is trite law that the *forum internum* is subject to unqualified protection in all the key international instruments (Article 18 of the Universal Declaration on Human Rights ('Universal Declaration'), Article 18 of the International Covenant on Civil and Political Rights (ICCPR), Article 9 of the European Convention for the Protection of Human Rights and Fundamental Freedoms ('European Convention) and Article 1(1) of the Declaration on the Elimination of all Forms of Intolerance and of Discrimination Based on Religion or Belief (1981 Declaration).[1]

---

[1] For discussion on the distinction between the internal and external freedoms in other contexts, such as the US Religious Clauses in the First Amendment, see M. McConnell, 'Religious Participation in Public Programs', 59 U Chicago L Rev (1992) 115. McConnell concludes that the religious freedom cases under the First Amendment have been distorted by the false choice between secularism and 'majoritarianism', neither of which faithfully reflects the philosophy of the such clauses. See also M. McConnell, 'Freedom From Persecution or Protection of the Rights of Conscience?: A Critique of Justice Scalia's Historical Arguments in City of Boerne v. Flores', 39(1) William Mary

Most commentators readily acknowledge certain specific components of the *forum internum* beyond the mere choice of religion or belief.
Harris, O'Boyle and Warbrick suggest, for example, that the first part of
Article 9(1) of the European Convention provides protection against
being required to reveal one's beliefs, protection against the imposition
of penalties for holding beliefs, and protection against indoctrination, at
least where indoctrination involves some positive action directed
against the individual. However, they suggest that Article 9(1) is not
violated by indoctrination if the individual is nevertheless left free to
hold his own beliefs.[2] Some of the practical difficulties in distinguishing
the inner from the outer realms of Article 9(1) are evident from the few
decisions which have attempted such a distinction but the real difficulty
for those claiming a *forum internum* violation lies in the lack of accepted
criteria for establishing interference. The standards which have been
proposed are such as to exclude all but the most exceptional claims.
Malcolm Evans suggests that the right to private thought does protect a
person from being subjected to actions intended to induce a change of
mind but that this threshold (couched in terms of 'indoctrination' in the
Danish Sex Education case)[3] would be so high as inevitably to amount to
conduct breaching other Convention Articles: 'Since the right to freedom of thought, conscience and religion is absolute, it might otherwise
be argued that advertising, or any other means of changing peoples'
opinions, might be covered.'[4]

In a summary of cases in which the individual is required to
act contrary to conscience by State-operated tax, social security and
similar schemes, Malcolm Evans adopted a threshold analogous to
that proposed by Harris, O'Boyle and Warbrick when he concluded:
'[p]rovided that the individuals are able to continue in their beliefs,
the *forum internum* remains untouched and there will be no breach
of Article 9(1)'.[5] Carolyn Evans, by contrast, suggests that a more
generous approach should be taken. In a review of European cases
concerning church tax (*Darby v. Sweden*)[6] and involving the forcible

L Rev (1998) 819, and G. Moens, 'The Action-Belief Dichotomy and Freedom of
Religion' 12 Sidney L Rev (1989) 195.

[2] D. J. Harris, M. O'Boyle and C. Warbrick, *Law of the European Convention on Human
Rights*, London: Butterworths (1995), at pp. 360–2.

[3] *Kjeldsen, Busk Madsen and Pedersen v. Denmark* (Ser. A) No. 23 (1976) ECtHR.

[4] M. D. Evans, *Religious Liberty and International Law in Europe*, Cambridge: Cambridge
University Press (1997), pp. 294–5.

[5] *Ibid.*, at p. 295.

[6] *Darby v. Sweden* (Ser. A) No. 187 (1990) ECtHR, annex to the decision of the Court.

participation of Jehovah's Witness children in military parades (*Valamis v. Greece*,[7] and *Efstratiou v. Greece*[8]), all of which concern the imposition of State requirements contrary to the beliefs of the individual, she observed that:

> '[i]n neither case did the action of the State go so far that it made impossible (or even particularly difficult) for the individuals to maintain their internal beliefs, but in each case the State required the individuals to act in a way that they felt was in direct contradiction to the requirements of those beliefs. They were in effect being asked to recant, by their behaviour, their religion. This conflict between the behaviour required of them and their beliefs was such that it arguably interfered with the internal as well as the external realm.'[9]

Although the European Court has reached inconsistent decisions in such cases, she argued that compulsion in matters of religion amounts to an interference with the *forum internum*, and that this point is underestimated in the practice of the Court.[10] Van Dijk and van Hoof similarly emphasised that the significance of the absolute guarantee of inner freedom of thought, conscience and religion:

> 'implies that one cannot be subjected to a treatment intended to change the process of thinking, that any form of compulsion to express thoughts, to change opinion, or to divulge a religious conviction is prohibited, and that no sanction may be imposed either on the holding of any view whatever or on the change of a religion or conviction: it protects against indoctrination by the State'.[11]

They also added that:

> '[t]he freedom to accept a religion or belief and to change one's religion or belief is unlimited. This freedom also includes the freedom not to have a religion or belief, and *not to be obliged to act in a way that entails the expression of the acceptation of a church, religion or belief that one does not share*'.[12]

---

[7] *Valamis v. Greece* (1997) 24 EHRR 294.   [8] *Efstratiou v. Greece* (1997) 24 EHRR 298.

[9] C. Evans, *Freedom of Religion Under the European Convention on Human Rights*, Oxford: Oxford University Press (2001), at pp. 77–8 (see pp. 72–9 and 170–98 for discussion of compulsion).

[10] *Ibid.*, at p. 102, noting particularly such cases as *Valamis v. Greece* (1997) 24 EHRR 294, *Efstratiou v. Greece* (1997) 24 EHRR 298.

[11] P. van Dijk and G. J. H. van Hoof, *Theory and Practice of the European Convention on Human Rights*, The Hague/London: Kluwer (1998), at pp. 541–2.

[12] *Ibid.*, at p. 547 (emphasis added).

A survey of European and United Nations jurisprudence does not reflect a coherent pattern of protection for the *forum internum* that enables the individual to resist compulsion to act contrary to belief generally. This is in no small part due to fears that by recognising that such compulsion raises issues of conscience, a basis will be provided for resisting basic civic obligations and the order of States would be thrown into chaos.[13] Attempts to reconcile apparently conflicting decisions have led some commentators such as Malcolm Evans to distinguish between compulsory involvement in activities taking place in the 'public sphere' (such as the obligation to pay general taxes, which are largely upheld) from those in the 'private sphere' (such as the obligation to support a particular religion to which one does not belong, which the European Commission has been willing to condemn).[14] Carolyn Evans has likewise distinguished between compulsory participation of a religious nature and compulsion that may be characterised as 'secular, general or neutral'.[15] However, such analyses do not alter the conclusion that so

---

[13] See generally, L. M. Hammer, *The International Human Right to Freedom of Conscience*, Aldershot: Ashgate (2001). Hammer focuses on the non-religious dimensions of freedom of conscience and its practical application independent of the right to freedom of religion. See also K. J. Partsch, 'Freedom of Conscience and Expression, and Political Freedoms', in L. Henkin (ed.), *The International Bill of Rights: The Covenant on Civil and Political Rights*, New York/Guildford: Columbia University Press (1981). Partsch suggests that 'perhaps issues of conscientious objection to civic duties are an aspect of "manifesting one's religion" covered by paragraph 3 of Article 18' (at p. 212). This view had most support in European jurisprudence and limited support in the Human Rights Committee, for example, among dissenting members of the Human Rights Committee in *Paul Westerman v. The Netherlands*, Communication No. 682/1996 (views of 3 November 1999) (2000) 7(2) IHRR 363), who considered that the author's objection to military service 'constituted a legitimate manifestation of his freedom of thought, conscience or religion under Article 18'. The majority held that 'the right to freedom of conscience does not as such imply the right to refuse all obligations imposed by law' (para. 9.3).

[14] M. D. Evans, *Religious Liberty and International Law in Europe*, p. 296, discussing *Darby v. Sweden*. See also Nowak who is one commentator who supports the 'manifestation' orientation of decisions concerning coercion, but only after actions leave the realm of privacy. 'The freedom to live and act in harmony with one's conscience enjoys the absolute protection of (private) freedom of conscience so long as these actions do not affect the rights and freedoms of others. Once they leave this sphere of privacy, as in the case of refusal to perform legal duties (e.g., duty to pay taxes or serve in the military), they are protected by Art. 18 only when they represent a practice or some other form of public manifestation of a religion or a belief. But even in this case, they are subject to the limitations found in para. 3.' (Nowak, *CCPR Commentary*, p. 315).

[15] C. Evans, *Freedom of Religion Under the European Convention on Human Rights*, Oxford: Oxford University Press (2001), Chapter 8.

far no adequate scheme of protection has yet been devised to cater for the inevitable conflict with the *forum internum* posed by certain forms of compulsion.

Although the *forum internum* consists of the full range of protection contemplated by the phrase 'the right to freedom of thought, conscience and religion' other than the right of external manifestation, the treaty organs have not fully established the scope of the *forum internum* beyond the conceptually straightforward freedom of choice of religion or belief. Recognition has been given to different strands of the *forum internum* without producing a coherent approach to the meaning or even scheme of protection for the *forum internum*. The purpose of this chapter is to determine the scope of the *forum internum* from an examination of the justifications for interference with the *forum internum* and the recognition given to the different means available for its protection by European and United Nations organs. This chapter will also examine whether the theoretical basis for past decision-making is sustainable.

It will be argued, first, that freedom from coercion to act contrary to one's religion or belief is protected within the *forum internum* even though an express general prohibition to that effect would be unacceptable because of its breadth. Repeated but superficial recognition is given to the *forum internum*, particularly by the Strasbourg organs when issues of compulsion to act contrary to belief are raised, but the practice has been to avoid affirming that such compulsion falls within the *forum internum* because of the consequence that it would not be subject to permissible limitations. The distinct preference of the European institutions (and to a lesser extent the Human Rights Committee) has been to decide such issues of coercion on the basis of manifestation (no matter how inappropriately) or discrimination, rather than on the basis of interference with the *forum internum*.

Secondly, a comparison will be made between the standard of recognition given to the *forum internum* when asserted by the applicant or author in 'direct' claims of *forum internum* violation (on the one hand) and (on the other) the 'indirect' recognition of *forum internum* rights when the *forum internum* is not the immediate subject matter of a claim but only arises incidentally, for example, in the interpretation of the limitation provisions that preserve the 'rights and freedoms of others'. The aim will be to highlight the manifest inconsistency between the habitual failure of the European institutions in particular to give due acknowledgement to the potential scope of the *forum internum* when 'directly' claimed within a core freedom of religion Article, by contrast to the readiness with which the *forum internum* is recognised 'indirectly' as a means of broadening the discretion available to States.

Private sources of intolerance and discrimination can have a profound effect on the enjoyment of *forum internum* rights which is often overlooked. The effect of discrimination in certain circumstances may be such as to impair the freedom to have or to adopt a religion or belief of choice and is often indistinguishable from punishment for holding particular beliefs. Furthermore, in an environment in which discrimination is practised, the right not to be compelled to reveal one's religion or belief becomes all the more critical. This chapter will also examine the impact of the development of principles relating to discrimination on the *forum internum*.

In short, this chapter will focus on coercion to act contrary to one's beliefs, compulsion to reveal one's beliefs and punishment for holding particular beliefs, as well as other elements that might form recognised constituents of the *forum internum*. Principles concerning coercion have undergone clearest development in the context of the core freedom of religion Articles and for the most part will be considered under the heading ' "Direct" protection for the *forum internum*'. The compulsory disclosure of religion or belief and punishment for holding particular beliefs, also widely considered to fall within the residual *forum internum*, arise in the context of both the 'direct' protection and 'indirect' protection for the *forum internum* and are discussed under all headings of this chapter.

'Direct' protection for the *forum internum*

Decisions concerning coercion to act contrary to one's beliefs illustrate the different approaches taken to the residual scope of the *forum internum*. Most of the detailed reasoning has been provided by the European, as opposed to United Nations, organs. The different approaches not surprisingly vary according to the nature of the legal obligation constituting such compulsion and fall into four groups. First, those in which applicable limitation provisions were invoked to restrict manifestation. Secondly, those in which the claim of coercion failed because of the element of choice available to the applicant, irrespective of the issue of manifestation. In such cases, the European Commission and the European Court have been more likely to acknowledge that protection against coercion falls within the *forum internum* without resorting to analysis based on manifestation and applicable limitations. Thirdly, those in which no reliance was placed on manifestation because specific provision had been made for the imposition of the legal obligation within the European Convention or ICCPR. The true basis of this third category of decisions is often rather obscure, particularly in European Convention decisions, and should in any event be reviewed in the light of wider acceptance at both European and Universal level that conscientious objection to military service does raise issues of conscience even though provision is specifically made for it in both the European Convention and ICCPR. Fourthly, are those decisions that importantly recognised that coercion to act contrary to one's beliefs constitutes interference with the *forum internum* within certain limits. It is this final group of cases that demonstrates the most interesting developments giving proper substance to the residual *forum internum*. Such decisions pose difficulties for States where it has to be concluded that States may not themselves rely on limitation provisions to justify coercion.

Taken together, these cases fail to provide an adequately reasoned basis for justifying coercive measures to act contrary to one's belief. A detailed analysis of the practice of the Human Rights Committee, the European Commission and the European Court reveals that the traditional approach to this subject needs revisiting. One of the aims of the discussion under this heading (' "Direct" protection for the *forum internum*') is to elicit a consistent foundation for decision-making in all such cases of coercion.

Decisions based on justified limitation on manifestation

Van Dijk and van Hoof note that the early decisions of the European Commission concerning the imposition of legal obligations against the individual's conscience were decided on the basis that Article 9 of the European Convention was applicable but so also was one of the limitation grounds.[16] This approach avoided determining whether coercion in such cases could constitute an interference with the *forum internum*. Instead, the European Commission decided that the limitation provisions in Article 9(2) justified the interference, paying close regard to the purpose of the legal obligation in question, as if each claim turned only upon the applicant's right to manifest. (Some early cases even avoided

---

[16] Van Dijk and van Hoof, *Theory and Practice of the European Convention*, p. 543.

the relevance of manifestation altogether even though it was a critical precondition to reliance on limitation provisions.)[17]

For example, in *X. v. The Netherlands*,[18] the applicant alleged that compulsory membership of the Health Service, as a condition for keeping cattle, required him to act contrary his religious conscience as a member of the Reformed Dutch Church and accordingly violated Article 9. The European Commission noted that the purpose of the Act for the Prevention of Tuberculosis among Cattle 1952, which imposed this requirement, was to provide safeguard against disease. Rather than explain how compulsion in such a scheme impinged upon Article 9, the European Commission merely commented that 'it is not necessary to determine this particular issue as the right invoked by the Applicant is, according to paragraph (2) of the Article, subject "to such limitations as are prescribed by law and are necessary in a democratic society . . . for the protection of health and morals" '.[19] The European Commission's reasoning was that even if the Act and its application were caught by Article 9(1), sufficient justification could be found in Article 9(2). However, it is only possible to take this approach if the Act and its application are seen to be restrictive of the *manifestation* of the applicant's religion or belief and therefore not an interference with the *forum internum*. No attempt was made to explain the nature of the applicant's manifestation. Manifestation would certainly be difficult to discern given that the action began with legal proceedings brought against the applicant under the Act, resulting in a fine (or prison sentence in default) for his failure to apply for membership of the Health Service after acquiring a cow.

Similarly, in a case concerning objections of conscience to compulsory motor insurance, the applicant in *X. v. The Netherlands*,[20] following his conviction for driving without insurance, claimed that according to his religious convictions prosperity and adversity are meted out to human beings by God and it is not permissible to attempt in advance to prevent or reduce the effects of possible disasters. Consistent with its earlier decisions,[21] the European Commission did not state precisely how the compulsion, in this case the enforcement of compulsory motor insurance schemes, raised issues within the scope of Article 9. It appears

---

[17] For example, *Reformed Church of X. v. The Netherlands*, App. No. 1497/62, 5 Yearbook (1962) 286.
[18] *X. v. The Netherlands*, App. No. 1068/61, 5 Yearbook (1962) 278.   [19] *Ibid.*, at 284.
[20] *X. v. The Netherlands*, App. No. 2988/66, 10 Yearbook (1967) 472.
[21] *X. v. The Netherlands*, App. No. 1068/61, 5 Yearbook (1962) 278; *Reformed Church of X. v. The Netherlands*, App. No. 1497/62, 5 Yearbook (1962) 286.

to have assumed at least that the facts may have given rise to a claim under Article 9(1) and continued, 'in so far as this provision is involved', justification may be found under Article 9(2). The purpose of the compulsory motor insurance scheme was to safeguard the rights of third parties who may become victims of motor accidents and, it noted, 'paragraph (2) of Article 9 expressly permits such limitations of the freedom to manifest one's religions or belief as are necessary in a democratic society "for the protection of the rights and freedoms of others" '.[22] Precisely what form the applicant's manifestation took was not stated, even though the finding that the application was manifestly ill-founded is obviously sensible. No effort was made to define the manifestation in question, nor, more importantly, to address the claim as framed by the applicant – in terms of interference with the *forum internum* within Article 9(1) through compulsory participation in an insurance scheme contrary to the practices of his religion and religious beliefs. In its review of previous decisions, and in this decision itself, the European Commission appears to have treated State measures to enforce compulsory participation in insurance schemes as justified restrictions on the *manifestation* of religion or belief. However, it is quite obvious that the applicant was not 'manifesting' his convictions by driving a motor vehicle and to suggest that driving a motor vehicle constitutes 'manifestation' of religion or belief would be stretching the meaning of that term.

The turning point for the examination of all Article 9 cases (not simply those concerned with coercion) came with *Arrowsmith v. United Kingdom*,[23] which led to a new (and better reasoned) emphasis on the nexus between the religion or belief in question and its expression or manifestation. Unfortunately, it also led to misapplication of notions of manifestation in subsequent claims based in substance upon coercion. The *Arrowsmith* case concerned claims under Articles 9 and 10 of the European Convention by a seasoned pacifist who had been convicted under the Incitement to Disaffection Act 1934 for circulating leaflets at an army base. The leaflets advised members of the armed forces in Northern Ireland of the options available to them in refusing to perform their duties. The European Commission decided that 'the term "practice" does not cover each act which is motivated or influenced by a religion or belief'[24]

---

[22] *X. v. The Netherlands*, App. No. 2988/66, 10 Yearbook (1967) 472, 476–8.
[23] *Arrowsmith v. United Kingdom*, App. No. 7050/75 (1978) 19 D&R 5.
[24] *Ibid.*, at 19–20, para. 71.

and refused to accept that her actions constituted a 'practice' within Article 9 because: 'when the actions of individuals do not actually express the belief concerned they cannot be considered to be as such protected by Article 9.1, even when they are motivated or influenced by it'.[25]

Although the facts in *Arrowsmith* justify such an analysis, the European Commission's reasoning is not appropriate to instances of State-imposed compulsion contrary to the individual's beliefs. Nevertheless, over-use of 'the *Arrowsmith* test' as it has become known (to determine whether a particular expression of belief is an eligible manifestation) has, on occasion, led applicants in cases concerning coercion to frame their own claims in terms of manifestation, somewhat artificially. Thus, in *C. v. United Kingdom*,[26] the applicant maintained, on the uncontested premise that pacifism was a belief, that as a Quaker his pacifist beliefs required him to oppose recourse to force and not to support (even indirectly) defence-related expenditure, as a 'necessary' manifestation of those beliefs. Accordingly, he resisted payment of the portion of his income tax attributable to military expenditure. The European Commission, referring to the formula established in *Arrowsmith*, commented as follows:

> 'Article 9 primarily protects the sphere of personal beliefs and religious creeds, i.e. the area which is sometimes called the *forum internum*. In addition, it protects acts which are intimately linked to these attitudes, such as worship and devotion which are aspects of the practice of religion or belief in a generally recognised form.
>
> However, in protecting this personal sphere, Article 9 does not always guarantee the right to behave in the public sphere in a way which is dictated by such a belief: – for instance by refusing to pay certain taxes because part of the revenue so raised may be applied for military expenditure.'[27]

The European Commission acknowledged the well known principle established in *Arrowsmith* that 'the term practice as employed in Article 9(1) does not cover each act which is motivated or influenced by a religion or belief' but then it invoked two entirely different additional principles, namely that the duty to pay general taxes is unrelated to issues of conscience, and that the State's right to raise such taxes is specifically authorised by the Convention. It commented:

---

[25] *Ibid.*, at 20, para. 71.
[26] *C. v. United Kingdom*, App. No. 10358/83 (1983) 37 D&R 142.   [27] *Ibid.*, at 147.

'The obligation to pay taxes is a general one which has no specific conscientious implications in itself. Its neutrality in this sense is also illustrated by the fact that no tax payer can influence or determine the purpose for which his or her tax contributions are applied, once they are collected. Furthermore, the power of taxation is expressly recognised by the Convention system and ascribed to the State by Article 1, First Protocol.

It follows that Article 9 does not confer on the applicant the right to refuse, on the basis of his convictions, to abide by legislation, the operation of which is provided for by the Convention, and which applies neutrally and generally in the public sphere, without impinging on the freedoms guaranteed by Article 9.'[28]

A blend of reasoning was therefore provided by the European Commission rendering it quite unclear whether the claim was inadmissible as a result of failure to make the necessary connection between private belief and external manifestation, as a result of the 'general' and 'neutral' nature of the law in question, or as a result of the fact that the State was exercising its power of taxation.[29] What is clear, however, is that in spite of readily acknowledging the *forum internum*, distinguishing it from external manifestation, the European Commission was not prepared to discuss the significance of the *forum internum* to the facts of the case. It is possible that it declined to do so because the applicant himself argued the matter on the basis of his right to manifest his beliefs.

Another issue influencing the European Commission, which is discussed in further detail below under the heading 'Decisions based on available alternatives', concerns the choice available to the applicant in avoiding conflict between matters of conscience and the legal requirements imposed on him. The European Commission noted that 'alternative methods of voicing his protest' were available to the applicant such as advertising his attitude and inviting others to support it through the democratic process.[30] It may be argued that the non-payment of taxes is not an 'available' manifestation in view of Article 1, First

---

[28] *Ibid.*, at 147.
[29] For a survey of case law on general and neutral laws, see C. Evans, *Freedom of Religion Under the European Convention*, pp. 179–86.
[30] Dignan correctly observed that the right to protest freely is not sufficient to justify compulsion to act against one's conscience: 'Forcing a man to act in contradiction to his conscience does constitute a denial of equal concern and respect which is not assuaged by allowing him to protest about it freely' J. Dignan, 'A Right Not to Render unto Caesar: Conscientious Objection for the Taxpayer' 34 Northern Ireland LQ (1983) 20, at 25.

Protocol and the wide-ranging powers of States in relation to taxation. The way the European Commission put it was as follows: 'It follows that Article 9 does not confer on the applicant the right to refuse, on the basis of his convictions, to abide by legislation, the operation of which is provided for by the Convention, and which applies neutrally and generally in the public sphere, without impinging on the freedoms guaranteed by Article 9.'[31]

Other cases of coercion have similarly invoked *Arrowsmith* principles in combination with the neutrality of the obligation in question. In V. *v. The Netherlands*,[32] the applicant, a doctor whose professional practice was founded on anthroposophical principles and whose fees were charged according to the patients' ability to pay, refused to participate in a compulsory professional pension scheme because contributions were determined by gross income, contrary to his anthroposophical beliefs. As with *C. v. United Kingdom*, the European Commission recited that primarily Article 9 protects the *forum internum*. It noted the *Arrowsmith* test and declared the claim inadmissible by stating that 'the refusal to participate in such a pension scheme, although motivated by the applicant's particular belief, cannot, in the view of the Commission, be considered as an actual expression of this belief'.[33] The rationale of the *Arrowsmith* test was once again stretched in order to render some connection between belief (giving rise to the refusal to join the pension scheme) and its expression. The European Commission also commented that 'the obligation to participate in a pension fund applies to all general practitioners on a purely neutral basis, and cannot be said to have any close link with their religion or beliefs'.[34] It therefore appears that the neutrality of the scheme was decisive, lending some weight to the suggestion that the aspect of neutrality was similarly decisive in *C. v. United Kingdom*. However, the dismissal of claims on the grounds of the neutrality of laws alone would involve the fallacy that neutral laws are incapable of giving rise to issues of conscience. Furthermore, any suggestion that neutral laws are incapable of being impugned where they are enacted under powers specifically recognised in the Convention would rest on another fallacy. In the case of *Mannoussakis and others v. Greece*,[35] a violation was found of Article 9 in the application of building control laws, which required the prior authorisation for the

---

[31] *Ibid.*, at 147.   [32] *V. v. The Netherlands*, App. No. 10678/83 (1984) 39 D&R 267.
[33] *Ibid.*, at 269.   [34] *Ibid.*, at 268.
[35] *Manoussakis and others v. Greece* 23 (1997) EHRR 387.

use of buildings for certain religious purposes, ostensibly within the express right of States provided for in Article 1 of Protocol 1 'to enforce such laws as it deems necessary to control the use of property in accordance with the general interest'. In practice it is extremely difficult to bring any claim successfully under Article 9 of the European Convention when *manifestation* of belief conflicts with laws that are general, neutral, or which fall within the burden which States are entitled to impose under particular Convention Articles, such as those relating to pensions, social security or taxation. However, it is even harder in cases involving coercion because of the inappropriateness of applying the *Arrowsmith* test of manifestation to interference by coercion.

The Strasbourg institutions have nevertheless demonstrated a marked tendency to focus on the manifestation of belief to the exclusion of other aspects of Article 9(1) of the European Convention. For example, a narrow focus only on the right to manifest religion and belief, ignoring altogether the *forum internum*, is reflected in the Opinion of Mr Schermers and Sir Basil Hall in *Darby v. Sweden*: 'The fact that the applicant had to pay a tax to defray expenditure incurred by church parish councils does not in our opinion infringe a right conferred on him by Article 9. He continued to have freedom to practise a religion, to manifest a religion, or to refrain from practising a religion.'[36]

Such reasoning would effectively confine the entirety of Article 9(1) only to the right of manifestation. The successful application of the *Arrowsmith* test depends on a particular connection between belief and its manifestation, when in reality the 'manifestation' of belief is rarely ever in play. Coercion applicants face an insurmountable hurdle when their claims are examined by reference to proper manifestation. They are required to maintain that their non-compliance with the law in question actually expresses the belief concerned and that the practice of their beliefs is unjustifiably restricted. It is in the nature of such claims that the applicant objects to being compelled to do something which, in particular, would *not* constitute a manifestation of his beliefs, is *alien* to such beliefs, and from which the applicant wishes to dissociate himself. The applicant does not assert that opposition to coercion (or non-compliance)

---

[36] *Darby v. Sweden* (Ser. A) No. 187 (1990) ECtHR, annex to the decision of the Court, p. 24. See also *Efstratiou v. Greece* (1997) 24 EHRR 298, para. 37. Mr Schermers and Sir Basil Hall dissented because they would have preferred the matter to be decided on the basis of a violation of Article 14 in conjunction with Article 1 of Protocol 1, thereby ruling out Article 9 altogether.

constitutes the practice of his religion or belief. For the same reason, the applicant also does not, in reality, maintain that the legal obligation in question comprises a *restriction* or limitation on the manifestation of belief forming part of the applicant's 'worship, teaching, practice and observance'. A legal requirement compelling the applicant to act in a particular way is not comparable to a restriction which limits the applicant's chosen outward manifestation of belief. Whenever *Arrowsmith* reasoning is applied to cases of coercion, analysis is based entirely upon the individual's reaction to State compulsion rather than on the issue of whether such compulsion is permissible *a priori*. Nevertheless, compulsion requiring an individual to act against his religion or belief raises issues of interference with the *forum internum* irrespective of the individual's reaction to such compulsion.

Examination of claims of coercion might instead begin with a determination of whether the activity compelled would be contrary to the beliefs concerned, assuming the beliefs in question are sufficiently recognised. There is a good level of consistency between the European and the United Nations institutions in the criteria to determine whether belief is eligible for protection. Not all beliefs are protected. For example, the Human Rights Committee in *M. A. B., W. A. T. and J.-A. Y. T. v. Canada*[37] concluded that a claim to 'belief' consisting of the worship and use of marijuana as the 'Sacrament' according to the tenets of the Assembly of the Church of the Universe, was outside Article 18 and inadmissible *ratione materiae*.[38] Similarly in the context of the European Convention, 'belief' includes pacifism (*Arrowsmith*), Communism (*Hazar, Hazar and Acik v. Turkey*),[39] atheism (*Angeleni v. Sweden*)[40] and pro-life anti-abortion beliefs (*Plattform 'Ärzte für das Leben' v. Austria*)[41] but excludes mere 'opinions' or 'ideas' (*Cambell and Cosans*).[42] Assuming the beliefs in question are eligible for protection, the next stage might be to examine the issue of manifestation. If non-compliance by the applicant does not constitute the *manifestation* of religion or belief, as the *Arrowsmith* test has been applied in that and subsequent

---

[37] *M. A. B., W. A. T. and J.-A. Y. T. v. Canada*, Communication No. 570/1993 (decision of 8 April 1994), UN Doc. A/49/40 vol. 2 (1994), p. 368.

[38] *Ibid.*, at p. 370, para. 4.2.

[39] *Hazar and Açik v. Turkey*, App. Nos. 16311/90, 16312/90 and 16313/90 (1992) 73 D&R 111 (settlement); (1992) 72 D&R 200 (admissibility).

[40] *Angeleni v. Sweden*, App. No. 10491/83 (1986) 51 D&R 41.

[41] *Plattform 'Ärzte für das Leben' v. Austria* (Ser. A) No. 139 (1988) ECtHR.

[42] *Campbell and Cosans v. United Kingdom* (Ser. A) No. 48 (1982) ECtHR.

cases,[43] then it may be concluded that the compulsion falls *prima facie* to be determined under Article 9(1) aside from questions of manifestation, as an interference with the *forum internum*.[44] This would avoid the application of the *Arrowsmith* test and the false premise on which limitation provisions are applied under Article 9(2) in claims based on coercion.

It would appear that the European Court has perpetuated the Commission's traditional analysis based on manifestation even when the Court has been prepared to find in favour of the applicant in clearly recognised instances of coercion. For example, in *Buscarini and others v. San Marino*[45] the applicants were elected to the General Grand Council (the parliament of the Republic of San Marino) in elections held in 1993. Upon taking parliamentary office they were required to swear an oath 'on the Holy Gospels', as required by section 55 of the Elections Act. The applicants claimed that this obligation, enforced by the General Grand Council, required them publicly to profess a particular faith in breach of Article 9. The Government maintained that the form of words in issue had lost its original religious character, as had certain religious feast days which the State recognised as public holidays. The European Court began by reciting its famous pro-pluralist statement in *Kokkinakis v. Greece*[46] and, as in that case, proceeded to address Article 9 by reference to manifestation after making only cursory reference to the fact '[t]hat

---

[43] In numerous cases since *Arrowsmith* it has been held that only manifestations that actually express the belief concerned will be protected forms of manifestation, not every act which is motivated and influenced by a religion or belief. So, in *Knudsen v. Norway* the protest at newly enacted abortion law by a priest refusing to undertake public functions 'did not actually express the applicant's belief or religious views and it cannot, therefore, be considered as such to be protected by Article 9 para. 1, even when it was motivated by it' (*Knudsen v. Norway*, App. No. 11045/84 (1983) 42 D&R 247, at p. 258). The Commission's statement that the 'applicant has not shown that he has been under any pressure to change his views or that he has been prevented from manifesting his religion or belief' (para. 258), demonstrates a focus on these particular elements to the exclusion of all others. See also *C. v. United Kingdom*, App. No. 10358/83 (1983) 37 D&R 142.

[44] For an alternative approach based on belief as the reason for action, see H. Gilbert, 'The Slow Development of the Right to Conscientious Objection to Military Service under the European Convention on Human Rights', 5 EHRLR (2001) 554, at 562–6.

[45] *Buscarini and others v. San Marino* (2000) 30(2) EHRR 208.

[46] 'As enshrined in Article 9, freedom of thought, conscience and religion is one of the foundations of a "democratic society" within the meaning of the Convention. It is, in its religious dimension, one of the most vital elements that go to make up the identity of believers and their conception of life, but it is also a precious asset for atheists, agnostics, sceptics and the unconcerned. The pluralism indissociable from a democratic society, which has been dearly won over the centuries, depends on it.' (*Kokkinakis v. Greece* (Ser. A) No. 260–A (1993) ECtHR, para. 31).

freedom entails, *inter alia*, freedom to hold or not to hold religious beliefs and to practise or not to practise a religion'. It immediately concluded that the requirement that the applicants 'take an oath on the Gospels did indeed constitute a limitation within the meaning of the second paragraph of Article 9, since it required them to swear allegiance to a particular religion on pain of forfeiting their parliamentary seats. Such interference will be contrary to Article 9 unless it is "prescribed by law", pursues one or more of the legitimate aims set out in paragraph 2 and is "necessary in a democratic society".'[47] On the basis that the requirement could not be regarded as 'necessary in a democratic society', the European Court concluded that Article 9 had been violated. This is in spite of the fact that the European Court recognised that, according to the applicants, 'the resolution requiring them to take the oath in issue was in the nature of a "premeditated act of coercion" directed at their freedom of conscience and religion. It aimed to humiliate them as persons who, immediately after being elected, had requested that the wording of the oath should be altered so as to conform with, *inter alia*, Article 9 of the Convention'.[48] The Court itself characterised the claim as 'requiring two elected representatives of the people to swear allegiance to a particular religion'.[49]

There could not be a clearer case of compulsion in the obligation to swear in accordance with religious beliefs that are not personally held, yet the European Court was treating that obligation as a restriction on manifestation. The requirement to swear an oath contrary to one's beliefs cannot sensibly be characterised as a restriction on the manifestation of one's own beliefs (still less a manifestation satisfying the close *Arrowsmith* nexus).

---

[47] *Buscarini and others v. San Marino* (2000) 30(2) EHRR 208, at para. 34.

[48] *Ibid.*, at para. 37.

[49] *Ibid.*, at para. 39. See also *McGuinness v. United Kingdom*, App. No. 39511/98 (unreported, decision of 8 June, 1999) in which the European Court rendered inadmissible the claim by a Sinn Fein Member of Parliament that the requirement to swear an oath of allegiance to the British monarchy violated Article 10. It distinguished the *Busarini* decision on the grounds that the consequences of refusal were less far-reaching, as the applicant was only deprived of access to the House of Commons and not restricted in Ministerial meetings outside the House. It held that the limitation on freedom of expression, the protection of the 'rights of others' in Article 10(2), should be interpreted as extending to the constitutional provision forming the basis of a democracy. As the United Kingdom is a constitutional monarchy, the requirement to take an oath of allegiance to the Queen could be construed as a reasonable condition. For further commentary, see 6 EHRLR (1999), page 639 and 70 BYBIL (1999) 366.

When the Human Rights Committee has examined issues of conflict with conscience stemming from a requirement that an oath be sworn in a particular form, the question of manifestation has not arisen. In its examination of State reports the Human Rights Committee noted with concern in relation to Ireland that the constitutional requirement that the President and judges must take a religious oath excluded some people from holding those offices.[50] In some instances discrimination may be the primary issue. For example, in relation to Estonia the Human Rights Committee was concerned that the automatic exclusion of persons unable to satisfy the requirements of the written oath of conscience concerning their previous activities (under the former Communist regime), when appointed to a State or local government agency, would give rise to an unreasonable restriction on the right of access to public service without discrimination.[51] The Human Rights Committee recommended that Estonia review the obligation to take an oath of conscience with a view to compliance with the non-discrimination provisions of the ICCPR and provide for the right to an effective remedy against a decision not to appoint or to dismiss a person in instances of refusal to take such an oath.[52] Similar concerns were expressed by the Committee in relation to Costa Rica[53] and Iraq.[54]

A review of Optional Protocol decisions based on facts similar to those in the *Arrowsmith* case unfortunately does not elicit detailed reasoning on the part of the Human Rights Committee. This is not surprising where the author has failed to assert the basis on which violation was claimed, as in *Leonardus Johannes Maria de Groot v. The Netherlands*.[55] The author had been convicted for participating in a criminal organisation when, as a peace activist, he attended a camp near a military base to demonstrate against militarism. He distributed

---

[50] UN Doc. A/48/40 (1993), para. 15 (Ireland). The Special Rapporteur also took up this issue with Pakistan, noting that the office of President must be held by a Muslim and, according to Article 42 of the Constitution, the President has to make an oath confirming this (UN Doc. E/CN.4/1996/95/Add.1 (1996), para. 17 (Pakistan), and with Greece, where the religious oath required to be given by the President of Greece means that only an Orthodox individual may occupy that office (UN Doc. A/51/542/Add.1 (1996), para. 17 (Greece).

[51] UN Doc. A/51/40 vol. 1 (1997), p. 21, para. 112 (Estonia).

[52] *Ibid.*, at pp. 22–3, para. 125.

[53] UN Doc. A/35/40 (1980), p. 78, para. 347 (Costa Rica).

[54] UN Doc. A/42/40 (1987), pp. 99–100, paras. 381–2 (Iraq).

[55] *Leonardus J. de Groot v. The Netherlands*, Communication No. 578/1994 (decision of 14 July 1995), UN Doc. A/50/40 vol. 2 (1999), p. 179.

leaflets explaining the purpose of the camp and painted a peace symbol on a military vehicle. The author claimed to be a victim of violation of Articles 17 and 18 but, fatally to his claim, did not sufficiently explain why.[56] The Human Rights Committee therefore considered that he had failed to substantiate for the purposes of admissibility that his rights under these Articles were violated. In a similar case concerning a protest against Dutch military policy, the author in *Gerrit van der Ent v. The Netherlands*[57] claimed that because the Dutch policy with regard to the sale of weapons and warplanes was in violation of international law, he should not have been convicted for public violence and damaging public property. The Human Rights Committee ruled his claim inadmissible following its earlier jurisprudence that the procedure laid down in the Optional Protocol was not designed for conducting public debate over matters of public policy.[58] As a result, it is difficult to make parallels with the *Arrowsmith* line of cases based on similar facts.

The Human Rights Committee, like the European Commission, has occasionally preferred to characterise coercive measures as limitations on manifestation, rather than interference with the *forum internum*, but on the facts of the cases before it there appear to be a better grounds for doing so than in many European Commission decisions. For example, in *K. Singh Bhinder v. Canada*,[59] a Sikh employee of the Canadian National Railway Company was obliged to wear safety headgear instead of a turban and was dismissed for his failure to do so. The Human Rights Committee explained that it did not matter whether it approached its decision on the basis of Article 18 or Article 26 as the conclusion reached would be the same. In a statement that bears all the hallmarks of the early European Commission decisions (that if Article 9 applies then so also does a limitation provision) the Human Rights Committee stated that,

> '[i]f the requirement that a hard hat be worn is regarded as raising issues under article 18, then it is a limitation that is justified by reference to the grounds laid down in article 18, paragraph 3. If the requirement is seen as

---

[56] *Ibid.*, at p. 182, para. 4.5.

[57] *Gerrit van der Ent v. The Netherlands*, Communication No. 657/1995 (decision of 3 November 1995), UN Doc. A/51/40 vol. 2 (1997), p. 276.

[58] *Ibid.*, at p. 277, para. 4.2. See also *E.W. et al. v. The Netherlands*, Communication No. 429/1990 (decision of 8 April 1993), UN Doc. A48/40 vol. 2 (1993), p. 198.

[59] *K. Singh Bhinder v. Canada*, Communication No. 208/1986 (views of 9 November 1989), UN Doc. A/45/40 vol. 2 (1990), p. 50.

a discrimination de facto against persons of the Sikh religion under article 26, then applying criteria now well established in the jurisprudence of the Committee, the legislation requiring that workers in federal employment be protected ... is to be regarded as reasonable and directed towards objective purposes that are compatible with the Covenant.'[60]

The Human Rights Committee was justified in treating this as a matter of manifestation (as the applicant himself claimed), rather than coercion, since this is consistent with General Comment No. 22,[61] which in paragraph 4 includes the wearing of distinctive clothing or head coverings within the meaning of the term 'the observance and practice of religion or belief'.[62] However, the conceptual distinction in this case is a fine one between restrictions on the manifestation of belief (the wearing of religious headdress), and the compulsory wearing of safety equipment contrary to religious mandate.

The merging of issues of manifestation and coercion was equally evident in the case of *A. R. Coeriel and M. A. R. Aurik v. The Netherlands*[63] when the authors claimed the right to observe the requirement to adopt Hindu names when seeking ordination as Hindu *pandits*. The authors claimed that a restriction on such a change of name violated their rights under Article 18 as it prevented them from furthering their studies for the Hindu priesthood. The claim under Article 18 failed. The Human Rights Committee considered that the regulation of surnames and name changes was eminently a matter of public order (to prevent the accidental use of offensive names or the deliberate use of the names of others) and restrictions were permissible under Article 18(3).[64] Moreover, the Human Rights Committee did not consider the State accountable for restrictions placed on the exercise of religious offices by religious leaders in another country. Instead, the Human Rights Committee decided the claim was admissible under Article 17 and found a violation on the basis that the notion of privacy refers to the

---

[60] *Ibid.*, at p. 54, para. 6.2.
[61] General Comment No. 22 (48), UN Doc. CCPR/C/21/Rev.1/Add.4 (1993). The text of General Comment No. 22 is at Annex 5.
[62] The Human Rights Committee did not apply reasoning based on the employee's voluntary choice in taking work that required him to wear safety headgear similar to that developed by the Commission and Court when applying Article 9 (see below under heading 'Decisions based on available alternatives', pp. 136–47).
[63] *A. R. Coeriel and M. A. R. Aurik v. The Netherlands*, Communication No. 453/1991 (views of 31 October 1994), UN Doc. A/50/40 vol. 2 (1995), p. 21.
[64] *Ibid.*, at p. 23, para. 6.1.

sphere of a person's life in which he or she can freely express his or her identity. It took the view that a person's surname constitutes an important component of their identity and cited as an example of arbitrary or unlawful interference the compulsion of foreigners to change their surnames.[65] It is questionable whether there was scope for the Human Rights Committee to have treated the author's name change in such circumstances as part of the 'inward' religious identity of the individual rather than the manifestation of religion – the individual opinion of Mr Ando (dissenting) suggests that the Committee's decision may be interpreted as being that 'the protection of one's privacy combined with the freedom of religion automatically entails the right to change one's family name', a view which he himself doubted.[66] On the appropriateness of treating the name change as the manifestation of religion he only went as far as agreeing with the 'manifestation formula' by saying that 'it is not impossible to argue that the request to change one's family name is a form of manifestation of one's religion, which is subject to the restrictions enumerated in paragraph 3 of article 18'.[67] The Committee has therefore been prepared to admit a name change for religious reasons as an important component of the individual's religious identity (albeit under Article 17) and to determine that State refusal to allow it exceeded the threshold of permissible interference. Even if it is accepted that a name change is an 'expression' of identity or of religion, the refusal to permit a change from one religious identity to another may still be equated with insistence that the individual retain a religious identity against their will (particularly if the name which is to be changed has particular religious significance), once again blurring the distinction between manifestation and coercion. The issue has enormous significance in view of allegations examined by the Special Rapporteur concerning compulsory name changes in Bulgaria to avoid Muslim nomenclature.[68]

A clearer case of coercion, rather than manifestation, is found in two cases concerning the forcible removal of beards from Muslim prisoners. In *Patterson Mathews v. Trinidad and Tobago*[69] the author, a prisoner,

---

[65] *Ibid.*, at p. 26, para. 10.2.

[66] *A. R. Coeriel and M. A. R. Aurik v. The Netherlands*, Communication No. 453/1991 (views of 31 October 1994), UN Doc. A/50/40 vol. 2 (1995), p. 28.

[67] *Ibid.*, at p. 28.

[68] UN Doc. E/CN.4/1990/46 (1990), para. 27; UN Doc. E/CN.4/1988/45 (1988) para. 32; UN Doc. E/CN.4/1991/56 (1991), para. 40 (Bulgaria).

[69] *Patterson Mathews v. Trinidad and Tobago*, Communication No. 569/1993 (views of 31 March 1998), UN Doc. A/53/40 (1998), p. 30.

was scheduled to be taken to an eye clinic for tests. He was told by wardens to shave off his beard which, as a Muslim, he refused to do. Prison officers then forcibly removed his beard. The author claimed that this amounted to a violation of his freedom of religion and of his right to privacy. The Human Rights Committee declared the claim inadmissible only by virtue of his failure to demonstrate that he had taken sufficient steps to bring this matter to the attention of the Trinidadian authorities. The more recent case of *Boodoo v. Trinidad and Tobago*[70] similarly concerned a claim by a prisoner who had forcibly had his beard removed despite his protestations that this was contrary to Muslim observance. He also claimed that he had been forbidden from worshipping at Muslim prayer services and that his prayer-books had been taken from him. The Human Rights Committee found a violation of Article 18, taking all these claims together, in the absence of any explanation from the State, and reaffirmed that the freedom to manifest religion or belief in worship, observance, practice and teaching encompasses a broad range of acts and that the concept of worship extends to ritual and ceremonial acts giving expression to belief, as well as various practices integral to such acts.[71] Although no greater reasoning was provided by the Human Rights Committee, the view may be taken that the enforced beard shaving in these cases is not religiously neutral since it required the author to forego practices that were dearly held and in their place exhibit practices consistent with a state of agnosticism, indifference or even opposition to his own beliefs. The denial of those beliefs may be intolerable to the individual.

There are doubtless many instances where issues of coercion and manifestation coincide but what is striking is the evident reluctance by the European Commission and the European Court, particularly in the early cases, to admit that coercion may constitute interference with the *forum internum*. In addition, the European and United Nations institutions have at times also avoided making a determination of interference with the *forum internum* where it has been possible to rely instead on the availability of choice, or on powers of State coercion expressly acknowledged by particular Convention or Covenant Articles (each of which will now be considered).

---

[70] *Boodoo v. Trinidad and Tobago*, Communication No. 721/1997 (views of 2 August 2002), UN Doc. A/57/40 vol. 2 (2002), p. 76.
[71] *Ibid.*, para. 6.6.

Decisions based on available alternatives

Exemption ruling out coercion

In the early cases concerning compulsory participation in tax and social security schemes, the European Commission avoided analysis of whether compulsion falls within the *forum internum* as well as analysis of issues of manifestation and appropriate limitations, and instead placed such schemes outside the ambit of Article 9 of the European Convention where, according to their terms, they contained any element of exemption for those who want to abstain on grounds of conscience.

In the European Commission case of *Reformed Church of X. v. The Netherlands*,[72] a pastor of the applicant Church objected to his compulsory participation in a pension scheme provided by the General Old Age Pensions Act, even though (aware of the position of adherents to the Dutch Reformed Church) the Netherlands Parliament had provided for exemption in the case of conscientious objectors – their contributions could be collected instead in the form of a tax which would be applied towards general revenue and not the pension fund. The applicant contended that the Bible makes it quite clear that imperative prescriptions have been given by God to all Christians to provide for old people who are in need, and particularly ministers of religion, such as the applicant, and that the authorities, in instituting the pension scheme, violated these divine prescriptions, which are overriding. The members of the Church had been compelled to participate in this scheme and were thereby prevented from living in accordance with God's prescriptions. The lower court in Denmark had attempted to describe the interrelation between manifestation and opposition to legal obligations,[73] and had concluded that resistance to such compulsory schemes could not amount to manifestation. The European Commission simply concluded that 'there has been no violation of any right which may have arisen under Article 9' on the sole ground that the Act does not oblige a person to apply for a pension and that section 36 of the Act expressly provides that conscientious objectors are exempt from paying direct contributions to the scheme, allowing them to make equivalent payments in lieu by way of tax so as to solve the religious dilemma which the Act might create for them. Implicit in such analysis is acceptance of the conscientious aspects of such a scheme without exemption.

---

[72] *Reformed Church of X. v. The Netherlands*, App. No. 1497/62, 5 Yearbook (1962) 286.
[73] *Ibid.*, at 290.

This decision was followed in *X. v. The Netherlands*,[74] based on similar facts but with the additional claim that the European Commission had failed, in *Reformed Church of X. v. The Netherlands*, to give due consideration to the fact that exemption in that case was only available to conscientious objectors resisting *all* forms of insurance. It was claimed that the terms of exemption could not avail those (such as the applicant) selectively opposed to this particular type of insurance. On this point, the European Commission merely concluded (in declaring the application inadmissible) that 'the provisions of law contested by the Applicant do not constitute a violation of any right that can be deduced from Article 9 of the Convention; whereas the European Commission refers in this respect to its decision on the admissibility of Application No. 1497/62'[75] (*Reformed Church of X. v. The Netherlands*). Once again, exemption constituted the sole basis of the decision.

The right of election is often decisive. In the context of church taxes, the European Commission indicated in *E. & G.R. v. Austria*[76] that the requirement to pay church taxes is not in itself contrary to freedom of religion provided that domestic law allows members to leave the church concerned if they so wish. The obligation to pay church contributions 'can be avoided if they choose to leave the church, a possibility which the State legislation has expressly provided for. By making available this possibility, the State has introduced sufficient safeguards to ensure the individual's freedom of religion'.[77] Accordingly, a Catholic Church levy could be enforced in civil courts against members of the Church and contributions were directly comparable to subscriptions payable for membership of a private association (akin to civil debts).[78]. The applicants claimed that, because State-conferred powers were used to enforce that levy, the State was directly or indirectly compelling the applicants to perform an act of religious relevance. The European Commission simply observed that Article 9 protects in particular the right to manifest one's religion 'in worship, teaching, practice and observance' and that the collection of financial contributions from its members by a church does not, as such, interfere with any of these activities. The focus on manifestation ignored the issues of coercion raised by the applicants (to which considerations of manifestation were not relevant).

---

[74] *X. v. The Netherlands*, App. No. 2065/63, 8 Yearbook (1965) 266.   [75] *Ibid.*, at 270.
[76] *E. & G. R. v. Austria*, App. No. 9781/82 (1984) 37 D&R 42.   [77] *Ibid.*, at 45.
[78] *Ibid.*, at 45.

The European Commission's recitation of the right to manifestation to the exclusion of other aspects of religious freedom seems particularly misplaced in decisions based on resistance to coercion, and misleading when it does not even constitute part of its ultimate reasoning. Nevertheless, these decisions demonstrate the ease with which claims of coercion may be dismissed as a result of the element of choice available to the applicant, and in such cases the European Commission has generally had less reason to resort to unnecessary and inappropriate notions of 'manifestation' even if it has done so in one or two instances.

Employment

The element of voluntary choice in taking employment or resigning appears similarly to be decisive in cases where the employer requires the applicant to act contrary to his beliefs, although once again the European Commission has readily appealed to principles of manifestation, rather than coercion, to conclude that the applicant's rights have been voluntarily relinquished.

In the religious context, the case of *X. v. Denmark*[79] concerned the refusal by a clergyman to baptise a child unless the parents underwent a number of sessions of instruction on baptism, a condition imposed by him as a matter of personal conscience which resulted in disciplinary action by his employer. The applicant's complaint, couched very clearly in terms of coercion to perform christenings without allowing him to provide such instruction, was that, 'as a clergyman in the State Church of Denmark, he has been requested by the Church Ministry under threat of sanctions to abandon a certain practice of christening'.[80] The European Commission summarised the entirety of Article 9 and conceded that it is conceivable that a dismissal for disobedience could raise an issue under this Article. However, the European Commission argued,

---

[79] *X. v. Denmark*, App. No. 7374/76 (1976) 5 D&R 157. Similar issues of conscientious objection in the workplace are discussed in: W. Durham, M. Wood, and S. Condie, 'Accommodation of Conscientious Objection to Abortion: A Case Study of the Nursing Profession' Brigham Young UL Rev (1982) 253; A. Grubb, 'Participating in Abortion and the Conscientious Objector' Cambridge LJ (1988) 162. Grubb comments on the scope of the 'conscience clause' in section 4(1) of the United Kingdom Abortion Act 1967. See also L. Hammer, 'Abortion Objection in the United Kingdom within the Framework of the European Convention on Human Rights and Fundamental Freedoms' EHRLR (1999) 564. Hammer argues that the scope of the right should be broadened to include ancillary personnel.

[80] *X. v. Denmark*, App. No. 7374/76 (1976) 5 D&R 158.

unusually, in terms of the *employer's* right of manifestation, noting that the church's right to manifest its beliefs through uniform practice prevails over that of the employee:

> 'A church is an organised religious community based on identical or at least substantially similar views. Through the rights granted to its members under Art. 9, the church itself is protected in its rights to manifest its religion, to organise and carry out worship, teaching, practice and observance, and it is free to act out and enforce uniformity in these matters. Further, in a State church system its servants are employed for the purpose of applying and teaching a specific religion. Their individual freedom of thought, conscience or religion is exercised at the moment they accept or refuse employment as clergymen, and their right to leave the church guarantees their freedom of religion in case they oppose its teachings.'[81]

References to the employer's right of manifestation were otiose, given the reliance placed by the European Commission on the employee's choice, and this represents a different (and uncommon) emphasis on manifestation over inner issues of conscience.

In another employee claim of coercion, *Knudsen v. Norway*,[82] greater stress was placed by the Commission upon certain aspects of the *forum internum*. The applicant, a priest, protested at a newly enacted abortion law by refusing to undertake public functions which he was employed to perform (such as the celebration of marriages) while otherwise still considering himself to be a true clergyman of the parish. He claimed his dismissal contravened Article 9 of the European Convention as his views on abortion were the same as those of the church to whom his duty was primarily owed, though contrary to those of the State. The European Commission framed its response according to four parallel questions, even though only the first was decisive. These were: first, whether the applicant was free to leave his employment; secondly, whether the applicant's refusal to perform certain public functions actually expressed the applicant's belief or religious views; thirdly, whether the applicant had been under any pressure to change his views (an issue commonly recited in cases of conflict of conscience in the employment context); and, fourthly, whether the applicant was restricted in his right to manifest his beliefs (irrespective of whether the refusal constituted manifestation). As to the first, the European Commission found:

---

[81] *Ibid.*, at 158.   [82] *Knudsen v. Norway*, App.No. 11045/84 (1985) 42 D&R 247.

'that a clergyman within a State Church system, has not only religious duties, but has also accepted certain obligations towards the State. If the requirements imposed upon him by the State should be in conflict with his convictions, he is free to relinquish his office as a clergyman within the State Church, and the Commission regards this as an ultimate guarantee of his right to freedom of thought, conscience and religion.'[83]

The European Commission decided that he was justifiably dismissed for refusing to perform functions that were administrative duties of his office. However, if the applicant's freedom to surrender his position constituted an ultimate guarantee of his freedom, it was unnecessary to continue with the three remaining questions but the European Commission nevertheless answered them as follows. It applied the *Arrowsmith* test and concluded that the applicant's refusal did not actually express his belief or religious views. It then observed that, '[t]he applicant has not shown that he has been under any pressure to change his views or that he has been prevented from manifesting his religion or belief. It follows that the applicant's dismissal did not in any way interfere with the exercise of his rights under Article 9 of the Convention.'[84]

What is useful about this passage is that it suggests that if the applicant had been put under such pressure to change his views then Article 9 of the Convention would have applied.

In *Knudsen v. Norway* the European Commission reinforced principles that it had already established in *Karlsson v. Sweden*,[85] concerning a job application made by a clergyman antagonistic towards the ordination of women. His job would require him to work with ordained women. The only substantive difference is that in *Karlsson*, instead of focusing on whether the applicant's protest satisfied the *Arrowsmith* test, the European Commission focused on the justification for measures taken by a State employer in order to satisfy itself that a job applicant possesses the necessary personal qualifications. The applicant was asked by the Diocesan Chapter (who knew his views) whether he would be prepared to co-operate with a woman clergyman. The applicant questioned their right to ask such hypothetical questions and replied that he would carry out his task to the best of his ability. He was disqualified as a candidate. The European Commission commented that freedom of religion does not include the right of a clergyman, within the framework

[83] *Ibid.*, at 257.   [84] *Ibid.*, at 258.
[85] *Karlsson v. Sweden*, App. No. 12356/86 (1988) 57 D&R 172.

of a church in which he is working or to which he applies for a post, to practise a special religious conception,[86] and it emphasised the applicant's freedom to leave his office as 'the ultimate guarantee', should the job requirements be in conflict with his convictions. The European Commission decided that the applicant's views did not disqualify him but his lack of necessary qualifications for the post did (his ability to work alongside women priests), thereby taking the matter outside Article 9.[87] The redundancy of three out of four of the European Commission's lines of reasoning in *Knudsen v. Norway* is emphasised by its focus in *Karlsson v. Sweden* only on the central issue of employer choice.

Even if the European Commission's unnecessary repetition of familiar and irrelevant issues (particularly those relating to manifestation) may be misleading, these decisions do serve to emphasise that as far as the *forum internum* is concerned, in the absence of the necessary freedom of choice, pressure to change an individual's views would constitute a violation. However it is disappointing that the European Commission has generally relied on the context of particular claims and has avoided the development of principles for the protection of the *forum internum* when dealing with issues of coercion.

In the military context it has been concluded that members of the armed forces undoubtedly call for different treatment from civilians and that for those who choose to pursue a military career certain restrictions may be imposed on them that could not be imposed on civilians. Thus, in *Yanasik v. Turkey*,[88] a case concerning an officer cadet who suffered considerable antagonism for the duration of his alleged participation in a fundamentalist religious movement, the European Commission relied on the military context of the claim. The applicant asserted that the accusations of fundamentalist activity and propaganda were unfounded and were designed to punish him for his beliefs. It was alleged that he had visited the premises of the movement, read their publications and attended ideological meetings. Although this was denied by him, it was accepted that the applicant had been free to manifest his religion, as he was entitled to. He was disciplined by successive reductions of his exemplary good conduct mark into a negative figure over a period of two months (coinciding with the adoption of his religious views) until it was recommended he be expelled with the opinion expressed

---

[86] *Ibid.*, at 175. See also *X. v. Denmark*, App. No. 7374/76 (1976) 5 D&R 157, at 158.
[87] *Ibid.*, at 175.   [88] *Yanasik v. Turkey*, App. No. 14524/89 (1993) 74 D&R 14.

that he did not have the makings either of a Military Academy cadet or an officer.

The State's position was that the applicant was incapable of submitting to military discipline (incorporating the principle of secularity within the Turkish army), which did not impede his ability to practise his religion. The European Commission recited the *Arrowsmith* formula and moved immediately to ascertain whether the measure constituted an interference with the exercise of the freedom of religion. Fundamental to its decision was the applicant's voluntary enrolment and the fact that military 'regulations may make cadets' freedom to practise their religion subject to limitations as to time and place, without however negating it entirely in order to ensure that the army functions properly'.[89] Applying the principle established in *Engel v. The Netherlands*[90] that military discipline implies, by its very nature, the possibility of placing certain limitations on the rights and freedoms of members of the armed forces which could not be imposed on civilians,[91] the European Commission concluded that appropriate limitations may include a duty for military personnel to refrain from participating in a Muslim fundamentalist movement whose aim and programme is to ensure the pre-eminence of religious rules. What stands out in this case is the European Commission's unnecessary focus on manifestation when the applicant could still practise his religion.[92] The applicant himself did not maintain that his freedom to manifest his religion was restricted and any alleged manifestation of fundamentalist beliefs through participation in the movement were denied. Likewise, the State affirmed that the applicant was able to observe his religious practices freely and commented that he had not made any allegation to the contrary. The applicant's claim therefore focused entirely on the *forum internum* (that the nature of the disciplinary action against him was punitive and coercive, aimed at convincing him to abrogate his religious interest) yet it was met by reasoning on the part of the

---

[89] *Ibid.*, at 26.   [90] *Engel v. The Netherlands* (Ser. A) 22 (1976) ECtHR.

[91] *Ibid.*, at para. 57.

[92] It is, however, consistent with similar decisions in the civil context where onerous professional duties may on occasion be compelled without this constituting forced or compulsory labour under Article 4(2) (*X. and Y. v. Germany*, App No. 7641/76 (1976) 10 D&R 224 (legal aid counsel was required to incur considerable costs without being paid an advance of his fees)). See also *X. v. Federal Republic of Germany*, App. No. 8682/79 (1981) 26 D&R 97.

European Commission confined solely to justifications for restricting the manifestation of religion in the military context.[93]

Any hope that such analysis might have developed only within the European Commission was dashed in the light of the European Court's decision in the case of *Kalaç v. Turkey*.[94] The European Court upheld the compulsory retirement of a military judge on the grounds that his conduct and his attitude were inconsistent with his military position, requiring the voluntary submission to a system of military discipline in a country dedicated to the principle of secularism. This was based upon allegations that he had 'revealed that he had adopted unlawful funda-mentalist opinions'[95] and had 'participated' in the Süleyman sect by providing occasional legal assistance on behalf of a community 'which was known to have unlawful fundamentalist tendencies'.[96] These allega-tions were readily accepted by the European Court, which added that States may adopt for their armies disciplinary regulations 'forbidding this or that type of conduct, in particular an attitude inimical to an established order reflecting the requirements of military service'.[97] The European Court concluded on the basis of these allegations that com-pulsory retirement was 'not based on Group Captain Kalaç's religious opinions and beliefs or the way he had performed his religious duties but on his conduct and attitude'.[98] It is questionable whether the State's assertions entitle the European Court to draw that conclusion. The distinction between 'religious opinions and beliefs' and 'conduct and attitude' is not convincing, and certainly not sufficient to distinguish interference with manifestation from interference with the *forum inter-num* through punishment for merely holding particular beliefs. Moreover, the European Court also commented that 'the applicant's compulsory retirement did not amount to an interference with the right guaranteed by Article 9 (art. 9) since it was not prompted by the way the applicant manifested his religion'.[99] This diverted attention from the real question whether the applicant's retirement was prompted by his choice of beliefs. There is little doubt, however, that the military context of this decision was critical, but even if the applicant had voluntarily accepted the system of military discipline in choosing to pursue a

---

[93] For a discussion on some unforeseen effects of military discipline on religious mani-festation, see L. S. Sheleff, 'Rabbi Captain the Goldman's Yarmulke, Freedom of Religion and Conscience, and Civil (Military) Disobedience' 17 Isr YB Hum Rts (1987) 197.

[94] *Kalaç v. Turkey* (1999) 27 EHRR 552.   [95] *Ibid.*, at para. 8.   [96] *Ibid.*, at para. 25.

[97] *Ibid.*, at para. 28.   [98] *Ibid.*, at para. 30.   [99] *Ibid.*, at para. 31.

military career,[100] interference with the *forum internum* may not be justified in any circumstances.

The European Commission has undoubtedly placed excessive reliance upon disciplinary regulations in order to uphold State measures. It has done so even in the university environment where, for example, in *Karaduman v. Turkey*,[101] a degree certificate was not made available to the applicant who refused to remove her Muslim headscarf for the purpose of a photograph attached to her degree certificate.

In the secular and non-military context, the freedom of choice in assuming (as well as leaving) employment was emphasised by the European Commission in the Article 9 case of *Stedman v. United Kingdom*, when the applicant claimed religious reasons for not working a Sunday shift at a travel agency.[102] The element of choice operated in that case even in relation to changes unilaterally imposed by the employer.[103] Likewise in *X. v. United Kingdom*,[104] which (unlike many cases in which the *Arrowsmith* test has been applied) directly concerned the applicant's freedom to manifest his religion in worship, the European Commission decided that a Muslim school teacher was not entitled to take time off for prayer on a Friday afternoon, as he had accepted the terms of employment (requiring his full-time attendance) without mentioning his religious requirements. A part-time position was available for him which would accommodate them. He claimed that his Muslim religion required attendance at a mosque or, failing that, worship with three or more other Muslims at school or, as a last resort, on his own. The European Commission did not apply the *Arrowsmith*

---

[100] *Ibid.*, at para. 28.
[101] *Karaduman v. Turkey*, App. No. 16278/90 (1993) 74 D&R 93.
[102] *Stedman v. United Kingdom*, App. No. 29107/95, 89–A (1997) D&R 104, at 107–8. See also *Konttinen v. Finland*, App. No. 24949/94 (1996) 87 D&R 68.
[103] For a review of European Convention case law under Article 9 in the employment context, see J. Bowers, 'The European Convention on Human Rights – The Employment Consequences of Articles 9 and 10', 42 Emp. Lawyer (2000) 16. J. Balfour examines whether the requirement that job applicants must hold a certain beliefs is compatible with Article 9 when applying for positions within religious associations and charities: J. Balfour, 'The European Convention and Religious Associations and Charities in Scotland', 1 HR & UKP (2000) 19. See also G. Quinn, 'Written Communication on Conscientious Objection in Labour Relations', in Council of Europe, *Freedom of Conscience*, (proceedings of a seminar organised by the Secretariat General of the Council of Europe in co-operation with the F. M. van Asbeck Centre for Human Rights Studies of the University of Leiden), Strasbourg: Council of Europe (1993).
[104] *X. v. United Kingdom*, App. No. 8160/78 (1981) 22 D&R 27.

test but noted that Article 9 is wider merely than manifestation: the 'object of Article 9 is essentially that of protecting the individual against unjustified interference by the State, but that there may also be positive obligations inherent in an effective "respect" for the individual's freedom of religion'.[105] The European Commission, however, went on to adapt the reasoning established in *X. v. Denmark* (that the freedom of religion of servants of a State Church 'is exercised at the moment they accept or refuse employment as clergymen, and their right to leave the church guarantees their freedom of religion in case they oppose its teachings').[106] It took from that decision that 'it may, as regards the modality of a particular religious manifestation, be influenced by the situation of the person claiming that freedom'.[107] In both cases the applicant had special contractual obligations but the European Commission distinguished this case in two respects: 'firstly, it does not concern religious manifestations in the course of the performance of professional functions, but absence from work for the performance of such manifestations; secondly, it does not relate to a religious dispute but to a coincidence of teaching obligations and religious duties'.[108] It was decisive that the issue of mosque attendance was not raised at his interview, nor for the following six years of his employment. Paraphrasing this rather unclear passage, the right to manifestation was sought to be exercised outside the employee's functions, which do not (but for timetabling) give rise to a conflict of conscience. The issue of conflict with conscience was therefore avoided. The wider aspects of Article 9 than manifestation and the scope of positive obligations that may burden States were, however, unfortunately avoided by the European Commission deciding as a matter of policy that in view of the complexities of the education system and the adaptations made in United Kingdom society, it was not prepared to assess the situation but only to consider 'whether the school authorities, in relying on the applicant's contract, arbitrarily disregarded his freedom of religion'.[109]

The approach taken to such issues by the Human Rights Committee is reflected in its comment in the case of *Delgado Paez v. Colombia*,[110]

---

[105] *Ibid.*, at 33.   [106] *X. v. Denmark*, App. No. 7374/76 (1976) 5 D&R 157, at 158.
[107] *X. v. United Kingdom*, App. No. 8160/78 (1981) 22 D&R 27, at 35.
[108] *Ibid.*, at 35.   [109] *Ibid.*, at 37.
[110] W. *Delgado Páez v. Colombia*, Communication No. 195/1985 (views of 12 July 1990), UN Doc. A/45/40 vol. 2 (1990), p. 43.

concerning the dismissal of the applicant from a denominational school, that 'Colombia may, without violating [Article 18], allow the Church authorities to decide who may teach religion and in what manner it should be taught'.[111] Although little supporting justification was provided, the Human Rights Committee focused on the author's right to profess or manifest his religion, which had not been violated by his dismissal from his teaching position for his 'progressive ideas in theological and social matters' (namely his liberation theology) where his duties involved the teaching of the Roman Catholic faith in its Orthodox form, in keeping with the beliefs of Catholic parents who chose to send their children to that school. The Human Rights Committee was not specific in the particular ground of limitation which it applied to support the restriction on the manifestation of his beliefs, although it may have been the rights and freedoms of others, namely the right of parents under Article 18(4) (discussed below under the heading 'Education'). However, the author's substantive claim in relation to threats on his life, protracted confrontation by the authorities in which they brought groundless charges, and other threats as part of a campaign to discredit the author resulted in a finding of violation of Article 9 of the ICCPR.

In another claim under the Optional Protocol, *G.T. v. Canada*,[112] the author realised that his personal convictions conflicted with those of his Catholic employer only after his employment had begun, so as to prevent him discussing certain health issues such as contraception, abortion and AIDS with students. He was therefore unable to take advantage of a procedure in Canada permitting job applicants to be allocated to non-Catholic schools on grounds of conscience only before starting their employment. The Human Rights Committee, however, declared the claim inadmissible for the author's failure to exhaust domestic remedies.

From these employment cases it may be concluded that where employment duties themselves give rise to conflicts of conscience, the employee's convictions must give way to employment duties since they were relinquished by contract. It is interesting to note that in the Optional Protocol case of *K. Singh Bhinder v. Canada*, referred to

---

[111] *Ibid.*, at p. 48, para. 5.7.
[112] *G.T. v. Canada*, Communication No. 420/1990 (decision of 22 March 1990) (1994) 1(1) IHRR 46.

above, Canada claimed that it was open to the Sikh author to avoid the operation of the hard-hat requirement by seeking other employment, and referred to the European Commission's decision in *X. v. United Kingdom*, in particular its emphasis on special contractual obligations and the option available to the applicant to resign from his employment if he considered it to be incompatible with his religious duties. The Human Rights Committee did not find it necessary to adopt an approach based on employee choice but instead on principles of manifestation. Having said that, there is nothing to indicate that the Human Rights Committee would reach any conclusion different from that of the European Commission if faced only with the issue of employee choice.[113]

What is clear about the cases based on employee choice is that there is widespread recognition that, even though they may be decided narrowly on issues of employee election and manifestation, a basis exists under the core freedom of religion provisions for the protection of the *forum internum* in claims based on coercion to act contrary to the individual's conscience, pressure to change belief, and punishment for holding particular beliefs. Unfortunately recognition for such *forum internum* rights is insufficiently developed in the supporting reasoning of the European and United Nations institutions. Instead there has been unsatisfactory and redundant reliance upon principles of manifestation in such claims.

Decisions based on provision for interference in the relevant Convention

The ICCPR and European Convention both acknowledge the State's ability to require military (or alternative) service. The power of taxation is expressly recognised by the European Convention (Article 1, First Protocol) though not by the ICCPR. The question that remains unanswered is the extent to which compulsory military service and certain forms of taxation raise issues of conscience within the core freedom of religion Articles. The issue has been obscured by the European and United Nations institutions because of a predominant focus on

---

[113] For discussion concerning consent to relinquish rights in the employment context, see, for example, UN Doc. A/39/40 (1984), p. 66, para. 356 (Gambia).

manifestation. Also, there still remains some controversy over the extent to which conscience, as distinct from religion or belief, extends to a right of manifestation or, as Malcolm Evans puts it, 'actualisation'.[114] Having said that, trends under both the European Convention and the ICCPR increasingly recognise the conscientious implications of certain forms of compulsion.

Military service

The Human Rights Committee and the Strasbourg organs have emphasised in numerous cases with some consistency that there is no right to conscientious objection to military service.[115] The State's ability to require military service is expressly recognised in Article 8(3)(c)(ii) of the ICCPR and Article 4(3)(b) of the European Convention, each excluding from the term 'forced or compulsory labour' military service or, in countries where conscientious objection is recognised, alternative service. These Articles are concerned with freedom from slavery.[116]

---

[114] M. D. Evans, *Religious Liberty and International Law in Europe*, p. 293. For a review of European Convention cases on conscientious objection to military service, see Gilbert, *The Slow Development of the Right to Conscientious Objection*, p. 554. Gilbert summarises the current debate on whether there is a right to manifest one's conscience at p. 556, n. 5. See also H. Gilbert, *The Right to Freedom of Belief: a Conceptual Framework*, unpublished PhD thesis, Essex University (2001).

[115] For Human Rights Committee decisions, see: *Brinkhof v. The Netherlands*, Communication No. 402/1990 (decision of 27 July 1993), UN Doc. A/48/40 vol. 2 (1993), 14 HRLJ (1994) 410; *L.T.K. v. Finland*, Communication No. 185/1984 (decision of 9 July 1985), UN Doc. A/40/40 (1985), p. 240; *Richard Maille v. France*, Communication No. 689/1996 (views of 10 July 2000) (2000) 7(4) IHRR 947; *Frederic Foin v. France*, Communication No.666/1995 (views of 3 November 1999) (2000) 7(2) IHRR 354; *Paul Westerman v. The Netherlands*, Communication No. 682/1996 (views of 3 November 1999) (2000) 7(2) IHRR 363. For European Convention decisions, see: *X. v. Austria*, App. No. 5591/72 (1973) 43 CD 161; *Conscientious Objectors v. Denmark*, App. No. 7565/76 (1978) 9 D&R 117; *X. v. Germany*, App. No. 7705/76 (1977) 9 D&R 196; *N. v. Sweden*, App. No. 10410/83 (1984) 40 D&R 203; *Johansen v. Norway*, App. No. 10600/83 (1985) 44 D&R 155; and *Autio v. Finland*, App. No. 17086/90 (1991) 72 D&R 245.

[116] For further reading, see: European Consortium for Church–State Research, *Conscientious objection in the EC countries* (Proceedings of the meeting, Brussels-Leuven, 7–8 December 1990, European Consortium for Church–State Research), Milan: Giuffrè (1992); K. Greenawalt, *Religious Convictions and Political Choice*, New York/Oxford: Oxford University Press (1988); S. Rodatà, 'Written Communication on Conscientious Objection to Military Service', in Council of Europe, *Freedom of Conscience*.

Certain statements in the European Convention case of *Grandrath v. Germany*[117] pose the question whether the imposition of military service (or alternative service) contrary to the individual's conscience and religion, and punishment for refusal to perform that service, violate Article 9 of the European Convention. The applicant in that case was a Jehovah's Witness leader who had been given dispensation to allow him to substitute military service with civilian service, which he refused to perform, and was sentenced to a term of imprisonment. He maintained that his beliefs were derived from Thomas Aquinas and Cardinal Newman and that his imprisonment was a violation of Article 9. However, the European Commission did not consider the issue further under Article 9 but instead relied on Article 4(3)(b) arguing that because

> 'civilian service may be imposed on conscientious objectors as a substitute for military service, it must be concluded that *objections of conscience do not, under the Convention, entitle a person to exemption* from such service. In these circumstances, the Commission finds it superfluous to examine any questions of the interpretation of the term "freedom of ... conscience and religion" as used in Article 9 of the Convention.'[118]

In *Grandreth v. Germany*, Mr Eusthadiades provided a convincing concurring opinion that Article 4(3)(b) does not rule out the application of Article 9.[119] Unfortunately, the precise basis on which Article 9 applies, but might be obviated by Article 4(3)(b), is unclear, whether (as suggested by van Dijk and van Hoof)[120] the manifestation of religion or belief, or some other basis. Nevertheless, a number of cases do confirm the application of Article 9 of the European Convention to situations of conscientious objection even though the European Convention does not guarantee as such a right to conscientious objection.[121] There have been some initiatives towards the recognition of a right to conscientious objection within Article 9 of the European Convention particularly by

---

[117] *Grandrath v. Germany*, App. No. 2299/64, 10 Yearbook (1967) 626.
[118] *Ibid.*, at 674 (emphasis added).   [119] *Ibid.*, at 690.
[120] Van Dijk and van Hoof, *Theory and Practice of the European Convention*, p. 545.
[121] *N. v. Sweden*, App. No. 10410/83 (1985) 40 D&R 203; *Autio v. Finland*, App. No. 17086/90 (1992) 72 D&R 245; and *Raninen v. Finland*, App. No. 20972/92, 84–A (1996) D&R 17. For further discussion see: B. P. Vermeulen, *Report on Scope and Limits of Conscientious Objection*, in Council of Europe, *Freedom of Conscience*, and E. Marcus, 'Conscientious Objection as an Emerging Human Right', 38 Virginia J Int'l L (1998) 507 (Marcus argues for the need to codify conscientious objection as an international human right).

the Parliamentary Assembly of the Council of Europe[122] and the Council of Ministers,[123] as well as in recent case law.

In her partly dissenting opinion, Commissioner Liddy in *Tsirlis and Kouloumpas v. Greece*[124] argued that Article 9 taken by itself should be the basis of a finding of violation as claimed by Jehovah's Witness ministers who were detained for refusing to perform compulsory military service (which would have been fundamentally contrary to their religion). She suggested that Article 4 of the European Convention does 'not mean that Article 9 is inapplicable, but rather that the necessity for compulsory military or alternative service falls to be considered under Article 9(2), and that the margin of appreciation is extended as a result of Article 4(3)(b)'.[125] She was of the opinion that the exclusions listed in Article 4(3) only affect Article 4 and do not operate (in the case of conscientious objectors) to limit the scope of other Articles.

Growing recognition for issues of conscientious objection within Article 9 is matched by similar developments at Universal level in the Human Rights Committee and the Commission on Human Rights.

Early decisions by the Human Rights Committee were not definitive. In line with the approach taken by the European Commission, the Human Rights Committee initially considered, in *L. T. K. v. Finland*,[126] that Article 18 does not provide for the right to conscientious objection

---

[122] Van Dijk and van Hoof refer in *Theory and Practice of the Human Convention*, (at p. 544), as non-binding authority, to Resolution 337 (1967) of the Parliamentary Assembly of the Council of Europe and reiterated in a European Parliament resolution of 7 February 1983, which reads as follows:

> '1. Persons liable to conscription for military service who, for reasons of conscience or profound conviction arising from religious, ethical, moral, humanitarian, philosophical or similar motives, refuse to perform armed service shall enjoy a personal right to be released from the obligation to perform such service.
> 2. This right shall be regarded as deriving logically from the fundamental rights of the individual in democratic Rule of Law States which are guaranteed in Article 9 of the European Convention on Human Rights.'

[123] Council of Ministers Recommendation No. R (87)8 (9 EHRR (1987) 529), elaborated in Explanatory Report to Recommendation No. R (87)8, para. 13. For further discussion on the emerging recognition of military conscientious objection within Article 9 of the European Convention and Article 18 of the ICCPR, see Hammer, *Freedom of Conscience*.

[124] *Tsirlis and Kouloumpas v. Greece*, App. No. 19234/91 (1996) 21 EHRR CD 30; *Tsirlis and Kouloumpas v. Greece* (1998) 25 EHRR 198.

[125] *Tsirlis and Kouloumpas v. Greece*, App. No. 19234/91 (1996) 21 EHRR CD 30 at CD 47.

[126] *L.T.K. v. Finland*, Communication No. 185/1984 (decision of 9 July 1985), UN Doc. A/40/40 (1985), p. 240.

to military service 'especially taking into account paragraph 3(c)(ii) of article 8'[127] but otherwise was not more specific. Similarly, in *J. P. K. v. The Netherlands*[128] and *T. W. M. B. v. The Netherlands*[129] when the coercive nature of compulsory military service against the individual's conscience was characterised by the authors as forcing them to become accomplices to the crime of genocide and crimes against peace, the Human Rights Committee observed that the ICCPR did not preclude the institution of compulsory military service[130] and that consequently the authors had not substantiated any claim by reference to the requirement to do military service. The Human Rights Committee merely recalled the provisions of Article 8(3)(c)(ii) and commented that the authors could not claim violation of Articles 6 or 7.

Since then, however, the Human Rights Committee in General Comment No. 22 has addressed the conflict between the obligation in military service to use lethal force and beliefs that prohibit it. Initially there may have been doubt whether conscientious objection should give rise to issues under Article 18 of the ICCPR when the proposal for inclusion of a right to conscientious objection in that Article was considered and not adopted.[131] However, in paragraph 11 of General Comment No. 22 the Human Rights Committee made explicit reference to Article 18, rather than Article 8, and it confirmed that compulsory military service would interfere with both the first and second part of Article 18(1) of the ICCPR, even though coercion in matters of military service is acknowledged to be permissible under Article 8(3)(c)(ii) of the ICCPR:[132] 'The

---

[127] *Ibid.*, at p. 242, para. 5.2.

[128] *J.P.K. v. The Netherlands*, Communication No. 401/1990 (decision of 7 November 1991), UN Doc. A/47/40 (1994), p. 405.

[129] *T.W.M.B. v. The Netherlands*, Communication No. 403/1990 (decision of 7 November 1991), UN Doc. A/47/40 (1994), p. 411.

[130] Respectively, p. 409, para. 6.5 and p. 415, para. 6.5.

[131] For the debates of the Commission on Human Rights as to whether to include such a right in Article 18, see UN Doc. E/CN.4/SR. 116 (1949) and UN Doc. E/CN.4/SR. 161 (1950). Although not adopted in Article 18, it was contemplated in Principle 11 of the Draft Principles on Freedom and Non-Discrimination in the Matter of Religious Rights and Practices prepared by the Sub-Commission on Prevention of Discrimination, UN Doc. E/CN.4/800, UN Doc. E/CN.4/Sub.2/206 (1960).

[132] Paragraph 11 was explicit in departing from earlier decisions such as *L.T.K. v. Finland* (that on the basis of Article 8(3)(c)(ii), Article 18 does not support the right to conscientious objection). A revised statement was considered necessary to effect this reversal in view of the General Comment's status as an authoritative pronouncement – see UN Doc. CCPR/C/SR. 1237 (1993), p. 3, para. 10 (Mr Dimitrijevic), and p. 7, para. 36 (Mrs Evatt).

Covenant does not explicitly refer to a right of conscientious objection, but the Committee believes that such a right can be derived from Article 18 inasmuch as the obligation to use lethal force may seriously conflict with the freedom of conscience and the right to manifest one's religion or belief.'[133]

As far as both the *forum internum* and manifestation are concerned, the test appears from this to be one of 'serious conflict'. In line with such developments within the Human Rights Committee, successive resolutions of the Commission on Human Rights serve to put the matter beyond question that conscientious objection to military service is a matter firmly within the ambit of Article 18 of the ICCPR.[134]

Case law developments at both European and Universal levels suggest that so long as a clear basis is thought to exist for conceding a right to conscientious objection (in this case in the Articles concerned with freedom from slavery), less reliance need be placed upon inappropriate appeals to manifestation as a means of supporting State interference.

---

[133] Confirmed recently in: *Frederic Foin v. France*, Communication No. 666/1995 (views of 3 November 1999) (2000) 7(2) IHRR 354, para. 10.3; *Paul Westerman v. The Netherlands*, Communication No. 682/1996 (views of 3 November 1999) (2000) 7(2) IHRR 363. See also R. Brett, *General Comment of the Human Rights Committee on Article 18 of the International Covenant on Civil and Political Rights: Developments on Conscientious Objection to Military Service*, Geneva: Quaker United Nations Office (1993). Following CHR Res. 1989/59, the Special Rapporteur recommended that States with a system of compulsory military service introduce for conscientious objectors various forms of alternative service if they had not already done so (UN Doc. E/CN.4/1997/91 (1996), para. 82).

[134] For example, see CHR Res. 1987/46 (1987). (This supported conscientious objection to military service as 'a legitimate exercise of the right to freedom of thought, conscience and religion recognized by the Universal Declaration of Human Rights and the International Covenant on Civil and Political Rights'). The point has been reiterated in CHR Res. 1989/59 (1989), CHR Res. 1995/83 (1995) (para. 4 reaffirmed General Comment No. 22, paragraph 11), CHR Res.1998/77 (1998), and CHR Res. 2000/34 (2000). CHR Res. 1998/77 (1998) affirmed in the preamble that 'conscientious objection to military service derives from principles and reasons of conscience, including profound convictions, arising from religious, moral, ethical, humanitarian or similar motives'. Weissbrodt provided a commentary on the adoption of CHR Res. 1987/46: D. S. Weissbrodt, 'The United Nations Commission on Human Rights Confirms Conscientious Objection to Military Service as a Human Right', 35 Neth Int'l L Rev (1988) 53. McPherson also provided a brief overview of the historical developments relating to conscientious objection within the UN, particularly those in the 43rd session of the Commission (1987) when it passed CHR Res.1987/46 – M. McPherson, 'The United Nations and Conscientious Objection', 1(1) Con & Lib (1989) 8. See also A. Eide and M. Chama, *Conscientious Objection to Military Service*, UN Doc. E/CN.4/Sub.2/30/Rev.1 and UN Doc. E/CN.4/Sub.2/1982/24 (1982).

The conclusion reached in early cases that manifestation is generally not relevant to conscientious objection is sound (and avoids the unnecessary shoe-horning of manifestation and State limitations of the type discussed above under the heading 'Decisions based on justified limitation on manifestation' when dealing with matters of compulsion). However, the early reasoning appears to be incorrect in suggesting that conscientious objection does not fall within the core freedom of religion Articles. The widespread acceptance of conscientious objection to military service within the freedom of religion Articles is a significant advance when seen as part of a general scheme of protection for the *forum internum* which includes freedom from coercion to act contrary to recognised aspects of conscience. It is submitted that all forms of compulsion to act contrary to one's beliefs *prima facie* raise issues for the *forum internum* where the necessary connection is established between a protected form of belief and compulsion contrary to that belief – a principle which could apply equally to the imposition of tax and social security schemes.

Taxation and social security

The fact that the power of taxation is expressly recognised by the European Convention system and ascribed to the State by Article 1, First Protocol does not of itself remove conscientious objection to the payment of taxes from the realm of Article 9. No equivalent recognition is given in the ICCPR to the power of States to secure the payment of taxes yet the Human Rights Committee has reached almost identical conclusions to those of the Strasbourg institutions. This suggests that reliance on Articles apart from those concerned with freedom of conscience is not necessary.[135]

The European Commission has not made a clear distinction in its dismissal of claims of conscience against taxation schemes between, on the one hand, the State's power recognised in the European Convention and, on the other, the failure of such claims adequately to exemplify

---

[135] Dignan argues for recognition of the right of tax diversion: Dignan, *A Right Not to Render unto Caesar*, p. 20. See also: K. Boyle, 'Freedom of Thought, Freedom of Conscience, Freedom of Religion and Freedom of Belief as Internationally Protected Rights: What is Agreed and What is Not Agreed', in E. Cotran and A. O. Sherif (eds.), *Democracy, the Rule of Law and Islam*, London: CIMEL and Kluwer Law International (1999); K. Boyle, *Report on Freedom of Conscience in International Law*, in Council of Europe, *Freedom of Conscience*; C. A. Gray, 'The World Peace Tax Fund Act: Conscientious Objection for Taxpayers', 74 Northw UL Rev (1979) 76 (Gray considers the US and international law arguments against the enforced payment of war taxes and viable legal alternatives).

issues of conscience. In the case of general taxes it is inevitably difficult to support the necessary connection between protected beliefs and the payment of taxes such as to raise serious implications for the individual's conscience, which is probably why in European Commission decisions the two issues are collapsed when referring to Article 1, First Protocol. Thus, in the case of *C. v. United Kingdom*,[136] the European Commission noted that:

> '[t]he obligation to pay taxes is a general one which has no specific conscientious implications in itself. Its neutrality in this sense is also illustrated by the fact that no tax payer can influence or determine the purpose for which his or her contributions are applied, once they are collected. Furthermore, the power of taxation is expressly recognised by the Convention system and is ascribed to the State by Article 1, First Protocol.'[137]

A similar approach been taken to social security payments. In *Reformed Church of X. v. The Netherlands*,[138] concerning the tax raised by way of alternative to compulsory participation in a pension scheme, the European Commission had no hesitation in treating payments by way of tax in lieu of social security as falling within Article 1 of Protocol 1. In doing so, the European Commission followed *Gudmundsson v. Iceland*[139] in which it had held that 'it is undoubtedly within the sovereign power of a State to enact legislation for the purpose of imposing taxes or other contributions the proceeds of which are to be appropriated to public purposes'.[140] It was sufficient in *Reformed Church of X. v. The Netherlands* that the tax raised was 'clearly assessed on the basis of valid law', it equalled the contributions which non-conscientious objectors were required to pay into the compulsory pension scheme, and was levied in the public interest 'to preserve equality and prevent evasion'. The tax thereby imposed was 'in every way, consistent with what are contemplated in paragraph (1) of Article 1 of the Protocol as permissible interferences with a person's right to the peaceable peaceful enjoyment of his possessions'.[141] In short, the distinction in substance between payment into a pension scheme and payment by way of tax was

---

[136] *C. v. United Kingdom*, App. No. 10358/83 (1983) 37 D&R 142.   [137] *Ibid.*, at 147.
[138] *Reformed Church of X. v. The Netherlands*, App. No. 1497/62, 5 Yearbook (1962) 286.
[139] *Gudmundsson v. Iceland*, App. No. 511/59, 3 Yearbook (1960) 394.   [140] *Ibid.*, at 422.
[141] *Reformed Church of X. v. The Netherlands*, App. No. 1497/62, 5 Yearbook (1962) 286, at 298–300.

of little practical importance and the application was declared inadmissible.

In *X. v. The Netherlands*,[142] the applicant in similar circumstances claimed that the forcible payment of contributions towards a compulsory old age insurance scheme was a violation of the right to property, as there was no question of them constituting either 'taxes' or 'other contributions' within the meaning of Article 1 of the Protocol. The European Commission disagreed, predictably, but offered very little explanation beyond a recitation of its earlier decisions.

A broadly similar approach has been taken by the Human Rights Committee, which declared inadmissible a number of claims based on conscientious objection to taxes, falling entirely outside the scope of Article 18 of the ICCPR.[143] In *J.P. v. Canada*[144] the Human Rights Committee observed that the scope of protection of the right to freedom of conscience and religion, as covered by Article 18, did not entail a right for conscientious objectors to refuse to pay taxes, part of which would be used to defray military expenditures. It concluded that the facts as submitted did not raise issues under any of the provisions of the ICCPR and declared the claim inadmissible, commenting as follows:

> 'The Committee notes that the author seeks to apply the idea of conscientious objection to the disposition by the State of the taxes it collects from persons under its jurisdiction. Although article 18 of the Covenant certainly protects the right to hold, express and disseminate opinions and convictions, including conscientious objection to military activities and expenditures, the refusal to pay taxes on grounds of conscientious objection clearly falls outside the scope of the protection of this article.'[145]

A similar conclusion was reached in *J.v.K. and G.M.G.v.K.-S. v. The Netherlands*,[146] and in *K.V. and C.V. v. Germany*[147] which also concerned the refusal to pay taxes on the basis of military expenditure.

---

[142] *X. v. The Netherlands*, App. No. 2065/63, 8 Yearbook (1965) 266.

[143] See M. Scheinin, 'The Right to Say "No": A Study Under the Right to Freedom of Conscience', 75 *Archiv für Rechts-und Sozialphilosophie* (1989) 345.

[144] *J.P. v. Canada*, Communication No. 466/1991 (decision of 7 November 1991), UN Doc. A/47/40 (1994), p. 426.

[145] *Ibid.*, at p. 427, para. 4.2.

[146] *J.v.K. and C.M.G.v.K.-S. v. The Netherlands*, Communication No. 483/1991 (decision of 23 July 1992), UN Doc. A/47/40 (1994), p. 435.

[147] *K.V. and C.V. v. Germany*, Communication No. 568/1993 (decision of 8 April 1994), UN Doc. A/49/40 vol. 2 (1994), p. 365.

In all of these cases, applications were dismissed solely on the basis of the neutrality of the obligation in question, supported (in the case of claims under the European Convention) by the power given to States to raise taxes. It may be concluded both from the rationale applied and from the fact that the power to raise taxes is not explicitly recognised in the ICCPR that ultimately these decisions turn on a failure to invoke issues of conscience on the particular facts, rather than any principle that taxation schemes are incapable of conflicting with the individual's conscience. More recent decisions, particularly in the European context, demonstrate the clear potential for such conflict. They also indicate a trend away from inappropriate reliance on principles of manifestation as a means of upholding State limitations, towards a more general recognition that coercion to act contrary to one's beliefs indeed raises issues of conscience, albeit within certain limits.

Recognition that coercion does not constitute manifestation

The clearest recognition that resistance to coercion does not constitute manifestation is found in the European Commission's opinion in *Darby v. Sweden*.[148] The applicant was a non-resident of Sweden and opposed the imposition of a church tax (collected together with ordinary municipal tax) designated specifically for the Lutheran Church. Exemption of 70 per cent was available for residents, but not non-residents. The residual 30 per cent covered the public functions of the church in maintaining registers of births, marriages and deaths and in attending to cemeteries, rather than the religious activities of the church. Although the European Court ultimately decided that the failure to grant exemption constituted a violation of Article 14, taken together with Article 1, First Protocol, the European Commission explained its position as follows.

> 'The Commission considers that the applicant's payment of church tax, on the basis of the legal obligation incumbent upon him, cannot be characterised as a "manifestation" of his religion. What is at issue here is thus the applicant's general right of freedom of religion under the first limb of Article 9 § 1.
>
> In the Commission's view this right protects everyone from being compelled to be involved directly in religious activities against his will without being a member of the religious community carrying out those activities. The paying of taxes to a church for its religious activities in the

---

[148] *Darby v. Sweden* (Ser. A) No. 187 (1990) ECtHR, annex to the decision of the Court.

circumstances described above (paragraph 48) must be seen as such involvement.'[149]

The European Commission's conclusion that Article 9(1) was violated on the basis of interference with the *forum internum* marks a clear rejection of its previous manifestation-oriented approach and provides a basis for claiming interference with the *forum internum* in cases of compulsion, without any reference to manifestation. At the same time, the European Commission managed to preserve its position in *C. v. United Kingdom* in the case of general taxes, as opposed to specific church taxes, by clearly delineating the two. It dismissed the Government's argument that the two should be treated similarly (such that the State must be free to use all taxes collected for purposes to which the individual may object).[150] That argument was, in the European Commission's view, relevant only to general taxes where there is insufficient link between the individual taxpayer and the State's Treasury expenditure. Insufficient linkage in the case of general taxes would defeat the suggestion that the taxpayer is required to act contrary to his conscience. The European Commission also achieved consistency with those cases concerning the element of choice available to the applicant, by restating the requirement that no one may be forced to enter, or be prohibited from leaving, a State Church.[151]

The European Commission also went out of its way to condemn the lengths that were suggested should be undertaken by applicants in order to avoid conflicts of conscience. In answer to the Government's argument that the applicant could have avoided the full church tax by becoming resident in Sweden, the European Commission refused to accept 'that an individual should be forced to move from his home and take up residence in the State concerned before he could enjoy the right to have his freedom of religion respected by the State'.[152] (The Commission could have followed this approach in the employment

---

[149] *Ibid.*, at pages 18–19, paras. 50–1.
[150] See also *Ortega Moratilla v. Spain*, App. No. 17522/90 (1992) 72 D&R 256. The applicant, a registered religious association, was refused exemption from property tax which had been granted to the Catholic Church. In answer to the applicant's claim that its property tax payments indirectly contribute to funding of the Catholic Church on account of the allowances the latter receives from the State, the Commission reaffirmed the principle in *C. v. United Kingdom* concerning the neutrality of general taxation and noted that 'the applicants have by no means established or even alleged that property tax is a tax used for a particular purpose' (at p. 262).
[151] *Darby v. Sweden*, at 18, para. 45.   [152] *Ibid.*, at para. 52.

cases discussed above[153] to determine that an employee is entitled to claim violation of Article 9 against an employer who wishes to impose new working restrictions which conflict with the employee's religious convictions.)

More recently, in *Refah Partisi (the Welfare Party) and others v. Turkey*,[154] the European Court supported the dissolution of a political party which advocated the application of some of Sharia's private law rules to the Muslim population in Turkey. The Grand Chamber upheld the lower Chamber's characterisation of this as coersive in that it would oblige individuals to obey rules of law imposed by religion, rather than those settled by the State in the exercise of its function as the impartial guarantor of individual rights and freedoms.[155] Accordingly, the Court rejected the applicants' claim that dissolution of the party amounted to discrimination against Muslims who wished to live their private lives in accordance with the precepts of their religion. The operation of religious private law was taken to constitute coercion on a sizeable part of the population.

Although the Human Rights Committee has not been faced with a claim similar to that of *Refah*, it has (in line with European practice) been vigilant in its review of State reports about the payment of church taxes by non-members.[156] In particular, it noted that in Finland a church tax was payable by members of a State-recognised religion and it asked 'whether this did not amount to discrimination contrary to the Covenant and might not be inconsistent also with freedom of religion inasmuch as a person who does not want to pay or cannot afford to pay could be led to renounce his religious faith'.[157]

---

[153] *Stedman v. United Kingdom*, App. No. 29107/95, 89–A (1997) D&R 104, at 107–8; *Konttinen v. Finland*, App. No. 24949/94, (1996) 87 D&R 68.
[154] *Refah Partisi (the Welfare Party) and others v. Turkey* (2003) 37 EHRR 1.
[155] *Ibid.*, at para. 119.
[156] UN Doc. A/38/40 (1983), p. 24, para. 113 (Iceland); UN Doc. A/41/40 (1986), p. 31, para. 146 (Sweden); UN Doc. A/41/40 (1986), p. 44, para. 212 (Finland).
[157] UN Doc. A/34/40 (1979), p. 97, para. 412 (Finland). For potentially discriminatory tax measures reported by the Special Rapporteur, see UN Doc. E/CN.4/2000/65 (2000), para. 80 (in Peru, following an order amending the legislation on exemption from property tax for religious organisations recognised by the State, a number of Christian congregations reportedly ceased their activities because of the absence of financial resources needed to pay taxes), and UN Doc. E/CN.4/2001/63 (2001), p. 18, para. 52 (in Hungary, tax and customs legislation was reportedly amended to limit the tax exemptions available to churches having contracts with the State, allegedly stripping most religious communities (such as Seventh Day Adventists, evangelicals, Methodists and Pentecostalists) of their tax-exempt status).

Summary

What is noticeable from all of the cases so far considered (of State compulsion in opposition to the individual's beliefs) is the initial reluctance on the part of both the European and United Nations organs to invoke the protection that is available to the individual within the first part of Article 9(1) of the European Convention and Article 18(1) of the ICCPR. Instead, reliance has been placed on the repetitive application of formulae relevant principally to manifestation, though with less force when other specific features of the claim permit State interference on other grounds – such as the element of choice, or the recognition of particular State powers within certain human rights instruments. The avoidance of findings of violation within the unrestricted *forum internum* is undoubtedly attributable to fears for the consequences of a blanket acknowledgement that compulsion to act contrary to one's beliefs raises issues of conscience. At worst, such an approach may invite wholesale challenges against States in their reliance on legal obligations necessary for the proper functioning of society. However, it may be argued that it would be preferable to aim for consistent treatment of protection for the *forum internum* without resorting to inappropriate notions of manifestation, reliance on the recognition of State powers of taxation or armament or even justifications based on the generality of laws when faced with situations which produce genuine conflicts of conscience. The practice of the Human Rights Committee is less open to criticism than that of the Strasbourg organs principally because the reasoning provided in individual decisions is less detailed but also because the Committee has taken the opportunity outside Optional Protocol claims to give due acknowledgement to certain *forum internum* rights.

Recent trends towards greater recognition of issues of conscience are visible but it is too early to conclude that such trends represent an intended shift in favour of broader recognition for the *forum internum*. The suggestion that the European Court might in future take a more forthright approach to issues of compulsion is constrained by the fact that the European Court in *Buscarini* reverted to the much-criticised 'manifestation' diagnosis even though it was perfectly clear that the applicants were not in any way 'manifesting' their beliefs but, on the contrary, were refusing to manifest beliefs which were not theirs.

'Indirect' protection for the *forum internum*

The European Commission in *Darby v. Sweden* importantly invoked the notion of 'respect' for the religious convictions of individuals by stipulating that 'Article 9 § 1 of the Convention requires that a State respects the religious convictions of those who do not belong to the church, for instance by making it possible for them to be exempted from the obligation to make contributions to the church for its religious activities'.[158] Although the European Commission's comments in *Darby v. Sweden* were rooted firmly in the idea of respect for the religious convictions of the individual, the fact that the beliefs are religious in nature should be immaterial.[159]

The notion of 'respect' for the beliefs of others is an increasingly important one and will now be considered in three different contexts: first, within the limitation ground 'the rights and freedoms of others' (continuing discussion of limitation grounds in Chapter 2 in the context of proselytism); secondly (but only incidentally), the application of those Articles in both the European Convention and the ICCPR which prevent any activity aimed at the destruction of the enjoyment of any recognised rights of others; and, thirdly, the right of parents to ensure that their own beliefs are 'respected' in the education of their children. The conscience or belief 'respected' for these purposes is not that of the applicant or author, except in the case of parents concerning the education of their children. Because the beneficiary of this type of protection is not generally the claimant, for present purposes this type of safeguard is described as constituting 'indirect' protection for the *forum internum*. The European Commission's comments in *Darby v. Sweden* are striking in that they refer to 'respect' for the applicant's beliefs, rather than respect owed to the beliefs of someone other than the applicant. Case law supporting the notion of respect for the applicant's own beliefs is sparse.

Detailed consideration will also be given to discrimination as another 'indirect' means of protection against coercion, where 'indirect' is used

---

[158] *Darby v. Sweden* (Ser. A) No. 187 (1990) ECtHR, annex to the decision of the Court, para. 58.

[159] In *Van den Dungen v. The Netherlands*, App. No. 22838/93 (1995) 80 D&R 147, the rationale justifying restrictions on the activities of the anti-abortionist outside an abortion clinic was 'the protection of others' against coercive tactics (inspired by the applicant's own religious beliefs) that would offend the *non-religious* beliefs of women attending the clinic.

to refer to the fact that the applicant does not (and need not) rely on a core freedom of religion Article in the European Convention or ICCPR. It is necessary to give discrimination particular attention given that the bulk of cases concerning discrimination relate to the application of coercive measures contrary to the individual's conscience, and given also that discriminatory measures are often claimed to constitute punishment for holding particular beliefs.

The remainder of this chapter will therefore be devoted to consideration of all such 'indirect' forms of protection for the *forum internum* to assist in building a consistent approach to the treatment of coercion to act contrary to one's beliefs, to arrive at a meaningful interpretation of the term 'respect', and to determine the scope of the other residual constituents of the *forum internum*. The purpose will be to observe, in particular, whether principles applicable to such indirect means of protection can be reconciled with the hesitancy on the part of both the Strasbourg and United Nations institutions, illustrated in the first part of this chapter, to give due recognition to the full scope of the *forum internum* when claimed directly within a core freedom of religion Article. Each of the 'indirect' means of protection against coercion will now be examined in turn.

The rights and freedoms of others as a ground of limitation

Protection for 'the rights and freedoms of others' (or equivalent terminology) appears as a ground of limitation in Articles 8, 9, 10 and 11 (and in Article 2 of the Fourth Protocol) of the European Convention, and in Articles 18, 19, 21 and 22 of the ICCPR, in each case operating, where appropriate, to justify State restriction of the exercise of the freedoms guaranteed in those Articles.

The 'rights of others' have, for example, justified restrictions under Article 10(2) of the European Convention on neo-Nazi activities ('aimed at impairing the basic order of freedom and democracy'),[160] and have justified the dismissal of a private employee on account of his membership of a party (and political activities within that party) which espoused racist views inimical to the aims of the employer.[161] The 'rights of others' have even been invoked in the allocation of broadcasting

---

[160] *Kühnen v. Germany*, App. No. 12194/86 (1988) 56 D&R 205, at 209. Restrictions on neo-Nazi activities were upheld under Article 10(2).

[161] *Van de Heijden v. The Netherlands*, App. No. 11002/84 (1985) 41 D&R 264.

frequencies, so that in *Groppera Radio AG and others v. Switzerland*[162] a ban on cable retransmission in Switzerland of programmes broadcast from Italy had a legitimate aim in ensuring pluralism, in particular of information, by allowing a fair allocation of frequencies internationally and nationally.[163]

However, appropriate limits to the 'rights of others' must be observed. It was argued in Chapter 2, in a review of Article 10 cases which invoked general notions of respect for the religious feelings of others within this ground of limitation, that such respect was not itself a right found within the text of Article 9(1) of the European Convention and that there was a risk that limitation provisions could be unduly extended by inappropriate reference to such notions.[164] If (contrary to this conclusion) it may successfully be argued that the individual is entitled to 'respect' for religious beliefs as a constituent of Article 9, then it must also surely be the case that such 'respect' falls within the *forum internum* of the beneficiary since, of the two hemispheres of the freedom of religion, 'respect' cannot easily be said to belong within the beneficiary's right of manifestation. The development, in the interpretation of limitation provisions, of a right to have one's beliefs 'respected' (particularly when it does not appear in the text of Article 9) would be at odds with the apparent lack of 'respect' for matters of individual conscience discussed above under the heading '"Direct" protection for the forum internum' and the more general failure by the European institutions to give proper recognition to *forum internum* rights.

Consistency with the traditionally recognised content of Article 9 may instead easily be achieved by an interpretation of 'respect' which is confined to ensuring that the *effect* of the exercise of freedom of expression does not impinge on known Article 9 freedoms (or indeed other freedoms). This is quite different from a right to 'respect for one's religious feelings' as such. The European Court's analysis in

---

[162] *Groppera Radio AG and others v. Switzerland* (Ser. A) No. 173–A (1990) ECtHR.

[163] *Ibid.*, at para. 69.

[164] This entailed in Chapter 2 under the headings 'Coercion' and 'Blasphemy, disparagement and gratuitous offence' at pp. 73–7 and 84–111, a review of the interpretation of paragraph 48 of the European Court's judgment in *Kokkinakis v. Greece* (Ser. A) No. 260–A (1993) ECtHR in the light of parallel developments in Article 10 jurisprudence beginning with the European Commission's decision in *Gay News Ltd and Lemon v. United Kingdom*, App. No. 8710/79 (1982) 5 EHRR 123 and subsequent decisions of the European Court in *Otto-Preminger-Institut v. Austria* (Ser. A) No. 295–A (1994) ECtHR; *Wingrove v. United Kingdom* (1997) 24 EHRR 1; and *Murphy v. Ireland* (App. No. 44179/98) (2004) 38 EHRR 212.

Otto-Preminger-Institut v. Austria[165] of the Government's assertion that the 'rights of others' includes the right to respect for one's religious feelings is particularly interesting. The example provided by the European Court of the impact on Article 9 freedoms in the case of extreme forms of expression focused firmly on established freedoms within Article 9: 'Indeed, in extreme cases the effect of particular methods of opposing or denying religious beliefs can be such as to inhibit those who hold such beliefs from exercising their freedom to hold and express them.'[166]

In this example the 'rights of others' affected by the expression included both the *forum interim* right to hold opinions and right of external manifestation, both well recognised rights within Article 9. The same paragraph of the *Otto-Preminger* judgment also referred to paragraph 48 of the judgment in *Kokkinakis v Greece*,[167] which in turn mentioned incompatibility with 'respect' for freedom of thought, conscience and religion in the case of improper forms of proselytsim.[168] The suggestion made in Chapter 2, that such 'respect' as developed in *Kokkinakis* was no more than a reference to the need to avoid interference with established Article 9 rights – in particular, freedom from coercion in religious choice – is consistent with the illustration of the *effect* of extreme forms of expression in *Otto-Preminger*. In short, the recognition that certain extreme forms of expression may have the effect of interfering with established Article 9 rights does not mean that a right exists, within Article 9, 'of citizens not to be insulted in their religious feelings by the public expression of views of other persons' (as asserted by the Government in *Otto-Preminger*).

Such protection might instead be said to rest more generally on the 'duties and responsibilities' to which freedom of expression is subject, according to the terms of Article 10(2). (Article 19 of the ICCPR carries a similar reference to 'special duties and responsibilities'.) This is consistent with the emphasis given recently in *Murphy v. Ireland*[169] on 'duties and responsibilities' when referring to the 'requirement to ensure the peaceful enjoyment of the rights guaranteed under Article 9 to the holders of such beliefs',[170] discussed extensively in Chapter 2 under the heading 'Blasphemy, disparagement and gratuitous offence', pp. 84–102.

---

[165] *Otto-Preminger-Institut v. Austria* (Ser. A) No. 295–A (1994) ECtHR, at para. 46.
[166] *Ibid.*, at para. 47.
[167] *Kokkinakis v. Greece* (Ser. A) No. 260–A (1993) ECtHR, at para. 48, discussed above at pp. 72–7.
[168] *Ibid.*, at para. 48.   [169] *Murphy v. Ireland* (App. No. 44179/98) (2004) 38 EHRR 212.
[170] *Ibid.*, at para. 65.

It is in this context that tolerance plays such an important role but not so as to restrict freedom of expression unduly. The balance is encapsulated in the familiar principle that freedom of expression applies 'not only to "information" or "ideas" that are favourably received or regarded as inoffensive or as a matter of indifference, but also to those that offend, shock or disturb; such are the demands of pluralism, tolerance and broadmindedness without which there is no "democratic society"'.[171] It is also important to observe the State's duty, as outlined by the European Court in *Serif v. Greece*,[172] and affirmed in *Supreme Council of the Muslim Community v. Bulgaria*[173] 'to ensure that the competing groups tolerate each other'.[174]

Nevertheless, the disparity is a stark one between, on the one hand, the potentially generous scope of limitations under Article 10 in the interests of avoiding religious offence and, on the other hand, the reluctance (particularly on the part of the European institutions) to give formal recognition to what is suggested above should fall within the *forum internum*.

One final observation concerns the position of minority religious groups. Both *Otto-Preminger* and *Wingrove* involved blasphemous offence to the majority religion (in the case of *Otto-Preminger* the Catholic majority in the Tyrol region representing as much as 87 per cent of the local population, and in the case of *Wingrove* the majority Protestant population of the United Kingdom). This begs the question whether the decisions were in fact based upon latitude in favour of State measures, and begs (more rhetorically) whether protection against religious attacks may benefit minority religious groups in equal measure. Protection available equally to minority groups would be consistent with the rejection by the European Court in *Kokkinakis* of the Greek Government's claim that public order limitations should justify restrictions on proselytism given that if the State remained indifferent to attacks on freedom of religious belief against the majority State Church, major unrest would be

---

[171] *Handyside v. United Kingdom* (Ser. A) No. 24 (1976) ECtHR, para. 49, approved, for example, in *Murphy v. Ireland* (App. No. 44179/98) (2004) 38 EHRR 212.

[172] *Serif v. Greece* (1999) 31 EHRR 561.

[173] *Supreme Holy Council of the Muslim Community v. Bulgaria* (App. No. 39023/97), Judgment of 16 December 2004, at para. 96.

[174] 'Although the Court recognises that it is possible that tension is created in situations where a religious or any other community becomes divided, it considers that this is one of the unavoidable consequences of pluralism. The role of the authorities in such circumstances is not to remove the cause of tension by eliminating pluralism, but to ensure that the competing groups tolerate each other' (*ibid.*, at para. 53).

caused that would probably disturb the social peace.[175] Unless the vulnerable position of minority groups is safeguarded, according to genuine notions of pluralism and tolerance, the use of 'respect' in limitation provisions would merely have the effect of allowing States to impose restrictions that support public and private sources of intolerance of minority religions.

It is for this reason that limits on the misuse of rights, coupled with guarantees against discrimination, are valuable as further 'indirect' means of protection. Guarantees against discrimination will be considered in detail later in this chapter but it is worth noting in passing that Article 5(1) of the ICCPR and Article 17 of the European Convention are most commonly used by States to justify the denial of Convention rights to individuals who claim them as a means or an end involving the destruction or limitation of the full enjoyment of guaranteed rights by others.[176] These provisions may also be used against States to constrain the misuse of State discretion.[177]

Education

A quite different, and more explicit, concept of 'respect' for religious convictions is found in the context of the protection enjoyed by parents in relation to the State education of their children. Parents are entitled to ensure that their own religious and philosophical convictions are respected in their children's education by virtue of Article 18(4) of the ICCPR, and

---

[175] *Kokkinakis v. Greece* (Ser. A) No. 260–A (1993) ECtHR, para. 46.

[176] For examples of European decisions, see: *Kommunistische Partei Deutschland v. Germany*, App. No. 250/57, 1 Yearbook (1955–7) 222; *Glimmerveen and Hagenbeek v. The Netherlands*, App. No. 8348/78 and 8406/78 (1979) 18 D&R 187; *East African Asians cases*, App. No. 4403/70 etc, (1981) EHRR 76, 36 CD 92. For Optional Protocol decisions, see: *Robert Faurisson v. France*, Communication No. 550/1993 (views of 8 November 1996), UN Doc. A/52/40 vol. 2 (1999), p. 84; and on related Articles, see *Tae-Hoon Park v. Korea*, Communication No. 628/1995 (views of 20 October 1998) (1999) 6(3) IHRR 623.

[177] In addition, positive duties on States to 'respect and to ensure' or to 'secure' guaranteed rights and freedoms play a significant role. Pocar emphasises the positive guarantees of the enjoyment of religious freedom in the ICCPR, the UN Charter and the Universal Declaration – F. Pocar, 'Religious Freedom in the System of the United Nations', 1(2) Con & Lib (1989) 14. See also: T. Buergenthal, 'To Respect and to Ensure: State Obligations and Permissible Derogations', in L. Henkin (ed.), *The International Bill of Rights: The Covenant on Civil and Political Rights*, New York/Guildford: Columbia University Press (1981); O. Schachter, 'The Obligation to Implement the Covenant in Domestic Law', in L. Henkin (ed.), *ibid.*

Protocol 1, Article 2 of the European Convention.[178] Issues affecting the *forum internum* arise principally in relation to the content of teaching on religious or philosophical matters within the school curriculum and, to a lesser extent, compulsion in administering school discipline.[179] The focus of discussion under this heading is whether the principles applicable to such Articles are consistent with those discussed above in this chapter and whether they contribute to an analysis of the scope of the *forum internum*. The position under the European Convention (which provides much material for discussion) will be considered first.

'Respect' for parental convictions based on indoctrination

The requirement to 'respect' parental wishes in Protocol 1, Article 2 of the European Convention has substantive content. In *Campbell and Cosans v. United Kingdom*,[180] the European Court indicated that it means more than 'acknowledge' or 'take into account' – 'in addition to a primarily negative undertaking, it implies some positive obligation on the part of the State'.[181] This concept of respect therefore stands in contrast to those references to 'respect' discussed earlier in this chapter which do not have clear authority, still less, authority within a Convention Article. However, the question is whether this concept of respect (given the nature and origin of Protocol 1, Article 2) has an impact on related provisions such as Articles 9 and 10.

Although the burden of the State in offering any form of education is confined, this of itself does not limit the State's obligations under Protocol 1, Article 2 which apply not only to religious education but other aspects of State education, such as sex education[182] and

---

[178] For the origins and drafting of Protocol 1, Article 2, see J. E. S. Fawcett, *The Application of the European Convention on Human Rights*, Oxford: Clarendon Press (1987), pp. 411–16. See also 1981 Declaration Article 5(2), and Vienna Concluding Document, para. 16(k), January 1989, 28 ILM (1989) 531, para. 16.7.

[179] See D. M. Clarke, 'Freedom of Thought in Schools: A Comparative Study', 35 Int'l & Comp Law Q (1986) 271. Clarke provides a review of the secular/neutral models for religious education in the United States and France, compared with that in Ireland (where there is no network of secular schools). He places particular emphasis on the role of State funding and risks of indoctrination. For discussion concerning the return of religious teaching in the educational system of the Federal Republic of Yugoslavia to rectify the historical exclusion from the educational system of any religious teaching, see B. Milosavljevic, 'Relations Between the State and Religious Communities in the Federal Republic of Yugoslavia', Brigham Young UL Rev (2002) 311.

[180] *Campbell and Cosans v. United Kingdom* (Ser. A) No. 48 (1982) ECtHR.

[181] *Ibid.*, at para. 37.

[182] *Kjeldsen, Busk Madsen and Pedersen v. Denmark* (Ser. A) No. 23 (1976) ECtHR.

the infliction of corporal punishment against the wishes of parents.[183] The context in which such obligations arise, however, is specific to parental duties and responsibilities: 'It is in the discharge of a natural duty towards their children – parents being primarily responsible for the "education and teaching" of their children – that parents may require the State to respect their religious and philosophical convictions.'[184]

Accordingly, the right belongs only to parents and not to their children.[185] That said, the European Court has suggested that a prior obligation is owed to children in their right to education, to which the right of parents is seen as an adjunct.[186] An appropriate balance therefore needs to be maintained between parental wishes and the State's obligation to provide education, which necessarily spans a broad range of religious and philosophical issues. The European Court considered this question in *Kjeldsen, Busk Madsen and Pederson v. Denmark (the Danish sex education* case),[187] a case which concerned parental objection (on grounds of religious belief) to compulsory sex education when integrated into the general curriculum. The curriculum comprised a variety of subjects, distinct from those classes dedicated to sex education from which exemption was possible. The European Court explained that Protocol 1, Article 2 permits the State to impart information or knowledge of a directly or indirectly religious or philosophical kind, since to avoid doing so would be unfeasible in the school curriculum. Prompted by the requirement stipulated in the *Belgian Linguistics* case[188] that the provisions of the Convention and Protocol must be read as a whole, the European Court attempted an interpretation consistent with Protocol 1, Article 2, and Articles 8 to 10 of the European Convention (and with the general spirit of the Convention itself as an instrument designed to

---

[183] *Campbell and Cosans v. United Kingdom* (Ser. A) No. 48 (1982) ECtHR; *X,Y and Z v. United Kingdom*, App. No. 8566/79, (1982) 31 D&R 50; *Seven Individuals v. Sweden*, App. No. 8811/79 (1982) 29 D&R 104; *B. and D. v. United Kingdom*, App. No. 9303/81 (1986) 49 D&R 44.

[184] *Kjeldsen, Busk Madsen and Pedersen v. Denmark* (Ser. A) No. 23 (1976) ECtHR 26, para. 52.

[185] *Eriksson v. Sweden* (Ser. A) No. 156 (1989) ECtHR, para. 93.

[186] *Kjeldsen, Busk Madsen and Pedersen v. Denmark* (Ser. A) No. 23 (1976) ECtHR 26, para. 52.

[187] *Kjeldsen, Busk Madsen and Pedersen v. Denmark* (Ser. A) No. 23 (1976) ECtHR.

[188] *Case relating to certain aspects of the laws on the use of languages in education in Belgium (the Belgian Linguistics case)* (Ser. A) No. 6 (1968) ECtHR 30, para. 1.

maintain and promote the ideals and values of a democratic society).[189] It defined the boundaries of such expediency in the following terms:

> 'The second sentence of Article 2 implies ... that the State, in fulfilling the functions assumed by it in regard to education and teaching, must take care that information or knowledge included in this curriculum is conveyed in an objective, critical and pluralistic manner. The State is forbidden to pursue an aim of indoctrination that might be considered as not respecting parents' religious and philosophical convictions. This is the limit that must not be exceeded.'[190]

It is doubtful whether the European Court would make such a simple statement of interpretation today, without further explanation. It is also unlikely that the European Court would make the following reference to 'proselytism', in the light of the distinction made in *Kokkinakis v. Greece* between acceptable and improper proselytism, when it went on to comment as follows:

> 'Certainly, abuses can occur as to the manner in which the provisions in force are applied by a given school or teacher and the competent authorities have a duty to take the utmost care to see to it that parents' religious and philosophical convictions are not disregarded at this level by carelessness, lack of judgment or misplaced proselytism.'[191]

The European Court readily accepted that it was not concerned with proselytism in this particular case and, more importantly, it did not suggest that lack of judgment or misplaced proselytism would constitute 'indoctrination'. It merely observed that the manner in which educational policy is implemented may require monitoring of school teachers against such practices. It would be exceedingly unlikely that isolated instances of proselytism could in reality amount to indoctrination although on a sufficient scale within a school or across a particular country, or possibly by the persistent forceful habits of a single teacher, the cumulative result may be that parental wishes are ultimately not respected. Furthermore, when the Greek Government in *Kokkinakis* cited the *Danish sex education* case as authority that proselytism as practised by Mr Kokkinakis constituted indoctrination, the European Court gave no support to that argument either in its reasoning or its ultimate decision.[192]

---

[189] *Ibid.*, at para. 52.   [190] *Ibid.*, at para. 53.   [191] *Ibid.*, at para. 54
[192] *Kokkinakis v. Greece* (Ser. A) No. 260–A (1993) ECtHR, para. 30.

Interference with the *forum internum* under Article 9 and indoctrina-tion for the purposes of Protocol 1, Article 2 may be expected to have in common a high threshold for violation. A strict threshold must be inferred from the Court's choice of the term 'indoctrination' in the *Danish sex education* case, supported by the fact that, according to the terms of Protocol 1, Article 2, no State discretion or justification is permitted to justify any failure to respect parental wishes. Consistency would be achieved with Article 9 if 'indoctrination' for the purposes of Protocol 1, Article 2 constituted interference with the *forum internum* of the child.[193] Although both Article 9 and Protocol 1, Article 2 contain safeguards against indoctrination, it is difficult to discern whether the same standard is applied to indoctrination under both Article 9 and Protocol 1, Article 2. In *Angeleni v. Sweden*,[194] parents claimed that their rights under Protocol 1 Article 2, and those of their child (the second applicant) under Articles 9 and 14 had been violated as a result of the child's enforced participation in Christian religious teaching contrary to the parents' atheistic wishes. The parents' claim was dismissed owing to reservations entered against Protocol 1, Article 2 but the European Commission examined the child's claims under Articles 9 and 14. It expressly acknowledged that protection against indoctrination of reli-gion is within Article 9(1):

> 'The Commission is of the opinion that Article 9 of the Convention affords protection against indoctrination of religion by the State, be it in education at school or in any other activity for which the State has assumed responsibility. The main issue to be determined in the present case is, accordingly, whether it has been established that the second applicant has been subjected to indoctrination of religion at school which would involve a disrespect for her right to freedom of religion as guaranteed by Article 9 para. 1 of the Convention.'[195]

The fact that the child's claim under Article 9 was used as a substitute for the parents' claim under Protocol 1, Article 2, leads to speculation whether the standards of indoctrination applicable to the latter were

---

[193] In cases of indoctrination the child would be entitled to claim violation of Article 9 (in addition to the parents' claim under Protocol 1, Article 2). In the event of conflict between the choice of the child and that of the parents, Malcolm Evans suggests that the wishes of the child should prevail – M. D. Evans, *Religious Liberty and International Law in Europe*, p. 346. For a contrary view, see R. Goy, 'La Garantie Européene de la Liberté de Religion', 107 *Revue du Droit Public* (1991) 5.

[194] *Angeleni v. Sweden*, App. No. 10491/83 (1986) 51 D&R 41.   [195] *Ibid.*, at 48.

substituted, and if so whether they are any different. It was accepted that the child was obliged to take part in lessons on the subject 'religious knowledge', but the European Commission found that she had only received a minor part of that teaching, having been given extensive exemption from the remainder. The European Commission found that although most of the instruction in religious knowledge focused on Christianity (provided by a teacher well-versed in Christianity but less so in other religions) this did not mean that the child had been under religious indoctrination in violation of Article 9. Nevertheless, it would have been useful if the European Commission had clarified whether the standard of indoctrination is to be the same 'in education at school' as 'in any other activity'.

The reference to 'disrespect' in *Angeleni v. Sweden* is not considered to mean anything other than 'violation' though given the variety of ways in which the term 'respect' had already developed so as to avoid 'offence', particularly in the context of the limitation ground 'protection of the rights of others' under Article 10, the European Commission might well be criticised for adding to the resulting uncertainty. For example, in *X. v. United Kingdom*[196] the dismissal of a teacher for expressing his personal (pro-life) beliefs to his classes and through posters and stickers was justified under Article 10(2) for the 'protection of the rights of others'. The European Commission made only passing reference to the rights of parents under Protocol 1, Article 2 but when applying the law to the facts focused on the offence that the applicant's views may cause to female staff, which may also be disturbing to children. This represents possibly the widest use of the term 'protection of the rights of others', and the most uncertain in scope. None of the rights of others in question was clearly identified and it is difficult to discern such rights within the European Convention except those relating to indoctrination in the context of education. Yet the facts do not remotely suggest indoctrination, and much of the applicant's behaviour for which he was criticised related to activities outside the classroom. There is therefore much to be gained from more careful use of the terms 'respect', 'disrespect' and 'offence'.

Nevertheless, it would appear that to the extent that the applicant in *X. v. United Kingdom* was criticised for instructing his classes in his personal views, the European Commission noted that these were classes from which the children could not absent themselves. In the *Danish sex*

---

[196] *X. v. United Kingdom*, App. No. 8010/77 (1979) 16 D&R 101.

education case it was only in relation to compulsory integrated sex education that Protocol 1, Article 2 could be invoked, rather than voluntary specific sex education, which was conducted in parallel. This reflects a degree of consistency with those cases discussed above under the heading 'Decisions based on available alternatives', pp. 136–45, that focused on the element of choice to defeat a claim of violation based upon coercion to act contrary to one's beliefs. The same must also surely be true of proselytism, so that the opportunity to absent oneself from unwanted proselytism must prevent even extreme forms of proselytism being treated as indoctrination. It is difficult to imagine proselytism in which the subject has no freedom of choice to decline the proselytiser's offer of persuasion (except perhaps the military context considered in *Larissis and others v. Greece*[197]).

It should not be forgotten that the true context for evaluating the scope of Protocol 1, Article 2 is its underlying aim to prevent indoctrination by at worst totalitarian governments, as supplemented by the requirements of pluralism. As the European Court stressed in the *Danish sex education* case, the second sentence of Protocol 1, Article 2 'aims in short at safeguarding the possibility of pluralism in education which possibility is essential for the preservation of the "democratic society" as conceived by the Convention. In view of the power of the modern State, it is above all through State teaching that this aim must be realised'.[198] Marked emphasis on pluralism is also evident in the European Commission's decision in *W. & D.M. and M. and H.I. v. United Kingdom*,[199] in which the European Commission affirmed that 'the essence of Art. 2 of Protocol No. 1 is the safeguarding of pluralism and tolerance in public education and the prohibition on indoctrination'.[200] However, if too low a threshold of indoctrination were to be applied for the purpose of Protocol 1, Article 2, the result could stifle a wider range of personal expressions by State teachers than intended (including those

---

[197] *Larissis and others v. Greece* (Ser. A) No. 65 (1998–V) ECtHR 363.

[198] *Kjeldsen, Busk Madsen and Pedersen v. Denmark* (Ser. A) No. 23 (1976) ECtHR, at para. 50.

[199] *W. & D.M. and M. and H.I. v. United Kingdom*, App. Nos. 10228/82 and 10229/82 (joined) (1984) 37 D&R 96.

[200] *Ibid.*, at 99. See also H. Cullen, 'Education Rights or Minority Rights?' 7 Int JLP & F (1993) 143. Cullen suggests that the only way of resolving what seem to be contradictory claims is by deciding whether minority education rights are a species of the right to education or of minority rights – she argues that the former allows for a fuller solution but that in the event of conflict between equality of opportunity and pluralism, equality of opportunity should prevail.

outside the classroom) and engender intolerance. The parental right, as explained by the European Court in the *Danish sex education* case, was 'to guide their children on a path in line with the parents' own religious or philosophical convictions',[201] which does not require immunisation against all contrary beliefs. The European Court's rationale in *Dahlab v. Switzerland*[202] for supporting the prohibition on a teacher wearing an Islamic headscarf in a State school sadly illustrates the error of applying too low a threshold. The potential harm of wearing a headscarf was described as follows:

> 'The Court accepts that it is very difficult to assess the impact that a powerful external symbol such as the wearing of a headscarf may have on the freedom of conscience and religion of very young children. The applicant's pupils were aged between four and eight, an age at which children wonder about many things and are also more easily influenced than older pupils. In those circumstances, it cannot be denied outright that the wearing of a headscarf might have some kind of proselytising effect, seeing that it appears to be imposed on women by a precept which is laid down in the Koran and which, as the Federal Court noted, is hard to square with the principle of gender equality. It therefore appears difficult to reconcile the wearing of an Islamic headscarf with the message of tolerance, respect for others and, above all, equality and non-discrimination that all teachers in a democratic society must convey to their pupils.'

The message which the children are more likely to note is one of the State's intolerance not only towards Muslim dress but Islam more generally as crudely characterised by the Court, and cannot easily be squared with 'the safeguarding of pluralism and tolerance in public education and the prohibition on indoctrination'. The appeal to the merest speculation of the possibility of 'some kind of proselytising effect' demonstrates the strength of stigma attached to proselytism which Chapter 2 strove to correct. Religious dress merely reflects genuine pluralism in a society in which teachers might be expected to come from a variety of religious traditions or, as with the applicant in this case, might be expected to convert to a religion different from the one in which they grew up.

Principles relating to compulsion within Protocol 1, Article 2 were tested in *Valsamis v. Greece*,[203] in which it was claimed that compulsory

---

[201] *Kjeldsen, Busk Madsen and Pedersen v. Denmark* (Ser. A) No. 23 (1976) ECtHR, para. 54.
[202] *Dahlab v. Switzerland* (App. No. 42393/98), Judgment of 15 February 2001.
[203] *Valsamis v. Greece* (1997) 24 EHRR 294.

attendance by a Jehovah's Witness child at a school procession on a national holiday marking a military event was contrary to the beliefs of her and her parents.[204] The beliefs in question were undoubtedly pacifist (acknowledged to be within the term 'conviction' following *Campbell and Cosans v. United Kingdom*),[205] which the applicants claimed, as Jehovah's Witnesses, they were bound to practise in daily life by opposition to any event with military overtones. (Identical claims and identical judgments are found in *Valsamis v. Greece* and *Efstratiou v. Greece*.)[206] The claim failed on two grounds. First, the Court could discern nothing, either in the purpose of the parade or in the arrangements for it, which could offend the applicants' pacifist convictions (noting that such commemorations of national events serve, in their way, both pacifist objectives and the public interest). In effect, the necessary connection between the act compelled and the belief in question had not been established. The circumstances were not comparable, for example, to compulsory school attendance on a recognised religious holiday.[207] This essential connection is analogous to that required between belief and

---

[204] *Ibid.*, at 306, para. 40. Note that Protocol 1, Article 2 has much in common with the protection against compulsion to act contrary to one's beliefs suggested by Article 5(b) of the Convention against Discrimination in Education (1960), which provides that 'no person or group of persons should be compelled to receive religious instruction inconsistent with his or their convictions'. The Convention was adopted 14 December 1960, 429 UNTS 93 and entered into force 22 May 1962. Note also that in the drafting of the 1981 Declaration the representative of Brazil proposed: 'No child shall be compelled to receive teaching on religion or belief against the wishes of his parents or legal guardians', UN Doc. E/1980/13; UN Doc. E/CN.4/1408 (Supp. No. 3) (1980), p. 115, para. 35.

[205] *Campbell and Cosans v. United Kingdom* (Ser. A) No. 48 (1982) ECtHR, at 16, para. 36.

[206] *Efstratiou v. Greece*, No. 24 EHRR (1997), p. 298. See also *Martins Casimiro v. Luxembourg* (App. No. 44888/98), unreported, decision of 27 April 1999, in which the European Court ruled as manifestly ill-founded a claim by Seventh Day Adventist parents to total dispensation from their child's education on Saturday. The denial of special dispensation was upheld on the basis that it is only available for one-off celebrations rather than general objection to Saturday attendance, which would cause grave disruption to the timetable of the child as well as other pupils and staff. However, the Court accepted that this might constitute a restriction on the applicant's right to manifest their religion (without considering the child's right to manifestation). In the event of a conflict between the child's right to education and the parents' right to freedom of religion, the interests of the child must prevail, on application of the limitation ground of 'the rights and freedoms of others' (70 BYBIL (1999) 364).

[207] In many countries this would be recognised as an interference – in Trinidad and Tobago, for example, school attendance may not be made compulsory on religious holidays of the creed to which the child's parents belong – K. Boyle and J. Sheen, *Freedom of Religion and Belief: A World Report*, London: Routledge (1997), p. 150.

its manifestation articulated in the formula developed in *Arrowsmith v. United Kingdom*[208] (discussed earlier in this chapter at pp. 121–30). In *Valsamis* the Court did not elaborate an equivalent formula but simply disagreed with the assertion that attendance at the procession constituted coercion against the applicant's conscience.[209]

Secondly, and quite separately, the European Court found no violation of Protocol 1, Article 2 in view of the State's competence and discretion in its broad educational function in the setting and planning of the curriculum.[210] Given the questions of expediency that this involves, which may vary across States, the European Court was not prepared to intervene where the exercise of this discretion fell short of indoctrination. However, the European Court did register surprise that pupils could be required, on pain of suspension from school, to parade outside the school precincts on a holiday,[211] but referred to the *Campbell and Cosans* dictum that the imposition of disciplinary penalties 'is an integral part of the process whereby a school seeks to achieve the object for which it was established, including the development and moulding of the character and mental powers of its pupils'.[212]

Thus, even within the development of principles applicable to the unrestricted right of parents under Protocol 1, Article 2, the European Court has developed a means of allowing broad State discretion in the setting and planning of the curriculum which is only constrained by the presumably high threshold of indoctrination. This is comparable to

---

[208] *Arrowsmith v. United Kingdom*, App. No. 7050/75 (1978) 19 D&R 5.

[209] This is to be contrasted with *Bernard and others v. Luxembourg*, App. No. 17187/90 (1993) 75 D&R 57, in which the applicants who objected to compulsory moral and social education within the school curriculum failed even to claim that by participating in these lessons their children would be exposed to religious indoctrination or any other form of indoctrination, and did not claim that the lessons, as taught, conflicted with their philosophical convictions either. They also did not describe the nature of their philosophical convictions in any detail which is critical given that the word 'convictions' denotes views that attain a certain level of cogency, seriousness, cohesion and importance following *Campbell and Cosans v. United Kingdom*.

[210] *Valsamis v. Greece* (1997) 24 EHRR 294, at 315, para. 27. The Court referred to its decision in *Young, James and Webster v. United Kingdom* (Ser. A) No. 44 (1981) ECtHR, in which at para. 63 it had commented that 'although individual interests may on occasion be subordinated to those of a group, democracy does not simply mean that the views of a majority must always prevail: a balance must be achieved which ensures the fair and proper treatment of minorities and avoids any abuse of a dominant position'.

[211] *Ibid.*, at para. 31.

[212] *Campbell and Cosans v. United Kingdom* (Ser. A) No. 48 (1982) ECtHR, para. 33.

other devices developed by the Strasbourg organs, in the context of the *forum internum* protection of Article 9, to permit latitude in State interference.

Alternative approaches: manifestation and coercion to act contrary to one's beliefs

Claims by children under Article 9 of the European Convention often arise out of the same facts on which parental claims under Protocol 1, Article 2 are based. Decisions under Protocol 1, Article 2 generally make little reference at all to manifestation.[213] By contrast, the approach of the European Commission to Article 9 claims by children demonstrates marked consistency with those claims of compulsion considered above under the heading, 'Decisions based on justified limitation on manifestation', pp. 121–30, in allowing for discretion in State interference through reliance on manifestation and applicable limitations. More recent decisions by the European Court, however, suggest some reluctance to continue that approach.

Each child in *Valsamis v. Greece* and *Efstratiou v. Greece*[214] claimed violation of Article 9 in terms specifically invoking freedom from coercion, namely 'the negative freedom not to manifest, by gestures of support, any convictions or opinions contrary to her own'[215] and challenged the necessity and the proportionality of the punishment which stigmatised and marginalised them. The Government maintained that Article 9 only protects 'aspects of religious practice in a generally recognised form that were strictly a matter of conscience' and was not under an 'obligation to take positive measures to adapt its activities to the various manifestations of its citizens' philosophical or religious beliefs'. The European Commission maintained that Article 9 did not exempt the applicant from disciplinary rules applied generally and neutrally, and in addition (reminiscent of the European Commission's formulaic approach to issues of coercion) noted that the applicant had not been restricted in her freedom to manifest her religion or belief.[216] The European Court did not follow the European Commission's line of reasoning and disallowed the claim on the Court's finding that the parade was not contrary to the applicant's convictions. The Court also

---

[213] See, for example, *Bernard and others v. Luxembourg*, App. No. 17187/90 (1993) 75 D&R 57.

[214] *Valsamis v. Greece* (1997) 24 EHRR 294.   [215] *Ibid.*, at para. 34.

[216] *Ibid.*, at paras. 35–6.

noted that the applicant had already been granted fairly extensive exemption from religious education and the Orthodox Mass on the grounds of her own religious beliefs.[217] The Court therefore appears to have avoided any reasoning under Article 9 based upon manifestation. If this constituted a rejection of the European Commission's previous approach, it would have been better if this had been stated unequivocally, particularly as it marked a clear departure from previous decisions.

For example, in *C.J., J.J. & E.J. v. Poland*,[218] claims were made under Articles 3, 9 and 14 based on the alleged indoctrination of a twelve-year-old girl (the second applicant) whose exemption from Catholic instruction required her instead to wait in a corridor and be subjected to detailed questioning from those in authority. The European Commission accepted that the child might have felt emotional distress (though not sufficient to substantiate her claim under Article 3) but decided the Article 9 claim of indoctrination was inadmissible by virtue of the exemption from religious instruction that was available to her. The European Commission pointed to the fact that the applicant herself decided to attend religious instruction, without giving due consideration to whether this may have been the result of the coercive effect of stigmatisation which she had suffered. The threshold applicable to indoctrination in the case of Article 9 claims therefore appears to be extremely high. More importantly for present purposes the European Commission's approach in *C.J., J.J. & E.J. v. Poland* to Article 9 claims of interference with the *forum internum* is striking for its focus on manifestation. In addition to the claim of indoctrination, Article 9 claims were also made in relation to the compulsory disclosure of non-religious convictions through school reports, which indicated that religious instruction was omitted from the subjects chosen. The European Commission focused on Article 8, rather Article 9, recognising that the rights protected under Article 8 are subject to limitations, and it concluded that the applicant had failed to show that she had suffered inconveniences which would reach a sufficient degree of seriousness

---

[217] For discussions on accommodating the requirements of minority religious groups, see: J. Bell, 'Religious Observance in Secular Schools: A French Solution', 2 Ed & Law (1990) 121; M. Anwar, 'Young Muslims in Britain: Their Educational Needs and Policy Implications', in M. W. Khan (ed.), *Education and Society and the Muslim World*, Saudi Arabia: Hodder and Stoughton (1981); S. A. Ashraf, 'A View of Education – An Islamic Perspective', in B. O'Keeffe (ed.), *Schools for Tomorrow: Building Walls or Building Bridges*, London: Falmer (1988).

[218] *C.J., J.J. & E.J. v. Poland*, App. No. 23380/94, 84–A (1996) D&R 46.

for the purposes of Article 8. Yet most commentators would consider the compulsory revelation of one's convictions to be within the *forum internum* protection of Article 9. Even though all claims of violation of Article 9 were based on rights within the *forum internum*, the European Commission recited its understanding of the full breadth of Article 9, including protection given to aspects of the practice of a religion or belief. It then gave individual consideration to whether each applicant was prevented from expressing their religious beliefs.[219]

In short, the quest of the European institutions appears to be that of making appropriate discretion available to States whenever possible. However, this is inappropriate in the case of those provisions which are intended to be free of any limitation, such as the rights of parents to have their beliefs respected in the education of their children, the freedom from compulsion to reveal one's beliefs and, of course, other aspects of the *forum internum* within the core freedom of religion Articles. Any appeal to limitation provisions in Article 9 claims of indoctrination or coercion, when directly comparable to parental claims under Protocol 1, Article 2, is likely to produce striking inconsistency in the outcome of decisions made under each of the two provisions.

At Universal level, no equivalent attempt is evident in the practice of the Human Rights Committee, which throughout appears to have maintained a strict approach to Article 18(4) of the ICCPR. The Human Rights Committee has confirmed in paragraph 6 of General Comment No. 22 that the right in Article 18(4) of the ICCPR is related to the guarantees of the freedom to teach a religion or belief stated in Article 18(1),[220] and accordingly (in line with European jurisprudence) benefits parents alone in relation to the upbringing of their children.[221] However, such a right cannot be equated with manifestation of religion or belief through teaching since it would then be subject to the limitations in Article 18(3) and inconsistent with paragraph 8 of General Comment No. 22 which affirms that 'the liberty of the parents and

---

[219] See also X. *v. United Kingdom*, App. No. 8160/78 (1981) 22 D&R 27. When the applicant submitted that the United Kingdom should not operate a system in which a job applicant must indicate his religion and thus risk not being appointed because of his religious obligations, the Commission observed that 'the present case does not raise the general issue of the confidentiality of information concerning one's religion, but the question of whether an employee should inform his employer in advance that he will be absent during a part of the time for which he is engaged' (p. 36, para. 14).

[220] UN Doc. CCPR/C/SR. 1207 (1993), p. 6, para. 39 (Mr Dimitijevic).

[221] UN Doc. CCPR/C/SR. 1207 (1993), p. 9, para. 51 (Mr Sadi).

guardians to ensure religious and moral education cannot be restricted'.[222] (Although paragraph 6 of the General Comment No. 22 refers only to State rather than private schools, the issue is of less relevance to the private sector given the freedom of parents to choose between different schools.[223] However, it is still necessary to distinguish between schools with and those without a primary religious mission.)[224]

In its Optional Protocol decisions the Human Rights Committee has not invoked measures which permit State discretion in restricting parental rights under Article 18(4). In *Hartikainen v. Finland*[225] the Human Rights Committee considered the status of compulsory teaching of history of religion and ethics as an alternative to religious instruction for children whose parents were atheists. The author claimed that because the textbooks used in such classes were written by Christians, the teaching was unavoidably religious in nature. The Human Rights Committee did not consider that such compulsory instruction was itself incompatible with Article 18(4) of the ICCPR provided the alternative instruction was 'given in a neutral and objective way and respects the beliefs of the parents and guardians who do not believe in any religion'.[226] The requirements established by the Human Rights Committee in this case have been supplemented by General Comment No. 22 in paragraph 6 which notes that 'instruction in a particular religion or belief is inconsistent with article 18(4) unless provision is made for non-discriminatory exemptions or alternatives that would accommodate the wishes of parents and guardians'.

Similarly, in *A. and S.N. v. Norway*[227] the authors, who were humanists, contended that their daughter had been exposed to Christian influences in her nursery education in violation of Articles 18(1), (2), (4) and 26 the ICCPR. They challenged the Norwegian Day Nurseries Act of 1975 as amended in 1983 which contained a clause providing that 'the day

---

[222] For a claim that violation of Article 18(4) amounts to a restriction on the parents' manifestation, see *Arieh Hollis Waldman v. Canada*, Communication No. 694/1996 (views of 3 November 1999) (2000) 7(2) IHRR 368, para. 3.2.

[223] UN Doc. CCPR/C/SR. 1207 (1993), p. 7, para. 45 (Mr Prado Vallejo); *ibid.*, at p. 8, para. 46 (1993) (Mr Aguilar); UN Doc. CCPR/C/SR. 1209 (1993), p. 3, para. 6 (Mr Pocar).

[224] UN Doc. CCPR/C/SR. 1209 (1993), p. 3, para. 10 (Mrs Higgins); *ibid.*, at p. 4, para. 14 (Mr Ndiaye).

[225] *Hartikainen v. Finland*, Communication No. 40/1978 (views of 9 April 1981), UN Doc. A/36/40 (1981), p. 147.

[226] *Ibid.*, at para. 10.4.

[227] *A. and S.N. v. Norway*, Communication No. 224/1987 (decision of 11 July 1988), UN Doc. A/43/40 (1988), p. 246.

nursery shall help to give the children an upbringing in harmony with basic Christian values', as well as the implementing guidelines which note that 'Christian festivals are widely celebrated in our culture. Therefore, it is natural that day nurseries should explain the meaning of these festivals to the children'.[228] The authors objected to such practices as singing grace at all meals (because even if not obligatory, a six-year-old would follow the other children).[229] The Human Rights Committee ruled the claim inadmissible only on the grounds that domestic remedies had not been exhausted.

In neither case did the Human Rights Committee refer to any concept of 'indoctrination' or other strict hurdle below which State discretion is permitted in the interests of expediency in setting and planning the school curriculum. Also in neither case did the Human Rights Committee resort to analysis based on the manifestation of religion or belief. The Human Rights Committee appears to be unequivocal in its view that limitation provisions are inappropriate to Article 18(4) claims. (It did not have the opportunity to consider parallel claims by children under Article 18(1) on the same facts as those arising under Article 18(4) since, in the case of *Hartikainen v. Finland*, the claim was made by the author and other members of the Union of Free-Thinkers, rather than affected children.)

The issue of manifestation was, however, raised by the author in *Arieh Hollis Waldman v. Canada*,[230] based on a claim that by singling out Roman Catholic schools in Ontario for full State funding when none was available for other non-secular schools, such as the private Jewish school to which he was required to send his children, he was impaired, in a discriminatory fashion, in the enjoyment of the right to manifest his religion, including the freedom to provide a religious education for his children.[231] He also made a similar claim in relation to Article 18(4)

---

[228] *Ibid.*, at para. 2.1.
[229] See also P. Cumper, 'School Worship: Praying for Guidance', EHRLR (1998) 45. Cumper explores collective worship in schools and whether this is contrary to international human rights obligations and considers proposals for reform. For a comparison between United Kingdom and United States practice towards Christian education and worship in State schools, see J. W. Montgomery, 'Christian Education and Worship in State Schools: The American Perspective', 144 *Law & Justice* (2000) 41.
[230] *Arieh Hollis Waldman v. Canada*, Communication No. 694/1996 (views of 3 November 1999) (2000) 7(2) IHRR 368.
[231] Para. 3.2. For further discussion on the issue of State financial support, see B. Basdevant-Gaudement, 'Le Régime Juridique de l'École Privée et les Autônomiers dans l'Enseignement Public en France', in European Consortium for Church–State Research, *Church and State in Europe. State Financial Support. Religion and the School,*

taken together with Article 2. The Human Rights Committee confirmed that the ICCPR does not impose any obligation on States to fund religious schools but if it decides to do so, the funding must be made available without discrimination (unless the differentiation is justified by reasonable and objective criteria).[232] The Committee found a violation of Article 26 in that the traditional distinction made in public education to protect Roman Catholics in Ontario did not justify the present preferential treatment given to Roman Catholic schools. Accordingly, the Human Rights Committee did not need to address the author's claims based on Article 18 but in view of the indications given previously by the Human Rights Committee (for example in General Comment No. 22) it is unlikely that the Human Rights Committee would attempt to invoke limitation provisions to justify State measures. More will be said of discrimination below but it is worth noting in this context the emphasis placed by the Human Rights Committee on issues of discrimination within Article 18(4), reflected in the following statement of Mr Scheinin (concurring): 'In general, arrangements in the field of religious education that are in compliance with article 18 are likely to be in conformity with article 26

Milan: Giuffrè (1992), pp. 139–70. See also *Nam v. Korea*, Communication No. 693/1996 (decision of 28 July 2003), UN Doc. A/58/40 vol. 2 (2003) 390. The author was a national language (Korean literature) teacher in a Seoul middle school and representative of an organisation concerned with improving national language education. He claimed that the prohibition of non-governmental publication of middle school national language textbooks prevented him from pursuing publication of his curricular textbook in violation of Article 19. He pointed out that middle school teachers and students studying Korean as a national language rely almost exclusively on textbooks, and that writing such a curricular textbook was the only effective way of communicating his ideas concerning middle school national language education. He disputed that State authorship of textbooks is a better safeguard for 'political and religious neutrality' than if the authorship was granted to citizens (*ibid.*, para. 9.3). The Committee observed that the communication did not relate to a prohibition of non-governmental publication of textbooks but rather related to the author's allegation that there is no process of scrutiny in place for the purpose of submitting non-governmental publications for approval by the authorities, for their use as school textbooks. This therefore fell outside the scope of Article 19 (*ibid.*, para. 10).

[232] For further discussion on the role of religion in public education and alternative methods of preserving the denominational character of schools in a secular society, see R. A. Baer, and J. C. Carper, ' "To the Advantage of Infidelity", or How Not To Deal With Religion In America's Public Schools', 14(5) *Educational Policy* (2000) 600, and J. C. Carper, 'History, Religion and Schooling: A Context for Conversation', in J. T. Sears and J. C. Carper (eds.), *Curriculum, Religion and Public Education: Conversations for an Enlarging Public Square*, New York: Teachers' College Press (1998).

as well, because non-discrimination is a fundamental component in the test under Article 18(4).'[233]

The breadth of the Human Rights Committee's concerns under Article 18(4) is apparent in its examination of State reports. At the most general level, questions have frequently been asked with a view to determining whether parental wishes are respected in the education of their children[234] and whether any compulsion exists.[235] Conscious that the position of religion in schools may be pervasive, the Committee has been keen to evaluate the effect of a dominant religion in society.[236] It has emphasised that if instruction is provided in a particular religion against parental convictions then it must either be made optional, or an alternative according with those convictions must be provided.[237] The 'non-compulsory' option available to States means they will not have the burden or cost of having to provide the alternative instruction. The Committee has asked how easily alternative religious education could be obtained[238] and, in answer to questions raised by the Committee, States have on occasion emphasised the importance of providing suitably qualified teachers when alternative religious education is offered.[239]

The Special Rapporteur has also observed that in Brunei restrictions were allegedly imposed on the teaching of the history of religions and other religious subjects,[240] that in Pakistan[241] and the Maldives[242] school curricula included mandatory Islamic instruction for Muslim

---

[233] *Arieh Hollis Waldman v. Canada*, Communication No. 694/1996 (views of 3 November 1999) (2000) 7(2) IHRR 368, at 379, para. 3.

[234] UN Doc. A/33/40 (1978), p. 72, para. 425 (USSR); UN Doc. A/37/40 (1982), p. 33, para. 146 (Morocco); UN Doc. A/38/40 (1983), p. 24, para. 113 (Iceland); UN Doc. A/41/40 (1986), p. 90, para. 398 (Hungary); UN Doc. A/45/40 (1990), p. 26, para. 109 (USSR); UN Doc. A/45/40 (1990), p. 37, para. 156 (Portugal).

[235] UN Doc. A/34/40 (1979), p. 31, para. 127 (Bulgaria).

[236] UN Doc. A/34/40 (1979), p. 97, para. 412 (Finland); UN Doc. A/34/40 (1979), p. 47, para. 199 (Spain); UN Doc. A/35/40 (1980), p. 29, para. 135 (Iraq); UN Doc. A/41/40 (1986), p. 31, para. 145 (Sweden); UN Doc. A/44/40 (1989), p. 18, para. 82 (Norway).

[237] UN Doc. A/33/40 (1978), p. 40, para. 240 (Norway); UN Doc. A/34/40 (1979), p. 62, para. 263 (Ukrainian SSR); UN Doc. A/35/40 (1980), p. 29, para. 135 (Iraq); UN Doc. A/35/40 (1980), p. 11, para. 54 (Poland); UN Doc. A/47/40 (1994), p. 89, para. 377 (Colombia).

[238] UN Doc. A/35/40 (1980), p. 71, para. 314 (Hungary).

[239] UN Doc. A/35/40 (1980), p. 72, para. 315 (Hungary).

[240] UN Doc. E/CN.4/1998/6 (1998), para. 63(e) (Brunei).

[241] UN Doc. E/CN.4/2000/65 (2000), para. 79 (Pakistan).

[242] UN Doc. E/CN.4/2001/63 (2001), p. 28, para. 99 (Maldives).

students, that in Romania there were reports that members of the Baha'i community had been told by their religious teacher that they would be put in a lower class if they continued to follow lessons on the Baha'i religion,[243] and that in Greece, primary and secondary school curricula included compulsory instruction in the Orthodox religion for members of that faith but with questionable exemption for those who were non-observant, atheist or who had converted to another religion.[244] There were also said to be almost daily religious sermons in Greece hostile to the faith of the Jehovah's Witnesses, causing psychological trauma among young Jehovah's Witness children.[245]

Summary

It would appear that the Human Rights Committee adopts a stricter approach to the parental guarantee within Article 18(4) than the European institutions under Protocol 1, Article 2, which find a basis for accommodating State restrictions wherever possible. The Human Rights Committee's approach more readily suggests that the unrestricted nature of Article 18(4) is upheld. It has not yet had to decide parallel claims by parents (under Article 18(4)) and children (under Article 18(1)) so as to bear out any distinction between the rights in question. Nevertheless, there cannot be any logical basis, in the case of parallel claims, for subjecting the rights of children to limitation provisions and not the rights of parents.

For so long as the Strasbourg organs continue in their reluctance to uphold the absolute nature of unrestricted rights greater importance may attach to the use of other indirect means of protection, perhaps the most readily available being protection against discrimination.

The use of anti-discrimination measures to protect the forum internum

In appropriate circumstances, guarantees against discrimination may provide an effective means of protection for freedom of thought, conscience and religion regardless of whether there has been a violation of a substantive Article. It is well settled that no violation of a substantive

---

[243] UN Doc. E/CN.4/2004/63/Add.2 (2004), p. 13, para. 56 (Romania).
[244] UN Doc. E/CN.4/2001/63 (2001), p. 17, para. 49 (Greece).
[245] UN Doc. A/51/542/Add.1 (1996), paras. 93–5 (Greece).

Article need be established at all in cases involving discrimination, either under Article 14 of the European Convention[246] or Articles 2(1) and 26 of the ICCPR.[247] This is particularly important in view of the difficulties of establishing a violation of the *forum internum* discussed above.[248] There also appears to be far greater recognition, in the context of discrimination, for the right to enjoy the freedoms guaranteed without interference from private (as well as public) sources.

The array of anti-discrimination instruments that have been ratified can leave no doubt as to the widespread support for European and United Nations measures which condemn discrimination.[249] Of those

---

[246] The clearest statement to that effect still remains that of the Court in the *Belgian Linguistics case* in which it summarised the status of the Article 14 guarantee as follows: 'While it is true that this guarantee has no independent existence in the sense that under the terms of Article 14 it relates solely to "rights and freedoms set forth in the Convention", a measure which in itself is in conformity with the requirements of the Article enshrining the right or freedom in question may however infringe this Article when read in conjunction with Article 14 for the reason that it is discriminatory' (*Case relating to certain aspects of the laws on the use of languages in education in Belgium* (*the Belgian Linguistics case*) (Ser. A) No. 6 (1968) ECtHR at 33, para. 9).

[247] *S. W. M. Broeks v. The Netherlands*, Communication No. 172/1984 (views of 9 April 1987), UN Doc. A/42/40 (1987), p. 139; *L. G. Danning v. The Netherlands*, Communication No. 180/1984 (views of 9 April 1987), UN Doc. A/42/40 (1987), p. 151; *F. W. Zwaan-de Vries v. The Netherlands*, Communication No. 180/1984 (views of 9 April 1987), UN Doc. A/42/40 (1987), p. 160. For an illustration of discrimination based on the beliefs of the author, see *Ivan Somers v. Hungary*, Communication No. 566/1993 (views of 23 July 1996), UN Doc. A/51/40 vol. 2, (1997), p. 144. It concerned the confiscation of family property because of the anti-Communist beliefs of the author's parents and their membership of the local Jewish community with alleged 'Zionist connections'. The Human Rights Committee declared the claim inadmissible as far as Articles 14, 18, 19, 21, 22 and 24 were concerned but admissible in so far as it appeared to raise issues under Article 26: the failure to provide adequate compensation for a clearly recognisable group of individuals on the basis of political opinion. However on the facts no violation was found as the criteria applied were held to be objective and reasonable.

[248] The use of claims of discrimination without violation of a core freedom of religion Article is illustrated by the European Commission case of *Iglesia Bautista 'El Salvador' and Ortega Moratilla v. Spain*, App. No. 17522/90 (1992) 72 D&R 256.

[249] They include (in addition to the 1981 Declaration, the ICCPR (Article 26), and European Convention (Article 14)): the Convention on Equal Remuneration for Men and Women Workers for Work of Equal Value (1951) (Geneva, 29 June 1951, in force 23 May 1953), 165 UNTS 257; the Discrimination (Employment and Occupation) Convention (1958) (Geneva, 25 June 1958, in force 15 June 1960), 362 UNTS 31; the UNESCO Convention against Discrimination in Education (1960) (Paris, 15 December 1960, in force 22 May 1962), 429 UNTS 93; the International Convention on the Elimination of All Forms of Racial Discrimination (1965)

provisions relevant to the immediate discussion (Article 14 of the European Convention, Articles 2(1) and 26 of the ICCPR and Article 2 of the 1981 Declaration), the differences between them are significant.[250] Article 14 of the European Convention itself only provides assurance against discrimination in the enjoyment of rights and freedoms set out in the substantive Articles in Section I of the European Convention on the listed grounds, which includes religion. As the European Commission put it in *X. v. Germany*,[251] 'Article 14 is not directed against discrimination in general but only against discrimination in relation to the rights and freedoms guaranteed by the

(New York, 21 December 1965, in force 4 January 1969), 660 UNTS 195; the International Convention on the Suppression and Punishment of the Crime of Apartheid (1973) (New York, 30 November 1973, in force 18 July 1976), 1015 UNTS 243; and the Convention on the Elimination of All Forms of Discrimination against Women (1979) (New York, 18 December 1979, in force 3 September 1981), 1249 UNTS 13. See also the conclusion of the United Nations Seminar on the Encouragement of Understanding, Tolerance and Respect in Matters Relating to Freedom of Religion or Belief, held at Geneva between 3 and 14 December 1984: 'Each State, in accordance with its own constitutional system should provide, if necessary, adequate constitutional and legal guarantees for freedom of religion or belief consistent with the provisions of the Universal Declaration of Human Rights, the International Covenants on Human Rights and the Declaration on the Elimination of All Forms of Intolerance and of Discrimination Based on Religion and Belief with a view to ensuring that freedom of religion or belief is assured in a concrete manner, that discrimination on grounds of religion or belief is proscribed, and that adequate safeguards and remedies are provided against such discrimination' – UN Doc. ST/HR/ SER.A/16 (1984), para. 102.

[250] For general discussion on non-discrimination provisions, see: D. McGoldrick, *The Human Rights Committee: Its Role in the Development of the International Covenant on Civil and Political Rights*, Oxford: Clarendon Press (1994), pp. 281–300; A. F. Bayefsky, 'The Principle of Equality or Non-Discrimination in International Law', 11 HRLJ (1990) 1; W. McKean, *Equality and Discrimination Under International Law*, Oxford: Clarendon Press (1983); M. S. McDougal, H. D. Lasswell and L. Chen, *Human Rights and World Public Order*, New Haven/London: Yale University Press (1980) (Chapter 11 considers religious discrimination); J. Greenberg, 'Race, Sex and Religious Discrimination', in T. Meron (ed.), *Human Rights in International Law: Legal and Policy Issues*, Oxford: Clarendon Press (1984); B. G. Ramcharan, 'Equality and Nondiscrimination', in L. Henkin (ed.), *The International Bill of Rights The Covenant on Civil and Political Rights*, New York/Guildford: Columbia University Press (1981); M. J. Bossuyt, *L'Interdiction de la Discrimination dans le Droit International des Droits de l'Homme*, Brusssels: Établishment Émile Bruylant (1976); K. J. Partsch, 'Fundamental Principles of Human Rights: Self-Determination, Equality and Non-Discrimination', in K. Vasak and P. Alston (eds.), *The International Dimensions of Human Rights*, Westport, Conn.: Greenwood (1982); M. Banton, *International Action Against Racial Discrimination*, Oxford: Clarendon Press (1996).

[251] *X. v. Germany*, App. No. 8410/78 (1980) 18 D&R 216.

Convention'.[252] The European Convention does not contain a provision guaranteeing equality of law comparable to Article 26 of the ICCPR.[253] Article 14 of the European Convention is of equivalent scope to Article 2 of the ICCPR. The 1981 Declaration of course, unlike the European Convention and ICCPR, is declaratory and non-binding but is specific to religious intolerance. However, all such measures are significant in providing a basis for resisting discriminatory interference with the *forum internum*, perhaps the most common being punishment for holding particular beliefs and compulsion to reveal one's beliefs.

The greatest difference between European and Universal practice relates to the concept of the margin of appreciation which allows wider discretion to States under the European Convention than is permitted under the ICCPR. Within European jurisprudence, the margin of appreciation allows States latitude in interpreting and applying certain European Convention obligations (for reasons explained in *Handyside v. United Kingdom*)[254] such as when relying on the limitation provisions in Articles 8 to 11 of the European Convention, as well as when exercising discretion within Article 14. The margin of appreciation operates in applying the criterion of 'reasonable relationship of proportionality' under Article 14 when determining whether the differentiation constituting discrimination is justified. The test, as first stated in the *Belgian Linguistics* case is that,

> 'the principle of equality of treatment is violated if the distinction has no objective and reasonable justification. The existence of such a justification must be assessed in relation to the aim and effects of the measure under consideration, regard being had to the principles which normally prevail in democratic societies. A difference of treatment in the exercise of a right laid down in the Convention must not only pursue a legitimate aim: Article 14 (art. 14) is likewise violated when it is clearly established

---

[252] *Ibid.*, at 220.

[253] For the distinction between Articles 2 and 26 of the ICCPR, see para. 12 of General Comment No. 18 (37), UN Doc. CCPR/C/21/Rev 1./Add.1 (1989), reprinted in UN Doc. A/45/40 vol. 1, Annex VI (1990), p. 174.

[254] *Handyside v. United Kingdom* (Ser. A) No. 24 (1976) ECtHR: 'By reason of their direct and continuous contact with the vital forces of their countries, State authorities are in principle in a better position than the international judge to give an opinion on the exact content of these requirements as well as on the "necessity" of a "restriction" or "penalty" intended to meet them' (para. 48).

that there is no reasonable relationship of proportionality between the means employed and the aim sought to be realised.'[255]

As noted by Harris, O'Boyle and Warbrick, States are given a wide margin of appreciation in the evaluation of the evidence on which to base the decision whether an objective and rational justification exists.[256] However, recognised 'suspect categories' of discrimination will be difficult for States to justify, such as those based on illegitimacy,[257] sex,[258] and race[259] but religion has, surprisingly, so far not been placed in a suspect category. International human rights instruments may serve as authority for claiming such status although reliance has so far not been placed on the 1981 Declaration for that purpose.

Although the margin of appreciation doctrine developed by the European Court is a familiar part of European jurisprudence, attracting much criticism and comment,[260] the Human Rights Committee, by contrast, has rarely ever adopted such a concept and it is generally considered not to form part of the Human Rights Committee's repertoire. One reason suggested by Schmidt is the fear of reliance on arguments of cultural relativism by States drawn from ideologically and economically diverse societies.[261] The only clear instance of such use occurred in the context of Article 19 of the ICCPR in *Hertzberg and*

---

[255] *Case relating to certain aspects of the laws on the use of languages in education in Belgium (the Belgian Linguistics case)* (Ser. A) No. 6 (1968) ECtHR, para. 10. See also *Chassagnou and others v. France* (2000) 29 EHRR 615, for the application of this test concerning the use of land in accordance with one's conscience.

[256] D. J. Harris, M. O'Boyle and C. Warbrick, *Law of the European Convention on Human Rights*, London: Butterworths (1995), at p. 479.

[257] *Marckx v. Belgium* (Ser. A) No. 31 (1979) ECtHR; *Inze v. Austria* (Ser. A) No. 126 ECtHR (1988).

[258] *Abdulaziz, Cabales and Balkandali v. United Kingdom* (Ser. A) No. 94 (1985) ECtHR.

[259] *East African Asians cases*, App. No. 4403/70 etc, (1981) 3 EHRR 76, 36 CD 92.

[260] For further discussion, see: S. Prebensen, 'The Margin of Appreciation and Articles 9, 10 and 11 of the Convention', 19 HRLJ (1998) 13 (Prebensen provides a general survey of the manner in which the doctrine has been applied in recent years); H. C. Yourow, *The Margin of Appreciation Doctrine in the Dynamics of European Human Rights Jurisprudence*, The Hague/London: Kluwer Law International (1996); T. A. O'Donnell, 'The Margin of Appreciation Doctrine: Standards in the Jurisprudence of the European Court of Human Rights', 4 HRQ (1982) 474.

[261] M. Schmidt, 'The Complementarity of the Covenant and the European Convention on Human Rights – Recent Developments', in D. J. Harris and S. Joseph (eds.), *The International Covenant on Civil and Political Rights and United Kingdom Law*, Oxford: Clarendon Press (1995), p. 657. See also P. R. Ghandhi, *The Human Rights Committee and the Right of Individual Communication, Law and Practice*, Aldershot: Ashgate (1998), pp. 311–14.

others v. Finland[262] and is isolated. Schmidt nevertheless suggests that a margin of appreciation of sorts may be evidenced by statements such as that made by the Human Rights Committee in *J.H.W. v. The Netherlands*[263] that 'social security legislation usually lags behind socio-economic developments'.[264] Without allowing States a margin of appreciation, the Human Rights Committee applies a test entailing 'reasonable and objective criteria' (*S.W.M. Broeks v. The Netherlands*),[265] which has been explained in General Comment No. 18 (37) as follows: '[T]he Committee observes that not every differentiation of treatment will constitute discrimination, if the criteria for such differentiation are reasonable and objective and if the aim is to achieve a purpose which is legitimate under the Covenant.'[266]

In reality, a number of differences may be discerned between European and Universal practice concerning the approach taken first, to differential treatment, and secondly, the application of the 'reasonable' and 'objective' criteria, both of which have significance to issues affecting the *forum internum*.

Differential treatment

The European Commission has typically taken a fairly literal approach to the issue of differential treatment as a basis for rendering claims inadmissible, comparable to that of the Human Rights Committee. This has only recently been softened by the European Court's increased willingness to admit more widely than before claims based on differential treatment, as well as those based on the failure of States to make appropriate differentiation.[267]

---

[262] *Hertzberg and others v. Finland*, Communication No. R.14/61 (views of 2 April 1982), UN Doc. A/37/40 (1982), p. 161: 'It has to be noted, first, that public morals differ widely. There is no universally applicable common standard. Consequently, in this respect, a certain margin of appreciation must be accorded to the responsible national authorities' (para. 10.3).

[263] *J.H.W. v. The Netherlands*, Communication No. 501/1992 (decision of 16 July 1993) (1994) 1(2) IHRR 39.

[264] *Ibid.*, at para. 5.2.

[265] *S.W.M. Broeks v. The Netherlands*, Communication No. 172/1984 (views of 9 April 1987), UN Doc. A/42/40 (1987), p. 139, at para. 13.

[266] Para. 13 of General Comment No. 18 (37), UN Doc. CCPR/C/21/Rev 1./Add.1 (1989), reprinted in UN Doc. A/45/40 vol. 1, Annex VI (1990), p. 174.

[267] For further discussion on differential treatment, see: J. Edwards, 'Preferential Treatment and the Right to Equal Consideration', in P. Cumper and S. Wheatley (eds.), *Minority Rights in the 'New' Europe*, The Hague/Boston: Martinus Nijhoff (1999); S. Fredman, 'Equality Issues', in B. S. Markesinis (ed.), *The Impact of the Human Rights Bill on*

A number of European Commission decisions reflect a mechanical approach to differential treatment. In *Van den Dungen v. The Netherlands*,[268] the applicant's claim under Article 14 (in conjunction with Articles 9 and 10) was directed against an injunction granted to prevent him pressing his religious views in a manner likely to offend those attending an abortion clinic. He based his Article 14 claim on the fact that in Holland it is normal to be addressed and handed leaflets by all kinds of people without the Dutch authorities taking measures to stop this. However, it was fatal to his claim that he did not allege that activities similar to those carried out by him in the vicinity of the clinic would not have been subject to an injunction if carried out by other people, as he had therefore failed to demonstrate differential treatment.[269] Similarly, in *X. v. United Kingdom*,[270] the European Commission noted in connection with the Muslim school teacher's claim under Article 14 (in conjunction with Article 9) that he had not claimed that he

> 'was either individually or as a member of his religious community treated less favourably by the education authorities than individuals or groups of individuals placed in comparable situations. The applicant refers in his submissions to the position of Jewish *children*, but he has not shown that other *teachers* belonging to religious minorities, e.g. Jewish teachers, received a more favourable treatment than he himself.'[271]

Although this suggests that differential treatment should be measured carefully across analogous minority groups, the European Commission has generally concluded that all religious communities are comparable, without much reference to the unusual effect that the uniform application of a given restriction may have on a particular group. The claim in *Konttinen v. Finland*[272] concerned the dismissal of a Seventh Day Adventist by the State Railways for occasionally leaving his Friday afternoon shift at sunset, in accordance with his Sabbath beliefs. This

---

English Law, Oxford: Oxford University Press (1998); S. L Carter, 'The Resurrection of Religious Freedom', 107.1 Harv L Rev (1993–4) 118.

[268] *Van den Dungen v. The Netherlands*, App. No. 22838/93 (1995) 80 D&R 147.

[269] *Ibid.*, at 152.

[270] *X. v. United Kingdom*, App. No. 8160/78 (1981) 22 D&R 27.

[271] *Ibid.*, at 38. See also the comments of Mr Wennergren in the drafting of para. 5 of General Comment No. 22, pointing out that certain forms of employment, such as jobs involving constant supervision, could not be performed by those who were required by their beliefs to stop every hour for prayer (UN Doc. CCPR/C/SR. 1166 (1992), p. 12, para. 80).

[272] *Konttinen v. Finland*, App. No. 24949/94 (1996) 87 D&R 68.

followed the employer's refusal to assign him to an earlier shift. The European Commission noted that the Finnish legislation providing for a weekly day of rest on Sunday does not guarantee to members of all religious communities any absolute right to have a particular day regarded as their holy day, and ruled that the applicant had not been treated differently from members of other religious communities.[273] It may be said that such an approach understates the differential impact of legislation applied uniformly, as emphasised by the applicant in *Stedman v. United Kingdom*,[274] who was an evangelical Christian who resisted the imposition of Sunday duties in her employment in a travel agency. The European Commission accepted that the applicant was dismissed for refusing to work on a Sunday. It attributed the dismissal not to her religious convictions as such but her refusal to agree to newly proposed contractual terms. The Commission concluded that there was no appearance that the applicant was treated in any way differently from employees of any other religious conviction.[275]

However, a new approach appears to be heralded by the European Court in the case of *Thlimmenos v. Greece*.[276] A Jehovah's Witness challenged his exclusion from the Greek Institute of Chartered Accountants as a result of his felonious conviction and imprisonment some years before for his conscientious objection to wearing a uniform at a time of military mobilisation. The applicant's claim was not based on differential treatment between convicted criminals and others, but the lack of appropriate distinction in Article 22(1) of the Civil Servants Code in barring the appointment of all convicted felons. As the European Court noted, he was treated like any other person convicted of a felony even though his criminal conviction resulted from the exercise of his freedom of religion. The European Court did not consider it necessary to examine whether his original conviction amounted to violation of Article 9. Instead, it focused on Article 14 and introduced an important distinction between discrimination through differential treatment and discrimination through failure to differentiate appropriately:

> 'The Court has so far considered that the right under Article 14 not to be discriminated against in the enjoyment of the rights guaranteed under the Convention is violated when States treat differently persons in analogous situations without providing an objective and reasonable justification.

---

[273] *Ibid.*, at 76.
[274] *Stedman v. United Kingdom*, App. No. 29107/95, 89–A (1997) D&R 104.
[275] *Ibid.*, at 109.   [276] *Thlimmenos v. Greece* (2001) 31 EHRR 411.

> However, the Court considers that this is not the only facet of the prohibition of discrimination in Article 14. The right not to be discriminated against in the enjoyment of the rights guaranteed under the Convention is also violated when States without an objective and reasonable justification fail to treat differently persons whose situations are significantly different.'[277]

Accordingly, since a criminal conviction for conscientious objection to wearing the military uniform does not imply any moral turpitude, the applicant's exclusion on the ground that he was an unfit person was not justified. The imposition of a further sanction beyond the term of imprisonment he had already served was disproportionate and did not pursue a legitimate aim. As a result, the European Court found that there existed no objective and reasonable justification 'for not treating the applicant differently from other persons convicted of a felony'.[278]

The European Commission's traditional analysis may therefore require reconsideration. The European Court's approach to discrimination based on identical treatment may, for example, assist applicants in a similar position to those in *Christians against Racism and Fascism v. United Kingdom* in which all street demonstrations were prohibited because of the public order risks of a violent counter-demonstration, even though the applicants' demonstration on its own would have been peaceable. This might also be supported by the positive obligations on States to protect Convention rights against interference from private sources recognised by the European Commission, *inter alia*, in *Scientology Kirche Deutschland v. Germany*.[279]

In Optional Protocol decisions the Human Rights Committee has traditionally applied similar principles of differential treatment under Article 26 of the ICCPR and Article 2(1) to those of the European Commission.[280] Thus, in *M.J.G. v. The Netherlands*,[281] the author

---

[277] *Ibid.*, at para. 44.   [278] *Ibid.*, at para. 47.
[279] *Christians against Racisim and Fascism v. United Kingdom*, App. No. 8440/78 (1980) 21 D&R 138; *Scientology Kirche Deutschland v. Germany*, App. No. 34614/96, 89–A (1997) D&R 163. See also *Plattform 'Ärzte für das Leben' v. Austria* (Ser. A) No. 139 (1988) ECtHR. For the treatment of the Church of Scientology in various countries, see M. Browne, 'Should Germany Stop Worrying and Love the Octopus? Freedom of Religion and The Church of Scientology in Germany and the United States', *Indiana International and Comparative Law Review* (1998) 155.
[280] McGoldrick takes the view that the Human Rights Committee applies the same criteria in the context of Article 2(1) as Article 26: McGoldrick, *The Human Rights Committee*, at p. 284.
[281] *M.J.G. v. The Netherlands*, Communication No. 267/1987 (decision of 24 March 1988), UN Doc. A/43/40 (1988), p. 271.

unsuccessfully claimed to be a victim of discrimination on the ground of 'other status' because, 'being a soldier during the period of his military service, he could not appeal against a summons like a civilian'. The Human Rights Committee declared the claim inadmissible noting (in line with early European Commission decisions) that the author had not claimed that the State penal procedures were not being applied equally to all citizens serving in the Netherlands armed forces.[282] This was followed in *H.A.E.d.J. v. The Netherlands*[283] in which the author claimed discrimination because as a conscientious objector he was not treated as a civilian but rather as a conscript and was thus ineligible for supplementary allowances under the General Assistance Act. The Human Rights Committee confirmed that there is no entitlement to be paid as if one were still in private civilian life and that Article 26 does not extend to differences that result from the uniform application of laws in the allocation of social security benefits. This would be consistent with the European Commission's line of reasoning.

One of the most conservative statements on the uniform application of general laws was provided in *K. Singh Bhinder v. Canada*:[284] 'the concept of freedom of religion only comprises freedom from State interference but no positive obligation for States Parties to provide special assistance to grant waivers to members of religious groups which would enable them to practise their religion'. However, in General Comment No. 18 (37), the Human Rights Committee went out of its way to emphasise that the principle of equality is not synonymous with equal treatment but requires differentiation in certain circumstances:

> 'the principle of equality sometimes requires States parties to take affirmative action in order to diminish or eliminate conditions which cause or help to perpetuate discrimination prohibited by the Covenant. For example, in a State where the general conditions of a certain part of the population prevent or impair their enjoyment of human rights, the State should take specific action to correct those conditions.'[285]

---

[282] *Ibid.*, at para. 3.2.

[283] *H.A.E.d.J. v. The Netherlands*, Communication No. 297/1988 (decision of 30 October 1989), UN Doc. A/45/40 vol. 2 (1990), p. 176. See also *B.d.B. et al. v. The Netherlands*, Communication No. 273/1988 (decision of 30 March 1989), UN Doc. A/44/40 (1989), p. 286.

[284] *K. Singh Bhinder v. Canada*, Communication No. 208/1986, (views of 9 November 1989), UN Doc. A/45/40 vol. 2 (1990), p. 50, at para. 4.5.

[285] Para. 10 of General Comment No. 18 (37), UN Doc. CCPR/C/21/Rev 1./Add.1 (1989), reprinted in UN Doc. A/45/40 vol. 1, Annex VI (1990), p. 174. A stict concept of 'aggravated discrimination' has been devised, applicable to situations where the effects

This is consistent with what Krishnaswami noted in the Universal context when he observed that 'since each religion or belief makes different demands on its followers, a mechanical approach to the principle of equality which does not take into account the various demands will often lead to injustice and in some cases even to discrimination'.[286]

'Reasonable' and 'objective' criteria

In the context of discriminatory exemption from religious education, the European Commission has invariably found objective and reasonable justification for distinctions between pupils belonging to those religious communities which have received Government permission to provide substitute religious education and those which have not (*Angeleni v. Sweden*),[287] as well as distinctions between children with religious convictions and those with non-religious convictions (*Bernard and others v. Luxembourg*).[288] A strict approach by the Human Rights Committee appears to be reflected in its examination of State reports,[289] as well as under Optional Protocol decisions, having had opportunity recently to examine the potential for State funding of denominational schools to constitute discrimination against other religions in *Arieh Hollis Waldman v. Canada*.[290] The Human Rights Committee concluded that the differences in treatment between Roman Catholic religious schools, which are publicly funded as a distinct part of the public education system, and Jewish schools, which are private by necessity, could not be considered reasonable and objective.[291]

There appear to be a number of points of departure between European and United Nations practice when considering conscientious

---

of discrimination are exacerbated by multiple identities (race, religion, membership of a minority) – see the study by the Special Rapporteur entitled 'Racial and religious discrimination: identification and measures' UN Doc. A/CONF.189/PC.1/7 (2000) (also at UN Doc. A/55/280, paras. 111–17 (2000)), provided to the Preparatory Committee for The World Conference Against Racism, Racial Discrimination, Xenophobia and Related Intolerance.

[286] A. Krishnaswami, 'Study of the Discrimination in the Matter of Religious Rights and Practices', 11 NYUJ Int'l L & Pol (1978) 227, at 230.

[287] *Angeleni v. Sweden*, App. No. 10491/83 (1986) 51 D&R 41.

[288] *Bernard and others v. Luxembourg*, App. No. 17187/90 (1993) 75 D&R 57.

[289] UN Doc. A/35/40 (1980), p. 37, para. 169 (Canada); UN Doc. A/49/40 vol. 1 (1994), p. 32, para. 158 (Costa Rica); UN Doc. A/36/40 (1981), p. 76, para. 360 (Norway); UN Doc. A/36/40 (1981), p. 17, para. 82 (Denmark); UN Doc. A/51/40 vol. 1 (1997), p. 31, para. 204 (Zambia).

[290] *Arieh Hollis Waldman v. Canada*, Communication No. 694/1996 (views of 3 November 1999) (2000) 7(2) IHRR 368.

[291] *Ibid.*, at para. 10.5.

objection to military service, and these have yielded interesting conclusions for certain aspects of the *forum internum*. On the extent to which differentiation may be made between separate categories of conscientious objectors (for example, to favour Jehovah's Witnesses whose objections are well recognised), the practice of the Human Rights Committee is at variance with that of the European Commission. In *N. v. Sweden*,[292] the European Commission upheld the pragmatic requirement of membership of a particular religious community as a precondition to exemption from military service, on the grounds that being a Jehovah's Witness constitutes strong evidence that objections to compulsory service are based on genuine religious convictions where no comparable evidence exists in regard to others.[293] Contrary to this approach, the Human Rights Committee stated in *Brinkhof v. The Netherlands*[294] that 'the exemption of only one group of conscientious objectors and the inapplicability of exemptions for all others cannot be considered reasonable' and that 'when a right of conscientious objection to military service is recognised by a State, no differentiation shall be made among conscientious objectors on the basis of the nature of their particular beliefs'.[295] The Human Rights Committee was also of the opinion that States should 'give equal treatment to all persons holding equally strong objections to military and substitute service'.[296]

Furthermore, the Human Rights Committee's approach to the duration of alternative service appears to have undergone revision recently to a tighter standard than that under Article 14 of the European Convention. At one time, both the European Commission (in such cases as *N. v. Sweden* and *Autio v. Finland*)[297] and the Human

---

[292] *N. v. Sweden*, App. No. 10410/83 (1985) 40 D&R 203.

[293] See also *Tsirlis and Kouloumpas v. Greece* (1998) 25 EHRR 198; *Raninen v. Finland*, App. No. 20972/92, 84–A (1996) D&R 17; *Grandrath v. Germany*, App. No. 2299/64, 10 YBECHR (1967), page 626; *Suter v. Switzerland*, App. No. 11595/85, 51 (1986) D&R 160.

[294] *Brinkhof v. The Netherlands*, Communication No. 402/1990 (decision of 27 July 1993), UN Doc. A/48/40 vol. 2 (1993), (1994) 14 HRLJ 410.

[295] *Ibid.*, at para. 9.3.

[296] *Ibid.*, at para. 9.4. This is reinforced in para. 11 of General Comment No. 22: 'When this right [of conscientious objection] is recognized by law or practice, there shall be no differentiation among conscientious objectors on the basis of the nature of their particular beliefs; likewise, there shall be no discrimination against conscientious objectors because they have failed to perform military service.' See also UN Doc. A/58/296 (2003), p. 13, paras. 71–2 (Kyrgyzstan).

[297] *N. v. Sweden*, App. No. 10410/83 (1985) 40 D&R 203; *Autio v. Finland*, App. No. 17086/90 (1991) 72 D&R 245.

Rights Committee (in *Aapo Jarvinen v. Finland*)[298] considered that a longer term of substitute service benefited the individual in not having to demonstrate the genuineness of his convictions. However, in *Frederic Foin v. France*,[299] the Human Rights Committee decided that where the sole aim of a term of alternative service of twice the length of military service is to test the sincerity of the individual's convictions, it is not based on reasonable and objective criteria.[300] However, it would allow differences applying such criteria as the nature of the specific service concerned or the need for special training in order to accomplish that service. The individual view of Mr Bertil Wennergren in *Aapo Jarvinen v. Finland* is particularly interesting in that he considered the effect of compelling conscientious objectors to sacrifice twice as much of their liberty in comparison to those who are able to perform military service on the basis of their belief to be not only unjust and counter to the requirement of equality before the law laid down in Article 26 but, in his view, it also failed to comply with the provisions of Article 18(2). Obliging conscientious objectors to perform 240 extra days of national service on account of their beliefs is to impair their freedom of religion or to hold beliefs of their choice. In his view, therefore, such discrimination could constitute interference with the *forum internum*.

Paradoxically, a narrowing of State discretion in distinguishing between the duration of military and civilian service would have the unexpected effect of increasing the likelihood of interference with the *forum internum*. Those dissenting in *Frederic Foin v. France* (Mssrs Ando, Klein and Kretzmer) preferred States to be free to adopt mechanisms which did not require the individual examination of applications for exemption, as this inevitably would involve intrusion

---

[298] *Aapo Jarvinen v. Finland*, Communication No. 295/1988 (views of 25 July 1990), UN Doc. A/45/40 vol. 2 (1990), p. 101.

[299] *Frederic Foin v. France*, Communication No. 666/1995 (views of 3 November 1999), (2000) 7(2) IHRR 354. See also: *Richard Maille v. France* Communication No. 689/1996 (views of 10 July 2000), (2000) 7(4) IHRR 947; *Paul Westerman v. The Netherlands*, Communication No. 682/1996 (views of 3 November 1999), (2000) 7(2) IHRR 363.

[300] See also the comments of the Human Rights Commmittee in examining State reports: UN Doc. A/57/40 vol. 1 (2002), p. 56, para. 78(18) (Georgia); UN Doc. A/58/40 vol. 1 (2003), p. 44, para. 79(15) (Estonia); UN Doc. A/59/40 vol. 1 (2004), p. 23, para. 64(17) (Russian Federation), p. 28, para. 65(15) (Latvia), p. 38, para. 67(17) (Colombia), p. 56, para. 71(17) (Lithuania), and p. 72, para. 75(21) (Serbia and Montenegro).

into matters of privacy and conscience. This serves as a reminder of the strict standard laid down by the Human Rights Committee in relation to compulsion to reveal one's beliefs, reflected in paragraph 3 of General Comment No. 22, which stipulates that '[i]n accordance with Articles 18(2) and 17, no one can be compelled to reveal his thoughts or adherence to a religion or belief'.[301] It is also reflected in the Human Rights Committee's examination of State reports.[302] The issue has also been monitored closely by the Special Rapporteur on religious intolerance.[303]

---

[301] For the preparation of para. 3 of General Comment No. 22, see UN Doc. CCPR/C/SR. 1166 (1992). Mr Sadi believed that freedom from compulsion to reveal one's thoughts or adherence to a religion or belief might cause a real problem in some societies where, for example, schools had to be informed of a child's religion in order to plan his education, the authorities frequently needed to know a citizen's religion in order to prepare his identity documents, and medical care sometimes had to take into account a patient's religion (for example the use of blood transfusions). States parties in his view could therefore be authorised to request such information when necessary and provided that it did not violate the fundamental rights of individuals (p. 2, para. 5), a view supported in principle by Mr El Shafei (p. 4, para. 15). However, there is an important gulf between a right to request details of someone's beliefs and compulsion to reveal their beliefs. Mrs Higgins suggested inclusion of reference to Article 17 of the ICCPR, since the right to freedom of thought, religion or belief was clearly a private matter (pp. 2–3, para. 6). Mr Dimitrijevic had no objection to mentioning Article 17 although as history had demonstrated that authorities had always sought to force individuals to reveal their thoughts or beliefs, he felt that it was preferable to guarantee the right of each individual to decline to reveal his thoughts or beliefs if he so desired, adding that there were circumstances in which a person could be compelled by law to reveal his opinions and in which he would run a risk if he revealed that he held a particular opinion. Such was the case, for example, in Korea if a person was a communist (p. 3, para. 7 and p. 4, para. 17). Mr Prado Vallejo wanted it to be specified that States were not entitled to require individuals to indicate, for example on administrative forms, their adherence to a particular religion (p. 4, para. 13). Although appreciating that religion was a private matter, like thought, a person could, in the opinion of Mr Lallah, be obliged to divulge his thoughts or beliefs in order to take an oath before testifying in court, when the wording of the oath varied depending on whether a person was an atheist or a believer for example, or in a tax declaration when a contribution was levied for churches. It was thus desirable to define the meaning of 'arbitrary or unlawful interference' if those notions were placed in the context of Article 18 (pp. 4–5, para. 20).

[302] UN Doc. A/47/40 (1992), p. 57, para. 247 (Ecuador). Members asked in which legal cases individuals were required to declare their religion or belief.

[303] The Special Rapporteur noted that Greece had voted in a law making it compulsory for citizens to declare their religion on their identity cards (UN Doc. E/CN.4/1995/91 (1992), p. 42; UN Doc. E/CN.4/1993/62 (1993), p. 78, para. 48 (Greece)). The Special Rapporteur drew to the attention of Greece the resolution of the European Parliament on the compulsory mention of religion on identity cards which states: 'C. whereas the compulsory mention of religion on identity documents violates the fundamental

The significance of recognising such a right within the *forum internum* was highlighted by Harris, O'Boyle and Warbrick when commenting as follows:

> 'Perhaps the explanation for this very strong protection of freedom of thought, conscience and religion is that there is no good reason why the state needs the information (though there are bad ones). If there were conceivably good reasons, possibly in the context of national security, for the state to know what a person believes, the resistance to giving it the power to do so reflects the shade of the Inquisition and the coercive investigations of modern totalitarian regimes.'[304]

freedoms of the individual set out in the Universal Declaration of Human Rights and the European Convention on Human Rights ... E. recalling that freedom of opinion and religious freedom are part of the foundations of a constitutional State and are the exclusive province of human conscience ... 1. Calls on the Greek government to amend the current legal provisions once and for all to abolish any mention, even optional, of religion on new Greek identity cards and not to bow to pressure from the Orthodox hierarchy ... 2. Considers that the role which religion has played or still plays in any society, however important it may be and without value judgements, in no way justifies the requirement to mention religion on an identity card' (UN Doc. A/51/542/Add.1 (1996), para. 30 (Greece)). In Pakistan, the decision to have the religion of all citizens indicated on their identification cards was met with real concern on the part of minority religious groups in Pakistan (UN Doc. E/CN.4/1995/91/Add.1 (1994), p. 52, para. 19 (Pakistan)). See also UN Doc. E/CN.4/1996/95/Add.1 (1996), paras. 22–3 and 85 (Pakistan). In Syria, identity cards of the members of the Jewish community were said to be marked in blue and to contain the word Mousawi (Jew) while no such indications exist on the identity cards of members of the Syrian Muslim and Christian communities (UN Doc. E/CN.4/1993/62 (1993), p. 98, para. 63 (Syria)). On a visit to Iran, the Special Rapporteur observed that non-Muslim owners of grocery shops are required to indicate their religious affiliation on the front of their shops, which he recommended be eliminated (UN Doc. E/CN.4/1996/95/Add.2 (1996), paras. 44 and 100 (Iran). The Special Rapporteur also sent an urgent appeal to Afghanistan asking the Supreme Chief of the Taliban not to issue a decree requiring non-Muslims to wear a distinctive emblem on their clothing, because of its discriminatory nature (UN Doc. A/56/253 (2001), p. 9, para. 30 (Afghanistan)). Finally, the Special Rapporteur observed that in Egypt identity cards may only be issued to followers of one of the three religions recognised by the Constitution and pointed out 'that the mention of religion on an identity card is a controversial issue and appears to be somewhat at variance with the freedom of religion or belief that is internationally recognized and protected. Moreover, even supposing that it was acceptable to mention religion on an identity card, it could only be claimed that the practice had any legitimacy whatsoever if it was non-discriminatory: to exclude any mention of religions other than Islam, Christianity or Judaism would appear to be a violation of international law' (UN Doc. E/CN.4/2004/63 (2004), p. 10, para. 42 (Egypt)).

[304] Harris, O'Boyle and Warbrick, *Law of the European Convention*, at p. 361.

In practice, protection against discrimination is one of the most effective safeguards for minorities.[305] Concerns about possible discrimination towards minority religious groups have frequently been expressed by the Human Rights Committee, particularly in countries with a dominant State religion, such as Sri Lanka[306] (when members of the Committee wished to know whether Buddhism enjoyed privileged treatment as compared with other religious denominations), Panama[307] (where the issue was whether the special status accorded to Christianity did not in fact constitute discrimination against other religions), Argentina[308] (when members of the Committee wished to know what the procedures for legal recognition of religious denominations were, how many non-Catholic denominations had been registered, and whether, once registered they were equal under the law with the Roman Catholic Church), and Syria[309] (where questions were put on measures taken to guarantee freedom of religion and belief so as to avoid discrimination against Christianity and Judaism). Similar issues have been raised with Israel,[310] Norway,[311] Iraq,[312] Peru[313] and Jordan,[314] and with those countries with a dominant atheist tradition.[315]

---

[305] For further reading generally on the position of religious minority groups as targets of discrimination, see: D. Fottrell and B. Bowring (eds.), *Minority and Group Rights in the New Millennium*, The Hague/London: Martin Nijhoff (1999); B. P. Vermeulen, 'The Freedom of Thought, Conscience and Religion. Reflections on Article 9(1) of the European Convention on Human Rights, in Particular with Regard to the Position of Minorities', in J. A. Smith and L. F. Zwaak (eds.), *International Protection of Human Rights Selected Topics: A Compilation of Contributions for Training Courses*, Utrecht: Utrecht Studie en Informatiecentrum Mensenrechten (1995); K. Rimanque, 'Report on Freedom of Conscience and Minority Groups', in Council of Europe, *Freedom of Conscience*; European Consortium for Church–State Research, *The Legal Status of Religious Minorities in the Countries of the European Union* (Proceedings of the meeting in Thessaloniki, 19–20 November 1993, European Consortium for Church–State Research, Milan: Giuffrè (1994); J. Bengoa, 'Existence and Recognition of Minorities', UN Doc. E/CN.4/Sub.2/AC.5/2000/WP.2 (2000); P. Thornberry, *International Law and the Rights of Minorities*, Oxford: Clarendon Press (1991); F. Capotorti, *Study on the Rights of Persons Belonging to Ethnic, Religious and Linguistic Minorities*, New York: United Nations Sales No. E. 91. XIV.2 (1991).

[306] UN Doc. A/46/40 (1991), p. 121, para. 480 (Sri Lanka).

[307] UN Doc. A/46/40 (1991), p. 112, para. 446 (Panama).

[308] UN Doc. A/45/40 (1990), p. 51, para. 224 (Argentina).

[309] UN Doc. A/32/44 (1977), p. 20, para. 115(i) (Syrian Arabic Republic).

[310] UN Doc. A/53/40 (1998), p. 49, para. 320 (Israel).

[311] UN Doc. A/44/40 (1989), p. 18, para. 81 (Norway).

[312] UN Doc. A/42/40 (1987), p. 99, para. 381 (Iraq).

[313] UN Doc. A/38/40 (1983), p. 63, para. 269 (Peru).

[314] UN Doc. A/37/40 (1982), p. 40, para. 180 (Jordan).

[315] UN Doc. A/33/40 (1978), p. 22, para.128 (Czechoslovakia); *ibid*., at p. 63, para. 379 (Yugoslavia).

More broadly, the Human Rights Committee has enquired about registration requirements for religious organisations in Lithuania and the distinctions made between different religious groups which could result in discrimination on religious grounds,[316] the discriminatory restrictions on certain religious groups in Morocco on the profession and practise of their beliefs,[317] legal discrimination against non-Muslims in Tunisia with respect to eligibility for public office,[318] and the unequal status of the Coptic community in Egypt.[319]

Summary

Non-discrimination provisions offer valuable indirect means of resisting interference with *forum internum* rights, indirect in the sense that the reliance is not placed on any direct guarantee (which has proved difficult under Article 9 of the European Convention because of the absolute nature of the *forum internum*).

The most obvious differences between United Nations and European standards in the area of discrimination lie, first, in the European concept of a margin of appreciation, which allows greater latitude to States and has no established counterpart in the ICCPR and, secondly, in the fact that the European Convention does not contain a provision guaranteeing equality of law comparable to Article 26 of the ICCPR. Trends at both United Nations and European levels indicate a degree of convergence towards greater acceptance of the conscientious implications of certain forms of compulsion, most notably compulsory military service. However, there are one or two points of departure in the context of conscientious objection to military service concerning the differentiation that may be made between separate categories of conscientious objectors and the duration of alternative service.

Conclusion

A review of European and Universal practice concerning protection for the *forum internum* demonstrates the habitual resolve on the part of the Strasbourg organs to allow States wide discretion, even in the case of interference with one of the most fundamental unrestricted rights. It has

---

[316] UN Doc. A/53/40 (1998), p. 32, para.175 (Lithuania).
[317] UN Doc. A/50/40 (1996), p. 27, para. 120 (Morocco).
[318] UN Doc. A/50/40 (1996), p. 23, para. 96 (Tunisia).
[319] UN Doc. A/39/40 (1984), p. 57, para. 301 (Egypt).

been argued in this chapter that this is partly attributable to a failure to develop a comprehensive regime relating to compulsion to act contrary to one's beliefs (whether in relation to military service, taxation, social security or other generally applicable laws). This, in turn, is grounded in fears of the consequences for the enforcement of generally applicable laws and the expectation that social disorder might result if all civic obligations were potentially open to challenge. Nevertheless, there is growing recognition that certain forms of compulsion to act contrary to one's belief that have long been considered to raise no implications for freedom of thought, conscience and religion (such as those concerning military service) fall squarely within Article 9 of the European Convention.

The early focus on manifestation by the European institutions had certain limited parallels within the practice of the Human Rights Committee although the number of cases coming before the European Commission and the consistency with which principles of manifestation were inappropriately applied to claims based on interference with the *forum internum* leave no doubt as to rationale for such European decisions (which cannot be said to operate within the Human Rights Committee), namely to allow State reliance on limitation provisions. In those cases of interference with the *forum internum* where it proved possible in the circumstances to avoid appealing artificially to principles of manifestation, such as where the applicant had an element of choice in avoiding the conflict of conscience, or where the compulsion in question appeared to have the sanction of a Convention Article, the European Commission deployed reasoning based fundamentally on available choice or the endorsement provided by that Article, combined with assertions of the neutrality of the compulsion. The decisions that have been most criticised in this chapter are those in which the European Commission faced a binary choice between recognising the *forum internum* and characterising the applicant's position in some way, no matter how inappropriately, as a form of manifestation. The European Court does not appear to have followed such a slavish approach to manifestation although it was disappointing at a time when the European Commission was seen to adopt a more realistic stance to the conscientious implications of tax payments in *Darby v. Sweden*, that the European Court in *Buscarini v. San Marino* missed a perfect opportunity to address in a coherent way the straightforward issue of compulsion to swear an oath according to beliefs that were not personally held.

The Human Rights Committee has less frequently and less obviously resorted to analysis based on manifestation to avoid upholding claims of *forum internum* violation and has taken the opportunity outside Optional Protocol claims to give due acknowledgement to certain *forum internum* rights. Consistent with the Human Rights Committee's greater willingness to admit that coercion to act contrary to belief falls within the *forum internum*, the Human Rights Committee has been prepared to acknowledge (in its examination of State reports) that the compulsory payment of church taxes from a person who does not want to pay or cannot afford to pay could lead them to renounce their religious faith. Similarly, when considering conscientious objection to military service, a member of the Committee considered that the effect of a prolonged term of alternative service could contravene the prohibition in Article 18(2) of the ICCPR.

Although there appears to be growing recognition of the *forum internum* in a variety of circumstances, particularly at United Nations level, this falls far short of a comprehensive, cohesive pattern of protection. In general, protection against coercion to act contrary to one's beliefs is undermined by Strasbourg organs, first, by a reluctance to recognise it as a right free of limitation provisions, secondly, by the insurmountable hurdle of framing claims in terms of manifestation (when this is patently not the substance of such claims), and thirdly, by a wide margin of appreciation in favour of States.

The preoccupation of the Strasbourg organs with State discretion is also evident in the approach taken to the limitation ground concerning protection of the rights of others and the developing notion of 'respect' for the religious beliefs of others. There remains a marked disparity between the willingness of the European institutions to give 'indirect' recognition to *forum internum* rights (or even to rights which are not traditionally acknowledged) when such rights are not the immediate subject matter of a claim but only arise incidentally in the context of 'the rights of others', and the apparent blindness to perceive issues relating to interference with the *forum internum* when asserted by the applicant in 'direct' claims of *forum internum* violation.

Furthermore, when faced with the unrestricted right of parents to have their convictions respected in the upbringing of their children (which the Human Rights Committee unequivocally treats as an absolute, unqualified right), a framework of protection was constructed around the concept of 'indoctrination' under the European Convention which confers extensive latitude upon States in relation to the school curriculum in all matters falling short of indoctrination. The higher the threshold for achieving indoctrination, the greater the discretion available to States.

It is therefore necessary to consider parallel means of protection when *forum internum* rights are at issue. Freedom from discrimination provides a useful basis on which to defend against interferences with the *forum internum*, without having artificially to establish an eligible form of manifestation. No violation need be established of a substantive Article in either the European Convention or the ICCPR and claims of discrimination are examined quite independently of limitation provisions that might be applicable in the case of violation of a substantive Article. In addition, when such limitation provisions do apply, discrimination claims might still arise if States discriminate in the reliance they place on those limitation provisions. Within European jurisprudence, the European Court's decision in *Thlimmenos v. Greece* is a significant landmark, particularly for extending discrimination principles to a failure to make appropriate differentiation.

In addition, the Court's consideration of the sanction imposed on the applicant in *Thlimmenos v. Greece* (by being excluded from a professional body in addition to his earlier term of imprisonment), touches on the important issue of interference with the *forum internum* through punishment for one's beliefs. This has proved notoriously difficult for applicants to assert, and no such claim has succeeded under Article 9 of the European Convention even though made on several occasions.[320] It is especially difficult to demonstrate that State interference is directed against particular beliefs when military discipline[321] or school regulations[322] require conformity to particular standards which are interpreted, as a matter of European jurisprudence, to fall within the discretion conferred on States. Punishment for membership of prohibited organisations is generally treated by both European and Universal organs under Articles relating to freedom of expression,[323] rather than freedom of conscience, supplemented where necessary (in view of the

---

[320] For example: *Kokkinakis v. Greece* (Ser. A) No. 260–A (1993) ECtHR; *Kalaç v. Turkey* (1999) 27 EHRR 552; *Yanasik v. Turkey*, App. No. 14524/89 (1993) 74 D&R 14.

[321] *Kalaç v. Turkey* (1999) 27 EHRR 552; *Yanasik v. Turkey*, App. No. 14524/89 (1993) 74 D&R 14.

[322] *Kjeldsen, Busk Madsen and Pedersen v. Denmark* (Ser. A) No. 23 (1976) ECtHR; *Valsamis v. Greece* (1997) 24 EHRR 294.

[323] *Vogt v. Germany* (Ser. A) No. 323–A (1995) ECtHR.

risks posed to democratic freedoms) by those Articles that prevent the misuse of guaranteed freedoms.[324]

Even compulsion to reveal one's beliefs, widely considered by commentators to fall within the *forum internum*, has been subjected to limitation provisions by the Strasbourg institutions, whether under Article 9(2) (*Gottesmann v. Switzerland*),[325] or other Articles (*C.J., J.J. & E.J. v. Poland*).[326] This may be contrasted with the stricter approach reflected by the Human Rights Committee in paragraph 3 of General Comment No. 22.

In short, the single most striking point that emerges in the discussion of the *forum internum* in this chapter is that the absolute, unimpugnable and fundamental nature of the *forum internum* has been undermined by European institutions through persistent avoidance of principles that permit the *forum internum* rights to be asserted by applicants.

---

[324] See, for example: *Kommunistische Partei Deutschland v. Germany*, App. No. 250/57, 1 Yearbook (1955–7) 222; *Glimmerveen and Hagenbeek v. The Netherlands*, App. No. 8348/78 and 8406/78 (1979) 18 D&R 187.

[325] *Gottesmann v. Switzerland*, App. No. 10616/83 (1984) 40 D&R 284.

[326] *C.J., J.J. & E.J. v. Poland*, App. No. 23380/94, 84–A (1996) D&R 46.

4

The right to manifest religious belief and applicable limitations

Introduction

This chapter will examine the scope of protection given to manifestations of religion or belief, as well as the corresponding limitation provisions that may be relied on by States to restrict such manifestations. It will highlight some of the differences between European and Universal jurisprudence, in particular, in the threshold at which manifestations of belief qualify for protection and in the breadth given to limitation provisions.

Although there is no established hierarchy distinguishing the variety of recognised forms of manifestation, there is no doubt that some (such as worship) are given greater importance than others (the wearing of religious headdress), at least in European practice. Certain forms of manifestation appear to be given little protection at all by the European organs even though clearly acknowledged at United Nations level. The causes of such apparent disparity deserve critical examination in the light of the widest available range of sources. The list of manifestations given in Article 6 of the Declaration on the Elimination of all Forms of Intolerance and of Discrimination based on Religion or Belief ('1981 Declaration') provides a useful framework for measuring current standards and assists a thematic analysis of different forms of manifestation. The chapter offers an evaluation of the scope of recognised expressions of religion or belief, stripped of considerations peculiar to the particular circumstances of individual cases.

Beliefs and their manifestation

The Universal Declaration on Human Rights ('Universal Declaration'), the International Covenant on Civil and Political Rights ('ICCPR'), the 1981 Declaration and European Convention for the Protection of Human Rights and Fundamental Freedoms ('European Convention') all give protection in the core freedom of religion Articles to the manifestation of beliefs according to a similar formula, namely 'freedom, either alone/individually or in community with others and in public or private, to manifest his religion or belief in teaching, practice, worship and observance'. In each Article, limitations on manifestation must be prescribed by law and be necessary to protect public safety, order, health or morals or the fundamental rights and freedoms of others.

Virtually no guidance on the nature of protected belief is provided in these Articles. In practice, a wide range of religious and non-religious beliefs is accommodated and the emphasis of decision-making is more on the existence of a proper connection between the religion or belief claimed and its manifestation through 'teaching, practice, worship and observance'. The detailed content of Article 6 of the 1981 Declaration represents the most precise articulation of different forms of religious manifestation in any international instrument and serves to identify the clearest instances of disparity between United Nations and European practice in the recognition given to different types of manifestation.

In the discussion that follows in this part of the chapter, a critique will be provided of the scope of beliefs qualifying for protection ('Protected beliefs'), the nexus that must be established between a belief and its manifestation ('Nexus between religion or belief and its manifestation'), the criteria for determining whether a State restriction constitutes interference ('Determination of whether there has been an interference'), and the activities that are habitually recognised to fall within the term 'teaching, practice, worship and observance' ('The scope of recognised manifestations of religion or belief').

Protected beliefs

The differences in drafting between the internal and external limbs of the key freedom of religion Articles (where the former refer to freedom of 'thought, conscience and religion' while the latter only refer to 'religion or belief') have caused some to speculate that the consequence is to exclude from the scope of manifestations of 'religion or belief' any expression of 'thought' or 'conscience'. For example, Malcolm Evans lucidly tabled the issue in the following way when commenting on Article 9 of the European Convention:

> 'Everyone has the right to freedom of thought, conscience and religion under Article 9. Article 9 also protects manifestations of religion or belief. Expressions of thought and conscience are protected by Article 10, as would

be any form of expression of a religion or belief which was not a "manifestation" for the purposes of Article 9. In the interests of clarity, it is best to reserve the term "manifestation" to describe a particular form of expression which is only relevant to "religion or belief". This means that whereas a religion or belief can be both expressed or manifested, a pattern of "thought" or "conscience" can only be "expressed". Therefore, there can be no question of manifesting or "actualizing" thought or conscience under Article 9. Expressions of thought or conscience are the exclusive preserve of Article 10.'[1]

Evans clearly considers the terminology of Article 9 to be critical to the interrelation between Articles 9 and 10 but whether this is merely a theoretical distinction (rooted only in the fact that 'religion or belief' – and not 'thought' or 'conscience' – are linked to the right to manifestation) or one that is meaningfully and consciously applied in practice is open to question. On any view it must not be forgotten that Article 9 of the European Convention derived its text from Article 18 of the Universal Declaration and was to be based as far as possible on that Article to reduce the risk of producing definitions that were inconsistent with those in United Nations instruments.[2] Liskofsky suggests that in the Universal Declaration the juxtaposition of 'thought' and 'conscience' with 'religion' was only a drafting compromise aimed at embracing non-religious (as well as religious) beliefs.[3] If this is the case, the dissociation of 'thought' and

---

[1] M. D. Evans, *Religious Liberty and International Law in Europe*, Cambridge: Cambridge University Press (1997), p. 285. Malcolm Evans advances similar arguments in the context of the ICCPR – M. D. Evans, 'The United Nations and Freedom of Religion: The Work of the Human Rights Committee', in R. J. Adhar (ed.), *Law and Religion*, Aldershot: Ashgate (2000), p. 40. However, not all commentators view the issue of importance. See, for example, C. D. de Jong, *The Freedom of Thought, Conscience and Religion or Belief in the United Nations (1946–1992)*, Antwerp/Groningen/Oxford: Intersentia-Hart (2000), pp. 20–34 and 78–80, in which de Jong (in the light of drafting history) separately examines the range of the terms 'thought, conscience and religion' and 'worship, observance, practice and teaching' protected in Article 18 of the Universal Declaration and Article 18 of the ICCPR but pays little attention to the more limited phraseology 'religion or belief' when considering manifestation. See also M. Nowak, *CCPR Commentary*, Kehl: N. P. Engel (1993), pp. 308–35. See also C. Evans, *Freedom of Religion Under the European Convention on Human Rights*, Oxford: Oxford University Press (2001), pp. 52–3 and pp. 133–67 for extensive discussion on manifestation and State discretion.

[2] See Chapter 1 under the heading 'Interrelation between the UN and European systems', pp. 7–9.

[3] In the context of the Universal Declaration, Liskofsky suggests that '[c]ombining "thought" and "conscience" with "religion", terms not defined nor even extensively discussed in the drafting, was a compromise intended, without saying so explicitly, to embrace atheists and other non-believers' (S. Liskofsky, 'The UN Declaration on the Elimination of Religious Intolerance and Discrimination: Historical and Legal

'conscience' from 'religion or belief' is of little consequence. Similarly, Lillich commented on Article 18 of the ICCPR that '[f]reedom of "thought" and "conscience", closely connected with freedom of "religion", are read as supporting the latter rather than as separate concepts worthy of independent analysis and development'.[4] It is at least arguable then that the phrase 'religion or belief' is to be broadly construed in light of the words 'thought' and 'conscience' that precede it. If it is not possible to go so far as to conclude that 'thought' and 'conscience' are sufficiently close to the concept of 'belief' as to be synonymous with 'belief' (an interpretation which would produce complete consistency with subsequent references in the Article to 'religion or belief'), it may still be possible to argue that the 'inner' realm, entitled to absolute protection, should be broader than formal 'belief', and would include intermediate results of belief formation that might be called 'thought' or 'conscience'.[5] It is also noteworthy that when Krishnaswami commented on Article 29 of the Universal Declaration in a progress report to the Sub-Commission he distinguished thought, conscience and religious belief from its outward manifestation without any narrowing only to religion or belief for that purpose:

> 'It will be noted that paragraph 2 of Article 29 admits of limitations of the freedoms set forth therein only for the purpose of protecting the rights and freedoms of others and the paramount interests of society as a whole. Freedom of thought, conscience and religious belief – as distinct from its outward manifestation – cannot affect the interests of third parties and society. The right to freedom of thought, conscience and religion is therefore an absolute right, and the limitations are applicable only to its outward manifestation.'[6]

Perspectives', in J. E. Wood (ed.), *Religion and the State: Essays in Honour of Leo Pfeffer*, Waco, Texas: Baylor University Press (1985), p. 456.

[4] R. B. Lillich, 'Civil Rights' in T. Meron (ed.), *Human Rights in International Law: Legal and Policy Issues*, Oxford: Clarendon Press (1984), at p. 159, n. 243. For further discussion, see B. G. Tahzib, *Freedom of Religion or Belief: Ensuring Effective International Legal Protection*, The Hague/London: Martinus Nijhoff Publishers (1996), pp. 72–3.

[5] P. W. Edge similarly does not draw a clear distinction between 'thought' or 'conscience' and 'belief' – 'It seems improbable that the categories of belief in the Article are to be defined and protected as separate entities. At the very least, the structure of the Article makes this difficult. Article 9(1) refers to "thought, conscience and religion", while Article 9(2) refers to "religion or belief". While part of this difference – the omission of thought from the qualifying second article – ensures that freedom of thought is an absolute right, it would seem difficult to argue that the change in wording from "conscience and religion" to "religion and belief" is important.' (P. W. Edge, 'Current Problems in Article 9 of the European Convention on Human Rights', *Juridical Review* (1996), 42, at 43).

[6] UN Doc. E/CN.4/Sub.2/SR.228 (1957), at p. 9.

In short, it may be wrong to make too much of the failure to repeat the terms 'thought' and 'conscience' in the 'manifestation' limb of Article 18 of the Universal Declaration, Article 18 of the ICCPR and Article 9 of the European Convention.

Indeed the European Court on occasion fails to observe the strict linguistic distinctions between Articles 9 and 10 of the European Convention. For example, it commented in *Pretty v. United Kingdom*[7] that 'not all opinions or convictions constitute beliefs in the sense protected by Article 9(1) of the Convention',[8] indicating that some 'opinions' (adopting a term found in Article 10 but not Article 9) might. Clearly there is some overlap between Articles 9 and 10 of the European Convention but it is important, as Malcolm Evans indicates, to reserve the term 'manifestation' to describe a particular form of expression which is only relevant to 'religion or belief'. What matters for the purpose of Article 9 is whether the claim involves a form of manifestation of a religion or belief through 'worship, teaching, practice or observance'. The European Court has usefully confirmed that whenever 'the exercise of the right to freedom of expression consists in the freedom to manifest one's religion or belief in worship, teaching, practice or observance, it is primarily the right guaranteed by Article 9 of the Convention which is applicable'.[9] This assists in determining the interrelation between Articles 9 and 10 of the European Convention and it is to be contrasted with the Human Rights Committee's tendency to make findings under both Articles 18 and 19 of the ICCPR even if it gives priority to one (*Malcolm Ross v. Canada*[10]).

As to the scope of the term 'religion or belief', in the context of the European Convention case law it is undoubtedly wide, so as to include pacifism (*Arrowsmith v. United Kingdom*),[11] Communism (*Hazar,*

---

[7] *Pretty v. United Kingdom* (2002) 35 EHRR 1.   [8] *Ibid.*, at para. 82.
[9] *Kokkinakis v. Greece* (Ser. A) No. 260–A (1993) ECtHR para. 79. In many cases, the Article 9 complaint may be subsumed by the complaint under Article 10, such as in *Incal v. Turkey*, where the applicant was convicted of disseminating separatist propaganda by virtue of his participation in the decision to distribute a leaflet criticising measures taken by the local authorities (*Incal v. Turkey* (2000) 29 EHRR 449). The European Court commented as follows: 'The applicant further complained of an infringement of his rights to freedom of thought, guaranteed by Article 9 of the Convention. Like the Commission, the Court considers that this complaint is subsumed by the complaint under article 10 and that it is not necessary to examine it separately' (*ibid.*, at 483, para. 60). This was followed in *Baskaya and Okçuoglu v. Turkey* (2001) 31 EHRR 292, para. 44.
[10] *Malcolm Ross v. Canada*, Communication No. 736/1997 (views of 18 October 2000), UN Doc. A/56/40 vol. 2 (2001), p. 69, at paras. 11.6 and 11.7.
[11] *Arrowsmith v. United Kingdom*, App. No. 7050/75 (1978) 19 D&R 5, at 19, para. 69.

Hazar and Acik v. Turkey),[12] atheism (*Angeleni v. Sweden*),[13] pro-life anti-abortion beliefs (*Plattform 'Ärzte für das Leben' v. Austria*),[14] and even beliefs of agnostics, sceptics and the unconcerned (*Kokkinakis v. Greece*).[15] In practice, followers of non-traditional religions and beliefs once bore the burden of proving the existence of the religion (or belief) in question (for example, Wicca)[16] though more recent decisions suggest more generous acknowledgement of non-mainstream religions (such as The Divine Light Zentrum,[17] The Moon Sect[18] and Druidism[19]). This is in contrast to the relative ease with which traditional religions have always been accepted as falling within Article 9. Recent examples have included minority or splinter groups from such religions.[20] The term 'belief' encompasses non-religious convictions and 'denotes views that attain a certain level of cogency, seriousness, cohesion and importance', such as parental opposition to corporal punishment (*Campbell and Cosans v. United Kingdom*).[21] However, a 'strong personal motivation' to have one's ashes scattered at home, in opposition to being buried in a cemetery among Christian memorials, fell outside Article 9 in *X. v. Germany*[22] as it did not appear to constitute the expression of 'a coherent view on fundamental problems'.[23] Similarly, in *Pretty v. United Kingdom*,[24] a belief in and support for the

---

[12] *Hazar and Açik v. Turkey*, App. Nos. 16311/90, 16312/90 and 16313/90 (1991) 72 D&R 200, at 213.

[13] *Angeleni v. Sweden*, App. No. 10491/83 (1986) 51 D&R 41, at 48.

[14] *Plattform 'Ärzte für das Leben' v. Austria*, App. No. 10126/82 (1985) 44 D&R 65, at 71.

[15] *Kokkinakis v. Greece* (Ser. A) No. 260–A (1993) ECtHR at 17, para. 31.

[16] In *X. v. United Kingdom*, App. No. 7291/75 (1977) 11 D&R 55, the Commission indicated that the burden is on the applicant to establish the existence of the Wicca religion (at p. 56).

[17] *Omkarananda and the Divine Light Zentrum v. United Kingdom*, App. No. 8188/77 (1981) 25 D&R 105.

[18] *X. v. Austria*, App. No. 8652/79 (1981) 26 D&R 89.

[19] *A. R. M. Chappell v. United Kingdom*, App. No. 12587/86 (1987) 53 D&R 241.

[20] See, for example, *Serif v. Greece* (1999) 31 EHRR 561; *Metropolitan Church of Bessarabia and others v. Moldova* (2002) 35 EHRR 306.

[21] *Campbell and Cosans v. United Kingdom* (Ser. A) No. 48 (1982) ECtHR, para. 36. Principled opposition to corporal punishment constituted a conviction for the purposes of Protocol 1, Article 2 (but not opposition to corporal punishment only in certain circumstances: *X., Y. and Z. v. United Kingdom*, App. No. 8566/79 (1982) 31 D&R 50).

[22] *X. v. Germany* App. No. 8741/79 (1981) 24 D&R 137.

[23] *Ibid.*, at 138. 'The Commission does not find that it is a manifestation of any belief in the sense that some coherent view on fundamental problems can be seen as expressed thereby'.

[24] *Pretty v. United Kingdom* (2002) 35 EHRR 1.

notion of assisted suicide for the applicant, in spite of the firmness of her views (which were not doubted), did not constitute beliefs in the sense protected by Article 9(1).[25]

A broad notion of 'belief' might similarly be said to be applied by the Human Rights Committee in Optional Protocol decisions, though its reasoning is less detailed. In *M.A.B., W.A.T. and J.-A.Y.T. v. Canada*,[26] for example, the authors claimed the protection of Article 18 of the ICCPR for the propagation and worship of marijuana as the 'Sacrament', or 'God's tree of life'. The Human Rights Committee not surprisingly assessed the content of the convictions and concluded that 'a "belief" consisting primarily or exclusively in the worship and distribution of a narcotic drug cannot conceivably be brought within the scope of article 18 of the Covenant'.[27] It is difficult to discern whether the beliefs in question were incapable of protection or whether the genuineness of the belief held by the authors was not established. Scepticism concerning the status of the 'belief' itself is hinted at in the use of inverted commas by the Human Rights Committee, coupled with the suggestion that the assertion of 'belief' in this case was no more than a device for legitimising criminal activity. This is in spite of the fact that the range of protected beliefs within Article 18 is undoubtedly broad, as confirmed in General Comment No. 22, para. 2:

> 'Article 18 protects theistic, non-theistic and atheistic beliefs, as well as the right not to profess any religion or belief. The terms belief and religion are to be broadly construed. Article 18 is not limited in its application to traditional religions or to religions and beliefs with institutional characteristics or practices analogous to those of traditional religions.'[28]

Even fascist beliefs[29] and anti-Semitic beliefs[30] are seemingly protected, as well as 'enemy-benefiting' beliefs (as demonstrated in

---

[25] *Ibid.*, at para. 82.
[26] *M.A.B., W.A.T. and J.-A.Y.T. v. Canada*, Communication No. 570/1993 (decision of 8 April 1994), UN Doc. A/49/40, vol. 2 (1994), p. 368.
[27] *Ibid.*, at para. 4.2.
[28] General Comment No. 22 (48), UN Doc. CCPR/C/21/Rev.1/Add.4 (1993). The text of General Comment No. 22 is at Annex 5. Malcolm Evans surveys the beliefs that are protected within Article 18 – M. D. Evans, 'The United Nations and Freedom of Religion', pp. 39–44.
[29] *M.A. v. Italy*, Communication No. 117/81 (decision of 10 April 1984), UN Doc. A/39/40 (1984), p. 190.
[30] *Malcolm Ross v. Canada*, Communication No. 736/1997 (views of 18 October 2000), UN Doc. A/56/40 vol. 2 (2001), p. 69 (Article 18 was considered at p. 85, para. 11.7).

Tae-Hoon Park v. Korea,[31] which concerned the author's criminal conviction for membership and participation in the activities of Young Koreans United, an organisation composed of young Koreans for the purpose of discussing peace and unification between North and South Korea).

The requirements of protected 'religion or belief' are therefore generally easily met within both Universal and European practice, though more could be done to clarify the basis on which certain beliefs are excluded from the protection of Article 18 of the ICCPR. However, the European Commission, and to a lesser extent the European Court, have adopted an additional hurdle, not conspicuous in the repertoire of the Human Rights Committee or other United Nations organs, requiring a particular nexus to be established between the qualifying religion or belief and its manifestation.

Nexus between religion or belief and its manifestation

The forms of manifestation mentioned in each of the core freedom of religion Articles are 'worship', 'teaching', 'practice' and 'observance'. Faced with the enormous theoretical breadth of activities that might be claimed to fall within the term 'practice', the European Commission in *Arrowsmith v. United Kingdom*[32] developed a means of confining the range of eligible manifestations. This approach has been followed in subsequent decisions, even those which do not concern the term 'practice'. The case centred upon the claim that an acknowledged pacifist was manifesting her beliefs when distributing leaflets to British soldiers in Northern Ireland, which explained to them the options for avoiding armed service. 'Pacifism' readily qualified as a 'belief'.[33] The question was whether the distribution of those leaflets constituted the manifestation of her pacifist beliefs through 'practice'. As a basic ground rule, the Commission considered that 'the term "practice" as employed in Article 9.1 does not cover each act which is motivated or influenced by a religion or belief'.[34]

---

[31] *Tae-Hoon Park v. Korea*, Communication No. 628/1995 (views of 20 October 1998) (1999) 6(3) IHRR 623.

[32] *Arrowsmith v. United Kingdom*, App. No. 7050/75 (1978) 19 D&R 5.

[33] *Ibid.*, at 19, para. 68: a 'commitment in both theory and practice, to the philosophy of securing one's political or other objectives without resorting to the threat or use of force against another human being under any circumstances, even in response to the threat or use of force'.

[34] *Ibid.*, at 19, para. 71.

It accepted that 'public declarations proclaiming generally the idea of pacifism and urging the acceptance of a commitment to non-violence may be considered as a normal and recognised manifestation of pacifist belief' but added the essential prerequisite that 'when the actions of individuals do not actually express the belief concerned they cannot be considered to be as such protected under Article 9.1, even if they are influenced by it'.[35]

The European Commission concluded that the distribution of leaflets did not constitute the manifestation of pacifist beliefs because the leaflets did not advocate pacifism – instead, it constituted anti-government protest which may have been motivated or influenced by pacifism. The leaflets did not themselves manifest pacifist belief and were such that they could in fact have been written by non-pacifists. The result of this reasoning, on its face, is to rule out activities that are simply 'motivated' or 'influenced' by a belief if they 'do not actually express the belief concerned'. *Arrowsmith* undoubtedly marked a turning point in Article 9 jurisprudence by formalising a strict connection between beliefs and their manifestation, principally as a means of coping with the difficulties of defining the term 'practice' and of controlling the range of imaginative claims based on that form of manifestation.

A survey of those cases in which the European Commission has applied the *Arrowsmith* test reveals some variation in its stringency, at times suggesting that the European Commission had tightened the 'actual expression' test to become one where the manifestation to be protected must be 'necessitated' by the religion or belief claimed. These cases must be treated with some caution.

For example, in *X. v. United Kingdom*[36] the issue of 'necessity' only arose because of the way in which the parties couched their arguments over whether the applicant's mosque attendance on Friday (on school days) was required by Islam.[37] The Commission did not raise the subject of 'necessity' on its own initiative: 'The parties' submissions in the present case concerning the "necessity" of the applicant's attendance at the mosque are connected with their discussion of his special contractual obligations as a teacher.'[38] The Government asserted that the

---

[35] *Ibid.*, at 20, para. 71. [36] *X. v. United Kingdom*, App. No. 8160/78 (1981) 22 D&R 27.
[37] *Ibid.*, at 34, para. 6: 'It is ... disputed between the parties whether the applicant's attendance of Friday prayers at the mosque on school days was during the relevant period ... required by Islam and thus a "necessary part" of his religious practice.'
[38] *Ibid.*, at 34, para. 7.

applicant's attendance was not 'necessary', drawing on the suggestion that this was a requirement under Article 9 following the pre-*Arrowsmith* decision of *X. v. United Kingdom*.[39] (That case concerned a Buddhist prisoner who lost his claim under Article 9 because 'he ha[d] failed to prove that it was a necessary part of this practice that he should publish articles in a religious magazine'.[40]) The Commission responded to the Government's submission by clarifying 'that its decision in Application No. 5442/74 took into account that applicant's situation as a detained person. In the case of a person at liberty, the question of the "necessity" of a religious manifestation, as regards time and place, will not normally arise under Article 9'.[41] The issue of necessity therefore has particular application to the manifestation of beliefs by prisoners, and it may be observed that most of these prison cases are relatively early ones.[42]

The military context also justifies the imposition of constraints on the manifestation of religion which would not be appropriate to civilians, so that military rules may make an officer cadet's 'freedom to practise their religion subject to limitations as to time and place, without however negating it entirely'.[43] However, it is doubtful that any test of 'necessary expression' (rather than the 'actual expression' formula developed in *Arrowsmith*) may be said to apply generally outside the prison and military contexts. In other cases concerning restrictions imposed by employment, not dissimilar to that concerning the Muslim teacher in *X. v. United Kingdom*, the European Commission has invoked the *Arrowsmith* test. For example, in *Knudsen v. Norway*,[44] when a clergyman protested against a newly enacted abortion law by refusing to carry out State functions (but continued to regard himself as a servant of the Church and continued with all other duties associated with being a

---

[39] *X. v. United Kingdom*, App. No. 5442/72 (1975) 1 D&R 41.   [40] *Ibid.*, at 42.

[41] *X. v. United Kingdom*, App. No. 8160/78 (1981) 22 D&R at 34, para. 7. In view of extra work and administrative difficulties of checking all material that might be sent out by prisoners for the purposes of publication, and the potential security risk involved, the rule that limited such publication was found to be necessary for the maintenance of prison discipline and therefore necessary in a democratic society for the purposes of Article 10(2) (*X. v. United Kingdom*, App. No. 5442/72 (1975) 1 D&R 42). For allegations of the denial of access to the prisoners' choice of religious literature reported by the Special Rapporteur, see UN Doc. E/CN.4/2005/61/Add.1 (2005), p. 82, para. 327 (Uzbekistan).

[42] Most notably *X. v. Austria*, App. No. 1753/63, 8 Yearbook (1965) 174, and *X. v. United Kingdom*, App. No. 5442/72 (1975) 1 D&R 41.

[43] *Yanasik v. Turkey*, App. No. 14524/89 (1993) 74 D&R 14, at 26. See also *Kalaç v. Turkey* (1999) 27 EHRR 552, at para. 27.

[44] *Knudsen v. Norway*, App. No. 11045/84 (1985) 42 D&R 247.

clergyman of the parish), the Commission (citing *Arrowsmith*) found that his refusal 'did not actually express the applicant's belief or religious views and it cannot, therefore, be considered as such to be protected by Article 9, para. 1, even when it was motivated by such views or belief'.[45]

Some claims are dealt with on the basis that Article 9 is inapplicable altogether. For example, in *Khan v. United Kingdom*,[46] the applicant claimed that his being charged with abduction and unlawful sexual intercourse as result of his marriage to a fourteen-year-old girl, as permitted under Islamic law, prevented him from manifesting his religion. Although there is some suggestion that the European Commission agreed that the question of manifestation should be determined according to *Arrowsmith* principles (because it commented that 'the term "practice" as employed by Article 9, para. 1 does not cover each act which may be motivated or influenced by a religion or belief'), it actually rendered the claim entirely outside Article 9: 'While the applicant's religion may allow the marriage of girls at the age of 12, marriage cannot be considered simply as a form of expression of thought, conscience or religion, but is governed specifically by Article 12.'[47]

The mere fact that an activity is permitted by a religion does not give it the status of manifestation (and in this case it did not even fall within Article 9).

In many cases, the European Commission need not examine the nexus between a belief and its manifestation simply because the case raises no issue connected with a religion or belief. In *D. v. France*,[48] the applicant could not satisfy the European Commission that being ordered to grant a letter of repudiation of a Jewish marriage to his ex-wife would oblige him to act against his conscience. He claimed that he manifested his religion or belief in observance or practice when refusing to do so.

> 'In this respect, the Commission notes that the applicant does not allege that in handing over the letter of repudiation he would be obliged to act against his conscience, since it is an act by which divorce is regularly established under Jewish law; he alleges only that by reason of his family's special status he would forfeit for all time the possibility of re-marrying his ex-wife, for the Mosaic law provides that a Cohen may not marry a divorced woman, whether his own ex-wife or anyone else's.'[49]

---

[45] *Ibid.*, at 258. However, the overriding consideration in this case was the freedom that the applicant had at all times to leave the church.

[46] *Khan v. United Kingdom*, App. No. 11579/85 (1986) 48 D&R 253.   [47] *Ibid.*, at 255.

[48] *D. v. France*, App. No. 10180/82 (1983) 35 D&R 199.   [49] *Ibid.*, at 202.

The issue of conscience would only arise at the time that he wished to remarry his ex-wife, but not otherwise. It would be wrong to jump to the conclusion that the European Commission was thereby establishing as the appropriate threshold that the applicant must 'be *obliged* to act against his conscience' in order for his actions to constitute proper manifestation. It was merely making the point that the applicant failed to allege any issue of conscience.

A more common illustration of neutrality in matters of conscience, as characterised by the European Commission, would be the case of *C. v. United Kingdom*,[50] concerning a Quaker opposed to the obligation to pay the portion of his taxes attributable to military expenditure. He claimed 'that it is a necessary part of the manifestation of his Quaker belief in practice and observance that forty per cent of his income tax be diverted to different, peaceful purposes. This step is not merely consistent with the Quaker beliefs, but necessary to their manifestation.'[51] The Commission disagreed with the applicant's assessment that there arose any issue of conscience to bring the claim within Article 9: 'The obligation to pay taxes is a general one which has no specific conscientious implications in itself. Its neutrality in this sense is also illustrated by the fact that no tax payer can influence or determine the purpose for which his or her tax contributions are applied, once they are collected.'[52]

Accordingly, the Commission did not apply the *Arrowsmith* test to determine whether the manifestation claimed actually expressed the underlying belief. The *Arrowsmith* test was, however, cited to lend weight to the following statement (that strictly speaking was redundant if the Commission was to determine the case on the neutrality of the obligation to pay taxes):

> 'Article 9 primarily protects the sphere of personal beliefs and religious creeds, i.e. the area which is sometimes called the *forum internum*. In addition, it protects acts which are intimately linked to these attitudes, such as acts of worship and devotion which are aspects of the practice of religion or belief in a generally recognised form.
>
> However, in protecting this personal sphere, Article 9 of the Convention does not always guarantee the right to behave in the public sphere in a way which is dictated by such belief: – for instance by refusing to pay certain taxes because part of the revenue so raised may be applied for military expenditure. The Commission so held in Application No. 7050/75 (Arrowsmith

---

[50] *C. v. United Kingdom*, App. No. 10358/83 (1983) 37 D&R 142.
[51] *Ibid.*, at 147.   [52] *Ibid.*, at 147.

v. the United Kingdom, Cmm Report, para 71, D.R. 19, p. 5) where it stated
that the term "practice" as employed in Article 9(1) does not cover each act
which is motivated or influenced by a religion or belief.'[53]

This dictum is an important one if it is intended to suggest that the
manifestation of religion or belief under Article 9 is fully encapsulated by
the formula 'acts which are intimately linked to these attitudes, such as acts
of worship or devotion which are aspects of the practice of a religion or a
belief in a generally recognised form'. The European Commission condensed the terms 'practice' and 'worship' (even though they appear separately in Article 9) and imposed the requirement that they be 'intimately
linked' to the underlying attitudes, which seems unduly restrictive.

The summary of Article 9 given in this passage has been repeated in
other cases where the neutrality of a generally imposed State obligation has been at issue, such as in *V. v. The Netherlands*,[54] when the
anthroposocial principles of a doctor caused him to refuse to participate
in a compulsory professional pension scheme.[55] However, whether it is
intended to impose an additional limitation beyond the *Arrowsmith*
nexus is debatable. It was certainly used in *Karaduman v. Turkey*[56] to
answer the applicant's claim that covering her head with a headscarf
was one of the 'observances' and 'practices' 'prescribed by' her religion,
which had been restricted by the requirement that she must provide
an identity photograph showing her bare-headed for the purpose of
a degree certificate. The Commission did not discuss whether head-
covering was a manifestation of the applicant's belief. It only commented that it had previously ruled that Article 9 'does not always
guarantee the right to behave in the public sphere in a way which
is dictated by such a belief', citing *Arrowsmith* and *C. v. United
Kingdom*.[57] This would certainly appear to be an inadequate answer
to the applicant's claim to be manifesting a religion (when her religion
actually prescribes the wearing of a headscarf) and amounts to avoidance of a proper *Arrowsmith* analysis of manifestation rather than a
refinement upon it.

It is more likely that the reference in *C. v. United Kingdom* to 'acts of
worship or devotion' as illustrations of proper forms of manifestation
was not so much intended to impose limits additional to the *Arrowsmith*
test as to emphasise the applicant's error in claiming that his resistance

---

[53] *Ibid.*, at 147.   [54] *V. v. The Netherlands*, App. No. 10678/83 (1984) 39 D&R 267.
[55] *Ibid.*, at 268.   [56] *Karaduman v. Turkey*, App. No. 16278/90 (1993) 74 D&R 93.
[57] *Ibid.*, at 108.

to State compulsion contrary to his beliefs constituted a form of manifestation. It would have been better still if the Commission had decided instead to give more concrete recognition to the risk of interference with *forum internum* associated with State compulsion. As argued in Chapter 3 under the heading 'Decisions based on justified limitation on manifestation', pp. 121–35, the *Arrowsmith* analysis is not appropriate to such claims and over-use of the *Arrowsmith* formula by the European Commission itself has led applicants to frame their own claims in terms of manifestation, somewhat artificially.

The European Court has not placed such extensive, repetitive reliance on *Arrowsmith* principles as the European Commission, although occasional use of the same warning does suggest that the former European Commission's jurisprudence has some support within the European Court. Certainly one of the most direct invocations of *Arrowsmith* was in the case of *Pretty v. United Kingdom*,[58] although the European Court, unlike the Commission in *Arrowsmith*, did not specify whether the Article 9 claim failed because of the nature of the belief asserted or because that belief did not involve a form of manifestation through 'worship, teaching, practice or observance':

> 'The Court does not doubt the firmness of the applicant's views concerning assisted suicide but would observe that not all opinions or convictions constitute beliefs in the sense protected by Article 9(1) of the Convention. Her claims do not involve a form of manifestation of a religion or belief, through worship, teaching, practice or observance as described in the second sentence of the first paragraph. As found by the Commission, the term "practice" as employed in Article 9(1) does not cover each act which is motivated or influenced by a religion or belief.'[59]

The reason why this may not have been elaborated further is that the Article 9 claim in substance amounted to a restatement of the applicant's Article 8 claim (to the extent that it concerned her commitment to the principle of personal autonomy) which had already been dealt with.

---

[58] *Pretty v. United Kingdom* (2002) 35 EHRR 1. In the UN context, see *Sanlés Sanlés v. Spain*, Communication No. 1024/2001 (decision of 30 March 2004), UN Doc. A/59/40 vol. 2 (2004), p. 505. This involved the alleged violation of Article 18(1) and the right to manifest personal beliefs through practices or deeds, as a result of the State's refusal to allow the author's assisted suicide, which reduced the author to 'enslavement to a morality he did not share, imposed by the power of the State, and forced [him] to exist in a state of constant suffering' (at para. 3.4) (declared inadmissible).

[59] *Ibid.*, at para. 82.

The European Court, like the Commission, has resorted to the *Arrowsmith* formula even when the issue of manifestation has not been in contention but instead the central claim has been interference with the *forum internum*. This begs the question precisely what role it is intended to play in such circumstances. In *Kalaç v. Turkey*,[60] the applicant maintained that compulsory retirement from his position as a military judge advocate infringed Article 9 because it was based on his religious beliefs and practices. It was not contested that he was able to fulfil all of the obligations associated with religious practice, yet the Court still reiterated the parameters of manifestation, in particular, the *Arrowsmith* warning that Article 9 'does not protect every act motivated or inspired by a religion or belief'.[61] The Court then went on to decide that his retirement was not based on his religious opinions and beliefs or, more importantly for these purposes, the way he had performed his religious duties (confirming that manifestation was irrelevant) but instead was based on his 'conduct and attitude' (a term that was not explained except through the reference to 'an attitude inimical to an established order reflecting the requirements of military service').[62] The suggestion left by the inclusion of the *Arrowsmith* warning is that his conduct and attitude constituted manifestations of his religion or belief that were outside the range of protection of Article 9. Yet the real shortcoming of this decision (as discussed in Chapter 3, 'Employment') is that the European Court was simply using the formula as an imprecise means of dismissing the claim. This is reminiscent of the shortcomings of the decision in *Yanasik v. Turkey*,[63] in which the Commission focused unnecessarily on manifestation when the parties agreed that the manifestation of the applicant's religion was not restricted. The Commission did so as a means of obviating the applicant's claim that focused entirely on the *forum internum* (that he was punished in order to persuade him to drop his religious interests).

Even in cases in which the claim clearly depends on whether the manifestation falls within the terminology of 'worship, teaching, practice and observance', the European Court has a tendency to be conservative to a point that prevents it from clarifying the scope of these activities. For example, in *Kokkinakis v. Greece*[64] it commented on the freedom to manifest religion by stating that '[b]earing witness in words and deeds is bound

[60] *Kalaç v. Turkey* (1999) 27 EHRR 552.   [61] *Ibid.*, at para. 27.   [62] *Ibid.*, at paras. 29–30.
[63] *Yanasik v. Turkey*, App. No. 14524/89 (1993) 74 D&R 14, discussed in Chapter 3 under the heading 'Education', pp. 165–82.
[64] *Kokkinakis v. Greece* (Ser. A) No. 260–A (1993) ECtHR.

up with the existence of religious convictions' and that manifestation 'includes in principle the right to try to convince one's neighbour, for example through "teaching"'.[65] It was enough for the Court's purposes that certain forms of proselytism could in principle constitute 'teaching' and therefore a legitimate manifestation of religion.[66] However, the real issue was the extent to which proselytism constitutes manifestation beyond the narrow meaning of 'teaching'. Similarly, in *Serif v. Greece*,[67] the European Court cited 'worship and teaching' as appropriate forms of manifestation, restricted by the criminal conviction of the applicant for having usurped the functions of a minister of a 'known religion' and for having publicly worn the dress of such a minister. All the applicant had done was to issue a message about the religious significance of a feast, deliver a speech at a religious gathering, issue another message on the occasion of a religious holiday and appear in public wearing the dress of a religious leader.[68] It is difficult to see the connection between these acts and 'worship'. Interestingly, in neither *Serif* nor *Kokkinakis* was the *Arrowsmith* formula cited in any form.

Even in cases turning on the scope of 'practice' (from which the *Arrowsmith* principle was derived), the Court's emphasis on the *Arrowsmith* principle is sometimes confined only to recalling that the term 'does not cover each act which is motivated or influenced by a religion or belief' without the stringent application of the 'expression' test found in *Arrowsmith* itself.[69] It certainly has some application outside the term 'practice', extending to 'observance', but in such instances evidence of the principle is only indirect. For example, in *Cha'are Shalom Ve Tsedek v. France*,[70] it is only possible to trace the reference to *Arrowsmith* through the broad statement of principle that 'Article 9 lists a number of forms which manifestation of one's religion or belief may take, namely worship, teaching, practice and observance (see the Kalaç v. Turkey judgment of 1 July 1997, *Reports* 1997-IV, p. 1209, § 27)'. Paragraph 27 of *Kalaç* merely contains the basic *Arrowsmith* summary given above. The simplicity of analysis may in part be due to the fact that in *Cha'are Shalom Ve Tsedek v. France* it was uncontested that ritual slaughter constituted a rite that provided Jews with

---

[65] *Ibid.*, at para. 31.   [66] *Ibid.*, at para. 31.

[67] *Serif v. Greece* (1999) 31 EHRR 561. See also *Agga v. Greece*, (App. Nos 50776/99 and 52912/99), Judgment of 7 October 2002.

[68] *Ibid.*, at para. 39.

[69] *Pretty v. United Kingdom* (2002) 35 EHRR 1, at para. 82; *Kalaç v. Turkey* (1999) 27 EHRR 552, at para. 27.

[70] *Cha'are Shalom Ve Tsedek v. France* (App. No. 27417/95), Judgment of 11 July 2000.

meat from slaughter in accordance with their religious prescriptions and was an essential aspect of practice of the Jewish religion within Article 9 'namely the right to manifest one's religion in observance'.[71] The nexus between belief and observance was therefore already established. Instead, the emphasis shifted on to whether there was an interference with this settled form of observance. The European Court decided that such observance would only be interfered with 'if the illegality of performing ritual slaughter made it impossible for ultra-orthodox Jews to eat meat from animals slaughtered in accordance with the religious prescriptions they considered applicable'.[72] In view of the applicant's ability to obtain supplies of ritually slaughtered meat from Belgium, there was no interference.

By way of summary of the European practice when establishing the connection between a qualifying religion or belief and its manifestation, although the *Arrowsmith* case concerned only manifestation through 'practice', its impact has also extended to limit available forms of 'worship', 'observance' and possibly also 'teaching' within Article 9.[73] The European approach may be criticised for not providing detailed explanations of the concepts of 'worship', 'teaching', 'practice' and 'observance' (even though the range of acts constituting manifestation is critical). Instead, the tendency of the European Commission in particular has been to recite rather mechanically the connection required by *Arrowsmith* between an alleged manifestation and the belief from which it is claimed to stem. In those cases where constraints are justified by reason of military or prison regulations, the reasoning provided to support them has suggested inadvertently that a stricter test than that formulated in *Arrowsmith* itself applies even outside the environment of military and prison regulation.[74]

---

[71] *Ibid.*, at para. 74.   [72] *Ibid.*, at para. 80.

[73] For a detailed analysis of the *Arrowsmith* test see C. Evans, *Freedom of Religion Under the European Convention*, pp. 111–25, and for the application of *Arrowsmith* outside the term 'practice', pp. 117–19.

[74] For example, Malcolm Evans discerns alternative approaches taken by the European Commission when determining what constitutes protected 'manifestation' for the purposes of Article 9(1) – M. D. Evans, *Religious Liberty and International Law in Europe*, pp. 307–13. The first is that the Commission accepts only 'necessary expressions' of religion or belief, evidenced by cases involving prisoners, questioning whether, for example, a prayer chain was 'an indispensable element in the proper exercise of the Buddhist religion' (*X. v. Austria*, App. No. 1753/63, 8 Yearbook (1965) 174, at 184) and upholding the refusal to grant a prisoner permission to publish in a Buddhist magazine on the basis that he had 'failed to prove that it was a necessary part of [Buddhist] practice that he should publish articles in a religious magazine' (*X. v. United Kingdom*, App. No. 5442/72 (1975) 1 D&R 41, at 42). The alternative approach to determining whether a manifestation is protected is to consider whether it is intended to 'give

The 'actual expression' test does not appear to have been adopted by the European Court with detailed precision although this may be attributed to the paucity of European Court cases in which the *Arrowsmith* nexus has been in contention. Even when *Arrowsmith* is cited, it is only to reiterate that Article 9 'does not cover each act which is motivated or influenced by a religion or belief', without a more detailed reminder of the 'actual expression' test. Most commonly, a particular form of manifestation (whether it be 'worship', 'teaching', 'practice' or 'observance') has readily been accepted by the Court without much clear substantiation. The resulting impression of European Commission decisions in particular is that the European criteria for determining the connection between protected beliefs and their manifestation (as enshrined in the *Arrowsmith* nexus) represents an obstacle which is not found at Universal level.

The illustrations of manifestation provided by the Human Rights Committee in paragraph 4 of General Comment No. 22 are generally conservative, in that they focus principally on ritual and ceremonial aspects of manifestation. However, there is nothing to suggest that the Human Rights Committee requires such a direct connection between beliefs and their manifestation as that mandated in the jurisprudence of the European Commission. On the contrary, in *J.P. v. Canada* (on facts very similar to those in the European Commission decision in *C. v. United Kingdom*) the Human Rights Committee suggested a generous range of eligible manifestations when affirming that '[a]lthough article 18 of the Covenant certainly protects the right to hold, express and disseminate opinions and convictions, including conscientious objection to military activities and expenditures, the refusal to pay taxes on grounds of conscientious objection clearly falls outside the scope of the protection of this article'.[75] As with *M.A.B., W.A.T. and J.-A.Y.T. v. Canada*, the Human Rights Committee did not explain the basis of its

expression' to religion or belief, such as in the case of *Knudsen v. Norway*, in which the dismissal of a minister whose refusal to conduct public functions as a protest at a recent Abortion Act, 'did not actually express the applicant's belief or religious view and it cannot, therefore, be considered as such to be protected by Article 9(1), even when it was motivated by it' (*Knudsen v. Norway*, App. No. 11045/84 (1985) 42 D&R 247, at 258). Carolyn Evans analyses what she characterises as the 'necessity approach' of general application following *Arrowsmith* – C. Evans, *Freedom of Religion Under the European Convention*, p. 116.

[75] *J.P. v. Canada*, Communication No. 466/1991 (decision of 7 November 1991), UN Doc. A/47/40 (1994), p. 426, at para. 4.2. See also *J.v.K. and C.M.G. v. K.-S. v. The Netherlands*, Communication No. 483/1991 (decision of 23 July 1992), UN Doc. A/47/40 (1994), p. 435, at para. 4.2.

decision either in terms of an examination of whether a belief qualifies for protection as such or in terms of an appropriate connection between a protected belief and its manifestation.

However, more recently, the Human Rights Committee in *Malcolm Ross v. Canada*,[76] was faced with the State's claim that the author's denigration of the Jewish faith was outside the scope of Article 18 because his opinions 'do not express religious beliefs and certainly do not fall within the tenets of Christian faith'. The State claimed that the author had 'cloaked his views under the guise of the Christian faith but in fact his views express hatred and suspicion of the Jewish people and their religion', and pointed to the fact that anti-Semitic views are not part of the Christian faith. The State also claimed that the author's expressions did not constitute the manifestation of a religion, 'as he did not publish them for the purpose of worship, observance, practice or teaching of their religion'.[77] The Human Rights Committee dealt with the matter primarily under Article 19 but, in concluding that Article 18 had not been violated, commented that the actions taken against the author in restricting his speech were not aimed at his thoughts or beliefs as such, but rather at the manifestation of those beliefs within a particular context.[78] Accordingly, a looser connection between beliefs and their manifestation appears to be accepted by the Human Rights Committee than for the purposes of Article 9 of the European Convention.

At the Universal level, a generous, inclusive approach to qualifying manifestations is reflected in the detail of Article 6 of the 1981 Declaration (considered in detail below under the heading 'The scope of recognised manifestations of religion or belief', pp. 235–92). Similarly, the Krishnaswami study suggests that because the term 'teaching, practice, worship and observance' was originally devised in the Universal Declaration with a view to bringing all religions or beliefs within its compass, with varying weight attached to forms of manifestation by different religions, 'it may be safely assumed that the intention was to embrace all possible manifestations of religion or belief with the terms "teaching, practice, worship and observance".[79]

---

[76] *Malcolm Ross v. Canada*, Communication No. 736/1997 (views of 18 October 2000), UN Doc. A/56/40 vol. 2 (2001), p. 69.

[77] *Ibid.*, at p. 78, para. 6.5.   [78] *Ibid.*, at p. 85, para. 11.7.

[79] A. Krishnaswami, 'Study of Discrimination in the Matter of Religious Rights and Practices', 11 NYUJ Int'l L & Pol (1978) 227, at 233.

It may be speculated whether greater recognition by the European Court of the full range of manifestations listed in Article 6 of the 1981 Declaration would result in less reliance on the *Arrowsmith* test to determine whether those activities actually express a religion or belief.

Determination of whether there has been an interference

It would appear that the criteria for assessing whether there has been State interference with the manifestation of religion or belief are not unduly rigid, at both European and Universal levels.

The Human Rights Committee, for example, decided in *Malcolm Ross v. Canada*[80] that the removal of the author from his teaching position, for expressing strongly anti-Semitic opinions entirely outside the performance of his duties as a teacher, constituted a restriction on his freedom of expression:

> 'The loss of a teaching position was a significant detriment, even if no or only insignificant pecuniary damage is suffered. This detriment was imposed on the author because of the expression of his views, and in the view of the Committee this is a restriction which has to be justified under article 19, paragraph 3, in order to be in compliance with the Covenant.'[81]

It was sufficient that detriment was brought upon the author. (The Committee found there to be no violation of Article 18 on substantially the same grounds as under Article 19.)

A similarly broad approach is reflected in the European Court's decision in *Metropolitan Church of Bessarabia and others v. Moldova*.[82] It concerned the impediments to 'worship' and a wide range of collective aspects of enjoyment of the freedom of religion posed by non-recognition. The applicants (the Metropolitan Church of Bessarabia and a number Moldovan nationals who were members of the *eparchic* council of the Church) alleged that the Moldovan authorities infringed Article 9 since the Religious Denominations Act required religious denominations active in Moldova to be recognised by means of a Government decision, which the authorities had refused to grant to the Metropolitan Church. Only religions recognised by the Government could be practised in Moldova. Accordingly, the applicants claimed that their freedom to manifest their religion in community with others was frustrated by

---

[80] *Malcolm Ross v. Canada*, Communication No. 736/1997 (views of 18 October 2000), UN Doc. A/56/40 vol. 2 (2001), p. 69.
[81] *Ibid.*, at p. 83, para. 11.1.
[82] *Metropolitan Church of Bessarabia and others v. Moldova* (2002) 35 EHRR 306.

the fact that they were prohibited from gathering together for religious purposes and by the complete absence of judicial protection of the Church's assets.[83] The applicants did not object to registration formalities as such, except where the lack of authorisation under those registration procedures made it impossible to practise their religion.[84] The European Court had no difficulty in establishing a violation of Article 9 for all applicants:

> 'The Court notes that under the Moldovan Law of 24 March 1992 only religions recognised by Government decision may be practised.
>
>   In the present case, the Court observes that the applicant Church may not pursue its activities since it is not recognised. In particular, its priests may not hold services, its members may not meet to practise their religion and, since it has not legal status, it is not entitled to judicial protection of its property.
>
>   Hence the Court holds that the refusal by the Moldovan Government to recognise the applicant Church, upheld by the decision of the Supreme Court of Justice of 9 December 1997, is an interference in the right of that church and of the other applicants to freedom of religion, as safeguarded by Article 9 of the Convention.'[85]

Four essential principles reaffirmed by this decision are: first, that the right of manifestation relates solely to one's own choice of religion or belief and is satisfied by no other available form of manifestation; secondly, that the right to manifest 'in community with others' is an essential, self-standing limb of Article 9; thirdly, that *locus standi* for legal entities (as opposed to individuals) is an obvious but critical prerequisite for many claims based on collective manifestation; and fourthly, and most importantly, the European Court was astute to the range of restrictions on manifestation that were imposed by non-recognition of religious entities. These will now each be taken in turn.

A State cannot claim the absence of interference merely by asserting that a close alternative is available to the form of manifestation restricted. In *Metropolitan Church of Bessarabia and others v. Moldova* the European Court rejected the Government's argument that the refusal to recognise the applicant Church did not amount to a prohibition of its activities or

---

[83] The lack of legal personality meant that the Church could not, for example, challenge the decision by the Government to grant conflicting land usage rights over a site where a chapel had been built for the celebration of mass, authorisation was refused for entry into the country of humanitarian aid from an overseas church, etc.

[84] The applicants appealed to the reasoning of the European Court in *Manoussakis and others v. Greece* (1997) 23 EHRR para. 37.

[85] *Metropolitan Church of Bessarabia and others v. Moldova* (2002) 35 EHRR 306, at para. 105.

those of its members since they retained their freedom to manifest their beliefs through worship and practice in the Metropolitan Church of Moldova, which was identical 'from the religious point of view'.[86] Instead, the European Court accepted the applicants' claim that any group of believers who considered themselves to be different from others should be able to form a new church, and that it was not for the State to determine whether or not there was a real distinction between these different groups or what beliefs should be considered distinct from others.[87] This emphasises something which is self-evident in the wording of Article 9 but all too easily overlooked, namely that Article 9(1) refers to the right of everyone 'to manifest *his* religion or belief' and not another's. This also has consequences for the decisions discussed at greater length in Chapter 3 under the heading '"Direct" protection for the forum internum', at pp. 121–36, in which claims against State coercion were determined on the basis that manifestation was at issue.

Of course, if appropriate means existed for the applicants to practise their own religion, there would have been no interference, even applying the strict test for establishing interference expressed in *Cha'are Shalom Ve Tsedek v. France*,[88] which determined that there would *only* be an interference if the restriction *made it impossible* for adherents to manifest according to their choice. In both *Cha'are Shalom* and *Metropolitan Church* the European Court upheld the applicants' particular choice of practice and observance even though apparently close alternatives were readily available. This is to be contrasted with the early European Commission case of *X. v. Germany*,[89] in which a prisoner detained in Germany complained that Article 9 was infringed by reason of inadequate facilities for Anglican worship and the denial of access to an Anglican priest (according to the rites of the Church of England) – even though other Protestant facilities were made available. The European Commission attached little importance to the applicant's denomination by observing 'that there is no evidence that a Protestant pastor or facilities for worship in the Protestant religion are not available to the Applicant; whereas, therefore, an examination of the case as it has been submitted does not disclose any appearance of a violation of the rights and freedoms set forth in the Convention and in particular in Article 9'.[90]

---

[86] *Ibid.*, at paras. 97 and 98.

[87] *Ibid.*, at para. 96. See also para. 117: 'The Court recalls also that in principle, the right to freedom of religion as understood in the Convention rules out any appreciation by the State of the legitimacy of religious beliefs or of the manner in which these are expressed.'

[88] *Cha'are Shalom Ve Tsedek v. France* (App. No. 27417/95), Judgment of 11 July 2000.

[89] *X. v. Germany*, App. No. 2413/65 (1966) 23 CD 1.   [90] *Ibid.*, at 8.

The failure on the part of the Commission to distinguish between the conditions applicable to prisoners and those at liberty (if that was relevant) and to appreciate the importance of denomination may be attributed to the fact that this was a 1966 decision. There is little doubt, following *Metropolitan Church*, that denominational choice is critical to the right of manifestation.

Secondly, although the collective aspect of religious manifestation has never seriously been questioned, it was usefully affirmed in *Metropolitan Church*. Even the European Commission has emphasised that freedom to manifest religion on one's own is not an adequate substitute for collective manifestation if sought by the applicant. Thus in *X. v. United Kingdom*[91] the Government tried unsuccessfully to suggest that the applicant's wish to observe Muslim worship could be satisfied by the possibility of private, solitary worship. The European Commission clarified that the two are not interchangeable:

> 'the right to manifest one's religion "in community with others" has always been regarded as an essential part of freedom of religion and finds that the two alternatives "either alone or in community with others" in Article 9(1) cannot be considered as mutually exclusive, or as leaving a choice to the authorities, but only as recognising that religion may be practised in either form'.[92]

Similarly, in *Kokkinakis v. Greece*[93] the European Court emphasised the principle that has been reiterated in numerous decisions since, that '[a]ccording to Article 9 (art. 9), freedom to manifest one's religion is not only exercisable in community with others, "in public" and within the circle of those whose faith one shares, but can also be asserted "alone" and "in private"'.[94]

The collective element of manifestation is therefore beyond question.

Thirdly, it is worth remembering the fundamental principle that the basis on which any religious entity exercises its rights under Article 9 in its own capacity is on behalf of and as a representative of its members or

---

[91] *X. v. United Kingdom*, App. No. 8160/78 (1981) 22 D&R 27.
[92] *Ibid.*, at 34.   [93] *Kokkinakis v. Greece* (Ser. A) No. 260–A (1993) ECtHR.
[94] *Ibid.*, at para. 31. Nowak suggests that purely private religious exercise is protected by the right to privacy under Article 17 and may not therefore be subject to any of the limitations provided by Article 18(3) for so long as it does not touch upon the sphere of privacy of others (Nowak, *CCPR Commentary*, p. 319).

adherents.[95] In *Metropolitan Church* this was addressed with little passing discussion.[96] The principle extends to church bodies and associations with religious and philosophical objectives[97] (even those associated with criminal activities),[98] although not to a company functioning on a commercial basis,[99] and with the further qualification that freedom of conscience (unlike freedom of religion) cannot be exercised by such a legal person.[100] (By contrast, no organisation has personal standing to submit communications to the Human Rights Committee under the Optional Protocol,[101] which represents an anomaly in the light of Article 6(b) of the 1981 Declaration.)

The fourth issue raised by the *Metropolitan Church* concerns the range of restrictions on manifestation that are imposed by non-recognition of religious entities such as to constitute interference. In *Metropolitan Church* the applicants did not object to registration formalities as such, though they did

---

[95] *X. and the Church of Scientology v. Sweden*, App. No. 7805/77 (1979) 16 D&R 68, at 70. See also: *Cha'are Shalom Ve Tsedek v. France* (App. No. 27417/95), Judgment of 11 July 2000, para. 72; *Canea Catholic Church v. Greece* (1999) 27 EHRR 521, para. 31. See generally L. S. Lehnhof, 'Freedom of Religious Association: The Right of Religious Organizations to Obtain Legal Entity Status Under the European Convention, Brigham Young UL Rev (2002) 561.

[96] *Metropolitan Church of Bessarabia and others v. Moldova* (2002) 35 EHRR 306, para. 101.

[97] See H. Cullen, 'The Emerging Scope of Freedom of Conscience', 22 Eur L Rev (1997) 32. Cullen discusses the status of churches at p. 36, and at p. 44 comments on the 'narrow holdings' of the European Court in the Greek cases preceding *Manoussakis and others v. Greece*. For further discussion on the scope for collective claims, see: J. Crawford (ed.), *The Rights of Peoples*, Oxford: Clarendon Press (1988); P. Alston (ed.), *Peoples' Rights*, Oxford: Oxford University Press (2001); B. Kingsbury, 'Claims by Non-State Groups in International Law', 25 Cornell Int'l LJ (1992) 481; C. Brolmann et al. (eds.), *Peoples and Minorities in International Law*, Dordrecht/London: Martinus Nijhoff (1993); N. Lerner, *Group Rights and Discrimination in International Law*, Dordrecht/London: Martinus Nijhoff (1991).

[98] *Omkarananda and the Divine Light Zentrum v. United Kingdom*, App. No. 8188/77 (1981) 25 D&R 105, at 117.

[99] *Kustannus Oy Vapaa Ajattelija AB and others v. Finland*, App. No. 20471/92, No. 85–A (1996) D&R 29, at 38.

[100] *Ibid.*, at 38; *Verein Kontakt-Information-Therapie and Hagen v. Austria*, App. No. 11921/86 (1988) 57 D&R 81, at 88.

[101] *A group of associations for the defence of the rights of disabled and handicapped persons in Italy, and persons signing the communication, on 9th January 1984 v. Italy*, Communication No. 163/1984 (decision 10 April 1984), UN Doc. A/39/40 (1984), p. 197; *J.R.T. and the W. G. Party v. Canada*, Communication No. 104/1981 (decision of 6 April 1983), UN Doc. A/38/40 (1983), p. 231. However, Nowak argues that 'religious societies as juridical persons are also entitled to a subjective right to the exercise of their belief, enabling them to submit an individual communication in the event this is violated' – Nowak, *CCPR Commentary*, p. 313.

allege that the refusal to recognise, coupled with the authorities' stubborn persistence in holding to the view that the applicants could practise their religion within another denomination, infringed their freedom of association, contrary to Article 11 of the Convention.[102] They also invoked Article 6 because recognition was a prerequisite to assuring legal protection for the religious community and its members against repeated assaults and instances of intimidation, as well as legal protection for its assets. This issue was never separately determined because Articles 6 and 11 'were taken into account in the context of Article 9'.[103] The interrelation between Articles 6, 9 and 11 was expressed by the European Court as follows:

> '[S]ince religious communities traditionally exist in the form of orga-
> nised structures, Article 9 must be interpreted in the light of Article 11 of
> the Convention, which safeguards freedom of association against unjus-
> tified interference by the State. This being so, the right of believers to
> freedom of religion, which includes the right to manifest one's religion
> collectively presupposes that believers may associate freely, without arbi-
> trary interference by the State. The autonomy of religious communities is
> in fact indispensable to pluralism in a democratic society and is thus an
> issue at the very heart of the protection afforded by Article 9.
>
> Moreover, one of the ways in which the right to manifest one's religion
> may be exercised, especially in the case of a religious community, is the
> opportunity to seek legal protection for the community, its members and
> its property, so that Article 9 must be seen not only in the light of Article 11,
> but also in the light of Article 6.'[104]

---

[102] *Metropolitan Church of Bessarabia and others v. Moldova*, (2002) 35 EHRR 306, para. 141.

[103] *Ibid.*, at para. 142.

[104] *Ibid.*, at para. 118. A comparable interrelation has been expressed by the Court in the case of political association: 'The Court reiterates that notwithstanding its autono-mous role and particular sphere of application, Article 11 must also be considered in the light of Article 10. The protection of opinions and the freedom to express them is one of the objectives of the freedoms of assembly and association as enshrined in Article 11 ... That applies all the more in relation to political parties in view of their essential role in ensuring pluralism and the proper functioning of democracy ... As the Court has said many times, there can be no democracy without pluralism. It is for that reason that freedom of expression as enshrined in Article 10 is applicable, subject to paragraph 2, not only to "information" or "ideas" that are favourably received or regarded as inoffensive or as a matter of indifference, but also to those that offend, shock or disturb. The fact that their activities form part of a collective exercise of freedom of expression in itself entitles political parties to seek the protection of Articles 10 and 11 of the Convention' – *Freedom and Democracy Party (ÖZDEP) v. Turkey* (2001) 31 EHRR 674, para. 37. See also *United Communist Party of Turkey and others v. Turkey* (1998) 26 EHRR 121, paras. 42–3.

Article 11 guarantees freedom of association as an end in itself. However, Article 9 is seemingly extended by Article 11 when the claim concerns safeguarding associative religious life against State interference. The Court made clear that the right to manifest one's religion 'encompasses the expectation that believers will be allowed to associate freely', without considering association merely as a means to the realisation of other forms of manifestation. It also prized the straightforward autonomous 'existence' of religious communities as indispensable for pluralism.

The European Court may therefore be taken to have revised the European Commission's restrictive interpretation of the scope of Article 9 in *X. v. Austria*,[105] concerning the dissolution by the State of an association founded by the applicant as the organisational vehicle for the Moon sect. The Commission decided that the applicant had not sufficiently demonstrated for the purposes of Article 9:

> 'that there has been any interference with his freedom of religion as a follower of the Moon sect; in particular it has [not] been shown that the dissolution of the association in which the sect wanted to organise itself did as such interfere with the manifestation of his religion or belief in worship, teaching, practice and observance. As the Government have stressed, the practice even of a non-recognised religion is fully guaranteed in Austria by Article 63(2) of the Treaty of St Germain independently from any form of registration.'[106]

Nevertheless, there is some consistency between this case and the European Court's reasoning in the *Metropolitan Church* case in that the only applicant in *X. v. Austria* was the individual claimant and not the association formed by him, and it would appear that the dissolution of the applicant's association did not have the impact on him that the refusal to recognise the Metropolitan Church of Bessarabia had on that Church and its members.

The importance of the associative aspects of religious manifestation has also been underscored in recent decisions such as *Hasan and Chaush v. Bulgaria*,[107] affirmed in *Supreme Holy Council of the Muslim Community v. Bulgaria*,[108] in which organised structure was regarded as

---

[105] *X. v. Austria*, App. No. 8652/79 (1981) 26 D&R 89.

[106] *Ibid.*, at 92–3. The word 'not' is omitted from the English text by a typographical error, made evident from the French text. As the headnotes put it there were '[n]o factors showing that the legal structure of an organisation was necessary for the manifestation of the religion in question'.

[107] *Hasan and Chaush v. Bulgaria* (2002) 34(6) EHRR 1339.

[108] *Supreme Holy Council of the Muslim Community v. Bulgaria* (App. No. 39023/97), Judgment of 16 December 2004, at para. 73. The Court found that there had been

central to the existence of religious communities,[109] and *Sidiropoulos v. Greece*,[110] in which the Court (in the context of Article 11) reiterated that the right of association is not to be construed narrowly and that convincing and compelling reasons are required to justify restriction of the right.[111] In *Refah Partisi (the Welfare Party) and others v. Turkey*,[112] this was put even more emphatically: 'Drastic measures, such as the dissolution of an entire political party and a disability barring its leaders from carrying on any similar activity for a specified period, may be taken only in the most serious cases.'[113] Nevertheless, it is notable that the Court in *Metropolitan Church* chose Article 9 to embrace all of the allegations, particularly as commentators typically focus more on freedom of association and discrimination when concerned with the misuse of registration requirements as a means of preventing the emergence of religious associations.[114]

---

an interference with the applicant organisation's right under Article 9 in that the relevant law, as applied in practice, required all believers belonging to a particular religion and willing to participate in the community's organisation, to form a single structure, headed by a single leadership even if the community is divided, without the possibility for those supporting other leaders to have an independent organisational life and control over part of the community's assets (paras. 81 and 85). The law thus left no choice to the religious leaders but to compete in seeking the recognition of the government of the day, each leader proposing to 'unite' the believers under his guidance.

[109] 'The Court recalls that religious communities traditionally and universally exist in the form of organised structures. They abide by rules which are often seen by followers as being of a divine origin. Religious ceremonies have their meaning and sacred value for the believers if they have been conducted by ministers empowered for that purpose in compliance with these rules. The personality of the religious ministers is undoubtedly of importance to every member of the community. Participation in the life of the community is thus a manifestation of one's religion, protected by Article 9 of the Convention.' (*Ibid.*, at para. 62).

[110] *Sidiropoulos v. Greece* (1999) 27 EHRR p. 633.

[111] 'The Court points out that the right to form an association is an inherent part of the right set forth in Article 11, even if that Article only makes express reference to the right to form trade unions. That citizens should be able to form a legal entity in order to act collectively in a field of mutual interest is one of the most important aspects of the right to freedom of association, without which that right would be deprived of any meaning … the exceptions set out in Article 11 are to be construed strictly; only convincing and compelling reasons can justify restrictions on freedom of association.' (*Ibid.*, at para. 40). See also *United Communist Party of Turkey and others v. Turkey* (1998) 26 EHRR 121, para. 46.

[112] *Refah Partisi (the Welfare Party) and others v. Turkey* (2003) 37 EHRR 1.

[113] *Ibid.*, at para. 100.

[114] See, for example, H. Clayson Smith, '*Liberte, Egalite et Fraternite* at Risk for New Religious Movements in France', Brigham Young UL Rev. (2000) 1099, at 1127. For an account of the importance of legal personality and entity structure to religious

The Special Rapporteur has also tended to focus on discrimination when drawing attention to the refusal to grant recognition in numerous countries such as Bulgaria,[115] the Russian Federation,[116] Kazakhstan,[117] Uzbekistan,[118] the Ukraine,[119] Turkmenistan,[120] Azerbaijan,[121] Nauru,[122] Greece,[123] Sudan,[124] Turkey,[125] Argentina,[126] Armenia,[127] Romania,[128] Slovakia[129] and Moldova.[130] The Court in *Metropolitan Church* was able to avoid examining the Article 14 claim as it amounted to no more than a repetition of the Article 9 assertions.

The European Court in *Metropolitan Church* also supported the need to ensure judicial protection for the community, its members and its assets – apparently extending to all church property, including humanitarian aid sent from the United States. This is more generous than the European Court's decision in *Holy Monasteries v. Greece*,[131] which confined the scope of protection under Article 9 only to 'objects intended for the celebration of divine worship'.[132] As the confiscation of monastery property applied to agricultural land, pastures and forest, it fell under the protection of Article 1 of the First Protocol even though the applicants claimed that it 'deprived them of the means necessary for pursuing their religious objectives and preserving the treasures of

organisations, see ODIHR, *Freedom of Religion or Belief: Laws Affecting the Structuring of Religious Communities*, Review Conference, September 1999, ODIHR (1999).

[115] UN Doc. E/CN.4/1997/91 (1996), para. 19(b) (Bulgaria); UN Doc. A/58/296 (2003), p. 7, para. 28 (Bulgaria).
[116] UN Doc. E/CN.4/1998/6 (1998), para. 58(b) (Russian Federation).
[117] UN Doc. E/CN.4/2000/65 (2000), para. 60 (Kazakhstan); UN Doc. A/58/296 (2003), p. 12, paras. 67–8 (Kazakhstan).
[118] UN Doc. E/CN.4/2000/65 (2000), para. 75 (Uzbekistan); UN Doc. E/CN.4/2004/63 (2004), p. 14, para. 76 (Uzbekistan).
[119] UN Doc. E/CN.4/2000/65 (2000), para. 98 (Ukraine).
[120] UN Doc. E/CN.4/2001/63 (2001), pp. 34–5, paras. 133 and 138 (Turkmenistan).
[121] UN Doc. A/57/274 (2002), p. 4, para. 14 (Azerbaijan).
[122] UN Doc. E/CN.4/2001/63 (2001), p. 29, para. 104 (Nauru).
[123] UN Doc. A/51/542/Add.1 (1996), para. 57 and paras. 71–4 (Greece).
[124] UN Doc. A/51/542/Add.2 (1996), para. 58 (Sudan).
[125] UN Doc. A/55/280/Add.1 (2000), pp. 27–9, paras. 157–64 (Turkey).
[126] UN Doc. E/CN.4/2002/73/Add.1 (2002), p. 33, para. 155 (Argentina).
[127] UN Doc. A/58/296 (2003), p. 5, para. 11 (Armenia).
[128] UN Doc. E/CN.4/2004/63/Add.2 (2004), p. 8, para. 28 (Romania) and p. 19, paras. 94–5 (Romania).
[129] UN Doc. E/CN.4/2004/63 (2004), p. 16, para. 90 (Slovakia).
[130] UN Doc. A/57/274 (2002), p. 10, para. 51 (Moldova).
[131] *Holy Monasteries v. Greece* (Ser. A) No. 301 (1995) ECtHR.   [132] *Ibid.*, at para. 87.

Christendom' and 'would impede the carrying out of their ascetic mission'.[133]

The *Metropolitan Church* case is undoubtedly of enormous contemporary significance given the prevalence of the practice of so many States in requiring registration of religious groups as a precondition to their official recognition. It also serves to heighten awareness of the way in which issues of discrimination and minorities are inextricably linked to religious manifestation. Probably more than any other human rights body, the OSCE has emphasised the importance of official recognition for religious bodies.[134] Registration requirements affect religious groups acutely, as reflected in Dinstein's observation that 'freedom of religion, as an individual right, may be nullified unless complemented by a collective human right of the religious group to construct the infrastructure making possible the full enjoyment of that freedom by individuals'.[135] The Special Rapporteur has consistently stressed that all religions or belief-based movements, regardless of their length of existence, geographical origin or ideological foundations, must benefit from all the guarantees attaching to respect for the right to freedom of thought, conscience, religion and belief.[136] The Special Rapporteur has added greatly to the appreciation of just how widespread is the abuse of the registration process and the consequences for religious entities, pointing out that in many countries, recognition gives religious groups the legal personality necessary to enter into contracts, without which they could not function or be permitted to claim allowances or tax benefits[137] (a point echoed by the Human Rights Committee when asking States about the availability of financial support and other

---

[133] *Ibid.*, at para. 86.

[134] See in particular the ODIHR, 'The Human Dimension Seminar on Constitutional, Legal and Administrative Aspects of the Freedom of Religion' held in Warsaw, 16–19 April 1996, *Consolidated Summary*, ODIHR (1996); 'Guidelines for Review of Legislation Pertaining to Religion or Belief' prepared by the OSCE/ODIHR Advisory Panel of Experts on Freedom of Religion and Belief, in consultation with the Council of Europe's Commission for Democracy Through Law (Venice Commission), adopted by the Venice Commission at its 59th plenary session (Venice, 18–19 June 2004).

[135] See, for example, UN Doc. E/CN.4/2005/61/Add.1 (2005), p. 39, para. 154 (Kyrgyzstan). See also Y. Dinstein (ed.), *The Protection of Minorities and Human Rights*, Dordrecht/London: Martinus Nijhoff (1992), p. 158.

[136] See, for example: UN Doc. E/CN.4/1988/45 (1988), p. 2, para. 8; UN Doc. E/CN.4/1989/44 (1989), p. 4, para. 17.

[137] K. Krassimir, *Religious Freedom in Southeastern and Central Europe*, Vienna/Sofia: International Helsinki Federation for Human Rights (2001) ('IHF 2001 Report'), at p. 10.

benefits derived by recognition).[138] Protection for mainstream religions is among the motivations for banning certain religious groups, to maintain 'religious harmony',[139] to avoid disturbances,[140] to prevent non-nationals from preaching,[141] to prevent certain mainstream religions from being practised at all (even privately),[142] and to prevent proselytism.[143] The registration process often places excessive discretion in the hands of States and has been used widely, for example, to prevent groups meeting unless registered,[144] to prevent evangelism or charitable work, to restrict religious seminars, the printing of religious materials and participation in church meetings,[145] and to prevent the building or use of places of worship.[146] The Human Rights Committee, in reviewing State reports, has understandably closely scrutinised legislation giving discretion to States in the registration of religious communities.[147]

Registration criteria are often devised to exclude those groups that are small in membership or are newly-established. Some countries merely formulate criteria in such a way that the submissions of the historical churches would automatically conform (Hungary).[148] Others (the Russian Federation) have denied registration for trivial reasons, such as spelling mistakes.[149] Krishnaswami was critical both of numerical

---

[138] UN Doc. A/36/40 (1981), p. 76, para. 359 (Norway); UN Doc. A/43/40 (1988), p. 112, para. 480 (Belgium). See also the Special Rapporteur's comments on Romania – UN Doc. E/CN.4/2004/63/Add.2 (2004), p. 8, paras. 31–3 (Romania).

[139] UN Doc. E/CN.4/1990/46 (1990), p. 19, para. 49 (Indonesia).

[140] UN Doc. E/CN.4/1993/62 (1993), p. 40, para. 36 (Indonesia).

[141] UN Doc. E/CN.4/1995/91 (1995), p. 20 (Belarus).

[142] UN Doc. E/CN.4/1995/91 (1995), pp. 21–3 (Bhutan).

[143] UN Doc. E/CN.4/1995/91 (1995), p. 65 (Nepal).

[144] UN Doc. A/58/296 (2003), p. 6, para. 24 (Belarus); UN Doc. E/CN.4/2005/61/Add.1 (2005), p. 10, para. 31 (Belarus) and p. 83, para. 332 (Uzbekistan).

[145] UN Doc. E/CN.4/1988/45 (1988), p. 6 (USSR).

[146] UN Doc. E/CN.4/2004/63/Add.2 (2004), p. 12, para. 53 (Romania); UN Doc. E/CN.4/2005/61/Add.1 (2005), p. 10, para. 33 (Belarus), p. 39, para. 153 (Kyrgyzstan) and p. 4, para. 12 (Azerbaijan).

[147] UN Doc. A/41/40 (1986), p. 44, para. 210 (Finland); UN Doc. A/41/40 (1986), p. 14, para. 73 (Luxembourg); UN Doc. A/36/40 (1981), p. 12, para. 57 (Venezuela); UN Doc. A/42/40 (1987), p. 83, para. 329 (Romania). See also: UN Doc. A/43/40 (1988), p. 42, para. 181 (Denmark); UN Doc. A/45/40 vol. 1 (1990), p. 116, para. 526 (Tunisia); UN Doc. A/46/40 (1991), p. 112, para. 446 (Panama); UN Doc. A/47/40 (1994), p. 15, para. 65 (Morocco); UN Doc. A/47/40 (1994), p. 47, para. 206 (Iraq).

[148] International Helsinki Federation for Human Rights (IHF), *Religious Intolerance in Selected OSCE Countries in 2000: Report to the Seminar on Freedom of Religion or Belief in the OSCE Region*, The Hague: IHF (2001) ('IHF 2000 Report'), at p. 18.

[149] IHF 2000 Report, at p. 23. See also I. Basova, 'Freedom Under Fire: The New Russian Religious Law', *Temple International and Comparative Law Journal*, (2000) 181.

limits for recognition as well as unnecessary restrictions on function that may follow recognition:

> '[W]here the law prescribes a minimum membership for forming a religious association, but the religion itself considers fewer members to be sufficient for this purpose, a small group may be handicapped in its desire to organize. In a country where the right to organize a religious group is recognized only if the sole purpose of the group is to hold religious services, this would constitute a severe limitation upon those religions for whom propagation of their faith, social, cultural or humanitarian activities, or the distribution of alms, are essential.'[150]

Numerical criteria were also condemned by the European Court in *Manoussakis and others v. Greece* when it was left to leaders of the dominant religion to examine whether the Jehovah's Witnesses' planning application arose from genuine religious need, represented by support from at least fifty families from more or less the same neighbourhood.[151]

Even if criteria for registration are not discriminatory, discrimination is often practised in procedural delays lasting several years and in the strictness with which registration requirements are enforced, as evidenced, for example, by allegations received by the Special Rapporteur concerning Zaire,[152] Iran,[153] and Cameroon.[154]

The Human Rights Committee has likewise repeatedly stressed concern for minority religions in General Comment No. 22 (as well as in State reports), expressing particular concern for minorities that are newly-established and even those that oppose State ideology.[155] Similarly, with regard to Article 27, the Human Rights Committee emphasised that the denial to religious minorities of benefits or privileges within the gift of the State constitutes discrimination prohibited under Articles 18, 26 and 27,[156] a point reaffirmed in its examination

---

[150] Krishnaswami, 'Study of Discrimination', 227, at 265.
[151] *Manoussakis and others v. Greece* (1997) 23 EHRR 387.
[152] UN Doc. E/CN.4/1990/46 (1990), p. 54, para. 92 (Zaire).
[153] UN Doc. E/CN.4/1992/52 (1992), p. 34, para. 50 (Iran).
[154] UN Doc. E/CN.4/1994/79 (1994), p. 38, para. 40 (Camaroon).
[155] Paras. 2, 9 and 10 of General Comment No. 22. See also T. S. Orlin, 'Religious Pluralism and Freedom of Religion: Its Protection in the Light of Church/State Relationships', in A. Rosas and J. E. Helgesen (eds.), *The Strength of Diversity – Human Rights and the Pluralist Democracy*, Dordrecht/London: Martinus Nijhoff (1992), p. 89.
[156] See General Comment No. 23 (50) on Article 27: UN Doc. CCPR/C/21/Rev.1/Add.5 (1994), reprinted in UN Doc. A/49/40 (1994), p. 107.

of State reports.[157] It has enquired about the prohibition of sects in some countries,[158] as well as obstacles to the legal recognition of sects.[159] The Human Rights Committee has also been keen to discern the procedures that exist in various countries for the legal recognition and authorisation of religious denominations and whether, once registered, they benefit from equal protection with those that enjoy State privilege.[160]

Krishnaswami added a different dimension to the potential impact of discrimination in the recognition of religions when commenting that it could constitute interference with the *forum internum*:

> '[I]f the State has discretionary power to grant or to refuse recognition, and if the privileges accorded to recognized religions, or to their followers, are very different from those accorded to unrecognized ones, this may lead to discrimination. Where the cumulative impact of such arrangements is severe – as in countries where to a large extent the personal status of each individual is regulated by the religious law of his community – even the basic right of an individual to change his religion or belief may be seriously impaired.'[161]

The issue of legal recognition is therefore one of vital topical importance, not only when assessing whether there has been State interference but also because of its coincidence with concerns for discrimination. The *Metropolitan Church* case gave the European Court opportunity to determine that there had been interference with a wider range of manifestations than was possible in previous decisions. However, the European institutions still appear to have been slow in giving acknowledgement to the complete range of manifestations of religion or belief that have long been recognised at United Nations level, as the following discussion will aim to illustrate.

---

[157] UN Doc. A/48/40 (1993), pp. 57–61, para. 22 (Iran).

[158] UN Doc. A/44/40 (1989), p. 106, para. 470 (Camaroon).

[159] UN Doc. A/42/40 (1987), p. 69, para. 270 (Zaire); UN Doc. A/43/40 (1988), p. 19, para. 71 (Trinidad and Tobago).

[160] UN Doc. A/53/40 (1998), p. 32, para. 175 (Lithuania); UN Doc. A/45/40 vol. 1 (1990), p. 51, para. 212 (Argentina); UN Doc. A/45/40 vol. 1 (1990), p. 68, para. 309 (Costa Rica); UN Doc. A/47/40 (1994), p. 74, para. 316 (Peru); UN Doc. A/57/40 vol. 1 (2002), p. 78, para. 84(13) (Moldova).

[161] Krishnaswami, 'Study of Discrimination', 227, at 262.

The scope of recognised manifestations of religion or belief

The degree to which different forms of manifestation of religion or belief have been given recognition in the practice of the United Nations and European institutions will now be considered, taking as the framework for analysis Article 6 of the 1981 Declaration. Extensive use will be made of the reports of the Special Rapporteur on freedom of religion or belief because of their value in illustrating the range of religious manifestations throughout the world.[162] In addition, the influential study by Krishnaswami[163] is of direct relevance since it comprises a review of those manifestations which he believed fell under the protection of Article 18 of the Universal Declaration. United Nations materials are of importance even in the context of European Convention claims, as Carolyn Evans has rightly pointed out:

'These studies could be taken in conjunction with the claims of applicants to demonstrate some of the types of behaviour that are internationally accepted as manifestations of religion or belief. Thus an applicant who could show that the State restricted one of the types of manifestation outlined in internationally recognised studies as a manifestation of belief, and who made a reasonable claim that such a manifestation was an important part of his or her religion, should be presumed to have a case under Article 9 (1) unless his or her claim can be shown to be fraudulent ...

These United Nations materials could be a valuable resource for the Court as they draw on studies and input from the wider international community. While the overwhelming majority of judges on the Court come from States that are predominantly Christian, the United Nations studies incorporate comments from States with a far wider range of religious demographics. Groups such as Muslims, Hindus, or Buddhists, which are minorities in most Council of Europe States, form majorities in other United Nations member States. Because of this, an issue such as the wearing of religious apparel, which a number of Western authors and judges consider marginal to religion, has been given greater prominence in international materials. Reference to such materials could prove useful to members of the Court in helping to ensure that majoritarian concepts of what it is to manifest a religion do not gain inappropriate significance in the Court's case law.'[164]

---

[162] For a summary of the work of the Special Rapporteur to 1995, see B. Dickson, 'The United Nations and Freedom of Religion', 44 Int'l & Comp Law Q (1995) 327. See also R. Amor, 'The Mandate of the UN Special Rapporteur', 12 Emory Int'l L Rev (1998) 10.
[163] Krishnaswami, 'Study of Discrimination', 227.
[164] C. Evans, *Freedom of Religion Under the European Convention*, pp. 125–7.

Of course, neither the European Court nor the Human Rights Committee is obliged to take United Nations studies or Article 6 of the 1981 Declaration into account in decision-making but it would be imprudent to ignore such materials, particularly on the issue of what constitutes the proper manifestation of religion or belief. There is also a tendency for European cases to be cited in Optional Protocol communications before the Human Rights Committee.[165] Perhaps of even greater value than the United Nations studies are the practical illustrations provided by the Special Rapporteur's reports, since they highlight recurring patterns of violation worldwide with which the European Court in its regional context may be less familiar but which the Court (and the Human Rights Committee) should nevertheless be astute to acknowledge. These reports are of importance, for immediate purposes, in cementing the discussion which has gone before in this chapter concerning the realisation of different forms of manifestation and the nature of restrictions frequently imposed by States. Once particular forms of manifestation win fuller acceptance, less reliance may need to be placed in the European context on such devices as the *Arrowsmith* test as a means of circumscribing broad notions of 'practice'. The Special Rapporteur's reports do not address extensively the application of the limitation provisions (which will be discussed later in this chapter) beyond offering a valuable warning of the range of inappropriate State claims routinely made to justify violation, as found in the responses to the allegations transmitted by the Special Rapporteur.

It also noteworthy that the list of recognised forms of manifestation given in Article 6 of the 1981 Declaration is a conservative one given that the ambitions of many countries remained unfulfilled in the face of tremendous opposition from Communist and Islamic countries in the drafting of the Declaration. The path leading up to the adoption of the 1981 Declaration was tortuous,[166] but an early milestone was the draft

[165] See, for example: K. *Singh Bhinder v. Canada*, Communication No. 208/1986 (views of 9 November 1989), UN Doc. A/45/40 vol. 2 (1990), p. 50 (Canada appealed, at para. 4.3, to the European Commission's reasoning in *Ahmad v. United Kingdom* (1982) 4 EHRR 126, paras. 11 and 13 (*X. v. United Kingdom*, App. 8160/78 (1981) 22 D&R 27)); *Malcolm Ross v. Canada*, Communication No. 736/1997 (views of 18 October 2000), UN Doc. A/56/40 vol. 2 (2001) 69, at para. 5.3, (Canada cited *Vogt v. Germany* (Ser. A) No. 323–A (1995) ECtHR).

[166] For the drafting history of the 1981 Declaration, see: Liskofsky, 'The UN Declaration on the Elimination of Religious Intolerance'; M. S. McDougal, H. D. Lasswell and L. Chen, *Human Rights and World Public Order*, New Haven/London: Yale University

declaration on the elimination of all forms of religious intolerance prepared by the Sub-Commission on Prevention of Discrimination and Protection of Minorities (the 'Sub-Commission's Draft Declaration'). This was presented to the Commission on Human Rights at its 20th session 'as representing its general views consistent with the principles adopted in 1960, regarding the substance which should be taken into account in preparing a draft declaration'.[167] Excruciatingly slow progress was then made while attention was intermittently focused on the Draft International Convention on the Elimination of All Forms of Religious Intolerance and then, between 1972 and 1981, on the equivalent Draft Declaration until the adoption by the General Assembly in November 1981 of the Declaration on the Elimination of All Forms of Intolerance and of Discrimination Based on Religion or Belief. The resulting text for the 1981 Declaration was therefore the product of a long and hard fought battle. Article 6 has been described as 'probably the most significant in the Declaration, because of its particularity'.[168] The sub-headings in the remainder of this discussion reproduce the text of each paragraph of Article 6 and provide the framework for detailed consideration of the standards applied at Universal and European levels to different forms of manifestation.

(a) 'To worship or assemble in connection with a religion or belief, and to establish and maintain places for these purposes'

Worship or assemble The term 'worship' as understood by the Human Rights Committee and explained in paragraph 4 of General

---

Press (1980), pp. 667–84 (1980); E. Schwelb, 'The International Convention on the Elimination of All Forms of Racial Discrimination 1965', 15 Int'l & Comp Law Q (1966) 996; H. A. Jack, *Eliminating All Forms of Religious Intolerance: What the United Nations Has Done and Can Do*, New York: WCRP (1972); H. A. Jack, *New Progress Toward a U.N. Declaration Against Religious Intolerance*, New York: WCRP (1973); H. A. Jack, *238 Words Towards Religious Freedom*, New York: WCRP (1975); H. A. Jack, *58 Words, Two Commas: Snail-Like Motion Toward a U.N. Declaration for Religious Freedom*, New York: WCRP (1976); H. A. Jack, *Slow Motion, Religiously*, New York: WCRP (1978); H. A. Jack, *U.N. Action Against Religious Discrimination*, New York: WCRP (1979); H. A. Jack, *The U.N. Declaration for Religious Freedom: The Result of Two Decades of Drafting*, WCRP, New York (1981) (H. A. Jack works cited by Tahzib, *Freedom of Religion or Belief*, p. 155).

[167] UN Doc. E/CN.4/873 (1964), para. 142, Resolution 3 (XVI), p. 63. The Draft Declaration is at the Annex, p. 64.

[168] S. Liskofsky, 'The UN Declaration on the Elimination of Religious Intolerance', p. 468.

Comment No. 22 clearly embraces, but is not confined to, institutional forms of worship: 'The concept of worship extends to ritual and cere-monial acts giving direct expression to belief, as well as various practices integral to such acts, including the building of places of worship, the use of ritual formulae and objects, the display of symbols, and the obser-vance of holidays and days of rest.' Although paragraph 4 falls short of providing illustrations of worship within non-traditional beliefs, there is no doubt that worship pursuant to such beliefs (which paragraph 2 reminds us are to be broadly construed) is included. This part of para-graph 4 is not directed at a detailed description of worship but is aimed instead at extending the term 'worship' to cover the essential prerequi-sites or means of worship, such as buildings and liturgical objects. Inevitably, the Human Rights Committee will need to assess the genu-ineness of the forms of worship claimed for any particular belief, and the rejection of the claim in *M.A.B., W.A.T. and J.-A.Y.T. v. Canada*,[169] that the propagation and worship of marijuana as the 'Sacrament' or 'God's tree of life' fell within Article 18, is not inconsistent with this conclusion. The Human Rights Committee certainly appears to be favourably inclined to non-institutional worship at sites of unique ceremonial importance.[170]

Consistent with a generous interpretation of the term 'worship' and the need to secure the preconditions for free worship, in examining State reports the Human Rights Committee has focused on freedom of

---

[169] *M.A.B., W.A.T. and J.-A.Y.T. v. Canada*, Communication No. 570/1993 (decision of 8 April 1994), UN Doc. A/49/40, vol. 2 (1994), p. 368.

[170] For example, in *Francis Hopu and Tepoaitu Bessert v. France* the Human Rights Committee found that the planned development of an ancestral burial ground in Tahiti constituted an arbitrary interference with privacy and family rights (in violation of Articles 17(1) and 23(1) of the ICCPR) – *Francis Hopu and Tepoaitu Bessert v. France*, Communication No. 549/1993 (views of 29 July 1997), UN Doc. A/52/40 vol. 2 (1999), p. 70. In a similar claim under Article 18, *Mathieu Vakoumé and others v. France*, the authors were members of the Touété tribe inhabiting a reservation on the Isle of Pines, where customary rights were exercised on land on which the State had granted development rights for the construction of a hotel complex. The authors claimed that they, 'like all Melanesians, live in a natural environment founded on a network of ties to their parents, their families and their dead. Veneration of the dead is a manifestation of religion and tradition inherent in their lifestyle, beliefs and culture' – *Mathieu Vakoumé and others v. France*, Communication No. 822/1998 (decision of 31 October 2000), UN Doc. A/56/40 vol. 2 (2001), p. 249, at p. 251, para. 3.6. Accordingly, they claimed that the 'destruction of the sacred site violated their freedom to manifest their religion or beliefs in worship and the observance of rights'. The issue unfortu-nately never came to be considered substantively as the communication was declared inadmissible for failure to exhaust all available domestic remedies.

worship as practised individually and collectively, both inside and out-side places designated for worship,[171] with concern for the practical consequences of restrictions on worship (prompting the Committee to ask Korea, for example, whether Koreans not only had free access to houses of worship but continued to attend them).[172] Unlike freedom of assembly, which Clapham suggests is only protected in the public realm and does not extend to private assembly,[173] the right to worship is qualified with the words, 'in public or private'. The need for this to be stated explicitly is evident from the Special Rapporteur's reports of restrictions in many countries on private and public worship.[174]

The Human Rights Committee's concern for securing freedom to worship extends also to restrictions on worship in particular circum-stances, such as in prison. The Human Rights Committee has empha-sised in paragraph 8 of General Comment No. 22 that '[p]ersons already subject to certain legitimate constraints, such as prisoners, continue to enjoy their rights to manifest their religion or belief to the fullest extent compatible with the specific nature of the constraint'. In *Boodoo v. Trinidad and Tobago*[175] a prisoner claimed that he had been forbidden from worshipping at Muslim prayer services and that his prayer-books had been taken from him. The Human Rights Committee found a violation of Article 18, taking all these claims together in the absence of any explanation from the State. As to the constraints of prison regulation, the European Commission has supported State restrictions on chapel worship in prison, heavily influenced by the need for prison discipline.[176] It is uncertain whether the position taken in

---

[171] UN Doc. A/38/40 (1983), p. 15, para. 74 (Mexico).

[172] UN Doc. A/39/40 (1984), p. 70, para. 382 (Korea). See also UN Doc. A/43/40 (1988), p. 69, para. 304 (Central African Republic); UN Doc. A/35/40 (1980), p. 29, para. 135 (Iraq).

[173] A. Clapham, *Human Rights in the Private Sphere*, Oxford: Clarendon Press (1993), p. 238.

[174] See, for example: UN Doc. E/CN.4/1995/91 (1995), pp. 14 and 17 (Saudi); UN Doc. E/CN.4/2005/61/Add.1 (2005), p. 25, para. 97 (Eritrea).

[175] *Boodoo v. Trinidad and Tobago*, Communication No. 721/1997 (views of 2 August 2002), UN Doc. A/57/40 vol. 2 (2002), p. 76.

[176] *Childs v. United Kingdom* (App. No. 9813/82), unpublished, decision of 1 March 1983, Council of Europe Digest of Strasbourg Case-Law relating to the European Convention on Human Rights, Section 9.2.1.1, p. 1. Robillard explores the exercise of religious freedom in prisons in the United Kingdom consistent with Article 9 standards: St. J. A. Robillard, 'Religion in Prison', 130 NLJ (1980) 800. See also N. S. Rodley, *The Treatment of Prisoners Under International Law*, Oxford: Clarendon Press (1999).

X. v. Germany,[177] in upholding the State's refusal to provide facilities for Anglican worship chosen by the prisoner, has been revised in light of the European Court's emphasis on denominational choice of worship in *Metropolitan Church of Bessarabia and others v. Moldova*.[178]

Restrictions on worship in other circumstances have been upheld by the European Commission, such as in *A. R. M. Chappell v. United Kingdom*,[179] when the closure of Stonehenge impeded midsummer solstice celebrations. The closure did not prevent solstice ceremonies at other sites, even though Stonehenge was of unique importance for Druidic worship and no alternative festival site could be found in that vicinity. This is not necessarily at odds with the Human Rights Committee's sensitivity to sites of unique ceremonial importance in *Francis Hopu and Tepoaitu Bessert v. France*,[180] or indeed its concern for minority religions,[181] but relates more to the application of limitation provisions in particular circumstances than the recognition of the right to worship generally.

In the context of restrictions on worship resulting from employment obligations, as discussed above in Chapter 3 under the heading 'Decisions based on available alternatives' at pp. 136–47, the element of choice in accepting and leaving employment appears readily to defeat claims under the European Convention so as to permit, in *X. v. United Kingdom*,[182] wide discretion to States in timetabling classes even if the effect is to exclude the possibility of a Muslim teacher worshipping at a nearby mosque on a Friday. Such decisions have some parallel with the Human Rights Committee's decision in *K. Singh Bhinder v. Canada*[183] (where the Sikh author had chosen employment that required a hard hat to be worn) although this case did not entail any restriction on the author's worship, on which the Committee would undoubtedly have placed a premium. It is perhaps surprising that the issue of worship did

---

[177] *X. v. Germany*, App. No. 2413/65 (1966) 23 CD 1.
[178] *Metropolitan Church of Bessarabia and others v. Moldova* (2002) 35 EHRR 306.
[179] *A. R. M. Chappell v. United Kingdom*, App. No. 12587/86 (1987) 53 D&R 241.
[180] *Francis Hopu and Tepoaitu Bessert v. France*, Communication No. 549/1993 (views of 29 July 1997), UN Doc. A/52/40 vol. 2 (1999), p. 70. See also *Mathieu Vakoumé and others v. France*, Communication No. 822/1998 (decision of 31 October 2000), UN Doc. A/56/40 vol. 2 (2001), p. 249.
[181] See *Kitok v. Sweden*, Communication No. 187/1985 (views of 27 July 1988), UN Doc. A/43/40 (1988), p. 221.
[182] *X. v. United Kingdom*, App. No. 8160/78 (1981) 22 D&R 27.
[183] *K. Singh Bhinder v. Canada*, Communication No. 208/1986 (views of 9 November 1989), UN Doc. A/45/40 vol. 2 (1990), p. 50.

not arise in the European Commission's decisions of *Stedman v. United Kingdom*[184] and *Konttinen v. Finland*,[185] concerning observance of days of rest, since these generally provide the only opportunity for collective worship,[186] and the European Commission in *X. v. United Kingdom*[187] had already rejected the State's claim that the right to worship alone or in community with others were mutually exclusive.[188]

The key to understanding these European decisions (other than those concerning prisoners) is that the outcome in each case did not prevent worship by the applicant in other circumstances than those specifically claimed. In reality and unsurprisingly worship is so readily recognised as a form of manifestation by both the European Commission[189] and the European Court[190] that claims based on restriction of the freedom to worship are generally accepted as such with little discussion. The European decisions focus predominantly on the grounds of limitation and might be criticised for allowing excessive discretion in favour of States (as discussed below under the heading 'Permissible limitations on the right to manifestation', at pp. 292–3) but without conspicuous departure from United Nations practice in relation to recognising the right to worship.

It is also worth mentioning that none of the European or Human Rights Committee decisions resulted in restrictions comparable to those on worship found in so many countries examined by the Special Rapporteur, which put the issue in context. These include the jailing

---

[184] *Stedman v. United Kingdom*, App. No. 29107/95 No. 89–A (1997) D&R p. 104.

[185] *Konttinen v. Finland*, App. No. 24949/94 (1996) 87 D&R 68.

[186] As D. J. Harris has pointed out in the context of the European Social Charter (signed 18 October 1961, 529 UNTS 89), 'immigrant or other minority group workers may be at a disadvantage if it is assumed that a part of the purpose of the day at rest is to allow a worker to practise his religion'. – D. J. Harris, *The European Social Charter*, Charlottesville: University Press of Virginia (1984), p. 43. See also D. Gomien, D. J. Harris and L. Zwaak, *Law and Practice of the European Convention on Human Rights and the European Social Charter*, Strasbourg: Council of Europe (1996).

[187] *X. v. United Kingdom*, App. No. 8160/78 (1981) 22 D&R p. 27.

[188] *Ibid.*, at p. 34, para. 5. See also *Logan v. United Kingdom*, App. No. 24875/94 (1996) 22 EHRR CD 178, concerning a claim that failure to take account of travel expenses when ordering child support payments meant that the applicant could not afford to travel to his Buddhist place of worship. The Commission commented that visits to places of worship were not an indispensable element of the applicant's religious worship (at p. CD 181).

[189] See, for example: *C. v. United Kingdom*, App. No. 10358/83 (1983) 37 D&R 142; *X. v. United Kingdom*, App. No. 8160/78 (1981) 22 D&R 27; *ISCON and others v. United Kingdom*, App. No. 20490/92 (1994) 90 D&R 90.

[190] See, for example: *Manoussakis and others v. Greece* (1997) 23 EHRR 387; *Metropolitan Church of Bessarabia and others v. Moldova* (2002) 35 EHRR 306.

and exclusion from places of worship of monks in China for demonstrating in protest at the State's conduct towards them,[191] as well as the forcible removal of hundreds of worshippers in the middle of religious services.[192] Measures restricting worship in some countries are very specific, such as in Viet Nam where religious services are effectively confined to those conducted by State-sponsored religious associations,[193] or in Burundi where the celebration of Mass has been forbidden on weekdays.[194] OSCE initiatives have also been valuable in pointing out restrictions on worship such as those in Armenia which require denominations other than the Armenian Apostolic Church to worship within their respective buildings only,[195] and those in Bulgaria, where peaceful meetings of religious communities are often disturbed violently.[196] However, it would appear that the most extreme attacks on worshippers have been by private actors.[197]

Establish and maintain places of worship and assembly   The right to build places of worship was recognised in paragraph 4 of General Comment No. 22 to be integral to worship, observance, practice and teaching, and by necessary implication includes also the right to maintain them. However, the need for sensitivity in the siting of religious buildings was acknowledged in the drafting of paragraph 4.[198] Restrictions on the use of buildings have, for the most part, historically been imposed by means of planning regulations, although in recent years registration procedures have taken centre stage in the means by which States constrain the structural aspects of religious practice.

Planning legislation has generally been allowed a wide margin of appreciation in European Convention cases under Article 8,[199] but in

---

[191]   UN Doc. E/CN.4/1995/91 (1995), p. 131 (China).

[192]   UN Doc. E/CN.4/1995/91/Add.1 (1995), p. 5, para. 8 (China).

[193]   UN Doc. E/CN.4/1994/79 (1994), p. 113, para. 79 (Viet Nam).

[194]   UN Doc. E/CN.4/1988/45 (1988), p. 4, para. 15 (Burundi).

[195]   IHF 2000 Report, p. 4.   [196] *Ibid.*, at p. 10.

[197]   For examples of attacks on congregations, see: UN Doc. E/CN.4/1995/91 (1995), p. 58 (Liberia); UN Doc. E/CN.4/2003/66 (2003), p. 13, para. 64 (Pakistan); UN Doc. A/57/274 (2002), p. 9, para. 46 (Pakistan); UN Doc. A/57/274 (2002), p. 9, para. 49 (Pakistan); UN Doc. A/57/274 (2002), p. 6, para. 29 (Egypt); and UN Doc. A/58/296 (2003), p. 11, para. 56 (India).

[198]   Mr Sadi emphasised the need to avoid provocation by building in the vicinity of rival places of worship (UN Doc. CCPR/C/SR. 1166 (1992), p. 5, para. 27). Mrs Higgins, referred to a recent project to set up a Carmelite convent at the entrance to the former Auschwitz concentration camp (*ibid.*, at p. 6, para. 31).

[199]   *Chapman v. United Kingdom* (2001) 33 EHRR 399, para. 92; *Buckley v. United Kingdom* (1997) 23 EHRR 101, para. 75.

Manoussakis and others v. Greece[200] the European Court took a more interventionist approach under Article 9 to the obstructions posed by the need for planning authorisation for the use of a rented room as a place of worship, since such restrictions 'call for very strict scrutiny by the Court'.[201] The potential for planning restrictions to operate as a preventive measure against religious minorities was made more prominent by the International Helsinki Federation for Human Rights ('IHF') when examining the use of planning restrictions in Germany to deny the building of a Turkish–Islamic centre,[202] and in Macedonia to prevent the reconstruction of a Jehovah's Witness Kingdom Hall on the basis that an urban plan did not 'provide for a location of a religious building on that very site'.[203] The Special Rapporteur has similarly scrutinised the use of planning regulations in numerous countries: Romania, where the Baptist Church at Comanesti was under threat of demolition because it had been built without permission;[204] Tajikistan, where it was alleged that three 'non-approved' mosques in the Frunze district had been destroyed;[205] Georgia, following pressure applied by the Georgian Orthodox Church on the authorities to make it difficult for Protestant and Armenian Orthodox communities to secure a permit to build places of worship;[206] Viet Nam, where permission was refused for a building which was then destroyed;[207] Bhutan, where the Seventh Day Adventist Church complained that the authorities refused to allow it to build a church even for its own citizens;[208] China, where several Buddhist institutes were allegedly destroyed on the grounds of contravention of health and safety regulations;[209] and Turkey, where formal notifications

---

[200] *Manoussakis and others v. Greece* (1997) 23 EHRR 387. See also *ISCON and others v. United Kingdom*, App. No. 20490/92 (1994) 90 D&R 90; *Beard v. United Kingdom* (2001) 33 EHRR 442.

[201] *Ibid.*, at para. 44.

[202] International Helsinki Federation for Human Rights (IHF), *Religious Discrimination and Related Violations of Helsinki Commitments, Report to the OSCE Supplementary Human Dimension Meeting on Freedom of Religion Vienna*, Vienna: IHF (1999), p. 11 (IHF 1999 Report).

[203] *Ibid.*, at p. 16.

[204] UN Doc. E/CN.4/1990/46 (1990), p. 37, para. 72 (Romania). See also UN Doc. A/42/40 (1987), p. 83, para. 331 (Romania).

[205] UN Doc. A/58/296 (2003), p. 16, para. 92 (Tajikistan).

[206] UN Doc. E/CN.4/2000/65 (2000), para. 40 (Georgia). See also UN Doc. E/CN.4/2004/63/Add.1 (2004), p. 11, para. 46 (Georgia).

[207] UN Doc. E/CN.4/2000/65 (2000), para. 99 (Viet Nam).

[208] UN Doc. E/CN.4/2001/63 (2001), p. 8, para. 19 (Bhutan).

[209] UN Doc. E/CN.4/2003/66 (2003), p. 7, paras. 21–3 (China).

were delivered to twenty-three congregations of Turkish Christians in Istanbul and other cities declaring that their rented or purchased places of worship were in a violation of municipal building laws.[210] In some countries, such as Saudi Arabia, the construction of Christian churches or chapels is allegedly prohibited altogether without the need to invoke planning or similar restrictions.[211] In other countries, the continued use of places of worship has simply been disallowed, such as Nigeria, where the authorities allegedly informed the Christian community that 150 buildings used as places of worship could not be used for that purpose,[212] and Myanmar, where the local authorities reportedly ordered Christians in various districts to stop conducting worship service in their churches.[213]

Recently, the Human Rights Chamber for Bosnia and Herzegovina in *The Islamic Community in Bosnia and Herzegovina v. The Republika Srpska*[214] assessed the inadequate facilities remaining for Muslims in Banja Luka following the destruction of mosques and desecration of graveyards during and after hostilities in 1993, compounded by a ban on the reconstruction of those mosques. The Chamber considered that the refusal to allow the rebuilding of the mosques was a violation of Article 9 of the European Convention but, significantly, it emphasised far more rigorously than the European institutions themselves ever have the positive obligation on States to protect these rights and freedoms by effective, reasonable and appropriate measures, and the need as a matter of urgency to remove the climate of fear to allow the practice of religion by all citizens in genuine freedom.[215] This contrasts with the permissive approach of the European Court when faced with opposing religious interests (at least until its decision in *Serif v. Greece*[216]).

Restrictions on carrying out repairs to existing buildings are common in some countries. In Egypt, a recurring issue faced by the Coptic Church concerns building and renovating restrictions under the 'Hamaiouni Decree' which resulted in delays of up to thirty years in the grant of permission for building or renovation work and the closure

---

[210] UN Doc. A/57/274 (2002), p. 10, paras. 52–3 (Turkey). See also UN Doc. A/57/274 (2002), p. 10, paras. 55–6 (Turkmenistan).

[211] UN Doc. E/CN.4/1990/46 (1990), p. 40, para. 74 (Saudi).

[212] UN Doc. E/CN.4/2000/65 (2000), para. 73 (Nigeria).

[213] UN Doc. A/57/274 (2002), p. 9, para. 40 (Myanmar).

[214] *The Islamic Community in Bosnia and Herzegovina v. The Republika Srpska*, Case No. CH/96/29, decision of 11 June 1999 (2000) 7(3) IHRR 833.

[215] *Ibid.*, at 859, para. 185.   [216] *Serif v. Greece* (1999) 31 EHRR 561.

of buildings in the interim.[217] A similar practice of delaying the grant of permits is alleged against Malaysia, where the aim is said to be opposition to the construction of places of Christian worship.[218] However, more commonly reported by the Special Rapporteur is the destruction of places of worship, such as in Indonesia, attributed to religious extremism affecting the Muslim and Christian communities,[219] in Chiapas, Mexico, where traditional rural leaders reportedly destroyed numerous Protestant churches,[220] and Moldova, where officials from the State Building Inspectorate allegedly gave the pastor of a Baptist church a new deadline for the enforced demolition of a church which had been erected illegally, even though the Baptists had reportedly paid a fine the previous year because of the illegal building work completed thirteen years earlier.[221]

Registration procedures are increasingly used to restrict minority religions in establishing or using places of worship. As discussed at length above under the heading 'Determination of whether there has been an interference', the European Court gave this issue some considerable prominence in *Metropolitan Church of Bessarabia and others v. Moldova*,[222] concluding succinctly that 'in the absence of recognition, the applicant Church may neither organise nor operate'.[223] In practice, registration formalities are most frequently used in the control of places of worship in a discriminatory way. For example, in the town of Belgorod, Russian authorities refused registration several times to the Catholic community because, once registered, they would demand the repatriation of the Catholic building which was given by the authorities to the Russian Orthodox Church.[224] Likewise, in Kyrgyzstan, it was

---

[217] See: S.E. Ibrahim et al., *The Copts of Egypt*, London: Minority Rights Group International (1996) at p. 23; UN Doc. E/CN.4/1990/46 (1990), p. 13, para. 40 (Egypt); UN Doc. E/CN.4/1992/52 (1992), pp. 15–17, para. 30 (Egypt). See also UN Doc. A/39/40 (1984), p. 57, para. 301 (Egypt) and UN Doc. A/57/274 (2002), p. 6, para. 29 (Egypt).

[218] UN Doc. E/CN.4/1995/91 (1995), p. 59 (Malaysia).

[219] UN Doc. E/CN.4/2000/65 (2000), para. 49 (Indonesia).

[220] UN Doc. E/CN.4/2000/65 (2000), para. 66 (Mexico).

[221] UN Doc. A/57/274 (2002), p. 9, para. 50 (Moldova).

[222] *Metropolitan Church of Bessarabia and others v. Moldova*, (2002) 35 EHRR 306.

[223] *Ibid.*, at para. 129.

[224] IHF 2000 Report, p. 24. For further discussion of the question of the return of religious property confiscated under the Communist regime, see UN Doc. E/CN.4/2004/63/Add.2 (2004), pp. 13–19, paras. 58–93 (Romania). See also *Palandjian v. Hungary*, Communication No. 1106/2002 (decision of 30 March 2004), UN Doc. A/59/40 vol. 2 (2004), p. 534.

announced that some 1,300 mosques would be subject to registration procedures in 2001 that would enable a special commission to evaluate the architectural, seismological and sanitary conditions of the mosques, so as to put many at risk of closure.[225] In other countries, the Special Rapporteur has noted that religious buildings have been at risk of selective destruction (Iraq)[226] or selective expropriation (Myanmar,[227] Iran,[228] Burundi,[229] Turkey[230] and China[231]).

The escalating use of registration and other formalities to obstruct the building and use of places of worship has therefore received attention at both Universal and European levels and, as illustrated by the Special Rapporteur, appears in a wide variety of guises. It is only in the light of the most recent European Court decision in *Metropolitan Church* that the European Convention may be seen to tackle this issue directly, in a manner consistent with the concern that has been voiced for some years by the Special Rapporteur. However, credit must also be given to the Human Rights Chamber for Bosnia and Herzegovina for its emphasis in *The Islamic Community in Bosnia and Herzegovina v. The Republika Srpska* on the positive obligation on States to protect places of worship and other sacred sites in a prevailing climate of hostility between religions.

(b) 'To establish and maintain appropriate charitable or humanitarian institutions'

General Comment No. 22 does not refer specifically to the right to establish and maintain charitable or humanitarian institutions, as recognised in Article 6(b) of the 1981 Declaration. However, paragraph 4 of General Comment No. 22 mentions that 'a broad range of acts' is encompassed within the freedom to manifest religion or belief and this may well be wide enough to admit the right to establish such charitable or humanitarian organisations.

Paragraph 4 also refers to ritual and ceremonial acts 'giving direct expression to belief' as well as various practices integral to such acts. It is doubtful whether the 'direct expression' formula is intended to impose

---

[225] *Ibid.*, at p. 20.
[226] UN Doc. E/CN.4/1989/44 (1989), p. 19, para. 44 (Iraq); UN Doc. E/CN.4/1993/62 (1993), p. 43, para. 39 (Iraq).
[227] UN Doc. E/CN.4/1994/79 (1994), p. 98, para. 64 (Myanmar).
[228] UN Doc. E/CN.4/1988/45 (1988), p. 5, para. 15 (Iran).
[229] UN Doc. E/CN.4/1988/45 (1988), pp. 4–5, para. 15 (Burundi).
[230] UN Doc. E/CN.4/1995/91 (1995), p. 104 (Turkey).
[231] UN Doc. E/CN.4/1995/91 (1995), p. 126 (China).

limits in the sense that the *Arrowsmith* test does in the context of Article 9 of the European Convention. In fact the *Arrowsmith* test might be said to represent a significant point of departure from Article 6 of the 1981 Declaration, if not also from the breadth of Article 18(1) of the ICCPR, particularly if the European Commission decision in *C. v. United Kingdom*[232] is to imply that protection under Article 9 is confined to 'acts of worship or devotion which are aspects of the practice of a religion or a belief in a generally recognised form'.[233] Against such a narrow interpretation of *C. v. United Kingdom* it may be argued that the European Commission's emphasis on conventional forms of manifestation was simply to stress the applicant's error in claiming that his resistance to 'neutral' State measures imposed generally (but contrary to his particular beliefs) constituted a form of manifestation. Similarly, the apparent hurdle of 'necessary' expression in such cases as *X. v. United Kingdom*[234] and *D. v. France*[235] may be said to be the result of the way in which the parties framed their Article 9 claims or was merely to emphasise the lack of any issue of conscience in the claim. If a stricter test of 'necessity' were to apply, the disparity between United Nations and European recognition of the right to establish and maintain appropriate charitable or humanitarian institutions would be all the more stark.

Fortunately, the more recent decision of the European Court in *Metropolitan Church of Bessarabia and others v. Moldova*[236] goes some way towards embracing such a right. Among the consequences of the State's refusal to recognise the applicant Church was that it was not entitled to judicial protection of its assets.[237] The European Court drew attention to the refusal of the Government Committee for Humanitarian Aid to authorise entry into Moldova of goods to the value of $9,000 sent from the United States, even though the goods had been given a transit visa by the Ukrainian authorities on the basis that they were a humanitarian gift. Ultimately the Deputy Prime Minister of Moldova intervened to classify the goods as humanitarian aid[238] but the Court's decision assists in supporting the inclusion within Article 9 of humanitarian practices if only by implication.

---

[232] *C. v. United Kingdom*, App. No. 10358/83 (1983) 37 D&R 142.
[233] *Ibid.*, at p. 144.
[234] *X. v. United Kingdom*, App. No. 5442/72 (1975) 1 D&R 41.
[235] *D. v. France*, App. No. 10180/82 (1983) 35 D&R 199.
[236] *Metropolitan Church of Bessarabia and others v. Moldova* (2002) 35 EHRR 306.
[237] *Ibid.*, at para. 105. [238] *Ibid.*, at paras. 85–7.

It is clear from the drafting of the 1981 Declaration that the right to establish certain 'educational' institutions is not within the realm of protection of Article 6(b), so that States are permitted to have sole responsibility in providing education.[239] It is necessary to distinguish three groups of educational institution because this principle only applies to one, namely, educational establishments provided by the State pursuant to its function as public educator. The limits to State discretion in matters of religion or belief have already been discussed in Chapter 3 under the heading 'Education', at pp. 165–75, and it is in relation to this function in particular that education was excluded from Article 6(b). Secondly, but quite separately, are educational establishments providing religious teaching, which are protected under Article 6(e). Thirdly, are charitable or humanitarian institutions established to provide education where the State is unable to do so. This latter category should in principle qualify as charitable or humanitarian institutions. As noted in Chapter 2 under the heading 'Social concern and inducements' at pp. 57–63, Krishnaswami considered that impressionable groups, such as children in orphanages or schools, run some risk of being subject to material inducement that might conceivably be regarded as coercive but he applauded the work of missionaries, who have achieved remarkable results in many parts of the world where children would not otherwise have been educated.[240] He also noted that it is sometimes argued that educational and social activities, such as the maintenance by a faith or by its missionaries of hospitals, schools and orphanages, 'constitute an unfair form of dissemination, since such activities are carried on amongst children – undoubtedly a particularly impressionable group'. However, he concluded that 'where the prior right of parents or guardians to decide whether or not their children shall attend religious instruction is conceded, and where the institutions in question advance social welfare, the advantages obtained by such educational and humanitarian activities can hardly be considered to constitute a material inducement to a change of religion or belief'.[241]

The right to establish and maintain appropriate charitable or humanitarian institutions has accordingly been the subject of attention by the Special Rapporteur when, for example, noting that the freedom to

---

[239] UN Doc. ESCOR, 1981, Supp. No. 5, at p. 144; UN Doc. E/1981/25 and UN Doc. E/CN.4/1475 (1981).
[240] Krishnaswami, 'Study of Discrimination', 227, at 242.   [241] *Ibid.*, at 255.

establish and maintain appropriate charitable or humanitarian institutions is brought into question when a religion or sect is banned by law.[242] He highlighted the position in Iran, where certain minorities had been deprived of the institutions necessary for the proper practice of their religion including those necessary for the maintenance of the social, educational and humanitarian activities of their community,[243] and in Viet Nam, where large numbers of humanitarian and religious institutions, including hospitals and orphanages had been forcibly closed or nationalised since 1975.[244]

The control of charitable or humanitarian institutions by the State or by the State Church has been a regular concern of the Special Rapporteur, even where such control exists for purely historical reasons. For example, the Special Rapporteur reported on the situation in Ireland involving the virtual monopoly of the Roman Catholic Church in the founding of hospitals. The Irish Government maintained that Article 6(b) of the 1981 Declaration clearly envisaged that hospitals, as charitable or humanitarian institutions, could be maintained by religious organisations if integrated by the State into its system of health-care delivery without discrimination.[245] By contrast, control of charitable and humanitarian institutions may be the result of discriminatory misappropriation, as was the case with property belonging to the Uniate Church in Romania (consisting of twenty schools, six hospitals, four orphanages, three retirement homes and other assets found in some 2,000 parishes), which had been applied to the Romanian Orthodox Church.[246] Control might also be achieved by granting the exclusive right to do charitable or humanitarian work to State institutions (such as in Armenia where this right had been conferred on the State-sponsored Armenian Apostolic Church)[247] or by denying the right to non-State institutions (such as Protestant organisations in Bulgaria).[248] Indirect means of controlling such work is sometimes achieved by more sweeping prohibitions, as in China, on carrying out any religious activities outside the Government recognised church.[249] Perhaps one of the

---

[242] UN Doc. E/CN.4/1987/35 (1986), p. 16, para. 51.

[243] UN Doc. E/CN.4/1988/45 (1988), p. 5, para. 15 (Iran).

[244] UN Doc. E/CN.4/1994/79 (1994), p. 113, para. 79 (Viet Nam).

[245] UN Doc. E/CN.4/1989/44 (1989), pp. 19 and 23, paras. 45 and 48 (Ireland).

[246] UN Doc. E/CN.4/1994/79 (1994), p. 103, para. 71 (Romania).

[247] IHF 2000 Report, at p. 4.

[248] IHF 2001 Report, p. 17. See also UN Doc. A/41/40 (1986), p. 14, para. 73 (Luxembourg).

[249] UN Doc. E/CN.4/1991/56 (1991), p. 69, para. 48 (China).

clearest threats to the establishment of charitable or humanitarian organisations is present in those countries like El Salvador where persecution (including extra-judicial execution) is directed on a large scale towards those belonging to religious denominations which are involved, out of social commitment, in work with the under-privileged classes of society.[250]

An accommodating approach to this issue has been taken in the Council of Europe Framework Convention for the Protection of National Minorities,[251] which contemplates in Article 8 obligations on the Parties 'to recognise that every person belonging to a national minority has the right to manifest his or her religion or belief and to establish religious institutions, organisations and associations'.

With these considerations in mind, the case law of the European Commission, which suggests that the establishment and maintenance of charitable or humanitarian institutions might be outside Article 9 (particularly on the application of the *Arrowsmith* test) should be re-examined. Only implicit recognition of such a right has been provided by the European Court (in the *Metropolitan Church* case).

(c) 'To make, acquire and use to an adequate extent the necessary articles and materials related to the rites or customs of a religion or belief'

The 1981 Declaration does not attempt to define the 'necessary articles and materials' contemplated in Article 6(c) although the Krishnaswami study gives an indication of items likely to fall within its scope when suggesting that,

> 'as a general rule the members of a religion or belief should not be prevented from acquiring or producing articles necessary for the performance of the rituals prescribed by their faith, such as prayer-books, candles, ritual wine and the like. And in cases where a country has adopted an exonomic system under which the Government controls

---

[250] UN Doc. E/CN.4/1992/52 (1992), p. 20, para. 33 (El Salvador).
[251] Council of Europe Framework Convention for the Protection of National Minorities, opened for signature 1 February 1995, 157 ETS. For further discussion on the Framework Convention, see: H. Klebes, 'Draft Protocol on Minority Rights to the ECHR', 14 HRLJ (1992) 140; H. Klebes, 'The Council of Europe's Framework Convention for the Protection of National Minorities' 16 HRLJ (1995) 92; A. Rönquist, 'The Council of Europe Framework Convention on for the Protection of National Minorities', 6(1) Helsinki Monitor (1995) 38.

means of production and distribution, the public authorities should make such articles, or the means of producing them, available to the groups concerned.'[252]

Although some States (Cuba) were reluctant to include express reference to the distribution and importation of 'articles and materials' proposed by the Sub-Commission,[253] both distribution and importation remain implicit within the expression 'acquire and use' as ultimately negotiated.

There is potential for overlap between Article 6(c) and other Articles of the 1981 Declaration but these are generally easily resolved. Given that separate protection is available under Article 6(d) to the freedom to write, issue and disseminate publications, it is likely that Article 6(c) was not itself intended to cover the activities of authors and publishers (nor even the use of published matter in seminaries – which Article 6(e) would cover – unless that use is for the purposes of devotion or worship).[254] It is unclear, however, whether Article 6(c) (or another Article) would protect against the seizure in Iraq of religious manuscripts and books from libraries or from private collections, including works of historical importance.[255] Interference with shrines is more likely to fall within Article 6(a), such as those in Iraq which were alleged to have been converted into Government offices.[256] When the use of 'articles and materials' relates less to worship than the celebration of particular ceremonies at sacred sites, that use is more likely to fall within Article 6(h).

Not all ceremonial items are protected by Article 6. The Human Rights Committee in *M.A.B., W.A.T. and J.-A.Y.T. v. Canada* dismissed as inadmissible *ratione materiae* a claim based on the use of marijuana as

---

[252] Krishnaswami, 'Study of Discrimination' 227, at 248.
[253] UN Doc. ESCOR, 1981, Supp. No. 5, p. 144; UN Doc. E/1981/25; UN Doc. E/CN.4/1475 (1981).
[254] However, the European Commission upheld (under Article 9(2)) the denial to a Tao Buddhist prisoner his request for religious text which contained illustrations of martial arts (*X. v. United Kingdom* App. No. 6886/75 (1976) 5 D&R 100).
[255] UN Doc. E/CN.4/1994/79 (1994), p. 79, para. 60 (Iraq).
[256] UN Doc. E/CN.4/1994/79 (1994), p. 79, para. 60 (Iraq). See also CHR Res. 2002/42, 'Elimination of all forms of religious intolerance', 23 April 2002, UN Doc. E/CN.4/2002/200 (2001): '4(e) To exert utmost efforts, in accordance with their national legislation and in conformity with international human rights standards, to ensure that religious places, sites and shrines are fully respected and protected and to take additional measures in cases where they are vulnerable to desecration or destruction' (this substantially follows the text of numerous previous resolutions of the Commission and General Assembly, for example, GA Res. 56/157 of 15 February 2002, UN Doc. A/56/583/Add.2 (2002)).

the 'Sacrament', as 'God's tree of life'.[257] In the context of the European Convention, the European Commission decided that the E-meter devised by the Church of Scientology only had commercial, rather than religious, significance.[258] Presumably even the narrow summary of Article 9 given in *C. v. United Kingdom*[259] concerning acts of worship and devotion would span the right to 'make, acquire and use to an adequate extent the necessary articles and materials related to the rites or customs of a religion or belief'. This is confirmed to some extent by the European Court's ruling in *Holy Monasteries v. Greece*,[260] which reaffirmed the protection given under Article 9 to 'objects intended for the celebration of divine worship'.[261]

Restrictions on the use of ritual articles and materials reported by the Special Rapporteur include the removal of crosses and other religious emblems from public places in Burundi,[262] Myanmar[263] and Armenia,[264] the prohibition in former Communist Albania against keeping religious symbols even privately (in the context of a wider ban on acts of worship such as making the sign of the cross or vocalising a prayer),[265] the arrest and detention in Saudi Arabia of those found possessing Christian pictures or the Bible in their home,[266] the threat of expulsion from Chamula lands in Mexico of those found reading the Bible,[267] and in Pakistan the arrest of Ahmadis wearing or displaying

---

[257] *M.A.B., W.A.T. and J.-A.Y.T. v. Canada*, Communication No. 570/1993 (decision of 8 April 1994), UN Doc. A/49/40, vol. 2 (1994), p. 368, at para. 4.2. See I. Loveland, 'Religious Drug Use as a Human Right?', 151 NLJ (2001) 41. Loveland comments on the futility of claims under the United Kingdom Human Rights Act 1998 by Rastafarians claiming possession and use of drugs in the manifestation of their religion.

[258] *X. and the Church of Scientology v. Sweden*, App. No. 7805/77 (1979) 16 D&R 68.

[259] *C. v. United Kingdom*, App. No. 10358/83 (1983) 37 D&R 142.

[260] *Holy Monasteries v. Greece* (Ser. A) No. 301 (1995) ECtHR.   [261] *Ibid.*, at para. 87.

[262] UN Doc. E/CN.4/1988/45 (1988), p. 4, para. 15 (Burundi).

[263] UN Doc. E/CN.4/2005/61/Add.1 (2005), p. 45, para. 172 (Myanmar).

[264] The Special Rapporteur transmitted to the Azerbaijani Government information on the systematic destruction of thousands of '*Khatchkars*' (stone crosses one metre wide by 2.5 metres long decorated with Christian symbols) in the Djulfa cemetery. Other '*Khatchkars*' were allegedly removed by truck to unknown destinations – UN Doc. A/58/296 (2003), p. 5, para. 16 (Armenia). (The Special Rapporteur drew attention to General Assembly Resolution 55/254 of 31 May 2001 on the protection of religious sites.)

[265] UN Doc. E/CN.4/1989/44 (1989), p. 7, para. 27 (Albania); UN Doc. E/CN.4/1990/46 (1990), p. 5, para. 23 (Albania).

[266] UN Doc. E/CN.4/1995/91 (1995), p. 17 (Saudi). See also UN Doc. E/CN.4/1999/58 (1999), paras. 31–2 (Saudi).

[267] UN Doc. E/CN.4/1995/91 (1995), p. 62 (Mexico).

articles which bear verses from the Koran.[268] In China, in June 2000, new regulations were allegedly proclaimed orally at Lhasa by the local authorities with a view to prohibiting the possession of altars and religious objects even in private homes.[269]

Article 6(c) may be taken to include protection for particular forms of dress and dietary regulations,[270] especially as no other Article of the 1981 Declaration is capable of embracing such widely recognised aspects of 'observance and practice of religion or belief', a term acknowledged in paragraph 4 of General Comment No. 22 to include 'not only ceremonial acts but also such customs as the observance of dietary regulations, the wearing of distinctive clothing or headcoverings' etc. While admitting the rationale for avoiding religious clothing in certain public institutions (for example schools[271] and possibly the armed forces[272]), Krishnaswami commented that it is 'desirable that persons whose faith prescribes such apparel should not be unreasonably prevented from wearing it'.[273]

The critical question is in what circumstances is the wearing of explicitly religious clothing acceptable? Certainly the European institutions limit such circumstances very narrowly. The European Commission in *Karaduman v. Turkey*[274] upheld the State's requirement that a photograph affixed to a degree certificate should depict the subject bare-headed and not, as the applicant wished, wearing a Muslim

---

[268] UN Doc. E/CN.4/1992/52 (1992), p. 75, para. 60 (Pakistan).

[269] UN Doc. E/CN.4/2001/63 (2001), p. 12, para. 27 (China).

[270] The origins are found in Article VI(5)(i) of the Sub-Commission Draft Declaration Article VI(5)(i) which is more explicit in its reference to dietary practice.

[271] This issue has been keenly felt in France. Steiner discusses the exclusion of Muslim girls from school for wearing a head-covering even though it does not interfere with their school work, and argues that France's treatment of the issue could be seen negatively (as the suppression of religious manifestation) or positively (as the toleration of multiculturalism, within certain limits): E. Steiner, 'The Muslim Scarf and the French Republic', 6 KCLJ (1995), 147. See also: S. Poulter 'Muslim Headscarves in Schools: Contrasting Legal Approaches in England and France', 17 Oxford J Leg Stud (1997) 43; F. Gaspard and F. Khosrokhavar, *Le Foulard et la République*, Paris: La Découverte (1995).

[272] Sheleff comments on the broad implications of the ban of the yarmulke in the armed forces for Jewish prayers: L. S. Sheleff, 'Rabbi Captain Goldman's Yarmulke, Freedom of Religion and Conscience, and Civil (Military) Disobedience', 17 Isr YB Hum Rts (1987) 197. See also G. Clayton and G. Pitt, 'Dress Codes and Freedom of Expression', EHRLR (1997) 54 – Clayton and Pitt argue that freedom to choose one's appearance is an aspect of freedom of expression deserving of protection.

[273] Krishnaswami, 'Study of Discrimination', 227, at 248.

[274] *Karaduman v. Turkey*, App. No. 16278/90 (1993) 74 D&R 93.

headscarf. The European Commission was influenced by a number of factors including the applicant's 'choice' in pursuing higher education in a secular university where it was necessary to ensure 'harmonious coexistence between students of different beliefs'. It also placed great store by the principle of secularity in Turkey and the apparent need, which was not substantiated, to restrict religious manifestations which 'may constitute pressure on students who do not practise that religion or those who adhere to another religion'. There was no evidence of such pressure, nor indeed any risk to public order (which the Commission also mentioned) from 'fundamentalist religious movements'.

The European Commission's concern was for the supposed risks and pressures that result from religious manifestation taking the form of straightforward religious observance or at most the expression of religious allegiance. To talk in terms of the principle of secularity in this secular university is not only to suggest that the applicant had a wide range of choice available to her but is to ignore the fact that the doctrine of secularity has been the source of widespread intolerance in Turkey. The degree of intolerance in Turkey against any form of religious dress is indicated by the ban imposed in July 2000 by the State Planning Organisation that prevented any civil servant or family member from wearing a headscarf at the organisation's rest and recreation facilities, and excluded those wearing 'beards, cloaks, turbans, skullcaps, headscarves or similar uncontemporary garb'.[275]

It is difficult to reconcile the decision in *Karaduman v. Turkey* with the importance given to religious dress by the Human Rights Committee. Although Krishnaswami expressed some support for the need to avoid religious clothing in certain public institutions, the European Court (like the Commission) appears to adopt an unduly rigid approach. In *Dahlab v. Switzerland*[276] the applicant was prohibited from wearing an Islamic headscarf in a State school where she taught, in reliance of Article 27(3) of the Federal Constitution, which made it compulsory to observe the principle of denominational neutrality in schools.[277] The applicant did not appear to have caused any obvious disturbance within the school. The Court accepted that during this

---

[275] IHF 2000 Report, p. 25.

[276] *Dahlab v. Switzerland* (App. No. 42393/98), Judgment of 15 February 2001.

[277] In a judgment of 26 September 1990 the Federal Court had held that the presence of a crucifix in State primary-school classrooms fell foul of this requirement of denominational neutrality (*ATF*, vol. 116 Ia, p. 252).

period there were no objections to the content or quality of her teaching. However, it went on to specify the potential harm of wearing a headscarf, in the following way:

'The Court accepts that it is very difficult to assess the impact that a powerful external symbol such as the wearing of a headscarf may have on the freedom of conscience and religion of very young children. The applicant's pupils were aged between four and eight, an age at which children wonder about many things and are also more easily influenced than older pupils. In those circumstances, it cannot be denied outright that the wearing of a headscarf might have some kind of proselytising effect, seeing that it appears to be imposed on women by a precept which is laid down in the Koran and which, as the Federal Court noted, is hard to square with the principle of gender equality. It therefore appears difficult to reconcile the wearing of an Islamic headscarf with the message of tolerance, respect for others and, above all, equality and non-discrimination that all teachers in a democratic society must convey to their pupils.

Accordingly, weighing the right of a teacher to manifest her religion against the need to protect pupils by preserving religious harmony, the Court considers that, in the circumstances of the case and having regard, above all, to the tender age of the children for whom the applicant was responsible as a representative of the State, the Geneva authorities did not exceed their margin of appreciation and that the measure they took was therefore not unreasonable.'

The Court considered the prohibition to be justified in principle and proportionate to the aim of protecting the rights and freedoms of others, public order and public safety. The supposed 'proselytising effects' were not clearly explained and it is unclear, for example, whether the underlying mischief opposed by the European Court lay in the fact that there was a clearly identifiable religious precept in which the form of dress originates, or in the possibility that the message conveyed by Muslim women's headdress was one of intolerance in view of popular claims to gender inequality. Even if a message at some level is conveyed by religious dress in these circumstances, the presence of teachers representing more than one religion must surely be symptomatic of genuine pluralism in a society. It may be questioned whether genuine pluralism exists in a country where teachers (whether in the classroom or outside) are not tolerated for disclosing their religious beliefs in simple forms of dress. If teachers, particularly of minority religions, are prohibited from wearing religious dress, the message is likely to be a powerful one of intolerance towards the religion concerned. Denominational neutrality is not thereby preserved. It is also odd that so much of the European Court's reasoning should turn upon a mere speculation 'that cannot be denied outright' about 'some kind of proselytising effect'. Nevertheless, the position of the European institutions is clear.[278]

The Special Rapporteur has addressed similar issues but with a strong accent on tolerance towards those wishing to adopt religious dress,[279] even in schools.[280]

But for these two European cases, most decisions concerning dress restrictions have been based on safety (for example, to require a Sikh motorcyclist in *X. v. United Kingdom*[281] to wear a crash helmet instead of a turban) or have been based on the level of control appropriate to the prison environment, to require a prison uniform to be worn (*X. v. United Kingdom*)[282] and prisoners to be clean-shaven (*X. v. Austria*).[283]

The Human Rights Committee has likewise supported safety restrictions to prevent a Sikh wearing a turban instead of safety headgear in an

---

[278] The issue is a live one in France, where on 10 February 2004 the National Assembly passed a bill on laicism with a special provision banning the conspicuous wearing of religious symbols such as crosses, headscarves and skullcaps in public places – International Helsinki Federation for Human Rights, country report on France (2004), p. 6.

[279] The Special Rapporteur noted that in Azerbaijan the Passports Department of the Ministry of the Interior has refused all photographs showing women wearing the *hijab* (UN Doc. E/CN.4/2001/63 (2001), p. 7, para. 17 (Azerbaijan)). The Special Rapporteur stressed that the wearing of the *hijab* or any other distinguishing elements causes a problem only in so far as it uses religion for other purposes, directly or indirectly expresses attitudes of intolerance towards others or can reasonably cause serious threats to the public order. If it blends in with the country's form of dress, and is observed normally, it should not give rise to limitations, reservations or objections, even where official documents are concerned (UN Doc. A/56/253 (2001), p. 48, para. 2 (Azerbaijan)).

[280] In the Special Rapporteur's Conclusions and Recommendations following a visit to Iran, the Special Rapporteur emphasised that the various community traditions and behaviour concerning dress should be respected, but believed that dress should not be turned into a political instrument and that flexible and tolerance attitudes should be shown so that the richness and variety of Iranian dress can be manifested without coercion. In particular, in the field of education, and especially in minority schools, the Special Rapporteur recommended freedom of dress on the understanding that this should obviously not be exercised in a manner contrary to its purposes (UN Doc. E/CN.4/1996/95/Add.2 (1996), para. 97 (Iran)).

[281] *X. v. United Kingdom* App. No. 7992/77 (1978) 14 D&R 234.

[282] *X. v. United Kingdom*, App. No. 8231/78 (1982) 28 D&R 5.

[283] *X. v. Austria*, App.No. 1753/63, 8 Yearbook (1965) 174.

industrial hard-hat area (*K. Singh Bhinder v. Canada*[284]). However, in *Riley et al. v. Canada*[285] the Human Rights Committee was unsympathetic to claims made by authors (who were both retired from the Royal Canadian Mounted Police ('RCMP') and were members of an organisation whose goal was to maintain tradition within the RCMP) who challenged the authorisation granted to a Khalsa Sikh officer to substitute a turban for the traditional wide brimmed 'mountie' stetson and forage cap. They claimed that the display of Khalsa Sikh symbols by Canada's national police implied RCMP–State endorsement of the exclusively male 'soldier-saint' Khalsa Sikh order and that in order to protect their rights under Article 18 the State should remain secular. They claimed that the concession which permits turbans to be worn introduces a denominational face to the most visible State agency. They also claimed violation of Articles 26 and 2(1) since this involved the RCMP in the advancement of Khalsa Sikh religious and political interests, which was denied to other groups.[286] The Committee concluded the claim was inadmissible since the authors had failed to show how the enjoyment of their rights under the Covenant had been affected by allowing Khalsa Sikh officers to wear religious symbols.[287]

As regards the wearing of beards as mandated by religious belief, the Committee recently found a violation of Article 18 in the forcible removal of a Muslim prisoner's beard (in conjunction with other claims) in *Boodoo v. Trinidad and Tobago*.[288]

Finally on the subject of dress, it should be remembered that just as secularity sometimes operates as a source of restriction when prohibiting religious dress, religious practice may on occasion raise issues of compatibility with human rights instruments when religious dress is expected to be worn. This is evident in both the Special Rapporteur's reports (of allegations that in Algeria women were threatened or killed for not respecting the Islamic dress code,[289] and that other forms of

---

[284] *K. Singh Bhinder v. Canada*, Communication No. 208/1986 (views of 9 November 1989), UN Doc. A/45/40 vol. 2 (1990), p. 50.

[285] *Riley et al. v. Canada*, Communication No. 1048/2002 (decision of 21 March 2002), UN Doc. A/57/40 vol. 2 (2002), p. 356.

[286] *Ibid.*, paras. 3.1, 3.3 and 3.5.   [287] *Ibid.*, para. 4.2.

[288] *Boodoo v. Trinidad and Tobago*, Communication No. 721/1997 (views of 2 August 2002), UN Doc. A/57/40 vol. 2 (2002), p. 76. See also *Patterson Mathews v. Trinidad and Tobago*, Communication No. 569/1993 (views of 31 March 1998), UN Doc. A/53/40 (1998), p. 30. (For further discussion, see Chapter 3 under the heading 'Decisions based on justified limitation on manifestation', pp. 121–36).

[289] UN Doc. E/CN.4/1995/91 (1995), p. 10 (Algeria).

public dress were strictly regulated in Afghanistan[290] and Sudan[291]) and in the Human Rights Committee's evaluation of State reports (most prominently in relation to Sudan).[292]

As to dietary restrictions, Krishnaswami pointed to the practical difficulties associated with dietary practices (so that, for example, it may be difficult in schools, hospitals, prisons or in the armed forces to meet the dietary requirements of all minority religions) and, at the same time, the need for public authorities to ensure that no one is prevented from observing the dietary practices prescribed by their religion or belief.[293] However, the strictness of the European Court's approach to the dietary requirements of certain minority Jews in *Cha'are Shalom Ve Tsedek v. France*[294] (in concluding that there had been no violation of Article 9 (no interference) owing to the availability of imported *glatt* meat), does not do complete justice to Krishnaswami's suggestion that where the means of production or distribution are under government control (as was the case in France), public authorities are 'under an obligation to place the objects necessary for observing dietary practices prescribed by particular faiths, or the means of producing them, at the disposal of members of those faiths'.[295] The European Court might at least have acknowledged the principles spelled out in the Universal context to indicate that it had considered them.

In short, the right to 'make, acquire and use to an adequate extent the necessary articles and materials related to the rites or customs of a religion or belief' in the 1981 Declaration is undoubtedly of uncertain scope and it is only by enlarging its literal meaning that it is possible to fit

---

[290] UN Doc. E/CN.4/1999/58 (1999), para. 26 and UN Doc. E/CN.4/2001/63 (2001), p. 4, para. 5 (Afghanistan).

[291] In the conclusions and recommendations following a visit to Sudan, the special Rapporteur commented: 'while emphasizing that traditions and customs, irrespective of their origins, are equally worthy of respect, urges that dress should not be the subject of political regulation and calls for flexible and tolerant attitudes in this regard, so as to allow the variety and richness of Sudanese garments to manifest themselves without constraint' (UN Doc. A/51/542/Add.2 (1996), para. 140 (Sudan)). This followed the Public Discipline and Conduct Act No. 2 (1992), which established the obligation of an Islamic dress code for women in public (*ibid.*, at para. 51). In addition, young Christians and animists in public schools allegedly faced pressure to comply with the Islamic dress code (*ibid.*, at para. 94).

[292] UN Doc. A/53/40 (1998), p. 25, para. 133 (Sudan).

[293] Krishnaswami, 'Study of Discrimination', 227, at 250–1.

[294] *Cha'are Shalom Ve Tsedek v. France* (App. No. 27417/95), Judgment of 11 July 2000.

[295] Krishnaswami, 'Study of Discrimination', 227, at 251.

practices concerning religious dress and the wearing of beards within Article 6(c). It is in the area of manifestation through the wearing of distinctive dress mandated by a religion that the practice of the European Commission and the European Court are most striking in accommodating State restrictions, and in accepting State assertions of the risks of allowing religious dress in certain contexts. A similarly permissive approach is reflected in the European Court's assessment of State restrictions concerning access to appropriately prepared food in accordance with religious dietary regulations. It is doubtful that the Human Rights Committee or the Special Rapporteur would support such an approach, at least without stressing the importance of such religious manifestations and without a rigorous assessment of State justifications for their restriction.

(d) 'To write, issue and disseminate relevant publications in these areas'

There is considerable potential for exaggerating the scope of this right unless due weight is given to two essential qualifications within Article 6(d), namely 'relevant', and 'in these areas'.[296] These two qualifications delineate religious manifestation from other forms of expression protected by Article 10 of the European Convention and Article 19 of the ICCPR. Since all of the Article 6 rights are to be read '[i]n accordance with Article 1 of the present Declaration',[297] Article 6(d) is directed at securing recognition for the right to publish only when it constitutes manifestation of religion or belief in worship, observance, practice and teaching. However, Article 6(d) is capable of encompassing a wide range of media beyond printed publications.[298]

---

[296] The word 'relevant' was intended to redress the mischief in a Byelorussian proposal that only 'appropriate' publications be protected, which would have given too much latitude to States – UN Doc ESCOR, 1981, Supp. No. 5, pp. 144–5; UN Doc. E/1981/25; UN Doc. E/CN.4/1475 (1981).

[297] See Article 6 of the 1981 Declaration.

[298] Although Article 6(d) of the 1981 Declaration refers only to 'relevant publications', it would be consistent with its purpose to include not only physical publications but other media, in line, for example, with Article 9 of the Council of Europe Framework Convention for the Protection of National Minorities (which guarantees national minorities freedom from discrimination in their access to the media, including printed media, sound radio and television broadcasting), and the Vienna Concluding Document of the OSCE (which refers to mass media in the context of the interests of religious minorities in public dialogue) – Vienna Concluding Document, para. 16(k), January 1989, 28 ILM (1989), p. 531.

There are few decisions that have analysed, as manifestations of religion or belief, publications of the type contemplated in Article 6(d). The European Commission was certainly not prepared in *X. v. United Kingdom*[299] to regard a prisoner's communication with other Buddhists through publication as a form of 'manifestation' even though he claimed it to be an important part of his religious practice.[300] The Commission was undoubtedly influenced by the security implications for the prison environment. Although not directly comparable, a rather more inclusive approach appears to be taken by the Human Rights Committee. In *Malcolm Ross v. Canada*,[301] the Committee made a surprisingly imprecise assessment of the author's anti-Semitic publications when accepting that he was restricted in his 'right to manifest religious belief' within Article 18 of the ICCPR.[302] This was in spite of the fact that the State stressed that his published opinions 'are not manifestations of a religion, as he did not publish them for the purpose of worship, observance, practice or teaching of a religion'.[303] The author himself certainly did not characterise his publications as 'teaching' (a suggestion he may have been keen to avoid given his insistence that the expressions of religious opinion were separate from his role as a teacher).

The Special Rapporteur certainly does not appear to adopt a restrictive interpretation of Article 6(d). For example, although Article 6(d) only refers to the right to 'write, issue and disseminate' publications, there is some suggestion in the Special Rapporteur's reports that the 'importation' of publications should also be protected, when close attention was given to whether in certain countries religious texts were available in contemporary language,[304] and may be imported.[305] The Special Rapporteur observed that in Morocco Muslims had allegedly been arrested because they had received literature from overseas.[306] It

---

[299] *X. v. United Kingdom*, App. No. 5442/72 (1975) 1 D&R 41.   [300] *Ibid.*, at 42.

[301] *Malcolm Ross v. Canada*, Communication No. 736/1997 (views of 18 October 2000), UN Doc. A/56/40 vol. 2 (2001), p. 69.

[302] *Ibid.*, at p. 83, para. 10.7.   [303] *Ibid.*, at p. 78, para. 6.5.

[304] UN Doc. E/CN.4/1989/44 (1989), p. 19, para. 31 (Bulgaria). See also UN Doc. E/CN.4/2003/66/Add.1 (2003), p. 19, para. 105 (Algeria) – religious books were only authorised in Arabic.

[305] UN Doc. E/CN.4/1989/44 (1989), p. 19, para. 31 (Bulgaria); UN Doc. E/CN.4/2004/63/Add.1 (2004), p. 12, para. 55 (Georgia).

[306] UN Doc. E/CN.4/1995/91 (1995), p. 60 (Morocco). See also: UN Doc. E/CN.4/1999/58 (1999), para. 76 (Morocco); UN Doc. E/CN.4/1998/6 (1998), para. 63(d) (Brunei).

was also noted that in China prison sentences had been imposed on three individuals for importing more than 33,000 Bibles into China.[307] The Special Rapporteur's attention has not been confined only to conventional forms of publication and, for example, it was noted that in Uzbekistan a Tashkent evangelist was reportedly interned in a psychiatric asylum after being warned several times that he should stop showing the film 'Jesus',[308] and that in Bulgaria a group of individuals headed by an Orthodox priest reportedly attacked three individuals who wanted to show the same film in a local community club.[309]

In practice, religious censorship takes a variety of forms. At worst it may be total, such as in former Communist Czechoslovakia where most religious literature was regarded as directed against the State, so that its duplication and distribution were prohibited.[310] Censorship may be directed against non-State religions, as in Afghanistan,[311] or it may be directed against minority religions religions, as in Iraq,[312] Turkey[313] or Azerbaijan.[314] Even partial censorship may have far-reaching results, illustrated by allegations that in Malaysia the use of certain words was prohibited except by Muslims, with the result that sales of the Bible in Malay were banned.[315] Allegations also suggest that in Malaysia religious publication easily carried the risk of State accusations of coercion or incitement to change religion.[316] In Bulgaria, registration requirements have facilitated the confiscation of religious publications (principally those of Jehovah's Witnesses, the Unification Church, and Protestant evangelicals).[317]

Even though the Special Rapporteur has highlighted examples of restrictions on this particular freedom, the Special Rapporteur has been equally quick to condemn the publication of statements of intolerance,

---

[307] UN Doc. A/57/274 (2002), p. 6, para. 26 (China). See also UN Doc. A/57/274 (2002), p. 6, para. 26 (China).
[308] UN Doc. E/CN.4/1995/91 (1995), p. 67 (Uzbekistan).
[309] UN Doc. E/CN.4/2001/63 (2001), p. 8, para. 20 (Bulgaria). See also UN Doc. A/56/253 (2001), p. 18, para. 68 (Turkmenistan).
[310] UN Doc. E/CN.4/1989/44 (1989), p. 39, para. 69 (Czechoslovakia).
[311] UN Doc. A/56/253 (2001), p. 8, para. 25 (Afghanistan).
[312] UN Doc. E/CC.4/1994/79 (1994), p. 80, para. 60 (Iraq).
[313] UN Doc. E/CN.4/2001/63 (2001), p. 35, para. 139 (Turkey).
[314] UN Doc. A/57/274 (2002), p. 4, para. 14 (Azerbaijan).
[315] UN Doc. E/CN.4/1995/91 (1995), p. 59 (Malaysia).
[316] UN Doc. E/CN.4/1995/91 (1995), pp. 59–60 (Malaysia).
[317] IHF 2001 Report, at p. 18.

particularly in the mass media.[318] The 1981 Declaration does not have a provision equivalent to Article 17 of the European Convention or Article 5 of the ICCPR (preventing the exercise of any right to destroy recognised rights and freedoms), although Article 2 clarifies the meaning of 'intolerance and discrimination based on religion or belief', which the 1981 Declaration sets out to eliminate. Sullivan examined the meaning of 'intolerance and discrimination' in view of their interchangeable use in Article 2(2) and concluded that 'intolerance is not a particular type of violation of religious freedom or of discrimination, but the attitudes that may motivate such violations'.[319] In keeping with this analysis, the Special Rapporteur has cited a number of allegations of the disparagement of minority religions in the mass media: in Mongolia, against Christians;[320] in Egypt, against Copts;[321] in Iraq, against Shia Muslims;[322] in Belgium, against new religions;[323] and in Azerbaijan, against Jehovah's Witnesses.[324] In Belarus, *Narodnaya Gazeta* was alleged to have published anti-Protestant articles claiming that 'Protestants push us to betray our ancestors' faith' (to lend support to the Belarus Exarchate of the Russian Orthodox Church).[325] However, most surprising, are the statements allegedly made in Georgia by the second most senior Orthodox bishop, Metropolitan Atanase, that all 'sectarians' in Georgia should be 'killed'. He named the Jehovah's Witnesses, the Baptists, the Anglicans and the Pentecostals among those who 'have to be shot dead'.[326]

The Human Rights Committee in reviewing State Reports has been unequivocal in its concern for the freedom to write, issue and disseminate religious publications and accordingly has asked States to indicate whether religious communities have the right to print and disseminate

---

[318] See also CHR Res. 2002/9 'Combating defamation of religion' (15 April 2002) UN Doc. E/CN.4/2002/200 (2002), in which concern was expressed at any role in which print, audio-visual or electronic media or any other means are used to incite acts of violence, xenophobia or related intolerance and discrimination towards Islam and any other religion.

[319] D. J. Sullivan, 'Advancing the Freedom of Religion or Belief through the UN Declaration of the Elimination of Religious Intolerance and Discrimination', 82 Am J Int'l L (1988) 487, at 505.

[320] UN Doc. E/CN.4/1995/91 (1995), p. 63 (Mongolia).

[321] UN Doc. E/CN.4/1994/79 (1994), p. 45, para. 44 (Egypt).

[322] UN Doc. E/CN.4/1994/79 (1994), p. 80, para. 60 (Iraq).

[323] IHF 2000 Report, p. 7.

[324] UN Doc. E/CN.4/2000/65 (2000), para. 14 (Azerbaijan).

[325] IHF 2000 Report, p. 5.

[326] UN Doc. A/57/274 (2002), p. 8, para. 36 (Georgia). See also UN Doc. E/CN.4/2004/63/Add.1 (2004), p. 15, para. 73 (Georgia).

religious materials and publications[327] and how this right is ensured.[328] It has also adopted a sympathetic interpretation of 'propaganda', asking whether religious propaganda was protected on an equal footing with atheistic propaganda in Communist countries[329] and non-Communist countries,[330] though at the same time expressing concern at provisions that permit anti-religious propaganda. One member, examining Article 53 of the Bulgarian constitution (which did permit anti-religious propaganda), commented that this amounted to non-existence of the freedom to disseminate religious propaganda and could be, according to another member, tantamount to intolerance. It was maintained that in a country where a particular (Communist) ideology was the guiding force in the State, anti-religious propaganda would be used with great force to the detriment of the principle of equality enshrined in the Covenant.[331] In addition, in Optional Protocol decisions, the Human Rights Committee has readily supported State restrictions on the dissemination of views of religious intolerance, such as *Malcolm Ross v. Canada*,[332] even if in that case the Committee was prepared to concede that such publication constituted the manifestation of religion or belief.

In short, the freedom to write, issue and disseminate relevant publications is best recognised, not surprisingly, by the Special Rapporteur, supported by the Human Rights Committee in a limited number of decisions and in its review of State reports. Recognition of such a right is also accompanied by uncompromising condemnation of all expressions of religious intolerance. The position under the European Convention, however, is not easy to discern given the paucity of decisions of general application.

(e) 'To teach a religion or belief in places suitable for these purposes'

As 'teaching' appears in the text of all the freedom of religion Articles, it goes without saying that it is a fundamentally recognised form of

---

[327] UN Doc. A/33/40 (1978), p. 63, para. 379 (Yugoslavia); UN Doc. A/37/40 (1982), p. 15, para. 70 (Japan).

[328] UN Doc. A/45/40 vol. 1 (1990), p. 26, para. 109 (USSR).

[329] UN Doc. A/33/40 (1978), p. 89, para. 535 (Byelorussian SSR); UN Doc. A/35/40 (1980), p. 22, para. 99 (Mongolia).

[330] UN Doc. A/35/40 (1980), p. 37, para. 169 (Canada); UN Doc. A/36/40 (1981), p. 27, para. 124 (Italy).

[331] UN Doc. A/34/40 (1979), p. 31, para. 126 (Bulgaria).

[332] *Malcolm Ross v. Canada*, Communication No. 736/1997 (views of 18 October 2000), UN Doc. A/56/40 vol. 2 (2001), p. 69. See also *J.R.T. and the W.G. Party v. Canada*, Communication No. 104/1981 (decision of 6 April 1983), UN Doc. A38/40 (1983), p. 231.

manifestation of religion or belief. Article 18 of the ICCPR underwent little analysis in General Comment No. 22 other than (in paragraph 4) the observation that 'the practice and teaching of religion or belief includes acts integral to the conduct by religious groups of their basic affairs, such as, *inter alia*, the freedom to choose their religious leaders, priests and teachers, the freedom to establish seminaries or religious schools and the freedom to prepare and distribute religious texts or publications'. These freedoms span Article 6(d), (e) and (g) of the 1981 Declaration but do little to clarify the extent of Article 6(e).

Article 6(e) refers to 'teaching' in 'suitable' places without being specific as to what criteria determine suitability. Article 6(e) would cover preaching at places of worship and (since teaching reaches beyond the immediate context of worship or assembly) education at seminaries and other training establishments designated for religious education, but it does not automatically permit the teaching of a religion or belief in State education which must, as discussed in Chapter 3 under the heading 'Education', at pp. 165–75, respect parental wishes within the constraints reiterated in Article 5 of the 1981 Declaration.[333] In his study, Krishnaswami referred not so much to the teaching as the dissemination of religion or belief, with particular concern for foreign missionaries who might impose a new culture that does not fit harmoniously with the existing order, but he added that claims to protect social stability and national security have been over-emphasised, 'with the result that the right to disseminate was unduly limited'.[334] Teaching clearly constitutes one form of dissemination although, as noted in Chapter 2 under the heading 'Blasphemy, disparagement and gratuitous offence', at pp. 105–9, poorly targeted legislation aimed at prohibiting speech on religious matters could impose serious unintended constraints on teaching.

Proselytism is also an acknowledged form of manifestation of religion or belief and, as it is not specifically contemplated by any other provision of Article 6, may be taken to fall within Article 6(e). In *Kokkinakis v. Greece*,[335] the European Court was guarded in its definition of 'teaching' but did firmly place persuasive forms of teaching within the realms of

---

[333] The wide range of eligible 'places' is illustrated by the acknowledgement that they would include State schools, which many countries would want to have a secular character, until Byelorussia successfully proposed the qualification 'suitable' UN Doc. ESCOR, 1981, Supp. No. 5, p. 145; E/1981/25; UN Doc. E/CN.4/1475 (1981).

[334] Krishnaswami, 'Study of Discrimination' 227, at 254–5.

[335] *Kokkinakis v. Greece* (Ser. A) No.260–A (1993) ECtHR.

acceptable proselytism: 'According to Article 9 ... freedom to manifest one's religion ... includes in principle the right to try to convince one's neighbour, for example through "teaching", failing which, moreover, "freedom to change [one's] religion or belief", enshrined in Article 9 ... would be likely to remain a dead letter.'[336] Even though there may be doubt as to what the European Court meant by its distinction between 'proper' and 'improper' proselytism, the former would certainly embrace 'teaching'. (The Special Rapporteur, however, has made no such distinction in reporting on restrictions on proselytism.[337]) The right to 'teach' is undoubtedly well recognised in both the European and United Nations systems.

As to the 'suitability' of the place in which the teaching is conducted, places of worship are among the most obvious fora for teaching and it may be assumed are 'suitable'. Nevertheless, the Special Rapporteur has reported on censorship in the government control of sermons in Viet Nam,[338] noting that teaching according to the precepts of individual denominations was compromised in Viet Nam by the aggregation of different denominations into State-sponsored religious associations (such as the Committee for the Solidarity of Patriotic Vietnamese Catholics, the Union of Patriotic Priests, the Protestant Association and the Viet Nam Buddhist Church).[339] In China, the concept of a formal place of worship is often absent outside State-controlled churches, with services and 'study groups' taking place in the homes of individual believers and where itinerant preachers proliferate,[340] and so it is suggested that 'suitable' should be given a wide meaning. In some countries, restrictions on religious teaching are more generalised, such as Turkey[341] and Uzbekistan,[342] where unauthorised religious education is punishable by fines and prison sentences.

---

[336] *Ibid.*, at para. 31, applied in *Larissis and others v. Greece* (Ser. A) No. 65 (1998–V) ECtHR 363 para. 45.

[337] See Chapter 2 under the heading 'Blasphemy, disparagement and gratuitions offence', pp. 109–11.

[338] UN Doc. E/CN.4/1993/62 (1993), p. 109, para. 68 (Viet Nam).

[339] UN Doc. E/CN.4/1994/79 (1994), p. 113, para. 79 (Viet Nam).

[340] UN Doc. E/CN.4/1994/79 (1994), p. 39, para. 41; p. 44, para. 42 (China); UN Doc. E/CN.4/1995/91 (1995), p. 125 (China). In China a local imam was also allegedly required to display a notice banning the teaching of religion privately and discouraging Islam from influencing family life and other activities – UN Doc. E/CN.4/2005/61/Add.1 (2005), p. 18, para. 67 (China).

[341] UN Doc. A/57/274 (2002), p. 10, para. 53 (Turkey).

[342] UN Doc. E/CN.4/2004/63 (2004), p. 14, para. 73 (Uzbekistan).

Seminaries are obviously suitable places for the teaching of religion yet the Human Rights Committee has had to ask certain countries to justify their actions in closing seminaries[343] or in not recognising qualifications acquired there.[344] The Special Rapporteur has also reported on the closure of Shia seminaries in Iraq (and the suppression of Shia literary works said to be of exceptional historic and cultural interest).[345] In China, there has not only been a marked contraction in the duration of theological teaching permitted in Catholic seminaries (apparently to alleviate the shortages of priests)[346] but teaching in many monasteries has also been endangered by the heavy labour schedule imposed by the Monastery Democratic Management Committee (which reportedly requires monks and nuns to work eight hours per day, six days per week). In addition, the age at which novices may be inducted was increased from seven or eight to eighteen years, and candidates were required to 'love' the country and the Communist Party and be approved by several State authorities.[347]

As far as teaching in schools and universities is concerned, personal preference is often keenly felt by individuals for religious foundations, even those aimed at secular qualifications, and a recurring issue of concern is discrimination in the closure of such institutions, appropriation by the State or refusal of permission to operate.[348] Discrimination in the provision of public funding is an increasingly common issue. In the Optional Protocol case of *Arieh Hollis Waldman v. Canada*,[349] the author claimed that Ontario's full funding of Roman Catholic schools, which was not available to Jewish schools, violated Article 18(1) of the ICCPR taken in conjunction with Article 2 because it meant that the author himself had to fund Jewish education for his children. He asserted that this financial

---

[343] UN Doc. A/38/40 (1983), p. 52, para. 234 (Nicaragua).

[344] UN Doc. A/38/40 (1983), p. 15, para. 74 (Mexico).

[345] UN Doc. E/CN.4/1993/62 (1993), p. 44, para. 39 (Iraq); UN Doc. E/CN.4/1994/79 (1994), p. 80, para. 60 (Iraq).

[346] UN Doc. E/CN.4/1994/79 (1994), p. 40, para. 41 (China).

[347] UN Doc. E/CN.4/1993/62 (1993), p. 14, para. 22 (China).

[348] See, for example: IHF 2001 Report, at p. 18 (in Bulgaria, between 1994 and 2000, numerous schools established by religious groups were closed or disbanded and the leases of premises were terminated or not renewed); UN Doc. E/CN.4/1993/62 (1993), p. 26, para. 25 (in Egypt, Islamic colleges, institutes and schools for the education of Muslim children proliferated in all parts of Egypt while permission was refused for the establishment of a Coptic university); UN Doc. E/CN.4/1993/62 (1993), p. 38, para. 34 (in India (Tamil Nadu) the Private Colleges Act meant that religious educational institutions founded by missionaries would be entirely controlled by the Government).

[349] *Arieh Hollis Waldman v. Canada*, Communication No.694/1996 (views of 3 November 1999) (2000) 7(2) IHRR 368.

burden significantly impaired, in a discriminatory fashion, the enjoyment of the right to *manifest* one's religion, including the freedom to provide a religious education for one's children, or to establish religious schools.[350] The Human Rights Committee accepted the author's claim under Article 26 and as a result did not consider Article 18(1) further. However, the case is interesting for its emphasis on the manifestation of religion or belief in the choice of denominational schools.

Another, unlikely, source of confirmation that manifestation through teaching includes teaching in the school curriculum is the dissenting opinion of Judge Valticos in *Kokkinakis v. Greece*. Although opposed to certain forms of proselytism, he commented that 'the term "teaching" in Article 9 ... undoubtedly refers to religious teaching in school curricula or in religious institutions, and not to personal door-to-door canvassing as in the present case'.

It is clear from decisions of both the Human Rights Committee and the European Commission that, in the school context, the rights of teachers to manifest their own religious or other beliefs is limited, but presumably only where their views are at odds with those of the school where they are employed. Greater freedom may be available to teachers in denominational schools to express beliefs consistent with the religious foundation of the school in question. In *W. Delgado Paes v. Colombia*[351] the author's views on 'liberation theology' differed from those of the church which supported his appointment. He was subjected to intense harassment and although his claim under Article 18 of the ICCPR failed, he successfully claimed violation of Article 25(c). The Human Rights Committee concluded that 'the author's right to profess or to manifest his religion has not been violated. The Committee finds, moreover, that Colombia may, without violating this provision of the Covenant, allow the church authorities to decide who may teach religion and in what manner it should be taught'.[352] A similar approach was taken by the European Commission in *X. v. United Kingdom*[353] when

---

[350] *Ibid.*, at paras. 3.2 and 5.3.

[351] *W. Delgado Páez v. Colombia*, Communication No. 195/1985 (views of 12 July 1990), UN Doc. A/45/40 vol. 2 (1990), p. 43.

[352] *Ibid.*, at para. 5.7. See also: *G.T. v. Canada*, Communication No. 420/1990 (decision of 22 March 1990) (1994) 1(1) IHRR 46 (the employee belatedly realised that his convictions conflicted with those of his Catholic employer, compromising his ability to teach on certain subjects); *Jansen-Gielen v. The Netherlands*, Communication No. 846/1999 (views of 3 April 2001), UN Doc. A/56/40 vol. 2 (2002), p. 158.

[353] *X. v. United Kingdom*, App. No. 8010/77 (1979) 16 D&R 101.

upholding the dismissal of a mathematics and English teacher in a non-denominational school for advertising his moral and religious beliefs through posters and stickers on school premises. The dismissal was held to be necessary in a democratic society under Article 10(2) (for the protection of the rights of others).[354] Profession of belief by teachers in the context of public education is therefore dealt with strictly unless fully in accordance with the denominational character of the school in question.[355]

It would also appear that restrictions on teaching religion or belief in the privacy of one's home might, according to European decision making, be justified in appropriate circumstances. For example, in *Seven Individuals v. Sweden*[356] the applicants believed that the traditional religious upbringing of their children necessitated corporal punishment, in spite of recent opposition to severe forms of corporal chastisement under Swedish law. The applicants maintained that this violated their rights under Articles 8, 9, and First Protocol, Article 2. In rejecting the claims under Articles 8 and 9, the European Commission observed that the law of assault and molestation was a normal measure for the control of violence and its extension to the ordinary physical chastisement of children by their parents was intended to protect potentially weak and vulnerable members of society. In addition, in rejecting the claim under First Protocol, Article 2, the European Commission noted that the children had not been subjected to any specific form of indoctrination in Swedish schools and that the law in question did not amount to criminalisation but mere guidance with no accompanying sanction.

Restrictions on teaching religious beliefs at home might also arise in child custody or access proceedings where the parents do not share the same beliefs. Thus, in the Optional Protocol case of *P.S. v. Denmark*,[357]

---

[354] For suggestions for a public education system that takes account of denominational requirements, see R. A. Baer, and J. C. Carper, '"To the Advantage of Infidelity", or How Not To Deal With Religion In America's Public Schools', 14(5) *Educational Policy* (2000) 600. For further discussion of separation of Church and State in the United States, see: M. McConnell, 'Religious Participation in Public Programs', 59 U Chicago L Rev (1992) 115; K. Sullivan, 'Religion and Liberal Democracy', 59 U Chicago L Rev. (1992) 195.

[355] See also *Dahlab v. Switzerland*, (App. No. 42393/98), Judgment of 15 February 2001.

[356] *Seven Individuals v. Sweden*, App. No. 8811/79 (1982) 29 D&R 104.

[357] *P.S. v. Denmark*, Communication No. 397/1990 (decision of 22 July 1992), UN Doc. A/47/40 (1992), p. 395.

the author claimed infringement of Article 18 of the ICCPR as a result of a restriction order that prevented him bringing up the subject of the Jehovah's Witness faith when exercising his right of access to his child. The restriction order prevented the child's participation in Jehovah's Witness rallies, gatherings, meetings, missions and any activities at which texts from the Bible were read aloud or interpreted or prayers were said. The claim was found inadmissible owing to failure to exhaust domestic remedies although, in an individual opinion, Mr Bertil Wennergren concluded that this raised issues under both Article 18 and Article 19 of the ICCPR.[358] The question of religious upbringing in custody matters has also arisen in European Convention cases. In *Palau-Martinez v. France*[359] an order was made by the State for children to reside with their father 'in order to remove them from the detrimental influence of their mother and her circle, who oblige them to practise the religion known as "Jehovah's Witnesses" [noting that] rules regarding child-rearing imposed by the Jehovah's Witnesses on their followers' children are open to criticism mainly on account of their strictness and intolerance and the obligation on children to proselytise'.[360] The European Court did not examine the issue under Article 9 (since it had already found in favour of the applicant under Article 14 in conjunction with Article 8 on grounds of lack of proportionality between the means employed and the legitimate aim pursued).[361] A similar conclusion was reached in *Hoffmann v. Austria*,[362] concerning the refusal of custody to the applicant on account of her religious beliefs. No decision has been made in relation to a substantive Article taken alone, dissociated from issues of discrimination. Nevertheless, these cases demonstrate the potential for far-reaching restrictions on religious teaching, even within the home.

---

[358] See also *Buckle v. New Zealand*, in which the author claimed that the authorities had taken her children away because she was a newborn Christian. The Human Rights Committee decided that she had failed to substantiate that her beliefs were the cause of her treatment by the State (*Buckle v. New Zealand*, Communication No. 858/1999 (views of 25 October 2000), A/56/40 vol. 2 (2001), p. 175).

[359] *Palau-Martinez v. France*, (App. No. 64927/01), Judgment of 16 December 2003.

[360] *Ibid.*, para. 13.

[361] In *Palau-Martinez v. France*, the European Court observed that the national court asserted only generalities concerning Jehovah's Witnesses and there was no direct, concrete evidence demonstrating the influence of the applicant's religion on her two children's upbringing and daily life, in particular, that the applicant took her children with her when attempting to spread her religious beliefs – *ibid.*, para. 42.

[362] *Hoffmann v. Austria* (Ser. A) No. 255–C (1993) ECtHR.

Finally, teaching religious beliefs in public places commonly falls to be determined according to principles of freedom of expression (rather than the *lex specialis* of freedom of religion Articles), although if it takes the form of a demonstration or procession then even the right to freedom of expression will be treated as subsidiary to freedom of assembly.[363] The degree of constraint on freedom of expression varies, under European jurisprudence, according to its context and place. In *Ahmet v. Greece*,[364] the distribution of inflammatory materials directed against a minority group was supported during the pre-election period. Even though a premium is put on the democratic value of freedom of expression,[365] the ease with which public order limitations are invoked in the case of public displays is illustrated by *X. v. Sweden*,[366] in which it was the applicant's disorderly behaviour, rather than his message, that was likely to provoke public indignation when he shouted loudly his views on pornography, fornication and alcohol. The manner of presentation in a public place appeared to be decisive.

In summary, the right to teach a religion spans a surprising range of issues beyond conventional teaching in places of worship and seminaries. The most strictly guarded arena, evident from European decisions, appears to be within State education, to prevent the secular curriculum from intrusion by teachers expressing their own personal beliefs in the course of their profession. At the same time, the denominational integrity of schools which offer a particular religious bias may be preserved by requiring individual teachers to conform to the religious precepts of the school, although most of the authority on this issue has come from the Human Rights Committee. The Human Rights Committee has also developed principles concerning discrimination in relation to the public funding of education (so as not to disadvantage denominational schools). Schools may therefore be suitable or quite unsuitable places for teaching depending on whether the teaching corresponds with the secular or denominational character of the school in question. However, it is doubtful whether the disciplining of children within the home and other aspects of domestic upbringing were ever intended to be brought

---

[363] *Plattform 'Ärzte für das Leben' v. Austria*, App. No. 10126/82 (1985) 44 D&R 65, at 71.

[364] *Ahmet Sadik v. Greece* (1997) 24 EHRR 323.

[365] See *Barthold v. Germany* (Ser. A) No. 90 (1985) ECtHR para. 58 – freedom of expression was described as 'one of the essential foundations of a democratic society and one of the basic conditions for its progress and for the development of every man and woman'.

[366] *X. v. Sweden*, App. No. 9820/82 (1984) 5 EHRR 297.

within the scope of Article 6(e) of the 1981 Declaration. The term 'teaching' for the purpose of that Article is perhaps best reserved to expressions of the content and substance of a belief system, even if intended to be persuasive, as in the case of proselytism.

(f) 'To solicit and receive voluntary financial and other contributions from individuals and institutions'

Fearful that contributions (particularly from overseas) might be used for political purposes to promote anti-State activities, the Soviet Union opposed this provision in the drafting of the 1981 Declaration in its entirety but overall only succeeded in adding the word 'voluntary'.[367] The right to solicit and receive voluntary financial and other contributions has received virtually no attention by the Human Rights Committee in its review of State reports, and only superficial reporting by the Special Rapporteur when, for example, noting that in Tibet, donations to Buddhist monasteries must be paid directly into a particular account and cannot be withdrawn or spent without the approval of an official body,[368] and that in Lao People's Democratic Republic a number of Christians were allegedly arrested at a Bible study meeting for creating divisions and undermining the Government, and for receiving funds from abroad.[369]

Legal recognition for religious bodies is essential to their ability to attract financial and other contributions and also to ensure that gifts are dealt with in accordance with the donor's wishes. If assets are received by individuals in a personal capacity then the absence of safeguards against misappropriation may deter such contributions. Most religious organisations depend for their existence on donations from members of the religious community or associated communities. Article 6(b) and (f) are therefore closely inter-related. Article 6(b) concerns the institutional framework for undertaking the charitable or humanitarian missions of a religion or belief, as well as for soliciting and receiving contributions. The decision in *Metropolitan Church of Bessarabia and others v. Moldova*[370] offers support for the rights under both Article 6(b) and (f) in that the European Court seized upon the lack of judicial protection of the Church's assets, which included humanitarian aid from the

---

[367] UN Doc. ESCOR, 1981, Supp. No. 5, p. 145; E/1981/25; UN Doc. E/CN.4/1475 (1981).
[368] UN Doc. E/CN.4/1988/45 (1988), p. 23, para. 45 (China).
[369] UN Doc. E/CN.4/1999/58 (1999), para. 86 (Lao People's Democratic Republic).
[370] *Metropolitan Church of Bessarabia and others v. Moldova* (2002) 35 EHRR 306.

United States, to illustrate the inevitable consequence of being denied legal personality.[371]

The wider, and perhaps better acknowledged implications of this right, include the need for protection against discrimination in the ability granted to different religious entities to receive contributions, and the need to avoid coercion, particularly in those countries in which the State Church is entitled to receive contributions by way of tax (as discussed, for example, in the European Commission's opinion in *Darby v. Sweden*).[372]

(g) 'To train, appoint, elect or designate by succession appropriate leaders called for by the requirements and standards of any religion or belief'

The autonomy of religious groups extends to the right to choose religious leaders, priests and teachers (recognised by paragraph 4 of General Comment No. 22 to be 'integral to the conduct by religious groups of their basic affairs'), the right to train them (especially since, as Krishnaswami noted, 'the lack of adequately trained leaders may make the performance of many practices and observances difficult, if not impossible'),[373] and the right to establish the appropriate requirements and preconditions for their appointment. (There may originally have been some doubt as to whether the right extended to atheistic organisations since the Soviet Union's proposed amendment that it do so was not accepted.)[374]

The draft produced by the working group of the Commission on Human Rights made provision for 'adequate numbers' of leaders until this qualification was removed from the 1981 Declaration at the suggestion of Nigeria.[375] Nevertheless, the Human Rights Committee[376] and the Special Rapporteur[377] have asked States to explain why the number of ministers of religious creeds is limited.

More generally in reviewing State Reports, the Human Rights Committee has asked States to justify government controls on the

---

[371] *Ibid.*, at para. 105.

[372] *Darby v. Sweden* (Ser. A) No. 187 (1990) ECtHR, annex to the decision of the Court.

[373] Krishnaswami, 'Study of Discrimination' 227, at 257.

[374] UN Doc. ESCOR, 1981, Supp. No. 5, p. 146, UN Doc. E/1981/25, UN Doc. E/CN.4/ 1475 (1981).

[375] UN Doc. ESCOR, 1981, Supp. No. 5, p. 146, UN Doc. E/1981/25; UN Doc. E/CN.4/ 1475 (1981).

[376] UN Doc. A/38/40 (1983), p. 15, para. 74 (Mexico).

[377] UN Doc. E/CN.4/1989/44 (1989), p. 33, para. 61 (Romania).

appointment of religious leaders, such as Roman Catholic bishops in Czechoslovakia[378] and the Grand Rabbi in Tunisia.[379] It has also enquired about the liability of ministers of religion to special penalties for making any attack on the Government or its actions,[380] and questioned the need for States to ensure that leaders possess appropriate theological credentials.[381] Similarly, the Special Rapporteur has reported on government control over Buddhist monks in Tibet by the Chinese authorities,[382] as well as indirect means of control, for example, alleged of the Emirate of Dubai which was said to have placed private mosques under the control of the Department of Islamic Affairs and Endowments so as to give it a significant say in the appointment of preachers.[383]

It was not until comparatively recently that the European Court had to consider restrictions in Bulgaria and Greece concerning the appointment of Muslim leaders, even though the European Commission has for some time been sensitive to the impact of the loss of a religious leader on a religious community.[384] *Hasan and Chaush v. Bulgaria*[385] concerned the forced removal of the leadership of the Muslim community in Bulgaria. The applicants (the appointed community leader and a representative of the community) claimed violation of Article 9. The Government argued that the issue did not fall within the rights of the individual applicants under Article 9 but instead solely Article 11. The European Court disagreed. It reiterated the now famous dictum from *Kokkinakis v. Greece* that 'freedom of thought, conscience and religion is one of the foundations of a democratic society ... [and that] ... the pluralism indissociable

---

[378] UN Doc. A/41/40 (1986), p. 80, para. 356 (Czechoslovakia).

[379] UN Doc. A/42/40 (1987), p. 36, para. 137 (Tunisia).

[380] UN Doc. A/41/40 (1986), p. 13, para. 69 (Luxembourg).

[381] UN Doc. A/42/40 (1987), p. 72, para. 285 (Zaire).

[382] UN Doc. E/CN.4/1993/62 (1993), p. 14, para. 22 (China).

[383] UN Doc. E/CN.4/1995/91 (1995), p. 36 (United Arab Emirates). See also UN Doc. E/CN.4/2005/61/Add.1 (2005), p. 39, para. 153 (Kyrgyzstan): in Kyrgyzstan several mosques were allegedly destroyed, even though registered, on the grounds that they had been built illegally on State-owned land – the head of the district declared that this would enable him to 'monitor the activities of the imams in [his] territory'.

[384] In *Omkarananda and the Divine Light Zentrum v. United Kingdom*, App. No. 8188/77 (1981) 25 D&R 105, at 118, the Commission indicated that Article 9 may be used to challenge a deportation order 'designed to' interfere with the exercise of Article 9 rights. In the circumstances, the deportation of a leader, though likely to shake the Divine Light Zentrum deeply could not be seen as an interference with the organisation's rights under Article 9.

[385] *Hasan and Chaush v. Bulgaria* (2002) 34(6) EHRR 1339.

from a democratic society, which has been dearly won over the centuries, depends on it',[386] before explaining the significance of the organisational life of religious organisations within Article 9 as follows:

> 'The Court recalls that religious communities traditionally and universally exist in the form of organised structures. They abide by rules which are often seen by followers as being of a divine origin. Religious ceremonies have their meaning and sacred value for the believers if they have been conducted by ministers empowered for that purpose in compliance with these rules. The personality of the religious ministers is undoubtedly of importance to every member of the community. Participation in the life of the community is thus a manifestation of one's religion, protected by Article 9 of the Convention.
>
> Where the organisation of the religious community is at issue, Article 9 must be interpreted in the light of Article 11 of the Convention which safeguards associative life against unjustified State interference. Seen in this perspective, the believer's right to freedom of religion encompasses the expectation that the community will be allowed to function peacefully free from arbitrary State intervention. Indeed, the autonomous existence of religious communities is indispensable for pluralism in a democratic society and is thus an issue at the very heart of the protection which Article 9 affords. It directly concerns not only the organisation of the community as such but also the effective enjoyment of the right to freedom of religion by all its active members. Were the organisational life of the community not protected by Article 9 of the Convention, all other aspects of the individual's freedom of religion would become vulnerable.'[387]

This has significance for the right to legal recognition as well as interference with the internal affairs of the community. The practical impact of replacing the legitimate leadership of the community and subsequently refusing recognition to the re-elected leadership was (according to the applicants) profound. It amounted to 'replacement of the whole organisational structure of the Muslim community and a complete destruction of the normal community life. All income was frozen, offices were seized by force, control over mosques was transferred, and any use

---

[386] *Ibid.*, at para. 60, applied in *Serif v. Greece* (1999) 31 EHRR 561, para. 49.
[387] *Ibid.*, at para. 62, (affirmed in *Supreme Holy Council of the Muslim Community v. Bulgaria* (App. No. 39023/97), Judgment of 16 December 2004, at para. 73).

of the community's documents and property by the leadership led by the first applicant was made impossible. Mr Hasan was thus compelled to continue his activities as head of the second largest religion in Bulgaria "from the street with zero financial resources".[388]

The European Court decided that a failure by the authorities to remain neutral in the exercise of their powers must lead to the conclusion that the State had interfered with the believers' freedom to manifest their religion.[389] But for very exceptional cases, the right to freedom of religion excludes any discretion on the part of the State to determine whether religious beliefs or the means used to express such beliefs are legitimate,[390] an issue of particular importance to new religions which are all too readily discredited for lack of doctrine or orthodoxy.

The empowering instrument was not 'prescribed by law' for the reasons given in more detail below under the heading 'Prescribed by law', pp. 293–301, owing principally to the degree of arbitrariness that could be applied by the State in exercising its discretion in appointing a leader. This may be seen as improving still further on the position the European Court had already taken in *Serif v. Greece*[391] when it relied heavily on principles of pluralism in a case concerning the criminal conviction of a religious leader for assuming the functions of a minister of a 'known religion'. The Court did not consider it necessary to rule on the question whether the interference was 'prescribed by law' in that case because it found incompatibility with Article 9 on other grounds, namely that his conviction for acting as a religious leader of a group that willingly followed him was not necessary in a democratic society to protect public order. The European Court rejected the Government's argument that it was necessary to accomplish unified leadership of divided religious communities to avoid religious disturbances. The European Court based its reasoning on the demands of religious pluralism in a democratic society:

> 'Although the Court recognises that it is possible that tension is created in situations where a religious or any other community becomes divided, it considers that this is one of the unavoidable consequences of pluralism. The role of the authorities in such circumstances is not to remove the

---

[388] *Ibid.*, at para. 66.   [389] *Ibid.*, at para. 78.   [390] *Ibid.*, at para. 78.
[391] *Serif v. Greece* (1999) 31 EHRR 561.

cause of tension by eliminating pluralism, but to ensure that the competing groups tolerate each other.'[392]

Serif v. Greece has since been closely followed in *Agga v. Greece*[393] in
a similar claim arising out of the conviction of the applicant for
having 'usurped the functions of a minister of a "known religion"' and
in *Supreme Holy Council of the Muslim Community v. Bulgaria.*[394]
Instances of interference with leadership are widespread and include
the removal from office in 1992 (by the Bulgarian Director of Religious
Affairs) of Bishop Yosif and Bishop Plovdiv, both of the Eastern
Orthodox Church for 'lack of activity', 'neglected obligations' and
'neglect of Christian traditions'. Bulgarian authorities also declared the
election of Bulgarian Patriarch Maxim to be invalid and the Holy Synod
of the Bulgarian Orthodox Church illegitimate, so that it could appoint
a new staff of leadership.[395] The Special Rapporteur reported similar
interference with Baptist leadership in Bulgaria[396] and with Orthodox
leadership in Albania.[397] Allegations of interference with religious leadership in other countries include the arrest followed by the disappear-
ance of Shia religious leaders in Iran,[398] the threat of deportation of
foreign clergy from Iraq,[399] the expulsion of Catholic priests and
Protestant ministers from Saudi Arabia,[400] the massacre of clergyman
in Rwanda,[401] repressive measures against Roman Catholic priests in
China who carry out religious activities outside the government-

---

[392] *Ibid.*, at para. 53, referring to *Plattform 'Ärzte für das Leben' v. Austria*, (Ser. A) No. 139
(1988) ECtHR, para. 32. Witte argues that religion must be seen as a vital dimension
of any legal regime of democracy and human rights: J. Witte, 'Religious Dimensions
of Law, Human Rights and Democracy', 26 Isr YB Hum Rts (1996) 87. See also
C. Gustafson and P. Juviler (eds.), *Religion and Human Rights: Competing Claims?*,
Armonk, New York/London: M. E. Sharpe (1999). Note that tolerance is also at the
heart of the commitments set out in the Framework Convention for the Protection of
National Minorities, in particular Article 6.

[393] *Agga v. Greece* (App. Nos 50776/99 and 52912/99), Judgment of 7 October 2002.

[394] *Supreme Holy Council of the Muslim Community v. Bulgaria* (App. No. 39023/97),
Judgment of 16 December 2004, at para. 96.

[395] IHF 2001 Report, at p. 20.

[396] UN Doc. E/CN.4/1990/46 (1990), p. 7, para. 30 (Bulgaria).

[397] IHF 2001 Report, at p. 19.

[398] UN Doc. E/CN.4/1993/62 (1993), p. 53, para. 39 (Iran).

[399] UN Doc. E/CN.4/1994/79 (1994), p. 79, para. 60 (Iraq).

[400] UN Doc. E/CN.4/1989/44 (1989), p. 7, para. 29 (Saudi).

[401] UN Doc. E/CN.4/1995/91 (1995), p. 77 (Rwanda).

organised church,[402] and the exile from Moldova of hundreds of priests of the Metropolitanate of Bessarabia.[403]

Subsidiary aspects of the right to appoint leaders include eligibility criteria based on gender (an issue of some importance in recent years to the ordination of women in Protestant churches) and citizenship. Citizenship has been a concern, for example, in Albania, where the requirement that religious leaders must be of Albanian citizenship in practice operated as a restriction on the eligibility of leaders from overseas. (In an attempt to restore the minority Greek Orthodox Church following forty-five years of repression, those appointed by the Ecumenical Patriarchate were inevitably not nationals yet they were still refused entry to Albania.)[404] In some countries, the head of the State Church fills that position *ex officio*, as in Great Britain where the sovereign as head of the established church must not be a Catholic.[405] (In some countries, religious stipulations even apply to secular leadership, such as the President of Greece who, according to Article 33.2 of the 1975 Constitution, must be a Christian (though not necessarily Orthodox).)[406]

In short, the interventionist approach by the European Court in *Hasan and Chaush v. Bulgaria* and in *Serif v. Greece* is of real value in view of the significance of leadership to each religious community and the widespread controls on religious leadership illustrated by the Special Rapporteur's reports. These highlight the need for specific protection in the appointment of leaders, both for the community and the leaders themselves, which appears to be well recognised by Universal and European institutions. Most interesting of all was the European Court's emphasis in *Hasan and Chaush v. Bulgaria* on the importance to the life of a religious community of organised structures and its thorough grasp of the risk to which other aspects of the freedom of religion are put if the organisational life of the community is not protected. It marks the beginning of a new era in the collective dimension of freedom of religion (reinforced by the Court's more recent decision in *Bessarabia and others v. Moldova*[407]), by giving paramount

---

[402] UN Doc. E/CN.4/1991/56 (1991), p. 69, para. 48 (China).
[403] UN Doc. E/CN.4/1994/79 (1994), p. 101, para. 69 (Moldova).
[404] UN Doc. E/CN.4/1995/91 (1995), p. 9 (Albania).
[405] For further elaboration, see K. Boyle and J. Sheen, *Freedom of Religion and Belief: A World Report*, London: Routledge (1997), p. 316.
[406] *Ibid.*, at p. 334.
[407] *Metropolitan Church of Bessarabia and others v. Moldova* (2002) 35 EHRR, 306.

importance to the autonomous existence of religious communities on which the enjoyment of the rights by all its active members depends.[408]

(h) 'To observe days of rest and to celebrate holidays and ceremonies in accordance with the precepts of one's religion or belief'

Those practices mentioned in paragraph 4 of General Comment No. 22 that appear to fall within Article 6(h) (overlapping to some extent with other paragraphs of Article 6) include 'ritual and ceremonial acts giving direct expression to belief', 'the use of ritual formulae and objects', 'the display of symbols' and 'the observance of holidays and days of rest'. In paragraph 4 these are principally associated with worship, while 'rituals associated with certain stages of life' and 'the use of a particular language customarily spoken by a group' (also mentioned in paragraph 4) more generally constitute 'observance and practice'. This suggests that distinctions between 'worship, observance, practice and teaching' within the core freedom of religion Articles are not easy to make.

Much also depends on the context of the manifestation, so that the choice of a particular language in liturgy would fall under the protection of worship, rather than observance and practice. This right would provide a basis for opposing the prohibition alleged to exist in Macedonia against Vlach, Serb Orthodox and Turks using their language in religious services,[409] and for opposing pressure applied to Greek Orthodox priests in Albania to conduct their liturgy in Albanian rather than in Greek.[410] Recognition of such a right might be enhanced by the European Charter for Regional or Minority Languages.[411] On a country visit to Iran, the Special Rapporteur noted that Protestant ministers had been under pressure from the authorities to cease conducting services in Persian and to prevent Muslim converts attending, which extends the significance of this right to the right to change religion.[412]

---

[408] *Hasan and Chaush v. Bulgaria* (2002) 34(6) EHRR 1339, at para. 62.

[409] IHF 2001 Report, at p. 18; IHF 2000 Report, at p. 21.

[410] UN Doc. E/CN.4/1995/91 (1995), p. 9 (Albania).

[411] See Resolution 192 (1988) of the Standing Conference of Local and Regional Authorities of Europe and Parliamentary Assembly Opinion No. 142 (1988). For Optional Protocol claims made by an English-speaking Protestant population in Colombian islands where Spanish was made the official language, see *E.P. et al. v. Colombia*, Communication No. 318/1988 (decision of 15 July 1990) UN Doc. A/45/40 (1990), p. 184.

[412] UN Doc. E/CN.4/1996/95/Add.2 (1996), para. 74 (Iran).

The 'use of a particular language customarily spoken by a group' and 'the display of symbols' (mentioned in paragraph 4 of General Comment No. 22) are of direct relevance to the position in Pakistan where members of certain communities have allegedly been forbidden from 'posing as Muslims' (in accordance with Ordnance XX and sections 295c and 298c of the Penal Code), preventing the adoption of any Muslim practice, profession of the *Kalima*, and the use of Muslim epithets and verses on mosques, private premises, greeting cards and private correspondence.[413]

A related issue concerns the use of names of religious significance. Names are not mentioned at all in General Comment No. 22 nor Article 6 of the 1981 Declaration, although Article 11 of the Framework Convention for the Protection of National Minorities requires Parties to recognise the right of members of national minorities to use their surnames and first names in their minority language and to receive official recognition for those names. In *A. R. Coeriel and M. A. R. Aurik v. The Netherlands*,[414] the Human Rights Committee preferred to deal with restrictions on the adoption of a religious name under Article 17 of the ICCPR (privacy), rather than Article 18, although Article 18 of the ICCPR and Article 6 of the 1981 Declaration could conceivably be deployed to challenge measures such as those taken in Bulgaria requiring members of the Muslim community to change their Islamic names into Bulgarian names.[415]

Government interference with the ceremonial use of land or property is capable of falling within Article 6(h). Few cases have come before the European institutions[416] although typically when examined by the Human Rights Committee the emphasis has been on minority rights,[417] economic rights,[418] or rights to privacy and family

---

[413] UN Doc. E/CN.4/1988/45 (1988), p. 5, para. 15 (Pakistan); UN Doc. E/CN.4/1989/44 (1989), p. 29, para. 57 (Pakistan); UN Doc. E/CN.4/1993/62 (1993), p. 81, para. 48 (Pakistan); UN Doc. E/CN.4/1995/91/Add.1 (1995), pp. 53–4 (Pakistan).

[414] *A. R. Coeriel and M. A. R. Aurik v. The Netherlands*, Communication No. 453/1991 (views of 31 October 1994), UN Doc. A/50/40 vol. 2 (1999), p. 21.

[415] UN Doc. E/CN.4/1990/46 (1990), p. 6, para. 27 (Bulgaria); UN Doc. E/CN.4/1988/45 (1988), p. 20, para. 32 (Bulgaria); UN Doc. E/CN.4/1991/56 (1991), pp. 62–3, paras. 40–1 (Bulgaria).

[416] See, for example, *Holy Monasteries v. Greece* (Ser. A) No. 301 (1995) ECtHR.

[417] See *Jouni E. Länsman et al. v. Finland*, Communication No. 671/1995 (views of 30 October 1996), UN Doc. A/52/40 vol. 2 (1999), p. 191 concerning Sami reindeer herders and the threat posed by logging and road construction.

[418] *Kitok v. Sweden*, Communication No. 187/1985 (views of 27 July 1988), UN Doc. A/43/40 (1988), p. 221.

life,[419] rather than those associated with religion, even though the religious significance of land in many cases is inescapable. For example, mining has threatened sites regarded as holy by the *Punmu* and *Pangurr* Aboriginal communities in Australia[420] and by the *Hopi* and *Havasupai* Indians in the United States,[421] and logging in the United States has interfered with use of an American Indian sacred cemetery.[422] Following a visit to the United States, the Special Rapporteur pointed out that the position of Native Americans deserves better attention, particularly their collective property rights, the inalienability of sacred sites and secrecy with regard to their location.[423] Similarly, following a visit to Argentina the Special Rapporteur focused on the need for access by indigenous people to their holy sites and burial grounds of religious significance and recommended the return of human remains of religious importance (located in museums and similar institutions) to the indigenous people.[424] Needless to say, the destruction in Afghanistan of the Buddhist statues of Bamayan was condemned unequivocally by the Special Rapporteur.[425]

It would appear that not all rights within the scope of Article 6(h) are to be accorded equal priority. For example, in the case of days of rest and

[419] *Francis Hopu and Tepoaitu Bessert v. France*, Communication No. 549/1993 (views of 29 July 1997), UN Doc. A/52/40 vol. 2 (1999), p. 70 – concerning the planned development of ancestral burial ground in Tahiti. See also *Mathieu Vakoumé and others v. France*, Communication No. 822/1998 (decision of 31 October 2000), UN Doc. A/56/40 vol. 2 (2001), p. 249.

[420] UN Doc. E/CN.4/1988/45 (1988), p. 22, para. 42 (Australia).

[421] UN Doc. E/CN.4/1988/45 (1988), p. 22, para. 42 (United States). For the equivalent position in Canada, see UN Doc. E/CN.4/1990/46 (1990), p. 8, para. 33 (Canada). See R. B. Collins, 'Sacred Sites and Religious Freedom on Government Land', *University of Pennsylvania Journal of Constitutional Law* (January 2003). The paper, presented at a symposium on native Americans and the Constitution, aims to evaluate legal protection for indigenous religions when a sacred site is found on government land.

[422] UN Doc. E/CN.4/1989/44 (1989), p. 13, para. 38 (United States).

[423] 'Because of the economic and religious conflicts affecting in particular sacred sites, the Special Rapporteur wishes to point out that the freedom of belief, in this case that of the Native Americans, is a fundamental matter and requires still greater protection … The expression of the belief has to be reconciled with other rights and legitimate concerns, including those of an economic nature, but after the rights and claims of the parties have been duly taken into account, on an equal footing (in accordance with each party's system of values)' – UN Doc. E/CN.4/1999/58/Add.1 (1998), paras. 81–2 (United States).

[424] UN Doc. E/CN.4/2002/73/Add.1 (2002), p. 35, para. 163 (Argentina).

[425] UN Doc. A/56/253 (2001), p. 8, para. 27 (Afghanistan).

holidays, the protection allowed by Article 6(h) is fairly insubstantial and, as proposed in the Sub-Commission's Draft Declaration, was essentially limited to non-discrimination.[426] In the drafting of paragraph (h) there was predictable resistance from Communist countries to any right to observe religious holidays,[427] and, though holidays and days of rest were ultimately included in Article 6(h), they are recognised to be subject to control by the State as public sector employer, and a balance needs to be struck in a multi-religious society between the number of public holidays that may feasibly be declared and the variety of beliefs that would elect different holidays for religious celebration.[428] It is interesting to note that even days of rest coinciding with the beliefs of the majority have run the accusation of being coercive (such as in Israel where the enforcement of the Sabbath extended to a ban on public transport, road closures, and compulsory dietary observance in certain public buildings).[429] Public holidays seldom serve the purpose of enabling religious observance and so recognition for minority religious holidays has proved difficult.[430] Even when it is claimed that restrictions conflict with religious observance, the European Commission has been unsympathetic towards applicants who have voluntarily accepted

---

[426] The Sub-Commission's Draft Declaration included in Article VI(8): 'Due account shall be taken of the prescriptions of each religion or belief relating to holy days and days of rest, and all discrimination in this regard between persons of different religions or beliefs shall be prohibited'.

[427] Mr Mateljak (Yugoslavia) commented that 'since religion in Yugoslavia was a private matter and religious persons were free to observe religious holidays, those holidays were private and the right to days of rest could not be based on them' (UN Doc. A/C.3/36/SR. 35 (1981), p. 9, para. 31).

[428] Krishnaswami, 'Study of Discrimination', 227, at 250.

[429] Boyle and Sheen, *A World Report*, p. 439.

[430] The European Commission in *X. v. United Kingdom* observed: 'in respect of the general question of religious and public holidays ... that, in most countries, only the religious holidays of the majority of the population are celebrated as public holidays. Thus Protestant holidays are not always public holidays in Catholic countries and vice versa' (*X. v. United Kingdom*, App. No. 8160/78 (1981) 22 D&R 27, at 38). Compare with the decision of the Supreme Court of Canada in *O'Malley v. Simpson's Sears Ltd* [1985] 2 SCR 536 which held that an employer contravened the Ontario human rights code when it failed to make reasonable accommodation to the request of an employee not to work on Saturday because it was her day of religious observance – UN Doc. E/CN.4/1992/52 (1992), p. 110, para. 84. Notice also that Article 2(5) of the European Social Charter requires contracting parties to 'ensure a weekly rest period which shall, as far as possible, coincide with the day recognised by tradition or custom in the country or region concerned as a day of rest'.

obligations that compromise their observance (*Stedman v. United Kingdom*),[431] and has shown its reluctance to accept the applicant's characterisation of such conflict (*Valsamis v. Greece*).[432]

The reference to 'ceremonies in accordance with the precepts of one's religion or belief' in Article 6(h) is ambiguous in that it could be confined to ceremonial acts, or alternatively could extend to wider observances such as the celebration of religious festivals (even if they are not recognised as public holidays), pilgrimages,[433] and the performance of rituals associated with certain stages of life (such as baptisms, circumcisions, weddings and funerals). The Special Rapporteur has highlighted, for example, State intervention to prevent Christmas celebrations in China,[434] a Christian procession in Kazakhstan,[435] a traditional Buddhist holiday in Bangladesh,[436] celebration of the Monlam (Great Prayer) Festival in China,[437] and criticised the negative attitude towards Ramadan and practices of circumcision in Bulgaria.[438] Another example is found in Montenegro where Christmas celebrations by the Montenegran Orthodox Church were prohibited in 2000 because the Church had been refused registration.[439] Pilgrimages are not mentioned either in General Comment No. 22 or in the 1981 Declaration[440] but have been the subject of Special Rapporteur reports concerning Czechoslovakia (where the authorities allegedly obstructed the annual pilgrimage to Levoča),[441] China (where the twelve-yearly pilgrimage to Mount Kailash was disrupted by State restrictions on the movement of pilgrims,[442] and where ancient traditions such as the search for

---

[431] *Stedman v. United Kingdom*, App. No. 29107/95, 89–A (1997) D&R 104.

[432] *Valsamis v. Greece* (1997) 24 EHRR 294.

[433] See P. Mason, 'Pilgrimage to Religious Shrines: An Essential Element in the Human Right to Freedom of Thought, Conscience and Religion', 25 Case W Res J Int'l L (1993), 619.

[434] UN Doc. E/CN.4/1993/62 (1993), p. 23, para. 22 (China).

[435] UN Doc. E/CN.4/1999/58 (1999), para. 70 (Kazakhstan).

[436] UN Doc. A/58/296 (2003), p. 6, para. 19 (Bangladesh).

[437] UN Doc. E/CN.4/1993/62 (1993), p. 5, para. 18 (China).

[438] UN Doc. E/CN.4/1988/45 (1988), p. 19, para. 31 (Bulgaria).

[439] IHF 2000 Report, at p. 33.

[440] This is in spite of the fact that the Sub-Commission's Draft Declaration included in Article VI(6): 'Everyone has the right to make pilgrimage to sites held in veneration, whether inside or outside his country, and every State shall grant freedom of access to these places.'

[441] UN Doc. E/CN.4/1988/45 (1988), p. 23, para. 47 (Czechoslovakia).

[442] UN Doc. E/CN.4/1991/56 (1991), p. 78, para. 50 (China); UN Doc. A/58/296 (2003), p. 7, para. 32 (China).

reincarnations were conducted by a committee organised by the authorities).[443] Examples of interference with the rites associated with certain stages of life include the sentence of death for a priest in former Communist Albania for baptising a child at the parents' request,[444] the attack by ultra-Orthodox Jews in Israel against Messianic Jews intending to baptise Jewish children,[445] and jail sentences in Bulgaria for parents who arranged traditional circumcision for their male children.[446] The Human Rights Chamber for Bosnia and Herzegovina has also had to consider the stoning of believers participating in funeral processions.[447]

As to the celebration of marriage, in the drafting of the Convention on religious intolerance various countries emphasised freedom to enter into marriage without discrimination on the ground of religion or belief, the need for tolerance for mixed marriages and freedom from coercion to undergo a religious marriage ceremony.[448] In the 1981 Declaration no mention is made of the choice of religious marriage rites as a manifestation (even though included in the Sub-Commission's Draft Declaration).[449] In the context of the European Convention it is clear that the European Commission subjects the substantive right to marry under Article 12 of the European Convention to the internal laws of States, permitting the invalidation of marriages that are not in compliance with domestic law.[450] Similarly, issues of divorce are generally dealt with under Article 12 rather than Article 9.[451] In *D. v. France*,[452] the European Commission held that a husband's refusal to repudiate his marriage by providing a *guett* to his ex-wife to enable her to remarry under Jewish law did not constitute manifestation of religion because he was not obliged to do so against his conscience or under Hebrew law.[453]

[443] UN Doc. E/CN.4/1992/52 (1992), p. 5, para. 22 (China).

[444] UN Doc. E/CN.4/1988/45 (1988), p. 4 (Albania).

[445] UN Doc. E/CN.4/2000/65 (2000), para. 56 (Israel).

[446] UN Doc. E/CN.4/1988/45 (1988), p. 4 (Bulgaria).

[447] *The Islamic Community in Bosnia and Herzegovina v. The Republika Srpska*, Case No. CH/96/29, decision of 11 June 1999 (2000) 7(3) IHRR 833, at 859, para. 186.

[448] UN Doc. E/CN.4/891 (1965), pp. 67–8, paras. 288, 289 and 291.

[449] Sub-Commission's Draft Declaration Article VII. However, the Special Rapporteur has reported on the discriminatory disruption of religious weddings in Turkey – UN Doc. E/CN.4/1989/44 (1989), p. 40, para. 71 (Turkey).

[450] *Khan v. United Kingdom*, App. No. 11579/85 (1986) 48 D&R 253.

[451] *Johnston v. Ireland* (Ser. A) No. 112 (1987) ECtHR.

[452] *D. v. France*, App. No. 10180/82 (1983) 35 D&R 199.

[453] Cf. *X. v. Australia*, Communication No. 557/1993 (decision of 16 July 1996), UN Doc. A/51/40 vol. 2 (1997), p. 235 in which the author was a member of the Wiradjuri

The performance of marriage, burial and similar rites is primarily regarded as a civic function although authority may be conferred on religious leaders to undertake them. The 1981 Declaration does not include specific reference to burial rites (even though contemplated in the Sub-Commission's Draft Declaration).[454] Much of the Special Rapporteur's focus on this issue has concerned the denial of burial rites in accordance with particular religious beliefs (notably those of the Ahmadi in Pakistan,[455] Shia in Iraq[456] and Protestants in Ethiopia),[457] the disruption of wedding services (for example, in Eritrea),[458] the disruption of funeral services (for example, Christian funerals in Egypt[459] and Hindu funerals in the United Arab Emirates),[460] and the desecration of cemeteries (including Muslim graveyards in Bulgaria[461] and the United Kingdom,[462] non-Muslim cemeteries in Cyprus,[463] Jewish tombs in the Russian Federation[464] and Belarus[465] and cemeteries of all confessions in Bosnia and Herzegovina).[466] The Human Rights Chamber for Bosnia and Herzegovina decided in *Dzevad Mahmutovic v. The Republika Srpska*[467] that a burial in accordance with Muslim religious regulations and practice clearly fell within the ambit of Article 9 of the European Convention, and so did any interference with the grave such as

Aboriginal Nation of New South Wales and having undergone an aboriginal ceremony of marriage before a civil one claimed violation of Article 18(1), 26 and 27 of ICCPR when his wife was awarded custody of the children and division of property against the author contrary to aboriginal custom – ruled inadmissible as domestic remedies had not been exhausted.

[454] The Sub-Commission's Draft Declaration Article VIII. For discussion on issues of the compatibility with Article 9 of exhumation, see case comment by L. Yates on *re: Crawley Green Road Cemetery, Luton* [2001] 2 WLR 1175, in 6(29) Ecc LJ (2001) 168; see also case comment by L. Yates on a Jewish exhumation in (2001) 6(28) Ecc LJ 80.

[455] UN Doc. E/CN.4/1993/62 (1993), p. 82, para. 48 (Pakistan).

[456] UN Doc. E/CN.4/1994/79 (1994), p. 80, para. 60 (Iraq).

[457] UN Doc. E/Cn.4/1995/91 (1995), p. 37 (Ethiopia).

[458] UN Doc. E/CN.4/2005/61/Add.1 (2005), p. 25, para. 96 (Eritrea).

[459] UN Doc. E/CN.4/1991/56 (1991), p. 87, para. 58 (Egypt); UN Doc. E/CN.4/1992/52 (1992), p. 12, para. 27 (Egypt).

[460] UN Doc. A/56/253 (2001), p. 11, para. 37 (United Arab Emirates).

[461] UN Doc. E/CN.4/1988/45 (1988), p. 4 (Bulgaria).

[462] UN Doc. E/CN.4/2005/61/Add.1 (2005), p. 72, para. 282 (United Kingdom).

[463] UN Doc. E/CN.4/1999/58 (1999), para. 49 (Cyprus).

[464] UN Doc. E/CN.4/2000/65 (2000), para. 35 (Russian Federation).

[465] UN Doc. E/CN.4/2005/61/Add.1 (2005), p. 12, para. 43 (Belarus).

[466] IHF 2000 Report, at p. 8.

[467] *Dzevad Mahmutovic v. The Republika Srpska*, Case No. CH/98/892, decision of 8 October 1999 (2000) 7(3) IHRR 869.

exhumation. The approach of the European Commission to the disposal of the dead has not been supportive of individual wishes. In *X. v. Germany*[468] it upheld the State's refusal to permit the applicant to have his ashes scattered on his own land, on the basis that the applicant's wish, no matter how strongly motivated (to avoid burial in a cemetery with Christian symbols) did not constitute a belief protected within Article 9 of the European Convention. Even under Article 8, the European Commission found no violation because of the public interest justifications which included the need to secure a peaceful resting place for human remains. However, the European Commission's support for other public interest justifications (including urban planning and public health) suggests that respect for the dead should not be seen as the driving concern of the Commission.

The issue of coercion is a particularly important one in connection with Article 6(h). The Special Rapporteur has been concerned, for example, with the alleged enforcement of Muslim observances under section 306 of the Mauritanian Penal Code of 1983,[469] the alleged imprisonment of religious leaders in Myanmar for not attending the religious ceremonies organised by the authorities,[470] and the alleged enforcement of dietary and other restrictions in public places during Ramadan in Saudi Arabia.[471] The Human Rights Committee has also been concerned to ensure that cultural or religious ceremonies and practices are not forced upon individuals, such as the caste systems in Nepal and India, which are seen as discriminatory,[472] and other practices in Zimbabwe which involve coercion on those unable to consent.[473] (Other practices such as immolating a widow at the pyre of her deceased husband, dedicating a virgin girl of tender years to a god to function as a

---

[468] *X. v. Germany*, App. No. 8741/79 (1981) 24 D&R 137.

[469] UN Doc. E/CN.4/1992/52 (1992), p. 73, para. 57 (Mauritania).

[470] UN Doc. E/Cn.4/1995/91 (1995), p. 64 (Myanmar).

[471] UN Doc. E/CN.4/1992/52 (1992), p. 81, para. 65 (Saudi).

[472] UN Doc. A/50/40 (1996), p. 18, para. 66 (Nepal); UN Doc. A/52/40 (1997), p. 69, para. 430 (India).

[473] UN Doc. A/53/40 (1998), p. 36, para. 214 (Zimbabwe). The Committee was concerned about practices such as *kuzvarita* (pledging of girls for economic gain), *kuripa ngozi* (appeasement of the spirits of a murdered person), *lobola* (bride price) and female genital mutilation. E. K. Quashigah examines international standards against the compulsion of girls to serve fetish gods to atone for family transgressions, in E. K. Quashigah, 'Religious Freedom and Vestal Virgins: The Trokosi Practice in Ghana', 10 RADIC (1998) 193.

devadasi[474] and female circumcision[475] have received attention from other sources.)

In summary, the range of practices capable of falling within Article 6(h) is so broad and varied that there is little to be gained from trying to discern patterns of consistency in applicable standards. It is clear that paragraphs (a) to (i) of Article 6 are not mutually exclusive, and indeed the range of practices that may be embraced by Article 6 should not be limited to those particularised in its drafting. The terms of Article 6(h) on their own shed little light on the range of ceremonial practices that are critically important to so many religions. The contribution of the Human Rights Committee in paragraph 4 of General Comment No. 22 is useful in drawing attention to the significance of the display of symbols extending well beyond their use for purely ceremonial purposes. Likewise, the choice of a particular language is central to the liturgy of many religions, as pointed out in paragraph 4 of General Comment No. 22. However, by far the greatest assistance towards a detailed understanding of Article 6(h), in spite of its imprecision, comes from the Special Rapporteur's illustrations of interference with the ceremonial aspects of religious manifestation. Because the few petition decisions that have been made by the European institutions and the Human Rights Committee have been confined to limited aspects of burial and marriage, days of rest or the customary use of ancestral land, the numerous facets of this particular right would remain inscrutable without the vivid portrayal of restrictions throughout the world illustrated by the Special Rapporteur. In addition, the words 'in accordance with the precepts of one's religion or belief' in Article 6(h) have particular value in emphasising the freedom of the individual's own choice in matters of ceremonial manifestation, which is most obviously restricted by the coercive imposition of State alternatives.

---

[474] Per Sinha J. of the Supreme Court of India in *Saifuddin Saheb v. State of Bombay* (1962) 49 AIR 853, at 863, para. 17.
[475] General Recommendation. No. 14, 9th Sess., 1990 of the Committee on the Elimination of Discrimination against Women, UN Doc. A/45/38 (1990), p. 80; UN Doc. E/CN.4/SUB.2/1989/42 of 21 August 1989, 'Study on Traditional Practices Affecting the Health of Women and Children by the Sub-Commission on Prevention of Discrimination and Protection of Minorities'.

(i) 'To establish and maintain communications with individuals and communities in matters of religion or belief at the national and international levels'

When included in the Sub-Commission's Draft Declaration, the emphasis of this freedom was on extending the right to establish and maintain religious communities and institutions to the right to form territorial federations.[476] The international dimension was raised in the drafting of the Convention on religious intolerance[477] but when debated for inclusion in the 1981 Declaration discussion focused on the interrelation of such a right with domestic law.[478] One purpose of international liaison was described more recently in the context of OSCE commitments as being to 'engage in consultations with religious faiths, institutions and organizations in order to achieve a better understanding of the requirements of religious freedom'.[479]

The Special Rapporteur has reported on numerous measures restricting this freedom. One of the most striking was a communication addressed recently to China concerning tens of thousands of Ismaeli Muslims in the autonomous Tajik district in the Sinkiang-Uighur region, who were allegedly cut off from their fellow believers in Tajikistan and the rest of the world. According to the imam of the Ismaeli mosque in Tashkurgan, children under the age of eighteen were unable to go to the mosque and the fourth Aga Khan was prevented from providing assistance to the Ismaeli Muslims in the region.[480] More commonly, restrictions on this freedom are targeted at the propagation of overseas religions (Mongolia),[481] so as to prevent foreign religious bodies (particularly missionaries) establishing a presence (China,[482] and Zimbabwe[483]), and to regulate participation by nationals in activity overseas (China,[484] Moldova[485] and Iran[486]).

---

[476] Sub-Commission's Draft Declaration Article VI(2)(ii): 'Every religious community and institution has the right, in association with similar religious communities and institutions, to form territorial federations on a national, regional or local basis.'

[477] UN Doc. E/CN.4/891 (1965), p. 66, para. 283.

[478] See, for example, UN Doc. A/C.3/36/SR. 43 (1981), p. 9, para. 53 (Romania).

[479] Vienna Concluding Document, January 1989, ILM 28 (1989) 531, para. 16(e).

[480] UN Doc. E/CN.4/2004/63 (2004), p. 10, para. 39 (China).

[481] UN Doc. E/CN.4/1995/91 (1995), p. 62 (Mongolia). In Mongolia, Article 4.7 of the Constitution states that: 'The organized propagation of religion from outside are [sic] forbidden.'

[482] UN Doc. E/CN.4/1993/62 (1993), p. 11, para. 20; ibid., at p. 13, para. 22 (China).

[483] UN Doc. E/CN.4/1995/91 (1995), p. 109 (Zimbabwe).

[484] UN Doc. E/CN.4/1993/62 (1993), p. 13, para. 22 (China).

[485] IHF 1999 Report, at p. 17.

[486] UN Doc. E/CN.4/1996/95/Add.2 (1996), para. 77 (Iran).

There has been opposition to the presence of religious leaders and members from overseas denominations when not invited by the official church in the host country in Romania[487] and in Bulgaria (where the authorities even used troops to deny entry to a number of Swedish Protestants who arrived to attend an interdenominational conference of 3000 co-religionists in Sofia).[488] Likewise, in Iran, Christian conferences have allegedly been prohibited and Christian Iranian citizens urged 'not to contact the West'.[489] In Belarus, unregistered religious organisations have allegedly not been authorised to invite foreign religious personnel[490] and, in Greece, foreign religious personnel who do not come from the European Union reportedly encounter obstacles in connection with entry visas and the renewal of residence permits.[491] In Moldova, a Methodist leader was asked by the National Security Ministry to cease co-operating with international organisations.[492] However, far more restrictive are the punitive measures reported in other countries for maintaining contacts abroad, such as in Morocco (where nineteen Muslims were allegedly arrested for receiving Christian literature from a foreigner),[493] China (where a Catholic priest was allegedly sentenced to eleven years' imprisonment for his loyalty to the Vatican and for having maintained contacts abroad)[494] and former Communist Czechoslovakia (where a Czech priest was charged in connection with his contacts with members of religious orders and Polish Catholics).[495]

Restrictions on movement have taken a variety of forms. Limits have reportedly been put in place to prevent Ahmadis in Pakistan from travelling to Mecca to perform the *haj* and to prevent Shia Muslims in

---

[487] UN Doc. E/CN.4/1995/91 (1995), p. 77 (Romania); UN Doc. E/CN.4/1990/46 (1990), p. 36, para. 71 (Romania). See also UN Doc. E/CN.4/2005/61/Add.1 (2005), p. 65, para. 254 (Macedonia).

[488] UN Doc. E/CN.4/1994/79 (1994), p. 27, para. 37 (Bulgaria). For an example of the expulsion of four Muslims from Bulgaria for constituting a 'threat for national security', see IHF 2001 Report, at p. 15.

[489] UN Doc. E/CN.4/1992/52 (1992), p. 34, para. 50 (Iran).

[490] UN Doc. E/CN.4/2000/65 (2000), para. 16 (Belarus).

[491] UN Doc. A/51/542/Add.1 (1996), para. 62 (Greece).

[492] UN Doc. A/57/274 (2002), p. 10, para. 51 (Moldova). See also UN Doc. E/CN.4/2005/61/Add.1 (2005), p. 68, para. 263 (Turkmenistan) for allegations that a new law in Turkmenistan requires religious groups to 'co-ordinate' contacts with foreigners with the Government, and to gain permission before receiving foreign support such as funding and religious literature.

[493] UN Doc. E/Cn.4/1995/91 (1995), p. 60 (Morocco).

[494] UN Doc. E/CN.4/1995/91/Add.1 (1995), p. 9 (China).

[495] UN Doc. E/CN.4/1988/45 (1988), p. 23, para. 48 (Czechoslovakia).

Saudi Arabia from studying in Iran, Iraq and Syria, even though this is necessary for them to become religious leaders.[496] Leaders have also been prevented from entering countries such as Saudi Arabia (which stopped foreign Shia leaders with any public role from entering the country).[497] In some countries, only religious leaders have been prevented from travelling abroad (Burundi),[498] while in others all members of entire religious communities have been prevented from visiting overseas (for example, the Syrian Jewish community).[499] Restrictions have even been imposed on freedom of movement within a country (such as monks in China[500] and *zakirs* in Pakistan, to avoid inflaming sectarian feeling[501]).

In the European context, it is clear that the European Convention does not include freedom from expulsion for foreign nationals (*X. v. Denmark*),[502] nor freedom for foreign nationals to enter another country (*Church of X. v. United Kingdom*).[503]

In short, the international component of the right in Article 6(i) is seemingly not well recognised, even though it is frequently more important than the purely national dimension. Restrictions on international communication may be used as a means of denying to minorities the essential practice of their religion or at least to deprive them of support from the worldwide community. Once again, the Special Rapporteur's reports have helped place this right in the context of the denial of more fundamental freedoms. Those reports also bear out the underlying motivation in many countries to restrict religious dialogue as part of a wider pattern of opposition towards foreign missionary work and proselytism, as well as the institutionalised preservation of State religion.

---

[496] Krishnaswami commented that 'when a pilgrimage is an essential part of their faith, any systematic prohibition or curtailment ... would constitute a serious infringement of the right of the individual to manifest his religion or belief': Krishnaswami, 'Study of Discrimination', 227, at 247.

[497] IHF 2001 Report, at p. 15 (Bulgaria).

[498] UN Doc. E/CN.4/1988/45 (1988), p. 5 (Burundi).

[499] UN Doc. E/CN.4/1994/79 (1994), p. 112, para. 78 (Syria).

[500] UN Doc. E/CN.4/1993/62 (1993), p. 6, para. 18 (China).

[501] UN Doc. E/CN.4/1995/91/Add.1 (1995), p. 52 (Pakistan).

[502] *X. v. Denmark*, App. No. 7465/76 (1977) 7 D&R (1977) 153. Nevertheless, see *Lotter and Lotter v. Bulgaria* (App. No. 39015/97), Judgment of 19 May 2004, in which two Austrian nationals claimed that violation of Articles 9 and 14 was constituted by Bulgarian authorities ordering them to leave Bulgaria for the sole reason that they were Jehovah's Witnesses. A friendly settlement was reached.

[503] *Church of X. v. United Kingdom*, App. No. 3798/68 (1968) 29 CD 70. For wider reading, see A. Eide, 'Citizenship and the Minority Rights of Non-Citizens', UNDoc. E/CN.4/Sub.2/AC.5/1999/WP.3 (1999).

Summary

Article 6 of the 1981 Declaration provides an extremely useful framework for the analysis of different manifestations of religion or belief, even though neither the European Court nor the Human Rights Committee is bound to observe formally the content of the 1981 Declaration. It was surprising to find that certain forms of manifestation recognised by the Krishaswami study or General Comment No. 22 do not easily fit within any of the manifestations particularised in Article 6, such as 'the display of symbols', or 'the use of a particular language customarily spoken by a group'. Nevertheless, their full practical importance could be appreciated from the incidents reported by the Special Rapporteur. The religious significance of names is not mentioned at all in General Comment No. 22 or in Article 6. Other forms of manifestation are more obvious, such as 'the wearing of distinctive clothing or head coverings' as noted in General Comment No. 22, which has received attention in a number of claims though was not specifically included in the text of Article 6 of the 1981 Declaration. The wearing of beards as mandated by particular religions remains one of the most commonly practised manifestations but formal recognition has been obscured by the prison environment in which claims at both United Nations and European levels have arisen. Similarly, the educational context of the European cases concerning the wearing of Muslim headscarves has been integral to the reasoning of those decisions without giving sufficient emphasis to the practice as an obvious and straightforward manifestation. Individual decisions are not only few in number but often emerge from a particular background which limits the recognition given to certain practices. The use of different sources to identify accepted forms of manifestation of religion or belief is therefore important to help to avoid such distortions, particularly in European case law.

It has to be questioned whether the *Arrowsmith* test should continue to occupy the central place it has done in European jurisprudence once sufficient acknowledgement is given to a wide range of manifestations falling within the 'term worship, teaching, practice and observance'. It is to be hoped that the European Court will not try to determine the span of eligible manifestations simply from a crude formula but instead pay due regard to the recognition of different manifestations so clearly established in Article 6 of the 1981 Declaration. The result is likely to be a convergence of standards at United Nations and European levels.

One other aspect of the external right of manifestation stands out. The collective dimension of manifestation has rarely been challenged and is beyond question. The primary value of the decision in the recent European case of *Metropolitan Church of Bessarabia and others v. Moldova* is its emphasis on the need to safeguard associative life against State restriction through registration formalities, one of the most effective means by which States prevent the survival of minority or recently introduced religious denominations. Lack of legal personality eradicates almost every possible form of collective manifestation and threatens the very existence of religious groups. The focus of this particular case was on the structural prerequisites for most forms of collective manifestation, and is greatly welcomed for that, even though the collective right to 'manifest in community with others', 'in public or private' has always been fundamental to the external limb of all of the core freedom of religion Articles. The European Court usefully isolated the particular State interference which was responsible for preventing the enjoyment of numerous forms of collective manifestation.

Many types of manifestation of course may be enjoyed by the solitary individual as fully as in community with others. A review of the illustrations in Article 6 of the 1981 Declaration indicates that some forms of manifestation do generally contemplate collective enjoyment but no real distinction between individual and collective, or indeed private and public, manifestation is evident in Article 6. For example, the rights in Article 6(a) to worship and assemble and to establish and maintain places for that purpose, and in Article 6(g) to appoint appropriate leaders, must generally be taken to address collective enjoyment, although worship obviously includes private, solitary worship and so no clear division appears to have been intended. The right in Article 6(b) concerning charitable or humanitarian institutions at first sight also appears primarily to be for collective enjoyment although, once again, there is no reason to rule out the private individual from the right to establish such institutions. The same could also be said of Article 6(f) when an individual needs to solicit outside voluntary contributions. Likewise, the rights in Article 6(c) to have access to customary and ritual articles, and in Article 6(h) to observe religious holidays and ceremonies make no distinction between the collective and individual, or public and private options for their enjoyment. However the rights in Article 6(d) to publish, in Article 6(e) to teach, and in Article 6(i) to enjoy free communication at national and international levels obviously all depend sufficiently upon co-operation or dialogue with others to conclude that these are intended to be realised in community with others. In reality, such distinctions serve no real purpose when considering different forms of manifestation. Instead, the abiding and fundamental distinction to be observed at all times remains within the architecture of all of the core freedom of religion Articles between the *forum internum* and the right to external manifestation.

In summary, Article 6 of the 1981 Declaration is an invaluable tool in the better identification and appreciation of different forms of manifestation. It has been the springboard for the work of the Special Rapporteur who has supplied an encyclopaedic range of illustrations of restrictions on manifestation, enabling each type of manifestation under consideration to be seen in its worldwide context, with greater visibility of the State motivation for intolerance or discrimination. This has enabled a better grasp of the implications of interference for religious groups and individuals. Without this practical context the results of individual decisions offer an incomplete and inadequate picture of the priorities that should be given to accepting certain forms of expression of religion or belief as manifestations.

Permissible limitations on the right to manifestation

Introduction

The key features of the limitation provisions found in the Universal Declaration, the ICCPR, the 1981 Declaration and the European Convention are the preconditions of limitation and the grounds of limitation. The preconditions are that the State measure must be 'prescribed by law',[504] and must be 'necessary'.[505] The grounds of limitation are those which protect[506] 'public safety', 'order', 'health', or 'morals' or the 'fundamental rights and freedoms of others'. Although there are superficial differences between these provisions (the most conspicuous being that Article 18 of the Universal Declaration does not contain its own limitation clause but is subject to the general limitation provision in Article 29(2)),[507] the drafting differences are not substantive. The

---

[504] The Universal Declaration states 'determined by law'.
[505] The Universal Declaration and European Convention add 'in a democratic society'.
[506] The Universal Declaration refers to the purpose of 'meeting the just requirements of'.
[507] Article 29 of the Universal Declaration is given close consideration in a study by E. A. Daes, 'The Individual's Duties to the Community and the Limitations on Human Rights and Freedoms Under Article 29 of the Universal Declaration of Human Rights', UN Doc. E/CN.4/Sub.2/432/Rev.2 (1983).

limitation provisions in Article 1(3) of the 1981 Declaration are the same as those found in Article 18 of the ICCPR and are taken to bear identical meaning. Article 9(2) of the European Convention and Article 18(3) of the ICCPR are likewise almost identical. Each of these limitation provisions will be examined in detail to determine the precise scope of the latitude allowed by States.[508]

Reasonably detailed guidance has been provided in European Convention decisions concerning each of the preconditions and grounds of limitation. The Human Rights Committee in its Optional Protocol decisions, by contrast, tends to offer only an abbreviated analysis of the 'prescribed by law' precondition (as it is rarely a contested issue) and of whether the measures taken against the author are necessary for the purpose stated.[509] European Convention decisions on the subject of religion are far more numerous than Human Rights Committee decisions, which are sparse. In discerning the Universal position, reliance will therefore be placed on General Comment No. 22 and the *travaux préparatoires* to supplement the few available decisions of direct relevance.

Prescribed by law

In the drafting of Article 29 of the Universal Declaration, the words 'prescribed by law' were proposed to emphasise the need for legal form but it quickly became evident that it was also necessary to qualify the nature of the laws on which States could rely. In answer to the possibility that laws may be unjust, Venezuela proposed a reference to 'just' requirements,[510] which was ultimately adopted in preference to France's 'legitimate' requirements.[511]

---

[508] For detailed discussion on the scope of limitation provisions (including analysis of *travaux préparatoires*), see: A. Svensson-McCarthy, *The International Law of Human Rights and States of Exception*, The Hague/London: Martinus Nijhoff (1985); A. C. Kiss, 'Permissible Limitations on Rights', in L. Henkin (ed.), *The International Bill of Rights The Covenant on Civil and Political Rights*, New York/Guildford: Columbia University Press (1981), pp. 290–309; A. C. Kiss, 'Commentary by the Rapporteur on the Limitation Provisions', 7(1) HRQ (1985) 15.

[509] See, for example, *Tae-Hoon Park v. Korea*, Communication No. 628/1995 (views of 20 October 1998) 6(3) IHRR (1999) 623, at 628, para. 10.3 (Article 19(3) of the ICCPR).

[510] *Ibid.*, at p. 650 (Venezuela).

[511] *Ibid.*, at p. 643 (France). For further discussion on this aspect of the limitation provisions, see O. Garibaldi, 'General Limitations on Human Rights: The Principle of Legality', 17 Harv Int'l LJ (1976) 503.

Two preconditions acknowledged in the context of the European Convention for satisfying the 'prescribed by law' requirement law are that the law in question must be adequately accessible and must be formulated with sufficient precision that the consequences of a given action are foreseeable.[512] Consistent with this interpretation, the term has been construed so that it 'does not merely refer back to domestic law but also relates to the quality of law, requiring it to be compatible with the rule of law, which is expressly mentioned in the preamble to the Convention'.[513] After a number of unsatisfactory, uncourageous decisions in which the 'prescribed by law' precondition was too easily upheld by the European Court, a refreshingly interventionist decision was recently taken by the Court in *Hasan and Chaush v. Bulgaria*[514] when (for the first time in the history of Article 9) it determined that the 'prescribed by law' requirement had not been satisfied. This may have been the result of pressure from opinions in cases such as *Kokkinakis v. Greece*[515] and *Larissis v. Greece*,[516] in which the European Court upheld the anti-proselytism laws of Greece in spite of criticism that unverifiable criteria in relation to proselytism (such as 'respectable or not respectable' and 'misplaced') could not guarantee legal certainty,[517] nor afford protection against arbitrary measures when a

---

[512] *The Sunday Times Case* (Ser. A) No. 30 (1979) ECtHR, para. 48: 'In the Court's opinion, the following are two of the requirements that flow from the expression "prescribed by law". Firstly, the law must be adequately accessible: the citizen must be able to have an indication that is adequate in the circumstances of the legal rules applicable to a given case. Secondly, a norm cannot be regarded as a "law" unless it is formulated with sufficient precision to enable the citizen to regulate his conduct: he must be able – if need be with appropriate advice – to foresee, to a degree that is reasonable in the circumstances, the consequences which a given action may entail.'

[513] *Malone v. United Kingdom* (Ser. A) No. 82 (1984) ECtHR, para. 67 (on the same wording in Article 8). It also 'implies that there must be a measure of protection in domestic law against arbitrary interferences by public authorities with the rights safeguarded' – *Olsson v. Sweden* (Ser. A) No. 130 (1988) ECtHR, para. 61(b).

[514] *Hasan and Chaush v. Bulgaria* (2002) 34(6) EHRR 1339. Although the interference with the internal organisation of the Muslim community in *Supreme Holy Council of the Muslim Community v. Bulgaria* was based on the same legal provisions which allowed unfettered discretion to the executive in *Hasan and Chaush v. Bulgaria*, the Court observed that there were considerable differences in the authorities' approach in the *Supreme Holy Council* case (the authorities did not make use of their discretion), and the European Court decided not to rule on whether the interference was prescribed by law (*Supreme Holy Council of the Muslim Community v. Bulgaria* (App. No. 39023/97), Judgment of 16 December 2004, at para. 90).

[515] *Kokkinakis v. Greece* (Ser. A) No. 260–A (1993) ECtHR.

[516] *Larissis and others v. Greece* (Ser. A) No. 65 (1998–V) ECtHR 363.

[517] Partly concurring opinion of Judge Pettiti in *Kokkinakis v. Greece*.

believer who tries to spread his religious beliefs can never be certain whether his conduct is illegal or not.[518]

Hasan and Chaush v. Bulgaria is also important for its focus on the range of discretion available to the State, rather than simply the legal measure which bestowed it. The case concerned the decision by the Council of Ministers and Directorate of Religious Denominations to substitute their own choice of leader for the one selected by the Muslim community. In reviewing the legal provisions which conferred the discretion to make such a decision, the European Court noted the following factors: that the relevant law did not dictate any substantive criteria for registering religious denominations and changes of their leadership; the absence of procedural safeguards against arbitrary exercise of the discretion left to the executive; that the relevant law and the decisions of the Directorate were not notified to those directly affected; that those decisions lacked necessary reasoning and were unclear in not referring to the first applicant even though he was the Chief mufti removed from position; and that the effect of refusing to recognise his leadership was arbitrarily to favour one faction of the divided religious community. Accordingly, the interference with the internal organisation of the Muslim community and the applicants' freedom of religion was not 'prescribed by law' in that it was arbitrary and was based on legal provisions which allowed an unfettered discretion to the executive so that it did not meet the required standards of clarity and foreseeability.[519]

The coincidence of this decision with the more demanding approach of the European Court towards discrimination, as reflected in *Tlimmenos v. Greece*[520] (discussed above in Chapter 3 under the heading 'Differential treatment', pp. 187–92, may suggest a policy shift away from the Court's traditional 'deference' towards State measures (as Carolyn Evans describes it) that interfere with freedom of religion. In particular, the Court's criticism of poorly targeted legislation in *Thlimmenos v. Greece* (in failing to distinguish between criminals of conscience and other felons in the admission of Chartered Accountants for the purposes of Article 14) constitutes an important development which may also have implications for the preconditions under Article 9

---

[518] Partly dissenting opinion of Judge Repik in *Larissis and others v. Greece*, (Ser. A) No. 65 (1998–V) ECtHR 363.
[519] *Hasan and Chaush v. Bulgaria* (2002) 34 EHRR 1339, at para. 86.
[520] *Thlimmenos v. Greece* (2001) 31 EHRR 411.

if it represents a willingness on the part of the Court to attack repressive legislation. Certainly this is suggested by the European Court's criticism of the legal provisions in *Hasan and Chaush v. Bulgaria*, resulting in a failure of the 'prescribed by law' requirement, and it may be speculated that the Court might in future more readily use the 'prescribed by law' precondition to condemn State measures that that are essentially preventive in regulating the practices of religious minorities.

More recently, in *Maestri v. Italy*,[521] the European Court examined the quality of a law which formed the basis of a disciplinary sanction imposed on a judge for belonging to the Freemasons. Although the law satisfied the condition of accessibility (because it was public and accessible to the applicant on account of his profession) it was not foreseeable as to its effects. It 'was not sufficiently clear to enable the applicant, who, being a judge, was nonetheless informed and well-versed in the law, to realise ... that his membership of a Masonic lodge could lead to sanctions being imposed on him'.[522] Accordingly, the interference was not prescribed by law and there was a violation of his right to freedom of assembly and association.

The inappropriate targeting of legislation and the misuse of excessive discretion are increasingly important issues given the trend in the domestic legislation of certain European countries since the late 1990s to be openly antagonistic towards non-State religions or denominations. The French About-Picard law came into force in May 2001 to allow courts to dissolve a religious association if it or its representatives have been convicted of more than one criminal offence.[523] Proposals for the

---

[521] *Maestri v. Italy* (App. No. 42393/98), Judgment of 17 February 2004.

[522] *Ibid.*, para. 41. Note also the joint dissenting opinion of Judges Bonello, Strážnická, Bîrsan, Jungwiert and Del Tufo which took issue with the appropriateness of the applicant's claim based on forseeability (when, in the Italian courts, the applicant accepted that the Italian system contains norms prohibiting judges from joining the Freemasons). The opinion also criticised the European Court's approach of interfering in a limited way, to enquire whether domestic law, *as established by the national authorities*, is compatible with the Convention. It also observed the functional incompatibility between the holding of judical office and membership of Italian Masonic lodges, which may require the exercise of judicial power to be distorted to the advantage of the association or its individual members. In the UN context, see *Arenz v. Germany*, Communication No. 1138/2002 (decision of 24 March 2004), UN Doc. A/ 59/40 vol. 2 (2004), p. 548. This concerned the authors' expulsion from a political party based on their affiliation with Scientology, which they alleged deprived them of their right to take part in their communities' political affairs (declared inadmissible).

[523] International Helsinki Federation for Human Rights, country report on France (2004), p. 6. The Council of Europe's Parliamentary Assembly appointed a special rapporteur

law were for criticised for the vague and apparently low threshold for entitling the State to dissolve religious organisations.[524] In one proposal, power was to be given to a single judge to dissolve any religious group deemed to be a 'sect'.[525] The loose definition of 'sect' was reflected in the sheer number already identified by the authorities (173), including such long-established entities as the Free Baptist Church.[526] Anti-sect laws have also been enacted in Austria.[527] Similarly, the Belgian Parliament in

to investigate whether the law is in accordance with Convention standards – Council of Europe, Rapporteur Cevdet Akcali, 'Freedom of religion and religious minorities in France', Doc. 9612, 31 October 2002.

[524] Senat, Proposed Law No. 131 of 14 December 1999: 'Proposition de loi tendant a renforcer le dispositif penal a l'encontre des associations ou groupements constituant, par leurs agissements delictueux, un trouble à l'ordre public ou un peril majeur pour la personne humaine'. For a detailed critique of early proposals, see: H. Clayson Smith, '*Liberte, Egalite et Fraternite*', 1099; K. A. Dunne, 'Addressing Religious Intolerance in Europe: The Limited Application of Article 9 of the European Convention of Human Rights and Fundamental Freedoms', *California Western International Law Journal* (1999) 117.

[525] '*Proposition de loi tendant a renforcer la prevention et la repression a l'entcontre des groupements a caractere sectaire*' – International Helsinki Federation for Human Rights (IHF), *Religious Intolerance in Selected OSCE Countries in 2000: Report to the Seminar on Freedom of Religion or Belief in the OSCE Region*, The Hague: IHF (2001) ('IHF 2000 Report').

[526] The issue of new religious movements and treatment of sects has attracted much controversy. See: P. Cumper, 'The Rights of Religious Minorities: The Legal Regulation of New Religious Movements', in P. Cumper and S. Wheatley (eds.), *Minority Rights in the 'New' Europe*, The Hague/Boston: Martinus Nijhoff (1999); European Consortium for Church – State Research, '*Le Statut constitutionnel des Cultes dans les Pays de l'Union Européennes*', Actes du Colloque, Université de Paris XI, 18–19 November 1994, European Consortium for Church-State Research, Paris: Litec (1995); I. C. Ibán, 'Religious Tolerance and Freedom in Continental Europe', 10 Rat Jur (1997) 90; I. C. Ibán, 'Nuovi Movimenti Religiosi: Problemi Giuridici', in S. Ferrari (ed.), *Diritti dell'Uomo e Libertà dei Gruppi Religiosi. Problemi Giuridici dei Nuovi Movimenti Religiosi*, Padua: Cedam (1989). Ibán speculates on the means by which tolerance between different European religions may be achieved in the light of the emergence of new religious movements but does not believe that equality means that every religion deserves protection. In his opinion the focus should remain on the legitimate expression of the individual's free will and not the group or religion or even belief concerned. See also H. Clayson Smith, '*Liberte, Egalite et Fraternite*', 1099.

[527] In 1997, Austria enacted legislation distinguishing traditional religions (of which twelve were initially recognised) from 'Confessional Communities' which will only qualify if they meet numerical criteria such as membership of 16,000 and retain that status for a period of ten years (twenty years in the case of communities newly applying for recognition). For further discussion, see C. J. Miner, 'Losing My Religion: Austria's New Religion Law in Light of International and European Standards of Religious Freedom', Brigham Young UL Rev (1998). Similarly, under the Russian Federation's Law of Freedom of Conscience and Religious Associations passed in 1997 a religious organisation must prove prior existence in Russia for fifteen years to satisfy registration

1997 voted on its own anti-sect report and has taken measures to monitor the activities of sects.[528] The list of sects appended to the report included reference to a Christian Fellowship operating at the European Parliament, believed to be an interdenominational prayer group participated in by (among others) members of the European Parliament.[529]

The broadly drafted anti-sect legislation in certain countries will undoubtedly mean that both the 'prescribed by law' and 'necessary in a democratic society' preconditions are likely to be tested in the near future for their effectiveness in regulating State intolerance, particularly those measures that are preventive in nature and do not criminalise specific acts.[530]

Concerns have also been voiced by the Special Rapporteur over the level of discretion reserved to the State on matters central to the existence and organisation of religious groups. For example, following a visit to Viet Nam the Special Rapporteur criticised various measures which gave the authorities excessive direct control over the activities of religious congregations, requiring permission for religious retreats and meditation periods, periodic congresses and national meetings, the ordination of leaders, dealings between Vietnamese clergy and their counterparts

---

requirements. See: I. Basova, 'Freedom Under Fire', 181; A. Lekhel, 'Leveling the Playing Field for Religious "Liberty" in Russia: A Critical Analysis of the 1997 Law "On Freedom of Conscience and Religious Associations"', 32 Vand J Transnat'l L (1999) 167. For similar developments in other countries, see: A. Krussteff, 'An Attempt at Modernization: The New Bulgarian Legislation in the Field of Religious Freedom', Brigham Young UL Rev (2001) 575; E. A. Clark, 'Church–State Relations in the Czech Republic: Past Turmoil and Present Transformation', Brigham Young UL Rev (1996) 1019.

[528] IHF 2000 Report, at pp. 6–7; International Helsinki Federation for Human Rights, country report on Belgium (2004), p. 5.

[529] The list of sects was not itself the subject of a vote by the Belgian Parliament.

[530] A strong preference for criminalising particular acts is commonly expressed. For example, see the (partly concurring) Opinion of Judge Pettiti in *Kokkinakis v. Greece* in which he advocated the use of 'specific criminal offences covering coercive acts and the activities of certain sects which truly attack human freedom and dignity' rather than 'legislation that provides for vague criminal offences which leave it to the court's subjective assessment whether a defendant is convicted or acquitted'. A similar concern was also expressed in the context of freedom of expression under the ICCPR by Nisuke Ando (concurring) in *Faurisson v. France* when voicing his fears that the Gayssot Act might unduly encroach upon the right to freedom of expression: 'In order to eliminate this possibility it would probably be better to replace the Act with a specific legislation prohibiting well-defined acts of anti-semitism or with a provision of the criminal code protecting the rights or reputations of others in general' (*Robert Faurisson v. France*, Communication No. 550/1993 (views of 8 November 1996), UN Doc. A/52/40 vol. 2 (1999), p. 84, at p. 97).

abroad, the repair of places of worship, and the opening of training schools. The Special Rapporteur concluded that several provisions were so vague and imprecise that excessive discretionary powers could permit the authorities to arrest, detain and imprison individuals for religious activities that were in full conformity with international law.[531]

A stricter approach to the 'prescribed by law' requirement by European Court may provide a valuable means for impugning legislation directed against the continued existence and functioning of religious groups. In *Metropolitan Church of Bessarabia and others v. Moldova*,[532] the applicants could not persuade the European Court to take up the issue in this way. The applicants accepted that the stipulation that religious denominations be recognised by a government decision was prescribed by the Religious Denominations Act (Law no. 979-XII of 24 March 1992) but, focusing instead on the use of State discretion following *Hasan and Chaush v. Bulgaria*, maintained that the procedure laid down by the Act had been misapplied: 'the true reason for refusal of registration had been political; the Government has in fact neither claimed nor proved that the applicant Church contravened the laws of the Republic'.[533]

Although the European Court understood that the applicants were framing this part of their claim around the arbitrariness of the Government's decision rather than the underlying Act, the Court declined to answer them specifically but instead was prepared to accept that the 'prescribed by law' requirement had been satisfied so that it could base its decision on other, broader, grounds.[534] It is not at all unusual for the Court to avoid determining whether an impugned provision is prescribed by law. For example, in *Manoussakis and others v. Greece*,[535] the European Court similarly avoided the applicants' claim directed at a general policy of obstruction pursued in relation to Jehovah's Witnesses when they wished to set up a church or place of worship – because the Court was prepared to find that there had been a violation on other grounds.[536] However, it is particularly important that the Court should issue strong and unambiguous messages in view of the prevalence of laws which are essentially preventive in nature, aimed at criminalising religious movements rather than individual criminal acts,

---

[531] UN Doc. E/CN.4/1999/58/Add.2 (1998), para. 107 (Viet Nam).
[532] *Metropolitan Church of Bessarabia and others v. Moldova* (2002) 35 EHRR 306.
[533] *Ibid.*, at para. 107.   [534] *Ibid.*, at para. 110.
[535] *Manoussakis and others v. Greece* (1997) 23 EHRR 387.   [536] *Ibid.*, at para. 38.

or aimed at depriving groups of legal recognition necessary for their survival.

The practice of the Human Rights Committee is reflected in paragraph 8 of General Comment No. 22 which emphasises that '[l]imitations imposed must be established by law and must not be applied in a manner that would vitiate the rights guaranteed in article 18'. The two limbs of this sentence represent two cumulative requirements yet in practice the Human Rights Committee often assesses them together. For example, in *Robert Faurisson v. France*,[537] when considering whether the restriction on the author's freedom to express doubts concerning the existence of extermination gas chambers was provided by law (the Gayssot Act 1990), the Human Rights Committee observed that the author's criminal conviction

> 'did not encroach upon his right to hold and express an opinion in general, rather the court convicted Mr Faurisson for having violated the rights and reputation of others. For these reasons the Committee is satisfied that the Gayssot Act, as read, interpreted and applied to the author's case by the French courts, is in compliance with the provisions of the Covenant.'[538]

Obviously the Human Rights Committee will find in favour of the author and need not examine the matter further if, as in *Auli Kivenmaa v. Finland*,[539] the State party does not refer to a law allowing the freedom in question to be restricted.[540] However, it would appear that the Human Rights Committee, like the European Court, is generally willing to make a finding that a restriction has been prescribed by law, even if it does so by indirect means. For example, *Malcolm Ross v. Canada*[541] concerned the author's removal from his teaching position for denigrating the Jewish faith in off duty comments. The Committee relied on the existence of a complicated legal framework surrounding the proceedings which led to his dismissal, and determined that the restriction had been prescribed by law. A Board of Inquiry held that the School Board was vicariously liable for the discriminatory conduct of its employee. The

---

[537] *Robert Faurisson v. France*, Communication No. 550/1993 (views of 8 November 1996), UN Doc. A/52/40 vol. 2 (1999), p. 84.

[538] *Ibid.*, at para. 9.5.

[539] *Auli Kivenmaa v. Finland*, Communication No. 412/1990 (views of 31 March 1994) (1994) 1(3) IHRR 88.

[540] *Ibid.*, at para. 9.4 (concerning the conviction of a protester for organising a public meeting).

[541] *Malcolm Ross v. Canada*, Communication No. 736/1997 (views of 18 October 2000), UN Doc. A/56/40 vol. 2 (2001), p. 69.

School Board was found to have discriminated against the Jewish students in the school district by failing to take action soon enough to prevent the employee's comments, which adversely affected the school environment. The School Board was ordered by the Board of Inquiry to remedy the discrimination by removing the author from his teaching position, and it was this that formed the basis of the applicant' claim. Although there was vagueness about the criteria relating to the provisions that were applied against the School Board and which were used to remove the author from his teaching position, this was made good in the Committee's opinion by the fact that the domestic Supreme Court had found that sufficient basis existed in Canadian law for upholding parts of the Board of Inquiry's order. The Committee would therefore not re-evaluate the findings of the Supreme Court but instead regarded the restriction as provided by law, through rather indirect and constructed reasoning.

Finally, before moving on to consider the requirements concerning the pursuit of a legitimate aim of State restrictions, it is worth observing one further danger of measures that although prescribed by law are widely scoped:

> '[E]ven when provided for by the law, a restriction is permissible only if it has in view one of the objects limitatively enumerated by the texts concerned. It is noteworthy that the wider a law is, the less its constitutive elements are defined, the more difficult it is to monitor respect for this second criterion which one could call "legitimacy", and the easier it is for a State to claim to have one of these objectives in view or to divert laws from the objective which they claim to pursue. From this point of view, the control of legitimacy is far from illusory; it is the natural extension of that of legality.'[542]

Legitimate aim

When examining whether a legitimate aim has been pursued (i.e. whether the aim of the restriction is properly directed at the protection of 'public safety', 'order', 'health', or 'morals' or the 'fundamental rights

---

[542] D. Türk and L. Joinet, 'The Right to Freedom of Opinion and Expression: Current Problems of its Realization and Measures Necessary for its Strengthening and Promotion', in S. Coliver (ed.), *Striking a Balance: Hate Speech, Freedom of Expression and Non-discrimination*, London: University of Essex, Human Rights Centre (1992), at p. 40.

and freedoms of others') both the European and United Nations institutions tend to accept rather than challenge the aim claimed by the State,
and accordingly pass over this precondition with little detailed analysis.

The European Court's rather superficial analysis of this precondition
is reflected, for example, in *Manoussakis and others v. Greece*,[543] when
determining whether a legitimate aim was pursued by planning restrictions affecting places of worship.[544]

> 'Like the applicants, the Court recognises that the States are entitled to
> verify whether a movement or association carries on, ostensibly in pursuit
> of religious aims, activities which are harmful to the population.
> Nevertheless, it recalls that Jehovah's Witnesses come within the defini-
> tion of "known religion" as provided for under Greek law (see the
> Kokkinakis v. Greece judgment of 25 May 1993, Series A no. 260-A,
> p. 15, para. 23). This was moreover conceded by the Government.
>
> However, having regard to the circumstances of the case and taking
> the same view as the Commission, the Court considers that the impugned
> measure pursued a legitimate aim for the purposes of Article 9 para. 2 of
> the Convention (art. 9-2), namely the protection of public order.'[545]

More recently, in *Buscarini and others San Marino*,[546] when the
legitimate aim claimed by the State had as its basis 'the need to preserve
public order, in the form of social cohesion and the citizens' trust in
their traditional institutions',[547] the Court declined to address the issue
at all since it found that compulsion to take a religious oath could not be
regarded as 'necessary in a democratic society'.[548] It would not have
been difficult for the Court to condemn this aim given that the Court
had earlier, in *Sidiropoulos v. Greece*,[549] emphatically rejected the State's
suggestion that the refusal to register an organisation named the 'Home
of Macedonian Civilisation' could pursue a similar aim of 'the upholding of Greece's cultural traditions and historical and cultural symbols'[550]

---

[543] *Manoussakis and others v. Greece* (1997) 23 EHRR 387.   [544] *Ibid.*, at para. 44.
[545] *Ibid.*, at para. 40. See also *Stankov and the United Macedonian Organisation Ilinden v. Bulgaria* (1998) 26 EHRR CD p. 103.
[546] *Buscarini and others San Marino* (2000) 30(2) EHRR 208.
[547] *Ibid.*, at para. 36.
[548] For further discussion, see C. Evans, *Freedom of Religion Under the European Convention*, pp. 147–9.
[549] *Sidiropoulos v. Greece* (1999) 27 EHRR 633.
[550] *Ibid.*, at para. 38. The refusal to register was based on the State's belief that the applicants intended to dispute the Greek identity of Macedonia and its inhabitants and undermine Greece's territorial integrity. However, the European Court did accept that the refusal was intended to protect 'national security and prevent disorder' for the

The Court in *Metropolitan Church of Bessarabia and others v. Moldova* followed *Manoussakis and others v. Greece* in recognising that States are at least 'entitled to verify whether a movement or association carries on, ostensibly in pursuit of religious aims, activities which are harmful to the population'.[551] Accordingly, the Court upheld the State's claim that refusing to recognise the applicant Church was intended to protect public order and public safety. The State put its argument as follows:

> 'The Moldovan State, the territory of which has oscillated in the course of history between Romania and Russian, has a population that is ethnically and linguistically varied. In these circumstances, there are few factors likely to guarantee the the the long-term survival of the young Republic of Moldova, which had been independent since 1991. One of these factors is religion, the majority of the population being of the Orthodox Christian religion. In consequence, recognition of the Orthodox Church of Moldova, subordinated to the Patriarchate of Moscow, has enabled the entire population to remain within that Church. Were the applicant

---

purposes of Article 11 in view of the situation prevailing in the Balkans at the time – *ibid.*, at para. 39.

[551] Religious organisations all too often run the risk of being characterised as conducting harmful political activity, as exemplified by countless allegations reported by the Special Rapporteur. See, for example: UN Doc. E/CN.4/1999/58 (1999), para. 48 (China claimed that the Dalai Lama used religion to pursue separatist activities); UN Doc. E/CN.4/2001/63 (2001), p. 32, para. 123 (in Lao People's Democratic Republic, Christian organisations were accused of representing an alien religion controlled by enemy forces); UN Doc. E/CN.4/1999/58 (1999), para. 90 (in Korea, the authorities reportedly discourage all religious activities apart from those that serve the interests of the State); UN Doc. E/CN.4/2000/65 (2000), para. 69 (in Nepal it was alleged that the police executed two Christian leaders of the Taka Church whom they suspected of belonging to the Maoist organisation waging a civil war in remote areas of the country); UN Doc. E/CN.4/2000/65 (2000), para. 99 (in Viet Nam the Bonze Thich Nhat Ban was reportedly arrested twice by the police on charges of belonging to an illegal organisation, the United Buddhist Church of Vietnam, and trying to overthrow the government although the purpose of the organisation was explained to be to enjoy freedom of religion not to undermine the State); UN Doc E/CN.4/1996/95/Add.2 (1996), para. 20 (the Iranian Government pointed out that the Baha'is are not a religious minority, but a political organisation which was associated with the Shah's regime, is against the Iranian Revolution and engages in espionage activities); UN Doc. A/55/280/Add.1 (2000), p. 26, paras. 146–7 (with regard to Turkey, the Special Rapporteur understood the legitimate concerns of the authorities in the face of religious extremism, but nevertheless believed that the active role played by the State in religious affairs constituted excessive interference not only in the way people manifest their belief but also against the very concept of freedom of religion and belief – the Special Rapporteur especially noted the position of non-Muslims, whose situation posed a problem in terms of the principles of tolerance and non-discrimination, and was a direct result of State policies on secularism and nationalism).

Church to be recognised, this cohesion would be in danger of being destroyed, and the Orthodox Christian population would be split between more than one Church; furthermore, there would be political forces at work behind the applicant Church, which is subordinated to the Patriarchate of Bucharest, that were closely connected with Romanian interests favouring reunion between Bessarabia and Romania. Recognition of the applicant Church would therefore revive long-standing rivalries in the population between Russia and Romania, thereby endangering the social peace, and even the territorial integrity of Moldova.'[552]

It made little difference that the State had not shown that the applicant Church had actually constituted a threat to public order and public safety but more surprising is the resonance of this State aim with that firmly rejected in *Sidiropoulos v. Greece*.[553]

The ease with which the 'legitimate aim' threshold is surmounted is also illustrated strikingly by cases such as *Dahlab v. Switzerland*[554] (in which a legitimate aim was found to have been pursued when prohibiting a schoolteacher from wearing a headscarf in 'the protection of the rights and freedoms of others, public safety and public order', even though it is particularly difficult to discern the relevance of public order and safety), and in *Murphy v Ireland*,[555] in which cursory consideration was given to the issue, as already discussed extensively above in Chapter 2 under the heading 'Blasphemy, disparagement and gratuitous offence', pp. 89–94, and in Chapter 3 under the heading 'The rights and freedoms of others as a ground of limitation' at pp. 161–5.

Although the European Court generally offers only a brief assessment of whether an impugned measure has been prescribed by law and pursues a legitimate aim, this is often no less than that provided by the Human Rights Committee. In some cases the Human Rights Committee's analysis is extensive. For example, in *Malcolm Ross v. Canada*,[556] in finding that the restrictions imposed on the author were

---

[552] *Ibid.*, at para. 111.
[553] For recent decisions centred on the dissolution of political parties, in which the the European Court has settled on 'national security' as the only legitimate aim pursued, see *Freedom and Democracy Party (ÖZDEP) v. Turkey* (2001) 31 EHRR 674, and *United Communist Party of Turkey and others v. Turkey* (1998) 26 EHRR 121.
[554] *Dahlab v. Switzerland*, App. No. 42393/98, decision of 15 February 2001.
[555] *Murphy v. Ireland*, App. No. 44179/98 (2004) 38 EHRR 212.
[556] *Malcolm Ross v. Canada*, Communication No. 736/1997 (views of 18 October 2000), UN Doc. A/56/40 vol. 2 (2001), p. 69.

for the purpose of protecting the 'rights or reputations' of others within Article 19 of the ICCPR, the Human Rights Committee's took account of earlier case law that extended the meaning of 'others' to cover a community as a whole,[557] it touched on the derivation of the aim of such restrictions in Article 20(2) (concerning religious hatred) and applied these principles directly to the facts in order to find a very clear aim of 'protecting the "rights or reputations" of persons of Jewish faith, including the right to have an education in the public school system free from bias, prejudice and intolerance'.[558]

In short, it may be said that the level of detail given to examining whether a legitimate aim has been pursued by State measures may vary from case to case both at European and United Nations levels (and the legitimacy of the aim is at times combined with other issues), but in general this precondition is easily satisfied and only rarely is the State's declared aim rejected.

Necessary (in a democratic society)

Verdoodt noted that the emphasis on 'a democratic society' is to provide the environment in which human rights may truly prosper,[559] yet it became clear in the early debates that the notion of 'democracy' in the Universal Declaration was capable of a diverse interpretation, with the Soviet Union, for example, defining 'democratic State' in terms which denote 'the obligation for a minority to submit to the majority of the people'.[560] The resulting draft limitation Article of the Universal Declaration refers to 'democratic society', firmly rejecting the Soviet Union's proposal for 'democratic State'. In order to root democracy in the purpose of the Declaration, France asserted (with the support of Lebanon) that 'the criterion of

---

[557] *Robert Faurisson v. France*, Communication No. 550/1993 (views of 8 November 1996), UN Doc. A/52/40 vol. 2 (1999), p. 84.

[558] *Malcolm Ross v. Canada*, Communication No. 736/1997 (views of 18 October 2000), UN Doc. A/56/40 vol. 2 (2001), p. 69, at p. 84, para. 11.5.

[559] A. Verdoodt, *Naissance et Signification de la Déclaration Universelle des Droits de l'Homme*, Lourain: Paris Société d'Études Morales, Socials et Juridiques, Editions Nauwelaerts (1964), at p. 271. See also P. T. Vegleris, 'Valeur et Signification de la Clause "dans une Société Démocratique" dans la Convention Européenne des Droits de l'Homme' 1(2) HRJ (1968) 219.

[560] UN Doc E/CN.4/SR. 51 (1948), p. 7 (USSR). See also UN Doc A/C.3/3/SR. 154 (1948), p. 657 (USSR) in which reference was made to the need to guarantee the community against any abuse of rights by the individual.

democracy in any nation was the extent to which human rights were really respected'.[561] France also referred to 'the purposes and principles of the United Nations' as the plumb-line for the limitation Article and to emphasise membership of the international community.[562] According to Chile, Article 29 reflects the 'true character of the declaration' and it 'proclaimed the need for a just social order'.[563] It contemplates 'a conception of society, which excludes all non-democratic regimes and provided a criterion for distinguishing between true and false forms of democracy'.[564] As Svensson-McCarthy has observed, there was agreement in principle among most countries that the basic criterion of a democratic society is whether or not it genuinely represents the will of the people and respects the human rights proclaimed in the Universal Declaration. Although it might appear circular to define democracy by reference to human rights, she concluded that we cannot ignore the fact that this is how the drafters explained a 'democratic society'.[565] This was reiterated in the Draft Principles on Freedom and Non-Discrimination in the Matter of Religious Rights and Practices prepared by the Sub-Commission on Prevention of Discrimination and Protection of Minorities which state that '[a]ny limitations which may be imposed shall be consistent with the purposes and principles of the United Nations'.[566]

The necessity of any restriction must be considered in conjunction with the particular ground of limitation claimed by the State. In assessing whether a State may rely on a limitation provision, the restriction in question must not only be justified in principle in pursuing a legitimate aim, it must also be 'necessary', according to Article 18 of the ICCPR, or 'necessary in a democratic society' according to Article 9 of European Convention. Given the discussion above under the heading 'Introduction', the discrepancies in terminology are not significant, although certain key differences do exist between the way in which the Human Rights Committee and the European Court determine whether a restriction is 'necessary'.

---

[561] UN Doc. E/CN.4/SR. 51 (1948), pp. 9 and 10 (France).

[562] UN Doc. A/C.3/3/SR. 155 (1948), p. 667 (France).

[563] UN Doc. A/PV/SR. 180 (1948), pp. 863–4 (Chile).

[564] *Ibid.*, (Chile).   [565] A. Svensson-McCarthy, *States of Exception*, p. 101.

[566] Part III, para. 2 (a), corresponds with rule 16(4)(b) of Krishnaswami's basic rules except that the latter emphasised that 'the freedom of everyone to manifest his religion or belief ... must be ensured as widely as possible. Any limitation imposed upon that freedom should be exceptional, should be confined within the narrowest possible bounds ... and should not be exercised in a manner contrary to the purposes and principles of the United Nations.'

The Human Rights Committee generally does not provide elaborate justification for its position on this question in Optional Protocol decisions. Certainly it appears reluctant to substitute its own analysis when none has been advanced either by the author[567] or the State party.[568] Sometimes the reasoning is so abbreviated as to be undiscernible,[569] although recent decisions have corrected this tendency. For example, in *Malcolm Ross v. Canada*,[570] the Committee carefully weighed the role of the school system, the influence of teachers of young children, the special duties and responsibilities that attach to the exercise of freedom of expression and the need for the school to ensure that the expression of discriminatory views is not legitimised by it. The Committee also took account of the author's statements made outside his school duties and the 'poisoned school environment' that affected Jewish children in the wider school district. The restriction was accordingly necessary to protect Jewish children in the school system from bias, prejudice and intolerance and the impact on the author in achieving the purpose of the restriction was minimal.[571] The clearest guidance from the Human Rights Committee concerning principles of 'necessity' is found in paragraph 8 of General Comment No. 22 which stresses that '[l]imitations may be applied only for those purposes for which they were prescribed and must be directly related and proportionate to the specific need on which they are predicated'. Furthermore, '[i]n interpreting the scope of permissible limitation clauses, States parties should proceed from the need to protect the rights guaranteed under the Covenant, including the right to equality and non-discrimination specified in articles 2, 3 and 26'.

The way in which the European Court assesses the notion of 'necessity' marks a significant departure from Human Rights Committee practice in that it allows a margin of appreciation to States in

---

[567] *Robert Faurisson v. France*, Communication No. 550/1993 (views of 8 November 1996), UN Doc. A/52/40 vol. 2 (1999), p. 84, at para. 9.7.

[568] *Auli Kivenmaa v. Finland*, Communication No. 412/1990 (views of 31 March 1994) (1994) 1(3) IHRR 88, at para. 9.3.

[569] See, for example, *K. Singh Bhinder v. Canada*, Communication No. 208/1986 (views of 9 November 1989), UN Doc. A/45/40 vol. 2 (1990), p. 50. The Human Rights Committee concluded that if the requirement that a Sikh wear safety headgear rather than a turban is regarded as raising issues under Article 18, then it is a limitation that is justified by reference to the grounds laid down in Article 18(3) (para. 6.2).

[570] *Malcolm Ross v. Canada*, Communication No. 736/1997 (views of 18 October 2000), UN Doc. A/56/40 vol. 2 (2001), p. 69.

[571] *Ibid.*, at pp. 84–5, para. 11.6.

determining the extent of the necessity of an interference (as discussed above in Chapter 3 under the heading 'The use of anti-discrimination measures to protect the forum internum', pp. 185–7). This was explained as follows in *Handyside v. United Kingdom*:

> 'By reason of their direct and continuous contact with the vital forces of their countries, State authorities are in principle in a better position than the international judge to give an opinion on the exact content of these requirements as well as on the "necessity" of a "restriction" or "penalty" intended to meet them. The Court notes at this juncture that, whilst the adjective "necessary" ... is not synonymous with "indispensable", neither has it the flexibility of such expressions as "admissible", "ordinary", "useful", "reasonable" or "desirable". Nevertheless, it is for the national authorities to make the initial assessment of the reality of the pressing social need implied by the notion of "necessity" in the context.'[572]

However, this margin of appreciation available to States is subject to European supervision. The task of the European Court is to determine whether the measures taken at national level were justified in principle – that is, whether the reasons adduced to justify them appear 'relevant and sufficient' and are proportionate to the legitimate aim pursued.[573] The way in which the Court routinely approaches the issue of proportionality is well illustrated by the following analysis by the Court in *Metropolitan Church of Bessarabia and others v. Moldova*:[574]

> 'The role of the Court is to inquire into whether the measures taken at national level are justified in principle and are proportionate.
>
> In order to determine the breadth of the margin of appreciation in this case the Court must take into account what is at stake, namely the need to maintain true religious pluralism, which is inherent in the notion of a democratic society. Similarly, great weight should be given to this need where it must be decided, as required by Article 9(2), whether the interference meets a "pressing social need" and is "proportionate" to the legitimate aim pursued. In exercising its power of control, the Court must consider the impugned interference on the basis of the file as a whole.'[575]

There was a tendency in early decisions of the European Court to make the narrowest possible finding of violation. Thus, in *Kokkinakis v. Greece*,[576]

---

[572] *Handyside v. United Kingdom* (Ser. A) No. 24 (1976) ECtHR, at para. 48.
[573] *The Sunday Times v. United Kingdom (No. 2)* (1992) 14 EHRR 229, at para. 50.
[574] *Metropolitan Church of Bessarabia and others v. Moldova* (2002) 35 EHRR 306.
[575] *Ibid.*, at para. 119.   [576] *Kokkinakis v. Greece* (Ser. A) No. 260–A (1993) ECtHR.

when purporting to weigh the requirements of the protection of the rights and liberties of others against the conduct of which the applicant was accused, in reality the European Court only focused its finding of violation on the wrongdoing of the national court in specifying insufficiently the way in which the anti-proselytism laws had been applied to the applicant, rather than on the law itself or the discretion available to the authorities in prosecuting the applicant in the first place.[577] Much depends on the context of the manifestation in question, so that in *Larissis and others v. Greece*[578] the peculiar characteristics of military life meant that the European Court found there was no violation in the case of proselytism directed at civilians but there was in the case of proselytism directed at lower-ranking fellow airmen because the confines of military life meant that proselytism could be viewed as a form of harassment or the application of undue pressure.[579]

The Court is also conscious of the impact of the particular medium chosen for exercising the freedom of expression, and is especially sensitive to the use of broadcast media. In *Murphy v. Ireland*[580] the Court upheld a blanket prohibition on religious advertising on an independent commercial radio station. In determining whether the reasons relied on by Ireland to justified the prohibition were 'relevant and sufficient' for the purposes of Article 10(2),[581] the Court was influenced by the potential impact of the audio-visual media, which have a more immediate, invasive and powerful effect than the print media, even on the passive recipient.[582] It was also significant that the applicant was free to advertise the same matter in other media and during public meetings and other assemblies and that the prohibition related only to advertising. The Court also accepted as relevant the Government's claim that purchased advertising time would lean in favour of unbalanced usage by religious groups with larger resources (causing conflict with the principle of neutrality in broadcasting), and noted that a complete or partial relaxation of the blanket prohibition so as to prohibit only unacceptable or excessive religious advertising would be difficult to apply fairly, objectively and coherently.[583]

---

[577] *Ibid.*, at paras. 47 and 49.
[578] *Larissis and others v. Greece* (Ser. A) No. 65 (1998–V) ECtHR 363.
[579] *Ibid.*, at paras. 50–1.
[580] *Murphy v. Ireland*, App. No. 44179/98 (2004), 38 EHRR 212.
[581] *Ibid.*, at para. 68, following *Wingrove v. United Kingdom* (1997) 24 EHRR 1, paras. 53 and 58–9.
[582] *Ibid.*, at para. 69, following *Jersild v. Denmark* (Ser.A) No. 289 (1995) ECtHR, para. 31.
[583] *Ibid.*, at paras. 77–8.

High among the factors to be taken into consideration in all cases is the nature of the manifestation restricted. This goes hand in hand with the more fundamental principle which the Court has consciously cherished in recent Article 9 decisions and that is the role of religious pluralism in a truly democratic society.[584] Thus in *Manoussakis and others v. Greece*,[585] the Court suggested that when determining whether a restriction on worship or observance is proportionate to the legitimate aim pursued, it will be subjected to 'very strict scrutiny' given the nature of the manifestation in question. It went on to say that 'in delimiting the extent of the margin of appreciation in the present case the Court must have regard to what is at stake, namely the need to secure true religious pluralism, an inherent feature of the notion of a democratic society'.[586] The European Court in *Manoussakis* ruled that the applicants' criminal conviction for setting up a church or place of worship without prior authorisation was effectively the creation of the State's own delays in handling the application. Given that the restriction had such a direct effect on the applicants' freedom of religion it could not be regarded as proportionate to the legitimate aim of that law in imposing planning conditions on the opening of places of

---

[584] See also in the UN context CHR Res. 2002/55 entitled 'Tolerance and pluralism as indivisible elements in the promotion and protection of Human Rights', (25 April 2002, UN Doc. E/CN.4/2002/200 (2002)), which recognised that tolerance and pluralism strengthen democracy, facilitate the full enjoyment of all human rights and thereby constitute a sound foundation for civil society, social harmony and peace, and that cultural diversity is a cherished asset for the advancement and welfare of humanity at large and should be valued, enjoyed, genuinely accepted and embraced as a permanent feature which enriches all societies. For discussion of religious pluralism in Spain and the challenges in balancing protection for religious minorities within Spain's constitutional framework, see A. Motilla, 'Religious Pluralism in Spain: Striking the Balance Between Religious Freedom and Constitutional Rights', Brigham Young UL Rev (2004) 575.

[585] *Manoussakis and others v. Greece* (1997) 23 EHRR 387.

[586] *Ibid.*, at para. 44. See also *Kokkinakis v. Greece* (Ser. A) No. 260–A (1993) ECtHR para. 31: 'As enshrined in Article 9 (art. 9), freedom of thought, conscience and religion is one of the foundations of a 'democratic society' within the meaning of the Convention. It is, in its religious dimension, one of the most vital elements that go to make up the identity of believers and their conception of life, but it is also a precious asset for atheists, agnostics, sceptics and the unconcerned. The pluralism indissociable from a democratic society, which has been dearly won over the centuries, depends on it.' It may be added that in Article 9 cases the European Court should perhaps also take more account of its statement in *Dudgeon v. United Kingdom* that if what is at stake is 'a most intimate aspect of private life' then 'there must exist particularly serious reasons before interferences on the part of the public authorities can be legitimate' – *Dudgeon v. United Kingdom* (Ser. A) No. 45 (1982) ECtHR para. 52.

worship.[587] The discretion available to the authorities had been used by the State to impose rigid, indeed prohibitive, conditions on the practice of religious beliefs by Jehovah's Witnesses which was inimical to principles of pluralism.

Interference with the organisational life of a religious community is also strictly viewed by the Court, not only for its strangulating effect on the activities of the community and its individual members[588] but also because it eliminates the essential preconditions that allow for genuine pluralism. In *Hasan and Chaush v. Bulgaria*[589] the applicants pointed to the serious legal and practical consequences of removing the legitimate leadership of the Muslim community and replacing it by leaders politically associated with the Government of the day. The Court found that the State had effectively put an end to the first applicant's functions as Chief Mufti, removing the community's own recognised leadership and disallowing its statute and by-laws. The profound effects of this to the leader and the community have already been discussed above at pp. 273–5. As part of its assessment, the Court recalled the importance of organised structures to religious communities and every constituent member. It then stressed that:

> '[w]here the organisation of the religious community is at issue, Article 9 must be interpreted in the light of Article 11 of the Convention which safeguards associative life against unjustified State interference. Seen in this perspective, the believer's right to freedom of religion encompasses the expectation that the community will be allowed to function peacefully free from arbitrary State intervention. Indeed, the autonomous existence of religious communities is indispensable for pluralism in a democratic society and is thus an issue at the very heart of the protection which Article 9 affords. It directly concerns not only the organisation of the community as such but also the effective enjoyment of the right to freedom of religion by all its active members. Were the organisational life of the

---

[587] *Ibid.*, at paras. 48–53.

[588] Although the Moldovan government tried to understate the effect of the State's refusal by pointing out that church members could meet, pray together and manage assets, the Court observed that in the absence of recognition it could neither organise itself nor operate: 'Lacking legal personality, it cannot bring legal proceedings to protect its assets, which are indispensable for worship, while its members cannot meet to carry on religious activities without contravening the legislation on religious denominations.' Even if the State had shown tolerance towards the church (which the Court did not accept), it could not be regarded as a substitute for recognition, since recognition alone was capable of conferring rights on those concerned (para. 53).

[589] *Hasan and Chaush v. Bulgaria* (2002) 34(6) EHRR 1339.

community not protected by Article 9 of the Convention, all other aspects of the individual's freedom of religion would become vulnerable.'[590]

The freedom of religious communities to enjoy autonomous existence is seen as indispensible for pluralism (as well as the precondition for the enjoyment of freedom of religion by individuals in their choice of collective expression). In *Metropolitan Church of Bessarabia and others v. Moldova*,[591] the Court asserted more explicitly than in *Hasan and Chaush v. Bulgaria* that when a State fails to observe its duty to remain neutral and impartial in such matters, '[w]hat is at stake here is the preservation of pluralism and the proper functioning of democracy'.[592]

Furthermore, the State cannot rely on the supposed adverse consequences of pluralism to justify eliminating it, but must instead fulfil its duty to ensure tolerance even on the part of private actors. In *Serif v. Greece*,[593] the Government sought to justify the criminal conviction of the applicant (for having usurped the functions of a minister of a 'known religion' and for having publicly worn the dress of such a minister) on the grounds that there were two muftis in Rodopi at the time, and the courts had to convict the spurious one in order to avoid creating tension among Muslims, tension between Muslims and Christians and tension between Turkey and Greece. The European Court responded with less emphasis on safeguarding the necessary preconditions for pluralism to flourish but in explicit terms of the State's duty when faced with the inevitable reality and consequence of pluralism. It is to ensure tolerance:

> 'Although the Court recognises that it is possible that tension is created in situations where a religious or any other community becomes divided, it considers that this is one of the unavoidable consequences of pluralism. The role of the authorities in such circumstances is not to remove the cause of tension by eliminating pluralism, but to ensure that the competing groups tolerate each other.'[594]

---

[590] *Ibid.*, at para. 62.

[591] *Metropolitan Church of Bessarabia and others v. Moldova* (2002) 35 EHRR 306.

[592] *Metropolitan Church of Bessarabia and others v. Moldova* (App. No. 45701/99), Judgment of 13 December 2001, para. 116. (This initial Council of Europe text is more explicit than the EHRR report.)

[593] *Serif v. Greece* (1999) 31 EHRR 561. See also *Agga v. Greece* (App. Nos 50776/99 and 52912/99), Judgment of 7 October 2002.

[594] *Ibid.*, at para. 53 – affirmed in *Supreme Holy council of the Muslim Community v. Bulgaria* (App. No. 39023/97), Judgment of 16 December 2004, at para. 96.

As the evidence for such tension was no more than a very remote possibility, the Court had no difficulty in rejecting any claim to 'a pressing social need', but the message given by the Court is clear. Even if tension is itself the consequence of pluralism, the State has a duty not to eliminate pluralism. This duty may be regarded as analogous to the duty of the State in the political sphere which the Court in *United Communist Party of Turkey and others v. Turkey*[595] referred to when recalling the description of the State 'as the ultimate guarantor of the principle of pluralism'.[596] Religious pluralism is not merely symptomatic of democracy – the full enjoyment and realisation of the freedom of religion depends on the removal of all obstacles to religious pluralism. The Court in *Metropolitan Church of Bessarabia and others v. Moldova* was conscious of the need to allow differences in denominational belief their own autonomous expression. If certain belief systems have no organised expression within a State, inevitably the choice of collective religious manifestation is limited. At the heart of pluralism is neutrality on the part of the State in permitting the existence and open practice of religious belief.

Certainly in the context of Article 9 the Court in the *Metropolitan Church* case went out of its way to entreat States to resort to democratic dialogue rather than lose their neutrality in their dealings with different factions, denominations or religions:[597]

> 'However, in the exercise of its regulatory power in the matter, and in its relations with the various religions, religious bodies and faiths, the State must remain neutral and impartial. The same applies to the maintenance of pluralism and the proper functioning of democracy, one of the principle characteristics of which is the possibility it offers of resolving a country's problems through dialogue, without recourse to violence, even when they are irksome.'[598]

The duty of neutrality and impartiality does not, however, mean that the State may not verify whether the declared aims of an organisation in its manifesto or other official publications are merely a smokescreen for activities which might justify restriction within the permissible grounds of limitation or, in extreme cases, under Article 17 (where intended to

---

[595] *United Communist Party of Turkey and others v. Turkey* (1998) 26 EHRR 121.
[596] *Ibid.*, at para. 44. See also paras. 25, 31 and 43 and *Refah Partisi (the Welfare Party) and others v. Turkey* (2003) 37 EHRR 1, at para. 89.
[597] *Metropolitan Church of Bessarabia and others v. Moldova* (2002) 35 EHRR 306.
[598] *Ibid.*, at para. 116.

314 THE RIGHT TO MANIFEST RELIGIOUS BELIEF

destroy Convention rights or freedoms). Certainly it means that the State may not assess the legitimacy of religious beliefs,[599] and given that there is little practical action on which to judge an organisation if a State dissolves or refuses legal recognition shortly following formation, there is greater risk to the State that it is not acting impartially if it does so.[600] Although this question most commonly arises in the context of the dissolution of political parties,[601] it is equally applicable to the dissolution of religious groups or the refusal to grant them legal recognition.[602] The Court should scrutinise the issue with care and, as suggested by the Court in the *Metropolitan Church* case, the onus is on the State to demonstrate that the applicant carries on activities other than those openly declared by it.[603] In the case of Article 11, it has been accepted that the way in which national legislation enshrines this freedom and its practical application by the authorities reveal the state of democracy in the country concerned, and '[c]onsequently, the exceptions set out in Article 11 are to be construed strictly; only convincing and compelling reasons can justify restrictions on freedom of association'.[604] Furthermore, as indicated by the Court in *United Communist Party of Turkey and others v. Turkey*, where there are suggestions of the existence of a particular threat within a country, the State would have to be able to demonstrate that the applicant bore responsibility for the problems which that threat posed in that country.[605]

These principles were tested recently in *Partisi (the Welfare Party) and others v. Turkey*[606] following the dissolution of the political party *Refah* on the basis of the statements made and stances adopted by its chairman and some of its members, rather than on what was apparent in its constitution. There was lengthy debate as to precisely what was intended

---

[599] *Cha'are Shalom Ve Tsedek v. France* (App. No. 27417/95), Judgment of 11 July 2000, at para. 84.

[600] *United Communist Party of Turkey and others v. Turkey* (1998) 26 EHRR 121, at para. 58.

[601] *United Communist Party of Turkey and others v. Turkey* (1998) 26 EHRR 121, at para. 58; *Sidiropoulos v. Greece* (1999) 27 EHRR 633, at para. 46.

[602] *Metropolitan Church of Bessarabia and others v. Moldova* (2002) 35 EHRR 306, at para. 125.

[603] *Ibid.*, at para. 125.

[604] *Sidiropoulos v. Greece* (1999) 27 EHRR 633, at para. 40. See also para. 41, insisting that 'the existence of minorities and different cultures in a country was a historical fact that a "democratic society" had to tolerate and even protect and support according to the principles of international law'.

[605] *United Communist Party of Turkey and others v. Turkey* (1998) 26 EHRR 121, at para. 59.

[606] *Refah Partisi (the Welfare Party) and others v. Turkey* (2003) 37 EHRR 1.

by such statements and whether they could be imputed to the party as a whole but the Grand Chamber of the European Court ultimately upheld the dissolution of *Refah* for its aim of instituting a plurality of legal systems (in which each religious group would be governed by a legal system in conformity with its members' religious beliefs) and its aim of establishing a theocratic society based on the application of Sharia to the internal or external relations of the Muslim community within the context of this plurality of legal systems. The Court also examined whether *Refah* might employ force as a political method. Although there was some ambiguity surrounding the word '*jihad*', reference was made in speeches by members of the party (from which leaders did not dissociate themselves) to resorting 'legitimately' to force in order to meet *Refah*'s objectives in gaining and retaining power.

The Grand Chamber supported the lower Chamber's conclusion that a plurality of legal systems would be incompatible with the Convention. The lower Chamber characterised it as coercive and discriminatory: coercive in that it would oblige individuals to obey, not rules laid down by the State in the exercise of its function as the impartial guarantor of individual rights and freedoms, but static rules of law imposed by religion; discriminatory in the difference in treatment between individuals in all fields of public and private law according to their religion or beliefs, which could not maintain a fair balance between, on the one hand, the claims of certain religious groups who wish to be governed by their own rules and, on the other, the interest of society as a whole, which must be based on peace and on tolerance between the various religions and beliefs.[607]

Far more controversially, however, the Grand Chamber followed the lower Chamber's conclusion that Sharia is difficult to reconcile with the fundamental principles of democracy, as conceived in the Convention taken as a whole.[608] Turkey's religious history was the unusual backdrop

---

[607] *Ibid.*, at para. 119. See S. Ferrari, 'The New Wine and the Old Cask, Tolerance, Religion and the Law in Contemporary Europe', 10 Rat Jur (1997) 75. Ferrari argues that the common European model of the relationship between church and religious faiths (based on the secularity of the State) should be founded on tolerance. See also P. W. Edge and G. Harvey (eds.), *Law and Religion in Contemporary Society*, Aldershot: Ashgate (2000).

[608] *Refah Partisi (the Welfare Party) and others v. Turkey* (2003) 37 EHRR 1, at para. 123: '72. Like the Constitutional Court, the Court considers that sharia, which faithfully reflects the dogmas and divine rules laid down by religion, is stable and invariable. Principles such as pluralism in the political sphere or the constant evolution of public freedoms have no place in it. The Court notes that, when read together, the offending

to this particular case and pivotal to the European Court's decision. The existing republican secular regime replaced an Ottoman Islamic theocratic system that accommodated non-Islamic communities through a plurality of legal systems. Under the secular system all religions became limited to what the Grand Chamber described as 'the sphere of private religious practice'.[609] The Grand Chamber accepted that the principle of secularism was important for the very survival of that democratic regime, and it saw that *Refah*'s policy had passed a critical threshold at which the introduction of Sharia in the manner proposed was inconsistent with Convention principles. The role of private law sought by *Refah* concerned the organisation and functioning of society as a whole. Since *Refah*'s policy was to apply some of Sharia's private law rules to the sizeable Muslim population in Turkey, it went beyond the freedom of individuals to observe the precepts of their religion. The Court explained that:

> 'freedom of religion, including the freedom to manifest one's religion by worship and observance, is primarily a matter of individual conscience, and stresses that the sphere of individual conscience is quite different from the field of private law, which concerns the organisation and functioning of society as a whole.
>
> It has not been disputed before the Court that in Turkey everyone can observe in his private life the requirements of his religion. On the other hand, Turkey, like any other Contracting Party, may legitimately prevent the application within its jurisdiction of private law rules of religious inspiration prejudicial to public order and the values of democracy for Convention purposes (such as rules permitting discrimination based on the gender of the parties concerned, as in polygamy and

statements, which contain explicit references to the introduction of sharia, are difficult to reconcile with the fundamental principles of democracy, as conceived in the Convention taken as a whole. It is difficult to declare one's respect for democracy and human rights while at the same time supporting a regime based on sharia, which clearly diverges from Convention values, particularly with regard to its criminal law and criminal procedure, its rules on the legal status of women and the way it intervenes in all spheres of private and public life in accordance with religious precepts ... In the Court's view, a political party whose actions seem to be aimed at introducing sharia in a State party to the Convention can hardly be regarded as an association complying with the democratic ideal that underlies the whole of the Convention.' In the UN context, see the comments of the Human Rights Committee on the application of Shariah law, for example, in Gambia: 'The State party should take appropriate measures to ensure that domestic laws (including decrees) and customary law, as well as certain aspects of the Shariah, are interpreted and applied in ways compatible with the provisions of the Covenant' UN Doc. A/59/40 vol. 1 (2004), p. 77, para. 76(16) (Gambia).

[609] *Ibid.*, at para. 125.

privileges for the male sex in matters of divorce and succession). The freedom to enter into contracts cannot encroach upon the State's role as the neutral and impartial organiser of the exercise of religions, faiths and beliefs.'[610]

Accordingly, the Court rejected the applicants' claim that State action against *Refah* amounted to discrimination against Muslims who wished to live their private lives in accordance with the precepts of their religion.

As to whether preventive intervention was justified, the Grand Chamber decided that this was 'consistent with Contracting Parties' positive obligations under Article 1 of the Convention to secure the rights and freedoms of persons within their jurisdiction'. The Court supported the lower Chamber's finding that the dissolution of *Refah* was proportionate to a pressing social need, since only 5 (out of a total of 157) MPs temporarily lost parliamentary office and incurred no significant pecuniary damage through the loss of the party's assets. Nevertheless, the lower Chamber observed the principle that 'the dissolution of a political party accompanied by a temporary ban prohibiting its leaders from exercising political responsibilities was a drastic measure and that measures of such severity might be applied only in the most serious cases'.[611] Some key distinctions need be maintained in order to understand this case fully. It principally addressed an attempt to impose a new system of law which would affect the organisation and functioning of society as a whole. It is therefore quite different from most of the cases arising under Article 9 which concern what the Grand Chamber at one point referred to as the sphere of 'individual conscience'.[612] Of course, the imposition of a new system of law would impinge upon individual conscience through various facets of the law identified by both Chambers. However, there is an important distinction between an attempt to affect society as a whole through the introduction of law inspired by a particular religion and what the Grand Chamber at another point described as 'the sphere of private religious practice'.[613] The references to 'individual conscience' and the 'sphere of private religious practice' may be understood to have direct parallels with the protection

---

[610] *Ibid.*, at para. 128.
[611] *Ibid.*, at para. 133. See also *Socialist Party and others v. Turkey* (1999) 27 EHRR 51.
[612] *Refah Partisi (the Welfare Party) and others v. Turkey* (2003) EHHR 1 at para. 128.
[613] *Ibid.*, at para. 125. The Grand Chamber did, however, reiterate the conditions in which a political or indeed religious party may promote a change in the law or constitutional structures of the State: 'first, the means used to that end must be legal and democratic; secondly, the change proposed must itself be compatible with fundamental democratic principles' (*ibid.*, at para. 98).

given to the *forum internum* and the right to manifest one's religion or belief.[614]

What the Grand Chamber did stress is that the principle of secularism in Turkish society was essential to the survival of its democratic regime and that this principle (accepted as being in harmony with the rule of law and respect for human rights and democracy) coloured not only this but earlier decisions of the Court upholding limitations on manifestation[615] such as *Kalaç v. Turkey*,[616] *Yanasik v. Turkey*,[617] and *Karaduman v. Turkey*,[618] which have already been discussed (especially in Chapter 3 under the heading 'Employment', pp. 141–4, and earlier in this chapter at pp. 215–18). In the case of Turkey, the principle of secularism and the role it plays in preserving the State's democratic regime therefore had an important and direct bearing on whether the interference in each case corresponded to a 'pressing social need' and was 'proportionate to the legitimate aim pursued'. Nevertheless, these decisions involving Turkey appear to stand apart from the decisions involving other countries discussed above which were notable for their emphasis on pluralism. Turkey must abide by its function as the impartial guarantor of individual rights and freedoms yet it may be argued that the principle of secularity in practice operates to deny the pluralist expressions of religion which might be expected in a truly democratic society. The case of *Refah Partisi (the Welfare Party) and others v. Turkey* demonstrated more clearly than any other decision concerning Turkey the unusual nature of its democratic system but it would appear that the role of pluralism in the circumstances which obtain in Turkey (with a singular lack of religious pluralism) still needs to be clarified. In spite of the need to observe some caution in evaluating cases concerning Turkey (in view of its political history), pluralism is undoubtedly high among the ideals and values of a democratic society and consistently forms an essential part of the Court's reasoning when determining the necessity of restrictions on manifestation.

The criteria used in the European context to determine whether an interference corresponds to a 'pressing social need' and is

---

[614] Although the words 'individual' and 'private' are misleading, they can not be taken to exclude the community or public aspects of manifestation, which are explicit in the wording of Article 9. This is obvious from the Grand Chamber's review of its previous case law on Article 9 – see, for example, para. 92.

[615] *Ibid.*, at paras. 93–5.   [616] *Kalaç v. Turkey* (1999) 27 EHRR 552.

[617] *Yanasik v. Turkey*, App. No. 14524/89 (1993) 74 D&R 14.

[618] *Karaduman v. Turkey*, App. No. 16278/90 (1993) 74 D&R 93.

'proportionate to the legitimate aim pursued' go a long way, in theory, towards addressing the comparatively recent phenomenon of antagonism towards supposedly dangerous sects, illustrated most vividly by recent developments in France and Belgium, as well as more widespread practices of dissolution and non-recognition. Assertions of necessity and proportionality should be difficult to substantiate when the State action is preventive, directed at the elimination of religious entities on the strength of their supposed harm. The principles of pluralism enunciated above emphasise not only the types of manifestation to which the European Court should give particular weight but also the expectations of a truly democratic society. These include the need for States to secure true religious pluralism and to create conditions of tolerance even when pluralism itself produces conflict. At the same time, the State must throughout maintain a position of neutrality and impartiality. The autonomous existence of a religious community, regardless of whether it is a so called 'sect', goes to the heart of the organisational dimension of the freedom of religion and is essential to the proper enjoyment of rights of manifestation by individual members. In the case of those organisations whose true aims are concealed, the onus remains on the State to demonstrate that the applicant carries on activities other than those openly declared by it, and even then the limitation provisions are to be construed strictly, with only convincing and compelling reasons admitted to justify restrictions on the freedom.

The earliest in-depth analysis of religious freedom and sects by the Special Rapporteur began by noting the negative use of the term 'sect', so as to differentiate sects from traditional religions and to justify the limited protection available to sects. The Special Rapporteur rejected any categorisation of sects on the basis of quantitative considerations and criticised any condemnation of sects for their eccentricity in doctrine or practice, on grounds of inherent subjectivism and arbitrariness.[619] The Special Rapporteur concluded that the distinction between a religion and a sect is too contrived to be acceptable, and explained that widespread hostility towards sects was commonly a tendency amongst the major religions to resist any departure from orthodoxy. At the same time, the Special Rapporteur reaffirmed that sects are obviously not above the law and so the State must ensure that the law is respected. Given that the law is capable of adequately protecting against false pretences and misdirection, beyond that it is not the business of the

---

[619] UN Doc. E/CN.4/1997/91 (1996), paras. 94–7.

State or any other group or community to act as the guardian of people's consciences.[620] However, the Special Rapporteur equally accepted that sects not only raise issues concerning the violation of the freedom of religion and belief but also of exploiting that freedom. Following a visit to Germany, where the issue of sects was given detailed attention, the Special Rapporteur concluded as follows:

> 'Generally speaking, and in conformity with international law, State intervention in the field of religion and belief cannot involve taking responsibility for people's consciences and promoting, imposing or censuring a particular faith or belief. And no group or community may arrogate to itself responsibility for the conscience of individuals. The State is, however, responsible for ensuring observance of the law, and in particular of criminal legislation relating to the preservation of public order, embezzlement, breach of trust, assault and battery, failure to assist a person in danger, indecent behaviour, procuring, unlawfully practising medicine, kidnapping and abducting of minors, etc. In other words, the State possesses a sufficiently broad range of legal instruments to combat the various guises adopted by groups and communities cloaking themselves under religion, and to deal with any misunderstandings that arise in respect of groups and communities involved in matters of religion and belief. The various legal instruments must be rigorously enforced, particularly in the social and tax spheres, in a substantiated and non-discriminatory manner.'[621]

Widespread hostility towards religious groups classified as sects or dangerous is evident from the range of countries considered by the Special Rapporteur including China,[622] the Syrian Arab Republic,[623] Egypt,[624] Kazakhstan,[625] Papua New Guinea,[626] Greece[627] and

---

[620] *Ibid.*, at paras. 98–9. The Special Rapporteur recently reported allegations that in Indonesia a draft bill drawn up by the Religious Affairs Ministry would prohibit people from attending religious ceremonies of a different faith and would ban teachings that 'deviate from the main teachings of that religion' UN Doc. E/CN.4/2005/61/Add.1 (2005), p. 34, para. 132 (Indonesia).

[621] UN Doc. E/CN.4/1998/6/Add.2 (1997), para. 101 (Germany).

[622] UN Doc. E/CN.4/2000/65 (2000), para. 27 (China); UN Doc. A/56/253 (2001), p. 52, para. 8 (China); UN Doc. E/CN.4/2001/63 (2001), pp. 11–12, para. 26 (China).

[623] UN Doc. E/CN.4/2000/65 (2000), para. 84 (Syrian Arab Republic).

[624] UN Doc. E/CN.4/2001/63 (2001), p. 13, para. 33 (Egypt).

[625] UN Doc. E/CN.4/2001/63 (2001), p. 25, para. 88 (Kazakhstan).

[626] UN Doc. E/CN.4/2001/63 (2001), p. 31, para. 119 (Papua New Guinea).

[627] UN Doc. A/51/542/Add.1 (1996), para. 7 (Greece).

Germany.[628] The difficulties facing them, as summarised by the Special Rapporteur in a survey of the treatment of sects, include an outright ban on the community, denial of registration, prohibitions against certain expressions of freedom of religion or belief (such as the refusal to allow the building of places of worship), direct attacks on freedom of religion or even belief (such as actions aimed at forcing a person to renounce their faith or belief) and arrests and convictions, ill-treatment and even expulsions.[629]

The broad principles canvassed above are as important to observe as the precise boundaries of the individual grounds of limitation on which the State may rely when imposing restrictions on manifestation, which will now be considered. The grounds of limitation generally receive fairly limited attention from both the European institutions and the Human Rights Committee. Frequently, more than one ground of limitation is operative and the differences between them do not appear to be precisely scoped.

Grounds of limitation

Public interest grounds of limitation

Public interest grounds of limitation within Article 18 of the ICCPR, Article 1(3) of the 1981 Declaration and Article 9 of the European Convention include 'public safety', 'public health' and 'public order', but exclude 'national security'. Article 29(2) of the Universal Declaration refers to 'public order and the general welfare in a democratic society'.

Public health and safety   Even though 'safety' and 'health' appear as separate grounds of limitation, the distinction between them seems to have been of little importance in decisions by the Human Rights Committee (when supporting the dismissal of a Sikh railway maintenance electrician who refused to wear safety headgear)[630] and in decisions by the European Commission (when considering the requirement that Sikh motorcyclists wear crash helmets,[631] that Sikh prisoners clean their cells,[632] and when

---

[628] UN Doc. E/CN.4/1998/6/Add.2 (1997), para. 101 (Germany).

[629] UN Doc. A/55/280 (2000), p. 23, para. 93.

[630] *K. Singh Bhinder v. Canada*, Communication No. 208/1986 (views of 9 November 1989), UN Doc. A/45/40 vol. 2 (1990), p. 50.

[631] *X. v. United Kingdom* App. No. 7992/77 (1978) 14 D&R 234, at 235.

[632] *X. v. United Kingdom*, App. No. 8231/78 (1982) 28 D&R 5.

addressing the enforced participation by farmers in a compulsory health scheme for the prevention of tuberculosis in cattle).[633]

Public safety and public health appear to be readily supported as grounds of limitation and little accompanying reasoning is considered necessary at both Universal and European levels.

The Human Rights Committee has on a few occasions enquired about issues of public safety in its examination of State reports, with the purpose of ensuring that religious practices do not put the safety of any person at risk.[634] It has focused both on religious practices which might pose health risks (such as female genital mutilation)[635] and unwarranted restrictions on religious practices on the grounds of public safety.[636]

In *Cha'are Shalom Ve Tsedek v. France*,[637] the Government maintained before the European Court that the refusal to approve the applicant as a regulated slaughterhouse pursued the legitimate aim of protecting order and public health, embracing issues such as public hygiene and the avoidance of animal suffering. Although the Court did not need to examine the limitations (because it found there was no interference), it confirmed the legitimate aim of the measure, namely 'protection of public health and public order, in so far as organisation by the State of the exercise of worship is conducive to religious harmony and tolerance'.[638] The Court therefore readily supported the public health aims and gave unusual breadth to the notion of public order.

Public safety is sometimes combined with public order in order to provide greater substance to justifications yet it is obviously important

---

[633] *X. v. The Netherlands*, App. No. 1068/61, 5 Yearbook (1962) 278.

[634] UN Doc. A/46/40 (1991), p. 74, para. 302 (India). In the context of protection of the family and children, members of the Committee enquired about the main features of the Commission of Sati (Prevention) Act 1987. Information was sought on any reported cased of *sati* since the passage of the Act. Questions were also asked about the Dowry Prohibition (Amendment) Act 1986, in particular, the number of dowry deaths before and after enactment of such legislation.

[635] UN Doc. A/53/40 (1998), p. 36, para. 214 (Zimbabwe); UN Doc. A/53/40 (1998), p. 23, para. 121 (Sudan); UN Doc. A/59/40 vol. 1 (2004), p. 49, para. 70(10) (Uganda), and p. 76, para. 76(10) (Gambia). For further reading see: K. Boulware-Miller, 'Female Circumcision: Challenges to the Practice as a Human Rights Violation', 8 Harv WLJ (1985) 155; K. Hayter, 'Female Circumcision – Is there a Legal Solution?' J Soc Wel Law (1984) 323; M. Davies (ed.), *Third World-Second World Sex: Women's Struggles and National Liberation: Third World Women Speak Out*, London: Zed (1983).

[636] UN Doc. A/37/40 (1982), p. 33, para. 146 (Morocco).

[637] *Cha'are Shalom Ve Tsedek v. France* (App. No. 27417/95), Judgment of 11 July 2000.

[638] *Ibid.*, at para. 84.

to differentiate the two according to their intended scope since public order is particularly susceptible to misuse through the labelling of religious activities (or the political activities of religious groups) as subversive.[639]

Order   In the drafting of the public order limitation in the ICCPR, in order to avoid the implication that public policy could constitute too wide a basis of restriction under Article 18 of the ICCPR, the United Kingdom proposed the formula 'the prevention of disorder'[640] with the accompanying explanation that 'if public policy could be invoked to restrict freedom of religion, the restrictions could be stringent indeed'.[641] Lebanon supported the United Kingdom on the basis that if 'the maintenance of order included action by the courts and enforcement of respect for the general principles governing a society, it was far too broad a basis for limitations of freedom of religion',[642] especially where those principles are in conflict with the enjoyment of the freedom. The ICCPR limitation refers only to 'order' (or in French, '*la protection de l'ordre*'), and not 'public order' or '*ordre public*', so as to avoid notions of social policy and to position it in line with the phrase 'prevention of disorder'.[643]

In the European context, high priority has been given to the risks of public disorder, for example to justify restrictions on the peaceful assembly by the applicant organisation in *Christians against Racism and Fascism v. the United Kingdom*[644] (under Article 11(2)) even though the source of such disorder was the undemocratic National Front which had planned a violent counter-demonstration.[645] The public order ground of limitation is given a broad interpretation so that, for example,

---

[639] See: UN Doc. E/CN.4/1987/35 (1987), p. 13; UN Doc. E/CN.4/1987/SR. 25, p. 7, para. 15 (Viet Nam). See also UN Doc. A/45/40 vol. 1 (1990), p. 84, para. 375 (Dominican Republic). The role of religious groups in the political process is an important one discussed by J. E. Wood, 'Church Lobbying and Public Policy', 28 J Church & St (1986) 183.

[640] UN Doc. E/CN.4/L.143 (1952) and UN Doc. E/CN.4/SR. 319 (1952), p. 4 (United Kingdom).

[641] UN Doc. E/CN.4/SR. 319 (1952), p. 12 (United Kingdom).

[642] UN Doc. E/CN.4/SR. 319 (1952), p. 13 (Lebanon).

[643] See K. J. Partsch 'Freedom of Conscience and Expression, and Political Freedoms', in L. Henkin (ed.), *The International Bill of Rights The Covenant on Civil and Political Rights*, New York/Guildford: Columbia University Press (1981), p. 213.

[644] *Christians against Racism and Fascism v. United Kingdom*, App. No. 8440/78 (1980) 21 D&R 138.

[645] *Ibid.*, at 152.

in *Manoussakis and others v. Greece*[646] public order was the proper basis for planning restrictions.[647]

In the prison context, not surprisingly the decisions of the European Commission evidence an interpretation of public order favourable to States, for example, to support restrictions on a violent convicted murderer attending chapel services in prison,[648] and those preventing a prisoner from acquiring a book on the subject of his religion because it contained a chapter on martial arts.[649] The European Commission tends to give little weight to certain forms of religious manifestation when invoking prison order and discipline, such as in *X. v. Austria* when a prisoner was prevented from receiving a prayer chain and from growing a beard in spite of his assertions that both were required for the practice of his Buddhist religion,[650] and in *X. v. United Kingdom* when the publication of articles by a prisoner in religious magazines was prohibited.[651] A preferable approach would be to give greater formal recognition to a wider range of manifestations, as noted above at pp. 290–2, and to require stringent justifications for restrictions on manifestation, even when considering the prison environment.

In *Metropolitan Church of Bessarabia and others v. Moldova*,[652] the Court accepted that the refusal to recognise the applicant Church pursued a legitimate aim, namely the 'protection of public order and public safety' because States are entitled to verify whether a religious organisation is a cloak for activities which are harmful to the population or to public safety.[653] This was arguably not the aim asserted by the State and

---

[646] *Manoussakis and others v. Greece* (1997) 23 EHRR 387, para. 40. Aware of the potential misuse of public order claims, Judge Martens commented in his concurring opinion in *Manoussakis and others v. Greece* that 'where freedom of religion is at stake ... public order arguments may easily disguise intolerance ... as a matter of principle the requested authorisation should always be given, unless very exceptional, objective and insuperable grounds of public order make that impossible.'

[647] Stavros considers public order issues to be exaggerated – S. Stavros, 'Freedom of Religion and Claims for Exemption from Generally Applicable, Neutral Laws: Lessons From Across The Pond?' EHRLR (1997) 607.

[648] *Childs v. United Kingdom* (App. No. 9813/82), unpublished, decision of 1 March 1983, Council of Europe Digest of Strasbourg Case-Law relating to the European Convention on Human Rights, Section 9.2.1.1, p. 1.

[649] *X. v. United Kingdom* App. No. 6886/75 (1976) 5 D&R 100.

[650] *X. v. Austria*, App. No. 1753/63, 8 Yearbook (1965) 174.

[651] *X. v. United Kingdom*, App. No. 5442/72 (1974) 1 D&R 41.

[652] *Metropolitan Church of Bessarabia and others v. Moldova* (2002) 35 EHRR 306.

[653] *Ibid.*, at para. 113 (following *Manoussakis and others v. Greece* (1997) 23 EHRR 387, para. 40).

suggests willingness on the part of the Court to support a legitimate aim simply by reciting principles established in earlier cases. (This was also a criticism of the Court's analysis in *Murphy v. Ireland*[654] discussed in Chapter 2 under the heading 'Blasphemy, disparagement and gratuitous offence.') at pp. 89–94. The Moldovan Government claimed instead to be protecting public order and public safety in uniting the entire Moldovan population within the rival Moldovan Orthodox Church and it considered that recognition of the applicant Church would revive old Russo-Romanian hostilities within the population, thus endangering social stability and even Moldova's territorial integrity.

Similarly, in *Serif v. Greece*[655] the State claimed that in protecting the authority of the lawful mufti the domestic courts sought to preserve order in the particular religious community and in society at large. In accepting that a legitimate aim was pursued in protecting public order the Court merely noted that the applicant was not the only person claiming to be the religious leader of the local Muslim community.[656]

National security   The intentional omission of the 'national security' ground of limitation in Article 18 of the ICCPR was because the term is 'not sufficiently precise to be used as a basis for the limitation of the exercise of the rights guaranteed'.[657] Frequently, issues under Article 18 of the ICCPR interrelate or overlap with those under Articles 19, 21 and 22 yet if the choice is made to determine a case under one of those latter Articles, it opens the way for national security to be pleaded by States as a permissible ground of limitation not available under Article 18. For example, in *Tae-Hoon Park v. Korea*,[658] the author alleged violation of Articles 18, 19 and 26 as a result of his conviction under National Security Law for belonging to an 'enemy benefiting' organisation. The Human Rights Committee disposed of the matter under Article 19 although it said it could equally have done so under Article 18.[659] There is thus potential for conflict with the Human Rights

---

[654] *Murphy v. Ireland* (App. No. 44179/98) (2004) 38 EHRR 212.
[655] *Serif v. Greece* (1999) 31 EHRR 561. See also *Agga v. Greece* (App. Nos 50776/99 and 52912/99), Judgment of 7 October 2002.
[656] *Serif v. Greece* (1999) 31 EHRR 561, at paras. 45.
[657] UN Doc. A/2929 Annexes, Agenda item 28 (part II) at p. 49 (1955). National security was also rejected as a ground of limitation in the 1981 Declaration, which faithfully reflects Article 18(3) of the Covenant.
[658] *Tae-Hoon Park v. Korea*, Communication No. 628/1995 (views of 20 October 1998) (1999) 6(3) IHRR 623.
[659] *Ibid.*, at para. 10.3.

Committee's clear statement in paragraph 8 of General Comment No. 22 that 'restrictions are not allowed on grounds not specified there [Article 18(3)], even if they would be allowed as restrictions to other rights protected in the Covenant, such as national security'.

In the European context, failure to distinguish those Articles to which the national security limitation may apply from those to which it may not (notably Article 9) is evident in the European Commission's early case law, such as *X. v. Austria*,[660] in which the applicant claimed that his conviction for activities aimed at the reintroduction into Austria of National Socialistic activities infringed Articles 9 and 10. The European Commission supported the measure as 'necessary in a democratic society in the interests of public safety and national security and for the protection of the rights and freedoms of others'.[661] This error appears to be isolated and has been discontinued.[662]

Nevertheless, scope exists for the European Court to admit national security grounds of limitation by means of too restrictive an approach to the nexus between protected beliefs and their manifestation. This may occur where the result of applying the test in *Arrowsmith v. United Kingdom*[663] too rigidly is to remove certain forms of religious expression from consideration under Article 9, instead requiring them to be dealt with under Articles 10 or 11, to which limitation grounds of national security may then apply (see the discussion above at pp. 210–20).[664]

The sensitivity of this recurrent topical issue is reflected in justifications advanced by various countries that fail to distinguish between public order and national security, such as in China (with claims that riots in Lhasa were instigated by the Dalai Lama clique, aimed at splitting the country),[665]

---

[660] *X. v. Austria*, App. No. 1747/62 (1963) 13 CD 42.

[661] *Ibid.*, at 54.

[662] See, for example, *X. v. United Kingdom*, App. No. 6084/73 (1975) 3 D&R, at 65.

[663] *Arrowsmith v. United Kingdom*, App. No. 7050/75 (1980) 19 D&R 5.

[664] For further discussion of recent developments in Europe, see S. Ferrari, 'Individual Religious Freedom and National Security in Europe After September 11', Brigham Young UL Rev (2004) 357.

[665] UN Doc. E/CN.4/1989/44 (1989), p. 12, para. 37 (China). See also UN Doc. E/CN.4/2004/63 (2004), p. 9, para. 35 (China) and UN Doc. E/CN.4/2005/61/Add.1 (2005), p. 18, para. 65 (China) on the Chinese Government's characterisation of Falun Gong as a violent 'anti-social, anti-science, anti-human sect', not a religion, and 'a heretical organisation'. The Special Rapporteur recently criticised an 'anti-subversion' law submitted by the Hong Kong Special Administrative Region of the People's Republic of China, whose vague and broad definition of terms such as 'subversive activities', 'treason' and 'sedition' were thought likely to undermine freedom of religion and belief – UN Doc. A/58/296 (2003), p. 7, para. 28 (China). See also A. S. Y. Cheung, 'In Search

Yugoslavia (where, in the process of democratisation there existed acute tensions among individual religious groups and political parties using religion to assert principles of nationalism),[666] Malaysia (where certain teachings were perceived to be injurious to national security and the unity of Muslims),[667] Viet Nam (where 'the policies of the State' determined the scope of limitation provisions),[668] and Turkey (where certain constitutional limitations contained vague expressions that could lead to extensive intervention by the State for 'violating the indivisible integrity of the State with its territory and nation').[669]

The Special Rapporteur is conscious that in response to terrorist threats States have increasingly used the pretext of security to limit the exercise of the right to freedom of religion or belief.[670] Relating this to states of emergency, the Special Rapporteur pointed out that States have clearly misinterpreted Article 4 of the ICCPR, which specifies that even in times of public emergency which threatens the life of the nation no derogation is permitted from Article 18.[671] Similarly, the Human Rights Committee expressed concern that freedom of religion could be threatened by a state of emergency in Ukraine[672] and Azerbaijan.[673]

Protection of morals

There is no universally applicable common standard of 'public morals'.[674] However, consistent with developing emphasis on pluralism, the Human Rights Committee has indicated that the term is not to be judged by reference to a single religion or culture. Paragraph 8 of General Comment No. 22 specifies that 'limitations on the freedom to manifest a religion or belief for the purpose of protecting morals must be based on principles not deriving exclusively from a single tradition'. This avoids any suggestion that Article 18(3) may be interpreted to mean that public morality is dictated by State religion or even the popular religion of a country. Accordingly, when examining State

of a Theory of Cult and Freedom Of Religion in China: The Case of Falun Gong', 13 Pac Rim L & Pol'y J (2004) 1.

[666] UN Doc. E/CN.4/1991/56 (1991), p. 12, para. 21 (Yugoslavia).
[667] UN Doc. E/CN.4/1999/58 (1999), para. 72 (Malaysia).
[668] UN Doc. E/CN.4/1999/58/Add.2 (1998), paras. 102–04 (Viet Nam).
[669] UN Doc. A/55/280/Add.1 (2000), p. 23, para. 125 (Turkey).
[670] UN Doc. A/58/296 (2003), p. 23, para. 139.
[671] UN Doc. A/58/296 (2003), p. 22, para. 134.
[672] UN Doc. A/57/40 vol. 1 (2002), p. 33, para. 74(11) (Ukraine).
[673] UN Doc. A/57/40 vol. 1 (2002), p. 48, para. 77(8) (Azerbaijan).
[674] *Hertzberg and others v. Finland*, Communication No. R.14/61 (views of 2 April 1982), UN Doc. A/37/40 (1982), p. 161, at para. 10.3.

reports the Human Rights Committee has expressed concern at a subjective or single tradition view of morality.[675]

There is some authority for the proposition that 'morals' for the purposes of Article 9 of the European Convention should similarly not be dictated by the religious or moral precepts of the majority population. In *Manoussakis and others v. Greece*[676] (in the context of public order considerations) the European Court rejected the Government's submission that, because of the position of the Orthodox Church in the national conscience, the substance of the notion of public order should vary on account of national characteristics.[677]

It has been recognised that there is no common concept of 'morals' for the purposes of Article 10 of the European Convention with the result that a wide margin of appreciation was applied in *Wingrove v. United Kingdom* because of the lack of uniformity of any conception of morals in the legal and social orders of the Contracting States.[678] There is certainly scope to argue that future application of the 'morals' ground of limitation should take better account of the demands of pluralism rather than the threats posed by pluralism (following *Serif v. Greece*),[679] and should involve better particularisation of the factors that justify a wide margin of appreciation.[680]

Fundamental rights and freedoms of others

The significance of the reference in Article 18(3) of the ICCPR to the '*fundamental* rights and freedoms of others' is not clear when other

---

[675] UN Doc. A/35/40 (1980), p. 57, para. 253 (Colombia); UN Doc. A/37/40 (1982), p. 40, para. 180 (Jordan); UN Doc. A/38/40 (1983), p. 42, para. 194 (Austria); UN Doc. A/39/40 (1984), p. 75, para. 416 (Panama).

[676] *Manoussakis and others v. Greece* (1997) 23 EHRR 387, para. 47.

[677] *Ibid.*, at para. 39. See also *Sidiropoulos v. Greece* (1999) 27 EHRR 633.

[678] *Wingrove v. United Kingdom* (1997) 24 EHRR 1, para. 58 and *Otto-Preminger-Institut v. Austria* (Ser. A) No. 295-A (1994) ECtHR, para. 50, both citing *Müller v. Switzerland* (Ser. A) No. 133 (1988) ECtHR, para. 35 (in turn referring to *Handyside v. United Kingdom*, (Ser. A) No. 24 (1976) ECtHR, para. 48).

[679] *Serif v. Greece* (1999) 31 EHRR 561.

[680] See P. W. Edge, 'The European Court of Human Rights and Religious Rights', 47 Int'l & Comp Law Q (1998) 680. When referring to the wide margin of appreciation in religious matters, Edge commented that 'it remains for the Convention organs to identify issues which they will take into account when determining the breadth of the margin of appreciation in a particular case. Without such development, there is a danger that the broad margin of appreciation justified by European diversity in religious issues could become no more than a mechanism by which the Court and Commission can avoid the political sensitivities which follow from that diversity' (at p. 685).

provisions (such as Articles 12(3), 21 and 22(2)) refer merely to 'the rights and freedoms of others'. Although there is some suggestion that the term as used in Article 18 is to be construed more narrowly than in those other Articles,[681] Meron argues against such a conclusion given the interchangeable use of the terms 'human rights' and 'fundamental rights', coupled with the lack of any hierarchy of rights (beyond the primacy of certain *jus cogens* rights).[682] The only reference made in the 1981 Declaration to 'the fundamental rights and freedoms of others' is in the limitation Article 1(3), which is a deliberate replica of Article 18 of the ICCPR.[683] Article 9 of the European Convention refers to 'the rights and freedoms of others'.

The limitation provisions applicable to freedom of expression refer to the 'rights' and 'reputation(s)' of others (rather that the 'rights and freedoms of others'). Also, 'duties and responsibilities' attach to the exercise of the freedom of expression but not the freedom of thought, conscience and religion. In many instances the factual background is such as to produce the same outcome whether relying on freedom of expression or freedom of religion. For example, in *Malcolm Ross v. Canada*[684] the Human Rights Committee included within the 'rights and reputations' of persons of Jewish faith, 'the right to have an education in the public school system free from bias, prejudice and intolerance'.[685] The Human Rights Committee determined the claim under Article 19 of the ICCPR and stressed the special duties and responsibilities that the exercise of freedom of expression carries, particularly in

---

[681] See UN Doc. E/CN.4/SR. 319 (1952) at pp. 4 and 14 for proposals to delete the word 'fundamental'.

[682] T. Meron, *Human Rights Law-Making in the United Nations: A Critique of Instruments and Process*, Oxford: Clarendon Press (1986), pp. 181–2; T. Meron, 'On a Hierarchy of International Human Rights', 80 Am J Int'l L (1986) 1.

[683] The 1961 Draft Principles on Freedom and Non-Discrimination in the Matter of Religious Rights and Practices (UN Doc. E/CN.4/800, UN Doc. E/CN.4/Sub.2/206, Annex (1960)) suggested a general approach for the resolution of conflicting religious interests by which 'public authorities shall endeavour to find a solution reconciling these demands in a manner such as to ensure the greatest measure of freedom to society as a whole'. See the debates of the Sub-Commission on Prevention of Discrimination and protection of Minorities (UN Doc. E/CN.4/Sub.2/SR. 299 (1960); UN Doc. E/CN.4/Sub.2/SR. 301 (1960); UN Doc. E/CN.4/Sub.2/SR. 302 (1960)). The text of the Draft Principles may be found in Krishnaswami, 'Study of Discrimination', 227, Annex 1.

[684] *Malcolm Ross v. Canada*, Communication No. 736/1997 (views of 18 October 2000), UN Doc. A/56/40 vol. 2 (2001), p. 69.

[685] *Ibid.*, at p. 84, para. 11.5.

the school system, but also commented in relation to Article 18 that in considering the 'fundamental rights and freedoms of others' under Article 18 the issues are substantially the same as those under Article 19 in this case.[686] There is little doubt that the two grounds of limitation coincided in the need to provide Jewish children with public education free from naked anti-Semitism. However, in other cases the 'rights' and 'reputation' of others and 'duties and responsibilities' (peculiar to the exercise of the freedom of expression) may be decisive. Accordingly, the discussion in Chapter 2 under the heading 'Blasphemy, disparagement and gratuitous offence', at pp. 84–102, and Chapter 3 (*The rights and freedoms of others as a ground of limitation*) questioned the extent to which the principles developed by the European Court in decisions such as *Otto-Preminger-Institut v. Austria*,[687] *Wingrove v. United Kingdom*[688] and *Murphy v. Ireland*[689] would have direct application to cases under Article 9 of the European Convention, particularly in the analysis of the rights of others.

Under Article 9, 'the protection of the rights and freedoms of others' was successfully relied upon in *Kokkinakis v. Greece*,[690] when the European Court observed a need 'to place restrictions on this freedom [proselytism] in order to reconcile the interests of the various groups and to ensure that everyone's beliefs are respected'.[691] An approach was suggested in Chapters 2 and 3 that might lead to the consistent development of the notion of 'respect' under both Articles 9 and 10 and prevent the 'the protection of the right and freedoms of others' being given indeterminate scope.

Certainly the context, as well as the manner of presentation, have a bearing on the rights of others under both Article 9 and Article 10. The school environment is an extremely sensitive one but the European institutions appear to have accepted uncritically State assertions made in reliance of the limitation grounds that invoke the rights of others. For

---

[686] *Ibid.*, at p. 85, para. 11.7.
[687] *Otto-Preminger-Institut v. Austria* (Ser. A) No. 295–A (1994) ECtHR.
[688] *Wingrove v. United Kingdom* (1997) 24 EHRR 1.
[689] *Murphy v. Ireland* (App. No. 44179/98) (2004) 38 EHRR 212.
[690] *Kokkinakis v. Greece* (Ser. A) No. 260–A (1993) ECtHR.
[691] *Ibid.*, at para. 33. See also *United Christian Broadcasters Ltd v. United Kingdom* (App. No. 44802), Judgment of 7 November 2000, in which the denial of access to the limited national broadcasting spectrum was to satisfy as many radio listeners as possible, and to protect the rights of others within the meaning of Article 10(2).

example, *X. v. United Kingdom*[692] concerned the dismissal of a Christian teacher of mathematics and English in a non-denominational school for refusing to comply with instructions not to advertise his beliefs, and his opposition to abortion, through posters and stickers. The European Commission merely accepted for the purposes of Article 10(2) the Government's bare assertion that this was considered offensive to female members of staff and disturbing to children. More recently, the European Court in *Dahlab v. Switzerland*[693] supported the prohibition on the applicant wearing an Islamic headscarf in a State school on the grounds of protecting the rights and freedoms of others, public order and public safety, 'weighing the right of a teacher to manifest her religion against the need to protect pupils by preserving religious harmony ... having regard, above all, to the tender age of the children for whom the applicant was responsible as a representative of the State'.

As to the manner of presentation, the limitation ground 'the rights and freedoms of others' was used, for example, in *X. v. Sweden*[694] to justify intervention against the noisy and disorderly manner in which a religious message was portrayed (likely to provoke indignation from the public), although no objection was taken to its content. Given that the European Commission supported the legitimate aim of protecting public order, one wonders what exactly was meant by the 'protection of the rights and freedoms of others' in addition. The unnecessary duplication of grounds of limitation serves to hide the true significance of each although it is accepted that on many occasions different grounds apply concurrently. Thus, in *A. R. M. Chappell v. United Kingdom*,[695] the European Commission upheld the denial of access to Stonehenge for a solstice ceremony in order to protect the monument and to avoid extreme chaos resulting from hippy convoys, 'in the interests of public safety, for the protection of public order or for the protection of the rights and freedoms of others'.

---

[692] *X. v. United Kingdom*, App. No. 8010/77 (1979) 16 D&R 101. For further criticism of this case, see Chapter 3 under the heading '"Respect" for parental convictions based on indoctrination', pp. 166–75.

[693] *Dahlab v. Switzerland*, (App. No. 42393/98), Judgment of 15 February 2001.

[694] *X. v. Sweden*, App. No. 9820/82 (1984) 5 EHRR 297 cf. the concerns of one member of the Human Rights Committee with the limitation ground concerned with 'public indignation' – UN Doc. A/33/40 (1978), p. 13, para. 79 (Sweden); UN Doc. A/41/40 (1986), p. 31, para. 146 (Sweden).

[695] *A. R. M. Chappell v. United Kingdom*, App. No. 12587/86 (1987) 53 D&R 241. See also *ISCON and others v. United Kingdom*, App. No. 20490/92 (1994) 90 D&R 90.

There appears to be some ambiguity as to whether 'protection of the rights and freedoms of others' may interfere with the choice of individuals to put themselves at risk.[696] The Human Rights Committee was not specific as to which ground of limitation operated in the case of *Singh Bhinder v. Canada*[697] to justify the dismissal of the author for not wearing a hard hat but it did not accept the author's contention that his own interests alone were at risk. In *X. v. United Kingdom*,[698] the European Commission did, however, single out 'the protection of health' when upholding the applicant's punishment for failing to wear a crash helmet when riding a motorcycle, presumably referring to his own health. It is rather more obvious that the 'protection of the rights and freedoms of others' (as victims entitled to compensation) should apply in the case of the criminal conviction of motorists for driving without compulsory motor insurance, as the European Commission decided in *X. v. The Netherlands*[699] when the applicant refused to insure because of his belief in absolute divine providence. It has yet to be determined whether such a ground of limitation may apply in the case of voluntary brainwashing although in *Riera Blume and others v. Spain*,[700] when a number of young individuals who had voluntarily joined a group called *Centro Esotérico de Investigaciones* were detained for 'reprogramming' by the State, they successfully claimed that their detention was arbitrary and hence unlawful under Article 5. The element of personal choice in such circumstances seemed to prevail, and this may be of relevance to the regulation of supposedly dangerous sects.[701]

In summary, when applying limitation grounds, areas of greatest commonality between Universal and European practice concern the extensive latitude available to States in matters of public safety, although

---

[696] The issue is of relevance to the refusal of blood transfusions by Jehovah's Witnesses though no decision has yet been made on the subject by either the European or UN institutions. Fineschi discusses the absolute duty on physicians in Italy to respect the refusal of blood transfusions by Jehovah's Witnesses: V. Fineschi, 'The Jehovah's Witnesses' Refusal for Blood Transfusions: The Jurisprudence and Medico-Legal Debate in Italy', 41 Med Sc & L (2001) 141.

[697] *K. Singh Bhinder v. Canada*, Communication No. 208/1986 (views of 9 November 1989), UN Doc. A/45/40 vol. 2 (1990), p. 50.

[698] *X. v. United Kingdom*, App. No. 7992/77 (1978) 14 D&R 234.

[699] *X. v. The Netherlands*, App. No. 2988/66, 10 Yearbook (1967) 472.

[700] *Riera Blume and others v. Spain* (2000) 30 EHRR 632.

[701] See J. T. Richardson, '"Brainwashing" Claims and Minority Religions Outside the US: Cultural Diffusion of a Questionable Concept in the Legal Arena', Brigham Young UL Rev (1996) 873.

when safety straddles public order there is greater risk of erosion of democratic freedoms. By far the greatest difference remains that of the margin of appreciation allowed in the European context. However, the principles developed by the European Court in the context of the duties and responsibilities of those exercising their freedom of expression, based on notions of 'respect', should be treated with some caution.

Although it was speculated above, at pp. 210–20 and 326, that the stringent connection between beliefs and their manifestation might effectively narrow the scope of the *lex specialis* of Article 9 in favour of other Articles (such as Articles 10 and 11, depending on the facts of each case) there is little evidence to support that concern in relation to the misuse of national security grounds of limitation, except under the European Commission's early case law (for example, *X. v. Austria*).[702] It is nevertheless extremely important to ensure that the distinctions between Article 9 and related Articles are preserved, especially given the indistinct boundaries between public order and national security in the claims made by States to justify restrictions on religious manifestation.

Conclusion

In this survey of the right to manifest religion or belief, a number of patterns in the practice of the European institutions and the Human Rights Committee need to be observed in order to appreciate the scope of any differences between the European and United Nations systems.

Within the European context the criteria for satisfying the so-called *Arrowsmith* test are at risk of being interpreted too restrictively. Terminology such as 'necessity', rather than 'actual expression' should be reserved to claims in which these terms were coined, bearing in mind their specific context (such as the military or prison environment) where the justifications for greater interference were widely accepted. Care should also be taken with those cases where no issue of conscience arose and statements that suggest a narrow application of the *Arrowsmith* test (for example, that the applicant was not *obliged* to act against his conscience) were merely pointing out the absence of a conflict. The nexus between a religion or belief and its manifestation under the *Arrowsmith* test should therefore not be overstated, otherwise the disparity between European and United Nations practice in

---

[702] *X. v. Austria*, App. No. 1747/2262 (1963) 13 CD 42.

determining this link would be exaggerated. Increasingly, the European Court makes reference to *Arrowsmith* (usually indirectly) as little more than a reminder of the principle that Article 9 'does not cover each act which is motivated or influenced by a religion or belief'.

The Human Rights Committee has not burdened itself with equivalent principles by which appropriate forms of manifestation will qualify for protection. It should be remembered that the *Arrowsmith* test arose principally as a means of imposing suitable limits on the scope of the term 'practice', where the belief in question was not a religious one. Its purpose was best served when the form of manifestation was not readily acknowledged. This led to the suggestion in this chapter that if the European Court were to give due attention to the full range of well recognised forms of religious manifestation enunciated in Article 6 of the 1981 Declaration, less reliance might need to be placed on the *Arrowsmith* test. Reference is frequently made to European materials in Human Rights Committee decisions, and vice versa, yet no reference has explicitly been made to Article 6 of the 1981 Declaration by the European Court in determining whether an alleged form of manifestation should qualify for protection. Presumably the European Court does not dissent from the list of manifestations given in Article 6. If it does dissent, this certainly deserves open explanation. The cementing of common standards that would result from acknowledgement of the content of Article 6 of the 1981 Declaration by the Court would also serve as a warning to States before unduly restricting uniformly accepted religious practices.

It is especially important that more widespread recognition be given to different religious manifestations since their significance is often obscured by individual decisions which have as their focus a particular context, such as the military, prison or school environment. Examples include *Larissis and others v. Greece*[703] (where proselytism directed at lower ranking airmen may constitute undue pressure in the confines of military life), *Dahlab v. Switzerland*[704] (where the denominational neutrality of schools was paramount) and *X v. United Kingdom*[705] (where the denial of certain rights to a Buddhist was justified by prison rules). It would also seem that many of the cases involving Turkey belong within a

---

[703] *Larissis and others v. Greece* (Ser. A) No. 65 (1998–V) ECtHR 363, at paras. 50–1.
[704] *Dahlab v. Switzerland* (App. No. 42393/98), Judgment of 15 February 2001.
[705] *X. v. United Kingdom*, App. No. 5442/72 (1975) 1 D&R 41, as clarified by the Commission in *X. v. United Kingdom*, App. No. 5442/72 (1975) 1 D&R 41.

special category, owing to the pecularities of the historical development of democracy in that country and the role of the driving principle of secularity, as explained in *Partisi (the Welfare Party) and others v. Turkey*.[706] It is therefore necessary to be aware of the special context of certain findings of no violation.

Although the European institutions were criticised for providing only cursory reasoning when examining the legitimacy of the aim of a State measure and the associated grounds of limitation (and for applying a threshold which is strikingly low), the statements of principle that accompany the analysis of whether an interference is 'necessary in a democratic society' demonstrate recent willingness by the European Court to give prominence to a number of significant issues. The Court has shown a consistently high regard for the essential preconditions to enable pluralism to flourish and a new emphasis has been placed on the State's duty to cope with tensions that inevitably stem from the co-existence of different religions in a pluralist society. Examples of such cases include *Kokkinakis v. Greece*,[707] *Manoussakis and others v. Greece*,[708] *Serif v. Greece*,[709] *Hasan and Chaush v. Bulgaria*[710] and *Metropolitan Church of Bessarabia and others v. Moldova*.[711] However, these statements contrast vividly with the narrow grounds on which certain decisions were made, most notably in *Kokkinakis v. Greece*,[712] and this begs the question whether recent European Court decisions reflect a change towards a broader, more interventionist approach.

Recent developments certainly indicate a marked willingness on the part of the European Court to impugn State legislation where it has habitually been used to perpetuate religious intolerance, going beyond mere criticism of the law (*Manoussakis and others v. Greece*) to the important finding that a legal measure was not prescribed by law (*Hasan and Chaush v. Bulgaria* and more recently *Maestri v. Italy*[713]). The case of *Hasan and Chaush v. Bulgaria* in particular represents a positive response to the use of arbitrary power or excessive discretion by

---

[706] *Refah Partisi (the Welfare Party) and others v. Turkey* (2003) 37 EHRR 1.
[707] *Kokkinakis v. Greece* (Ser. A) No. 260–A (1993) ECtHR at para. 31.
[708] *Manoussakis and others v. Greece* (1997) 23 EHRR at para. 44.
[709] *Serif v. Greece* (1999) 31 EHRR 561, at para. 53.
[710] *Hasan and Chaush v. Bulgaria* (2002) 34(6) EHRR at para. 62.
[711] *Metropolitan Church of Bessarabia and others v. Moldova* (2002) 35 EHRR 306, at paras. 116 and 119.
[712] *Kokkinakis v. Greece* (Ser. A) No. 260–A (1993) ECtHR at para. 49.
[713] *Maestri v. Italy* (App. No. 42393/98), Judgment of 17 February 2004.

States, and the impact of that case may extend to other issues, such as the registration obstacles facing many religious communities.

Even the pragmatic support for State restrictions in such cases as *Christians against Racism and Fascism v. United Kingdom*[714] may need to be reconsidered in view of the Court's new emphasis in *Serif v. Greece* on the State's duty to ensure tolerance in the midst of inter-religious tension.

The scope for discrimination in granting legal recognition, as well as the motivation of States in administering the processes of registration and legal recognition, were ably illustrated by the Special Rapporteur's reports, emphasising the inseparability of discrimination and manifestation in practice. Krishnaswami even went so far as to highlight the risks to the *forum internum* of extensive discrimination in the grant of legal status. The issues canvassed in this chapter do not therefore bear solely upon the individual or collective right to manifest religion or belief but are inextricably linked to issues of discrimination and even concerns for the *forum internum*.

A significant recent landmark in the battle against discrimination was the requirement in *Thlimmenos v. Greece*[715] for better targeting of legal measures that are discriminatory, following the failure of national law to distinguish felons of conscience from those guilty of dishonesty or moral turpitude. The potential has yet to be realised for development of this principle in opposing anti-sect laws (which are now an abiding feature of the European landscape yet fail to make fully justifiable distinctions between religions), as well as laws such as those historically found in Greece that prohibit proselytism, both 'proper' or 'improper'.

Important conclusions were drawn in this chapter from a thematic analysis of different forms of manifestation, according to the categorisation provided by Article 6 of the 1981 Declaration. It revealed differences in the standards applied at European and Universal levels to the same form of manifestation, as well as discrepancies in the priority given to separate types of manifestation. Of the well recognised rights, the right to worship only appears to be subject to a lower standard at European level if it is not appreciated that the cases which upheld State restrictions on worship do not interfere with worship in general but only at certain

---

[714] *Christians against Racism and Fascism v. United Kingdom*, App. No. 8440/78 (1980) 21 D&R 138.

[715] *Thlimmenos v. Greece* (2001) 31 EHRR 411. See Chapter 3, under the heading 'Differential treatment', pp. 187–92.

times or locations (*ARM Chappell v. United Kingdom*[716] and *X. v. United Kingdom*[717]). The right to establish and maintain charitable and humanitarian organisations did not have the same level of recognition under the European Convention as at Universal level, at least until *Metropolitan Church of Bessarabia and others v. Moldova*,[718] but even then only by implication. This right suffers to some extent from the stigma associated with missionary work even though it is commonly expressed in straightforward social action. The right to teach has generally been uniformly acknowledged, although residual doubt remains at European level as to the interrelation between teaching and proselytism. A related issue concerns the anti-vilification and religious harassment legislation which is emerging in some countries, comparable in their effect to legislation in various parts of the world aimed at safeguarding the orthodoxy of religious belief. Such laws could conceivably raise issues of conflict with even the most basic right to teach the tenets of one's faith.

Of those rights which are less well-recognised, the right to make, acquire and use the necessary articles and materials related to the rites and customs of a religion or belief is seemingly not well acknowledged, principally because its scope is not clearly defined. Although practices concerned with diet and distinctive clothing are thought to be included, they are not specified and, in the case of religious headdress, the right has not been given high priority by the European institutions (*Karaduman v. Turkey*[719] and *Dahlab v. Switzerland*[720]) – similarly with the wearing of beards in spite of obvious significance to the Muslim religion. In relation to the dissemination of relevant publications, statements by the Human Rights Committee suggest a higher level of recognition for this particular right than European institutions although this could be a reflection of the fact that the only European authority concerns the right of prisoners to publish in the face of the administrative burden on States in preserving prison security (*X. v. United Kingdom*).[721] The right to solicit and receive contributions is possibly the most neglected of all rights in Article 6 of the 1981 Declaration, having been given little attention from the Human Rights Committee and even the Special

---

[716] *A. R. M. Chappell v. United Kingdom*, App. No. 12587/86 (1987) 53 D&R 241.
[717] *X. v. United Kingdom*, App. No. 8160/78 (1981) 22 D&R 27.
[718] *Metropolitan Church of Bessarabia and others v. Moldova* (2002) 35 EHRR 306.
[719] *Karaduman v. Turkey*, App. No. 16278/90 (1993) 74 D&R 93.
[720] *Dahlab v. Switzerland* (App. No. 42393/98), Judgment of 15 February 2001.
[721] *X. v. United Kingdom*, App. No. 5442/72 (1975) 1 D&R 41.

Rapporteur, and receiving only indirect support in *Metropolitan Church of Bessarabia and others v. Moldova*. The right to observe days of rest and to celebrate holidays and ceremonies in accordance with the precepts of one's religion or belief is not clearly defined beyond ceremonial acts usually accompanying worship and the performance of ceremonies associated with particular stages of life. There have been few European decisions to support this right – most have concerned worship or conflict between a day of rest and employment obligations. Most of the Human Rights Committee's Optional Protocol decisions on such issues have not fallen directly within the scope of this right but instead have arisen from the use of land, particularly land of ceremonial significance which has been under threat for commercial reasons. As such it has not acquired prominence.

The work of the Special Rapporteur has been illuminating in underscoring the significance of all forms of manifestation of religion. This added greatly to an understanding of those rights which have so far been given little attention in the decisions of the European institutions and the Human Rights Committee. More generally the Special Rapporteur's reports could be of invaluable help in enabling the European Court to apprehend more fully the right to manifest religion or belief in the global context and in the light of the recurring threats to such practices.

Finally, it is salutary to heed the warning of the Human Rights Committee when balancing the right to manifestation against applicable limitation provisions, that 'the extent to which a State exercised its right under the Covenant to limit various fundamental freedoms not only by law but also in practice, was a reflection of the true scope of those freedoms in a society'.[722]

---

[722] UN Doc. A/37/40 (1982), p. 50, para. 227 (Rwanda). It is also important to remember the warning from the General Assembly, reiterating a point already stressed by the Human Rights Committee, that restrictions on the freedom to manifest religion or belief are permitted only if they 'are applied in a manner that does not vitiate the right to freedom of thought, conscience and religion', GA Res 49/188 of 23 December 1994, para. 7, UN Doc. A/49/49 vol. 1 (1995), p. 207. See also Siracusa Principle 2: 'The scope of a limitation referred to in the Covenant shall not be interpreted so as to jeopardise the essence of the right concerned' ('Siracusa Principles on the Limitation and Derogation Provisions in the International Covenant on Civil and Political Rights', 7(1) HRQ (1985) 3).

5

Conclusion

The myth surrounding the nature of coercion to change religion or belief

This work began by considering freedom of choice in religion and the intention behind those provisions which offer protection against coercion that would impair that freedom of choice. The discussion touched upon an issue which, perhaps more than any other, bears out the conspicuous disparity between Universal and European practice – the strictness of standards maintained by the Human Rights Committee and the Special Rapporteur over decades contrasts with the accommodating approach of the Strasbourg institutions in supporting State restrictions on critical aspects of the freedom of thought, conscience and religion. This has so far only partially been corrected in important recent decisions.

In spite of opposition from numerous States to an explicit right to change religion, which even threatened the existence of the Declaration on the Elimination of all Forms of Intolerance and of Discrimination Based on Religion or Belief ('the 1981 Declaration') at a crucial stage of its drafting, the Human Rights Committee has constantly interpreted Article 18 of the International Covenant on Civil and Political Rights ('ICCPR') so as to embrace fully the right freely to change or to maintain religion at will. The Human Rights Committee's position has most clearly been stated in General Comment No. 22, fully conscious of the weight of opposition to that interpretation from States expressed as early as 1947 in the drafting of the Universal Declaration on Human Rights ('Universal Declaration'), repeated again in the drafting of the ICCPR and reiterated, arguably with greater effect, in the preparation of the 1981 Declaration. In addition to General Comment No. 22, the Human Rights Committee has unequivocally confirmed its position on the right to change religion in its review of State reports, and the Special Rapporteur has also provided

information on a wide range of circumstances in which that right has
been denied. The Human Rights Committee therefore managed to
regain ground that had ostensibly been lost in the drafting of the
ICCPR (in not making express mention of the right to change religion
found in the Universal Declaration) and the drafting of the 1981
Declaration (in losing the reference in the ICCPR to the right to adopt
a religion of one's choice, in favour of freedom to have a religion of one's
choice). In doing so, the Human Rights Committee has allowed no
compromise with States on a fundamental issue, notwithstanding
immense pressure from numerous politically powerful countries.
Although it may seem surprising that the Human Rights Committee
did not address proselytism and missionary work in General Comment
No. 22, this may be understood in terms of its rejection of those arguments advanced in the early debates that such activities readily constitute coercion within the meaning of Article 18(2) of the ICCPR. If so, it
would represent still further lack of compromise with States. In any
event, the characterisation of proselytism and missionary work as coercive was not accepted in those debates.

The approach of the Human Rights Committee is to be contrasted
with a consistent pattern which emerges from decisions by the European
Court and the former European Commission across a range of issues,
amounting to a policy of concession in favour of State interference. It is
illustrated by the European Court's response when first confronted with
issues touching upon proselytism and coercion to change religion. The
European Court in *Kokkinakis v. Greece*[1] gave nominal endorsement to
the principle that proselytism represents a legitimate manifestation of
religion but created a distinction between 'improper proselytism' and
other forms of proselytism. This allowed the Court to support the
legitimate aim of Greece's anti-proselytism law in the possibility that
there might exist certain extreme forms of proselytism that warrant
constraint. Quite apart from the other criticisms that might be made
of the judgment in that case, the European Court unwittingly and quite
unnecessarily rekindled arguments against proselytism and missionary
activity long since rejected at Universal level for being exaggerated or
misplaced. The European Court did so principally by providing a basis
for enabling the aim of anti-proselytism laws to be supported, in protecting the rights and freedoms of others, by virtue of a supposed need to
reconcile the interests of various groups and ensure that everyone's

[1] *Kokkinakis v. Greece* (Ser. A) No. 260–A (1993) ECtHR.

beliefs are 'respected'.[2] It then made a finding of violation on the narrowest conceivable ground, namely the inadequately reasoned application of this anti-proselytism law to the facts of the case. The Court then stood by this approach in the subsequent proselytism case concerning Greek airmen in *Larissis v. Greece*,[3] yet was unable in *Kokkinakis* or *Larissis* to clarify the distinction between protected and improper forms of proselytism, nor provide an adequate explanation of improper proselytism (even though 'not compatible with respect for the freedom of thought, conscience and religion of others').[4] This is a particularly important omission given that in *Larissis* the Court evidently found instances of both proper and improper proselytism. The European Court may be criticised for taking such an approach to proselytism when it was the unwarranted characterisation of proselytism as coercive that lay at the heart of the earliest debates in the preparation of Article 18 of the Universal Declaration and in the formulation of Article 18(2) of the ICCPR, and which to this day still has real significance in many parts of the world. The European Court, in short, gave ground to the claims, that were firmly rejected in those earliest United Nations debates, that proselytism may so readily impair religious choice and amount to interference with the *forum internum*.

For separate but related reasons, the *Kokkinakis* decision was also criticised in Chapter 1 for giving insufficient importance to the fundamental right to change one's religion and for not heeding the principle that it is not the State's concern if somebody attempts to induce another to change their religion. Similar concerns were voiced that the European Commission's decision in *Gottesmann v. Switzerland*[5] (though much earlier) had also given insufficient attention to the implications of freedom to change religion, by boldly asserting that States have a wide discretion to decide on the conditions on which an individual may be regarded as having decided to leave a religious denomination. This illustrates a more widespread failure on the part of the Strasbourg organs to appreciate the recurrent challenges to the freedom to change religion found in the global context. By contrast, when confronted with issues of clear importance, the Human Rights Committee is ready to assert their significance in terms which do not erode earlier standards.

---

[2] *Ibid.*, at paras. 33 and 44.
[3] *Larissis and others v. Greece* (Ser. A) No. 65 ECtHR (1998–V) 363.   [4] *Ibid.*, at para. 48.
[5] *Gottesmann v. Switzerland*, App. No. 101616/83 (1984) 40 D&R 284.

Developing recognition of issues of conscience

Although Article 18(2) of the ICCPR offers explicit protection against coercion in religious choice, there remains an awkward vacuum in all core freedom of religion Articles concerning protection against other forms of coercion, notably coercion to act contrary to one's religion or belief, punishment for holding particular beliefs and compulsion to disclose one's beliefs. A survey of those cases in which the individual was coerced into acting contrary to belief drew attention to the need for an approach to be developed to all cases of coercion impinging directly on the individual's conscience that is consistent with the growing recognition of issues of conscience affecting compulsory military service and even certain forms of taxation. The significance of this issue has largely been obscured by the specific provision made for compulsory military service in both the ICCPR and European Convention, and the recognition given in the European Convention to the State's powers of taxation, as well as the fact that most cases in which State powers are exercised as a matter of welfare and social policy do not generally give rise to issues of conscience.

The treatment given to claims of compulsion to act contrary to one's beliefs by both the European Commission and the European Court discloses resolute consistency in characterising such claims in terms of manifestation. The purpose has been clear: to provide a means by which States may readily rely upon limitation provisions. This entailed an interpretation of manifestation beyond credible bounds when the applicant could not in any meaningful sense be said to be manifesting belief. This is partly explained by the understandable need in the case of much generally applicable law to find a basis for justifying compulsion. However, the manner in which decisions have been reasoned, especially by the European Commission, has been particularly unsatisfactory. Frequently, decisions have entailed little more than a formulaic recitation of the multiple, often redundant, grounds on which claims have historically been decided against applicants (derived from claims based largely on manifestation). Only limited statements (such as those in *Darby v. Sweden*)[6] suggest any true acknowledgement of the effects of compulsion on the *forum internum* and these require further development.

---

[6] *Darby v. Sweden* (Ser. A) No. 187 (1990) ECtHR, annex to the decision of the Court.

Nevertheless, at both United Nations and European levels there has been growing awareness in recent years of the conscientious implications of compulsory military service and taxation levied for the benefit of the State Church. Whatever direction such developments take, attention to the implications of compulsion for the *forum internum* served to highlight an area where a more positive, consistent approach might be taken at European level, with due recognition that compulsion gives rise to issues of conscience more frequently than has previously been appreciated. It is possible that, in line with a growing acceptance of the conscientious implications of compulsory military service, other forms of compulsion will not so readily be dismissed as raising no issues for the *forum internum*, and that this in turn may provoke a more critical, comprehensive reassessment of the range of rights generally considered to fall within the *forum internum*.

The widening of State discretion in European jurisprudence

The European Court has indicated an apparent willingness over many years to allow States wide discretion through, among other means, the Court's broad interpretation of limitation provisions. This is evident most recently in the introduction of the notion of 'respect' for the religious beliefs or feelings of others as a way of supporting State restrictions on the exercise of Article 9 and Article 10 freedoms.

This particular development began with the European Court's reference in *Kokkinakis v. Greece* to the need, in certain circumstances, to ensure that everyone's beliefs are 'respected', coupled with its finding of a legitimate aim of Greece's anti-proselytism law in the rights and freedoms of others. This was relied on in subsequent Article 10 decisions such as *Otto-Preminger-Institut v. Austria*,[7] *Wingrove v. United Kingdom*[8] and *Murphy v. Ireland*[9] but little guidance has been provided on the precise meaning of 'respect'. In *Otto-Preminger-Institut v. Austria*, the Court went so far as to equate 'respect for the religious feelings of believers' with the guarantees in Article 9 even thought it is not easy to find anything comparable to such a right within the traditionally recognised realm of Article 9. The notion of 'respect', as recently developed within the limitation provisions, is also difficult to reconcile

---

[7] *Otto-Preminger-Institut v. Austria* (Ser. A) No. 295–A (1994) ECtHR.
[8] *Wingrove v. United Kingdom* (1997) 24 EHRR 1.
[9] *Murphy v. Ireland*, App. No. 44179/98 (2004) 38 EHRR 212.

with the persistent failure on the part of the European institutions to recognise essential *forum internum* rights within Article 9 when asserted outside the limitation provisions, as discussed in Chapter 3. It is paradoxical that rights of doubtful origin may easily be invoked within limitation provisions, while certain rights more traditionally accepted as falling within the protection of Article 9 find limited recognition within European jurisprudence.

Suggestions were made in all chapters for an interpretation of 'respect' which would be consistent for the purposes of both Articles 9 and 10 and would give more certain scope to the limitation provisions in both Articles. It was proposed that 'respect' for Article 9 freedoms (as developed in *Otto-Preminger-Institut v. Austria, Wingrove v. United Kingdom* and *Murphy v. Ireland*) might refer to the assurance that Article 9 rights (both *forum internum* and *forum externum*) are to be preserved against interference where they may otherwise be put at risk by the exercise of the freedom of expression by others. This would go some way towards correcting the Court's lack of attention to *forum internum* rights discussed in Chapter 3. Equally it may be argued that principles of 'respect' stem from the special duties and responsibilities of those exercising their freedom of expression, to operate as an important constraint when the degree of offence caused to others reaches a particular degree of severity. In that way the traditional scope of Article 9 freedoms would be preserved. In any event, it is important to identify appropriate limits to an otherwise uncertain extension to grounds of limitation by the European Court.

However, if the proper interpretation of this development is that there has been a deliberate broadening of limitation grounds as applied by the European Court, the inescapable conclusion is that the European Court is more willing to accommodate State interference with religious freedom than affirm and uphold the measures of protection that have been entrusted to it. Added to this is the Court's confirmation of a wide margin of appreciation within the sphere of morals or religion, at least under Article 10. By contrast, no equivalent latitude has ever been granted to States by the Human Rights Committee, and no equivalent doctrine of 'respect' for the religious beliefs or feelings of others has been recognised by the Human Rights Committee.

Perhaps the most striking extension of latitude to States by the Strasbourg institutions is reflected in the use of limitation provisions in claims concerning certain key aspects of the unrestricted *forum internum*. The nature and scope of the *forum internum* was considered at length in Chapter 3 with particular reference to such issues as compulsion to act contrary to one's beliefs, compulsion to reveal one's beliefs and punishment for holding particular beliefs. Particularly surprising was the European Court's recent approach to compulsory religious oath-taking in *Buscarini v. San Marino*,[10] which the European Court characterised as a form of manifestation of the applicant's beliefs (when it was entirely unnecessary to make the limitation provisions available since the Court was prepared to make a finding of violation). This contrasts with the Human Rights Committee's treatment of the issue in its evaluation of State reports, which suggests nothing less than a strict approach to compulsory religious oath-taking. In relation to claims concerning punishment for holding particular beliefs, the European Commission's approach has remained consistent, but disappointing. It was illustrated by the inappropriate application of principles of manifestation in *Yanasik v. Turkey*[11] which avoided the real issue for the *forum internum* in the applicant's claim that he was punished for his beliefs. The applicant denied that he was manifesting his beliefs through participation in fundamentalist activity and conceded that he had otherwise not been restricted in manifesting his beliefs. Manifestation does not therefore appear to have been at issue. The military context was nevertheless said to subject cadets' freedom to practise their religion to certain limitations. Similar emphasis in *Kalaç v. Turkey*[12] by the European Court also avoided addressing the applicant's claim that he was punished for holding fundamentalist beliefs.

Taken as a whole, the practice of the Human Rights Committee in matters of compulsion against the individual's conscience and punishment for holding particular beliefs does not attract the same criticism. The Optional Protocol decisions in which such issues have arisen have been relatively few. When the Human Rights Committee has addressed the question of manifestation it has generally been appropriate to do so. When faced with claims that genuinely give rise to issues of conscience, the Human Rights Committee has taken the opportunity to advance standards in certain respects, particularly in the context of discrimination. For example, in *Brinkhof v. The Netherlands*,[13] it departed from

---

[10] *Buscarini and others San Marino* (2000) 30(2) EHRR 208.
[11] *Yanasik v. Turkey*, App. No. 14524/89 (1993) 74 D&R 14.
[12] *Kalaç v. Turkey* (1999) 27 EHRR 552.
[13] *Brinkhof v. The Netherlands*, Communication No. 402/1990 (decision of 27 July 1993), UN Doc. A/48/40 vol. 2 (1993), (1994) 14 HRLJ 410.

European practice in that the Committee did not permit differentiation between separate categories of conscientious objectors, and it emphasised that equal treatment should be given to all persons holding equally strong objections to military and substitute service. In *Frederic Foin v. France*[14] it even criticised its earlier practice of allowing a longer term of substitute service to test the genuineness of conscientious objectors' convictions. Admittedly this may necessitate an examination of each conscientious objector's beliefs but at the same time the decision does nothing to detract from the Human Rights Committee's clear statement in paragraph 3 of General Comment No. 22 that no one can be compelled to reveal their thoughts or adherence to a religion or belief. The European Commission's approach to claims based on compulsory revelation of beliefs in *C. J., J. J. & E. J. v. Poland*,[15] once again, suggests avoidance of Article 9, in favour of Article 5, in order to take advantage of limitation grounds that would not be available under Article 9.

Other means of widening State discretion in Strasbourg jurisprudence include the principles developed for giving effect to the absolute obligation of States to respect parental convictions in public education. This involved establishing a high threshold of indoctrination below which States are given discretion as a matter of necessary expediency in setting and planning the school curriculum. The Human Rights Committee, by contrast, does not refer to a concept of indoctrination or other strict hurdle below which State discretion is permitted. On the contrary, the Human Rights Committee has been unequivocal in its view that limitation provisions are inappropriate to Article 18(4) claims to eliminate State discretion.

The measures taken by the European Commission and European Court to dispose of claims of interference with the *forum internum*, by allowing States to rely on limitation provisions, has failed to give essential recognition to the *forum internum* that is required by Article 9(1) of the European Convention. Instead, the result has arguably been an erosion of standards that has not been matched at Universal level. The contrast between the lack of recognition given to the *forum internum* when directly claimed and the potential reach of the limitation grounds is striking. At the same time, the Human Rights Committee has upheld the absolute nature of *forum internum* rights and, in General

---

[14] *Frederic Foin v. France*, Communication No. 666/1995 (views of 3 November 1999) (2000) 7(2) IHRR 354.

[15] *C.J., J.J. & E.J. v. Poland*, App. No. 23380/94, No. 84–A (1996) D&R 46.

Comment No. 22 in particular, has done much to reassert the strictness of obligations imposed on States it relation to the *forum internum*.

The range of manifestations of religion or belief

There are a number of obvious differences between European and United Nations practice in determining the range of protected forms of manifestation of religion or belief. The first is that under Article 9 of the European Convention principles have developed requiring a strict nexus between religion or belief and its manifestation (stemming from principles first established in *Arrowsmith v. United Kingdom*).[16] The result has ostensibly been to admit a narrower range of manifestations of religion or belief under Article 9 than under both Article 18 of the ICCPR and Article 6 of the 1981 Declaration. The *Arrowsmith* test emerged as a device for coping with the indeterminate scope of the term 'practice'. It may be questioned whether that test would enjoy such a prominent role in European jurisprudence if greater recognition existed at European level for a wider range of manifestations of religion or belief than that established in individual decisions. In general, decisions under Article 9 of the European Convention have not resulted in extensive explicit recognition of different forms of manifestation because those decisions are confined by the particular issues in contention and are inevitably coloured by the factual background to each case. (Nevertheless, the decision in *Metropolitan Church of Bessarabia and others v. Moldova*[17] was both timely and welcomed in its endorsement of the collective aspects of religious manifestation, which have historically been understated in individual decisions.)

For this reason it was suggested that a suitable reference point for the European Court (and indeed the Human Rights Committee) might be the detailed range of manifestations already accepted at Universal level in Article 6 of the 1981 Declaration. The comparison was illuminating between the variety of manifestations reflected in the Special Rapporteur's reports (on the one hand) and (on the other) those represented in the individual decisions of the European institutions and the Human Rights Committee (supplemented by General Comment No. 22). A vivid portrayal was provided by the Special Rapporteur of religious practices worldwide, which are routinely

---

[16] *Arrowsmith v. United Kingdom*, App. No. 7050/75 (1980) 19 D&R 5.
[17] *Metropolitan Church of Bessarabia and others v. Moldova* (2002) 35 EHRR 306.

restricted according to patterns of violation which are not reflected in individual decisions. These reports might also usefully be heeded by the European Court to increase its sensitivity to the factors which threaten the enjoyment of fundamental freedoms in the wider context.

Meeting future challenges

A survey of violations of the freedom of thought, conscience and religion in the Universal context, particularly well illustrated by the Special Rapporteur, hints at the potential for escalation in the range of issues to be faced by the European Court in coming years. Those which are already evident in Europe but have not yet been fully examined by the European Court include the increasing incidence of laws which are essentially preventive of the emergence of new religious movements, laws prohibiting religious harassment and religious vilification (which could have far-reaching implications even for the teaching or simple presentation of one's own beliefs) and the excessive discretion reserved by the State in such matters as the regulation of sects.

The European Court's interpretation of the 'prescribed by law' requirement in *Hasan and Chaush v. Bulgaria*[18] is of particular importance in impugning those laws which confer excessive discretion and omit essential procedural safeguards against arbitrary abuse. The Court's unsatisfactory reluctance to make such findings had already been exposed in *Manoussakis and others v. Greece* in the concurring opinion of Judge Martens, who objected to the Court upholding the 'prescribed by law' requirement even when it seemed manifestly inappropriate to do so. A similar interventionist trend might also be seen in the area of discrimination, in the European Court's novel approach to differential treatment adopted in *Thlimmenos v. Greece*,[19] in finding a violation where States, without an objective and reasonable justification, fail to make appropriate differentiation in certain cases. This is more consistent with the Human Rights Committee's position in General Comment No. 18 in which it emphasised that the principle of equality is not synonymous with equal treatment but requires differentiation and, on occasion, affirmative action in order to diminish or eliminate conditions which perpetuate discrimination. Discrimination is seen as one of the most important avenues for addressing repressive legislation.

---

[18] *Hasan and Chaush v. Bulgaria* (2002) 34(6) EHRR 1339.
[19] *Thlimmenos v. Greece* (2001) 31 EHRR 411.

These developments represent important advances in the more effective supervision of European Convention obligations.

Another important development by the European Court concerns its assessment of the of the role of pluralism in determining whether a restriction is necessary in a democratic society. One of the historical shortcomings of the European approach was to interpret pluralism so as to justify State interference whenever there was a risk of conflict between the wishes of different religious groups (for example, in *Karaduman v. Turkey* restrictions were justified by the need to 'ensure harmonious co-existence between students of different beliefs').[20] In *Kokkinakis v. Greece* (decided at approximately the same time as *Karaduman v. Turkey*) a similar principle was expressed through the need to reconcile the interests of various groups and ensure that everyone's beliefs are 'respected'.[21] Appeals to lofty notions of pluralism, however, rang hollow when accompanied by a narrow finding of violation in *Kokkinakis* based only on the national court's lack of reasoning, and did not do justice to the Court's preamble that,

> '[a]s enshrined in Article 9 (art. 9), freedom of thought, conscience and religion is one of the foundations of a "democratic society" within the meaning of the Convention. It is, in its religious dimension, one of the most vital elements that go to make up the identity of believers and their conception of life, but it is also a precious asset for atheists, agnostics, sceptics and the unconcerned. The pluralism indissociable from a democratic society, which has been dearly won over the centuries, depends on it.'[22]

The *Kokkinakis* judgment highlighted as one of the European Court's most significant failings a yawning gap between the principles it espoused and the means by which it implemented them in substantive reasoning.

Signs that was being corrected first became visible in *Manoussakis and others v. Greece*[23] when the European Court found that the use of a planning restriction was not proportionate given what was at stake, 'namely the need to secure true religious pluralism, an inherent feature of the notion of a democratic society'.[24] There was still further improvement on the application of principles of pluralism when the European Court in *Serif v. Greece*[25] focused not so much on the possible grounds of

---

[20] *Karaduman v. Turkey*, App. No. 16278/90 (1993) 74 D&R 93, at 108.
[21] *Ibid.*, at para. 30.   [22] *Ibid.*, at para. 31.
[23] *Manoussakis and others v. Greece* (1997) 23 EHRR 387.   [24] *Ibid.*, at para. 44.
[25] *Serif v. Greece* (1999) 31 EHRR 561.

limitation on which States may rely in situations of conflict between religious groups but instead the role of States in promoting pluralism through tolerance. More recently still, in *Hasan and Chaush v. Bulgaria*,[26] the Court stressed that freedom for religious communities to enjoy autonomous existence is seen as a prerequisite for pluralism, not just a precondition for the enjoyment of freedom of religion.[27] This has obvious implications for measures that are aimed to hinder the emergence or the very survival of new religious movements. Of course, additional support for the role of pluralism to protect the interest of minority religions came with the Court's assertion in *Metropolitan Church of Bessarabia and others v. Moldova* that when a State fails to observe its duty to remain neutral and impartial in such matters, '[w]hat is at stake here is the preservation of pluralism and the proper functioning of democracy'.[28]

It remains to be seen whether these principles will be implemented by the European Court in future substantive reasoning (rather than simply invoked to furnish an impression that such fundamental principles have been adequately considered), in keeping with what appears to be an increasingly interventionist, if not uniform, trend.

Overview

By way of summary, in interpreting Article 18 of the ICCPR, the Human Rights Committee appears to have been far more consistent than the European institutions have been when applying Article 9 of the European Convention and, in particular, has not shown equivalent respect for State restrictions on religious freedom. Added to this there is a high level of consistency between the Human Rights Committee's position in General Comment No. 22, its practice in Optional Protocol decisions and its examination of State reports. Although Optional Protocol decisions tend to be fairly brief they are sufficient to elucidate basic substantive reasoning. The analysis of State reports provides useful additional authority for Committee opinion though this is confined by the factual limits of each situation addressed and by the practical constraint that issues affecting this particular freedom compete for space against questions relating to other ICCPR Articles which may have

---

[26] *Hasan and Chaush v. Bulgaria* (2002) 34(6) EHRR 1339.   [27] *Ibid.*, at para. 62.
[28] *Metropolitan Church of Bessarabia and others v. Moldova* (App. No. 45701/99), Judgment of 13 December 2001, para. 116.

higher priority. Nevertheless, the position of the Human Rights Committee is generally extremely clear.

In short, the Human Rights Committee may be said to have made a number of critical advances in standards affecting religious freedom in the face of substantial obstacles posed by the demands of States. The European institutions have undoubtedly accommodated clear instances of State intolerance (particularly against minority religions) in stark contrast to the position taken by the Human Rights Committee and the Special Rapporteur.

The European Court and European Commission have historically paid little attention to the global context and it is suggested that in future greater use might be made by the European Court of authoritative United Nations material in at least the following ways: to derive a greater appreciation of the significance to minority religions in European countries of different forms in which religious belief is manifested; to avoid any unnecessary departure from Human Rights Committee practice; and to forewarn the European Court of the significance of certain violations where they are better understood by reference to parallel situations in countries outside Europe.

The similarities between the text of Article 18 of the Universal Declaration and Article 9 of the European Convention belie one important difference between the Universal and the European systems. Among countries that are signatory to United Nations instruments, the differences in culture, domestic law, political ideology and even in the basic conception of freedom of thought, conscience and religion are reflected in the obstacles that prevented the development of a convention containing provisions comparable to those in the 1981 Declaration.[29] The consistency of the Human Rights Committee in its supervisory role and in strict standard-setting in the face of such obstacles has not been matched in European practice. Instead, Strasbourg organs have apparently followed a policy of least intervention and of accommodating State intolerance, even though greater scope exists in the development of European jurisprudence for strict and uniform application of principles than can be expected in the development of Universal standards. However, it is expected that recent interventionist trends of the European Court will continue to develop in response to the immediate demands facing the Court.

---

[29] T. van Boven discusses the universality of human rights in different ideological systems in 'Religious Liberty in the Context of Human Rights', 37 Ec Rev (1985) 345.

ANNEXES

Annex 1: Universal Declaration of Human Rights

Preamble

Whereas recognition of the inherent dignity and of the equal and inalienable rights of all members of the human family is the foundation of freedom, justice and peace in the world,

Whereas disregard and contempt for human rights have resulted in barbarous acts which have outraged the conscience of mankind, and the advent of a world in which human beings shall enjoy freedom of speech and belief and freedom from fear and want has been proclaimed as the highest aspiration of the common people,

Whereas it is essential, if man is not to be compelled to have recourse, as a last resort, to rebellion against tyranny and oppression, that human rights should be protected by the rule of law,

Whereas it is essential to promote the development of friendly relations between nations,

Whereas the peoples of the United Nations have in the Charter reaffirmed their faith in fundamental human rights, in the dignity and worth of the human person and in the equal rights of men and women and have determined to promote social progress and better standards of life in larger freedom,

Whereas Member States have pledged themselves to achieve, in co-operation with the United Nations, the promotion of universal respect for and observance of human rights and fundamental freedoms,

Whereas a common understanding of these rights and freedoms is of the greatest importance for the full realization of this pledge,

Now, Therefore,
THE GENERAL ASSEMBLY
proclaims

THIS UNIVERSAL DECLARATION OF HUMAN RIGHTS as a common standard of achievement for all peoples and all nations, to the end that every individual and every organ of society, keeping this Declaration constantly in mind, shall strive by teaching and education to promote respect for these rights and freedoms and by progressive measures, national and international, to secure their universal and effective recognition and observance, both among the peoples of Member States themselves and among the peoples of territories under their jurisdiction.

Article 1

All human beings are born free and equal in dignity and rights. They are endowed with reason and conscience and should act towards one another in a spirit of brotherhood.

Article 2

Everyone is entitled to all the rights and freedoms set forth in this Declaration, without distinction of any kind, such as race, colour, sex, language, religion, political or other opinion, national or social origin, property, birth or other status. Furthermore, no distinction shall be made on the basis of the political, jurisdictional or international status of the country or territory to which a person belongs, whether it be independent, trust, non-self-governing or under any other limitation of sovereignty.

Article 3

Everyone has the right to life, liberty and security of person.

Article 4

No one shall be held in slavery or servitude; slavery and the slave trade shall be prohibited in all their forms.

Article 5

No one shall be subjected to torture or to cruel, inhuman or degrading treatment or punishment.

Article 6

Everyone has the right to recognition everywhere as a person before the law.

Article 7

All are equal before the law and are entitled without any discrimination to equal protection of the law. All are entitled to equal protection against any discrimination in violation of this Declaration and against any incitement to such discrimination.

Article 8

Everyone has the right to an effective remedy by the competent national tribunals for acts violating the fundamental rights granted him by the constitution or by law.

Article 9

No one shall be subjected to arbitrary arrest, detention or exile.

Article 10

Everyone is entitled in full equality to a fair and public hearing by an independent and impartial tribunal, in the determination of his rights and obligations and of any criminal charge against him.

Article 11

1) Everyone charged with a penal offence has the right to be presumed innocent until proved guilty according to law in a public trial at which he has had all the guarantees necessary for his defence.
2) No one shall be held guilty of any penal offence on account of any act or omission which did not constitute a penal offence, under national or international law, at the time when it was committed. Nor shall a heavier penalty be imposed than the one that was applicable at the time the penal offence was committed.

Article 12

No one shall be subjected to arbitrary interference with his privacy, family, home or correspondence, nor to attacks upon his honour and reputation Everyone has the right to the protection of the law against such interference or attacks.

Article 13

1) Everyone has the right to freedom of movement and residence within the borders of each state.
2) Everyone has the right to leave any country, including his own, and to return to his country.

Article 14

1) Everyone has the right to seek and to enjoy in other countries asylum from persecution.
2) This right may not be invoked in the case of prosecutions genuinely arising from non-political crimes or from acts contrary to the purposes and principles of the United Nations.

Article 15

1) Everyone has the right to a nationality.
2) No one shall be arbitrarily deprived of his nationality nor denied the right to change his nationality.

Article 16

1) Men and women of full age, without any limitation due to race, nationality or religion, have the right to marry and to found a family. They are entitled to equal rights as to marriage, during marriage and at its dissolution.
2) Marriage shall be entered into only with the free and full consent of the intending spouses.
3) The family is the natural and fundamental group unit of society and is entitled to protection by society and the State.

Article 17

1) Everyone has the right to own property alone as well as in association with others.
2) No one shall be arbitrarily deprived of his property.

Article 18

Everyone has the right to freedom of thought, conscience and religion; this right includes freedom to change his religion or belief, and freedom, either alone or in community with others and in public or private, to manifest his religion or belief in teaching, practice, worship and observance.

Article 19

Everyone has the right to freedom of opinion and expression; this right includes freedom to hold opinions without interference and to seek, receive and impart information and ideas through any media and regardless of frontiers.

Article 20

1) Everyone has the right to freedom of peaceful assembly and association.
2) No one may be compelled to belong to an association.

Article 21

1) Everyone has the right to take part in the government of his country, directly or through freely chosen representatives.
2) Everyone has the right to equal access to public service in his country.
3) The will of the people shall be the basis of the authority of government; this shall be expressed in periodic and genuine elections which shall be by universal and equal suffrage and shall be held by secret vote or by equivalent free voting procedures.

Article 22

Everyone, as a member of society, has the right to social security and is entitled to realization, through national effort and international co-operation and in accordance with the organization and resources of each State, of the economic, social and cultural rights indispensable for his dignity and the free development of his personality.

Article 23

1) Everyone has the right to work, to free choice of employment, to just and favourable conditions of work and to protection against unemployment.
2) Everyone, without any discrimination, has the right to equal pay for equal work.
3) Everyone who works has the right to just and favourable remuneration ensuring for himself and his family an existence worthy of human dignity, and supplemented, if necessary, by other means of social protection.
4) Everyone has the right to form and to join trade unions for the protection of his interests.

Article 24

Everyone has the right to rest and leisure, including reasonable limitation of working hours and periodic holidays with pay.

Article 25

1) Everyone has the right to a standard of living adequate for the health and well-being of himself and of his family, including food, clothing,

housing and medical care and necessary social services, and the right to security in the event of unemployment, sickness, disability, widowhood, old age or other lack of livelihood in circumstances beyond his control.

2) Motherhood and childhood are entitled to special care and assistance. All children, whether born in or out of wedlock, shall enjoy the same social protection.

Article 26

1) Everyone has the right to education. Education shall be free, at least in the elementary and fundamental stages. Elementary education shall be compulsory. Technical and professional education shall be made generally available and higher education shall be equally accessible to all on the basis of merit.

2) Education shall be directed to the full development of the human personality and to the strengthening of respect for human rights and fundamental freedoms. It shall promote understanding, tolerance and friendship among all nations, racial or religious groups, and shall further the activities of the United Nations for the maintenance of peace.

3) Parents have a prior right to choose the kind of education that shall be given to their children.

Article 27

1) Everyone has the right freely to participate in the cultural life of the community, to enjoy the arts and to share in scientific advancement and its benefits.

2) Everyone has the right to the protection of the moral and material interests resulting from any scientific, literary or artistic production of which he is the author.

Article 28

Everyone is entitled to a social and international order in which the rights and freedoms set forth in this Declaration can be fully realized.

Article 29

1) Everyone has duties to the community in which alone the free and full development of his personality is possible.

2) In the exercise of his rights and freedoms, everyone shall be subject only to such limitations as are determined by law solely for

the purpose of securing due recognition and respect for the rights and freedoms of others and of meeting the just requirements of morality, public order and the general welfare in a democratic society.

3) These rights and freedoms may in no case be exercised contrary to the purposes and principles of the United Nations.

Article 30

Nothing in this Declaration may be interpreted as implying for any State, group or person any right to engage in any activity or to perform any act aimed at the destruction of any of the rights and freedoms set forth herein.

Annex 2: International Covenant on Civil and Political Rights

[Articles 1 to 27 only]

Preamble

The States Parties to the present Covenant,

Considering that, in accordance with the principles proclaimed in the Charter of the United Nations, recognition of the inherent dignity and of the equal and inalienable rights of all members of the human family is the foundation of freedom, justice and peace in the world,

Recognizing that these rights derive from the inherent dignity of the human person,

Recognizing that, in accordance with the Universal Declaration of Human Rights, the ideal of free human beings enjoying civil and political freedom and freedom from fear and want can only be achieved if conditions are created whereby everyone may enjoy his civil and political rights, as well as his economic, social and cultural rights,

Considering the obligation of States under the Charter of the United Nations to promote universal respect for, and observance of, human rights and freedoms,

Realizing that the individual, having duties to other individuals and to the community to which he belongs, is under a responsibility to strive for the promotion and observance of the rights recognized in the present Covenant,

Agree upon the following articles:

Part I

Article 1

1. All peoples have the right of self-determination. By virtue of that right they freely determine their political status and freely pursue their economic, social and cultural development.
2. All peoples may, for their own ends, freely dispose of their natural wealth and resources without prejudice to any obligations arising out of international economic co-operation, based upon the principle of mutual benefit, and international law. In no case may a people be deprived of its own means of subsistence.
3. The States Parties to the present Covenant, including those having responsibility for the administration of Non-Self-Governing and Trust Territories, shall promote the realization of the right of self-determination, and shall respect that right, in conformity with the provisions of the Charter of the United Nations.

Part II

Article 2

1. Each State Party to the present Covenant undertakes to respect and to ensure to all individuals within its territory and subject to its jurisdiction the rights recognized in the present Covenant, without distinction of any kind, such as race, colour, sex, language, religion, political or other opinion, national or social origin, property, birth or other status.
2. Where not already provided for by existing legislative or other measures, each State Party to the present Covenant undertakes to take the necessary steps, in accordance with its constitutional processes and with the provisions of the present Covenant, to adopt such legislative or other measures as may be necessary to give effect to the rights recognized in the present Covenant.
3. Each State Party to the present Covenant undertakes:
   a) To ensure that any person whose rights or freedoms as herein recognized are violated shall have an effective remedy, notwithstanding that the violation has been committed by persons acting in an official capacity;
   b) To ensure that any person claiming such a remedy shall have his right thereto determined by competent judicial, administrative or legislative authorities, or by any other competent authority

provided for by the legal system of the State, and to develop the
possibilities of judicial remedy;

c) To ensure that the competent authorities shall enforce such
remedies when granted.

Article 3

The States Parties to the present Covenant undertake to ensure the equal
right of men and women to the enjoyment of all civil and political rights
set forth in the present Covenant.

Article 4

1. In time of public emergency which threatens the life of the nation and
the existence of which is officially proclaimed, the States Parties to
the present Covenant may take measures derogating from their
obligations under the present Covenant to the extent strictly required
by the exigencies of the situation, provided that such measures are
not inconsistent with their other obligations under international law
and do not involve discrimination solely on the ground of race,
colour, sex, language, religion or social origin.

2. No derogation from articles 6, 7, 8 (paragraphs 1 and 2), 11, 15, 16
and 18 may be made under this provision.

3. Any State Party to the present Covenant availing itself of the right of
derogation shall immediately inform the other States Parties to the
present Covenant, through the intermediary of the Secretary-General
of the United Nations, of the provisions from which it has derogated
and of the reasons by which it was actuated. A further communication
shall be made, through the same intermediary, on the date on which
it terminates such derogation.

Article 5

1. Nothing in the present Covenant may be interpreted as implying for
any State, group or person any right to engage in any activity or
perform any act aimed at the destruction of any of the rights and
freedoms recognized herein or at their limitation to a greater extent
than is provided for in the present Covenant.

2. There shall be no restriction upon or derogation from any of the
fundamental human rights recognized or existing in any State Party
to the present Covenant pursuant to law, conventions, regulations or
custom on the pretext that the present Covenant does not recognize
such rights or that it recognizes them to a lesser extent.

Part III

Article 6

1. Every human being has the inherent right to life. This right shall be protected by law. No one shall be arbitrarily deprived of his life.
2. In countries which have not abolished the death penalty, sentence of death may be imposed only for the most serious crimes in accordance with the law in force at the time of the commission of the crime and not contrary to the provisions of the present Covenant and to the Convention on the Prevention and Punishment of the Crime of Genocide. This penalty can only be carried out pursuant to a final judgement rendered by a competent court.
3. When deprivation of life constitutes the crime of genocide, it is understood that nothing in this article shall authorize any State Party to the present Covenant to derogate in any way from any obligation assumed under the provisions of the Convention on the Prevention and Punishment of the Crime of Genocide.
4. Anyone sentenced to death shall have the right to seek pardon or commutation of the sentence. Amnesty, pardon or commutation of the sentence of death may be granted in all cases.
5. Sentence of death shall not be imposed for crimes committed by persons below eighteen years of age and shall not be carried out on pregnant women.
6. Nothing in this article shall be invoked to delay or to prevent the abolition of capital punishment by any State Party to the present Covenant.

Article 7

No one shall be subjected to torture or to cruel, inhuman or degrading treatment or punishment. In particular, no one shall be subjected without his free consent to medical or scientific experimentation.

Article 8

1. No one shall be held in slavery; slavery and the slave-trade in all their forms shall be prohibited.
2. No one shall be held in servitude.
3. a) No one shall be required to perform forced or compulsory labour;
   b) Paragraph 3 (a) shall not be held to preclude, in countries where imprisonment with hard labour may be imposed as a punishment

for a crime, the performance of hard labour in pursuance of a sentence to such punishment by a competent court;

c) For the purpose of this paragraph the term "forced or compulsory labour" shall not include:

(i) Any work or service, not referred to in subparagraph (b), normally required of a person who is under detention in consequence of a lawful order of a court, or of a person during conditional release from such detention;

(ii) Any service of a military character and, in countries where conscientious objection is recognized, any national service required by law of conscientious objectors;

(iii) Any service exacted in cases of emergency or calamity threatening the life or well-being of the community;

(iv) Any work or service which forms part of normal civil obligations.

Article 9

1. Everyone has the right to liberty and security of person. No one shall be subjected to arbitrary arrest or detention. No one shall be deprived of his liberty except on such grounds and in accordance with such procedure as are established by law.

2. Anyone who is arrested shall be informed, at the time of arrest, of the reasons for his arrest and shall be promptly informed of any charges against him.

3. Anyone arrested or detained on a criminal charge shall be brought promptly before a judge or other officer authorized by law to exercise judicial power and shall be entitled to trial within a reasonable time or to release. It shall not be the general rule that persons awaiting trial shall be detained in custody, but release may be subject to guarantees to appear for trial, at any other stage of the judicial proceedings, and, should occasion arise, for execution of the judgement.

4. Anyone who is deprived of his liberty by arrest or detention shall be entitled to take proceedings before a court, in order that court may decide without delay on the lawfulness of his detention and order his release if the detention is not lawful.

5. Anyone who has been the victim of unlawful arrest or detention shall have an enforceable right to compensation.

Article 10

1. All persons deprived of their liberty shall be treated with humanity and with respect for the inherent dignity of the human person.

2. a) Accused persons shall, save in exceptional circumstances, be seg-
      regated from convicted persons and shall be subject to separate
      treatment appropriate to their status as unconvicted persons;
   b) Accused juvenile persons shall be separated from adults and
      brought as speedily as possible for adjudication.
3. The penitentiary system shall comprise treatment of prisoners the
   essential aim of which shall be their reformation and social rehabilitation. Juvenile offenders shall be segregated from adults and be
   accorded treatment appropriate to their age and legal status.

Article 11

No one shall be imprisoned merely on the ground of inability to fulfil a
contractual obligation.

Article 12

1. Everyone lawfully within the territory of a State shall, within that
   territory, have the right to liberty of movement and freedom to
   choose his residence.
2. Everyone shall be free to leave any country, including his own.
3. The above-mentioned rights shall not be subject to any restrictions
   except those which are provided by law, are necessary to protect
   national security, public order (ordre public), public health or morals
   or the rights and freedoms of others, and are consistent with the other
   rights recognized in the present Covenant.
4. No one shall be arbitrarily deprived of the right to enter his own
   country.

Article 13

An alien lawfully in the territory of a State Party to the present Covenant
may be expelled therefrom only in pursuance of a decision reached in
accordance with law and shall, except where compelling reasons of
national security otherwise require, be allowed to submit the reasons
against his expulsion and to have his case reviewed by, and be represented for the purpose before, the competent authority or a person or
persons especially designated by the competent authority.

Article 14

1. All persons shall be equal before the courts and tribunals. In the
   determination of any criminal charge against him, or of his rights and
   obligations in a suit at law, everyone shall be entitled to a fair and

public hearing by a competent, independent and impartial tribunal established by law. The press and the public may be excluded from all or part of a trial for reasons of morals, public order (ordre public) or national security in a democratic society, or when the interest of the private lives of the parties so requires, or to the extent strictly necessary in the opinion of the court in special circumstances where publicity would prejudice the interests of justice; but any judgement rendered in a criminal case or in a suit at law shall be made public except where the interest of juvenile persons otherwise requires or the proceedings concern matrimonial disputes or the guardianship of children.

2. Everyone charged with a criminal offence shall have the right to be presumed innocent until proved guilty according to law.

3. In the determination of any criminal charge against him, everyone shall be entitled to the following minimum guarantees, in full equality:

    a) To be informed promptly and in detail in a language which he understands of the nature and cause of the charge against him;

    b) To have adequate time and facilities for the preparation of his defence and to communicate with counsel of his own choosing;

    c) To be tried without undue delay;

    d) To be tried in his presence, and to defend himself in person or through legal assistance of his own choosing; to be informed, if he does not have legal assistance, of this right; and to have legal assistance assigned to him, in any case where the interests of justice so require, and without payment by him in any such case if he does not have sufficient means to pay for it;

    e) To examine, or have examined, the witnesses against him and to obtain the attendance and examination of witnesses on his behalf under the same conditions as witnesses against him;

    f) To have the free assistance of an interpreter if he cannot understand or speak the language used in court;

    g) Not to be compelled to testify against himself or to confess guilt.

4. In the case of juvenile persons, the procedure shall be such as will take account of their age and the desirability of promoting their rehabilitation.

5. Everyone convicted of a crime shall have the right to his conviction and sentence being reviewed by a higher tribunal according to law.

6. When a person has by a final decision been convicted of a criminal offence and when subsequently his conviction has been reversed or he has been pardoned on the ground that a new or newly discovered fact

shows conclusively that there has been a miscarriage of justice, the person who has suffered punishment as a result of such conviction shall be compensated according to law, unless it is proved that the non-disclosure of the unknown fact in time is wholly or partly attributable to him.

7. No one shall be liable to be tried or punished again for an offence for which he has already been finally convicted or acquitted in accordance with the law and penal procedure of each country.

Article 15

1. No one shall be held guilty of any criminal offence on account of any act or omission which did not constitute a criminal offence, under national or international law, at the time when it was committed. Nor shall a heavier penalty be imposed than the one that was applicable at the time when the criminal offence was committed. If, subsequent to the commission of the offence, provision is made by law for the imposition of the lighter penalty, the offender shall benefit thereby.

2. Nothing in this article shall prejudice the trial and punishment of any person for any act or omission which, at the time when it was committed, was criminal according to the general principles of law recognized by the community of nations.

Article 16

Everyone shall have the right to recognition everywhere as a person before the law.

Article 17

1. No one shall be subjected to arbitrary or unlawful interference with his privacy, family, home or correspondence, nor to unlawful attacks on his honour and reputation.

2. Everyone has the right to the protection of the law against such interference or attacks.

Article 18

1. Everyone shall have the right to freedom of thought, conscience and religion. This right shall include freedom to have or to adopt a religion or belief of his choice, and freedom, either individually or in community with others and in public or private, to manifest his religion or belief in worship, observance, practice and teaching.

2. No one shall be subject to coercion which would impair his freedom to have or to adopt a religion or belief of his choice.
3. Freedom to manifest one's religion or beliefs may be subject only to such limitations as are prescribed by law and are necessary to protect public safety, order, health, or morals or the fundamental rights and freedoms of others.
4. The States Parties to the present Covenant undertake to have respect for the liberty of parents and, when applicable, legal guardians to ensure the religious and moral education of their children in conformity with their own convictions.

Article 19

1. Everyone shall have the right to hold opinions without interference.
2. Everyone shall have the right to freedom of expression; this right shall include freedom to seek, receive and impart information and ideas of all kinds, regardless of frontiers, either orally, in writing or in print, in the form of art, or through any other media of his choice.
3. The exercise of the rights provided for in paragraph 2 of this article carries with it special duties and responsibilities. It may therefore be subject to certain restrictions, but these shall only be such as are provided by law and are necessary:
   a) For respect of the rights or reputations of others;
   b) For the protection of national security or of public order (ordre public), or of public health or morals.

Article 20

1. Any propaganda for war shall be prohibited by law.
2. Any advocacy of national, racial or religious hatred that constitutes incitement to discrimination, hostility or violence shall be prohibited by law.

Article 21

The right of peaceful assembly shall be recognized. No restrictions may be placed on the exercise of this right other than those imposed in conformity with the law and which are necessary in a democratic society in the interests of national security or public safety, public order (ordre public), the protection of public health or morals or the protection of the rights and freedoms of others.

Article 22

1. Everyone shall have the right to freedom of association with others, including the right to form and join trade unions for the protection of his interests.

2. No restrictions may be placed on the exercise of this right other than those which are prescribed by law and which are necessary in a democratic society in the interests of national security or public safety, public order (ordre public), the protection of public health or morals or the protection of the rights and freedoms of others. This article shall not prevent the imposition of lawful restrictions on members of the armed forces and of the police in their exercise of this right.

3. Nothing in this article shall authorize States Parties to the International Labour Organisation Convention of 1948 concerning Freedom of Association and Protection of the Right to Organize to take legislative measures which would prejudice, or to apply the law in such a manner as to prejudice, the guarantees provided for in that Convention.

Article 23

1. The family is the natural and fundamental group unit of society and is entitled to protection by society and the State.

2. The right of men and women of marriageable age to marry and to found a family shall be recognized.

3. No marriage shall be entered into without the free and full consent of the intending spouses.

4. States Parties to the present Covenant shall take appropriate steps to ensure equality of rights and responsibilities of spouses as to marriage, during marriage and at its dissolution. In the case of dissolution, provision shall be made for the necessary protection of any children.

Article 24

1. Every child shall have, without any discrimination as to race, colour, sex, language, religion, national or social origin, property or birth, the right to such measures of protection as are required by his status as a minor, on the part of his family, society and the State.

2. Every child shall be registered immediately after birth and shall have a name.

3. Every child has the right to acquire a nationality.

Article 25

Every citizen shall have the right and the opportunity, without any of the distinctions mentioned in article 2 and without unreasonable restrictions:

a) To take part in the conduct of public affairs, directly or through freely chosen representatives;
b) To vote and to be elected at genuine periodic elections which shall be by universal and equal suffrage and shall be held by secret ballot, guaranteeing the free expression of the will of the electors;
c) To have access, on general terms of equality, to public service in his country.

Article 26

All persons are equal before the law and are entitled without any discrimination to the equal protection of the law. In this respect, the law shall prohibit any discrimination and guarantee to all persons equal and effective protection against discrimination on any ground such as race, colour, sex, language, religion, political or other opinion, national or social origin, property, birth or other status.

Article 27

In those States in which ethnic, religious or linguistic minorities exist, persons belonging to such minorities shall not be denied the right, in community with the other members of their group, to enjoy their own culture, to profess and practise their own religion, or to use their own language.

Annex 3: Declaration on the Elimination of all Forms of Intolerance and Discrimination Based on Religion or Belief

The General Assembly,

Considering that one of the basic principles of the Charter of the United Nations is that of the dignity and equality inherent in all human beings, and that all Member States have pledged themselves to take joint and separate action in co-operation with the Organization to promote and encourage universal respect for and observance of human rights and fundamental freedoms for all, without distinction as to race, sex, language or religion,

Considering that the Universal Declaration of Human Rights and the International Covenants on Human Rights proclaim the principles of non-discrimination and equality before the law and the right to freedom of thought, conscience, religion and belief,

Considering that the disregard and infringement of human rights and fundamental freedoms, in particular of the right to freedom of thought, conscience, religion or whatever belief, have brought, directly or indirectly, wars and great suffering to mankind, especially where they serve as a means of foreign interference in the internal affairs of other States and amount to kindling hatred between peoples and nations,

Considering that religion or belief, for anyone who professes either, is one of the fundamental elements in his conception of life and that freedom of religion or belief should be fully respected and guaranteed,

Considering that it is essential to promote understanding, tolerance and respect in matters relating to freedom of religion and belief and to ensure that the use of religion or belief for ends inconsistent with the Charter of the United Nations, other relevant instruments of the United Nations and the purposes and principles of the present Declaration is inadmissible,

Convinced that freedom of religion and belief should also contribute to the attainment of the goals of world peace, social justice and friendship among peoples and to the elimination of ideologies or practices of colonialism and racial discrimination,

Noting with satisfaction the adoption of several, and the coming into force of some, conventions, under the aegis of the United Nations and of the specialized agencies, for the elimination of various forms of discrimination,

Concerned by manifestations of intolerance and by the existence of discrimination in matters of religion or belief still in evidence in some areas of the world,

Resolved to adopt all necessary measures for the speedy elimination of such intolerance in all its forms and manifestations and to prevent and combat discrimination on the ground of religion or belief,

Proclaims this Declaration on the Elimination of All Forms of Intolerance and of Discrimination Based on Religion or Belief:

Article 1

1. Everyone shall have the right to freedom of thought, conscience and religion. This right shall include freedom to have a religion or whatever belief of his choice, and freedom, either individually or in community with others and in public or private, to manifest his religion or belief in worship, observance, practice and teaching.

2. No one shall be subject to coercion which would impair his freedom to have a religion or belief of his choice.
3. Freedom to manifest one's religion or belief may be subject only to such limitations as are prescribed by law and are necessary to protect public safety, order, health or morals or the fundamental rights and freedoms of others.

Article 2

1. No one shall be subject to discrimination by any State, institution, group of persons, or person on the grounds of religion or other belief.
2. For the purposes of the present Declaration, the expression "intolerance and discrimination based on religion or belief" means any distinction, exclusion, restriction or preference based on religion or belief and having as its purpose or as its effect nullification or impairment of the recognition, enjoyment or exercise of human rights and fundamental freedoms on an equal basis.

Article 3

Discrimination between human beings on the grounds of religion or belief constitutes an affront to human dignity and a disavowal of the principles of the Charter of the United Nations, and shall be condemned as a violation of the human rights and fundamental freedoms proclaimed in the Universal Declaration of Human Rights and enunciated in detail in the International Covenants on Human Rights, and as an obstacle to friendly and peaceful relations between nations.

Article 4

1. All States shall take effective measures to prevent and eliminate discrimination on the grounds of religion or belief in the recognition, exercise and enjoyment of human rights and fundamental freedoms in all fields of civil, economic, political, social and cultural life.
2. All States shall make all efforts to enact or rescind legislation where necessary to prohibit any such discrimination, and to take all appropriate measures to combat intolerance on the grounds of religion or other beliefs in this matter.

Article 5

1. The parents or, as the case may be, the legal guardians of the child have the right to organize the life within the family in accordance

with their religion or belief and bearing in mind the moral education in which they believe the child should be brought up.

2. Every child shall enjoy the right to have access to education in the matter of religion or belief in accordance with the wishes of his parents or, as the case may be, legal guardians, and shall not be compelled to receive teaching on religion or belief against the wishes of his parents or legal guardians, the best interests of the child being the guiding principle.

3. The child shall be protected from any form of discrimination on the ground of religion or belief. He shall be brought up in a spirit of understanding, tolerance, friendship among peoples, peace and universal brotherhood, respect for freedom of religion or belief of others, and in full consciousness that his energy and talents should be devoted to the service of his fellow men.

4. In the case of a child who is not under the care either of his parents or of legal guardians, due account shall be taken of their expressed wishes or of any other proof of their wishes in the matter of religion or belief, the best interests of the child being the guiding principle.

5. Practices of a religion or belief in which a child is brought up must not be injurious to his physical or mental health or to his full development, taking into account article 1, paragraph 3, of the present Declaration.

Article 6

In accordance with article 1 of the present Declaration, and subject to the provisions of article 1, paragraph 3, the right to freedom of thought, conscience, religion or belief shall include, inter alia, the following freedoms:

a) To worship or assemble in connection with a religion or belief, and to establish and maintain places for these purposes;

b) To establish and maintain appropriate charitable or humanitarian institutions;

c) To make, acquire and use to an adequate extent the necessary articles and materials related to the rites or customs of a religion or belief;

d) To write, issue and disseminate relevant publications in these areas;

e) To teach a religion or belief in places suitable for these purposes;

f) To solicit and receive voluntary financial and other contributions from individuals and institutions;

g) To train, appoint, elect or designate by succession appropriate leaders called for by the requirements and standards of any religion or belief;

h) To observe days of rest and to celebrate holidays and ceremonies in accordance with the precepts of one's religion or belief;

i) To establish and maintain communications with individuals and communities in matters of religion and belief at the national and international levels.

Article 7

The rights and freedoms set forth in the present Declaration shall be accorded in national legislation in such a manner that everyone shall be able to avail himself of such rights and freedoms in practice.

Article 8

Nothing in the present Declaration shall be construed as restricting or derogating from any right defined in the Universal Declaration of Human Rights and the International Covenants on Human Rights.

Annex 4: Convention for the Protection of Human Rights and Fundamental Freedoms

(EUROPEAN CONVENTION ON HUMAN RIGHTS)

[Articles 1 to 28 and First Protocol, Article 1]

The governments signatory hereto, being members of the Council of Europe, considering the Universal Declaration of Human Rights proclaimed by the General Assembly of the United Nations on 10th December 1948;

Considering that this Declaration aims at securing the universal and effective recognition and observance of the Rights therein declared;

Considering that the aim of the Council of Europe is the achievement of greater unity between its members and that one of the methods by which that aim is to be pursued is the maintenance and further realisation of human rights and fundamental freedoms;

Reaffirming their profound belief in those fundamental freedoms which are the foundation of justice and peace in the world and are best maintained on the one hand by an effective political democracy and on the other by a common understanding and observance of the human rights upon which they depend;

Being resolved, as the governments of European countries which are like-minded and have a common heritage of political traditions, ideals, freedom and the rule of law, to take the first steps for the collective enforcement of certain of the rights stated in the Universal Declaration,

Have agreed as follows:

Article 1 – Obligation to respect human rights

The High Contracting Parties shall secure to everyone within their jurisdiction the rights and freedoms defined in Section I of this Convention.

Section I – Rights and freedoms

Article 2 – Right to life

Everyone's right to life shall be protected by law. No one shall be deprived of his life intentionally save in the execution of a sentence of a court following his conviction of a crime for which this penalty is provided by law.

Deprivation of life shall not be regarded as inflicted in contravention of this article when it results from the use of force which is no more than absolutely necessary:

in defence of any person from unlawful violence;
in order to effect a lawful arrest or to prevent the escape of a person lawfully detained;
in action lawfully taken for the purpose of quelling a riot or insurrection.

Article 3 – Prohibition of torture

No one shall be subjected to torture or to inhuman or degrading treatment or punishment.

Article 4 – Prohibition of slavery and forced labour

No one shall be held in slavery or servitude.

No one shall be required to perform forced or compulsory labour.

For the purpose of this article the term "forced or compulsory labour" shall not include:

any work required to be done in the ordinary course of detention imposed according to the provisions of Article 5 of this Convention or during conditional release from such detention;
any service of a military character or, in case of conscientious objectors in countries where they are recognised, service exacted instead of compulsory military service;
any service exacted in case of an emergency or calamity threatening the life or well-being of the community;
any work or service which forms part of normal civic obligations.

Article 5 – Right to liberty and security

Everyone has the right to liberty and security of person. No one shall be deprived of his liberty save in the following cases and in accordance with a procedure prescribed by law:

the lawful detention of a person after conviction by a competent court;

the lawful arrest or detention of a person for non-compliance with the lawful order of a court or in order to secure the fulfilment of any obligation prescribed by law;

the lawful arrest or detention of a person effected for the purpose of bringing him before the competent legal authority on reasonable suspicion of having committed an offence or when it is reasonably considered necessary to prevent his committing an offence or fleeing after having done so;

the detention of a minor by lawful order for the purpose of educational supervision or his lawful detention for the purpose of bringing him before the competent legal authority;

the lawful detention of persons for the prevention of the spreading of infectious diseases, of persons of unsound mind, alcoholics or drug addicts or vagrants;

the lawful arrest or detention of a person to prevent his effecting an unauthorised entry into the country or of a person against whom action is being taken with a view to deportation or extradition.

Everyone who is arrested shall be informed promptly, in a language which he understands, of the reasons for his arrest and of any charge against him.

Everyone arrested or detained in accordance with the provisions of paragraph 1.c of this article shall be brought promptly before a judge or other officer authorised by law to exercise judicial power and shall be entitled to trial within a reasonable time or to release pending trial. Release may be conditioned by guarantees to appear for trial.

Everyone who is deprived of his liberty by arrest or detention shall be entitled to take proceedings by which the lawfulness of his detention shall be decided speedily by a court and his release ordered if the detention is not lawful.

Everyone who has been the victim of arrest or detention in contravention of the provisions of this article shall have an enforceable right to compensation.

Article 6 – Right to a fair trial

In the determination of his civil rights and obligations or of any criminal charge against him, everyone is entitled to a fair and public hearing within a reasonable time by an independent and impartial tribunal established by law. Judgment shall be pronounced publicly but the press and public may be excluded from all or part of the trial in the interests of morals, public order or national security in a democratic society, where the interests of juveniles or the protection of the private life of the parties so require, or to the extent strictly necessary in the opinion of the court in special circumstances where publicity would prejudice the interests of justice.

Everyone charged with a criminal offence shall be presumed innocent until proved guilty according to law.

Everyone charged with a criminal offence has the following minimum rights:

to be informed promptly, in a language which he understands and in detail, of the nature and cause of the accusation against him;

to have adequate time and facilities for the preparation of his defence;

to defend himself in person or through legal assistance of his own choosing or, if he has not sufficient means to pay for legal assistance, to be given it free when the interests of justice so require;

to examine or have examined witnesses against him and to obtain the attendance and examination of witnesses on his behalf under the same conditions as witnesses against him;

to have the free assistance of an interpreter if he cannot understand or speak the language used in court.

Article 7 – No punishment without law

No one shall be held guilty of any criminal offence on account of any act or omission which did not constitute a criminal offence under national or international law at the time when it was committed. Nor shall a heavier penalty be imposed than the one that was applicable at the time the criminal offence was committed.

This article shall not prejudice the trial and punishment of any person for any act or omission which, at the time when it was committed, was criminal according to the general principles of law recognised by civilised nations.

Article 8 – Right to respect for private and family life

Everyone has the right to respect for his private and family life, his home and his correspondence.

There shall be no interference by a public authority with the exercise of this right except such as is in accordance with the law and is necessary in a democratic society in the interests of national security, public safety or the economic well-being of the country, for the prevention of disorder or crime, for the protection of health or morals, or for the protection of the rights and freedoms of others.

Article 9 – Freedom of thought, conscience and religion

1. Everyone has the right to freedom of thought, conscience and religion; this right includes freedom to change his religion or belief and freedom, either alone or in community with others and in public or private, to manifest his religion or belief, in worship, teaching, practice and observance.
2. Freedom to manifest one's religion or beliefs shall be subject only to such limitations as are prescribed by law and are necessary in a democratic society in the interests of public safety, for the protection of public order, health or morals, or for the protection of the rights and freedoms of others.

Article 10 – Freedom of expression

Everyone has the right to freedom of expression. This right shall include freedom to hold opinions and to receive and impart information and ideas without interference by public authority and regardless of frontiers. This article shall not prevent States from requiring the licensing of broadcasting, television or cinema enterprises.

The exercise of these freedoms, since it carries with it duties and responsibilities, may be subject to such formalities, conditions, restrictions or penalties as are prescribed by law and are necessary in a democratic society, in the interests of national security, territorial integrity or public safety, for the prevention of disorder or crime, for the protection of health or morals, for the protection of the reputation or rights of others, for preventing the disclosure of information received in confidence, or for maintaining the authority and impartiality of the judiciary.

Article 11 – Freedom of assembly and association

Everyone has the right to freedom of peaceful assembly and to freedom of association with others, including the right to form and to join trade unions for the protection of his interests.

No restrictions shall be placed on the exercise of these rights other than such as are prescribed by law and are necessary in a democratic society in the interests of national security or public safety, for the prevention of disorder or crime, for the protection of health or morals or for the protection of the rights and freedoms of others. This article shall not prevent the imposition of lawful restrictions on the exercise of these rights by members of the armed forces, of the police or of the administration of the State.

Article 12 – Right to marry

Men and women of marriageable age have the right to marry and to found a family, according to the national laws governing the exercise of this right.

Article 13 – Right to an effective remedy

Everyone whose rights and freedoms as set forth in this Convention are violated shall have an effective remedy before a national authority notwithstanding that the violation has been committed by persons acting in an official capacity.

Article 14 – Prohibition of discrimination

The enjoyment of the rights and freedoms set forth in this Convention shall be secured without discrimination on any ground such as sex, race, colour, language, religion, political or other opinion, national or social origin, association with a national minority, property, birth or other status.

Article 15 – Derogation in time of emergency

In time of war or other public emergency threatening the life of the nation any High Contracting Party may take measures derogating from its obligations under this Convention to the extent strictly required by the exigencies of the situation, provided that such measures are not inconsistent with its other obligations under international law.

No derogation from Article 2, except in respect of deaths resulting from lawful acts of war, or from Articles 3, 4 (paragraph 1) and 7 shall be made under this provision.

Any High Contracting Party availing itself of this right of derogation shall keep the Secretary General of the Council of Europe fully informed of the measures which it has taken and the reasons therefor. It shall also inform the Secretary General of the Council of Europe when such measures have ceased to operate and the provisions of the Convention are again being fully executed.

Article 16 – Restrictions on political activity of aliens

Nothing in Articles 10, 11 and 14 shall be regarded as preventing the High Contracting Parties from imposing restrictions on the political activity of aliens.

Article 17 – Prohibition of abuse of rights

Nothing in this Convention may be interpreted as implying for any State, group or person any right to engage in any activity or perform any act aimed at the destruction of any of the rights and freedoms set forth herein or at their limitation to a greater extent than is provided for in the Convention.

Article 18 – Limitation on use of restrictions on rights

The restrictions permitted under this Convention to the said rights and freedoms shall not be applied for any purpose other than those for which they have been prescribed.

First Protocol

Article 1 – Protection of property

Every natural or legal person is entitled to the peaceful enjoyment of his possessions. No one shall be deprived of his possessions except in the public interest and subject to the conditions provided for by law and by the general principles of international law.

The preceding provisions shall not, however, in any way impair the right of a State to enforce such laws as it deems necessary to control the use of property in accordance with the general interest or to secure the payment of taxes or other contributions or penalties.

Article 2 – Right to education

No person shall be denied the right to education. In the exercise of any functions which it assumes in relation to education and to teaching, the State shall respect the right of parents to ensure such education and teaching in conformity with their own religious and philosophical convictions.

Annex 5: Text of General Comment No. 22

1. The right to freedom of thought, conscience and religion (which includes the freedom to hold beliefs) in article 18 (1) is far-reaching

and profound; it encompasses freedom of thoughts on all matters, personal conviction and the commitment to religion or belief, whether manifested individually or in community with others. The Committee draws the attention of States parties to the fact that the freedom of thought and the freedom of conscience are protected equally with the freedom of religion and belief. The fundamental character of these freedoms is also reflected in the fact that this provision cannot be derogated from, even in time of public emergency, as stated in article 4 (2) of the Covenant.

2. Article 18 protects theistic, non-theistic and atheistic beliefs, as well as the right not to profess any religion or belief. The terms belief and religion are to be broadly construed. Article 18 is not limited in its application to traditional religions or to religions and beliefs with institutional characteristics or practices analogous to those of traditional religions. The Committee therefore views with concern any tendency to discriminate against any religion or belief for any reasons, including the fact that they are newly established, or represent religious minorities that may be the subject of hostility by a predominant religious community.

3. Article 18 distinguishes the freedom of thought, conscience, religion or belief from the freedom to manifest religion or belief. It does not permit any limitations whatsoever on the freedom of thought and conscience or on the freedom to have or adopt a religion or belief of one's choice. These freedoms are protected unconditionally, as is the right of everyone to hold opinions without interference in article 19 (1). In accordance with articles 18 (2) and 17, no one can be compelled to reveal his thoughts or adherence to a religion or belief.

4. The freedom to manifest religion or belief may be exercised "either individually or in community with others and in public or private". The freedom to manifest religion or belief in worship, observance, practice and teaching encompasses a broad range of acts. The concept of worship extends to ritual and ceremonial acts given direct expression to belief, as well as various practices integral to such acts, including the building of places of worship, the use of ritual formulae and objects, the display of symbols, and the observance of holidays and days of rest. The observance and practice of religion or belief may include not only ceremonial acts but also such customs as the observance of dietary regulations, the wearing of distinctive clothing or headcoverings, participation in rituals associated with certain stages of life, and the use of a particular language customarily spoken by

a group. In addition, the practice and teaching of religion or belief includes acts integral to the conduct by religious groups of their basic affairs, such as, inter alia, the freedom to choose their religious leaders, priests and teachers, the freedom to establish seminaries or religious schools and the freedom to prepare and distribute religious texts or publications.

5. The Committee observes that the freedom to "have or to adopt" a religion or belief necessarily entails the freedom to choose a religion or belief, including, inter alia, the right to replace one's current religion or belief with another or to adopt atheistic views, as well as the right to retain one's religion or belief. Article 18 (2) bars coercions that would impair the right to have or adopt a religion or belief, including the use of threat of physical force or penal sanctions to compel believers or non-believers to adhere to their religious beliefs and congregations, to recant their religion or belief or to convert. Policies or practices having the same intention or effect, such as for example those restricting access to education, medical care, employment or the rights guaranteed by article 25 and other provisions of the Covenant are similarly inconsistent with article 18 (2). The same protection is enjoyed by holders of all beliefs of a non-religious nature.

6. The Committee is of the view that article 18 (4) permits public school instruction in subjects such as the general history of religions and ethics if it is given in a neutral and objective way. The liberty of parents or legal guardians to ensure that their children receive a religious and moral education in conformity with their own convictions, set forth in article 18 (4), is related to the guarantees of the freedom to teach a religion or belief stated in article 18 (1). The Committee notes that public education that includes instruction in a particular religion or belief is inconsistent with article 18 (4) unless provision is made for non-discriminatory exemptions or alternatives that would accommodate the wishes of parents and guardians.

7. According to article 20, no manifestation of religions or beliefs may amount to propaganda for war or advocacy of national, racial or religious hatred that constitutes incitement to discrimination, hostility or violence. As stated by the Committee in its General Comment 11 [19], States parties are under the obligation to enact laws to prohibit such acts.

8. Article 18 (3) permits restrictions on the freedom to manifest religion or belief only if limitations are prescribed by law and are necessary to protect public safety, order, health or morals, or the fundamental

rights and freedoms or others. The freedom from coercion to have or to adopt a religion or belief and the liberty of the parents and guardians to ensure religious and moral education cannot be restricted. In interpreting the scope of permissible limitation clauses, States parties should proceed from the need to protect the rights guaranteed under the Covenant, including the right to equality and non-discrimination on all grounds specified in articles 2, 3 and 26. Limitations imposed must be established by law and must not be applied in a manner that would vitiate the rights guaranteed in article 18. The Committee observes that paragraph 3 of article 18 is to be strictly interpreted: restrictions are not allowed on grounds not specified there, even if they would be allowed as restrictions to other rights protected in the Covenant, such as national security. Limitations may be applied only for those purposes for which they were prescribed and must be directly related and proportionate to the specific need on which they are predicated. Restrictions may not be imposed for discriminatory purposes or applied in a discriminatory manner. The Committee observes that the concept of morals derives from many social, philosophical and religious traditions; consequently, limitations on the freedom to manifest a religion or belief for the purpose of protecting morals must be based on principles not deriving exclusively from a single tradition. Persons already subject to certain legitimate constraints, such as prisoners, continue to enjoy their rights to manifest their religion or belief to the fullest extent compatible with the specific nature of the constraint. States parties' reports should provide information on the full scope and effects of limitations under article 18 (3), both as a matter of law and of their application in specific circumstances.

9. The fact that a religion is recognized as a State religion or that it is established as official or traditional or that its followers comprise the majority of the population, shall not result in any impairment of the enjoyment of any of the rights under the Covenant, including articles 18 and 27, nor in any discrimination against adherents of other religions or non-believers. In particular, certain measures discriminating against the latter, such as measures restricting eligibility for government service to members of the predominant religion or giving economic privileges to them or imposing special restrictions on the practice of other faiths, are not in accordance with the prohibition of discrimination based on religion or belief and the guarantee of equal protection under article 26. The measures contemplated

by article 20, paragraph 2, of the Covenant constitute important safeguards against infringements of the rights of religious minorities and of other religious groups to exercise the rights guaranteed by articles 18 and 27, and against acts of violence or persecution directed toward those groups. The Committee wishes to be informed of measures taken by States parties concerned to protect the practices of all religions or beliefs from infringement and to protect their followers from discrimination. Similarly, information as to respect for the rights of religious minorities under article 27 is necessary for the Committee to assess the extent to which the freedom of thought, conscience, religion and belief has been implemented by States parties. States parties concerned should also include in their reports information relating to practices considered by their laws and jurisprudence to be punishable as blasphemous.

10. If a set of beliefs is treated as official ideology in constitutions, statutes, proclamations of the ruling parties, etc., or in actual practice, this shall not result in any impairment of the freedom under article 18 or any other rights recognized under the Covenant nor in any discrimination against persons who do not accept the official ideology or who oppose it.

11. Many individuals have claimed the right to refuse to perform military service (conscientious objection) on the basis that such right derives from their freedoms under article 18. In response to such claims, a growing number of States have in their laws exempted from compulsory military service citizens who genuinely hold religious or other beliefs that forbid the performance of military service and replaced it with alternative national service. The Covenant does not explicitly refer to a right of conscientious objection, but the Committee believes that such a right can be derived from article 18, inasmuch as the obligation to use lethal force may seriously conflict with the freedom of conscience and the right to manifest one's religion or belief. When this right is recognized by law or practice, there shall be no differentiation among conscientious objectors on the basis of the nature of their particular beliefs; likewise, there shall be no discrimination against conscientious objectors because they have failed to perform military service. The Committee invites States parties to report on the conditions under which persons can be exempted from military service on the basis of their rights under article 18 and on the nature and length of alternative national service.

BIBLIOGRAPHY

Allan, J., *Shopping for a God. Fringe Religions Today*, Leicester: Intervarsity (1986).

Alston, P. (ed.), *Peoples' Rights*, Oxford: Oxford University Press (2001).

Alston, P. and C. Crawford (eds.), *The Future of UN Human Rights Treaty Monitoring*, Cambridge: Cambridge University Press (2000).

Amor, R., 'The Mandate of the UN Special Rapporteur', 12 Emory Int'l L Rev (1998) 10.

An-Na'im, A. A., 'Religious Minorities under Islamic Law and the Limits of Cultural Relativism', 9 HRQ (1987) 1.

Anwar, M., 'Young Muslims in Britain: Their Educational Needs and Policy Implications', in M. W. Khan (ed.), *Education and Society and the Muslim World*, Saudi Arabia: Hodder and Stoughton (1981).

Ashraf, S. A., 'A View of Education – An Islamic Perspective', in B. O'Keeffe (ed.), *Schools for Tomorrow: Building Walls or Building Bridges*, London: Falmer (1988).

Baer, R. A. and J. C. Carper, '"To the Advantage of Infidelity" or How Not To Deal With Religion In America's Public Schools', 14(5) *Educational Policy* (2000) 600.

Balfour, J., 'The European Convention and Religious Associations and Charities in Scotland', 1 HR & UKP (2000) 19.

Banton, M., *International Action Against Racial Discrimination*, Oxford: Clarendon Press (1996).

Basdevant-Gaudemet, B., '*Le Régime Juridique de l'École Privée et les Autônomiers dans l'Enseignement Public en France*', in European Consortium for Church–State Research, *Church and State in Europe. State Financial Support. Religion and the School*, Milan: Giuffrè (1992), pp. 139–70.

Basova, I., 'Freedom Under Fire: The New Russian Religious Law', *Temple International and Comparative Law Journal* (2000) 181.

Bayefsky, A. F., 'The Principle of Equality or Non-Discrimination in International Law', 11 HRLJ (1990) 1.

Beckford, J. A., *Cult Controversies, The Societal Response to the New Religious Movements*, London: Tavistock (1985).

Bell, J., 'Religious Observance in Secular Schools: A French Solution', 2 Ed & Law (1990) 121.

Bengoa, J., 'Existence and Recognition of Minorities', UN Doc. E/CN.4/Sub.2/AC.5/2000/WP.2 (2000).

Benito, E. O., *Elimination of all Forms of Intolerance and Discrimination Based on Religion or Belief*, Human Rights Study Series No. 2, UN Sales No. E. 89. XIV.3, Geneva: United Nations Centre for Human Rights (1989).

Berman, H., 'Religious Rights in Russia at a Time of Tumultuous Transition: A Historical Theory', in J. D. van der Vyver, J. D. Witte, *Religious Human Rights in Global Perspective: Legal Perspectives*, The Hague/London: Martinus Nijhoff (1996).

Bernhardt, R., 'Current Developments – Reform of Control Machinery under the European Convention on Human Rights: Protocol 11', 89 Am J Int'l L (1995) 145.

Bloed, A., 'Monitoring the CSCE Human Dimension: In Search of its Effectiveness', in A. Bloed et al. (eds.), *Monitoring Human Rights in Europe*, Dordrecht/London: Martinus Nijhoff in co-operation with the Helsinki Federation for Human Rights (1993).

Bloed, A., 'The OSCE and the Issue of National Minorities' in A. Phillips and A. Rosas (eds.), *Universal Minority Rights*, London: Minority Rights Group (International) (1995).

Boerefijn, I., *The Reporting Procedure under the Covenant on Civil and Political Rights: Practice and Procedures of the Human Rights Committee*, Antwerp: Hart Intersentia (1999).

Bossuyt, M. J., *Guide to the 'Travaux Préparatoires' of the International Covenant on Civil and Political Rights*, Dordrecht/Lancaster: Martinus Nijhoff (1987).

Bossuyt, M. J., *L'Interdiction de la Discrimination dans le Droit International des Droits de l'Homme*, Brusssels: Éstablishment Émile Bruylant (1976).

Boulware-Miller, K., 'Female Circumcision: Challenges to the Practice as a Human Rights Violation', 8 Harv WLJ (1985) 155.

Bowers, J., 'The European Convention on Human Rights – The Employment Consequences of Articles 9 and 10', 42 Emp Lawyer (2000) 16.

Boyle, K., 'Freedom of Thought, Freedom of Conscience, Freedom of Religion and Freedom of Belief as Internationally Protected Rights: What is Agreed and What is Not Agreed', in E. Cotran and A. O. Sherif (eds.), *Democracy, the Rule of Law and Islam*, London: CIMEL and Kluwer Law International (1999).

Boyle, K., 'Religious Intolerance and the Incitement of Hatred' in S. Coliver (ed.), *Striking a Balance: Hate Speech, Freedom of Expression and Non-discrimination*, London: University of Essex, Human Rights Centre (1992).

Boyle, K., 'Report on Freedom of Conscience in International Law', in Council of Europe, *Freedom of Conscience*, (proceedings of seminar organised by the Secretariat General of the Council of Europe in co-operation with the F. M. van Asbeck Centre for Human Rights Studies of the University of Leiden), Strasbourg: Council of Europe Press (1993).

Boyle, K. and J. Sheen, *Freedom of Religion and Belief: A World Report*, London: Routledge (1997).

Boyle, K. and A. Baldaccini, 'International Human Rights Approaches to Racism', in S. Fredman (ed.), *Discrimination and Human Rights: The Case of Racism*, Oxford: Oxford University Press (2001).

Bradney, A., *Religions, Rights and Laws*, Leicester: Leicester University Press (1993).

Brett, R., *General Comment of the Human Rights Committee on Article 18 of the International Covenant on Civil and Political Rights: Developments on Conscientious Objection to Military Service*, Geneva: Quaker United Nations Office (1993).

Brolmann, C. et al. (eds.), *Peoples and Minorities in International Law*, Dordrecht/London: Martinus Nijhoff (1993).

Browne, M., 'Should Germany Stop Worrying and Love the Octopus? Freedom of Religion and The Church of Scientology in Germany and the United States', *Indiana International and Comparative Law Review* (1998) 155.

Buergenthal, T., 'A Court and Two Consolidated Treaty Bodies', in A. F. Bayefsky (ed.), *The UN Human Rights Treaty System in the 21st Century*, The Hague/London: Kluwer Law International (2000).

Buergenthal, T., 'The CSCE and the Promotion of Racial and Religious Tolerance', 22 Isr YB Hum Rts (1992) 31.

Buergenthal, T., 'To Respect and to Ensure: State Obligations and Permissible Derogations', in L. Henkin (ed.), *The International Bill of Rights: The Covenant on Civil and Political Rights*, New York/Guildford: Columbia University Press (1981).

Capotorti, F., 'Study on the Rights of Persons Belonging to Ethnic, Religious and Linguistic Minorities', New York: United Nations Sales No. E. 91. XIV.2 (1991).

Carper, J. C., 'History, Religion and Schooling: A Context for Conversation', in J. T. Sears and J. C. Carper (eds.), *Curriculum, Religion and Public Education: Conversations for an Enlarging Public Square*, New York: Teachers' College Press (1998).

Carter, S. L., 'The Resurrection of Religious Freedom', 107.1 Harv L Rev (1993–4) 118.

Cassese, A., 'The General Assembly: Historical Perspective 1945–1989', in P. Alston (ed.), *The United Nations and Human Rights: A Critical Appraisal*, Oxford: Clarendon Press (1992).

Cassin, R., La Déclaration Universelle et la Mise en Oeuvre des Droits de l'Homme, 79 RCADI (1951) 241.

Cheung, A. S. Y., 'In Search of a Theory of Cult and Freedom of Religion in China: The Case of Falun Gong', 13 Pac Rim L & Pol'y J (2004) 1.

Clapham, A., *Human Rights in the Private Sphere*, Oxford: Clarendon Press (1993).

Clark, E. A., 'Church–State Relations in the Czech Republic: Past Turmoil and Present Transformation', Brigham Young UL Rev (1996) 1019.

Clark, R. S., 'The United Nations and Religious Freedom', 11 NYUJ Int'l L & Pol (1978) 197.

Clarke, D. M., 'Freedom of Thought in Schools: A Comparative Study', 35 Int'l & Comp Law Q (1986) 271.

Claydon, J., 'The Treaty Protection of Religious Rights: UN Draft Convention on the Elimination of All Forms of Intolerance and of Discrimination Based on Religion or Belief', 12 Santa Clara L Rev (1972) 403.

Clayson Smith, H., 'Liberte, Egalite et Fraternite at Risk for New Religious Movements in France', Brigham Young UL Rev (2000) 1099.

Clayton, G. and G. Pitt, 'Dress Codes and Freedom of Expression', EHRLR (1997) 54.

Cohen, C. P., 'Freedom of Religion or Belief: One of The Human Rights of Children', paper submitted at the conference on Building Understanding and Respect between People of Diverse Religions or Beliefs, Warsaw, 14–18 May 1989.

Cohen, C. P., 'United Nations Convention on the Rights of the Child: Introductory Note', 44 Int'l Comm'n Jurists Rev (1990) 36.

Collins, R. B., 'Sacred Sites and Religious Freedom on Government Land', University of Pennsylvania Journal of Constitutional Law (January, 2003).

Cooper, J. and A. M. Williams, 'Hate Speech, Holocaust Denial and International Human Rights Law', EHRLR (1996) 593.

Council of Europe, Collected Edition of The 'Travaux Préparatoires' of the European Convention on Human Rights, 8 vols., The Hague: Martinus Nijhoff (1975–85).

Council of Europe, Freedom of Conscience (proceedings of a seminar organised by the Secretariat General of the Council of Europe in co-operation with the F. M. van Asbeck Centre for Human Rights Studies of the University of Leiden), Strasbourg: Council of Europe (1993).

Council of Europe, In Our Hands, The Effectiveness of Human Rights Protection 50 Years after the Universal Declaration, Strasbourg: Council of Europe Press (1998).

Crawford, J. (ed.), The Rights of Peoples, Oxford: Clarendon Press (1988).

Cullen, H., 'Education Rights or Minority Rights?', 7 Int JLP & F (1993) 143.

Cullen, H., 'The Emerging Scope of Freedom of Conscience', 22 Eur L Rev (1997) 32.

Cumper, P., 'The Rights of Religious Minorities: The Legal Regulation of New Religious Movements', in P. Cumper and S. Wheatley (eds.), Minority Rights in the 'New' Europe, The Hague/Boston: Martinus Nijhoff (1999).

Cumper, P., 'School Worship: Praying for Guidance', EHRLR (1998) 45.

Davies, M. (ed.), Third World-Second World Sex: Women's Struggles and National Liberation: Third World Women Speak Out, London: Zed (1983).

Dickson, B., 'The United Nations and Freedom of Religion', 44 Int'l & Comp Law Q (1995) 327.

Dignan, J., 'A Right Not to Render unto Caesar: Conscientious Objection for the Taxpayer' 34 Northern Ireland LQ (1983) 20.

Dinstein, Y. (ed.), *The Protection of Minorities and Human Rights*, Dordrecht/ London: Martinus Nijhoff (1992).

Document of the Copenhagen Meeting of the Conference on the Human Dimension of the CSCE 1990 (1990) 29 ILM 1311.

Drzemczewski, A. and J. Meyer-Ladewig, 'Principal Characteristics of the New European Convention on Human Rights Mechanism, as established by Protocol 11, signed on 11th May, 1994', 15 HRLJ (1994) 81.

Dunne, K. A., 'Addressing Religious Intolerance in Europe: The Limited Application of Article 9 of the European Convention of Human Rights and Fundamental Freedoms', *California Western International Law Journal* (1999) 117.

Durham, W., M. Wood, and S. Condie, 'Accommodation of Conscientious Objection to Abortion: A Case Study of the Nursing Profession' Brigham Young UL Rev (1982) 253.

Edge, P. W., 'Current Problems in Article 9 of the European Convention on Human Rights', *Juridical Review* (1996) 42.

Edge, P. W., 'The European Court of Human Rights and Religious Rights', 47 Int'l & Comp Law Q (1998) 680.

Edge, P. W., 'Holy War on the Doorstep', 146 NLJ (1996) 190.

Edge, P. W., 'Kokkinakis v. Greece: A Response to Dr Juss', 2 J Civ Lib (1997) 41.

Edge, P. W. and G. Harvey (eds.), *Law and Religion in Contemporary Society*, Aldershot: Ashgate (2000).

Editorial, 'To Evangelize or Proselytize', 20 Int'l Bull Miss Res (1966) 1.

Edwards, J., 'Preferential Treatment and the Right to Equal Consideration', in P. Cumper and S. Wheatley (eds.), *Minority Rights in the 'New' Europe*, The Hague/Boston: Martinus Nijhoff (1999).

Eide, A., 'Citizenship and the Minority Rights of Non-Citizens', UN Doc. E/CN.4/Sub.2/AC.5/1999/WP.3 (1999).

Eide, A. and Chama, M., 'Conscientious Objection to Military Service', UN Doc. E/CN.4/Sub.2/30/Rev.1 and UN Doc. E/CN.4/Sub.2/1982/24 (1982).

European Consortium for Church–State Research, *Conscientious objection in the EC countries* (Proceedings of the meeting, Brussels-Leuven, 7–8 December 1990, European Consortium for Church–State Research), Milan: Giuffrè (1992).

European Consortium for Church–State Research, *The Legal Status of Religious Minorities in the Countries of the European Union* (Proceedings of the meeting in Thessalonikai, 19–20 November 1993, European Consortium for Church–State Research), Milan: Giuffrè (1994).

European Consortium for Church–State Research, '*Le Statut Constitutionnel des Cultes dans les Pays de l'Union Européennes*', Actes du Colloque, Université de Paris XI, 18–19 November 1994, European Consortium for Church–State Research, Paris: Litec (1995).

Evans, C., *Freedom of Religion Under the European Convention on Human Rights*, Oxford: Oxford University Press (2001).

Evans, M. D., *Religious Liberty and International Law in Europe*, Cambridge: Cambridge University Press (1997).

Evans, M. D., 'The United Nations and Freedom of Religion: The Works of the Human Rights Committee', in R. J. Adhar (ed.), *Law and Religion*, Aldershot: Ashgate (2000).

Fawcett, J. E. S., *The Application of the European Convention on Human Rights*, Oxford: Clarendon Press (1987).

Ferrari, S., 'Individual Religious Freedom and National Security in Europe After September 11', Brigham Young UL Rev (2004) 357.

Ferrari, S., 'The New Wine and the Old Cask, Tolerance, Religion and the Law in Contemporary Europe', 10 Rat Jur (1997) 75.

Fineschi, V., 'The Jehovah's Witnesses' Refusal for Blood Transfusions: The Jurisprudence and Medico-Legal Debate in Italy', 41 Med Sc & L (2001) 141.

Fottrell, D. and B. Bowring (eds.), *Minority and Group Rights in the New Millennium*, The Hague/London: Martin Nijhoff (1999).

Fredman, S., 'Equality Issues', in B. S. Markesinis (ed.), *The Impact of the Human Rights Bill on English Law*, Oxford: Oxford University Press (1998).

Garay, A., 'Liberté Religieuse et Proselytisme: l'Experience Européene', 17 *Revue Trimestrielle des Droits de l'Homme* (1994) 144.

Garibaldi, O., 'General Limitations on Human Rights: The Principle of Legality', 17 Harv Int'l LJ (1976) 503.

Gaspard, F. and Khosrokhavar, F., *Le Foulard et la République*, Paris: La Découverte (1995).

Genn, R., 'Legal developments – Helsinki Process – Advance in International Outlawing of Incitement to Racism and Religious Hatred', 24 Pat of Prej (1990) 97.

Ghandhi, P. R., *The Human Rights Committee and the Right of Individual Communication, Law and Practice*, Aldershot: Ashgate (1998).

Ghandhi, P. R. and J. James, 'The English Law of Blasphemy and the European Convention on Human Rights', EHRLR (1998) 430.

Gilbert, H., *The Right to Freedom of Belief: a Conceptual Framework*, Unpublished PhD thesis, Essex University (2001).

Gilbert, H., 'The Slow Development of the Right to Conscientious Objection to Military Service under the European Convention on Human Rights' 5 EHRLR (2001), 554.

Gomien, D., D. J. Harris and L. Zwaak, *Law and Practice of the European Convention on Human Rights and the European Social Charter*, Strasbourg: Council of Europe (1996).

Goy, R., 'La Garantie Européene de la Liberté de Religion' 107 *Revue Du Droit Public* (1991) 5.

Gray, C. A., 'The World Peace Tax Fund Act: Conscientious Objection for Taxpayers', 74 Northw UL Rev (1979) 76.

Greenawalt, K., *Religious Convictions and Political Choice*, New York/Oxford: Oxford University Press (1988).

Greenawalt, K., *Speech, Crimes and the Uses of Language*, Oxford: Oxford University Press (1989).

Greenberg, J., *Race, Sex and Religious Discrimination*, in T. Meron (ed.), *Human Rights in International Law: Legal and Policy Issues*, Oxford: Clarendon Press (1984).

Grubb, A., *Participating in Abortion and the Conscientious Objector*, Cambridge LJ (1988) 162.

Gunn, T. J., 'Adjudicating Rights of Conscience under the European Convention on Human Rights', in J. van der Vyver and J. Witte (eds.), *Religious Human Rights in Global Perspective: Legal Perspectives*, The Hague/London: Martinus Nifhoff (1996).

Gustafson, C. and P. Juviler (eds.), *Religion and Human Rights: Competing Claims?*, Armonk, New York/London: M. E. Sharpe (1999).

El Hajje, O., *Islamic Countries and the International Instruments on Human Rights*, 3(1) Con & Lib (1991) 46.

Hammer, L., 'Abortion Objection in the United Kingdom within the Framework of the European Convention on Human Rights and Fundamental Freedoms', EHRLR (1999) 564.

Hammer, L. M., *The International Human Right to Freedom of Conscience*, Aldershot: Ashgate (2001).

Harris, D. J., *The European Social Charter*, Charlottesville: University Press of Virginia (1984).

Harris, D. J., M. O'Boyle and C. Warbrick, *Law of the European Convention on Human Rights*, London: Butterworths (1995).

Hayden, P., 'Religiously Motivated "Outrageous" Conduct: Intentional Infliction of Emotional Distress as a Weapon Against "Other People's Faiths"', 34 William Mary L Rev (1993) 579.

Hayter, K., 'Female Circumcision – Is there a Legal Solution? J Soc Wel Law (1984) 323.

Helgesen, J., 'Between Helsinki and Beyond' in A. Rosas, J. Helgesen and D. Gomien (eds.), *Human Rights in a Changing East–West Perspective*, London: Pinter (1990).

Henkin, L., *Introduction*, in L. Henkin (ed.), *The International Bill of Rights: The Covenant on Civil and Political Rights*, New York/Guildford: Columbia University Press (1981).

Higgins, R., 'The United Nations Human Rights Committee' in R. Blackburn and J. Taylor (eds.), *Human Rights for the 1990s: Legal, Political and Ethical Issues*, London: Mansell (1991).

Ibán, I. C., '*Nuovi Movimenti Religiosi: Problemi Giuridici*', in S. Ferrari (ed.), *Diritti Dell'uomo e Libertà dei Gruppi Religiosi. Problemi Giuridici dei Nuovi Movimenti Religiosi*, Padua: Cedam (1989).

Ibán, I. C., 'Religious Tolerance and Freedom in Continental Europe', 10 Rat Jur (1997) 90.

Ibrahim, S. E. et al., *The Copts of Egypt*, London: Minority Rights Group International (1996).

International Helsinki Federation for Human Rights (IHF), *Religious Discrimination and Related Violations of Helsinki Commitments, Report to the OSCE Supplementary Human Dimension Meeting on Freedom of Religion Vienna*, Vienna: IHF (1999).

International Helsinki Federation for Human Rights (IHF), *Religious Intolerance in Selected OSCE Countries in 2000: Report to the Seminar on Freedom of Religion or Belief in the OSCE Region*, The Hague: IHF (2001).

Jack, H. A., *238 Words Towards Religious Freedom*, New York: WCRP (1975).

Jack, H. A., *58 Words, Two Commas: Snail-Like Motion Toward a U.N. Declaration for Religious Freedom*, New York: WCRP (1976).

Jack, H. A., *Eliminating All Forms of Religious Intolerance: What the United Nations Has Done and Can Do*, New York: WCRP (1972).

Jack, H. A., *New Progress Toward a U.N. Declaration Against Religious Intolerance*, New York: WCRP (1973).

Jack, H. A., *Slow Motion, Religiously*, New York: WCRP (1978).

Jack, H. A., *U.N. Action Against Religious Discrimination*, New York: WCRP (1979).

Jack, H. A., *The U.N. Declaration for Religious Freedom: The Result of Two Decades of Drafting*, New York: WCRP (1981).

Jones, T. D., *Human Rights: Group Defamation, Freedom of Expression and the Law of Nations*, The Hague/Boston/London: Martinus Nijhoff (1998).

de Jong, C. D., *The Freedom of Thought, Conscience and Religion or Belief in the United Nations (1946–1992)*, Antwerp/Groningen/Oxford: Intersentia-Hart (2000).

Juss, S. S., 'Kokkinakis and Freedom of Conscience Rights in Europe', 1 J Civ Lib (1996) 246.

Kandelia, S., *Implementing the OSCE's Human Dimension Since 1995*, Papers in the Theory and Practice of Human Rights, No. 26, London: University of Essex, Human Rights Centre (1999).

Kaufmann, B., *Das Problem der Glaubens- und Überzeugungsfreiheit im Völkerrecht*, Zürich: Schulthess Polygraphischer Verlag (1989).

Kearns, P., 'The Uncultured God: Blasphemy Law's Reprieve and the Art of Matrix', EHRLR (2000) 512.

Kingsbury, B., 'Claims by Non-State Groups in International Law', 25 Cornell Int'l LJ (1992) 481.

Kiss, A. C., 'Commentary by the Rapporteur on the Limitation Provisions', 7(1) HRQ (1985) 15.

Kiss, A. C., 'Permissible Limitations on Rights', in L. Henkin (ed.), *The International Bill of Rights: The Covenant on Civil and Political Rights*, New York/Guildford: Columbia University Press (1981).

Klebes, H., 'Draft Protocol on Minority Rights to the ECHR', 14 HRLJ (1992) 140.

Klebes, H., 'The Council of Europe's Framework Convention for the Protection of National Minorities' 16 HRLJ (1995) 92.

Krassimir, K., *Religious Freedom in Southeastern and Central Europe*, Vienna/Sofia: International Helsinki Federation for Human Rights (2001).

Krishnaswami, A., *Study of Discrimination in the Matter of Religious Rights and Practices*, UN Doc. E/CN.4/Sub.2/200/Rev.1 (1960), reprinted in 11 NYUJ Int'l L & Pol (1978) 227.

Krussteff, A., 'An Attempt at Modernization: The New Bulgarian Legislation in the Field of Religious Freedom', Brigham Young UL Rev (2001) 575.

Kurland, P. B., *Religion and the Law of Church and State and the Supreme Court*, Chicago: Aldine (1962).

Lehnhof, L. S., 'Freedom of Religious Association: The Right of Religious Organizations to Obtain Legal Entity Status Under the European Convention', Brigham Young UL Rev (2002) 561.

Lekhel, A., 'Leveling the Playing Field for Religious "Liberty" in Russia: A Critical Analysis of the 1997 Law "On Freedom of Conscience and Religious Associations"', 32 Vand J Transnat'l L (1999) 167.

Lerner, N., 'The Final Text of the UN Declaration against Intolerance and Discrimination Based on Religion or Belief' 12 Isr YB Hum Rts (1982) 185.

Lerner, N., *Group Rights and Discrimination in International Law*, Dordrecht/London: Martinus Nijhoff (1991).

Lerner, N., 'Proselytism, Change of Religion, and International Human Rights', 12 Emory Int'l L Rev (1998) 477.

Lerner, N., *Religion, Beliefs and International Human Rights*, Maryknoll, New York: Orbis (2000).

Lerner, N., 'Religious Human Rights under the United Nations' in J. van der Vyver and J. Witte (eds.), *Religious Human Rights in Global Perspective: Legal Perspectives*), The Hague/London: Martinus Nijhoff (1996).

Lerner, N., 'Toward a Draft Declaration Against Religious Intolerance and Discrimination, 11 Isr YB Hum Rts (1981) 82.

Lerner, N., *The U.N. Convention on the Elimination of All Forms of Racial Discrimination*, Alphen aan den Rijn: Sijhoff & Noordhoff (1980).

Lillich, R. B., 'Civil Rights', in T. Meron (ed.), *Human Rights in International Law: Legal and Policy Issues*, Oxford: Clarendon Press (1984).

Liskofsky, S., 'The UN Declaration on the Elimination of Religious Intolerance and Discrimination: Historical and Legal Perspectives', in J. E. Wood (ed.), *Religion and the State: Essays in Honour of Leo Pfeffer*, Waco, Texas: Baylor University Press (1985).

Little, D., J. Kelsay and A. Sachedina, *Human Rights and the Conflict of Cultures. Western and Islamic Perspectives on Religious Liberty*, Columbia SC: University of South Carolina Press (1988).

Lord, K. S., 'What Does Religious Liberty in the OSCE Mean in Practice?', 5(2) OSCE Bulletin (1997) 9.

Loveland, I., 'Religious Drug Use as a Human Right?', 151 NLJ (2001) 41.

Lynn, B. et al. (eds.), *The Right to Religious Liberty: The Basic ACLU Guide to Religious Rights*, Carbondale: South Illinois University Press (1995).

McConnell, M., 'Freedom From Persecution or Protection of the Rights of Conscience?: A Critique of Justice Scalia's Historical Arguments in *City of Boerne v. Flores*' 39(1) William Mary L Rev (1998) 819.

McConnell, M., 'Religious Participation in Public Programs' 59 U Chicago L Rev (1992) 115.

McDougal, M. S., H. D. Lasswell and L. Chen, *Human Rights and World Public Order* New Haven/London: Yale University Press (1980).

McGoldrick, D., 'The Development of the CSCE after the Helsinki 1992 Conference', 42 Int'l & Comp Law Q (1993) 411.

McGoldrick, D., *The Human Rights Committee: Its Role in the Development of the International Covenant on Civil and Political Rights*, Oxford: Clarendon Press (1994).

McGoldrick, D. and T. O'Donnell, 'Hate-Speech Laws: Consistency with National and International Human Rights Law', 18(4) *Legal Studies* (1998) 453.

McKean, W., *Equality and Discrimination under International Law*, Oxford: Clarendon Press (1983).

McPherson, M., *The United Nations and Conscientious Objection*, 1(1) Con & Lib (1989) 8.

Marcus, E., 'Conscientious Objection as an Emerging Human Right', 38 Virginia J Int'l L (1998) 507.

Marood, T., 'British Asian Muslims and the Rushdie Affair' 61 Pol Quart (1990) 143, in a collection of essays entitled 'The Political Revival of Religion: Fundamentalism and Others', p. 123.

Mason, P., 'Pilgrimage to Religious Shrines: An Essential Element in the Human Right to Freedom of Thought, Conscience and Religion', 25 Case W Res J Int'l L (1993) 619.

Meron, T., *Human Rights Law-Making in the United Nations: A Critique of Instruments and Process*, Oxford: Clarendon Press (1986).

Meron, T., 'On a Hierarchy of International Human Rights', 80 Am J Int'l L (1986) 1.

Milosaviljevic, B., 'Relations Between the State and Religious Communities in the Federal Republic of Yugoslavia', Brigham Young UL Rev (2002) 311.

Miner, C. J., 'Losing My Religion: Austria's New Religion Law in Light of International and European Standards of Religious Freedom', Brigham Young UL Rev (1998) 607.

Moens, G., 'The Action-Belief Dichotomy and Freedom of Religion 12 Sidney L Rev (1989) 195.

Montgomery, J. W., 'Christian Education and Worship in State Schools: The American Perspective', 144 *Law & Justice* (2000) 41.

Montgomery, J. W., 'When is Evangelism Illegal?', 148 NLJ (1998) 524.

Motilla, A., 'Religious Pluralism in Spain: Striking the Balance Between Religious Freedom and Constitutional Rights', Brigham Young UL Rev (2004) 575.

Mowbray, A. R., *Cases and Materials on the European Convention on Human Rights*, London: Butterworths (2001).

Mowbray, A. R., 'A New European Court of Human Rights', PL (1994) 540.

Nelson, G. K., *Cults, New Religions and Religious Creativity*, London: Routledge & Kegan Paul (1987).

Nowak, M., *CCPR Commentary*, Kehl: N. P. Engel (1993).

Nsereko, D., 'Religion, the State and the Law in Africa', 28 J Church & St (1986) 269.

ODIHR, *Freedom of Religion or Belief: Laws Affecting the Structuring of Religious Communities*, Review Conference, September 1999, ODIHR (1999).

ODIHR, 'The Human Dimension Seminar on Constitutional, Legal and Administrative Aspects of the Freedom of Religion' held in Warsaw, 16–19 April 1996, *Consolidated Summary*, ODIHR (1996).

O'Boyle, M., 'Reflections on the Effectiveness of the European System for the Protection of Human Rights' in A. F. Bayefsky (ed.), *The UN Human Rights Treaty System in the 21st Century*, The Hague/London: Kluwer Law International (2000).

O'Donnell, T. A., 'The Margin of Appreciation Doctrine: Standards in the Jurisprudence of the European Court of Human Rights', 4 HRQ (1982) 474.

Opsahl, T., 'The General Comments of the Human Rights Committee', in Jekewitz, Jürgen et al. (eds.), *Des Menschen Recht Zwischen Freiheit und Verantwortung: Festschrift für Karl Joseph Partsch*, Berlin: Dunker & Humblot (1989).

Opsahl, T., 'The Human Rights Committee', in P. Alston (ed.), *The United Nations and Human Rights: A Critical Appraisal*, Oxford: Clarendon Press, (1992).

Orlin, T. S., 'Religious Pluralism and Freedom of Religion: Its Protection in the Light of Church/State Relationships', in A. Rosas and J. Helgesen (eds.), *The Strength of Diversity – Human Rights and the Pluralist Democracy*, Dordrecht/London: Martinus Nijhoff (1992).

Parkinson, P. 'Enforcing Tolerance: Vilification Laws and Religious Freedom in Australia', paper given at the Eleventh Annual International Law and Religion Symposium: 'Religion in the Public Sphere: Challenges and Opportunities', Provo, Utah, 3–6 October 2004.

Partsch, K. J., 'Freedom of Conscience and Expression, and Political Freedoms' in L. Henkin (ed.), *The International Bill of Rights: The Covenant on Civil and Political Rights*, New York/Guildford: Columbia University Press (1981).

Partsch, K. J., 'Fundamental Principles of Human Rights: Self-Determination, Equality and Non-Discrimination', in K. Vasak and P. Alston (eds.), *The International Dimensions of Human Rights*, Westport, Conn.: Greenwood (1982).

Pfeffer, L., *Religious Freedom*, Skokie: National Textbook Company for the American Civil Liberties Union (1977).

Pocar, F., 'Religious Freedom in the System of the United Nations', 1(2) Con & Lib (1989) 14.

Poulter, S., 'Muslim Headscarves in Schools: Contrasting Legal Approaches in England and France', 17 Oxford J Leg Stud (1997) 43.

Prebensen, S., 'The Margin of Appreciation and Articles 9, 10 and 11 of the Convention', 19 HRLJ (1998) 13.

Quashigah, E. K., 'Religious Freedom and Vestal Virgins: The Trokosi Practice in Ghana', 10 RADIC (1998) 193.

Quinn, G., 'Written Communication on Conscientious Objection in Labour Relations', in Council of Europe, *Freedom of Conscience*, Strasbourg: Council of Europe (1993) (proceedings of seminar organised by the Secretariat General of the Council of Europe in cooperation with the F. M. van Asbeck Centre for Human Rights Studies of the University of Leiden).

Ramcharan, B. G., 'Equality and Nondiscrimination', in L. Henkin (ed.), *The International Bill of Rights: The Covenant on Civil and Political Rights*, New York/Guildford: Columbia University Press (1981).

Ramcharan, B. G., 'Religious Witness and Practice in Political and Social Life as an Element of Religious Liberty', in B. Lynn, et al. (eds.), *The Right to Religious Liberty: The Basic ACLU Guide to Religious Rights*, Carbondale: South Illinois University Press (1995).

Richardson, J. T., '"Brainwashing" Claims and Minority Religions Outside the US: Cultural Diffusion of a Questionable Concept in the Legal Arena', Brigham Young UL Rev (1996) 873.

Rigaux, F., 'L'Incrimination du Proselytism Face à la Liberté d'Expression', 17 *Revue Trimestrielle des Droits de l'Homme* (1994) 144.

Rimanque, K., 'Report on Freedom of Conscience and Minority Groups', in Council of Europe, *Freedom of Conscience*, (proceedings of seminar organised by the Secretariat General of the Council of Europe in cooperation with the F. M. van Asbeck Centre for Human Rights Studies of the University of Leiden) Strasbourg: Council of Europe (1993).

Robeck, C. M., 'Mission and the Issue of Proselytism', 20 Int'l Bull Miss Res (1996) 2.

Robertson, A. H., 'The Implementation System: International Measures', in L. Henkin (ed.), *The International Bill of Rights: The Covenant on Civil and Political Rights*, New York/Guildford: Columbia University Press (1981).

Robertson, A. H. and J. G. Merrills, *Human Rights in the World*, Manchester: Manchester University Press (1996).

Robillard, St. J. A., 'Religion in Prison', 130 NLJ (1980) 800.

Robinson, N., *Universal Declaration of Human Rights: Its Origins, Significance, Application and Interpretation*, New York: Institute of Jewish Affairs (1958).

Rodatà, S., 'Written Communication on Conscientious Objection to Military Service', in Council of Europe, *Freedom of Conscience* (proceedings of seminar organised by the Secretariat General of the Council of Europe in cooperation with the F. M. van Asbeck Centre for Human Rights Studies of the University of Leiden), Strasbourg: Council of Europe (1993).

Rodley, N. S., *The Treatment of Prisoners Under International Law*, Oxford: Clarendon Press (1999).

Rönquist, A., 'The Council of Europe Framework Convention on for the Protection of National Minorities', 6(1) *Helsinki Monitor* (1995) 38.

Rosas, A. and J. E. Helgesen (eds.), *The Strength of Diversity: Human Rights and Pluralist Democracy*, Dordrecht/Boston: Martinus Nijhoff (1992).

Roth, S., 'Denial of the Holocaust as an Issue of Law', 23 Isr YB Hum Rts (1993) 215.

Rumney, P., 'Incitement to Racial Hatred and the Problem of Social Exclusion', 5(2) CIL (2000/2001) 89.

Sandgren, M. L., 'Extending Religious Freedoms Abroad: Difficulties Experienced by Minority Religions', *Tulsa Journal of Comparative and International Law* (2001) 251.

Schachter, O., 'The Obligation to Implement the Covenant in Domestic Law', in Henkin, L. (ed.), *The International Bill of Rights: The Covenant on Civil and Political Rights*, New York/Guildford: Columbia University Press (1981).

Scheinin, M., 'Article 18', in A. Eide (ed.), *The Universal Declaration of Human Rights: A Commentary*, Oslo: Scandinavian University Press (1992).

Scheinin, M., 'The Right to Say "No": A Study Under the Right to Freedom of Conscience', 75 *Archiv für Rechts- und Sozialphilosophie* (1989) 345.

Schermers, H., 'The Eleventh Protocol to the European Convention on Human Rights', 19 Eur L Rev (1994) 367.

Schmidt, M., 'The Complementarity of the Covenant and the European Convention on Human Rights – Recent Developments', in D. J. Harris and S. Joseph (eds.), *The International Covenant on Civil and Political Rights and United Kingdom Law*, Oxford: Clarendon Press (1995).

Schwelb, E., 'Civil and Political Rights: the International Measures of Implementation', 62 Am J Int'l L (1968) 827.

Schwelb, E., 'The International Convention on the Elimination of All Forms of Racial Discrimination 1965', 15 Int'l & Comp Law Q (1966), p. 996.

Shaw, M., 'Freedom of Thought, Conscience and Religion', in St J. McDonald, F. Matscher and H. Petzold (eds.), *The European System for the Protection of Human Rights*, Dordrecht/London: Martinus Nijhoff (1993).

Sheleff, L. S., 'Rabbi Captain Goldman's Yarmulke, Freedom of Religion and Conscience, and Civil (Military) Disobedience' 17 Isr YB Hum Rts (1987) 197.

Sieghart, P., *The International Law of Human Rights*, Oxford: Clarendon Press (1990).

Sorabjee, S., 'Freedom of Expression in India, in Developing Human Rights Jurisprudence', *Commonwealth Secretariat* vol. 7 (1999).

Stavros, S., 'Freedom of Religion and Claims for Exemption from Generally Applicable, Neutral Laws: Lessons From Across The Pond?' EHRLR (1997) 607.

Steiner, E., 'Blasphemy and Incitement to Hatred under the European Convention', 6 KCLJ (1995) 143.

Steiner, E., 'The Muslim Scarf and the French Republic', 6 KCLJ (1995) 147.

Sullivan, D. J., 'Advancing the Freedom of Religion or Belief through the UN Declaration of the Elimination of Religious Intolerance and Discrimination', 82 Am J Int'l L (1988) 487.

Sullivan, D. J., 'Gender Equality and Religious Freedom: Toward a Framework for Conflict Resolution', 24 NYUJ Int'l L & Pol (1992) 795.

Sullivan, K., 'Religion and Liberal Democracy', 59 U Chicago L Rev (1992) 195.

Svensson-McCarthy, A., *The International Law of Human Rights and States of Exception*, The Hague/London: Martinus Nijhoff (1998).

Tahzib, B. G., *Freedom of Religion or Belief: Ensuring Effective International Legal Protection*, The Hague/London: Martinus Nijhoff Publishers (1996).

Thornberry, P., *International Law and the Rights of Minorities*, Oxford: Clarendon Press (1991).

Türk, D. and L. Joinet, 'The Right to Freedom of Opinion and Expression: Current Problems of its Realization and Measures Necessary for its Strengthening and Promotion', in S. Coliver (ed.), *Striking a Balance Hate Speech, Freedom of Expression and Non-discrimination*, London: University of Essex, Human Rights Centre (1992).

Urban Morgan Institute, 'Siracusa Principles on the Limitation and Derogation Provisions in the International Covenant on Civil and Political Rights', 7(1) HRQ (1985) 3.

Van Boven, T., 'Advances and Obstacles in Building Understanding and Respect between People of Diverse Religions and Beliefs' 13 HRQ (1991) 437.

Van Boven, T., *De Volkenrechtelijke Bescherming van de godsdienstvrijheid*, Assen, Netherlands: Van Gorcum (1967).

Van Boven, T., 'Discrimination and Human Rights Law: Combating Racism', in S. Fredman (ed.), *Discrimination and Human Rights: The Case of Racism*, Oxford: Oxford University Press (2001).

Van Boven, T., 'Religious Liberty in the Context of Human Rights', 37 Ec Rev (1985) 345.

Van Bueren, G., *The International Law on the Rights of the Child*, Dordrecht/London: Martinus Nijhoff (1998).

Van Dijk, P. and G.J.H. Van Hoof, *Theory and Practice of the European Convention on Human Rights*, The Hague/London: Kluwer (1998).

Vegleris, P.T., '*Valeur et Signification de la Clause "dans une Société Démocratique" dans la Convention Européenne des Droits de l'Homme*', 1(2) HRJ (1968) 219.

Verdoodt, A., *Naissance et Significance de la Déclaration Universelle des Droits de l'Homme*, Lourain: Paris Société d'Études Morales, Socials et Juridiques, Editions Nauwelaerts (1964).

Vermeulen, B.P., 'The Freedom of Thought, Conscience and Religion. Reflections on Article 9(1) of the European Convention on Human Rights, in Particular with Regard to the Position of Minorities', in J.A. Smith and L.F. Zwaak (eds.), *International Protection of Human Rights Selected Topics: A Compilation of Contributions for Training Courses*, Utrecht: Utrecht Studie en Informatiecentrum Mensenrechten (1995).

Vermeulen, B.P., 'Report on Scope and Limits of Conscientious Objection', in Council of Europe, *Freedom of Conscience* (proceedings of seminar organised by the Secretariat General of the Council of Europe in cooperation with the F.M. van Asbeck Centre for Human Rights Studies of the University of Leiden), Strasbourg: Council of Europe (1993).

Walkate, J.A., *The Right of Everyone to Change His Religion or Belief – Some Observations*, 30 Neth Int'l L Rev (1983) 146.

Walkate, J.A., 'The U.N. Declaration on the Elimination of All Forms of Intolerance and Discrimination Based on Religion or Belief (1981) – An Historical Overview', 1(2) Con & Lib (1989) 21.

Weigel, G. 'Religion as a Human Right', 77 *Freedom at Issue* (1984) 3.

Weissbrodt, D.S., 'The United Nations Commission on Human Rights Confirms Conscientious Objection to Military Service as a Human Right', 35 Neth Int'l L Rev (1988) 53.

Witte, J., 'Religious Dimensions of Law, Human Rights and Democracy', 26 Isr YB Hum Rts (1996) 87.

Wood, J.E., 'Church Lobbying and Public Policy', 28 J Church & St (1986) 183.

Yourow, H.C., *The Margin of Appreciation Doctrine in the Dynamic of European Human Rights Jurisprudence*, The Hague/London: Kluwer Law International (1996).

INDEX

religious choice, freedom of (cont.)
  right to change, 339
religious movements, new, 3, 297, 350
religious offences, 3, 104, 105, 106,
  108
Religious Offences Bill, 106
religious practice
  articles necessary for, 250
religious symbols, 238, 279, 286,
  290, 379
respect
  for the religious feelings of others,
    87, 88, 89, 160, 343
  right of community to live free from
    religious hatred, 82–4
Ress, Judge, 81
right to solicit and receive voluntary
    financial and other
    contributions, 271, 337
rights and freedoms of others, see
    limitations, rights and
    freedoms of others
  attempting to make converts, 72
  blasphemy, disparagement and
    gratuitous offence, 84–111
  coercion that impairs religious
    choice, 4, 73–7
  'conflict' between proselytiser and
    proselytised, 76–7
  duties and responsibilities, 86–96
  hate speech, 77
  offensive speech, 83–4
  'respect' for religious beliefs or
    feelings, 26–7, 75, 85–7,
    113, 330
ritual articles and materials, see
    ceremonial items
rituals associated with certain stages of
    life, 278, 282, 379
  baptisms, 138, 282
  ceremonies, 229, 240, 251, 274,
    278, 282, 285, 291, 338,
    372
  circumcision, 282, 283
    female, 286
  funerals, 282
  marriage, 30, 213, 283, 284,
    355, 377

pilgrimages, 282
weddings, 282
Robillard, 239
Romania, 65, 78, 182, 230, 232,
  243, 244, 245, 249, 272,
  287, 288
Russian Federation, 65, 110, 230,
  232, 245, 284, 297
Rwanda, 276

Sadi, 195, 242
Saudi, 29–31, 43, 45, 55–6, 64, 110,
  239, 244, 252, 276, 285,
  288
  1981 Declaration, 56
  ICCPR, 30, 43, 45, 55, 59
Scarman, Lord, 99
Scheinin, 180
Schermers, 127
Schwelb, 15
sects, 297–8, 319
secularity, 3, 142, 254, 257, 315, 318,
  335
sharia, 315
Sikh, 320
Slovakia, 230
Sorabjee, Soli, 108
Spain, 181, 310
Special Rapporteur, 5, 7, 10, 15–16,
  22, 37, 52–3, 64, 66,
  103, 109–11, 231,
  263, 271
  legal recognition of religious
    groups, 336
  missionary work, 56, 62
  publications, 260
  right to maintain communication
    with communities and
    individuals, 287
  sects, 319
Sri Lanka, 62, 197
State discretion, 343
State religion, xi, 3, 41, 45, 65, 197,
  289, 381
State Reports, 10, 12–15, 102
Steiner, 253
succession of appropriate leaders,
  272–8